RELIGIOUS HATRED AND INTERNATIONAL LAW

The UN International Covenant on Civil and Political Rights obliges State parties to prohibit any advocacy of religious hatred that constitutes incitement to discrimination or violence. This book traces the origins of this provision and proposes an *actus reus* for this offence. The question whether hateful incitement is a prohibition per se or also encapsulates a fundamental 'right to be protected against incitement' is extensively debated. Also addressed is the question of how to judge incitement. Is *mens rea* required to convict someone of advocating hatred, and if so, what degree of intent? This analysis also includes the paramount question if and to what extent content and/or context factors ought to be decisive. The author engages extensively with comparative domestic law and compares the workings of the UN Human Rights Committee with those of the UN Committee on the Elimination of Racial Discrimination and the European Court of Human Rights.

JEROEN TEMPERMAN is an associate professor of public international law at Erasmus University Rotterdam. He is also the editor-in-chief of *Religion and Human Rights*.

CAMBRIDGE STUDIES IN INTERNATIONAL AND COMPARATIVE LAW

Established in 1946, this series produces high quality scholarship in the fields of public and private international law and comparative law. Although these are distinct legal sub-disciplines, developments since 1946 confirm their interrelations.

Comparative law is increasingly used as a tool in the making of law at national, regional and international levels. Private international law is now often affected by international conventions, and the issues faced by classical conflicts rules are frequently dealt with by substantive harmonization of law under international auspices. Mixed international arbitrations, especially those involving state economic activity, raise mixed questions of public and private international law, while in many fields (such as the protection of human rights and democratic standards, investment guarantees and international criminal law) international and national systems interact. National constitutional arrangements relating to 'foreign affairs', and to the implementation of international norms, are a focus of attention.

The series welcomes works of a theoretical or interdisciplinary character, and those focusing on the new approaches to international or comparative law or conflicts of law. Studies of particular institutions or problems are equally welcome, as are translations of the best work published in other languages.

General Editors

James Crawford SC FBA
Whewell Professor of International Law, Faculty of Law, University of Cambridge
John S. Bell FBA
Professor of Law, Faculty of Law, University of Cambridge

A list of books in the series can be found at the end of this volume.

RELIGIOUS HATRED AND INTERNATIONAL LAW

The Prohibition of Incitement to Violence or Discrimination

By

JEROEN TEMPERMAN

CAMBRIDGE
UNIVERSITY PRESS

CAMBRIDGE
UNIVERSITY PRESS

University Printing House, Cambridge CB2 8BS, United Kingdom

Cambridge University Press is part of the University of Cambridge.

It furthers the University's mission by disseminating knowledge in the pursuit of education, learning and research at the highest international levels of excellence.

www.cambridge.org
Information on this title: www.cambridge.org/9781107124172

© Jeroen Temperman 2016

First published 2016

A catalogue record for this publication is available from the British Library

Library of Congress Cataloguing in Publication data
Temperman, Jeroen, author.
Religious hatred and international law : the prohibition of incitement to violence or discrimination / Jeroen Temperman.
pages   cm. – (Cambridge studies in international and comparative law)
Includes bibliographical references and index.
ISBN 978-1-107-12417-2 (hardback)
1. Freedom of religion (International law)   2. Freedom of expression.
3. Hate speech–Law and legislation   4. International law and human
rights.   5. International Covenant on Civil and Political Rights
(1966 December 16)   I. Title.
K3258.T46 2015
341.4'832–dc23   2015022585

ISBN 978-1-107-12417-2 Hardback

For Irene and Samuel

CONTENTS

FOREWORD

The prohibition of incitement in international human rights law has attracted enormous attention in the last couple of years. Previously, even many experts had only been dimly aware of the norm, which on the surface may look slightly strange in human rights documents, since it seems to serve a restrictive purpose rather than empowering human beings. While some observers continue to express unease about a human rights norm that obliges State parties to prohibit certain speech acts, others interpret this prohibition as the corollary to an implicit right of everyone to be free from incitement to acts of hatred, a right particularly significant for members of ethnic, religious or other minorities. Unsurprisingly, the precise contours of the prohibition of incitement – definitions, thresholds, remedies – remain contested, and the relationship of this particular provision to other human rights guarantees, in particular freedom of expression, continues to cause controversies.

Within UN fora, the new attention to incitement was preceded by a decade of emotional debates on how to deal with the issue of 'defamation of religions'. Between 1999 and 2010 the Organizations of the Islamic Conference (now: Organization of Islamic Cooperation (OIC)), regularly tabled resolutions titled 'combating defamation of religions', which repeatedly led to a split within the UN membership. In order to overcome an increasingly sterile antagonism, new formulas were proposed, with a view to facilitating more meaningful discussions. In all those new formulas, 'incitement' figures as a key term. In March 2011 the OIC tabled Human Rights Council Resolution 16/18 on (inter alia) incitement, which was adopted without a vote and has served as a main reference document in the UN. In October 2012 a series of expert seminars organized by the Office of the High Commissioner for Human Rights culminated in the Rabat Plan of Action on the prohibition of advocacy of national, racial or religious hatred that constitutes incitement to discrimination, hostility or violence.

Religious incitement is merely one kind of incitement alongside other forms. However, in the wake of a decade of controversies over 'defamation of religions', the new attention paid to incitement has much to do with hateful conflicts around (or ascribed to) religious differences. Many observers welcomed the move from 'defamation' to 'incitement' as an important step. Whereas the concept of defamation was linked to projects of protecting the reputations of certain religions, the prohibition of incitement focuses on human beings, individuals and communities, and thus seems to fit better with the general human rights approach. However, one should bear in mind that the Penal Codes of many states have overly broad anti-incitement laws, which can be as damaging to freedom of expression and other human rights as traditional anti-blasphemy laws. The Rabat Plan of Action therefore places great emphasis on the significance of freedom of expression as the *sine qua non* to public discourses. While defining a very high threshold for restrictive measures, in accordance with international human rights law, the Rabat Plan of Action encourages states and other stakeholders to invest mainly in 'positive speech' as the most promising strategy for countering incitement.

Jeroen Temperman's study on the prohibition of incitement in international law comes at the right moment. In view of highly politicized current debates, Temperman provides a detailed and comprehensive analysis with an unprecedented depth. When dealing with the *travaux préparatoires* of international incitement provisions, he reminds us of largely forgotten debates that took place generations ago. When taking stock of various individual cases and country assessment, he at the same time describes the learning curve in international courts and monitoring agencies. And by comparing global, regional and national developments, he further broadens the awareness of very different experiences in this area.

I hope that Jeroen Temperman's book will find many readers. The book will doubtless contribute to a more solid debate on a complicated human rights provision, which itself will certainly continue to trigger many controversies.

Heiner Bielefeldt, UN Special Rapporteur
on freedom of religion or belief

ACKNOWLEDGEMENTS

This monograph is the result of a four-year research project, most generously supported by the Erasmus University Rotterdam in the form of an EUR-Fellowship. I am grateful to the Fulbright Program for sponsoring an extended research leave, which enabled the final write-up. Thanks also to American University Washington College of Law, especially to Claudia Martin, for hosting me during my 2014 sabbatical. Thanks to Sander van de Laar for his help in finalizing the tables. Thanks to the team at Cambridge University Press, in particular Elizabeth Spicer, and to the copy editor Lorraine Slipper and project manager Rob Wilkinson, for their invaluable contributions during the production process. Special thanks go to Ellen Hey, chair of the Department of International and European Union Law at Erasmus School of Law, for stimulating this project and for providing me with the best possible research conditions.

Legal developments are reflected up until 1 January 2015.

TABLE OF INTERNATIONAL LAW

TABLE OF NATIONAL LAW

Brazil

Bulgaria

Canada

Chile

Colombia

Croatia

Cyprus

Czech Republic

Denmark

Ecuador

Estonia

Finland

France

Georgia

Germany

Romania

Russia

San Marino

Santa Lucia

Serbia

Singapore

Slovakia

United Kingdom

United States

Uruguay

TABLE OF INTERNATIONAL CASES

Human Rights Committee

Committee on the Elimination of Racial Discrimination

European Court of Human Rights (incl. decisions by the former European Commission of Human Rights)

Inter-American Court of Human Rights

TABLE OF NATIONAL CASES

Switzerland

United Kingdom

United States

1

Introduction

1.1 Background

Liberal states harbour a fundamental contradiction at their core.[1] On the one hand, they cherish the right to freedom of expression. On the other hand, they insist that citizens should be treated equally and protected from discrimination and violence. States wary of social hostility may be inclined to combat forms of 'extreme speech'. Indeed, some states have taken measures to outlaw sources of social unrest that are liable to upset, for example, the religious sensitivities of citizens by criminalizing speech through blasphemy laws, religious defamation laws or through hate speech laws. Critics of such policies respond that the only effective response to extreme speech is *more speech*.[2] That is, they suggest that the 'marketplace of ideas' should be permitted to do its work: in a liberal state publicly made extreme statements will trigger sufficient counter-balancing speech to ensure that fighting words will remain just that – fighting *words*.[3] Moreover, some would argue, if we rely on hate

---

[1] From the outset it should be noted that in this study we are concerned with a *liberal* dilemma. Regimes that themselves publicly incite discrimination or violence against religious minorities do not raise our dilemma in a meaningful way. Sections 1.1 and 1.2 of this introduction draw on Jeroen Temperman, 'Blasphemy Versus Incitement', in Christopher Beneke *et al.* (eds.), *Profane: Sacrilegious Expression in a Multicultural Age* (University of California Press, 2014), 401–25.

[2] As forcefully put by Justice Brandeis in his concurring opinion in the US Supreme Court decision in *Whitney* v. *California*, 274 U.S. 357 (1927), arguing that '[t]o courageous, self-reliant men, with confidence in the power of free and fearless reasoning applied through the processes of popular government, no danger flowing from speech can be deemed clear and present, unless the incidence of the evil apprehended is so imminent that it may befall before there is opportunity for full discussion. If there be time to expose through discussion the falsehood and fallacies, to avert the evil by the processes of education, the remedy to be applied is more speech, not enforced silence.'

[3] US Supreme Court Justice Oliver Wendell Holmes is credited with developing the notion of the marketplace of ideas. *Abrams* v. *United States*, 250 U.S. 616 (1919). In his dissenting opinion Justice Holmes argued that freedom of expression is best reached by 'free trade in ideas' in 'the competition of the market'.

speech laws, there is a risk that we lose our natural inclination to actively fight bad ideas. It was for the latter reason that John Stuart Mill defended a fierce form of freedom of expression:

> even if the received opinion be not only true, but the whole truth; unless it is suffered to be, and actually is, vigorously and earnestly contested, it will, by most of those who receive it, be held in the manner of a prejudice, with little comprehension or feeling of its rational grounds. And not only this, but ... the meaning of the doctrine itself will be in danger of being lost, or enfeebled, and deprived of its vital effect on the character and conduct: the dogma becoming a mere formal profession, inefficacious for good, but cumbering the ground, and preventing the growth of any real and heartfelt conviction, from reason or personal experience.[4]

The marketplace defence of free speech has it critics, though. One concern may be that counter-speech by the targeted groups or individuals themselves may be encumbered by the fact that they are oftentimes at a socially disadvantageous position, while, at the same time, not all such groups can count on others to speak up for them.[5] Still others would argue that unbridled free speech sounds all well and good in states with a strong constitutional tradition of fundamental rights protection, but that such absolute freedom is perilous in non-liberal or non-democratic states, or states with a history of religious or ethnic tensions. What, some ask, about genocidal societies?[6] William Schabas made this point forcefully when he wrote that '[a] well-read and well-informed *genocidaire* will know that at

---

[4] John Stuart Mill, *On Liberty* (London: John W. Parker & Sons, 1859), at chapter 2.

[5] See Ishani Maitra and Mary Kate McGowan, 'Introduction and Overview', in Ishani Maitra and Mary Kate McGowan (eds.), *Speech & Harm: Controversies Over Free Speech* (Oxford University Press, 2012), 1–23, at 9. Nielsen makes the point that the marketplace doctrine is premised on faulty empirical assumptions, showing that hate speech targets in particular, for various reasons, typically do not respond to verbal attacks and that the 'more speech' ideal (i.e. counter-speech) is often easier to invoke than actually carry out. Laura Beth Nielsen, 'Power in Public: Reactions, Responses, and Resistance to Offensive Public Speech', in Maitra and McGowan (eds.), *Speech & Harm*, 148–73. For that reason it has been proposed that hate speech policies, rather than penalizing hate speakers, could focus on empowering hate speech targets to speak up by providing them with the necessary institutional, educational and material support. See Katharine Gelber, '"Speaking Back": The Likely Faith of Hate Speech Policy in the United States and Australia', in Maitra and McGowan (eds.), *Speech & Harm*, 50–71. For concerns about the true potential of counter-speech, see also Caroline West, 'Words that Silence? Freedom of Expression and Racist Hate Speech', in Maitra and McGowan (eds.), *Speech & Harm*, 222–48.

[6] In the words of Schabas, '[t]he road to genocide in Rwanda was paved with hate speech.' William A. Schabas, 'Hate Speech in Rwanda: the Road to Genocide', (2000) 46 *McGill LJ* 141–71, at 144. See also Lynne Tirrell, 'Genocidal Language Games', in *Speech & Harm*, 174–221.

the early stages of planning of the "crime of crimes", his or her money is best spent not in purchasing machetes, or Kalashnikovs, or Zyklon B gas, but rather investing in radio transmitters and photocopy machines.'[7]

This is thus our liberal dilemma: a choice between absolute freedom of expression, albeit perpetually accompanied by the risk that the rights of minorities might be undermined by hateful, extremist factions;[8] *or* pro-active prevention of the undermining of minority rights through anti-incitement legislation, albeit at the sacrifice of absolute free speech.[9] As this book takes an international law perspective, and seeing as international law has made a tentative choice in favour of – albeit *high*-threshold – restrictions,[10] the dilemma for – many[11] – states is more

---

[7] Schabas, 'Hate Speech in Rwanda', at 171.

[8] See e.g. Ronald Dworkin, 'A New Map of Censorship' (2006) 1 *Index on Censorship* 130–3 and Ronald Dworkin, 'Foreword', in Ivan Hare and James Weinstein (eds.), *Extreme Speech and Democracy* (Oxford University Press, 2009), v–ix; Ivan Hare and James Weinstein, 'Free Speech, Democracy, and the Suppression of Extreme Speech Past and Present', in Hare and Weinstein (eds.), *Extreme Speech and Democracy*, 1–7; James Weinstein, *Hate Speech, Pornography, and the Radical Attack on Free Speech Doctrine* (Boulder: Westview Press, 1999); Eric Heinze, 'Viewpoint Absolutism and Hate Speech' (2006) 69:4 *Modern Law Review* 543–82; C. Edwin Baker, 'Autonomy and Hate Speech', in Hare and Weinstein (eds.), *Extreme Speech and Democracy*, 139–57; Kent Greenawalt, *Fighting Words* (Princeton University Press, 1996), particularly at 63 (he does, however, predict that US courts will shift more in the direction of the Canadian approach to hate speech, at 151) and more generally Kent Greenawalt, *Speech, Crime, and the Uses of Language* (Oxford University Press, 1989), for instance at 301; Miklos Haraszti, 'Hate Speech and the Coming Death of the International Standard Before It Was Born (Complaints of a Watchdog)', foreword in Michael Herz and Peter Molnar (eds.), *The Content and Context of Hate Speech: Rethinking Regulation and Responses* (Cambridge University Press, 2012), xiii–xviii; for an argument against religious hatred laws specifically, see Eric Barendt, 'Religious Hatred Laws: Protecting Groups or Belief?' (2011) 17 *Res Publica* 41–54.

[9] See e.g., Jeremy Waldron, *The Harm in Hate Speech* (Cambridge, MA: Harvard University Press, 2012) and Jeremy Waldron, 'Dignity and Defamation: The Visibility of Hate' (2010) 123 *Harvard Law Review* 1596–657. Further, see Eric Barendt, *Freedom of Speech* (2nd rev. edn, Oxford University Press, 2007), accepting the rationale of certain anti-racist hate speech laws (at 170–86) yet being critical of most religion-oriented incitement laws (at 189–92). See also Toby Mendel, 'Does International Law Provide for Consistent Rules on Hate Speech?', in Herz and Molnar (eds.), *The Content and Context of Hate Speech*, 417–29; Steven J. Heyman, 'Hate Speech, Public Discourse, and the First Amendment', in Hare and Weinstein (eds.), *Extreme Speech and Democracy*, 158–82; Bhikhu Parekh, 'Is there a Case for Banning Hate Speech', in Herz and Molnar (eds.), *The Content and Context of Hate Speech*, 37–56; Michael Rosenfeld, 'Hate Speech in Constitutional Jurisprudence: A Comparative Analysis' (2003) 24 *Cardozo Law Review* 1523–67; David Kretzmer, 'Freedom of Speech and Racism' (1986–1987) 8 *Cardozo Law Review* 445–513.

[10] See Art. 20(2) ICCPR, and Art. 4 ICERD.

[11] Yet not, for instance, the USA, which has made reservations to those internationally mandated restrictions on extreme speech.

nuanced than that. Our liberal dilemma proper, then, is *how to prevent abuses* emanating from the fact that, through international law, states are offered tools for restriction *whilst taking seriously* the goods those tools are supposed to protect: minority rights, freedom from violence and persecution, and freedom from discrimination.

This book explores what equilibrium between free speech on the one hand, and avoiding hatred-based marginalization of *religious* groups specifically on the other, international law envisages. The key contention is that international human rights law is increasingly distinguishing between (unacceptable) laws that combat blasphemy, religious defamation and unqualified forms of 'hate speech' on the one hand, and (acceptable) incitement laws that specifically target forms of hate propaganda likely to stir up violence and discrimination. The former set of laws look to the protection of targeted groups against 'direct harm' stemming from hate speech and other insulting forms of speech. Incitement laws look to 'indirect harm', that is, the extent to which extreme speech acts influence an audience to engage in actions – discrimination or violence – against a target group.

The underlying rationale of that particular development is that such unqualified insult and hate speech laws are liable to foster governmental abuse. Governments – potentially working in tandem with the country's dominant religion – could use, and some are indeed known to use,[12] such laws to stifle unpopular speech so as to retain the status quo. Incitement legislation, by contrast, could – in the abstract – offer an important contribution to two of international human rights law's foundational goals: equality and freedom from fear.

This book's objective is to scrutinize if and to what extent Article 20(2) of the International Covenant on Civil and Political Rights (ICCPR) helps to 'solve' our liberal dilemma.[13] The importance and relevance of further conceptualizing Article 20(2) ICCPR can hardly be overstated. Article 20(2) ICCPR is a rather cryptic provision. Whereas Article 4 of the International Convention on the Elimination of All Forms of Racial Discrimination (ICERD) has from the outset worked as a catalyst for the elimination of racial discrimination,[14] for the first forty years of its

---

[12] Paul Marshall and Nina Shea, *Silenced: How Apostasy & Blasphemy Codes are Choking Freedom Worldwide* (Oxford University Press, 2011).

[13] International Covenant on Civil and Political Rights, adopted by General Assembly Resolution 2200A (XXI) of 16 December 1966, entry into force 23 March 1976.

[14] International Convention on the Elimination of All Forms of Racial Discrimination, adopted by General Assembly Resolution 2106 (XX) of 21 December 1965, entry into force 4 January 1969.

existence Article 20(2) ICCPR certainly has not had a similar role in relation to eradicating religious discrimination or religious strife. Even *within* Article 20(2) one can see how international monitoring bodies as well as national policy makers and judges have hitherto focused on the grounds of *racial* and *national* hatred, not on *religious* hatred.[15]

Speech critical of race is, naturally, categorically abject and repugnant; speech critical of religion is not necessarily so. Discourse critical of religion may be perceived as hateful by religious adherents; however, such critical discourse in actual fact may very well amount to a *free exercise* of religion and ought to be protected, not combated, by states. Thus regulations in the area of religious speech or speech concerning religions may well have an unduly 'chilling effect' on free speech and may moreover constitute unjustifiable restrictions on freedom of religion.

That said, State parties to the ICCPR have pledged to take action with respect to any advocacy of religious hatred whenever that hate propaganda constitutes *incitement* to discrimination, hostility or violence. That is the red flag they have accepted. Yet without further benchmarking, that particular internationally mandated limit may and in fact does trigger a host of widely differing state practices on extreme speech. Louis-Léon Christians has observed that the current situation in Europe alone is for this reason highly complex: 'Although almost every European State legislates for the criminal offence of incitement to national, racial or religious hatred, the geometry of such offences is very variable both because of the wording used in each case and because there are alternative offences to be taken into account in every national system.'[16]

Indeed, as long as further benchmarks concerning the international incitement prohibition are lacking, data collection and fact-finding will be highly problematic.[17] Lacking sound definitions, conceptualizations, criteria in relation to such questions as the content, intent, or context of incitement, we cannot comparatively monitor incidents of incitement in the State parties to the ICCPR or other international agreements containing incitement prohibitions. We cannot compare and contrast successful prosecutions; nor can we flag situations where under the international standards state authorities should have acted more proactively (i.e. to

---

[15] Louis-Léon Christians, *Study for the European Expert Workshop on the Prohibition of Incitement to National, Racial or Religious Hatred* (OHCHR expert seminar on Article 20(2) ICCPR, 9–10 February 2011, Vienna) (hereafter *Study on Incitement*), at 2.

[16] Christians, *Study on Incitement*, at 5.

[17] Alexander Verkhovsky, *Data-Collection and Fact-Finding* (OHCHR expert seminar on Article 20(2) ICCPR, 9–10 February 2011, Vienna).

discharge their 'positive obligations': consider the role of victims to incitement, access to justice, but also proactively promote tolerance through, for instance, education, and liaise with the media). Also, importantly, lacking sound concepts makes it hard to condemn *abuses*. Incidents that have led to prosecutions and convictions that never should have, from an international law perspective, led to interferences with free speech must be consistently berated.

1.2   Our liberal dilemma embedded in wider international developments

With respect to the issue of extreme speech about or motivated by religion, we have recently witnessed two contradictory developments within the United Nations.[18] For over a decade, political bodies such as the General Assembly and the Human Rights Council (and the former Commission on Human Rights) have pushed for more rigorous international and national measures combating 'defamation of religion'.[19] These UN Resolutions, proposed by the Organization of Islamic Cooperation, have been vehemently criticized by legal scholars, who argue that combating defamation of religion would be tantamount to destroying not only the core right of freedom of expression, but also the right to freedom of religion.[20] The latter, after all,

---

[18] For a more comprehensive analysis, see Jeroen Temperman, 'Blasphemy, Defamation of Religions and Human Rights Law,' (2008) 26:4 *Netherlands Quarterly of Human Rights* 517–45; Jeroen Temperman, 'Freedom of Expression and Religious Sensitivities in Pluralist Societies: Facing the Challenge of Extreme Speech', (2011) 3 *Brigham Young University Law Review* 729–57; and Jeroen Temperman, 'The Emerging Counter-Defamation of Religion Discourse: A Critical Analysis', (2010) 4 *Annuaire Droit et Religion* 553–9.

[19] E.g. Commission on Human Rights, Resolution 1999/82 on 'Defamation of Religions' of 30 April 1999; Resolution 2001/4 on 'Combating Defamation of Religions as a Means to Promote Human Rights, Social Harmony and Religious and Cultural Diversity' of 18 April 2001; Resolution 2002/9 on 'Combating Defamation of Religions' of 15 April 2002; Resolution 2003/4 on 'Combating Defamation of Religions' of 14 April 2003; Resolution 2004/6 on 'Combating Defamation of Religions' of 13 April 2004; and Resolution 2005/3 on 'Combating Defamation of Religions' of 12 April 2005. This trend was subsequently continued by the Human Rights Council: see, e.g., Resolution 4/9 on 'Combating Defamation of Religions' of 30 March 2007; and Resolution 7/19 on 'Combating Defamation of Religions' of 27 March 2008. See also General Assembly Resolutions 60/150 of 16 December 2005, 61/164 of 19 December 2006 and 62/154 of 18 December 2007 (all on 'Combating Defamation of Religions').

[20] A selection: Temperman, 'Blasphemy, Defamation of Religions and Human Rights Law'; L. Bennett Graham, 'Defamation of Religions: The End of Pluralism?' (2009) 23

includes the right to manifest beliefs that may be heretical, defamatory or blasphemous to another person.

More recently, as of 2011, the tone of these Resolutions has been moderated to accommodate Western criticism: the Resolutions are now entitled 'Combating intolerance, negative stereotyping and stigmatization of, and discrimination, incitement to violence and violence against, persons based on religion or belief'.[21] On their face the revamped Resolutions – commencing with Human Rights Council Resolution 16/18 – accord better with standards of international human rights law, since they condemn more expressly incitement rather than plain defamation.[22] Scholars and human rights NGOs have indicated how this new focus on combating intolerance and incitement in practice could and should serve to promote *existing* international human rights standards (rather than introduce new, potentially harmful concepts).[23] Within legal scholarship there remains, at the same time, real anxiety that future political Resolutions, or misinterpretation of the existing ones, will serve as justifications for national practices that unduly stifle speech critical of majority religions.[24]

Emory International Law Review 69–84; Sejal Parmar, 'The Challenge of "Defamation of Religions" to Freedom of Expression and the International Human Rights System' (2009) 3 *European Human Rights Law Review* 353–75; Allison G. Belnap, 'Defamation of Religions: A Vague and Overbroad Theory that Threatens Basic Human Rights' (2010) *Brigham Young University Law Review* 635–85; Rebecca J. Dobras, 'Is the United Nations Endorsing Human Rights Violations?: An Analysis of the United Nations' Combating Defamation of Religious Resolutions and Pakistan's Blasphemy Laws' *Georgia Journal of International & Comparative Law* 37 (2009) 339–80; and most recently and comprehensively, Lorenz Langer, *Religious Offence and Human Rights* (Cambridge University Press, 2014).

[21] E.g. Human Rights Council Resolution 16/18, 'Combating intolerance, negative stereotyping and stigmatization of, and discrimination, incitement to violence and violence against, persons based on religion or belief' (UN Doc. A/HRC/RES/16/18, adopted on 24 March 2011). See also the parallel revamped General Assembly Resolutions: General Assembly Resolution 66/167, 'Combating intolerance, negative stereotyping, stigmatization, discrimination, incitement to violence and violence against persons, based on religion or belief' (UN Doc. A/RES/66/167, adopted on 19 December 2011); and General Assembly Resolution 67/178, 'Combating intolerance, negative stereotyping, stigmatization, discrimination, incitement to violence and violence against persons, based on religion or belief' (UN Doc. A/RES/67/178, adopted on 20 December 2012).

[22] E.g. A/HRC/RES/16/18, para. 3.

[23] Notably, see Universal Rights Group, *Combatting Global Religious Intolerance: The Implementation of Human Rights Council Resolution 16/18* (Policy Report, 2014).

[24] E.g. Robert C. Blitt, 'Defamation of Religion: Rumors of Its Death are Greatly Exaggerated' (2011) 62 *Case Western Reserve Law Review* 347–97. The Universal Rights Group report, mentioned in the previous note, shares these concerns and even speaks in terms of helping states to bring the implementation of this Resolution 'back on track' (at 4 and 7).

While the General Assembly and the Human Rights Council have pushed for restrictions on religious defamation, UN independent experts have been pushing states to affirm existing international norms – which standards imply that many states ought to narrow rather than widen definitions of punishable speech. The timing of these expert interventions suggests that they are in direct reaction to ongoing developments within the said political bodies of the UN. For instance, the UN Special Rapporteur on freedom of religion or belief, an independent expert, has held that defamation of religion does not in itself adversely impact the freedom of religion, and thus does not necessarily engage international law.[25] Indeed, the Special Rapporteur called national criminal bans on defamation of religion 'counter-productive'.[26] Further, the Human Rights Committee, which monitors compliance with the ICCPR, officially treats blasphemy and religious defamation bans as violations of international law and calls for their removal. Newly adopted General Comment No. 34 observes that: 'Prohibitions of displays of lack of respect for a religion or other belief system, including blasphemy laws, *are incompatible with the Covenant.*'[27] Thus, according to the Committee, unqualified forms of defamation of religion (blasphemy, disrespect of religion, gratuitously offensive speech, satire, religious criticism, etc.) shall not be combated by states.

The UN Special Rapporteur on freedom of expression has also warned against lowering free speech standards in the – alleged – interest of freedom of religion. Rapporteur Ligabo argued that:

> with increased frequency, particularly due to events that dominated international politics recently, an alleged dichotomy between the right to freedom of opinion and expression and the right to freedom of religion or belief has been purported. In particular, it has been argued that the dogmatic use of freedom of expression as a fundamental human right has undermined people's ability to fully enjoy other human rights, in particular freedom of religion. The Special Rapporteur strongly rejects such a view.[28]

---

[25] *Report of the Special Rapporteur on Freedom of Religion or Belief, Asma Jahangir, and the Special Rapporteur on Contemporary Forms of Racism, Racial Discrimination, Xenophobia and Related Intolerance, Doudou Diène, Further to Human Rights Council Decision 1/107 on Incitement to Racial and Religious Hatred and the Promotion of Tolerance* (UN Doc. A/HRC/2/3, 20 September 2006), paras. 36–39.

[26] A/HRC/2/3, para. 42.

[27] Human Rights Committee, *General Comment 34: Article 19: Freedoms of Opinion and Expression* (CCPR/C/GC/34, adopted at its 102nd session, Geneva, 11–29 July 2011), para. 48 (emphasis added).

[28] A/HRC/7/14, para. 63.

Indeed, freedom of expression and freedom of religion are not perpetually in conflict; nor are these fundamental freedoms automatically at odds any time someone says something critical or shocking about a religious belief.

In fact, international law already has norms in place for the most extreme forms of speech about religion or motivated by religion. The latter Special Rapporteur, too, emphasizes:

> that existing international instruments establish a clear limit on freedom of expression. In particular, the International Covenant on Civil and Political Rights provides that ... 'any advocacy of national, racial or religious hatred that constitutes incitement to discrimination, hostility or violence shall be prohibited by law'. The main problem thus lies in identifying at which point exactly these thresholds are reached.[29]

The latter problem is precisely what forms the problem statement of the present book: when is the threshold of incitement within the meaning of international human rights law reached, and what, then, marks the difference with low-threshold defamation of religion (protected by freedom of expression)? Moreover, how can a 'combating incitement' approach avoid the pitfalls of abuse that the 'combating defamation' approach so clearly fails to avoid? In the words of the Special Rapporteur on freedom of expression, our research into the question of punishable incitement:

> should meet a number of requirements. In particular, it should not justify any type of prior censorship, it should be clearly and narrowly defined, it should be the least intrusive means in what concerns limitations to freedom of expression and it should be applied by an independent judiciary ... [T]hese limitations are designed to protect individuals rather than belief systems, guaranteeing that every person will have all of his or her human rights protected.[30]

This book proposes to address this challenge in the following ways.

---

[29] A/HRC/7/14, para. 65.

[30] A/HRC/7/14, 65. In the next paragraph the Rapporteur notes that 'a broader interpretation of these limitations, which has been recently suggested in international forums, is not in line with existing international instruments and would ultimately jeopardize the full enjoyment of human rights.' This is a reference to the combating defamation of religion approach.

1.3   Outline

This book enquires into the legislative and judicial obligations that flow from the international prohibition on hateful incitement as enshrined in the International Bill of Rights. Some 160 states have,[31] by ratifying the ICCPR, pledged to 'prohibit by law' *any advocacy of national, racial or religious hatred that constitutes incitement to discrimination, hostility or violence* (Article 20, paragraph 2, ICCPR). The leading question is: which speech acts engage this prohibition and in respect of this ban what are the precise legislative and judicial obligations of State parties?

It should be noted from the outset that there is a consensus among stakeholders that Article 20(2) ICCPR presupposes civil and administrative law sanctions and measures in addition to criminal law responses to incitement; moreover, it is widely understood that any anti-incitement toolbox ought to include non-legal approaches as well as legal ones.[32] For

---

[31] I.e. all ICCPR State parties minus the seven states that have made reservations to Art. 20 ICCPR. Australia, Belgium, Luxembourg, Malta, New Zealand, United Kingdom and the United States have deposited reservations or interpretative declarations that limit their obligations under Art. 20(2), typically to the effect that no further national legislation shall be deemed to be required under the terms of this provision. A number of states have entered reservations to Art. 20(1) on war propaganda.

[32] *Rabat Plan of Action on the Prohibition of Advocacy of National, Racial or Religious Hatred that Constitutes Incitement to Discrimination, Hostility or Violence* (Conclusions and recommendations emanating from the four regional expert workshops organized by OHCHR in 2011 and adopted by experts in Rabat, Morocco on 5 October 2012), paras. 23–29; Committee on the Elimination of Racial Discrimination, *General Recommendation 35: Combating Racist Hate Speech* (UN Doc. CERD/C/GC/35, 83rd session, 12–30 August 2013), paras. 30–44, listing a comprehensive set of positive measures; Special Rapporteur on Freedom of Religion or Belief, *Tackling Manifestations of Collective Religious Hatred* (A/HRC/25/58, 26 December 2013), particularly paras. 31–53; Special Rapporteur on the Promotion and Protection of the Right to Freedom of Opinion and Expression, *Report of the Special Rapporteur to the General Assembly on Hate Speech and Incitement to Hatred* (A/67/357, 7 September 2012), particularly paras. 56–74; ARTICLE 19, *Prohibiting Incitement to Discrimination, Hostility or Violence: Policy Brief* (2012), at 41–45 ('Sanctions and other measures'). For scholarly accounts on non-legal approaches to incitement, see e.g. Peter Molnar, 'Responding to "Hate Speech" with Art, Education, and the Imminent Danger Test', in Herz and Molnar (eds.), *The Content and Context of Hate Speech*, 183–97; Maleiha Malik, 'Extreme Speech and Liberalism', in Ivan Hare and James Weinstein (eds.), *Extreme Speech and Democracy* (Oxford University Press, 2009), 96–120; David Richards, *Free Speech and the Politics of Identity* (Oxford University Press, 1999), particularly chapters 4 to 6, presenting ways to promote counter-speech as a remedy; Katrine Gelber, 'Reconceptualizing Counterspeech in Hate Speech Policy', in Herz and Molnar (eds.), *The Content and Context of Hate Speech*, 198–216; Arthur Jacobson and Bernhard Schlink, 'Hate Speech and Self-Restraint', in Herz and Molnar (eds.), *The Content and Context of Hate Speech*, 217–41.

instance, tolerance, pluralism, 'social consciousness', sensitization and inter-cultural dialogue can be promoted through soft-law policies in the areas of education, the media, civil society, and through the state liaising with inter-faith and other religious organizations, as well as religious and political leaders. Let us be clear, however, that this book ventures chiefly into the legal side of the debate and, more specifically, into the criminal law ramifications of Article 20(2) ICCPR.

The book's problem statement and its leading research question can be broken down into the following parts, sub-questions and specific issues.

The origins of the incitement prohibition. What is the genesis of the international prohibition of religion-based or religion-oriented hateful incitement? The first part of the book gives an overview of the historical debates that led to the adoption of Article 7 of the Universal Declaration of Human Rights (UDHR) and Article 20(2) of the ICCPR. We will chart the different drafting proposals and analyse how they differed from each other. By doing so, we will also get a sense of the main concerns and challenges that motivated the proponents and opponents of the provision against hateful incitement. From those debates it transpires that the original inception of the prohibition of advocacy of national, racial or religious hatred should be understood against the backdrop of the Second World War and the Holocaust, indicating the extreme nature of the type of 'incitement' the drafters had in mind. Notwithstanding that, we will see that the drafting history leaves many questions concerning the incitement provision unanswered. For starters, we do not find definitions of the clause's constituent terms such as 'advocacy', 'hatred' or 'incitement'. Neither do we find there answers to threshold questions on the required gravity of the speech. Also, in history alone we do not find answers to questions of national implementation, nor on evidentiary issues.

The legal nature of the incitement prohibition. Can a right to be protected against incitement be distilled from international law? Once we have a better understanding of the genesis of the international incitement prohibition, we will delve into its legal nature in Part II of the book. Article 20 is most certainly the odd one out in the ICCPR. In addition to establishing the mandatory nature of this provision, we will seek an answer to the question of whether the incitement prohibition can additionally be construed as a 'right'. On the face of it, this provision does not enumerate another fundamental right but rather merely a *sui generis* state obligation. What is more, that principle or obligation may be construed as a special limit on other fundamental rights, notably the right to freedom of expression. Article 20(2) ICCPR is one of the very few cases in international human rights law where international law a priori settles a human rights conflict: in favour of combating incitement – and hence in favour of non-discrimination, the right to life, physical integrity, freedom from fear, and such underlying norms[33] – and at the expense of unbridled free speech. Notwithstanding this peculiar nature of the incitement provision, by way of preliminary legal assessment this part of the book addresses the question as to whether a 'right to be free from incitement' can be distilled from Article 20(2) of the ICCPR. The question's relevance, among other issues, lies in the area of legal standing: should the incitement prohibition be just that – a 'mere' prohibition – then it will mostly if not exclusively function as a legitimizing factor for interfering with an alleged inciter's free speech. If the incitement prohibition has as its flip-side a fundamental right to be free from incitement, then an incitement *victim* may have a claim against a state that fails to combat incitement. In this regard the workings of the Human Rights Committee under Article 20(2) ICCPR are compared with the views of the Committee on the Elimination of Racial Discrimination and the European Court of Human Rights.

The *actus reus* of the incitement offence. Which acts amount to 'incitement' in the meaning of international law and what are the state's legislative duties in relation to this offence? This part of the book seeks to define and conceptualize incitement within the meaning of international law. Specifically, the *actus reus* of the incitement offence dictated by Article 20(2) of the ICCPR is determined. To that end, the meaning of the incitement prohibition's constituent terms – 'advocacy', *'religious* hatred',[34] 'incitement', 'discrimination', 'hostility' and 'violence' – will be unravelled. A careful examination of Article 20(2) ICCPR supports the view that the threshold of this extreme speech provision is very high. The article's qualified – if somewhat cryptic and convoluted – formulation

---

[33] Proponents of incitement laws have formulated different values that are in the balance, i.e. to be weighed with free speech. Waldron submits that what incitement laws seek to protect is 'dignity'. Waldron, *The Harm in Hate Speech*, at 105–43. Heyman formulates several rights that may deserve protection: 'personal security', 'rights of personality', and the 'right to recognition'. Heyman, 'Hate Speech', at 165–9.

[34] While this provision also refers to 'national' and 'racial' hatred, the focus of this book is chiefly on 'religious' hatred. It is the inclusion of 'religious hatred' that makes the ICCPR's incitement clause unique (*cf.* Article 4 ICERD). Also, it is this type of hatred that thus far is least conceptualized in international law.

leaves no doubt as to the extreme nature of the speech required to trigger the ban. One of the key contentions of this book is that Article 20(2) does not purport to ban 'hate speech'. The provision requires national prohibitions of certain *qualified* types of extreme speech, namely those that incite certain adverse responses: discrimination, hostility or violence. The drafters of the ICCPR realized that the community of states is hardly in a position to ban all expression of hatred, let alone 'hatred' per se. Given the qualified nature of the adopted prohibition, we must conclude that not all 'externalized' forms of hatred ought to be subject to prosecution, but only those externalizations that incite to one of the proscribed actions (discrimination, hostility or violence). Accordingly, the incitement offence will be construed as a triangular act. For Article 20(2) of the ICCPR to be engaged, it takes an inciter and a target group, as well as an audience likely to act imminently upon the inciteful speech act.

Judging incitement. Which implementation, judicial and evidentiary obligations flow from international standards on hateful incitement? In this part of the book the question as to how state authorities can legitimately convict someone of the incitement offence in the meaning of Article 20(2) of the ICCPR is addressed. First and foremost, how can state authorities prove that someone committed this offence? To that effect the question is addressed as to whether international standards on hateful incitement require proof of intent or another degree of *mens rea*. Again, the workings of the Human Rights Committee are compared and contrasted to that of other international monitoring bodies. Further (judicial) enforcement obligations lie in the area of proving that the impugned speech act in actual fact reached the level of gravity required under international law. Article 20(2) of the Covenant implores State parties to prohibit (only) those hateful speech acts that constitute incitement. Although the offence of incitement is by definition an inchoate crime, the question of the likelihood of harm, which can be distilled both from the necessity test as well as from the incitement definition itself, matters. And since the actual risk emanating from incitement is per definition a contextual matter, it will be argued that national judges are to ensure that 'context' factors are taken into account in addition to 'content' factors. Building on recent benchmarks, such as the *Rabat Plan of Action*, Human Rights Committee's *General Comment No. 34* and the Committee on the Elimination of Racial Discrimination's *General Recommendation No. 35* on racial hate speech, such context factors as the overall socio-political context, the position and role of the speaker, the extent of the speech, the position of the target group and likelihood/imminence are analysed.

Punishing incitement. What sanctions are envisaged by international standards against incitement? In the final part of the book we consider sanctions and aggravating factors. As for the latter, the question is addressed if it matters whether incitement is committed alone or in an organized capacity. The question of sanctions is twofold. First, there is the general question of what types of sanction are generally envisaged by the ICCPR and other international human rights treaties with respect to the offence of hateful incitement. Second, what penalties can judges mete out in concrete incitement cases? The latter question essentially asks what factors determine the necessity and proportionality of a penalty in a concrete incitement case.

1.4   A note on methodology

Seeking to conceptualize the prohibition of incitement in international law, this study's prime legal yardstick is the UN International Covenant on Civil and Political Rights. The Human Rights Committee's workings in the area of Article 20(2) of the ICCPR are, where possible and relevant, compared and contrasted with approaches adopted by the Committee on the Elimination of Racial Discrimination and the (regional) European Court of Human Rights. In addition, extensive comparative legal analysis provides us with insights into how parties to the ICCPR are discharging their obligations under Article 20(2). Comparative analysis provides a unique opportunity to take stock of the widely diverging forms of state practice – including both good and bad practice – in the area of incitement.

PART I

The genesis of the prohibition of religious hatred constituting incitement in international law

Pre-ICCPR developments

2.1 Introduction

One will find no clear predecessor of Article 20 ICCPR in the 1948 Universal Declaration of Human Rights,[1] although there are some first hints. Discussing those 'hints' in this chapter, first a brief overview of what the UDHR offers on freedom of expression and the issue of incitement is presented. Subsequently, we will delve into the most pertinent historical debates leading up to the adoption of the relevant UDHR articles. Finally, some of the unresolved legal questions flowing from the relevant UDHR articles are flagged.

2.2 The Universal Declaration of Human Rights and extreme speech

The final version of the UDHR, as adopted on 10 December 1948 by the General Assembly of the United Nations, contains in Article 19 the general right to freedom of expression:

> Everyone has the right to freedom of opinion and expression; this right includes freedom to hold opinions without interference and to seek, receive and impart information and ideas through any media and regardless of frontiers.

The later to be adopted Article 19 ICCPR distinguishes more clearly between the *freedom of opinion* and the *freedom of expression*,[2] and deems the former freedom more outspokenly absolute whilst subjecting the latter freedom to certain restrictions.[3] Where the drafters of the ICCPR later on saw it fit to gear multiple limitation clauses specifically toward the

---

[1] Universal Declaration of Human Rights, GA Res. 217A (III), UN Doc. A/810 at 71 (1948) (UDHR).

[2] See Art. 19(1) and Art. 19(2) ICCPR.

[3] See Art. 19(3) ICCPR.

different rights, the drafters of the UDHR opted for one generic limitation clause in Article 29(2):

> In the exercise of his rights and freedoms, everyone shall be subject only to such limitations as are determined by law solely for the purpose of securing due recognition and respect for the rights and freedoms of others and of meeting the just requirements of morality, public order and the general welfare in a democratic society.

Accordingly, from the system of the UDHR it follows that this limitation clause applies to freedom of expression too.

Turning to the issue of 'extreme speech', whereas, as we will see, in the 1966 ICCPR the general freedom of expression provision is immediately followed by the incitement prohibition – thus implying their interrelatedness and interplay – in the UDHR we have to look elsewhere, namely Article 7. This Article contains mere remnants of much more comprehensive hate speech clauses that were proposed – but voted down – in the UDHR drafting committees. Article 7 ostensibly deals with equality before the law, but ends with a note on incitement:

> All are equal before the law and are entitled without any discrimination to equal protection of the law. All are entitled to equal protection against any discrimination in violation of this Declaration *and against any incitement to such discrimination.*[4]

Two things are striking. First, unlike the later ICCPR, the protection against incitement appears to be formulated as an *individual right* ('entitled'). Second, the protection is limited to protection against incitement to *discrimination*, while the later ICCPR also proscribes incitement to violence or hostility. Thus, under the UDHR 'incitement' appears to be a narrower and a wider concept at the same time when compared to the later ICCPR. The exclusive focus on incitement to discrimination is narrow. Yet the UDHR provides much more explicitly than the ICCPR a *right to be free from incitement* to discrimination.[5]

The UDHR further contains a general *abuse of rights* clause in the final Article 30:

---

[4] UDHR, Art. 7 (emphasis added).
[5] In the ICCPR, as we will see, the norm is rather formulated as a command addressed to states: all State parties are obligated to prohibit certain forms of incitement. This does not mean that the latter norm may not be construed so as to imply a positive right too (for a comprehensive discussion of this question, see Chapter 5).

> Nothing in this Declaration may be interpreted as implying for any State, group or person any right to engage in any activity or to perform any act aimed at the destruction of any of the rights and freedoms set forth herein.

That general restriction may also have ramifications for free speech.[6] As we will see, many binding human rights conventions would later follow the UDHR's lead and include similar abuse of rights provisions.

2.3 Historic debates: to tolerate or not to tolerate the intolerant?

Accordingly, although the said 'protection against incitement' provision (Article 7) and the quoted 'abuse of rights' clause (Article 30) touch upon it, all in all the UDHR does not contain a clear-cut incitement prohibition.[7] Farrior argues that the history of the combined set of relevant UDHR rights 'indicates that most of the drafters understood them to allow restrictions on the advocacy of hatred'.[8] Indeed, notwithstanding the UDHR's eventual relative silence on the issue, the question of how tolerant states in the post-Second World War world ought to be vis-à-vis those who are in word or deed intolerant was repeatedly debated by the drafters of the UDHR. This was mostly due to USSR interventions and amendments in favour of restrictions forcing the drafters to reflect on this question.[9]

The discussion on extreme speech limitations took place at two different levels. One question was whether the freedom of expression clause itself should include a special limit on extremely intolerant speech – we just saw that it ultimately does not. The second question was whether the

---

[6] It may be noted at this point that abuse of rights provisions have been construed as a hate speech prohibition or have been employed by monitoring bodies as a special limit on freedom of expression (be it as a matter of admissibility or as a consideration on the merits of a free speech complaint), notably within the context of the regional European Convention on Human Rights, which otherwise lacks an incitement prohibition. See further section 6.6 of Chapter 6.

[7] While the ICCPR *travaux* research in the chapters to come is based on original primary source research, this UDHR *travaux* overview is largely based on a number of excellent secondary accounts, notably: Stephanie Farrior, 'Molding the Matrix: The Historical and Theoretical Foundations of International Law Concerning Hate Speech' (1996) 14:1 *Berkeley Journal of International Law* 1–98; Johannes Morsink, *The Universal Declaration of Human Rights: Origins, Drafting & Intent* (Philadelphia: University of Pennsylvania Press, 1999); and Manfred Nowak, *U.N. Covenant on Civil and Political Rights: CCPR Commentary* (2nd rev. edn, Kehl: N. P. Engel, 2005).

[8] Farrior, 'Molding the Matrix', at 12.

[9] Morsink, *UDHR*, at 65–72.

equality principle ought to say something about the issue of incitement to discrimination – we just saw that it ultimately does. Some states would have liked the UDHR to have contained a more robust incitement provision – something the ICCPR nearly two decades later would indeed include.

The UN Commission on Human Rights, the subsidiary body in charge of drafting the UDHR, created several sub-commissions, including a Sub-Commission on the Freedom of Information, which held its first session in May–June 1947, to advise on the complex issue of what rights and obligations should be incorporated into the overall freedom of expression provision.[10] An early British free-speech-clause proposal presented there – ironically, the UK would at later drafting stages become one of the most fervent opponents of an international hate speech prohibition[11] – held that freedom of expression must include a possibility for the state to restrict 'publications aimed at suppression of human rights and fundamental freedoms'.[12] The British delegation's rationale for this special restriction was that 'it would be inconsistent for a Bill of Rights whose whole object is to establish human rights and fundamental freedoms to prevent any Government, if it wished to do so, from taking steps against publications whose whole object was to destroy the rights and freedoms which it is the purpose of the Bill to establish'.[13] To their own proposal the British – somewhat noncommittally[14] – added that we must not forget that 'no Government is obliged by the Bill to make use of the powers of limitation which are provided in [the proposed incitement clause]'.[15] The question whether international standards on combating incitement *allow* or indeed rather *force* states to prohibit extreme speech would in fact become a recurring subject of heated debate.

---

[10] Morsink, *UDHR*, at 66–7.

[11] To add one more irony and show the full circle this country has made: the UK would half a century down the road become a pioneer by creating one of the most comprehensive hate speech bills.

[12] E/CN.4/Sub.1/38, at 11–13 and E/CN.4/21, Annex B at 35. Morsink, *UDHR*, 66 (at fn. 81); Farrior, 'Molding the Matrix', at 42.

[13] E/CN.4/21 at 36 para (b). Farrior, 'Molding the Matrix', at 13; Morsink, *UDHR*, at 67.

[14] Farrior 'Molding the Matrix', at 13 (fn. 60), observes that the clause is made in square brackets, indicating that the British themselves were not completely sure about the provision on hate publications. More reservations about vague choice of words can be found in E/CN.4/21, Annex B at 36 para b. It may be noted again that British representatives at other times and within other drafting committees argued and voted against any special restrictions on freedom of expression (e.g. within the Third Committee: proposed amendment E/CN.4, at 99; and explanation in E/CN.4/SR.52, at 13–14).

[15] E/CN.4/21, Annex B, at 36, para. c. Farrior, 'Molding the Matrix', at 13.

Despite the Commission's second attempt (December 1947) to have the Sub-Commission on the Freedom of Information brainstorm about the problem of intolerant speech, a specific restriction on extreme speech was again not adopted. The Sub-Commission convened in January–February 1948 for a second session, among other things to deal with the Commission's request to consider the possibility of excluding from the scope of the right to freedom of expression those 'publications and other media of public expression which aim or tend to inflict injury, or incite prejudice or hatred, against persons or groups because of their race, language, religion or national origin'.[16] The Sub-Commission, chaired by Archibald MacKenzie (the British delegate who made important contributions to founding the UN), voted by majority against that possibility.[17]

The USSR was adamant that special limits on free speech should be enshrined one way or another, so as to prevent extremists like the Nazis from abusing their rights.[18] This time they appealed, within the framework of the Third Committee, to states' anti-fascist sentiments to further this cause. Fascists, it was contended, ought not to have rights in the first place, and both the freedom of expression article and freedom of association/assembly article ought to reflect that.[19] 'War-mongering' and 'fascist speech' was to be outlawed for once and for all, considering that such extreme speech had fostered 'the horrors that the world had recently known'.[20] The twofold USSR proposal was that the freedom of expression clause explicate that this right 'should not be used for purposes of propagating fascism, aggression and for provoking hatred as between nations' whilst 'fascist or anti-democratic' organizations were to be excluded from the protection of the freedom of association.[21] After extensive discussions on the notion of 'fascism' – how to define it?; must we define it?; could anti-fascist measures not be abused by the state?; must we for the purposes of this historical Declaration single-out fascism at all?; and so on – the whole idea was voted down and abandoned.[22] One direct consequence of this discussion, though, was that the

---

[16] E/CN.4/77, at 12–13. Farrior, 'Molding the Matrix', at 18; Morsink, *UDHR*, at 67.
[17] E/CN.4/Sub.1/SR.27, at 1–5. Morsink, *UDHR*, at 67.
[18] Morsink, *UDHR*, at 67–9.
[19] E/800. Morsink, *UDHR*, at 68; see also Farrior, 'Molding the Matrix', at 18–19.
[20] UN General Assembly Official Records, 3rd Comm., 180th plen. mtg. (9 Dec. 1948) at 855. Farrior, 'Molding the Matrix', at 18.
[21] E/800. Morsink, *UDHR*, at 68. [22] Morsink, *UDHR*, at 68–69.

word 'peaceful' was inserted into the provision on the freedoms of assembly and association.[23]

The upshot of this part of the drafting discussions was that the freedom of expression clause itself would eventually not include any special reference to incitement or the need to tackle, combat or penalize it.[24] Indeed, the freedom of expression clause, like all other substantive UDHR rights, would not incorporate a specific limitation clause at all, as the drafters ultimately opted for the above quoted generic limitation clause (Article 30).

A separate debate on intolerant speech took place against the background of the to-be-drafted equality provision, Article 7. Here the Soviets had more success. The fact that the USSR proposals were to become partially successful may very well have had to do with the express twofold mission the second Sub-Commission was on: preventing discrimination and protection minorities.[25] In any event, credited for being the very first proposal for a comprehensive international hate speech provision,[26] in 1947 USSR representative Borisov tabled the following proposal to the Sub-Commission on the Prevention of Discrimination and the Protection of Minorities (hereinafter also the 'Borisov proposal'):

> Any advocacy of national, racial, and religious hostility or of national exclusiveness or hatred and contempt, as well as any action establishing a privilege of a discrimination based on distinctions of race, nationality or religion constitute a crime and shall be punishable under the law of the state.[27]

---

[23] GOAR, Third Session, Proceedings of the Third Committee, 445. Morsink, *UDHR*, at 69.

[24] Note that the fact that the words 'by any means whatsoever' were deleted from an early formulation of freedom of speech indicates, as Farrior observes, 'that the Commission believed that the right to freedom of expression does not include the right to incite racial or religious hatred'. This deletion may have been the result of interventions made by the Coordinating Committee of Jewish Organizations. Farrior, 'Molding the Matrix', at 14.

[25] Morsink, *UDHR*, at 70; Farrior, 'Molding the Matrix', at 15 fn. 73.

[26] Nowak, *CCPR Commentary*, at 469. Nowak considers this proposal as containing the origins of Art. 20 ICCPR. Note that at this stage (1947) the drafting processes of the Declaration and the Covenant(s) were still very much intertwined. In fact, initially the idea was to have one international bill of fundamental rights. At a later point in time (E/CN.4/21, 1 July 1947), it was decided to rather first adopt one general declaration of rights setting out the basic rights as such, and to subsequently adopt an international treaty giving further body to those same rights and more thought to their realization and implementation. Ultimately – significantly fuelled by Cold War dialectics over the meaning, importance and implications of the different categories of rights – no less than three documents were produced: the 1948 Universal Declaration and the 1966 International Covenants on Civil and Political Rights and Economic, Social and Cultural Rights respectively (the sum of them is referred to as the 'International Bill of Rights').

[27] E/CN.4/Sub.2/21. Morsink, *UDHR*, at 70; Nowak, *CCPR Commentary*, at 469.

This proposal was clearly crafted after laws that were at the time in place in the USSR, satellite states and fellow communist regimes. The 1936 Soviet Constitution – the 'Stalin Constitution' – similarly saw logic in merging an equality clause with a hate speech prohibition:

> Equality of rights of citizens of the U.S.S.R., irrespective of their nationality or race, in all spheres of economic, state, cultural, social and political life, is an indefeasible law. Any direct or indirect restriction of the rights of, or, conversely, any establishment of direct or indirect privileges for, citizens on account of their race or nationality, as well as any advocacy of racial or national exclusiveness or hatred and contempt, is punishable by law.[28]

While the Borisov proposal was not as such adopted – though one can see how it went on to in turn influence the later ICCPR advocacy of hatred clause that is not unlike this proposal[29] – a slimmed-down version made it into the UDHR eventually.

Before that happened, first a French proposal and then a joint Australian–Chinese proposal were voted down.[30] The French proposal sought to codify the notion that infringements of the non-discrimination principle must be punishable and redressable under national laws.[31] The Australian–Chinese proposal, suggested as an amendment to the Borisov proposal, had attempted to fine-tune the USSR proposal, and at the same time take on board the French ideas on redress. This led to the following incitement clause proposal:

> Any advocacy of national, racial and religious hostility and any action establishing a privilege or a discrimination based on distinctions of race, nationality or religion shall be prohibited by the law of the State.[32]

This text was only just rejected, there being 5 votes against and 5 votes in favour, with 1 abstention.[33]

While particularly the USA now wished the incitement proposals altogether off the table, due to joint Australian–Chinese–French efforts the Sub-Commission ultimately recommended to the Commission on Human Rights 'the inclusion in the proposed Convention or in the Declaration of Rights, at appropriate places, of clauses condemning

---

[28] Art. 123 of the 1936 Soviet Constitution. Morsink, *UDHR*, at 349 fn. 90.
[29] See also Nowak, *CCPR Commentary*, at 469.
[30] E/CN.4/52, at 6. Farrior, 'Molding the Matrix', at 15.
[31] E/CN.4/52, at 5.
[32] E/CN.4/52, at 5. Farrior, 'Molding the Matrix', at 15.
[33] E/CN.4/52, at 5. Farrior, 'Molding the Matrix', at 15.

incitement to violence against any religious groups, race, nation or minority'.[34]

What is striking in the Sub-Commission's advice is that at this stage of the crafting process the drafters focused exclusively on incitement to *violence*, while the ultimately adopted incitement clause is exclusively concerned with incitement to *discrimination*.[35] There is an irony in that the USA, rather than accepting the original incitement prohibition, had pushed for the subject to be dropped. For it was precisely that high-threshold incitement to violence ban that resonated fairly well with US legal reasoning reigning at the time. Specifically, the 1919 judicial 'clear and present danger' doctrine might have lent some support to an incitement to violence ban,[36] at least more so than to a much wider incitement to discrimination ban.

In addition to the Sub-Commission, communications from organizations and NGOs that were eligible for consultation during the drafting process, like the World Jewish Congress,[37] as well as other stakeholders, notably the Preparatory Commission for the International Refugee Organization, also insisted that the idea of inclusion of an incitement clause be seriously entertained. The latter body made the following intervention:

> equality before the law should, in national law, be safeguarded not only by the embodiment of positive rights to this effect, but also by the incorporation in civil and criminal law of adequate safeguards against discrimination, incitement to, and advocacy of, discrimination. Incitement to discrimination is frequently directed against national, religious and racial groups. Civil proceedings and criminal prosecutions against instigators of discrimination, or even violence, against such groups have sometimes failed in the past because the law provided only for the protection of individuals, but not of groups. It would, therefore ... be desirable that *municipal laws should contain adequate safeguards against discrimination, incitement to, and advocacy of, discrimination against individuals or groups of individuals*.[38]

[34] E/CN.4/52, at 5; and SR.7, at 8, adopted by 10 votes to 0, with 1 abstention. Morsink, *UDHR*, at 70.

[35] See Farrior, 'Molding the Matrix', at 15.

[36] *Schenck* v. *United States*, 249 U.S. 47 (1919), opinion of the Court delivered by Justice Oliver Wendell Holmes, Jr. With the benefit of hindsight it can further be said that the concepts that were then on the table, with their emphasis on violence, would have resonated even better with the 'imminent lawless action' test as developed some decades later. See *Brandenburg* v. *Ohio*, 395 U.S. 444 (1969).

[37] E/CN.4/51, at 2 ('Teaching of racial or religious intolerance must be prevented').

[38] E/CN.4/41, at 2 (italics in original).

Be that as it may, holding on to these partial victories, the Soviet representatives tried to get a USSR proposal accepted after all, this time within the Working Group of the Second Session of the Commission on Human Rights.[39] Delegate Bogomolov reiterated that '[f]reedom of the press and free speech could not serve as a pretext for propagating views which poisoned public opinion'[40] and went on to re-table the Borisov proposal.[41] Eleanor Roosevelt resented the idea. Roosevelt considered that 'her Government would be opposed to the introduction of the Soviet Union proposal in the declaration' and she 'did not think that a law such as that proposed by the Soviet Union representative could be applied in practice'.[42] The Soviet representative, however, demanded a vote: this proposal too was narrowly rejected.[43]

While some states were against this idea for substantive reasons,[44] it seems that other representatives, like René Cassin of France,[45] did not so much object to the general idea of a prohibition of incitement but felt that the Declaration was simply not the place for such a special norm. For such a norm would inevitably touch upon complex questions of national implementation. It was the Belgian representative, Professor Dehousse,[46]

---

[39] Morsink *UDHR*, at 70–71.

[40] AC.1/SR7, at 9. Morsink *UDHR*, at 70. Interestingly, a 'poisoned environment' is what half a century later indeed emerged as a relevant legal factor in applying the incitement provision. E.g., Human Rights Committee, *Malcolm Ross* v. *Canada*, Communication no. 736/1997 (18 October 2000), para. 11.6.

[41] E/CN.4/SR.34, at 9.   [42] E/CN.4/SR.34, at 10.

[43] AC.1/SR7, at 11. Morsink, *UDHR*, 71. Voting record: 2 in favour, 2 against, with 2 abstentions. Roosevelt is recorded to have stated that it 'did not seem necessary to consider the Soviet representatives' proposal'. Farrior, 'Molding the Matrix', at 16.

[44] The Chilean representative was against the proposal as 'it put all power in the hands of the state' (E/CN.4/SR.34, at 10).

[45] E/CN.4/SR.34, at 10. Morsink, *UDHR*, at 71.

[46] Who in passing (E/CN.4/SR.34, at 3) also accused the Soviets of hypocrisy since they were most of the time vehemently against inclusion in the Declaration of anything that touched upon implementation, yet now had come up with a norm that required all states to design legislation ensuring that hate speech 'constitutes a crime and shall be punishable under the law of the State' (see the Soviet proposal in E/CN.4/Sub.2/21). The UK representative, for his part, wondered why the Soviet proposal did not offer protection against discrimination on the grounds of one's political opinions: 'In accordance with [the Borisov] amendment a one-party Government would not be obliged to take measures to safeguard the freedom of those professing a different political opinion from its own' (E/CN.4/SR.34, at 3). It is not hard to see which actual one-party government was being provoked by these and similar comments. See also the comments made by Mr Cruz Coke from Chile (E/CN.4/SR.34, at 4). Before turning to the Belgian amendment, the Borisov amendment was voted down once and for all: 10 votes against, 4 in favour, with 3 abstentions.

who managed to nip this problem in the bud and overcome the apparent stalemate. He did so by means of subtly changing the nature and wording of the incitement provision. Rather than codifying an especial international prohibition of incitement with all its uncertainty as to domestic legislative requirements, it was proposed that the equality clause offer protection against incitement to discrimination in addition to protection against discrimination per se. For that purpose it would merely be necessary to add the words 'and against any incitement to such discrimination' to Article 7 of the Declaration.[47] In the second session of the Commission on Human Rights, the Belgian proposal was adopted by 10 votes, 0 votes against, with 6 abstentions.[48] In its summary report of the Second Session, which includes a draft Declaration, the combined equality incitement provision reads:

> All are equal before the law regardless of office or status and entitled to equal protection of the law against any arbitrary discrimination, or against any incitement to such discrimination, in violation of this Declaration.[49]

The added word 'arbitrary' can be traced back to a Philippine proposal.[50] It is unclear why in this draft the words 'in violation of this Declaration' were added;[51] in the version ultimately adopted by the UN General Assembly, the words are not deleted but moved forward slightly.[52]

Some debate and modest resistance was still to be encountered in the Third Session of the Commission on Human Rights – the fifth stage of the drafting of the UDHR – and within the Third Committee, that is the sixth and penultimate stage of the drafting process before the final adoption by the General Assembly. The UK argued that, based on experience in that state, measures against incitement to discrimination were not quite necessary: 'The force of public opinion had always proved sufficient to deal any

---

[47] E/CN.4/SR.35, at 3. Morsink, *UDHR*, at 71; Farrior, 'Molding the Matrix', at 16.

[48] E/CN.4/SR.35, at 5.   [49] E/600, at 17.

[50] E/CN.4/SR.35, at 5.

[51] The Commission on Human Rights was possibly inspired by an Australian amendment (E/CN.4/SR.35, at 7 and 10–11) that was meant to foster the discussions on the Draft Covenant rather than Draft Declaration. During that particular meeting some delegates appeared rather confused as to whether they were drafting a Convention or a Declaration or both (E/CN.4/SR.35, see the discussion at 7–12). That discussion reached a Babelic pinnacle when the Soviet representative Bogomolov exclaimed he hoped that they were not drafting a Bill of Rights for 'in Russian, "Bill of Rights" meant "English Law"' (E/CN.4/SR.35, at 11).

[52] They have been inserted after the first mention of 'discrimination' in the second sentence of Art. 7 UDHR.

with attempts at such incitement.'[53] In a joint proposal with India the UK urged the Commission to delete the incitement element from the equality clause.[54] Again, much debate ensued, with amongst others Chilean, French and Yugoslav representatives defending robust protection against incitement, and US and Uruguayan delegates arguing against.[55] The Lebanese delegate hoped to appease everyone by inserting 'systematic' before 'incitement', but that proposal was defeated.[56] A Chinese proposal to delete the evidently controversial incitement provision from the equality clause once and for all was, however, voted down by a minimal vote of 8 to 7.[57]

That meant that the final hurdle before adoption by the General Assembly was the necessary approval by the Third Committee. One might expect discussion here to have been fierce and adversarial again, but endorsing the protection-against-incitement part of the equality clause went surprisingly smoothly – albeit far from uneventfully. For the incitement clause's sudden acceptance was importantly 'helped' by South Africa's meddling in the debate. While apartheid was on the rise back at home, South Africa proposed to delete the entire second half of Article 7 ('All are entitled to equal protection against any discrimination in violation of this Declaration and against any incitement to such discrimination').[58] In the words of Morsink, this:

> caught everyone's attention ... the South African position on what rights to include in the Declaration lacked integrity and its proposal ... was soundly defeated ... The open discussion of the hatred and contempt on which the system of apartheid was based convinced many of the drafters that people have a right to be protected not just against discrimination, but also against incitement to it.[59]

Consequently, it was by collectively expressing their distaste about ongoing atrocity that enabled states to overcome their own hesitation and reluctance

---

[53] E/CN.4/SR.52, at 13–14.

[54] E/CN.4, at 99. Morsink, *UDHR*, at 71.

[55] E/CN.4, at 99. Morsink, *UDHR*, at 71.

[56] By 6 votes to 5, with 5 abstentions. Morsink, *UDHR*, at 71–72.

[57] With one abstention. Morsink, *UDHR*, at 72.

[58] Around the same time South African representatives started doubting the wisdom of including the incitement provisions in the draft Covenant. E/CN.4/82/Add.4, at 20: the incitement clause of the draft equality provision 'also requires that every person is to be protected against any incitement to arbitrary discrimination in violation of the Convention ... this would require legislation'. The hate propaganda article was 'perhaps premature' (E/CN.4/82/Add.4, at 20).

[59] Morsink, *UDHR*, at 72.

on the question of prohibiting incitement to discrimination (less well known, as we see later, is that apartheid also crucially influenced the wording of Article 20(2) ICCPR).[60]

Ultimately, Article 7 was adopted by the Third Committee by 45 votes to 0, with only South Africa abstaining; whereas the specific incitement aspect of the clause was carried by 41 votes to 3, with 2 delegates abstaining.[61]

2.4   Conclusion: the questions unanswered

The UDHR raised as many questions as it answered as to the nature, scope and practical ramifications of the treatment of 'incitement' under international law.

First of all, is the incitement prohibition a requisite or an option? What the UDHR ultimately provides on the question of incitement differs strikingly from the original Borisov proposal in at least one crucial respect: the Declaration does not contain obligatory language to the effect that states must ban incitement, but merely extends the protection offered by Article 7 – protection from discrimination – to incitement to discrimination. What 'protection against incitement to discrimination' means in terms of legal implementation is far from clear. Can such 'protection' only be achieved through the adoption of a priori restrictions on free speech? Considering the more far-reaching and more explicit proposals that were rejected, one could *a contrario* reason that the ultimate formulation does not require the adoption of such extreme speech legislation.[62] But if the incitement clause does not mean protection against incitement in the form of laws prohibiting incitement, then what exactly does the incitement provision purport to achieve?

Arguably, under the incitement element of Article 7 states are permitted – one may say, mildly encouraged yet not forced – to adopt incitement (to discrimination) legislation. In addition, Article 7 would appear to sanction free speech limitations applied in actual extreme speech cases by judges.[63] Farrior contends that 'the drafting history

---

[60] For more details, see section 3.2.1 of Chapter 3.

[61] Morsink, *UDHR*, at 72.

[62] As the UK argued, 'no Government is obliged by the Bill to make use of the powers of limitation which are provided in [the proposed clause]'. E/CN.4/21, Annex B at 36, para. c.

[63] Farrior likewise tentatively posits that the UDHR's equal protection clause 'arguably allows restrictions on hate speech'. Farrior, 'Molding the Matrix', at 14 (reiterated at 17: 'may be interpreted as allowing restriction on hate speech').

indicates [that] this clause was adopted with the understanding that it protected against propaganda of national, racial and religious hostility and hatred, as well as the understanding that although article 19 protected freedom of expression, it did not protect expression that incites discrimination'.[64]

Further, considering the fact that the incitement provision is incorporated into the separate equality clause and thus is not a specific proviso incorporated into the freedom of expression clause, the provision strictly speaking does not look exclusively to (limit) free speech. Consequently, Article 7, second sentence, potentially circumscribes all substantive UDHR rights, that is in a manner not unlike the general limitation clauses included in Articles 29 and 30. A more narrow reading is that Article 7 simply refines – in situations where the peculiar circumstances of the human rights balancing exercise so require – the general limitation clause of Article 29(2).[65] 'Protection against incitement to discrimination', then, purports to secure 'due recognition and respect for the rights and freedoms of others'.[66]

Be that as it may, the fact remains that the incitement provision is formulated as a *right* rather than a clear-cut limitation clause. Both the wording – 'all are entitled to protection against incitement to discrimination' – and its place within the UDHR – the first twenty-eight articles reflect fundamental rights, and the last two contain restrictions and caveats – support that view. In the chapters to come we will see that the ICCPR somewhat changed the nature of the incitement clause. This begs the question whether a right to protection against incitement exists under international law.[67]

Then there are the numerous questions of implementation. The drafters of the UDHR avoided questions of implementation and left those questions for the immediate follow-up exercise – the drafting of the binding human rights Covenants. These questions include but are certainly not limited to: what characterizes speech that constitutes incitement and how to distinguish such incitement from intolerant or extreme speech that

---

[64] Farrior, 'Molding the Matrix', at 14–15.

[65] Morsink, *UDHR*, at 72.

[66] Art. 29(2) of the UDHR states: 'In the exercise of his rights and freedoms, everyone shall be subject only to such limitations as are determined by law solely for the purpose of securing due recognition and respect for the rights and freedoms of others and of meeting the just requirements of morality, public order and the general welfare in a democratic society.'

[67] See Chapter 5.

qualifies as protected speech? How to prove such speech occurred? What does a law that protects against incitement look like? What punishment may be imposed on those who commit incitement? We will resume these debates in our discussion of the next major international, and legally binding, extreme speech provision – Article 20 ICCPR.

The drafting of Article 20(2) ICCPR

3.1 Introduction

The ICCPR drafters created a legal framework that provides for an absolute *right to hold opinions*; while the *freedom of expression* is subject to certain limitations: 'respect of the rights or reputations of others', 'protection of national security', 'public order' (*ordre public*), 'public health' or 'morals'. On top of that, Article 20(2) urges states to prohibit by law certain forms of extreme speech, thus not only allowing for a special restriction on free speech but in fact *obligating* State parties to fight certain forms of extreme speech through prohibitive efforts.[1] Article 5(1), finally, repeats the abuse of rights doctrine that we have previously encountered in Article 30 UDHR.

The relevant free and extreme speech provisions read in full as follows:

Article 5(1)

Nothing in the present Covenant may be interpreted as implying for any State, group or person any right to engage in any activity or perform any act aimed at the destruction of any of the rights and freedoms recognized herein or at their limitation to a greater extent than is provided for in the present Covenant.

Article 19

1. Everyone shall have the right to hold opinions without interference.
2. Everyone shall have the right to freedom of expression; this right shall include freedom to seek, receive and impart information and ideas of all kinds, regardless of frontiers, either orally, in writing or in print, in the form of art, or through any other media of his choice.
3. The exercise of the rights provided for in paragraph 2 of this article carries with it special duties and responsibilities. It may therefore

---

[1] Exactly if and to what extent Art. 20(2) is mandatory will be determined in Chapter 4.

be subject to certain restrictions, but these shall only be such as are provided by law and are necessary:

(a)   For respect of the rights or reputations of others;

(b)   For the protection of national security or of public order (ordre public), or of public health or morals.

Article 20

1.   Any propaganda for war shall be prohibited by law.[2]

2.   Any advocacy of national, racial or religious hatred that constitutes incitement to discrimination, hostility or violence shall be prohibited by law.

Until recent times the incitement provision of the ICCPR, Article 20(2), was not extensively engaged with – neither at the international level by international monitoring bodies,[3] nor at the domestic level by legislators or judges. Those two dimensions, naturally, reinforce each other. As long as no comprehensive guidance is provided by international monitoring bodies on what exactly is expected from states, implementation and enforcement at the national level – that is beyond generally expressing commitment to the norm – is bound to become encumbered. Also, as long as non-enforcement at the national level does not lead to consistent and firm condemnations at the international level, be it in the form of Concluding Observations flowing from the state reporting procedure or in the form of jurisprudential reproaches, vigorous implementation at the national level cannot be expected.

The original crafting of the prohibition of hateful incitement should be understood against the background of the Second World War. The horrors of the Holocaust had been fostered significantly by a hate-mongering state apparatus. Tackling the prevention of crimes against humanity at the roots, it was felt, implied a need for 'preventive prohibitions in the area of formation of public opinion'.[4] The

---

[2]   The subject of propaganda for war is beyond the scope of this book. For a comprehensive account, see Michael G. Kearney, *The Prohibition of Propaganda for War in International Law* (Oxford University Press, 2007).

[3]   It was not until 1983 that the Human Rights Committee first acknowledged Art. 20(2) ICCPR by devoting a – very brief – General Comment to this provision. Human Rights Committee, *General Comment 11: Article 20* (Nineteenth session, 1983). See also Dominic McGoldrick, *The Human Rights Committee: Its Role in the Development of the International Covenant on Civil and Political Rights* (Oxford: Clarendon Press, 1991), 484, observing that the Committee's 'considerations of article 20 have been more limited in scope' compared to the other substantive provisions of the Covenant.

[4]   Manfred Nowak, *U.N. Covenant on Civil and Political Rights: CCPR Commentary* (2nd rev. edn, Kehl: N.P. Engel, 2005), at 468.

drafters presumed a direct link between the incitement prohibition and the right to life,[5] a clear indication of the extreme type of speech that comes within the ambit of Article 20(2) ICCPR. Thus, what the drafters were talking about are the most abominable acts of dehumanizing or demonizing the other, affecting the latter's dignity, equality and integrity by way of actually inciting violence, hostility or discrimination against that 'otherness'. In a separate part of this book[6] we will return to such threshold questions in more detail and from a contemporary legal perspective.

For now, such links made in the *travaux* to underlying fundamental rights as rationale for the incitement prohibition, and the links made to the Third Reich's hate propaganda machinery, serves to explain why many liberal states have long considered that little if any implementation at the domestic level is required by Article 20(2) ICCPR. Twentieth-century gross and systematic human rights abuses have, however, sadly manifested that Article 20(2) ICCPR is perhaps not redundant. First of all, the Yugoslav Wars remind us that also in our day and age, the state apparatus may be hijacked for the purposes of war propaganda, dissemination of hateful messages and provoking the cleansing of one's neighbour.[7]

Second, as we will see in due course and notwithstanding its original association with the crimes of National Socialism and with state-instigated hate propaganda, the incitement prohibition certainly also impacts *horizontal types of incitement*: individual incitement against other individuals or groups. This is no rare scenario at all. This consequence of the incitement clause raises the crucial question of whether vulnerable minorities indeed need legal protection from extremely intolerant, inciteful speech. The drafters differed on that score.

---

[5] Nowak, *CCPR Commentary*, at 468.

[6] See Chapters 7 and 8.

[7] On 'incitement' offences in international criminal law, see Wibke Timmermann, 'Incitement in International Criminal Law' (2006) 864 *International Review of the Red Cross* 823–52. On incitement to genocide specifically, see Susan Benesch, 'Vile Crime or Inalienable Right: Defining Incitement to Genocide' (2008) 48:3 *Virginia Journal of International Law* 485–528; Toby Mendel, *Study on International Standards Relating to Incitement to Genocide or Racial Hatred for the UN Special Advisor on the Prevention of Genocide* (April 2006); and Irwin Cotler, 'State-Sanctioned Incitement to Genocide: The Responsibility to Prevent', in Michael Herz and Peter Molnar (eds.), *The Content and Context of Hate Speech: Rethinking Regulation and Responses* (Cambridge University Press, 2012), 430–55.

3.2   The drafters' views: renewed historic debates

Article 20 shares the same roots as the discussed UDHR provisions. In the early drafting years, the crafting of two pioneering international human rights instruments was on the agenda: a Declaration and a Covenant. The latter was to be split into two Covenants. Accordingly, those same early proposals – notably the 1947 Borisov proposal, tabled in the Sub-Commission on Prevention of Discrimination and Protection of Minorities[8] – also went on to influence the Covenant debates on hate propaganda. The Sub-Commission on Prevention of Discrimination and Protection of Minorities' advice (December 1947) to the Commission on Human Rights should be reiterated too, namely to include 'in the *proposed Convention* or in the Declaration of Rights, at appropriate places, [clauses] condemning incitement to violence against any religious groups, race, nation or minority'.[9]

In sum, the drafters had at this early stage already decided that incitement must somehow be reckoned with, but in what precise modality was far from decided. We have seen how these debates would ultimately have marginal effects on the final text of the UDHR – the discussions were to have a far more significant effect on the ICCPR.

3.2.1   The different proposals

Numerous amendments on the issue at hand have been proposed, adopted, amended, rejected, re-tabled, and so on, in the different committees in the course of the drafting of the ICCPR. In the same Commission on Human Rights meeting in which the 'Dehousse formula' – the Belgian amendment that inserted the words 'and against any incitement to such discrimination' into the equality provision of the Declaration – finally resolved the UDHR debate on extreme speech, several hate propaganda provisions were tabled with a view towards inclusion into the ICPPR, starting with a Chinese proposal. The Chinese amendment proposed by Dr Wu (Commission on Human Rights, Second Session) held that:

> Any advocacy of national, racial or religious hostility, designed to provoke violence, shall be forbidden under the law of the state.[10]

---

[8]   E/CN.4/Sub.2/21.
[9]   E/CN.4/52, at 5 (emphasis added); and SR.7, at 8.
[10]   E/CN.4/SR/35, at 3 and 11.

A number of things are striking. First, the clause speaks of advocacy of 'hostility', rather than advocacy of 'hatred'. Although perhaps equally vague, 'hatred' would later on become the preferred term in connection with the act of 'advocacy' (occasionally: 'propaganda'). Second, the clause omits the word 'incitement', although the descriptive alternative ('designed to provoke') arguably boils down to the same thing.[11] Third, only 'violence' is listed as a proscribed result, while later on the much broader categories of 'hostility' and 'discrimination' would be added. Again, this may have been a ploy to get the USA on board; however, we know already from our previous (UDHR) discussions that the USA started objecting to the incitement clause quite early on in the negotiations.

At any rate, the amendment was adopted.[12] It was also decided, as proposed by the Australian delegation – or else the text might 'throw' the clause on discrimination 'out of balance'[13] – that the provision should be an independent article. This was fine for Dr Wu, but then the new article should be inserted immediately after the discrimination article 'since it also related to one aspect of discrimination'.[14] In fact, the *travaux* show constant shifts: occasionally a nexus was perceived between hate propaganda and non-discrimination, at other times a link to freedom of expression – and its limitations – was deemed more natural.[15] At still other times the hate propaganda article was listed as the final substantive provision of the Covenant, indicating the *sui generis* character of the clause.[16]

Interestingly, despite the novelty of reserving an entire new article to the issue of hate propaganda, at this point in time (December 1947) 'incitement' was also still dealt with separately in the discrimination article. Professor Dehousse thought it only logical that his successful UDHR amendment was reintroduced in the Covenant.[17] The French and Australian delegates also wanted to anchor the nexus between equality and anti-incitement. Picking up on an idea formulated by René

---

[11] Indeed, subsequent drafts replace 'designed to provoke violence' with 'incitement to violence'.

[12] E/CN.4/SR/35, at 12 (7 votes in favour, 2 against, with 7 abstentions).

[13] E/CN.4/SR/35, at 11.   [14] E/CN.4/SR/35, at 11.

[15] Which is, as we have seen, also the preferred solution of the final ICCPR text: the incitement clause immediately follows the freedom of expression Article.

[16] The latter explains why in much of the drafting history the advocacy provision is numbered Article 26. 'Article 20' will generally be used throughout even when at the material time the Article had another number. 'Hate propaganda Article', 'incitement Article' or 'advocacy Article' are also used.

[17] E/CN.4/SR/35, at 6. The discrimination Article at this point in time was listed as Article 19; it would ultimately become Article 26.

Cassin, Colonel Hodgson of Australia argued that 'there was a great difference between the wording of the corresponding articles of the Declaration and of the Convention': whereas the non-discrimination article of the Declaration 'laid down a principle', the equivalent provision of the Convention 'involved an obligation on the part of the State'.[18] Therefore, 'in order to coordinate the two texts, whilst maintaining the binding character' of the Convention article, he proposed the following Convention-provision on discrimination:

> Every person, regardless of office or status, shall be entitled to equal protection under the law and shall be protected by the law against any arbitrary discrimination and against any *incitement to such discrimination* in violation of this [Convention].[19]

The French–Australian amendment was adopted.[20] This led to an interim result of having no less than two incitement provisions in the draft Covenant, which version was published by the Commission on Human Rights at the end of the Second Session (17 December 1947). In that draft, the discrimination article included the French–Australian amendment (verbatim).[21] The draft incitement article at this point read:

> Any advocacy of national, racial or religious hostility that constitutes an incitement to violence shall be prohibited by the law of the state.[22]

Less than half a year later both incitement provisions were deleted again by the Commission's Drafting Committee, a decision significantly fuelled by fierce opposition from Mrs Roosevelt of the USA and Mr Wilson of the UK.[23] This deletion, however, proved far from permanent since, due to

---

[18] E/CN.4/SR/35, at 6–7.

[19] E/CN.4/SR/35, at 7 and 10 (emphasis added). Note that the final word of the amendment is actually 'Declaration', but this was an apparent mistake as the meeting had already moved on to discussing the Covenant (see E/CN.4/SR/35 at 7–11). In E/600, at 35, this is corrected ('Covenant').

[20] E/CN.4/SR/35, at 11 (11 votes in favour, 1 against, with 4 abstentions).

[21] Inserted as the second sentence of what was now, after renumbering, Article 20. E/600, at 35.

[22] E/600, at 35. While 'incitement' had made its appearance, the provision still strikingly omitted any mention of 'hatred'. It may be recalled that the by now firmly defeated Borisov proposal had focused on 'exclusiveness or hatred and contempt'. Thus the drafters had somewhat strayed from the concept of 'hate speech' – they would later return to it.

[23] E/CN.4/AC.1/SR.28, at 2 and 4. The incitement element of the equality clause was defeated by 5 votes to 3. The hate propaganda Article was defeated by 4 votes to 3, with 1 abstention. A Chilean amendment, which read 'Any advocacy of national, racial or religious hostility that constitutes an incitement to violate the liberties and rights mentioned

joint USSR and French efforts, the debate on incitement was revitalized a year later (in the summer of 1949). The USSR amendment read:

> The propaganda in whatever form of Fascist-Nazi views and the propaganda of racial and national superiority, hatred and contempt shall be prohibited by law.[24]

René Cassin fully supported the gist of the USSR proposal. However, he thought that the angle and terminology used – especially the words 'Fascist-Nazi views' – were not general enough for an international human rights convention and went on to propose his own amendment:

> Any advocacy of national, racial or religious hostility that constitutes an incitement to violence and hatred shall be prohibited by the law of the State.[25]

With this proposal we are essentially back to where the drafting process stood at the end of the Second Session – the draft is almost identical to the version that was included in the full Covenant draft of December 1947.[26] Importantly, due to the joint Soviet–French efforts 'hatred' was now on the agenda – something already envisaged by Mr Borisov.

Discussion and voting on the two amendments was postponed until more clarity could be acquired on the status of the freedom of expression provision.[27] However, nothing prevented the representatives from starting a discussion on a general *abuse of rights* clause. Interestingly, this was one of the few agenda items that saw agreement between the USA and USSR representatives – they were both mildly against or at least did not find it truly necessary.[28] Most other delegates were, however, in favour of this particular – if peculiar – proviso.[29] The abuse of rights provision

---

in this Covenant shall be prohibited by the law of the State', was to no further avail (E/CN.4/AC.1/SR.28, at 4).

[24] E/CN.4/223. Other delegations joined in: Yugoslavia and Ukraine were in favour, some Western European states (e.g. Denmark) were concerned, while Uruguay was against (E/CN.4/223, at 5–6). The notion that the international human rights covenant ought to help eradicate 'fascism' popped up in different guises. For instance, at various times it was proposed that a prohibition of fascist organizations be included. E.g. A/AC.3/SR.291, para. 8 (Ukraine); E/SR.438, para. 59 (USSR); A/C.3/SR.569, para. 20 (Czechoslovakia).

[25] E/CN.4/SR.123, at 6.   [26] E/600, at 35.

[27] E/CN.4/223, at 6. This was to the dismay of the Soviet delegate, who regretted the 'tendency to postpone consideration of one article after another' (E/CN.4/223, at 6).

[28] E/CN.4/223, at 7 and 9 (although the latter would, with the right alterations, support it).

[29] E.g. Lebanon, India (by implication), Australia, France, Denmark, Chile (by implication) and the Philippines (by implication). E/CN.4/223, at 8–11.

would ultimately become enshrined in the Covenant in Article 5(1). The Covenant's abuse of rights clause is, according to the *travaux*, modelled after the Declaration's closing article on the same matter.[30] In the final drafting stages the adoption of Article 5 was further facilitated by the fact that an equivalent provision had made its way in the socio-economic counterpart of the ICCPR – the International Covenant on Economic, Social and Cultural Rights (ICESCR).[31] This made further debate super-fluous and the General Assembly's Third Committee adopted Article 5 ICCPR unanimously in 1962.[32]

Adoption of Article 20 would prove far more turbulent than that of the general abuse of rights clause. In 1950 both the USSR and the French proposals for a hate propaganda article were rejected due to a US cam-paign and motion against them.[33] In the case of the USSR proposal, this move was facilitated by the fact that the USSR had withdrawn from the Commission on Human Rights 'for political reasons'.[34] During the Sixth Session (1950) of the Commission on Human Rights one other amend-ment was tabled – a Philippine proposal – but it was never voted upon:

> Every act which tends to stir up hatred or violence against any person or groups of persons by reason of race, colour, sex, language, religion, polit-ical, economic or other opinion, national or social origin, property, edu-cational attainment, birth or other status, shall be prohibited by the law of the State.[35]

This is an interesting proposal, given the extensive list of prohibited grounds. In fact, the Philippine list is even more comprehensive than the one eventually included in Article 26 on equality before the law. The final

---

[30] A/2929, para. 55. In the *travaux*, both Art. 5(1) and Art. 5(2) are referred to as 'saving clauses', although only Art. 5(2) would appear to be a proper saving clause. The latter norm would, according to Nowak, have been more appropriate as part of Part V of the Covenant (containing other such *sui generis* caveats). Nowak, *CPPR Commentary*, at 111.

[31] International Covenant on Economic, Social and Cultural Rights, adopted and opened for signature, ratification and accession by General Assembly Resolution 2200A (XXI) of 16 December 1966, entry into force 3 January 1976.

[32] A/C.3/SR.1206, para. 55. For the several drafts proposed and discussed in the drafting committees leading up to this final draft, see Marc J. Bossuyt, *Guide to the 'Travaux Préparatoires' of the International Covenant on Civil and Political Rights* (Dordrecht/ Boston/Lancaster: Martinus Nijhoff Publishers, 1987), at 105–11.

[33] Nowak, *CPPR Commentary*, at 469. For the extensive discussion leading up to this, see E/ CN.4/SR.174.

[34] That is, in the words of the Chilean delegate. He argued, however, that this does not mean that no votes should be taken on that delegation's earlier proposals. After some debate on this point, the USSR amendments were rejected. E/CN.4/SR.175, at 6.

[35] E/CN.4/365. Bossuyt, *Guide to the Travaux Préparatoires'*, at 405.

Article 20(2) mentions solely 'national', 'racial' and 'religious' hatred, implying that hatred advocated in relation to, for instance, sex is not to be combated. This was the only proposal to mention sex as a prohibited ground.[36]

The – temporary – absence of any incitement provision from the draft Covenant was regretted by some delegations in the General Assembly's Third Committee[37] and in the Economic and Social Council (ECOSOC).[38] Civil society also criticized the omission. The World Jewish Congress rightly noted that a failure to introduce an incitement clause would cause discrepancy with the Declaration:

> Consistent and assiduous application of [UN] principles … cannot be achieved if propaganda would be permitted poisoning the minds of people by preaching false doctrine. Moreover, such propaganda would defeat the purpose of Article 7 of the Universal Declaration of Human Rights granting protection against any incitement to discrimination.[39]

It took a few years for the phenomenon to resurface.[40] In 1953 the problem of incitement was successfully revitalized through an intervention of the Sub-Commission on Prevention of Discrimination and Protection of Minorities, which urged the Commission on Human Rights to adopt an article dealing with the 'condemnation of incitement to violence against any religious group, nation, race or minority'.[41]

Rather than generally condemning such incitement – thus 'merely tackling its consequences' – the Polish representative felt it was necessary

---

[36] Stephanie Farrior, 'Molding the Matrix: The Historical and Theoretical Foundations of International Law Concerning Hate Speech' (1996) 14:1 *Berkeley Journal of International Law* 1–98, at 26.

[37] A/AC.3/SR.291, para. 8 (Ukraine) and para. 54 (Belarus).

[38] E/SR.438, paras. 55 and 59 (USSR): 'freedom of speech and of the Press should not be used for war propaganda, for the incitement of hatred among peoples, for racial discrimination, or for the dissemination of slanderous rumours. Furthermore, it should be stated that the law must prohibit all propaganda on behalf of fascist or nazi views and all propaganda directed against specific racial or national groups or intended to incite to hatred and contempt. [This proposal is] inspired by the tragic fate of millions of human beings before and during the Second World War.'

[39] E.CN.4/NGO/21, at 6. It further commented that '[i]ncitement to racial or religious hatred and intolerance by the Nazi Party in Germany led eventually to atrocities unparalleled in human history. Any propaganda of the Nazi type inciting to racial or religious hatred and intolerance should be prohibited by the Covenant.'

[40] During the Eighth Session of the Commission on Human Rights there was no mention of a hate propaganda provision whatsoever. See memorandum on the draft covenant of 1952: E/CN.4/528/Add.1.

[41] E/2256 at 54 and E/CN.4/L.269.

instead to go 'to the root of the evil', proposing the following amendment to the Sub-Commission's proposal:

> Any advocacy of national or racial exclusiveness, hatred and contempt or religious hostility, particularly of such a nature as to constitute an incitement to violence, shall be prohibited by the law of the state.[42]

The Sub-Commission's proposal had only looked to situations of incitement to 'violence'.[43] Mr Druto of Poland explained why that was not sufficient by recalling 'the widespread use by the Nazi regime in Germany of nationalist propaganda by which the constant repetition of the theory of racial domination had led not only to the curtailment of human rights, but to the destruction of entire peoples'.[44] The Polish amendment appears to be influenced by the early Borisov proposal, which had also focused on notions of 'exclusiveness' and 'contempt'. The rather convoluted formula was heavily debated. Most delegations felt that the Polish amendment – especially the peculiar 'particularly' construction[45] – made the provision actually less clear.[46] France, one of the Western states in favour of an incitement prohibition almost throughout the drafting process, mobilized Shakespeare to warn against vagueness when its representative stated that it was 'only too well aware that "striving to better, oft we mar what's well"'.[47]

The upshot was that the Sub-Commission's earlier incitement provision was adopted, albeit with alterations suggested by the Chilean representative.[48] The Chilean representative, Mr Diaz-Casanueva, had made a passionate presentation about the effects of modern-day hate propaganda:

> It must be recognized that propaganda was today a social phenomenon the effects of which were so enormously enhanced by modern techniques that it had become a very dangerous weapon and one that could

---

[42] E/CN.4/SR.377, at 4. The amendment was subsequently listed as E/CN.4/L.269.

[43] The Sub-Commission's own proposal read: 'Any advocacy of national, racial or religious hostility that constitutes an incitement to violence shall be prohibited by the law of the State.' E/2256, annex II.

[44] E/CN.4/SR.377.

[45] For criticism regarding this subordinate clause, see e.g. E/CN.4/SR.378, at 6–7.

[46] Mr Kriven of Ukraine liked it a lot, though (E/CN.4/SR.378 at 5–6), and was clearly one of the three delegates voting in favour of the Polish amendment, the two other likely candidates being Yugoslavia and the USSR.

[47] E/CN.4/SR.377, at 12 (quoting *King Lear*, Act 1, Scene 4). He went on stating that it 'is generally preferable to avoid unduly overloading a text with terms of vague connotation that were only liable to prove ambiguous'.

[48] E/CN.4/SR.379, at 13 (adopted by 8 votes to 5, with 4 abstentions).

be trained on specific targets. Everyone still remembered the propaganda campaigns conducted in certain countries before the last world war with the object of mentally conditioning the masses for war – campaigns so well organized that they had actually induced collective hypnosis ... Sociologists who had studied that modern phenomenon rightly claimed that skilfully directed propaganda could successfully nullify the effects or falsify the premises of education. Modern technical facilities for disseminating ideas, such as the press and wireless, were accessible to the young, they too were exposed to propaganda campaigns, which might be cleverly enough conducted to induce in the masses an attitude towards a nation, a case or a church that might end in an explosion of violence.[49]

The French delegate had read the same sociological literature on the possibility of 'mind-conditioning and spiritual rape of the masses' and joined in by arguing that '[t]here could be no doubt that certain forms of propaganda were so insidious that they ended by setting up veritable conditioned reflexes in the individual, and could thus be regarded as coming within the scope of the problems under consideration by the Commission'.[50]

The Sub-Commission/Chilean proposal read:

> Any advocacy of national, racial or religious hostility that constitutes an incitement to hatred and violence shall be prohibited by the law of the State.[51]

Although most of the key terms would still be shifted around, the novelty of inserting the words 'that constitutes an incitement' would influence most subsequent drafts – including the one finally adopted. Luckily Poland insisted on a roll-call vote, for the outcome is very telling indeed: almost all Communist and lesser-developed states voted in favour;[52] the UK, the USA and Australia voted against, while Sweden, Belgium and China abstained.

---

[49] E/CN.4/SR.377, at 5. Many delegates expressed support for this intervention (E/CN.4/SR.377, at 5–6 and at 10–11). The Yugoslav representative (E/CN.4/SR.377, at 6) was so convinced by these arguments that he now felt that 'the text proposed did not go far enough. Such an article ought to be directed ... against all propaganda that constituted incitement to hatred and intolerance in every sphere'.

[50] E/CN.4/SR.377, at 12.

[51] E/CN.4/SR.379, at 13. This proposal was made directly after the Polish amendment was formulated. See E/CN.4/SR.377, at 5. The Chilean amendment was later separately documented in E/CN.4/L.270. The adopted draft article is included in the Commission's 1953 report of the Ninth Session, which includes a full draft Covenant plus commentary: E/2477, at 9 and at 45.

[52] France, having casted a vote in favour too, being the exception here. E/CN.4/SR.379, at 13.

Due to said concerted efforts, the concept of 'hatred' resurfaced in the incitement provision. As the Commission on Human Rights formulated it in its summary of the Ninth Session (1953), it had been agreed by majority 'that any propaganda constituting an incitement to hatred was no less serious than that constituting an incitement to violence; both should be prohibited'.[53] One wonders, though, whether the drafters realized that they were moving in circles. What they had adopted was – verbatim[54] – René Cassin's 1949 amendment.

In the draft Covenant presented at the end of the Ninth Session (1953) by the Commission on Human Rights,[55] the incitement provision had been moved to the end of the section containing substantive human rights (Article 26).[56] In the Third Committee's Ninth and Tenth Sessions (1954–5), this led to renewed debate as to the article's ideal position – while its merits, too, were once again subject to intense debates. The inclusion/deletion debate was repeated, accompanied by largely the same opinions: from the USSR, Czechoslovakia and Poland wishing to maintain and preferably expand the incitement provisions;[57] to Canada observing that the incitement clause and the freedom of expression clause were internally 'inconsistent';[58] to the UK, France, Australia and Belgium calling the incitement prohibition too 'progressive';[59] to the USA wishing

---

[53] E/2447, at 9. Previously, the Uruguayan representative had already claimed that the 'indulgence of hatred must inevitably lead to violence'. E/CN.4/SR.379, at 8.

[54] E/CN.4/SR.123, at 6. The words are literally the same; the only difference is that 'violence' and 'hatred' swapped places.

[55] E/2477.

[56] The 1955 annotations on the full draft Covenant prepared by the UN Secretary-General discuss briefly the history of this provision. Though not mentioned by name, in the discussed accepted and rejected alternatives and voiced concerns one recognizes the Polish amendment, the Sub-Commission's proposal and the Chilean amendment, as well as the UK's concerns. A/2929, paras. 189–194.

[57] These states argued that Art. 19 on freedom of expression should include an additional incitement restriction. USSR: A/C.3/SR.565, para. 31 (while the merits of a separate incitement provision are defended in paras. 20, 25 and 27) and A/C.3/SR.576, para. 31 (including a frontal attack on the attitude of the USA on the issue at hand). Czechoslovakia: A/C.3/SR.569, para. 19. Poland: A/C.3/SR.571, para. 16. In fact, in the meetings in which Art. 19 was debated separately very similar discussions on the merits of a special incitement restriction were held; however, the 'school of thought' (in the words of the UN Secretary-General) that advocated a brief list of accepted limitations won that debate. A/2929, para. 128 and para, 134. Czechoslovakia and Poland, moreover, proposed a novel prohibition: a ban on propaganda for war. A/C.3/SR.569, para. 19 (Czechoslovakia); A/C.3/SR.571, para. 16 (Poland).

[58] A/C.3/SR.570, para. 4 (thus disagreeing with the former states).

[59] A/C.3/SR.575, para. 3 (thus advising its removal).

to delete the incitement clause altogether;[60] to, finally, Brazil trying to mediate by ingeniously proposing to merge the gist of the incitement article with the general restrictions listed in the freedom of expression article so as to 'avoid difficulties for States which were constitutionally unable to restrict freedom of expression in any way'.[61]

Albeit not as an integral part thereof, the incitement provision did in 1961 move back in the direction of the freedom of expression clause,[62] forming close partners ever since then. There were still a number of delegations that wished that both Article 19 on freedom of expression *and* a separate provision would condemn hate propaganda. In 1961, during the deliberations on freedom of expression it was definitively settled by the majority that the 'basic purpose of article 19 was to protect the right of the individual to freedom of opinion and expression and that the article should therefore contain as few restrictions as possible'.[63] It was decided that if further amendments for restrictions were formulated, those would be discussed in connection with the incitement clause, not in relation to the free speech clause.[64]

The Sixteenth Session of the Third Committee in 1961 saw three more proposals for an advocacy of hatred provision, including the one ultimately adopted. These three amendments have come to be known as the 'four-Power amendment', the 'nine-Power amendment' and the triumphant 'sixteen-Power amendment'.

On 20 October 1961 Lebanon, Philippines, Saudi Arabia and Thailand proposed the following article:

> Any propaganda for war and advocacy of national, racial and religious hatred inciting to violence shall be prohibited by law.[65]

Accordingly, the war and hate propaganda clauses were merged within one succinct provision. In addition, the emphasis is once again fully on incitement to violence – something that pleased the USA. Mrs Tillett, representing the USA, explained that they were still against any clause on incitement; yet among the alternatives now tabled she would support and

---

[60] Mrs Lord argued on behalf of the USA that the provision 'seriously threatened the principle of freedom of expression'. A/C.3/SR.568, para. 15.

[61] A/C.3/SR.580, para. 11. Amendment separately filed as A/C.3/L.413.

[62] Decision taken (upon a Chilean proposal) to insert the incitement clause directly after the freedom of expression clause in A/C.3/SR.1073, paras. 46 and 49.

[63] A/5000, para. 30.

[64] See also Nowak, *CCPR Commentary*, at 470; Bossuyt, *Guide to the Travaux Préparatoires'*, at 398.

[65] A/C.3/L.932.

vote for the four-Power amendment since her delegation remained 'interested in an appropriate wording ... that would safeguard ... article 19'.[66] Other delegations were content with this amendment too. The Congolese representative commented that 'the four-Power amendment was of an almost mathematical precision and was remarkably concise. Through the addition of the words "inciting to violence" ... the concept of advocacy of hatred acquired a much more specific meaning.'[67]

On that same day, nine other states (Brazil, Cambodia, Ghana, Guinea, Iraq, Mali, Morocco, United Arab Republic and Yugoslavia) proposed an alternative:

> Any advocacy of national, racial or religious hostility that constitutes an incitement to hatred, discrimination and violence, as well as war propaganda, shall be prohibited. This prohibition shall be incorporated in the law of the state.[68]

Most striking in this amendment is the addition of the word 'discrimination'.[69] While this may seem nothing spectacular at first glance – the first ever hate propaganda proposal, the 1947 Borisov proposal, had contained the word 'discrimination' – the *travaux* reveal that the timing of this term's reinsertion is loaded with political significance.[70] The main reason why some delegations insisted on 'incitement to discrimination' becoming punishable was the emergence of apartheid – 'a crime against humanity as great as the crimes of the Hitlerite fascists'.[71] Although some delegations pointed out that the insertion of the word 'discrimination' is superfluous (since 'advocacy of

---

[66] A/C.3/SR.1080, para. 19.   [67] A/C.3/SR.1081, para. 19.

[68] A/C.3/L.930/Rev.2. The creation of the nine-Power amendment was led by Brazil that had two days earlier worked on its own proposal, which reads: 'Any advocacy of national, racial or religious hostility that constitutes an incitement to hatred and violence, including war propaganda, shall be prohibited by the law of the State.' A/C.3/L.930. Clearly, Brazil had managed to get eight states on board in exchange for some minor alterations.

[69] The final sentence is odd and could easily have been merged with the main sentence. The Indian delegate, however, was pleased with this formulation as it 'forcefully indicated the intention of placing a categorical prohibition on the activities in question' (A/C.3/SR.1080, para. 3). Note further that war and hate propaganda are retained as one clause.

[70] While duly noting the correlation between South Africa's scandalous home affairs and the adoption of an incitement clause of sorts in the UDHR, other *travaux* studies appear not to have detected this point.

[71] I.e. in the words of Mrs Rousseau of Mali, one of the nine-Power amendment's masterminds. A/C.3/SR.1080. The Indian delegate stated that 'the nine-Power amendment introduced a very important word, "discrimination"'. A/C.3/SR.1080, para. 3.

hostility' would inherently incite discrimination),[72] it would prove to be a permanent addition.

Indonesia expressed the hope that the four plus nine states would join forces and draft a final joint proposal that could garner comprehensive support among the delegations.[73] Indonesia itself was willing to help out and with further assistance by Poland[74] and Congo (Leopoldville),[75] the sixteen-Power amendment became fact.[76] This amendment reads:

1. Any propaganda for war shall be prohibited by law.
2. Any advocacy of national, racial, or religious hatred that constitutes incitement to discrimination, hostility or violence shall be prohibited by law.[77]

This is the text as one finds it today in the ICCPR. Clearly, war and hate propaganda are more firmly separated again – albeit separate parts of one extreme speech provision – which may be relevant to threshold questions.[78] That is to say, it is not self-evident any longer that in order to engage Article 20(2) the advocacy of hatred must be carried out with the ultimate objective of causing armed conflict, as some drafters had previously maintained when the two notions were still tightly integrated.[79]

---

[72] Congo (Leopoldville) had, for instance, convincingly argued in the Third Committee that the 'word "discrimination" seemed superfluous, since any advocacy of national, racial or religious hostility generally involved discriminatory measures'. A/C.3/SR.1081, para. 18. Similarly, France argued that the term discrimination was 'unnecessary, since advocacy of national, racial or religious hatred could in fact be nothing else than advocacy of discrimination'. See also the remark made in respect of the later sixteen-Power amendment, which also contained 'discrimination'. A/C.3/SR.1083, para. 8.

[73] A/C.3/SR.1081, para. 3.

[74] Poland had already indicated to 'strongly' support the nine-Power amendment as 'it was completely in conformity with the views of her delegation and had the merit of going to the roots of the problem.' A/C.3/SR.1081, para. 31. Indeed, the nine-Power amendment was not too far removed from a proposal once (1953) made by the Polish delegation in the Commission. E/CN.4/SR.377, at 4; and E/CN.4/L.269.

[75] The latter had earlier urged the nine powers to reconsider their positions as the four-Power amendment would be much better than the nine-Power amendment. Having joined the drafting table, however, Congo signed off on an amendment that for all intents and purposes resembles the nine-Power amendment the closest.

[76] Prior to this, two proposals were made parenthetically and were never voted upon: A/C.3/SR.1081, para. 66: 'Any advocacy of national, racial and religious hatred that constitutes incitement to violence and war shall be prohibited by law' (Italy); and para. 80: 'Any propaganda for war, and any advocacy of national, racial or religious hostility inciting to intolerance, discrimination or violence shall be prohibited by law' (Indonesia).

[77] A/C.3/L.933.

[78] We will return to threshold questions in Chapter 7.

[79] E.g. A/C.3/SR.1079, para. 2 (Brazilian delegate).

Further, 'discrimination' is retained. It is worth noting that in this final formulation the word 'and' is changed into 'or' (discrimination, hostility *or* violence). The nine-Power amendment had used the word 'and' (hatred, discrimination *and* violence).[80] That would strictly speaking have implied that the clause is only engaged if the impugned 'advocacy of hostility', as that amendment formulated it, somehow constituted an incitement to all three evils at once – hatred, discrimination and violence. This change was most likely the doing of the Polish and Yugoslavian representatives.[81]

All these last-minute changes caused the USA to be vehemently against the provision once again.[82] France also now started distancing itself firmly from the provision.[83] After all the important work René Cassin had done in aiding the creation of an incitement provision, France's objections may come as a surprise. Apparently, the turn the sixteen-Power amendment had taken opened France's eyes to the inherent risks of incitement legislation. Another explanation could be that France was reluctant all along,[84] and that René Cassin worked on a far more personal title within the Commission on Human Rights than France's representative (Mr Bouquin) in the Third Committee could afford himself. That explanation is at least partly belied by the fact that France next declared that it would be willing to vote in favour of an earlier hate propaganda

---

[80] A/C.3/L.930/Rev.2. That said, there appears to have been a crucial discrepancy between the English, French and Spanish translations of the amendment. Only the English version used 'and', while the other versions employed 'or'. This mistake was pointed out by Yugoslavia: A/C.3/SR.1081, para. 9. Apparently no revised amendment was distributed despite the chairman's request to that effect (A/C.3/SR.1081, para. 10).

[81] The Polish delegation had previously (erroneously or at least prematurely – see previous footnote) praised the nine-Power amendment as it 'employed the conjunction "or". Thus the existence of any single one of those elements, all of which were very serious, would bring into play the ban on propaganda inciting to national, racial or religious hostility. The Polish delegation could not but approve such a formula without reservation.' A/C.3/SR.1081, para. 36. Probably upon noticing that (the English version of) the nine-Power amendment actually did not use 'or', Poland would have been the first to correct that mistake as per the sixteen-Power amendment. The Yugoslavian representative had a few meetings earlier already held a plea in favour of 'or' instead of 'and'. This intervention reads: 'The wording as it stood might make it possible to confine the application of the article to cases where advocacy of hatred finally led to violence, whereas it was just as important to suppress manifestations of hatred which, even without leading to violence, constituted a degradation of human dignity and a violation of human rights.' A/C.3/SR.1079, para. 9. See also Farrior, 'Molding the Matrix', at 26.

[82] A/C.3/SR.1083, paras. 14–17.

[83] A/C.3/SR.1083, paras. 6–13, containing extensive criticism of the clause.

[84] Note that years before (as early as 1954), France's General Assembly's Third Committee representative had already been under apparent governmental instructions to call the incitement provision too 'progressive'. A/C.3/SR.575, para. 3

draft article, namely the one that was drafted by the Sub-Commission and amended by Chile to be adopted by the Commission on Human Rights in its Ninth Session – nearly a decade previously.[85] States that were opposed to the new draft were further concerned by the fact that the incitement article was going to be inserted directly after the freedom of expression clause.[86] This might – as was felt by France, Uruguay and India, for instance – undermine or needlessly offset the right to freedom of expression.[87]

Despite these protests, the second paragraph of Article 20 ICCPR on incitement was adopted by 50 votes to 18, with 15 abstentions.[88] As the votes were taken by a roll-call (at the request of the USSR), it transpired that not a single Western industrialized state supported the incitement provision at the time of its adoption. The states that voted in favour include African, Eurasian Communist, Asian and South American states. Expressly against were, among others: Belgium, Canada, Denmark, Finland, Ireland, Japan, Netherlands, New Zealand, Norway, Sweden, the UK and USA, while states such as Australia, Austria, China, Cyprus, France, Greece, Italy, Portugal and Spain abstained from the vote on the second paragraph of Article 20 ICCPR. Most notable absentees amongst the yes-voters were Chile and France (both abstained),[89] two states whose delegates had in past times most passionately argued in favour of an incitement prohibition.[90]

At the voting meeting a most peculiar thing happened. Just before casting their votes, delegates had started – as was customary – the process of explaining for what precise reasons they were about to vote in favour

---

[85] A/C.3/SR.1083, para. 6.

[86] Even though that was not the doing of the sixteen powers. This had already been decided (by consensus) by the Third Committee some time before on a Chilean proposal to that effect. A/C.3/SR.1073, paras. 46 and 49. The sixteen-Power amendment merely confirms this. See second footnote in the text of A/C.3/L.933.

[87] A/C.3/SR.1083, paras. 7 and 20.

[88] A/C.3/SR.1083, para. 58. At the request of Chile, before proceeding to the vote on the entire second paragraph of Art. 20, a separate vote was taken on the insertion of the words 'to discrimination, hostility or'. That phrase was adopted by 43 votes to 21, with 19 abstentions. A/C.3/SR.1083, para. 57. The war propaganda sub-clause (Art. 20, para. 1) was adopted by 53 votes to 21, with 9 abstentions and can accordingly be considered to be the most popular half of Art. 20. Spain is the only Western European State voting in favour of this element. The Article as a whole – i.e. the two paragraphs dealing with war and hate propaganda respectively – was adopted by 52 votes to 19, with 12 abstentions. A/C.3/SR.1083, para. 58.

[89] Chile did, however, vote in favour of the overall article.

[90] See also Farrior, 'Molding the Matrix', at 40–41.

or against. Yet suddenly the representative from Mali asked the chairman whether it was not possible to just get the voting over and done with: those 'delegations that wished to do so could explain their votes after the voting.'[91] The Philippine chairman was further persuaded to proceed like that by the USSR and Bulgaria, while Australia thought this procedure was rather unfair to those who had not yet been able to speak their mind.[92] The chairman decided to comply with the request made by the delegate from Mali.[93] This sudden change of procedure did cause 'a certain amount of dissatisfaction', as the chairman mildly put it.[94] A separate meeting was convened – *ex post facto* – to repair this. The delegates that were still on the speakers list were almost all against the incitement provision.[95]

3.2.2 Key thematic debates

In discussing the different drafts proposed we have had a first taste of what drove the different delegations. Let us now highlight some of the fiercest thematic discussions that went to the heart of why the post-Second World War world truly needed anti-incitement legislation – or why we should not give in to the urge to ban extreme speech, as others vehemently argued. The following debates show that, from quite early on in the crafting process,[96] the drafters were no longer exclusively concerned with state-instigated hate propaganda. Both the proponents and the opponents show – through respectively their supporting comments and their concerns – that the incitement clause has horizontal ramifications, too.[97]

---

[91] A/C.3/SR.1083, para. 48. [92] A/C.3/SR.1083, paras. 49–53.

[93] A/C.3/SR.1083, para. 54. [94] A/C.3/SR.1084, para. 1.

[95] A/C.3/SR.1084, para. 3 (Norway, also speaking on behalf of the delegations of Denmark, Finland, Iceland, Sweden and Norway: against); para. 7 (Australia: against); para. 13 (Italy: against); para. 16 (Canada: against); para. 19 (Ecuador: against); para. 22 (UK: against); para. 31 (Colombia: against); para. 35 (Panama: against).

[96] Farrior, 'Molding the Matrix', at 23–24 has identified the 1950 amendment proposed by René Cassin (EICN.4/SR.174) as the decisive moment for this expansion of scope.

[97] Indeed, some discussion took place on this precise matter in the Commission on Human Rights, albeit in the context of drafting the freedom of expression provision. According to the USA, that fundamental freedom protects 'against governmental interference. Extension to the field of private infringements on freedom of information would create complications and give rise to many unpredictable situations' (E/CN.4/SR.160, at 10). The French representative rebutted this by reference to Article 2 of the draft Covenant on state obligations. Since State parties are both to 'respect and ensure' the Covenant rights to all individuals, they are under an obligation to protect both against governmental and horizontal interferences (E/CN.4/SR.160, at 13). Other states concurred with this view (e.g. E/CN.4/SR.160, at 12: Denmark; E/CN.4/SR.163 at 11: Lebanon) and it became the

3.2.2.1   All feared abuse

The debate on incitement was one dominated by fear. Essentially, all delegations feared abuse – some feared the abuse of unlimited speech while others feared abuse of a priori limits on free speech. Perfectly illustrating the controversial nature of an incitement ban, some states were very concerned with the risk that free speech may again be abused for fascist-like purposes, whilst other delegations were rather concerned that a priori restrictions on free speech might be abused by totalitarian states.

Accordingly, this agenda item caused the emergence of two vehemently opposing camps – those who argued that the Holocaust had proven that the international community must once and for all define the precise limits of free speech so as to prevent similar atrocities in the future, versus those who argued that the only medicine for extreme speech is more speech, and that the worst we could do at that junction in time was to fall into the trap of trying to circumscribe free speech and thus in one fell swoop provide tyrants with an excuse for repressing unpopular ideas or criticism.

The diametrically opposed positions led to much (mis)apprehension. Was the 'pro' (incitement legislation) lobby truly interested in eradicating hatred as the root of all evil? Then 'why … not prohibit evil itself', as the Uruguayan representative exclaimed in a Third Committee meeting.[98] Throughout the negotiations there was a sense – true or false – that the 'pro' camp was not wholly selfless in pushing for limitations, but were all too keen to put them to use back at home. Conversely, was the anti-lobby truly suggesting that, after all that had happened, fascists should be able to say what they wanted, thus continuing to poison the minds of people? For instance, in what appears to be all but an accusation against the naysayers, who kept calling incitement provisions either too vague or impracticable, the Polish representative stated that the 'vote on the Polish amendment would show which delegations were ready to tolerate the perpetuation of conditions which bred group hostility and permitted the subjection of one people to another'.[99] Western industrialized countries were sometimes perceived as overly dismissive or at any rate not

---

dominant view. Indeed, in contemporary human rights discourse and legal scholarship the view that human rights imply negative and positive state obligations, including due diligence obligations in horizontal relations among private parties, is well entrenched. Farrior, 'Molding the Matrix', at 23–4. See further the state representatives' interventions in the following sub-sections.

[98] A/C.3/SR.1083, para. 23   [99] E.g. E/CN.4/SR.378, at 10.

appreciative enough of incitement provisions. That was a position easy for them to maintain since those states had 'been particularly lucky not to have been threatened by totalitarian ideologies, [while] the rest of the world had not been so fortunate' – as a Chilean representative responded to a UK representative in the heat of the debate.[100] Similarly, a Yugoslavian delegate could not understand the fuss made about the supposed vagueness of the hate propaganda provision – the Yugoslav people 'knew what was meant by incitement to hatred'.[101] A fellow Yugoslav representative in a later meeting similarly lamented: 'It was probably necessary to have been a victim of such propaganda, as the people of Yugoslavia had been, to appreciate the importance of an article which ... should figure in all relevant international instruments.'[102] The Pakistani representative in the Third Committee somewhat pessimistically opined that 'any failure ... to adopt that article would imply approval of racial and religious hostility and discrimination. Moreover, any advocacy of national hostility, which was an outcome of hatred, could not fail to lead to violence and ultimately to war, which, if it became global, might well result in the destruction of humanity.'[103]

During the Sixteenth Session of the General Assembly's Third Committee (1961), during which the final version of the incitement clause was at long last adopted, Mrs Tillett of the USA and Lady Tweedsmuir of the UK once more – but to no avail – warned against abuse of the hate propaganda clause by (respectively) 'totalitarian' or 'unscrupulous' governments.[104] The USSR, instead, now wished to forbid all 'propaganda for national, racial or religious hostility' regardless of whether it constituted actual incitement to hatred and violence.[105] This intervention made the Japanese delegate first doubt the wisdom of the pending draft of the hate propaganda article. How about a situation in which advocacy of national, racial or religious hostility did not lead to violence? Could states then still take measures? In the words of this delegate, 'would such a ban not be very detrimental to freedom of expression?'[106]

---

[100] E/CN.4/AC.1/SR.28, at 3.   [101] E/CN.4/SR.174, at 9.

[102] E/CN.4/SR.379, at 12.   [103] A/C.3/SR.1081, para. 46.

[104] A/C.3/SR.1078, para. 6 (USA) and para. 17 (UK). The former held one last plea against the clause some days later during the meeting in which the final version was definitively adopted: A/C.3/SR.1083, paras. 14–17. Her last argument reflected all too transparently a feigned sense of miscomprehension. Also, this was perhaps not her strongest intervention: 'She wondered, for instance, whether the Press of most countries of the world, which had recently reported on the explosion of a high-power bomb ... could be accused of engaging in war propaganda.'

[105] A/C.3/SR.1079, para. 20.   [106] A/C.3/SR.1079, para 22.

3.2.2.2 The Cold War in the drafting chambers

Although the debate at times bordered on relativism, a majority of states ultimately managed to adopt an extreme speech provision. Farrior identifies another stumbling block that doubtless had slackened the process: 'many of the drafters were concerned not only about advocacy of hatred that would incite imminent violence, but also about the casual connection they saw between such advocacy and the problem of discrimination.'[107] This was clearly contrary to the experiences and wishes of the Americans. But even when the draft advocacy article only dealt with 'incitement to violence' (1947),[108] the USA objected to it, fearing abuse. Inciting violence and a 'clear and present danger' that violence will actually occur are two quite different things for an American lawyer.[109] Thus for the USA it was one thing to have its Supreme Court making only in the most extreme cases ad hoc exceptions to First Amendment-guaranteed free speech on the basis of jurisprudential doctrines revolving around real dangers; it was quite another thing to codify a priori exceptions in an international bill of rights, thus potentially providing suppressive regimes with the tools for their repression. In a governmental comment on one of the drafts, it beseeched fellow delegations to delete the incitement provision:

> The present laws of the United States prevent incitement to violence for any reason when there is a clear and present danger that *violence will actually result*. Long experience with the problem of free speech has led to the conclusion that any greater limitation would be liable to misuse for the purpose of suppressing free speech. It is felt that the utmost freedom of speech is a better safeguard against hostility and violence than general laws giving increased powers to suppress freedom of speech.[110]

In the drafting committee meeting, Mrs Roosevelt supported and explained her government's position by outlining her own: 'while some countries limited freedom of expression in this respect ... it was better

---

[107] Farrior, 'Molding the Matrix', at 22.

[108] I.e. the draft Covenant as it stood after the Second Session of the Commission on Human Rights (December 1947), see E/600, at 35 (see Article 21).

[109] By this time, the clear and present danger doctrine had already been developed by the US Supreme Court to determine if and when restrictions are possible on First Amendment rights, notably free speech and freedom of assembly. The tests stems from the First World War, see *Schenck* v. *United States*, 249 U.S. 47 (1919). The narrower test of 'imminent lawless action' was developed much later, indeed after the drafting process had come to completion. See *Brandenburg* v. *Ohio*, 395 U.S. 444 (1969).

[110] E/CN.4/82, at 12 (emphasis added); and E/CN.4/82/Rev.1, at 23.

to err on the side of too great freedom of speech … [T]his problem was best treated by individual self-discipline rather than by the enactment of law which played into the hands of those who would attempt to restrict freedom of speech entirely.'[111] The Soviet representative, Mr Pavlov, vehemently disagreed, arguing that the hate propaganda article:

> could place a powerful weapon in the hands of democracy, serving to restrict the dissemination of Nazi-Fascist propaganda … [T]he failure to restrict the dissemination of Nazi-Fascist theories had resulted, in recent times, in a terrible destruction of lives and in the elimination of human rights in Germany … [T]rue democrats could not but be anti-Fascist and anti-Nazi, and were therefore obliged to combat such theories.[112]

Other members supported this view,[113] but neither Mr Wilson of the UK nor Mrs Roosevelt was persuaded. The former reiterated that 'the only safe remedy was to let the people speak freely and clearly', while the latter held once more that 'people who are able to hear all sides of any given problem would usually come to wise conclusions'.[114]

In defence of the USSR 1949 amendment on hate propaganda,[115] Mr Pavlov opined that '[m]illions had perished because the propaganda of racial and national superiority, hatred and contempt, had not been stopped in time. Yet five years had hardly elapsed since the end of the war, and there were already signs of a revival of similar tendencies in various countries of the world.'[116] The US representative rebutted this by invoking the judicial practice of the US Supreme Court. For instance, in the case of *Terminiello* v. *Chicago* the US Supreme Court had held that an ordinance aiming at banning speech that 'stirs the public to anger, invites dispute, brings about a condition of unrest, or creates a disturbance' was unconstitutional.[117] Accordingly, 'the principle of democracy was better served by allowing individuals to create disputes and dissension than by suppressing their freedom of speech … nothing should be included in the Covenant which might serve to suppress that freedom.'[118] René Cassin,

---

[111] E/CN.4/AC.1/SR.28, at 2–3.   [112] E/CN.4/AC.1/SR.28, at 3.

[113] E/CN.4/AC.1/SR.28, at 2–4, Chilean interventions.

[114] E/CN.4/AC.1/SR.28, both recorded at 3.

[115] E/CN.4/223.   [116] E/CN.4/SR.123, at 4.

[117] *Terminiello* v. *Chicago*, 337 U.S. 1 (1949). Farrior, 'Molding the Matrix', at 23, spotted the historical link to this case. It may be noted that the US Supreme Court upheld a statute criminalizing group defamation as late as the 1950s. See *Beauharnais* v. *Illinois*, 343 U.S. 250 (1952). Though never formally overruled, that judgment was significantly revisited through subsequent jurisprudence.

[118] E/CN.4/SR.123, at 5.

however, agreed with the USSR that 'where freedom of speech was abused to provoke criminal acts, it should be curbed'; however, 'the difficulty was to determine where use became abuse.'[119]

In 1950 the USA, through Mrs Roosevelt, fought relentlessly against the incitement provision: 'It would be extremely dangerous to encourage Governments to issue prohibitions in that field, since any criticism of public or religious authorities might all too easily be described as incitement to hatred and consequently prohibited. [The article is] not merely unnecessary, it [is] also harmful'.[120] During the Sixth Session she therefore warned the Commission on Human Rights 'not to include in the draft covenant any provision likely to be exploited by totalitarian States for the purpose of rendering the other articles null and void'.[121] She illustrated her point by reference to Hungary, Bulgaria and Romania where the 'suppression of fascism' provided 'a loophole for those seeking to ignore their obligations and enabled them to consider themselves justified in their attitude'.[122] The Chilean representative in the Commission doubted the wisdom of an incitement prohibition by means of squarely challenging censorship in the USSR and other communist states.[123]

Yet it was a Chilean amendment that brought the issue of incitement back to everyone's attention some years later (1953) – and this time for good. Mr Hoare of the UK did not rejoice in the fact that the notion of incitement was on the table again:

> The Chilean amendment would ... necessitate a measure of control over thought such as had never been contemplated. It was interesting to note that its author [Mr Diaz-Casanueva] had invoked the analogy of preventive medicine ... The idea of prevention necessarily implied censorship. It was a very serious question whether United Nations authority should be lent to a proposal that would have the effect of imposing a censorship, and as far as the United Kingdom was concerned, the answer had been 'No!' ever since the days when Milton had written 'Areopagitica' and was 'No!' today.[124]

---

[119] E/CN.4/SR.123, at 6. This is the moment he proposed his own amendment.

[120] E/CN.4/SR.174, at 6.

[121] E/CN.4/SR.174, at 7. Netherlands and Belgium agreed.

[122] E/CN.4/SR.174, at 7.

[123] The criticism was particularly aimed at the USSR campaign against 'cosmopolitanism' (i.e. foreign influences): 'an unduly narrow conception of national dignity might induce some officials to take advantage ... to impose an unjustified censorship'. E/CN.4/SR.174, at 12.

[124] E/CN.4/SR.379, at 6.

Perhaps he should have limited his passionate intervention to these examples. At any rate, when Mr Hoare mentioned parenthetically that *Mein Kampf* was not prohibited in the UK, all of a sudden he became the one that had a lot to answer for.[125] All ensuing indignation, however, was eloquently rebutted by the UK delegate:

> [he] regretted that his casual observation that to the best of his beliefs Hitler's 'Mein Kampf' had not been banned in the United Kingdom should have shocked the Soviet Union representative. It was clear that the latter had no conception of what was meant in the United Kingdom by freedom of speech. That being so, it was less difficult to comprehend his inability to understand how the British people could have successfully fought Hitler unaided for a considerable and highly critical period of the war and at the same time allowed 'Mein Kampf' to circulate throughout the country. He would only say that the United Kingdom would maintain and fight for its conception of liberty as resolutely as it had fought against Hitler.[126]

Mrs Lord, arguing on behalf of the USA in the General Assembly's Third Committee, was most partial to the ideas of Mrs Roosevelt. She felt that the hate propaganda provision 'seriously threatened the principle of freedom of expression by requiring the prohibition of incitement to racial, religious and national hatred and hostility. While most members would condemn the advocacy of hostility of any kind, such a prohibition would entail acceptance of the principle of totalitarian control over all forms of expression.'[127] This attack on totalitarianism led to a counter-attack by the USSR: 'The sufferings caused by the racial theories of the Nazi criminals were well known, and the world had already paid too dearly for that so-called freedom of expression ... Freedom of expression should be restricted in certain cases, as it was in many countries, including the United States of America.'[128]

In 1955, when a full draft Covenant was realized after ten General Assembly sessions, the UN Secretary-General summarized the controversy and deadlock as follows:

> The question was debated whether the covenant should include an article prohibiting 'any advocacy of national, racial or religious hostility'. On the one hand, the opinion was expressed that legislation was not the most effective means to deal with the matter, and that if propaganda should constitute a menace to public peace, article 19 [freedom of expression],

---

[125] E/CN.4/SR.379, at 6.   [126] E/CN.4/SR.379, at 13.
[127] A/C.3/SR.568, para. 15.   [128] A/C.3/SR.576, para. 31.

paragraph 3 [restrictions], of the draft Covenant on Civil and Political Rights would be applicable. On the other hand, it was emphasized that the strong influence of modern propaganda on the minds of men rendered legislative intervention necessary and that the general provisions of article 19, paragraph 3, were not adequate, as they did not impose upon States parties any obligation to prohibit the advocacy of national, racial or religious hostility. Fears were expressed that an article prohibiting such advocacy might lead to abuse and would be detrimental to freedom of expression. It was proposed that only such advocacy of national, racial or religious hostility as 'constitutes an incitement to violence' should be prohibited by the law of the State. In discussing this proposal the view was expressed that no law would be effective if it did not go to the root of the evil.[129]

One recognizes the position as defended by Poland, the USSR and Chile, among other states, as sharply contrasted to the position, characterized by concerns and reluctance, voiced by chiefly the UK and the USA.

3.2.2.3 Genuine research and other protected public discourse

In the debates the problem of how to consider the compatibility of scientific – yet potentially controversial – pronouncements on relevant topics such as religion or race repeatedly popped up. This discussion of 'genuine contributions' to public discourse is as pertinent and relevant to human rights law today as it was to the drafters half a century ago.

For Mr Malik of Lebanon, the uncertainty as to whether such discourse could potentially come within the ambit of the incitement provision was one of the main reasons to be wary about this article. He argued that '[t]ruth stood above national peace. It would be a serious mistake to introduce a provision into the covenant prohibiting in effect the scientific and objective utterance of truth which was the best guarantee of human progress.'[130]

René Cassin also thought the incitement provision should be premised on a 'clear distinction between objective studies of a scientific nature and pure propaganda'.[131] He illustrated this point by reference to the works of racial demography by Arthur de Gobineau, 'which gave a prominent role to the Germanic race but were in the nature of a scientific study', something that 'should not be confused with the newspaper "*Der Sturmer*" which incited to murder'.[132]

---

[129] A/2929, paras. 189–191 [130] E/CN.4/SR.174, at 8.
[131] E/CN.4/SR.174, at 10. [132] E/CN.4/SR.174, at 10.

The Chilean representative in the Commission on Human Rights also found it most problematic that 'any publication or study which dealt objectively with ethnic matters might be interpreted as hostile propaganda'. Moreover, he foresaw major problems in the area of *religious* manifestations and religious discourse: 'all the religions based on the dogma of revelation believed they had an absolute and unquestionable monopoly of the truth; their propaganda was accordingly unfavourable or positively hostile towards other religions. [The draft provision] might have the effect of precluding all religious discussion.'[133]

One particular fear of backlash was related to the plight of *national liberation movements*. Seeing how the likes of Mahatma Gandhi, 'the greatest champion of non-violence',[134] could be imprisoned over incitement charges, the Egyptian representative in the Commission on Human Rights at some point felt urged to propose an amendment to the incitement clause, adding the words 'not aiming at the achievement or protection of the rights recognized in this Covenant' to the word 'violence'.[135] Despite the fact that there was some support for this notion,[136] the Egyptian delegate withdrew his motion first thing after lunch that same day, since he 'felt that it would be detrimental to the cause of human rights and detract from the value of the covenants to link the attainment of lawful objectives with hatred and violence'.[137]

3.2.2.4   National legislative potential

Closely related to the abuse debate, another key thematic thread running through the debates can best be described as 'definitional issues and legislative potential'. Time and again it was held by certain delegates that provisions concerning hate propaganda were simply too vague, that their key terms were imprecise and could never be conclusively defined – in sum, that the incitement clause was not practicable for states at the domestic legislative and judicial level.[138]

Mrs Roosevelt set the tone in that regard in the Second Session of the drafting committee of the Commission on Human Rights by stating that 'the expression of the words "incitement to such discrimination" was too

---

[133] E/CN.4/SR.174, at 13.   [134] E/CN.4/SR.378, at 7.

[135] E/CN.4/SR.378, at 13; amendment separately filed as E/CN.4/L.271.

[136] The Chilean delegation would be prepared to accept an amendment to that effect. E/CN.4/SR.378, at 11. The Egyptian intervention also led to scorn: E/CN.4/SR.378, at 8 (USSR).

[137] E/CN.4/SR.379, at 4.

[138] In addition to the examples mentioned shortly, see A/C.3/SR.1081, para. 66 (Italy); para. 67 (Ireland); and para. 72 (Greece); A/C.3/SR.1082, para. 18 (Cyprus) and para. 22 (Japan); A/C.3/SR.1084, para. 31 (Colombia).

vague and that its inclusion in the article, therefore, was not desirable'.[139] At a later stage of the drafting process she also deemed the term 'religious hostility' specifically too obscure.[140]

Delegates who shared this sense of ambiguity feared a backlash in the area of religious freedom. Mr Malik of Lebanon, for instance wondered whether the attempt to tackle religious hostility could legitimize states to act against a person preaching a religion not yet practised in the country.[141] Mr Hoare of the UK presented the same type of argument:

> In a country where a minority practised a religion different from that of the majority, there was room for a great deal of controversy. Supposing the religious leader of the minority put the case for his faith in violent and perhaps bitter words, the Government would then be able, on the strength of the proposed article, to evade its obligations to protect the minority.[142]

There were repeatedly expressed concerns regarding virtually every word of the draft incitement clause, including: 'advocacy',[143] 'religious hostility',[144] 'incitement',[145] 'violence'[146] and 'hatred'.[147] The difference between the key terms was also found unclear by some. One delegate, for instance, found it 'difficult to draw a distinction between *advocacy* and *incitement*. It was equally difficult to differentiate between various shades of feeling ranging from hatred to ill-feeling and mere dislike.'[148]

These challenges questioned the clause's potential for legislative and judicial implementation and enforcement. For instance, specifically on 'advocacy', a UK delegate in the Commission on Human Rights argued that the word:

> was not defined, and it was notoriously difficult to draw a line between advocacy and pernicious propaganda. Advocacy might be well-intentioned but overstep the bounds of the permissible; it might be misguided; or it might simply be foolish. It was impossible to express those shades of meaning in a text. After all, the words of Voltaire had been intended to incite religious hatred – and indeed they were still on the Index of the Roman Catholic Church.[149]

---

[139] E/CN.4/AC.1/SR.28, at 2. Similarly, E/CN.4/SR.174, at 13 (Chile).
[140] E/CN.4/SR.174, para. 27.
[141] E/CN.4/SR.174, at 8.   [142] E/CN.4/SR.379, at 5.
[143] E/CN.4/SR.174, at 11 (China) and 12 (Chile).
[144] E/CN.4/SR.174, at 10 (Lebanon) and 11 (China).
[145] E/CN.4/SR.174, at 13 (Chile); A/C.3/SR, para. 6 (USA).
[146] E/CN.4/SR.174, at 13 (Chile).
[147] E.g. E/CN.4/SR.174, at 13 (Chile); A/C.3/SR, para. 6 (USA).
[148] E/CN.4/SR.174, para. 26 (emphasis added).
[149] E/CN.4/SR.379, at 6.

Mrs Lord argued on behalf of the USA in the General Assembly that 'it was doubtful whether the terms themselves could be defined with sufficient precision for an international treaty'.[150]

Other delegations did not quite understand these hesitations. At some point the Chilean representative in the Commission on Human Rights lamented that it 'could as well be asked, how could [one] define such terms as "honour", "reputation" or "republic". Yet those terms certainly had their place in legislation.'[151] Similarly, in the Fifth Session of the Commission on Human Rights, the Yugoslav delegate – somewhat naively – argued: '[m]urder and arson were prohibited by national legislations, and fascist-nazi views and the propaganda of racial and national superiority constituted a similar crime at the international level. No person advocating such criminal views should be allowed protection under the Covenant.'[152] René Cassin sought to rebut the alleged unwieldy nature of the incitement provision by referring to relevant incitement prohibitions at the time already codified by France and the Netherlands – '[t]wo great democracies had thus been led to put into effect what some did not wish to have stipulated.'[153]

The World Jewish Community had already repeatedly lobbied for a hate propaganda provision, when in 1953 they made one more intervention with a view towards playing down this particular concern:

> Turning to the alleged difficulty of applying such an article … as a member of the minority which had suffered more than any other from the absence of provisions such as those under discussion and a third of whose members had suffered the supreme sacrifice during the Second World War, he would recall that for many years the words 'Down with the Jews' had appeared in the Nazi publication, the 'Stürmer', in letters over an inch high, and houses in Germany had been plastered with hundreds of thousands of posters calling for the death of the Jews or other minorities. It would be difficult to deny that such propaganda incited hatred or violence, and it would be doing the independent and enlightened judges of

---

[150] A/C.3/SR.568, para. 15

[151] E/CN.4/SR.377, at 14. Some eight years later, in 1961, the same Mr Diaz-Casanueva, this time in the Third Committee of the General Assembly, gave a comprehensive presentation on how (hate) 'propaganda' could be defined as a legal concept. See A/C.3/SR.1078, paras. 7–16.

[152] E/CN.4/SR.123, at 5. The final sentence is interesting. It is quite a different thing to adopt an international norm forcing all states to adopt hate legislation at the national level, than to bar the author of extreme views from protection under the Covenant. The latter resembles the 'abuse of rights' doctrine, a related but ultimately different matter.

[153] E/CN.4/SR.174, at 10.

the democratic nations an injustice to suppose that they would have any difficulty in applying an article prohibiting it.[154]

The 1953 draft incitement provision – that version which had resulted from a Sub-Commission on prevention of Discrimination and Protection of Minorities' intervention slightly amended by a Chilean proposal – effectively mediated in these definitional and threshold debates. While some delegations, notably the USA and the UK,[155] felt that only a ban on incitement to 'violence' could be conceptualized by domestic law-makers and judges, other representatives wished to go much further than that. One may recall how Poland at one point wished to prohibit advocacy of 'exclusiveness' and 'contempt';[156] while a Yugoslav representative felt that the provision 'ought to be directed … against all propaganda that constituted incitement to hatred and intolerance in every sphere'.[157] The Sub-Commission's proposal had focused on 'incitement to violence'; as a result of the adopted Chilean amendment it focused on advocacy of religious and other hostility 'that constitutes an incitement to hatred and violence'.[158] The 'and' is not without meaning. The *cumulative* effect was intended, thus finding middle ground between insisting that minimally imminent violence is required and insisting 'that any propaganda constituting an incitement to hatred was no less serious than that constituting an incitement to violence'.[159] Because of the 'and', the threshold was exceptionally high at that particular stage of the drafting.[160] Some years later, all of that would be renegotiated again – with a different outcome.

---

[154] E/CN.4/SR.378, at 5.

[155] Extreme speech limitations according to the UK representative in the Commission on Human Rights should only relate to 'conduct likely to cause a breach of the peace, that was to say, conduct which, whether or not it actually resulted in violence, a reasonable person would conclude to be likely to lead to violence'. E/CN.4/SR.377, at 8. As the Commission on Human Rights formulated it in its summary of the Ninth Session (1953), some delegations 'thought that while "an incitement to violence" was a definable legal concept, "an incitement to hatred" was a subjective notion that could not easily lend itself to legal action'. E/2447, at 9.

[156] E/CN.4/SR.377, at 4; and E/CN.4/L.269.

[157] E/CN.4/SR.377, at 6.   [158] E/2447, at 9.   [159] E/2447, at 9.

[160] Such also was the reading of the Polish representative in the Third Committee, who resented the fact that 'some delegations wished to restrict [the] prohibition to violence in the strict sense of the word and refused to extend it to other forms of hostility, although the latter were the most prevalent. That was the attitude of the sponsors of the four-Power amendment and of the authors of the original text. According to the latter, indeed, *only a combination of hatred and violence came within the prohibition; if one of those two elements were lacking, the prohibition could no longer apply.*' A/C.3/SR.1081, paras. 34–35 (emphasis added). This urged Poland to support the broader nine-Power amendment and to help draft the subsequent sixteen-Power amendment.

In 1961 the delegations that felt that the incitement article consisted of important *and* definable legal concepts were getting the upper hand in the General Assembly's Third Committee. This momentum was kicked off by an extensive discourse on the legal and judicial potential of incitement by Mr Diaz-Casanueva of Chile.[161] In the next meeting the Brazilian delegate joined in, postulating that he also:

> did not believe that that sort of propaganda was difficult to define. What it in fact meant was the repeated and insistent expression of an opinion for the purpose of creating a climate of hatred and lack of understanding between the peoples of two or more countries, in order to bring them eventually to armed conflict. That was an intention which any court should be able to establish as easily as it established *animus injuriandi* or *animus defendendi* in criminal law.[162]

Clearly, hate and war propaganda were taken in conjunction in this argument – fostering hatred so as to ultimately cause war.

In the later sixteen-Power amendment – the subsequently adopted final version of Article 20 – hate and war propaganda are again disentangled and presented as two separate paragraphs. Moreover, finally the formula 'religious (and other) hatred *that constitutes incitement* to discrimination, hostility or violence' was decided upon, which, many delegations thought, amounted to a definable legal concept. As the Brazilian delegate in the Third Committee argued, the sixteen-Power amendment 'included the word "hatred" as the point of departure and as the prime cause of violence. Naturally, the draft Covenant could not deal with the subjective aspects of hatred but must condemn incitement to hatred only when it was *externalized*, at which point it was quite readily determined by the courts.'[163]

A final point of contention regarding national implementation of the incitement clause concerned censorship. From the *travaux* it transpires that the incitement prohibition was by no means purported to authorize let alone require prior censorship. The final result (Article 20(2) ICCPR), however, is somewhat ambiguous. It requires hateful incitement to be 'prohibited by law' – how State parties precisely ought to go about that was not spelled out. Indeed, the final text does not even make it explicit whether that 'law' should be of a criminal/penal nature.[164] Commenting

---

[161]   A/C.3/SR.1078, paras. 7–16.

[162]   A/C.3/SR.1079, para. 2.

[163]   A/C.3/SR.1082, para. 5 (emphasis added).

[164]   Farrior, 'Molding the Matrix', at 48, argues that one of the main differences between Art. 4 ICERD and Art. 20(2) ICCPR is that only the former requires criminal laws and

on a French draft that does not differ much from the finally adopted text, Mr Cassin argued that the provision 'did not seek to promote the adoption of preventive and censorship measures but left the Governments free to choose the means by which they might prohibit certain kinds of harmful propaganda'.[165] Some years later, ever in favour of the adoption of an incitement provision, René Cassin wished:

> to reassure certain delegations which saw in the text an authorization for the establishment of a preventive censorship. The word "prohibited" did not mean *a priori* that a government should set up a system to stifle liberty. If an unlawful act could be punished in the criminal courts, it could also be the subject of civil liability actions, and one might well imagine a religious or alien group which was the object of propaganda constituting an incitement to violence suing the authors of such propaganda for damages in civil courts.[166]

The Polish representative in that same meeting 'failed to see' how the incitement clause 'could possibly be regarded as having any relationship with censorship in any form'.[167] According to the Pakistani delegate in the Commission on Human Rights, 'prohibition must be understood to include punishment but was not taken as being anticipatory or involving censorship.'[168] Some states challenged the provisions simply on account of the *risk* of states abusing the clause, arguing that because of potential censorship 'the remedy might be worse than the evil it sought to remove'.[169] Generally speaking, the supporters of the clause – the majority – rejected

---

sanctions, whereas the latter might be satisfied through civil or administrative laws and measures.

[165] E/CN.4/SR.174, at 5.   [166] E/CN.4/SR.379, at 9.

[167] E/CN.4/SR.379, at 10.

[168] Concluding with all but a sneer aimed at the UK delegation: 'On that point the United Kingdom's representative's objection was baseless'. E/CN.4/SR.379, at 12.

[169] E/CN.4/SR.377 at 7 (Australia). Farrior, 'Molding the Matrix', at 32. Curiously, the UN Secretary-General, in his 1955 annotations on the full draft Covenant, did not really get his head around the matter of censorship and limited himself to charting the variety of opinions on the matter: 'The words "shall be prohibited by the law of the State" were chosen in preference to the words "constitutes a crime and shall be punished under the law of the State". It was feared by some that the words "shall be prohibited by the law of the State" might encourage the establishment of governmental censorship. Another opinion was that the article could not be interpreted as suggesting that States should impose censorship. The view was expressed that States parties would be free to enact whatever legislation they deemed appropriate to put the article into effect' (A/2929, para. 194). Surely, State parties are not quite free to enact any legislation as they see fit on this issue and the latter position must be dismissed as a minority view among the drafters.

the notion that Article 20(2) authorizes censorship and downplayed the risk that ill-disposed states would abuse it to that effect.[170]

3.3   Concluding remarks

Certainly not all forms of 'hate speech' – let alone hatred – were to be banned as far as the drafters supporting the incitement clause were concerned, but only those forms of hatred that are *externalized* in the sense of actively appealing to adverse actions – be it 'discrimination', 'hostility' or 'violence' – against groups or individuals on account or their ethnicity or religion. While some delegations were not quite convinced,[171] this was the consensus concept the majority of drafters settled upon. The *travaux* are very illuminating on one thing: the incitement prohibition was a highly controversial clause. The recorded drafting history almost literally reads as: 'damned if you do, damned if you don't' (put international standards in place against incitement). Clearly, through the overstated and emotional considerations on Article 20 ICCPR we can see that the Cold War was being battled out around the drafting table. Yet at its core the debate was also a genuine human rights debate. As Nowak describes it, these historical discussions 'reflect the question of how far freedom of expression, which is so essential for the Western understanding of human rights and democracy, may or must be restricted in the interest of protecting other rights, such as the right to life and the prohibition of discrimination'.[172] Article 20(2) is indeed one of the rare provisions of international human rights law that – a priori – fixes a balance of sorts between a clash of rights. The majority of drafters settled in favour of the protection against violence and discrimination, indirectly in support of the right to life and the 'right to dignity', but in doing so they sacrificed the notion – or chimera – of absolute free speech.

The *travaux* also leave questions unanswered. Many of these questions are pursued in this book, for instance, how to actually define such key terms as 'advocacy', 'hatred', or 'incitement'. What type of speech acts engage Article 20(2) ICCPR, that is, what is the Article's precise legal threshold? Taking some of the drafters' concerns on domestic

---

[170] See also Nowak, *CCPR Commentary*, at 470 and 474.
[171] In addition to the usual suspects (USA and UK), Mr Cox of Peru may be added. He stated he was not 'happy' about what he called subjective and 'emotional elements' included in the incitement prohibition. A/C.3/SR.1082, para. 38.
[172] Nowak, *CCPR Commentary*, at 471.

implementation seriously, what should a domestic incitement law look like in order to be compatible with Article 20(2) ICCPR? And how does one prove incitement?

Two other questions are by no means answered. First, does Article 20(2) *oblige* State parties to have laws in place against incitement? Second, does Article 20(2) contain, in addition to a prohibition, a substantive *right*? It is with these two preliminary legal questions that we will jumpstart our conceptualization of the incitement prohibition in the next part of this book. To that effect we will delve into some additional drafting debates; however, more contemporary legal sources will be integrated into our analysis in order to yield definitive answers.

PART II

Preliminary matters

The mandatory nature of Article 20(2) ICCPR

4.1   Introduction

The United Nations General Assembly adopted the International Covenant on Civil and Political Rights on 16 December 1966. It took another decade for the ICCPR, including the incitement provision, to enter into effect in 1976.[1] The fact that those states in favour of the Covenant's incitement provision outnumbered the critics does not imply that thereafter the adopted provision led an easy life, free from criticism, obscurity or misunderstanding. Despite years of eventful drafting, debating, negotiating and renegotiating, 'the legal formulation of this provision is not entirely clear', as Nowak puts it in an understatement in his ICCPR treatise.[2] Indeed, the formulation is ambiguous precisely because it was subject to intense controversy, bargaining and fragile compromises.

The question that this part of the book poses to the incitement provision is very straightforward indeed – what is it? What is the legal nature of this provision, a provision that is so different from other Covenant articles? First, we establish if and to what extent Article 20(2) ICCPR is mandatory for State parties. Second, we will establish whether the provision is a prohibition per se, or if it also – despite its peculiar formulation – presupposes human rights (Chapters 5–6).

4.2   Textual analysis

The ICCPR's advocacy of hatred clause is, clearly, first and foremost a *prohibition*. To be precise, Article 20(2) orders State parties to prohibit advocacy of hatred that constitutes incitement. That is, the international norm

---

[1] Thirty-five ratifications were required. The ICCPR entered into force on 23 March 1976, three months after the thirty-fifth instrument of ratification was deposited with the Secretary-General of the United Nations.

[2] Manfred Nowak, *U.N. Covenant on Civil and Political Rights: CCPR Commentary* (2nd rev. edn, Kehl: N. P. Engel, 2005), at 474.

itself does not appear to be self-executing since it expressly calls for the adoption of national laws to achieve its purpose – banning incitement, both vertically (by state authorities) and horizontally (by private persons). Thus Article 20(2) is actually an 'international decree to prohibit' rather than a pure 'international prohibition'. The question that concerns us now is how mandatory this particular 'command' is for State parties.

The ordinary meaning of Article 20(2) in the light of the rationale of the Covenant leaves little doubt that it was intended to be a mandatory provision – incitement *shall be* prohibited by law.[3] The 'object and purpose' of the Covenant is to guarantee civil and political rights worldwide with a major emphasis on the promotion of equality.[4] When we consider the clause's 'context',[5] it is significant that the provision has been included in Part III of the Covenant. Part III lists the Covenant's substantive civil and political rights and standards, which are all considered to be mandatory. Furthermore, it is telling that the provision is codified as a separate article. Proposals to merge the provision with the freedom of expression clause were rejected during the drafting process. This signifies, first, that Article 20 may strictly speaking contain special limits not only for freedom of expression, but also in relation to other rights, such as the freedom of association.[6] Second and more important for our present purposes, its independent existence signifies that the provision is more than 'just' a limitation clause.

The difference from Article 13 of the International Convention on the Protection of the Rights of All Migrant Workers and Members of Their Families (CMW) is striking.[7] In that treaty, 'the purpose of preventing any advocacy of national, racial or religious hatred that constitutes incitement to discrimination, hostility or violence' is listed, among other aims, as a legitimate ground for limiting freedom of expression – nothing more, nothing less. Short of forcing states, that particular formulation authorizes State parties to combat incitement. Accordingly, State parties to the CMW *may*, under certain circumstances, employ the legitimate aim

---

[3] See also Sarah Joseph, Jenny Schultz and Melissa Castan, *The International Covenant on Civil and Political Rights* (Oxford University Press, 2000), 410, speaking of 'mandatory limitations' on free speech.

[4] See Art. 31(1) of the Vienna Convention on the Law of Treaties (VCLT), 1155 UNTS 331, 8 ILM 679, entered into force 27 January 1980. See ICCPR, Articles 2, 3, 4, 24, 26 and 27.

[5] VCLT, Art. 31(2).

[6] Nowak, *CCPR Commentary*, at 468.

[7] International Convention on the Protection of the Rights of All Migrant Workers and Members of Their Families, Adopted by General Assembly Resolution 45/158 of 18 December 1990, entry into force 1 July 2003.

of fighting incitement to justify a restriction on free speech. That limitation ground – the purpose of preventing incitement – does not, however, impose a duty to adopt anti-incitement legislation. The language on incitement of Article 20(2) ICCPR is totally different. It directly addresses State parties to the effect that they 'shall' prohibit incitement by law. Consequently, the text of the Covenant as such and when compared to other UN human rights treaties leads to the conclusion that Article 20(2) is a mandatory provision.

The compulsory nature of Article 20(2) also follows from a comparison between its formulation and that found in Article 7 of the UDHR. Under the Declaration, 'all are entitled to equal protection against any incitement to such discrimination'. This provision arguably *allows* laws safeguarding against incitement,[8] among other imaginable strategies, to guarantee such protection. It does, however, not quite follow from that formulation that incitement laws *must* be adopted. By contrast, the 'shall be' employed by Article 20(2) is rather adamant on this point.

The question whether states *may* or *must* take legislative measures against incitement is clearly a significant one. Especially during the early years of its mandate, the Human Rights Committee seemed quite reluctant to assess State parties' compliance with Article 20(2) ICCPR. The Committee on the Elimination of Racial Discrimination (CERD), on the contrary, frequently condemned and still condemns the lack of implementation of the hate propaganda clause enshrined in the International Convention on the Elimination of All Forms of Racial Discrimination (Article 4 ICERD).[9] That difference alone can of course hardly be construed as an argument against the mandatory nature of Article 20(2) ICCPR – it does say something about prioritization, though. For CERD, Article 4 ICERD has always been among the central provisions in the fight against racial discrimination. For the Human Rights Committee, Article 20(2) ICCPR was initially certainly not key to its efforts to promote civil and political rights worldwide. That said, in recent years the article is more frequently invoked by individual complainants (see Chapter 5), while it is also more actively engaged with by the Committee, for instance in its Concluding Observations on state reports and in a recent General

---

[8] See Stephanie Farrior, 'Molding the Matrix: The Historical and Theoretical Foundations of International Law Concerning Hate Speech' (1996) 14:1 *Berkeley Journal of International Law* 1–98, at 12. See also Robin Edger, 'Are Hate Speech Provisions Anti-Democratic? An International Perspective' (2010) 26:1 *American University International Law Review* 119–55, at 126–7.

[9] For details, see Chapter 6 (particularly sections 6.2– 6.4 thereof).

Comment (No. 34). The latter developments will shortly be discussed in this chapter, but first we briefly return to the drafting archives.

4.3   *Travaux préparatoires*

The conclusion that Article 20(2) ICCPR is mandatory is, albeit implicitly, corroborated by the *travaux*. It follows *a contrario* from the fears and critiques expressed by the opponents to the provision. The gist of these dismissive interventions was that while some states may already have adopted measures to combat extreme speech and be quite content with their efforts, other states saw no need for such restrictive laws and, more importantly, should not be forced by the rest of the world community into accepting them. For example, as early as during the drafting stages of the Declaration, in the Second Session (1948) of the drafting committee of the Commission on Human Rights, Mr Wilson of the UK was already fulminating against the mounting pressure to adopt a provision prohibiting something his country would never wish to prohibit. His intervention is recorded as follows: 'The United Kingdom had always relied, with success, on a well-informed public opinion to deal with the problem of incitement. He could not agree with [an amendment] which forbade "all incitement to establish arbitrary distinctions", since he considered that this would constitute an attempt to force the enactment of laws where countries were already adequately handling the problem.'[10] Some years later, Mr Hoare of the UK continued along the same lines and complained in the Commission on Human Rights that although the 'activities listed were clearly deserving condemnation',[11] no one particular course of action should be made compulsory for all states. Specifically, any 'proposal that States should be obliged to legislate against activities such as advocacy of exclusiveness or contempt must ... be examined with great care before being voted into the covenant'.[12] As far as he was concerned, '[i]t was for every government to deal with [hate] propaganda under its domestic law, and it did not need the authority of an international obligation to do so.'[13] He concluded that '[e]very state enjoyed the prerogative of passing any law that it liked, but it was another matter to impose on the society of States a requirement to enact legislation of a repressive character. Why should his own country, which was quite able to deal in its own

---

[10] E/CN.4/AC.1/SR.28, at 2.   [11] E/CN.4/SR.377, at 8.
[12] E/CN.4/SR.377, at 8.
[13] Words spoken at a later meeting: E/CN.4/SR.379, at 6.

way with [hate speech], be compelled to introduce into its law ... a conception foreign to its whole tradition?'[14] Seeing as an actual requirement to enact legislation – 'of a repressive character' – was precisely what was ultimately adopted, one understands the UK's reservation to the article made upon ratification.

Other representatives went as far as insinuating that their governments would and could not comply with this article. In response to the 1953 Sub-Commission/Chilean draft article on incitement, Mr Whitlam of Australia, for example, lamented that:

> the draft article had been extended to such an extent as to leave him rather at a loss ... [T]here was no likelihood whatever that a provision in that form would be embodied in Australian legislation ... [L]egislation was not the best means of achieving the desired result. It was axiomatic in Australia that people could not be legislated into morality. To be effective, legislation of the kind proposed would inevitably involve censorship and repressive police action – a system utterly abhorrent to the Australian way of life.[15]

Again, it comes as no surprise then that this country, too, entered a reservation to Article 20 upon ratification of the Covenant.

The summary of the Ninth Session (1953) of the Commission on Human Rights does not let these concerns go unnoticed. 'A number of representatives questioned the wisdom', the summary carefully states, 'of any mandatory requirement of legislation against [hate] propaganda.'[16]

Curiously, this deadlock could perhaps have been resolved had the representatives taken seriously a proposal made by the Brazilian delegation in the Third Committee of the General Assembly. Having already argued that the incitement provision 'was not a right, but a restriction of rights, particularly the right of freedom of expression',[17] an amendment was proposed by a Brazilian delegate with a view towards merging the gist of the incitement article with the general restrictions listed by the freedom of expression article. This would 'avoid difficulties for States which were constitutionally unable to restrict freedom of expression in any way'.[18] The provision might have garnered more final votes in the General Assembly, since an incitement restriction on free speech would have been an option

---

[14] E/CN.4/SR.379, at 6–7.

[15] E/CN.4/SR.377, at 6–7. To this day Australia has reserved the right not to introduce any further legislative provision on matters flowing from Art. 20 ICCPR. See section 4.4 for more details.

[16] E/2447, at 9.   [17] A/C3/SR.580, para. 11.

[18] A/C.3/SR.580, para. 11. Amendment separately filed as: A/C.3/L.413.

rather than an obligation. For the same reasons, that formulation might have prevented states from entering reservations.

4.4   Reservations

Seeing as some states were not pleased with the mandatory language of the ultimately adopted incitement provision, it is not surprising that a number of governments entered reservations to Article 20 upon ratification.[19] Different modalities can be distinguished. Those reservations purport to ensure that the state in question: (1) shall not be forced to act in ways contrary to constitutionally and internationally protected freedoms such as free speech, freedom of religion or freedom of association; (2) shall not be forced to adopt more (far-reaching) legislation, that is in addition to what is already in place in the state concerned; or (3) shall not be forced to adopt any legislation on the subject of extreme speech. Some reservations mix some or all of these angles.

Belgium made an interpretative declaration of the first kind: 'The Belgian Government declares … that article 20 as a whole shall be applied taking into account the rights to freedom of thought and religion, freedom of opinion and freedom of assembly and association proclaimed in articles 18, 19 and 20 of the Universal Declaration of Human Rights and reaffirmed in articles 18, 19, 21 and 22 of the Covenant.' Luxembourg made a very similar declaration.[20] Such declarations reflect concerns on the part of these governments that Article 20 is in actual fact, or can be, at odds with those fundamental rights.

Australia's reservation is an illustration of the second type. Australia, which repeatedly stated throughout the drafting process that it was perfectly content with its own ways of tackling the issue of extreme speech, indeed went on to reserve the following privilege: 'having legislated with respect to the subject matter of the article in matters of practical concern in the interest of public order (*ordre public*), the right is reserved not to introduce any further legislative provision on these matters.' New Zealand and the UK similarly reserved the right not to introduce

---

[19] Belgium, Denmark, Finland, France, Iceland, Ireland, Luxembourg, Netherlands, Norway, Sweden and Switzerland made a reservation to Art. 20(1) on banning war propaganda.

[20] Luxembourg: 'The Government of Luxembourg declares … that article 20 as a whole will be implemented taking into account the rights to freedom of thought, religion, opinion, assembly and association laid down in articles 18, 19 and 20 of the Universal Declaration of Human Rights and reaffirmed in articles 18, 19, 21 and 22 of the Covenant.'

any *further* legislation.[21] Reservations of this second type do not reject Article 20(2) outright. They rather aim to confirm that those domestic laws in place at the time of ratification are sufficient to discharge the obligations under the Covenant.

Malta and the USA, went significantly beyond that position, and entered reservations of the third category, that is to the effect that no legislation or action would be required under Article 20 at all.[22] The US reservation reads: 'article 20 does not authorize or require legislation or other action by the United States that would restrict the right of free speech and association protected by the Constitution and laws of the United States.' Like the Belgian reservation, a clash with free speech and freedom of association is considered inevitable. Moreover, in the face of that certain collision the First Amendment is prioritized. Accordingly, the best course of action under Article 20, this reservation purports, is no action at all.

What all these reservations and declarations have in common is that they do not reject Article 20(2) altogether. No state has entered a reservation to the effect that it 'does not consider itself bound' by Article 20(2) – a negating formulation some states have employed vis-à-vis some of the Covenant's articles.[23] It is open to dispute whether Article 20(2) is so tightly linked with the object and purpose of the Covenant that a reservation totally rejecting this provision would be invalid. Those who insist on the clause's inextricable link with such foundational Covenant standards as equality and the right to life may make such a case; others will emphasize the controversial status of the provision during the drafting process and the obscure life it led for the first few decades of its existence.

Be that as it may, states have not gone as far as a complete rejection of the article. What unites the different types of reservations is that, whatever

---

[21] New Zealand: 'The Government of New Zealand having legislated in the areas of the advocacy of national and racial hatred and the exciting of hostility or ill will against any group of persons, and having regard to the right of freedom of speech, reserves the right not to introduce further legislation with regard to article 20.' UK: 'The Government of the United Kingdom interpret article 20 consistently with the rights conferred by articles 19 and 21 of the Covenant and having legislated in matters of practical concern in the interests of public order (*ordre public*) reserve the right not to introduce any further legislation. The United Kingdom also reserve a similar right in regard to each of its dependent territories.'

[22] Malta: 'The Government of Malta interprets article 20 consistently with the rights conferred by Articles 19 and 21 of the Covenant but reserves the right not to introduce any legislation for the purposes of article 20.'

[23] E.g. Congo has made a reservation that reads: 'The Government of the People's Republic of Congo declares that it does not consider itself bound by the provisions of article 11.'

the precise meaning of Article 20(2), a state's own legal practice in the area of dealing with extreme speech will be maintained. Arguably, nowadays it requires such a reservation to perpetuate domestic practices that are not based on incitement laws. That is to say, all other states that would endeavour to comply with Article 20(2) by means short of a law expressly banning incitement are liable to get the UN Human Rights Committee on their case.

4.5   Human Rights Committee

The text of Article 20(2) ICCPR itself leaves little doubt that legislative action is necessary, since advocacy of hatred that constitutes incitement to discrimination, hostility or violence 'shall be prohibited by law'. Nevertheless, in the face of widespread reluctance on the part of State parties the Human Rights Committee had to convince states of the need for legislative action. First in 1983, in a General Comment on Article 20, the Human Rights Committee referred to the incitement bans flowing from this provision as 'required prohibitions'.[24] Specifically, according to the Committee, '[i]n view of the nature of article 20, States parties *are obliged* to adopt the necessary legislative measures prohibiting the actions referred to therein'.[25] Expressing its concern that many State parties still refrained from adopting the appropriate laws, the Committee reiterated in no uncertain terms that:

> [f]or article 20 to become fully effective *there ought to be a law* making it clear that propaganda and advocacy as described therein are contrary to public policy and providing for an appropriate sanction in case of violation. The Committee, therefore, believes that States parties which have not yet done so should take the measures necessary to fulfil the obligations contained in article 20, and should themselves refrain from any such propaganda or advocacy.[26]

In its 2011 General Comment No. 34 on freedom of expression, the Committee reiterates – in a section dedicated to the interplay between Articles 19 and 20 – that legislative action is required under Article 20. The Committee states: 'What distinguishes the acts addressed in article 20

---

[24] Human Rights Committee, *General Comment 11: Article 20* (Nineteenth session, 1983), para. 2. For an extensive drafting history of this Comment, see Dominic McGoldrick, *The Human Rights Committee: Its Role in the Development of the International Covenant on Civil and Political Rights* (Oxford: Clarendon Press, 1991), 484–90.

[25] HRC, *General Comment 11*, para. 1 (emphasis added).

[26] HRC, *General Comment 11*, para. 2 (emphasis added).

from other acts that may be subject to restriction under article 19, paragraph 3, is that for the acts addressed in article 20, the Covenant indicates the specific *response required* from the State: their prohibition by law.'[27] Earlier drafts of this General Comment were perhaps even more vehement on this point. Consider, for instance, this (dropped) excerpt:

> Article 20 is an important tool for the protection of persons from discrimination, hostility or attack because of their national, racial or religious identity. It imposes an obligation on States parties with regard to the prohibition of specific forms of extreme speech. It requires legislative action on the part of States parties. Such legislation should be reviewed as necessary to take account of contemporary forms and manifestations of national, racial and religious hatred. It is not compatible with the Covenant for the legislative prohibitions to be enacted by means of customary, traditional or religious law.[28]

The adopted text of the General Comment, in any event, is clear on the obligatory nature of the clause. The Committee adds once more in the final paragraph of the new freedom of expression Comment that 'with regard to the specific forms of expression indicated in article 20 … States parties *are obliged* to have legal prohibitions'.[29] Thus, for the Committee it is entirely clear that political commitment to this norm alone is not sufficient. Compliance requires national implementation, more particularly a law explicitly prohibiting advocacy of hatred that constitutes incitement to discrimination, hostility or violence.

Although the level of scrutiny in the relation to the incitement provision does not yet compare to that exhibited by CERD,[30] occasionally the Human Rights Committee has condemned the lack of appropriate legislation in the context of the state reporting procedure, being a further indication that as far as the Committee is concerned Article 20(2) is as mandatory as can be. For instance, Slovenia was summoned to 'adopt strong measures to prevent and prohibit the advocacy of hate and intolerance that constitutes prohibited incitement and fulfil the provisions of article 20'.[31] From some observations it transpires that the Committee

---

[27] Human Rights Committee, *General Comment 34: Article 19: Freedoms of Opinion and Expression* (CCPR/C/GC/34, adopted 102nd Session, 11–29 July 2011), para. 51.

[28] Human Rights Committee, *Draft General Comment No. 34* (UN Doc. CCPR/C/GC/34/CRP.2, dated 29 January 2010).

[29] HRC, *General Comment 34*, para. 52 (emphasis added).

[30] See Chapter 6 (particularly sections 6.2–6.4 thereof) for details on CERD's monitoring practice in relation to Art. 4 ICERD.

[31] A/60/40 vol. I (2005) 74, para. 93(13) (Slovenia).

assesses the texts of legislative developments quite closely. For example, the Committee reviewed New Zealand's practices in light of the Covenant and noted that although this country has a law generally corresponding to the obligations flowing from Article 20(2), it nonetheless needed to better ensure that the advocacy of *religious* hatred in particular was also covered.[32] Occasionally, the Committee also notes and welcomes legislative progress made under Article 20(2).[33] The relevant – albeit somewhat meagre – output from the state reporting procedure supports the view that Article 20(2) is mandatory.

Finally, some additional support for the position that Article 20(2) is mandatory can be found in the Committee's views on individual communications. Adversary proceedings taking place before the Committee are perhaps not the most logical source to search for an answer to the question whether or not Article 20(2) requires State parties to adopt prohibitions. Virtually all cases that directly or indirectly touch upon Article 20(2) have been brought by convicted inciters. In other words, in most cases in which Article 20(2) played a role revolve around persons – be it politicians, teachers or pamphleteers – claiming that states have unduly interfered with their freedom of expression. Thus those persons had made certain public statements, as a result of which the state interfered with their speech; those interferences came in the form of criminal sanctions or state-sanctioned job dismissals, and so on. Before the Committee the key question was every time whether Article 19 on freedom of expression was breached by the state or whether the limitations envisaged by that same article or by Article 20(2) were justly applied.

Accordingly, what we have seen very rarely until now are cases wherein an (alleged) hate speech *victim* complains about the fact that a State party either has no laws prohibiting incitement in place or that the State party concerned applies domestic laws contrary to the meaning of Article 20(2) of the ICCPR. Obviously, such a case would put pressure on the Committee to squarely address the mandatory nature of Article 20(2) ICCPR.[34]

---

[32] A/50/40 vol. I (1995) 38, para. 181 (New Zealand). See A/50/40 vol. I (1995) 57, para. 322 (Ukraine) for a somewhat similar observation. See also CCPR/C/RUS/CO/6 (2009), para. 24, and A/59/40 vol. I (2003) 20, para. 64(20) (Russia), assessing its law against 'extremist activity' in much detail, praising some aspects but extensively criticizing other elements.

[33] E.g. A/56/40 vol. I (2001) 34, para. 73(8) (Denmark): 'The amendment to the Danish Criminal Code to prohibit advocacy of national or racial hatred (art. 20) is welcomed.'

[34] In Chapter 5 we will see that a case of this type is pending, urging the Committee to pronounce on such matters as the mandatory nature of Art. 20(2) ICCPR and the concomitant issue of standing for incitement victims.

The current one-sided nature of Article 20(2) jurisprudence notwithstanding, the Committee has in fact already pronounced itself on the mandatory nature of Article 20(2) ICCPR in its case law. In *J.R.T. and W.G. Party* v. *Canada* the Committee considers that Canada had under the Covenant 'an obligation under article 20(2) of the Covenant to prohibit' the type of speech under discussion (namely telephonically disseminated hate messages).[35] In this case, this point is construed as a crucial argument in deeming the case, brought by a convicted inciter against Canada, to be inadmissible.[36]

4.6   Comparative law

Almost all State parties to the ICCPR, in one way or another, have adopted domestic laws that correspond – albeit certainly not always closely, as we will see in subsequent parts of this book – with Article 20(2) of the Covenant.[37] A few states, whilst not having entered reservations to this article, have, however, omitted to do so. Andorra and San Marino are among the Western states that do not prohibit incitement by law within the meaning of the Covenant.[38] In the light of the specific object of this book, it should be added that some states have codified a limited incitement offence excluding incitement based on *religious* hatred.[39]

---

[35] Human Rights Committee, *J.R.T. and the W.G. Party* v. *Canada*, Communication no. 104/1981 (6 April 1983), para. 8(b).

[36] The quoted sentence is immediately followed by the following conclusion: 'In the Committee's opinion, therefore, the communication is, in respect of this claim, incompatible with the provisions of the Covenant.' *J.R.T. and the W.G. Party* v. *Canada*, para. 8(b).

[37] The comparative law, comparative case law and comparative state practice analyses in this book are indebted to the studies providing relevant country-specific information published by the UN Office of the High Commission for Human Rights (www.ohchr .org/EN/Issues/FreedomOpinion/Articles19-20/Pages/ExpertsPapers.aspx). This data was gathered during the four 2011 Expert workshops (Workshop for Europe: Vienna, 9–10 February 2011; Workshop for Africa: Nairobi, 6–7 April 2011; Workshop for Asia Pacific: Bangkok, 6–7 July 2011; Workshop for the Americas: Santiago de Chile, 12–13 October 2011) on the prohibition of incitement.

[38] In Andorra, the act of publicly offending religious sentiments and disturbing religious rituals is criminalized by the Criminal Code. See Art. 301 of the Criminal Code of Andorra 1995. Clearly, neither of these bans resembles an incitement prohibition. San Marino prohibits religious insult and horizontal breaches of religious freedom. See Articles 260 and 261 of the Criminal Code of San Marino (1974) respectively. Again, these offences can certainly not be considered to correspond to Art. 20(2) ICCPR.

[39] E.g. Georgia, FYR Macedonia, Malta and Slovakia prohibit advocacy of only racial or ethnic hatred, not religious hatred. This will be discussed in more detail in Chapter 8.

It does not come as a surprise that states that have entered reservations to Article 20 ICCPR do not have in place incitement laws in the meaning of that provision. The USA would be the prime example here.[40] At the federal level there is no incitement law, while incitement laws adopted at the state level are liable to be struck down by the Supreme Court if they fail its 'imminent lawless action' test first adopted in *Brandenburg* v. *Ohio*.[41]

It has been observed already that while some reserving states quoted more principled – free speech – concerns about the incitement prohibition, most of the reservations are in fact to the effect that no (new) legislation shall be deemed to be required under Article 20(2) ICCPR. It may be recalled that Australia is among the states that reserved a right not to introduce further legislation on the matter of extreme speech. At the federal level it does ban hate speech (Racial Discrimination Act 1975), though only when motivated by ethnicity – not religion.[42] Interestingly, at state level legislation has been passed to also combat incitement on grounds of religion (e.g. Tasmania,[43] Queensland[44] and Victoria).[45] Upon ratification of the ICCPR, New Zealand, too, stipulated not to introduce further legislation with regard to Article 20. The Human Rights Act 1993 does tackle extreme speech,[46] but again incitement based on religious grounds is not covered. On account of intersecting hate grounds,

---

[40] For an interesting account on how the American population – as contrasted to European populations – feels about hate speech legislation, see Jamal Greene, 'Hate Speech and the Demos', in Michael Herz and Peter Molnar (eds.), *The Content and Context of Hate Speech: Rethinking Regulation and Responses* (Cambridge University Press, 2012), 92–115, describing a trend of ever-decreasing support for such legislation.

[41] *Brandenburg* v. *Ohio*, 395 U.S. 444 (1969). See, e.g., *R.A.V.* v. *City of St. Paul*, 505 U.S. 377, unanimously striking down a Minnesota crime ordinance that had led to the conviction of the applicant who had burned a cross on the lawn of a black person. See James Weinstein, 'An Overview of American Free Speech Doctrine and its Application to Extreme Speech', in Ivan Hare and James Weinstein (eds.), *Extreme Speech and Democracy* (Oxford University Press, 2009), 81–91, at 83, arguing that '[c]ontent-based regulations of public discourse are subject to "strict scrutiny", a test that almost always leads to the invalidation of the regulation.' See also Eric Barendt, *Freedom of Speech* (2nd rev. edn, Oxford University Press, 2007), 183–6.

[42] Racial Discrimination Act 1975, No. 52/1975 as amended through Act No. 96/2013 [Australia].

[43] Section 19(d) of the Anti-Discrimination Act 1998 [Tasmania].

[44] Section 124A of the Anti-Discrimination Act 1991 [Queensland].

[45] Section 8 of the Racial and Religious Tolerance Act 2001 [Victoria]. See e.g. *Islamic Council of Victoria* v. *Catch the Fire Ministries Inc* (Final) [2004] VCAT 2510 (22 December 2004), dismissing a religious vilification complaint.

[46] Section 131 of the Human Rights Act 1993 [New Zealand], prohibiting incitement based on grounds of 'colour, race, or ethnic or national origins'.

anti-hate speech laws have been deemed to be applicable to some instances of anti-Semitic speech.[47]

4.7   Concluding remarks

The text of Article 20(2) ICCPR itself, the considerations of the Covenant's drafters, the subsequent practice exhibited by State parties, and above all, the Human Rights Committee's views on the matter, all indicate that the incitement prohibition is mandatory and accordingly *requires* State parties to adopt legal prohibitions against incitement. Curiously, it does not indisputably follow from the text of Article 20(2) ICCPR that such a domestic law must be of a criminal nature. Quite to the contrary, Farrior has argued that one of the key differences between Article 20(2) ICCPR and Article 4 ICERD is that only the latter demands criminal prohibitions while the obligations flowing from the former norm could in theory be met through civil and administrative sanctions alone.[48] Indeed, Article 20(2) is increasingly viewed by stakeholders as urging states to adopt a comprehensive toolbox of anti-incitement measures, also including proactive measures promoting tolerance through, for instance, education, sensitization and awareness-raising.[49] That said, virtually all State parties to the ICCPR have opted for criminal incitement prohibition, be it exclusively or indeed in combination with other strategies.

---

[47] E.g. New Zealand Court of Appeal, *King-Ansell* v. *Police* [1979] 2 NZLR 531.

[48] Farrior, 'Molding the Matrix', at 48. Ivan Hare, 'Extreme Speech under International and Regional Human Rights Standards', in Hare and Weinstein (eds.), *Extreme Speech and Democracy*, observing the same at 71.

[49] E.g. OHCHR, CERD and ARTICLE 19. See, respectively, *Rabat Plan of Action on the Prohibition of Advocacy of National, Racial or Religious Hatred that Constitutes Incitement to Discrimination, Hostility or Violence* (Conclusions and recommendations emanating from the four regional expert workshops organized by OHCHR in 2011 and adopted by experts in Rabat, Morocco on 5 October 2012), paras. 23–29; CERD, *General Recommendation 35: Combating Racist Hate Speech* (UN Doc. CERD/C/GC/35, 83rd session, 12–30 August 2013), paras. 30–44; and ARTICLE 19, *Prohibiting Incitement to Discrimination, Hostility or Violence: Policy Brief* (2012), at 41–45. See also the literature mentioned in Chapter 1 (at footnote 32).

Article 20(2) ICCPR: prohibition per se or also a human right?

5.1 Introduction

Article 20 is most certainly the Covenant's odd one out.[1] On the face of it, this provision does not enumerate another fundamental right but rather a *sui generis* state obligation. What is more, that principle or obligation may be construed as a *special limit* on other fundamental rights, notably on the right to freedom of expression, but also for instance on the right to freedom of association. Accordingly, the hateful incitement prohibition can be considered an 'alien element in the system of the Covenant'.[2]

This anomaly leads us to the important question whether the provision indeed merely contains a special duty for states to prohibit extreme speech, or whether the norm presupposes a human right – the *right to protection against incitement*. The question is relevant because the position of incitement victims would be stronger if such an implied or underlying right could be inferred from Article 20(2).

First of all, should the advocacy clause contain an individual legal entitlement in addition to a mere command to prohibit extreme speech, State parties to the ICCPR would be bound to 'respect and ensure' this right to be free from prohibited forms of incitement.[3] Alleged victims, then, are or rather must be in a position to have a breach of their right determined by a competent judicial body and to receive an 'effective remedy' in case of a violation of their rights.[4] Arguably, remedies may also be provided if the provision boils down to a plain prohibition, yet this may be harder to achieve than in the event a breach of the norm can be construed

---

[1] This chapter draws on Jeroen Temperman, 'A Right to be Free from Religious Hatred? The Wilders Case in the Netherlands and Beyond', in Peter Molnar (ed.), *Free Speech and Censorship Around the Globe* (New York/Budapest: Central European University Press, 2014), 509–30.

[2] Manfred Nowak, *U.N. Covenant on Civil and Political Rights: CCPR Commentary* (2nd rev. edn, Kehl: N. P. Engel, 2005), at 468.

[3] ICCPR, Art. 2(1).   [4] ICCPR, Art. 2(3).

as an actual 'human rights violation'. In the case of a general prohibition without a clear human rights beneficiary it is unclear who has standing to bring the claim at the national level.

The relevance of the potential qualification as a 'right' extends to the international legal arena. Specifically, an affirmative answer could – after exhausting domestic venues – provide alleged incitement *victims* with international legal standing to complain about non-implementation of state obligations flowing from Article 20(2) ICCPR. This would mean standing before the Human Rights Committee.

5.2   Textual analysis

Again, the provision's context and the overall object and purpose of the Covenant are significant, particularly the fact that the article has been included in Part III of the Covenant listing the substantive civil and political rights. Part II, by contrast, contains general instructions on equal human rights promotion in addition to a couple of general caveats in relation to emergency situations and abuses of rights. Had the incitement standard been merged with the latter 'abuse of rights' doctrine, for instance, it would have been quite out of the question to construe the norm as an actual legal entitlement. The drafters, however, decided to insert this – albeit odd-looking – norm into the section dealing with substantive human rights.

Further, the fact that the provision is codified as a separate article is again telling. Significantly, proposals to merge the provision with the limitations paragraph of the freedom of expression article – Article 19 ICCPR – were rejected during the drafting process. Still, we must critically reflect on the 'ordinary meaning' to be given to the incitement clause in the context and in the light of the object and purpose of the ICCPR. Certainly, the text of Article 20 does not literally provide a right. At no point does it mention the words 'right' or 'freedom'. However, neither does the prohibition of torture: 'No one shall be subjected to torture or to cruel, inhuman or degrading treatment or punishment.'[5] Monitoring bodies nevertheless commonly speak of the 'freedom from torture',[6] thus *individualizing* the protection against torture. The protection the state

---

[5] ICCPR, Art. 7. See also, e.g., Art. 8(1): 'No one shall be held in slavery; slavery and the slave-trade in all their forms shall be prohibited.'

[6] E.g. Human Rights Committee, *General Comment 20: Article 7* (Forty-fourth session, 1992), para. 15 ('freedom from').

owes to its inhabitants is accordingly reformulated into an individual legal entitlement vis-à-vis the state.

What is striking about the incitement clause is that it is formulated as an express command addressed at State parties. They 'shall' prohibit by law any advocacy of national, racial or religious hatred that constitutes incitement to discrimination, hostility or violence. The fact that implementation laws are required at the national level seems to suggest that the provision is not self-executing. The non-self-executing nature of a human rights provision does not, however, rule out that the norm in question contains a fundamental right. Certain fundamental economic and social rights are deemed non-self-executing – they are still considered to be human rights.

At the risk of question-begging, there is a procedural argument to be made in favour of a rights interpretation. If the norm were to boil down merely to a 'command to prohibit', in extreme speech case law the provision would not add a single thing to Article 5 of the ICCPR on abuse of rights (together with Article 3 of the Optional Protocol to the ICCPR).[7] That is to say, the incitement prohibition would serve as an admissibility criterion in relation to those applicants – convicted inciters – who allegedly acted contrary to Article 20(2) ICCPR. The abuse of rights doctrine can serve that exact purpose,[8] making Article 20(2) ICCPR redundant procedurally speaking.

Be that as it may, based on a textual analysis we remain undecided on the question of implied rights. At best, we can conclude that a textual analysis does not rule out or positively resist an implied rights interpretation. Let us turn to the workings of the Human Rights Committee, but not before we let the Covenant's drafters speak on the matter.

5.3   Travaux préparatoires

The drafting history contains glimpses of what must have been the first discussion on the present issue: banning incitement – is that a *sui generis*

---

[7] The latter article reads: 'The Committee shall consider inadmissible any communication under the present Protocol which ... it considers to be an abuse of the right of submission of such communications or to be incompatible with the provisions of the Covenant.' Optional Protocol to the International Covenant on Civil and Political Rights, adopted and opened for signature, ratification and accession by General Assembly Resolution 2200A (XXI) of 16 December 1966, entry into force 23 March 1976.

[8] See e.g. Human Rights Committee, *M.A.* v. *Italy*, Communication no. 117/1981 (21 September 1981), for an example of such a procedural outcome based purely on Art. 5 ICCPR (abuse of rights).

state obligation or also human right? There were some states that felt that the international bill of rights did not quite lend itself to inclusion of what could – all things considered – best be deemed an ideal or a principle rather than a universal right. At an early point in the drafting process a New Zealand representative, for instance, hoped to free the Covenant from – whilst kindly burdening others with – the notion of incitement:

> It is a question whether the article, the aim of which will merit general approval, finds its correct place in a Covenant on Human Rights or whether it could not be included more appropriately in the proposed convention on genocide. As at present drafted, it does not conform to the general pattern of the rest of the Covenant, in that *it neither states nor is apparently intended to state the rights of an individual.*[9]

During the final drafting stages of the provision this type of criticism was mounting. A number of states wondered whether an international human rights covenant was the right place for an incitement provision since the latter was not clearly a 'right'. When discussing the hate propaganda clause in the Third Committee, the Belgian representative stated that it 'was not the Committee's task to draw up a list of social or moral principles, but to draft an international legal instrument'.[10] Similarly, during the Sixteenth Session (1961) of the Third Committee of the General Assembly both the Netherlands and Ireland stated that the norm was out of place.[11] For similar reasons, some delegations questioned the general *abuse of rights* provision (Article 5) – was that merely a principle or a right? Mr Simsarian of the USA, for instance, wished to see 'examples of cases in which it would prove to be an additional protection of a particular right'.[12] It may be reiterated that this particular clause did not end up among the substantive human rights in Part III of the Covenant, while the more specific advocacy clause did.[13]

---

[9] E/CN.4/82/Add.12, at 12 (emphasis added). Note that Art. III(c) of the Convention on the Prevention and Punishment of the Crime of Genocide went on to declare 'direct and public incitement to commit genocide' a punishable offence but that treaty omits hate propaganda offences. Convention on the Prevention and Punishment of the Crime of Genocide, 78 UNTS 277, 9 December 1948 (GA Res. 260), entered into force 12 January 1951.

[10] A/C.3/SR.1082, para. 27.

[11] A/C.3/SR.1081, paras. 14–15 (Netherlands) and para. 70 (Ireland).

[12] E/CN.4/223, at 8.

[13] Note that in the European Convention on Human Rights the abuse of rights provision (Art. 17) does form part of the section on fundamental rights. At the same time, it is clear there that the doctrine serves as a special admissibility criterion. See Art. 35(3)(a) [European] Convention for the Protection of Human Rights and Fundamental Freedoms, ETS No. 5 of 4 November 1950, entered into force 3 September 1953.

Throughout the drafting process it was remarked that the incitement provision did not constitute a right but a restriction. An early observation of this kind was made by the South African delegate in the Third Session (1948) of the Commission on Human Rights, during the drafting of the Declaration. He warned that the UDHR's draft-equality provision 'requires that every person is to be protected against any incitement to arbitrary discrimination in violation of the Convention ... this would require legislation. The necessary legislation, would constitute a further exception to freedom of expression ... and the latter article would have to be framed in such a way as to provide for such an exception'.[14] Later, largely for the same reasons, some states felt that there could be no place for such a restrictive provision in a binding covenant.[15] Even some of the states that were in favour of the norm conceded that the incitement prohibition did not amount to a clear right.[16]

A positive link between Article 20(2) and human rights was, however, made by some contributors to the drafting debates. There were delegates who considered norms against incitement a matter of *minority rights protection*,[17] while others deemed the incitement provision a matter of *group* or *collective rights*. Ghana, for instance, argued that 'there was a great difference between article 19 [on freedom of expression] and [article 20 on incitement], since the former set forth individual rights while the latter defined collective rights'.[18] Similarly, the Czechoslovakian representative in the Third Committee 'could not understand' those delegations that were of the opinion that the incitement clause 'did not protect a fundamental right',[19] implying that it was self-evident that the provision safeguarded a host of Covenant rights. A Philippines representative specified this. He regretted that some states felt that the incitement clause was out of place in this human rights instrument, for this provision 'in fact sanctioned the *right to life* and the *right to live in peace with one's neighbours*'.[20]

---

14 E/CN.4/82/Add.4, at 20. See, however, the caveats about the South African drafting contributions in section 2.3 of Chapter 2.
15 E/CN.4/SR.174, at 6 (USA and Netherlands). A/C.3/SR.570, para. 4 (Canada).
16 A/C.3/SR.580, para. 11. The Brazilian representative in the Third Committee noted that the incitement provision 'was not a right, but a restriction of rights, particularly the right of freedom of expression'.
17 E/CN.4/82/Add.4, at 20 (South Africa).
18 A/C.3/SR/1079, para. 53.   19 A/C.3/SR.1080, para. 14.
20 A/C.3/SR.1081, para. 23 (emphasis added).

Clearly, the *travaux* are only of limited help to our question. The proponents of the incitement provision outnumbered the opponents, yet not even the proponents were united in attributing rights status to this article. Let us now venture into the workings of the Human Rights Committee so as to ascertain whether a right to be free from incitement could be distilled from the Covenant.

5.4 Human Rights Committee

A number of Human Rights Committee sources shine a light on our question of whether Article 20(2) ICCPR contains besides a prohibition – or strictly, a state duty to prohibit – also a human right. In this section we will discuss the Committee's views as presented in its General Comments, its comments on state reports (specifically its conclusions or 'Concluding Observations') and its findings in case law ('Views').

5.4.1 General Comments

Both General Comment No. 11 on Article 20 ICCPR as well as the new General Comment No. 34 on Article 19 (and 20) ICCPR do not support the view that the incitement provision incorporates a right. These Comments speak exclusively in terms of 'prohibitions',[21] altogether ignoring the question of whether or not Article 20(2) also embodies a right to be free from incitement to discrimination, hostility or violence.

What General Comment No. 11 does say is that Article 20 is compatible with the freedom of expression,[22] thus contradicting concerns expressed by many delegations during the drafting process. General Comment 34 is more outspoken on the relationship between Articles 19 and 20. In the words of the Human Rights Committee, 'Articles 19 and 20 are compatible with and complement each other. The acts that are addressed in article 20

---

[21] Human Rights Committee, *General Comment 11: Article 20* (Nineteenth session, 1983), para. 1 ('legislative measures prohibiting the actions referred to'; 'prohibited by law'; 'prohibit') and para. 2 ('prohibited by law'; 'these required prohibitions'; 'For article 20 to become fully effective there ought to be a law making it clear that propaganda and advocacy as described therein are contrary to public policy and providing for an appropriate sanction in case of violation'). Human Rights Committee, *General Comment 34: Article 19: Freedoms of Opinion and Expression* (CCPR/C/GC/34, adopted at its 102nd session, Geneva, 11–29 July 2011), para. 51 ('prohibition by law') and para. 52 ('legal prohibitions').

[22] Human Rights Committee, *General Comment 11*, para. 2.

are all subject to restriction pursuant to article 19, paragraph 3. As such, a limitation that is justified on the basis of article 20 must also comply with article 19, paragraph 3.'[23] What this means is that impugned speech acts cannot be said to fall either in category 20(2) or in category 19(3). Thus there is no such thing as a priori unprotected speech. All speech, including speech acts that engage Article 20(2), is subject to the general rules on restrictions and the safeguards that come with Article 19's system of limitations. This means that restrictions that are supported by Article 20(2) must be 'provided by law', serve a 'legitimate aim' and must be 'necessary' to protect that aim.[24]

Be that as it may, this recent Comment, too, does not expressly invite communications under Article 20(2) by alleged victims of incitement. This was not an oversight. In the past individual Committee members have expressed (conflicting) views on this issue.[25] Accordingly, the current status quo in the Committee is reflected in its reluctance to make a general pronouncement on the status of Article 20(2) and, specifically, on the question of legal standing for incitement victims. We will see, though, that the Committee has shown more willingness to pronounce on this question in its case law.[26]

5.4.2   Concluding observations

In the state reporting procedure under the ICCPR, the Committee speaks almost exclusively in terms of a 'prohibition', avoiding the use of a 'right' to be free from incitement. That said, the Human Rights Committee's Concluding Observations have hinted at the need for domestic access to justice for victims of incitement. For instance, in relation to (then) Serbia and Montenegro the Committee expressed its concerns about the protection of Roma and other minorities. It urged this State party to take all measures to combat violence and incitement, including the establishment of 'mechanisms to receive complaints from victims and ensure investigation and prosecution' of cases of incitement to violence.[27] The necessary

---

[23] Human Rights Committee, *General Comment 34*, para. 50. First held in *Malcolm Ross v. Canada*, Communication no. 736/1997 (18 October 2000), para. 10.6.

[24] ICCPR, Art. 19(3).

[25] See section 5.4.3 below. Particularly, see the questions raised in the 2009 case of *Maria Vassilari et al. v. Greece*, Communication no. 1570/2007 (19 March 2009).

[26] See section 5.4.3 below.

[27] A/59/40 vol. I (2004) 68, para. 75(25) (Serbia and Montenegro).

protection furthermore entailed ensuring 'access to adequate remedies and compensation'.[28] The Committee has indicated the same in relation to instances of incitement against Roma in Slovakia.[29]

This shows that there is more to the prohibition of hateful incitement than meets the eye. Compliance with Article 20(2), apparently, does not merely entail having domestic hate speech bans in place – alleged victims must moreover be in a legal position to lodge complaints about instances of incitement. The step from accepting such derivative access to justice rights to concluding that the incitement provision itself embodies a human right is a small one.

In a number of other observations on state reports the Committee went even further and urged State parties to stringently enforce their incitement laws. For instance, the Human Rights Committee demanded that Switzerland 'ensure rigorous enforcement of its laws against racial incitement and discrimination'.[30] It gave very concrete guidelines how to go about this. Switzerland 'should consider broadening the mandate of the Federal Commission against Racism, or creating an independent human rights mechanism with the power to initiate legal action'.[31] Similarly, scrutinizing Israel's relevant practice, the Committee observed that 'public pronouncements made by several prominent Israeli personalities in relation to Arabs ... may constitute advocacy of racial and religious hatred constituting incitement to discrimination, hostility and violence'.[32] In a remark that seems to go even further than the Committee's own jurisprudence on incitement, it added that this 'State party should take the necessary action to *investigate, prosecute and punish* such acts in order to ensure respect for article 20, paragraph 2, of the Covenant'.[33] This actual 'duty to punish' was also formulated in the Committee's reflections on Egypt's compliance report. The Committee expressed itself to be 'deeply concerned at the State party's failure to take action following the publication of some very violent articles against the Jews in the Egyptian press, which in fact constitute advocacy of racial and religious hatred and

[28] A/59/40 vol. I (2004) 68, para. 75(25).
[29] CCPR/CO/78/SVK (2003), para. 17: 'The State party should take all necessary measures to combat racial violence and incitement, provide proper protection to Roma, and establish adequate mechanisms to receive complaints from victims and ensure adequate investigation and prosecution of cases of racial violence and incitement to racial hatred.'
[30] A/57/40 vol. I (2002) 44, para. 76(8) (Switzerland).
[31] A/57/40 vol. I (2002) 44, para. 76(8).
[32] A/58/40 vol. I (2003) 64, para. 85(20) (Israel).
[33] A/58/40 vol. I (2003) 64, para. 85(20) (emphasis added).

incitement to discrimination, hostility and violence'.[34] Therefore Egypt 'must take whatever action is necessary to *punish such acts* by ensuring respect for article 20, paragraph 2, of the Covenant'.[35] On another occasion the Committee called for 'sterner measures' to prevent individuals from promoting hatred in Belgium.[36] The Committee admonished Guyana to 'ensure strict compliance with article 20(2) of the Covenant by enforcing the prohibition of incitement to racial hostility'.[37] In relation to Burundi, the Committee demanded more action be taken against incitement by the media;[38] while in relation to Slovenia the Committee was concerned about manifestations of incitement in both the media and the 'public domain'.[39]

Accordingly, not only is Article 20(2) mandatory (see Chapter 4), it also imposes on State parties positive duties to investigate and, where necessary, to prosecute and punish perpetrators. Within the context of the state reporting procedure the Committee has not gone as far, however, as to distil a right to be protected against incitement from the Covenant. Also, none of the above observations conclusively shows that Article 20(2) ICCPR provides incitement victims with standing before the Human Rights Committee.

5.4.3   Views in individual communications

To date only a small number of cases have been decided in which Article 20(2) plays a more or less prominent role. This meagre output notwithstanding, these cases do show an interesting interpretative evolution of the legal nature of this provision. On the basis of the following jurisprudential overview, we can conclude that the Committee is gradually developing a right to be free from incitement in the meaning of Article 20(2) ICCPR.

Initially, Article 20(2) merely served as a bar to admissibility in cases brought by convicted inciters. The case of *J.R.T. and the W.G. Party v. Canada* revolved around the white supremacist Western Guard Party, established in 1972, and its leader, John Ross Taylor. Mr Taylor and his party had produced telephone answering machine messages that played

---

[34] A/58/40 vol. I (2002) 31, para. 77(18) (Egypt).
[35] A/58/40 vol. I (2002) 31, para. 77(18) (emphasis added).
[36] A/59/40 vol. I (2004) 56, para. 72(27) (Belgium).
[37] A/55/40 vol. I (2000) 53, para. 378 (Guyana).
[38] A/49/40 vol. I (1994) 58, para. 363 (Burundi).
[39] A/60/40 vol. I (2005) 74, para. 93(13) (Slovenia).

to those who called a number listed under 'White Power Message' in the Toronto telephone book. Callers were warned of 'the dangers of international finance and international Jewry leading the world into wars, unemployment and inflation and the collapse of world values and principles'.[40] The Canadian Human Rights Act 1985 prohibits precisely this type of telephonic hate messages.[41] Ignoring court orders to cease this message service, the Western Guard Party was fined and Taylor was sentenced to prison.[42] Taylor complained before the Human Rights Committee, alleging a breach of his freedom of expression (Article 19 ICCPR).[43] Canada's first and foremost objection concerned the admissibility of the case.[44] Canada argued that the impugned provision of the Canadian Human Rights Act does not breach the right to freedom of expression, 'but in fact gives effect to article 20(2) of the Covenant'.[45] This makes this case the first in which Article 20 was invoked, in this case by the responding party, the state. The intended effect of that particular argument was clear – to deny Taylor standing. Indeed, Canada argued that 'not only is the author's "right" to communicate racist ideas not protected by the Covenant, it is in fact

[40] Human Rights Committee, *J.R.T. and the W.G. Party* v. *Canada*, Communication no. 104/1981 (6 April 1983), para. 2.1.

[41] Human Rights Act 1985 (R.S.C., 1985, c. H6), Art. 13(1) [Canada]. Later amended and expanded through R.S., 1985, c. H6, s. 13; 2001, c. 41, s. 88. Comparable clauses can be found in the human rights codes of some of Canada's Provinces and Territories. See Section 2 of the Human Rights, Citizenship and Multiculturalism Act, R.S.A., 2000, c. H14 [Alberta]; Section 7 of the Human Rights Code, R.S.B.C., 1996, c. 210 [British Columbia]; Section 13 of the Consolidation of Human Rights Act, R.S.N.W.T., 2002, c. 18 [Northwest Territories]; and Section 14 of the Human Rights Code, R.S.S., 1979, c. S24.1 [Saskatchewan]. Richard Moon, *Report to the Canadian Human Rights Commission Concerning Section 13 of the Canadian Human Rights Act and the Regulation of Hate Speech on the Internet* (October 2008).

[42] He was sentenced to one year's imprisonment. Initially both were suspended sentences, but ultimately, after yet further messages were recorded, the suspension of these sentences was lifted on account of contempt of court and Taylor was committed to jail. For one of the domestic cases in which John Ross Taylor and his party were held to have breached the Canadian Human Rights Act, see Canadian Human Rights Tribunal, *Smith and Lodge* v. *Western Guard Party*, 1979 CHRT 1. On this case, see Robin Edger, 'Are Hate speech Provisions Anti-Democratic? An International Perspective' (2010) 26:1 *American University International Law Review*, 119–55, at 132.

[43] Complaints were brought on behalf of the W.G. Party too. However, as under the Optional Protocol to the ICCPR only individuals can bring complaints (preamble and Articles 1, 2 and 5), the association's complaints were inadmissible. Taylor's second complaint (also declared inadmissible) concerned an alleged violation of his freedom of correspondence, which will not be dealt with here.

[44] *J.R.T. and the W.G. Party* v. *Canada*, paras. 6.1–6.4.

[45] *J.R.T. and the W.G. Party* v. *Canada*, para. 6.2.

incompatible with its provisions, and therefore this part of the communication is in this respect inadmissible under articles 1, 2 and 3 of the Optional Protocol'.[46]

The Human Rights Committee agreed with Canada and, moreover, endorsed the suggested course of action: it declared that Mr Taylor's communication was 'incompatible with the provisions of the Covenant' and deemed it therefore inadmissible on the basis of Article 3 of the Optional Protocol to the ICCPR. The argument to support this view stated that 'the opinions which Mr. T. seeks to disseminate through the telephone system clearly constitute the advocacy of racial or religious hatred which Canada has an obligation under article 20(2) of the Covenant to prohibit'.[47]

Accordingly, Article 20(2) is construed as an admissibility criterion; that is in cases where impugned speech acts prima facie run counter to the spirit of the prohibition of Article 20(2), applicants may be deprived of legal standing.[48] Consequently, in this approach Article 20(2) essentially equates to the general abuse of rights doctrine of Article 5 ICCPR, which also functions as a bar to legal standing. This approach is questionable in the light of the object and purpose of the Covenant.[49] Article 3 of the Optional Protocol to the ICCPR does expressly refer back to the abuse of rights doctrine as an obstacle to admissibility; it does not, however, to that same effect refer back to Article 20(2).

What is more, in this early approach adopted by the Committee alleged inciters cannot count on the same protection as guaranteed to other persons – a form of 'content discrimination'. Actions that come within the ambit of Article 20(2), this questionable approach suggests, do not merit the protection guaranteed by Article 19 on freedom of expression. This view that an expression is either protected or altogether barred from protection on account of its running counter to the spirit of Article 20(2) must be firmly rejected. Although the Committee still adhered to this reading in a case as recent as 1993 (in an *obiter dictum*),[50] we will see that the Committee made a U-turn on this matter later on.

---

[46] *J.R.T. and the W.G. Party* v. *Canada*, para. 6.2.

[47] *J.R.T. and the W.G. Party* v. *Canada*, para. 8(b).

[48] Put differently, such cases may be deemed inadmissible *ratione materiae*. The latter rendition is Nowak's preferred reading of the case. Nowak, *CCPR Commentary*, at 476.

[49] See also Nowak, *CCPR Commentary*, at 454–5 and 476–7.

[50] Human Rights Committee, *Ballantyne, Davidson, McIntyre* v. *Canada*, Communications Nos. 359/1989 and 385/1989 (31 March 1993). One of the key questions in this case was whether commercial speech came within the ambit of the protection offered by Art. 19 ICCPR. Whereas Canada denied this (para. 8.9), the Committee argued that

Thus this either/or approach – speech would fall into either Article 19 or in the Article 20(2) category – implies that in the latter instance no scrutiny into the general rules on restrictions on free speech provided by Article 19(3) would be necessary. It is that restriction mechanism incorporated into Article 19 that offers additional protection to the core right of free speech. That system urges legal inquiries into such as issues as: is the restriction based on positive law? Does the law serve a recognized public good such as 'public order' or the 'respect of the rights or reputations of others'? Is the restriction necessary and proportionate to securing that legitimate aim?

The view that there are two categories of speech – protected speech and a priori unprotected speech – leads to the removal of those safeguards in cases brought by alleged inciters. If that were indeed what was required by Article 20(2), one would expect a very robust test determining that impugned speech acts do indeed prima facie amount to incitement within the meaning of that article.[51] Nothing of the sort can be discerned in *J.R.T. and the W.G. Party* v. *Canada*. It was simply assumed that Article 20(2) was engaged by both Canada and by the Committee. In fact, the Committee's conclusion, which holds that the telephonically disseminated messages 'clearly constitute the *advocacy of racial or religious hatred* which Canada has an obligation under article 20(2) of the Covenant to prohibit',[52] is very telling. For Canada faced no such obligation – this State party was in fact obliged to prohibit the 'advocacy of national, racial or religious hatred *that constitutes incitement to discrimination, hostility or violence*'.

Consequently, the approach taken in this early Article 20(2) case altogether deprived the applicant of the protection offered by the right to freedom of expression. The decision does not scrutinize whether the advocacy of hatred constituted incitement.[53] Also, since Article 19(3) was circumvented, the decision omits an assessment of the necessity of the

---

Art. 19 'must be interpreted as encompassing every form of subjective ideas and opinions capable of transmission to others, *which are compatible with article 20 of the Covenant*, of news and information, of commercial expression and advertising, of works of art, etc.; it should not be confined to means of political, cultural or artistic expression' (para. 11.3, emphasis added). *A contrario*, the Committee says here that speech that is incompatible with Art. 20 is per definition not subject to the rules and protection of Art. 19.

[51] See Nowak, *CCPR Commentary*, at 478, contending that '[b]y its very nature, this sort of review is substantive, and it is out of place in admissibility proceedings'.

[52] *J.R.T. and the W.G. Party* v. *Canada*, para. 8(b) (emphasis added).

[53] The question of how to prove incitement is addressed in Part III of this book.

restriction. It may be questioned whether the 'rights of others' were truly engaged. The Committee revised this approach in its next two decisions in extreme speech cases.

The case of *Robert Faurisson v. France* revolved around a British–French literature professor, who had publicly cast doubt as to the existence of gas chambers for extermination purposes at Auschwitz and in other Nazi concentration camps through various statements and writings from the 1970s onwards.[54] He had claimed that no decree ordering the extermination had ever been discovered and that it was never proven how so many people could be killed by gas-asphyxiation. Also after the adoption of the French Gayssot Act 1990, which prohibits the contestation of crimes against humanity as defined in the London Charter of 1945 (on the basis of which the Nazi leaders were tried at Nuremburg),[55] Mr Faurisson went on to express his negationist viewpoints. In one particular magazine interview he stated that:

> No one will have me admit that two plus two make five, that the earth is flat, or that the Nuremberg Tribunal was infallible. I have excellent reasons not to believe in this policy of extermination of Jews or in the magic gas chamber ... I would wish to see that 100 per cent of all French citizens realize that the myth of the gas chambers is a dishonest fabrication ('est une gredinerie'), endorsed by the victorious powers of Nuremberg ... with the approval of the 'court historians'.[56]

Following private criminal actions filed by associations of French resistance fighters and of deportees to German concentration camps, he was convicted and fined by a French court for the crime of '*contestation de crimes contre l'humanité*'.[57]

Robert Faurisson complained about the interferences with his right to freedom of expression, including his academic freedom, before the UN Human Rights Committee.[58] The French government invoked both the

---

[54] Human Rights Committee, *Robert Faurisson v. France*, Communication no. 550/1993 (19 July 1995).

[55] Law No. 90–615 of 13 July 1990 on the Punishment of Racist, Xenophobic or Anti-Semitic Acts, commonly referred to as the 'Gayssot Act'.

[56] *Robert Faurisson v. France*, para. 2.6 (the French is underlined in the original).

[57] *Robert Faurisson v. France*, para. 2.5.

[58] *Robert Faurisson v. France*, para 3.1. He had in fact not quite exhausted all local remedies (recourse to the Court of Cassation was still open), but the Committee forgave him that considering the fact that the decision in a related negationism case – the one against the editor-in-chief of the magazine that had published Faurisson's interview – already dealt with by that highest judicial body did not give Mr Faurisson much hope. See para. 2.9 (Faurisson on non-exhaustion), paras. 4.3–4.5 (France on non-exhaustion), and para. 6.1 (Committee's final say on exhaustion of remedies).

general abuse of rights doctrine of Article 5(1) and the incitement prohibition of Article 20(2) ICCPR.[59] In relation to the former provision, France argued that the European Court of Human Rights applies a similar approach – construing the abuse of right doctrine as an obstacle to admissibility – in this type of case.[60] In relation to the Covenant's incitement prohibition, France reminded the Committee that in previous case law (*J.R.T. and the W.G. Party* v. *Canada*) Article 20(2) had been employed to deny standing to a convicted inciter.

The fact that France 'invokes' Article 20(2),[61] as Canada had done in *J.R.T. and the W.G. Party* v. *Canada*, is interesting in its own right. Obviously, substantive human rights provisions tend to be invoked by the applicant. Article 20(2) contains legislative duties for State parties. For the time being, State parties also seem to consider themselves the main *beneficiaries* of Article 20(2) in contentious proceedings on extreme/free speech cases. That is, France obviously 'invokes' Article 20(2) so as to be let off easy, as Canada was pardoned in *J.R.T. and the W.G. Party* v. *Canada*. Indeed, France 'concludes that it merely complied with its international obligations by making the (public) denial of crimes against humanity a criminal offence'.[62]

What France further suggests by this invocation is that Article 20(2) must serve and be recognized, in the monitoring work of the Human Rights Committee, as a sweeping trump against freedom of expression claims made by extremists. Quoting from *J.R.T. and the W.G. Party* v. *Canada*, France endorsed the Committee's prior view that if a

---

[59] *Robert Faurisson* v. *France*, paras. 7.1–7.8. In addition, France argued that under Art. 4 ICERD it was obliged to declare the dissemination of such racist ideas a punishable offence. In fact, the Committee on the Elimination of Racial Discrimination had recently praised the newly adopted Gayssot Act in its Concluding Observations pertaining to France's state report. See A/49/18 (1994), para. 142. The Act is there mentioned under 'Positive aspects'. CERD more specifically 'noted with satisfaction' that 'measures have recently been adopted by the French authorities to prevent and intensify the fight against racial discrimination and xenophobia. In that connection, such measures as ... the establishment of the new offence regarding crimes against humanity under Act No. 90–615 of 30 July 1990 ... are welcomed'.

[60] *Robert Faurisson* v. *France*, para. 7.4. The European Convention on Human Rights enshrines 'abuse of rights' in Art. 17. At the time of the *Faurisson* decision, this doctrine has indeed already been applied to deny standing to the applicants in *Glimmerveen and Hagenbeek* v. *The Netherlands*, Application nos. 8348/78 and 8406/78 (European Commission of Human Rights decision of 11 October 1979). For this and other Art. 17 ECHR decisions, see Chapter 6 (particularly section 6.6 thereof).

[61] *Robert Faurisson* v. *France*, para. 7.7.

[62] *Robert Faurisson* v. *France*, para. 7.7.

statement comes within the ambit of Article 20(2), substantive scrutiny under Article 19 on freedom of expression is no longer necessary.

The Human Rights Committee, however, changed course. It abandoned the inadmissibility approach and decided the case on the merits. Although the Committee was certainly right to make this U-turn, it did not explain why it changed tack. Curiously moreover, it ignored the significance of Article 20(2) in its substantive assessment altogether.[63] In order to assess whether Faurisson's conviction amounted to a violation, the Committee exclusively applied Article 19, including this provision's regime of restrictions. The Committee found that the restrictions on Faurisson's free speech were permitted and necessary for the sake of ensuring 'respect of the rights or reputations of others' (Article 19, paragraph 3(a)). Crucially, in that respect the Committee reiterated that this ground for restriction may relate to both individuals as well as to a 'community as a whole'.[64] In the case at hand the Committee is, of course, referring to the Jewish community.

Accordingly, the Committee concluded that '[s]ince the statements made by the author, read in their full context, were of a nature as to raise or strengthen anti-semitic feelings, the restriction served the respect of the Jewish community *to live free from fear of an atmosphere of anti-semitism*'.[65] Arguably, the Committee should have spelled out which 'rights or reputations of others' were precisely at stake. This community right to live free from fear of discrimination and intimidation cannot be found literally in the Covenant, though it does generally resonate with Article 27 (minority rights), Article 26 (equality) and, indeed, Article 20(2) on laws against incitement. At that point in time the majority of Committee members apparently did not wish to go as far as to infer from Article 20(2) the existence of an independent 'freedom from incitement'.[66] It chose to avoid any mention of Article 20(2), yet thereby leaving this right to 'live free from fear' somewhat unsubstantiated.

[63] See also Nowak, *CCPR Commentary*, at 478.

[64] *Robert Faurisson* v. *France*, para. 9.6 (underlining in original). This was accepted by the Committee as early as 1983 in a (now replaced) General Comment. Human Rights Committee, *General Comment 10: Article 19* (Nineteenth session, 1983), para. 4: 'Paragraph 3 [of Article 19] expressly stresses that the exercise of the right to freedom of expression carries with it special duties and responsibilities and for this reason certain restrictions on the right are permitted which may relate either to the interests of other persons or to those of the community as a whole.'

[65] *Robert Faurisson* v. *France*, para. 9.6 (emphasis added).

[66] Taylor argues, however, that the Committee implicitly endorsed a 'right of a community to live free from religious hatred'. Paul M. Taylor, *Freedom of Religion: UN and European Human Rights Law and Practice* (Cambridge University Press, 2005), at 82.

From the individual (concurring) opinions it transpires that a number of Committee members would have preferred to apply Article 20(2) directly to the merits of this case. These appended opinions are also much more clear and specific as to which 'rights of others' were at stake in this case. Emphasizing both Article 7 UDHR and Article 20(2) ICCPR, members Elizabeth Evatt and David Kretzmer argued that '[e]very individual has the right to be free not only from discrimination on grounds of race, religion and national origins, but also from incitement to such discrimination'.[67] This 'right to be free from racial, national or religious incitement'[68] features a number of times in their individual opinion. Sometimes this notion is referred to as the 'right of a person to be free from incitement to discrimination on grounds of race, religion or national origins',[69] the 'right to be free from incitement to anti-semitism'[70] or 'the right to be free from incitement to racism or anti-semitism'.[71] Occasionally it is referred to as an express group right ('right of the Jewish community in France to live free from fear of incitement to anti-semitism'[72]). This suggests that the question as to whether we are dealing with a classic individual right or some type of group, collective or perhaps minority right was far from resolved; yet the bottom line is that these members distilled an actual right from Article 20(2) ICCPR.

Member Lallah also concluded that the case should have been considered in the specific light of Article 20, paragraph 2 of the Covenant.[73] Whereas the latter opinion does not elaborate on any right to be free from incitement, the individual concurring opinion by Prafullachandra Bhagwati does so, in so many words.[74]

---

[67] Individual opinion by Elizabeth Evatt and David Kretzmer, co-signed by Eckart Klein, para. 4. Cecilia Medina Quiroga in her separate opinion expresses support for this opinion.

[68] Opinion Evatt/Kretzmer/Klein, para. 7.

[69] Opinion Evatt/Kretzmer/Klein, para. 4.

[70] Opinion Evatt/Kretzmer/Klein, para. 9.

[71] Opinion Evatt/Kretzmer/Klein, para. 10.

[72] Opinion Evatt/Kretzmer/Klein, para. 7.

[73] Individual opinion by Rajsoomer Lallah, para. 11.

[74] Individual opinion by Prafullachandra Bhagwati. In his personal assessment of the case he concludes that the restrictive law justifiably served the 'purpose of respect for the right and interest of the Jewish community to live free from fear of an atmosphere of anti-semitism, hostility or contempt'. He further mentions 'the rights and interests of the Jewish community to live in society with full human dignity and free from an atmosphere of anti-semitism'. Admittedly, these formulations are closer to the plenary Committee's notion of a 'right to live free from fear'. Bhagwati's choice of words – 'rights and interests' – is striking, moreover, as it suggests that he was not wholly convinced that the notion concerned amounts to an actual right.

In sum, the Committee as a whole for the first time supported a community right 'to live free from fear of an atmosphere of [discrimination]';[75] individual members further fleshed out a 'right to be free from racial, national or religious incitement'. Accordingly, in *Faurisson* the 'freedom from incitement' for the first time saw the light of day, albeit merely in the opinions of individual Committee members. In this case, the main function of this freedom was to function as an actual 'right of others', thus as a limiting factor applicable to inciting speech. The *Faurisson* decision did not indicate whether or not this right to be free from incitement might be independently invoked by incitement victims.

Malcolm Ross v. Canada is also a case of Holocaust denial. Ross worked as a modified resource teacher for remedial reading in a school district of New Brunswick, Canada.[76] He had made negationist and other anti-Semitic remarks, though not in class but as part of his second life as a pamphleteer. Throughout the period of his teaching position, from 1976 to 1991, he had published and spread booklets or pamphlets with such titles as *Web of Deceit, The Real Holocaust, Spectre of Power* and *Christianity vs. Judeo-Christianity*, and he had made off-duty yet public statements, including through a television appearance and through letters sent to newspapers, all expressing his negationist and anti-Semitic views.[77] A Jewish parent – whose children actually attended another school, albeit in the same school district – filed a complaint with the Human Rights Commission of New Brunswick. Interestingly, the domestic procedures against Ross indicate what was likely the last straw for this parent. His daughter had wanted to go and watch a gymnastics competition at the school where Ross taught, but was advised that she probably should not go there because that was 'where the teacher who hates Jews works' (she eventually did go, but felt anxious for fear of being attacked).[78] In any event, in the parental complaint against the School Board it was argued that the school ought to take disciplinary action against Ross, since otherwise it would be implicitly condoning the latter's anti-Semitic attitude.[79] Specifically, the parent submitted that the School Board had breached a section of the New Brunswick Human Rights Code on equal access to

---

[75] In this case, a right to live free from fear of an atmosphere of *anti-Semitism*.
[76] Human Rights Committee, *Malcolm Ross v. Canada*, Communication no. 736/1997 (18 October 2000).
[77] *Malcolm Ross v. Canada*, paras. 2.1 and 4.2.
[78] According to the Supreme Court of Canada's judgment, *Ross v. New Brunswick School District No. 15*, [1996] 1 S.C.R. 825, para. 40.
[79] *Malcolm Ross v. Canada*, para. 2.3.

publicly provided educational services, which must be rendered without discrimination on the basis of religion or ancestry.[80] The Human Rights Commission established a Board of Inquiry to look into the complaint. On the nature of Mr Ross' statements, the Board of Inquiry stated that it had 'no hesitation in concluding that there are many references in these published writings and comments by Malcolm Ross which are *prima facie* discriminatory against persons of the Jewish faith and ancestry. It would be an impossible task to list every prejudicial view or discriminatory comment contained in his writings as they are innumerable and permeate his writings.'[81] It went on to argue that Ross' writings and remarks 'denigrate the faith and beliefs of Jews and call upon true Christians to not merely question the validity of Jewish beliefs and teachings but to hold those of the Jewish faith and ancestry in contempt as undermining freedom, democracy and Christian beliefs and values. Malcolm Ross identifies Judaism as the enemy and calls on all Christians to join the battle.'[82] Based on those findings the Board of Inquiry recommended a set of sanctions, including a relegation to a non-teaching position,[83] something eventually upheld by the Canadian Supreme Court.[84]

Malcolm Ross complained before the UN Human Rights Committee that both his freedom of expression and his freedom of religion – he asserted that his views were also religiously motivated – were violated by Canada. Among other arguments, Canada raised preliminary defences against the admissibility of the communication based on Article 20(2) ICCPR.[85] By drawing parallels between both cases Canada tried to persuade the Committee to stick to its admissibility approach as first formulated in *J.R.T. and the W.G. Party* v. *Canada*. Specifically, Canada argued that 'both communications concerned anti-Semitic speech' and 'both communications involved orders [restricting free speech] made pursuant to human rights legislation'.[86] Canada's holistic interpretation of Articles 19–20 ICCPR boils down to the 'either/or' variant. Either the speech act is protected as legitimate speech in principle protected by Article 19 (and deriving further protection from Article 18 in case

---

[80] *Malcolm Ross* v. *Canada*, para. 3.4.
[81] *Malcolm Ross* v. *Canada*, para. 4.2. See also *Ross* v. *New Brunswick School District No. 15*, para. 38.
[82] *Malcolm Ross* v. *Canada*, para. 4.2. See also *Ross* v. *New Brunswick School District No. 15*, para. 38.
[83] *Malcolm Ross* v. *Canada*, para. 4.3.
[84] *Malcolm Ross* v. *Canada*, paras. 4.6–4.8.
[85] *Malcolm Ross* v. *Canada*, para. 6.2.
[86] *Malcolm Ross* v. *Canada*, para. 6.4.

of religious speech); or the speech act falls squarely in the category of extreme Article 20 speech and must be deemed unprotected per se. In the words of the Government of Canada, 'freedom of religion and expression under the Covenant must be interpreted as not including the advocacy of national, racial or religious hatred that constitutes incitement to discrimination, hostility or violence.'[87] Further insisting on the inadmissibility of the case, Canada moreover invoked the general abuse of right doctrine of Article 5 ICCPR.[88]

The Human Rights Committee, however, made a drastic U-turn. It distanced itself from the admissibility approach taken in *J.R.T. and the W.G. Party* v. *Canada* much more outspokenly than it had done in the *Faurisson* case. In *Faurisson* the Committee for the first time decided an extreme speech case on the merits, but somewhat obscurely took Article 20(2) out of the equation. In *Malcolm Ross* the Committee reasoned that Article 20(2) did apply to extreme speech cases and at the same time conceded that such cases may very well be decided on the merits.[89]

A direct consequence of this reversal of *J.R.T. and the W.G. Party* v. *Canada* was enhanced clarity about the relationship between Article 19 and Article 20(2) ICCPR. For the first time it was made explicit that restrictions based on Article 20(2) must also always comply with the general rules on restriction of Article 19(3).[90] Previously, the 1983 General Comment (No. 11) on Article 20 had merely determined that Articles 19 and 20 are 'fully compatible'.[91] The reinterpretation of the link between the two articles as established in *Ross* would seem to be the only reading that can indeed vouch for full compatibility between Articles 19 and 20. Still, it is rather important that this case finally settles this seemingly obvious matter. The jurisprudential line adopted in *Ross* means that in Human Rights Committee proceedings an invocation of Article 20(2) by a responding state cannot exonerate a State party from its human rights obligations under Article 19, thus making Article 20(2) fundamentally different from Article 5(1) of the ICCPR. That is, if an impugned speech act prima facie comes within the ambit of Article 20(2), this does not

---

[87] *Malcolm Ross* v. *Canada*, para. 6.3.

[88] *Malcolm Ross* v. *Canada*, para. 6.3. Canada also argued that Mr Ross abused his rights with an aim of destroying religious and educational rights. *Malcolm Ross* v. *Canada*, para. 6.6.

[89] The reversal of *J.R.T. and the W.G. Party* v. *Canada* is described in much detail in *Malcolm Ross* v. *Canada*, paras. 10.5–10.6.

[90] *Malcolm Ross* v. *Canada*, para. 10.6.

[91] Human Rights Committee, *General Comment 11*, para. 2.

make the case *ipso facto* inadmissible. Given the principled interrelatedness of Articles 19 and 20, incitement cases would almost always need to be considered on the merits of the free speech complaint. The Committee needs to determine whether the restriction – albeit one that derives support from Article 20(2) – was permissible under Article 19(3). To that end, the Committee needs to look into the *legality* (was the anti-incitement measure provided by a law?), *legitimacy* (did the incitement law serve a legitimate aim?) and *necessity* (was the restriction imposed necessary to protect the conflicting aim?) of the restriction on free speech. While Article 20(2) – as is conceded by the Human Rights Committee[92] – comes to the help of State parties as far as the first two questions of this tripartite test are concerned, the third question in particular is subject to a contextual analysis in the light of the facts of the case.

Thus the fact that a state was carrying out anti-incitement legislation so as to give effect to Article 20(2) of the Covenant is only a partial answer to the question whether the restriction imposed can be justified. A State party discharging its Article 20(2) obligations will be in a strong position, it is true, to claim that the restriction was based on law. Also, the aim of the restriction would generally accord with the Covenant. The state would typically seek to protect the 'rights and reputations of others', being the group or individuals targeted by the inciting speech act. Assessment by the Committee would nevertheless be in order to determine first whether the restrictive law in question was truly of a type that corresponds with Article 20(2), and further so as to follow through on the legitimacy of the aim invoked by the State party. That being said, the necessity test will tend to be most significant. Due to the Committee's decision in *Ross*, the fact that the Covenant supports, indeed *orders* incitement legislation no longer amounts to a wholesale justification for incitement law-based restrictions. Post *Ross* it will need to be investigated whether the restriction, for instance a criminal law conviction or a job dismissal, was necessary in the light of the particulars of the case. Accordingly, the Committee is to substantively assess whether the actual enforcement of the incitement law in question was, all things considered, necessary to achieve the aim of protecting the rights of the incitement's target.[93] In sum, the Committee's

---

[92] *Malcolm Ross* v. *Canada*, para. 10.6: 'In applying those provisions [i.e. possible restrictions on freedom of expression formulated by Art. 19(3)], the fact that a restriction is claimed to be required under article 20 is of course relevant.'

[93] Part IV of this book is intended to comprehensively address the question of how incitement can be proven – or invalidated, as the case may be.

conclusion that Article 20(2) and Article 19(3) are interrelated has important legal ramifications.

In the case of *Malcolm Ross* v. *Canada* the Committee was ultimately of the view that the facts of the case did not disclose a violation of the Covenant. Among other reasons, it found that Ross had indeed incited against Jews and it considered it proven that his statements were of a nature as to negatively affect the rights of others.[94]

It is interesting to focus on the question of which 'rights' were at stake according to the Committee. Reiterating a formula first expressed in General Comment No. 10 and subsequently in *Faurisson*, the Committee posited that the rights or reputations of others within the meaning of Article 19(3), may relate to other persons but also to 'a community as a whole'.[95] Further advancing this point, it posited that 'restrictions may be permitted on statements which are of a nature as to raise or strengthen anti-semitic feeling, in order to uphold the Jewish communities' *right to be protected from religious hatred*. Such restrictions also derive support from the principles reflected in article 20(2) of the Covenant.'[96] Here the Committee goes significantly beyond its findings in *Faurisson*.[97] First, whereas in the latter case the plenary Committee had spoken in terms of a somewhat vague 'freedom from fear' of discrimination, here the Committee develops a more robust 'right to be protected from religious hatred'.[98] Second, the Committee expressly distils this right from Article 20(2), something it had refused to do in *Faurisson*.

---

[94] *Malcolm Ross* v. *Canada*, paras. 11.5–11.6.

[95] *Malcolm Ross* v. *Canada*, para. 11.5 (emphasis added).

[96] *Malcolm Ross* v. *Canada*, para. 11.5.

[97] While the Committee makes it seem like this was old news (*Malcolm Ross* v. *Canada*, para. 11.5: 'as held in *Faurisson v France*'), the following nuances, if not departures, are most remarkable.

[98] One could criticize this notion, too, since the keyword of Art. 20(2) is 'incitement', not 'hatred'. On the difference between protection against 'hate speech' and protection against 'incitement', see section 8.2.2 of Chapter 8. Somewhat confusing, furthermore, is the fact that in the same paragraph the Committee came up with a dissimilar type of 'rights and reputations of others'. That is, it further specified 'that the restrictions imposed on him were for the purpose of protecting the "rights or reputations" of persons of Jewish faith, including the *right to have an education in the public school system free from bias, prejudice and intolerance*' (*Malcolm Ross* v. *Canada*, para. 11.5, emphasis added). There is no such right in the Covenant. It must be noted, though, that this particular formulation appears to have been copied from the domestic proceedings. It is based on the equal access to public service principle and on equality before the law as codified by Art. 5 of the Human Rights Act, R.S.C., 1985, c. H6 [Canada] and Art. 15 of the Canadian Charter of Rights and Freedoms, which is part of the Constitution Act, 1982 (80), 1982, c. 11 (U.K.), Schedule B. A 'right to be educated in a school system that

The upshot of this is that *Ross* marks the first Human Rights Committee decision in which the plenary Committee recognized a right to be protected from religious hatred as distilled from Article 20(2) ICCPR.[99] The Committee seemed to suggest that the right to be protected from religious hatred is a group right when it accrues the right to Jewish communities.[100] Then again, the second reference to this right ('persons of Jewish faith') resonates well with the language of minority rights as codified by Article 27 – although the general rationale of those rights is to protect minorities, it is strictly speaking individual 'persons belonging to such minorities' who are regarded as the beneficiaries or rights holders.[101] In any event, in the *Malcolm Ross* case the main use of this Article 20-derived 'right' was to function as a limiting factor. That is, Jewish communities or Jewish persons were the holders of the 'rights of others' (Article 19, paragraph 3). Since the rights of a concrete minority (Jewish persons) were at stake, the inciter's speech acts were legitimately restricted. An interesting question is what the legal position of these communities or persons would have been had the Canadian authorities *not* taken measures against the inciter, Mr Ross. Would those same right-holders, Jews, then have legal grounds to complain about Canada's inaction? This discussion is continued after consideration of the next case, which was yet again brought by an extremist, not by an alleged incitement victim.

The *Zündel* case is essentially another Holocaust denial case, albeit somewhat dissimilar from the previous ones.[102] Ernst Zündel did not complain about anti-hate speech restrictions on his freedom of expression per se, but more specifically complained about the fact that he was not permitted to publicly challenge Canadian hate speech legislation in the way he saw fit. The applicant was a German citizen who resided from 1958 to 2000 in Canada. That year he was deported to Germany in relation to his neo-Nazi involvement and for allegedly being a danger to

is free from bias, prejudice and intolerance' is distilled from those domestic norms in paras. 80, 83 and 85 of *Ross* v. *New Brunswick School District No. 15*. Be that as it may, the Committee could have geared this part of its reasoning more towards the language of Art. 20(2) or stuck to its newly adopted 'right to be protected from religious hatred'.

99   Note that member Hipólito Solari Yrigoyen would have preferred to move Art. 20(2) even more to the centre of the Committee's reasoning. See Individual opinion of Hipólito Solari Yrigoyen. It may further be recalled that in *Faurisson* several individual members of the Committee were already of this view, as evidenced by their separate opinions.

100 *Malcolm Ross* v. *Canada*, para. 11.5 ('Jewish communities' right').

101 ICCPR, Art. 27.

102 Human Rights Committee, *Ernst Zündel* v. *Canada* (I), Communication no. 953/2000 (admissibility decision of 27 July 2003).

Canadian national security (in Germany he was arrested, prosecuted and jailed on charges of Holocaust denial).[103] His white supremacist activism was chiefly channelled through his work as a publicist and creator of the 'Zundelsite', a website – still up and running at the time of writing – dedicated to the dissemination of negationist publications and views. There he posted such works as *Did Six Million Really Die?*, a Holocaust denial booklet written by Richard Verrall, his own *The Hitler We Loved and Why*,[104] as well as the writings of Malcolm Ross, the anti-Semitic teacher discussed previously.[105]

A Holocaust survivor lodged a complaint with the Canadian Human Rights Commission against Zündel's website. The Canadian Human Rights Tribunal inquiring into the complaint denied Zündel the possibility of raising a defence of truth against the complaint of exposing Jews to hatred and contempt. According to the Tribunal this would only 'add a significant dimension of delay, cost and affront to the dignity of those who are alleged to have been victimized by these statements'.[106] Accordingly, the Canadian Human Rights Tribunal did not want to provide him with another stage to disseminate his hateful views.

Subsequently, Zündel booked the Canadian Parliamentary Press Gallery to hold a press conference, planning to discuss this interim ruling. However, the House of Commons passed a unanimous motion that Zündel be denied admittance to the parliamentary precincts. It is that particular motion that Zündel's complaints before the Human Rights Committee are related to. He complained that the exclusion from this press conference room violated his freedom of expression.[107]

Canada's main defence was that Article 19 can hardly be deemed to be breached as a result of said refusal. After all, Zündel was not barred from expressing his views outside the parliamentary precincts (in fact, he did

---

[103] Regional Court of Mannheim, *Zündel* judgment (14 February 2007). A separate Human Rights Committee case ensued over his detention and deportation: *Ernst Zündel v. Canada* (II), Communication no. 1341/2005 (admissibility decision of 20 March 2007).

[104] Before being unmasked by Canadian journalists, Zündel published anti-Semitic works under his pseudonym 'Christof Friedrich' (his middle names). He also published a book claiming that UFOs are secret Nazi weapons. Christof Friedrich, *UFOs – Nazi Secret Weapon?* (1974, published by his own Samisdat Publishers).

[105] The facts of the case before the Human Rights Committee only singles out '*Did Six Million Jews Really Die?*'. *Ernst Zündel v. Canada* (I), para. 2.1, slightly misquoting the title of this booklet.

[106] Canadian Human Rights Tribunal, *Citron v. Zündel* (interim decision of 25 May 1998). Cited in *Ernst Zündel v. Canada* (I), para. 2.2.

[107] Other complaints invoked Articles 3 and 26 on equality.

hold an informal press conference on the pavement in front of the parliamentary precincts).[108] Canada argued, moreover, that if the Committee nonetheless could discern an interference with Zündel's free speech, that such restriction was justified pursuant the Covenant. Canada invoked both the regular restrictions to freedom of expression (Article 19, paragraph 3) and Article 20(2) on incitement.[109]

It is clear that Canada had been following the trends and developments in the Committee's jurisprudence on these articles – predictably so, as some of the leading cases had involved Canada itself.[110] That is to say, Canada did not invoke Article 20(2) so as to deny the admissibility of the case, but rather so as to legitimize possible interferences it had made. Echoing the findings of the Committee in *Faurisson* and *Ross*, Canada posits that '[t]he restriction imposed on the author served the purpose of protecting the Jewish communities' right to religious freedom, freedom of expression, and their right to live in a society free of discrimination, and also found support in article 20, paragraph 2, of the Covenant'.[111] Further underscoring the relevance of Article 20(2) to the particulars of this case, Canada emphasized that the fact that 'the author had been active for almost thirty years in the worldwide distribution of materials that deny the Holocaust and other Nazi atrocities against the Jews sufficiently explained the House of Commons' concern that he would use the facilities of Parliament as a platform to disseminate Anti-Semitic views, thereby exposing the Jewish community to hatred and discrimination'.[112] Having duly taken note of the fact that, since *Malcolm Ross*, necessity of interferences with free speech must always be substantiated, even when those restrictions are generally supported by the obligations flowing from Article 20(2), Canada extensively elaborated on this matter.[113]

Notwithstanding Canada's readiness to discuss the merits of the case, the Human Rights Committee unanimously declared the case inadmissible. This can, however, by no means be seen as a departure from *Malcolm Ross*. Essentially what happened is that the Committee

---

[108] *Ernst Zündel* v. *Canada* (I), para. 5.3.
[109] *Ernst Zündel* v. *Canada* (I), paras. 5.4–5.5.
[110] In *Ross* Canada's strategy had still been to squarely challenge the admissibility on account of alleged hate speech. *Malcolm Ross* v. *Canada*, para. 6.2.
[111] *Ernst Zündel* v. *Canada* (I), para. 5.5.
[112] *Ernst Zündel* v. *Canada* (I), para. 5.5. Furthermore, Canada points out that besides Art. 20(2) of the ICCPR, Art. 4 of ICERD also obliged it to take measures against extreme speech.
[113] *Ernst Zündel* v. *Canada* (I), paras. 5.5–5.6.

agreed with Canada's main defence – the Covenant does not quite contain an unfettered right to freedom of expression within parliamentary precincts – making all of Canada's arguments based on Article 20(2) superfluous.

The case of *Kasem Said Ahmad and Asmaa Abdol-Hamid* v. *Denmark* could have been the very first communication triggering a decision on the merits of an actual Article 20(2) complaint, but was all but stillborn.[114] Since domestic remedies were not fully exhausted – one of the applicants was still involved in an appeal in relation to proceedings flowing from a private criminal prosecution – the Committee rendered it inadmissible.[115] In any event, the facts of the case hardly disclosed that the applicants suffered 'incitement' within the meaning of the Covenant given that their grievances concerned 'religious insult' rather than advocacy of religious hatred that constitutes incitement to discrimination or violence.[116] The complaint was made against the backdrop of the 'Danish cartoons'. In 2005 the Danish newspaper *Jyllands-Posten* invited members of the Danish Newspapers' Illustrators Union to depict the Prophet Mohammed 'as they saw him'.[117] While the Danish cartoons and the ensuing global row are infamous, less well known is the fact that this newspaper did not publish these cartoons without any context, but embedded them in a discussion – albeit a fairly sensationalist one – on freedom of expression. Thus on 30 September 2005, when the item appeared on the front page, one of the cartoons was published together with the caption 'Some Muslims reject modern, secular society. They demand a special position, insisting on special considerations of their own religious feelings. It is incompatible with secular democracy and freedom of expression, where one has to be ready to put up with scorn, mockery and ridicule.'[118] Further, inside the paper a full article was published discussing how freedom of expression in Denmark had come under threat by fears over religious sensitivities and potential reactions of Muslims. Another short article continued the debate by addressing the risk that Denmark may give in to these fears and yield to self-censorship. A final column then presented the twelve remaining cartoons.

---

[114] Human Rights Committee, *Kasem Said Ahmad and Asmaa Abdol-Hamid v. Denmark*, Communication no. 1487/2006 (admissibility decision of 1 April 2008).
[115] *Kasem Said Ahmad and Asmaa Abdol-Hamid v. Denmark*, paras. 2.18, 4.13 and 6.2.
[116] See also *Fatima Andersen v. Denmark* and *A.W.P. v. Denmark*, discussed in this section.
[117] *Kasem Said Ahmad and Asmaa Abdol-Hamid v. Denmark*, para. 2.1.
[118] *Kasem Said Ahmad and Asmaa Abdol-Hamid v. Denmark*, para. 2.1.

As the authors of the communication found seven illustrations to be particularly offensive, it is worth briefly highlighting those.[119] In the words of the Danish Director of Public Prosecutions,[120] the cartoons in question depicted the following:

- the face of a grim-looking bearded man with a turban shaped like an ignited bomb [cartoon 2];
- a bearded man wearing a turban, standing on clouds with arms outspread, saying: 'Stop, stop, we ran out of virgins!' Waiting in front of him is a row of men in tatters with plumes of smoke over their heads [cartoon 11];
- a bearded man wearing a turban, standing with a halo shaped like a crescent moon over his head [cartoon 4];[121]
- a bearded man wearing a turban and carrying a sword, standing with a black bar covering his eyes. Standing at his sides are two women wearing black gowns, with only their eyes visible [cartoon 10];
- two bearded men wearing turbans and armed with a sword, a bomb and a gun, running towards a third bearded man wearing a turban. He is reading a sheet of paper and gesturing them to hold off, with the words: 'Relax folks! It's just a sketch made by an unbeliever from southern Denmark' [cartoon 8];
- a bearded man wearing a turban, standing with the support of a staff and leading an ass with a rope [cartoon 6];
- five stylized female figures wearing headscarves, with facial features depicted as a star and a crescent moon. The caption reads: 'Prophet! You crazy bloke! Keeping women under the yoke!' [cartoon 5].[122]

Following criminal complaints alleging violations of the prohibition of religious insult and religious discrimination made by Muslim

---

[119] *Kasem Said Ahmad and Asmaa Abdol-Hamid* v. *Denmark*, para. 2.5 (n. 2).

[120] While using the terminology used by the Danish Director of Public Prosecutions, this quote follows the order of the applicant's own descriptions of the cartoons since the latter might indicate a particular hierarchy of concerns.

[121] These applicants, who offered their own descriptions of the cartoons in their communication, may have meant cartoon 1 here ('the face of a man whose beard and turban are drawn within a crescent moon, and with a star, symbols normally used for Islam', in the words of the Danish Director of Public Prosecutions). Just to be sure, let us also provide the applicants' own description of that cartoon: 'a man stands wearing a turban that has ambiguous pointed ends coming out of it, which could be viewed either as devil's horns or points of a crescent moon forming a halo'. *Kasem Said Ahmad and Asmaa Abdol-Hamid* v. *Denmark*, para. 2.5 (n. 2).

[122] *Kasem Said Ahmad and Asmaa Abdol-Hamid* v. *Denmark*, para. 2.5.

organizations, a public prosecution was instigated.[123] However, the regional public prosecutor decided to discontinue the investigation and, after appeal, the Director of Public Prosecutions also concluded to cease the criminal proceedings.[124] Subsequent private criminal proceedings by Muslim organizations led to a court decision indicating that the impugned speech acts aimed at social criticism and did not amount to the criminal offence of religious insult.[125]

It was the appeal to the latter judgment that was still pending when the applicants turned to the Human Rights Committee. There the authors of the communication complained of having been 'denied an effective remedy for incitement of hatred against Muslims, prohibited under article 20 of the Covenant, by acts and omissions of ... the Director of Public Prosecutions'.[126] They further claimed that this denial:

> has permitted and furthered violations of the Covenant related to protection against attacks on honour and reputation, of public order and safety, against racial and religious discrimination, and against incitement to racial and religious discrimination against Danish Arabs and Muslims, as well as the guarantee of equal protection before the law. The failure to prosecute resulted in serious injuries and trivialization of the controversy, while sending a message that incitement against Arabs and Muslims was acceptable.[127]

Denmark extensively dwelt on the nature of Article 20(2) ICCPR. It observed that:

> the Committee has yet to find a breach of article 20 of the Covenant. In the three cases in which it expressed views on this provision, the authorities had interfered with expressions of unambiguously anti-Semitic nature. In each case, the Committee concluded that the authors' rights had not been violated by the interferences because the expressions were so racist in character that they were covered directly by article 20, or were justified as a permissible limitation on freedom of expression under article 19, paragraph 3.[128]

Denmark was probably referring to the cases of *J.R.T. and the W.G. Party*, *Faurisson* and *Ross*. Indeed, as we have seen, the Committee has never found a breach of Article 20(2). If anything, Article 20(2) has served to

---

[123] Sections 140 and 266(b) of the Danish Criminal Code respectively.
[124] *Kasem Said Ahmad and Asmaa Abdol-Hamid* v. *Denmark*, paras. 2.9–2.15.
[125] *Kasem Said Ahmad and Asmaa Abdol-Hamid* v. *Denmark*, para. 2.18.
[126] *Kasem Said Ahmad and Asmaa Abdol-Hamid* v. *Denmark*, para. 3.1.
[127] *Kasem Said Ahmad and Asmaa Abdol-Hamid* v. *Denmark*, para. 3.1.
[128] *Kasem Said Ahmad and Asmaa Abdol-Hamid* v. *Denmark*, para. 4.7.

justify interferences with free speech. Denmark contended that there was no sufficient precedent to deal with cases brought by alleged incitement victims.[129]

Denmark further submitted that the impugned speech act did not engage Article 20(2). 'Article 20 sets a high threshold', according to the responding state, 'requiring not only such advocacy, but advocacy constituting incitement to discrimination, hostility or violence.'[130] In that regard, the Danish government argued that the applicants had failed to show how the impugned statements, or the decision not to prosecute specifically, had affected them directly (victim requirement),[131] that the impugned speech acts lacked a clear intention to incite violence or discrimination,[132] and that in any event the illustrations were not quite of a nature as to trigger Article 20(2), also emphasizing the *context* in which they were published.[133] On each of these issues – the threshold of Article 20(2), the question of intent on the part of the persons responsible for the speech act, the question of victim status, the question of the relevance of the speech act's context – it would have been extremely interesting to hear the Committee's Views.[134] While procedural flaws underlying this communication meant that the Committee was barred from answering them, we will address all these issues in the chapters to come.[135]

One year after the Committee's admissibility decision in *Kasem Said Ahmad and Asmaa Abdol-Hamid* v. *Denmark*, the Committee was faced with a communication in which it could hardly dodge the question of victim status under Article 20(2) ICCPR – or could it? While *Maria Vassilari et al.* v. *Greece* does not deal with incitement on religious grounds, it is an important communication with respect to our present discussion of

---

[129] *Kasem Said Ahmad and Asmaa Abdol-Hamid* v. *Denmark*, para. 4.7: 'The cases therefore provide no guidance on the interpretation of Art. 20 where, as presently, the State party has not interfered with freedom of expression.'

[130] *Kasem Said Ahmad and Asmaa Abdol-Hamid* v. *Denmark*, para. 4.7.

[131] *Kasem Said Ahmad and Asmaa Abdol-Hamid* v. *Denmark*, paras. 4.4–4.5.

[132] *Kasem Said Ahmad and Asmaa Abdol-Hamid* v. *Denmark*, para. 4.8.

[133] *Kasem Said Ahmad and Asmaa Abdol-Hamid* v. *Denmark*, para. 4.6.

[134] On this case, see also (Committee member) Abdelfattah Amor, 'Considérations sur le Paragraphe 3 de l'Article 19 du Pacte International Relative aux Droits Civils et Politique' (paper presented at the Expert seminar on 'Freedom of expression and advocacy of religious hatred that constitutes incitement to discrimination, hostility or violence – the links between Articles 19 and 20 of the International Covenant on Civil and Political Rights', organized by the Office of the United Nations High Commissioner for Human Rights, 2–3 October 2008, Geneva, Switzerland).

[135] For threshold questions, see Chapter 7. For the question of intent, see Chapter 9. For the relevance of context, see Chapter 10.

victim status under the Covenant's incitement provision.[136] The applicants alleged that Greece breached Article 20(2) by not combating incitement against Roma people. Thus the three applicants actually invoked
Article 20(2) on which to (partly) base their complaint. Accordingly, we
are again dealing with alleged incitement victims who claim that the state
did not do enough to restrict the inciter's free speech.

Specifically, four Greek citizens of Roma descent filed the communication with the Human Rights Committee, complaining about a letter that
was sent to the Rector and the Rector's Council of the University of Patras
and that was subsequently published in a newspaper called *Peloponnisos*.
The letter was entitled 'Objection against the Gypsies: Residents gathered
signatures for their removal'. The letter was composed by representatives of local associations of Patras and contained 1,200 signatures of
non-Roma residents living near Roma settlements. The letter's drafters
and signatories collectively accused the Roma of 'crimes, including physical assault, battery, and an arson attack on a car' and they 'demanded
that they be "evicted" from the settlement and failing eviction threatened
with "militant action".'[137]

Two of the applicants were residents of the Roma settlement in
question – the other two applicants joined the domestic case later on
as witnesses – and filed a twofold criminal complaint under the Greek
Anti-Racism Law.[138] First, they complained about the public expression of
offensive ideas against the Roma residents on account of their racial origin (Article 2 of said law). Second, they complained about public incitement to discrimination, hatred or violence against Roma on account of
their racial origin (Article 1 of said law). A preliminary judicial investigation was opened, but the incitement charges under Article 1 of the
Anti-Racism Law were dropped. While the writers of the letter were initially charged and the signatories of the letter and the owner and editor of
the newspaper indicted for publicly expressing offensive ideas in violation
of Article 2 of the Anti-Racism Law, the Misdemeanours Court of Patras
acquitted the defendants. This court concluded that the Anti-Racism
Law was not violated by the accused because 'doubts remained regarding
the … intention to offend the complainants by using expressions referred
to in the indictment'.[139]

---

[136] Human Rights Committee, *Maria Vassilari et al.* v. *Greece*, Communication
no. 1570/2007 (19 March 2009).
[137] *Maria Vassilari et al.* v. *Greece*, para. 2.1.
[138] Anti-Racism Law, no. 927/1979 [Greece].
[139] *Maria Vassilari et al.* v. *Greece*, para. 2.6.

According to the applicants, the domestic trial was larded with mistakes and ambiguities. For instance, the fact that the criminal offences of which the Roma community had been accused (in the impugned letter) were found to be unsubstantiated by the competent police authority was ignored by the Patras Court.[140] Further, the presiding judge of that court had apparently made comments during the proceedings indicating a prejudicial attitude vis-à-vis Roma.[141] Crucially, on the question of intent the Court's finding that the impugned letter merely intended to draw the authorities' attention to the plight of the Roma, and could not be said to incite discrimination or violence, was wholly unsubstantiated according to the authors of the communication to the Human Rights Committee.[142]

The applicants claimed, among other things, that Article 20(2) ICCPR had been breached 'because the Patras Court failed to appreciate the racist nature of the impugned letter and to effectively implement the Anti-Racism Law 927/1979 aimed at prohibiting dissemination of racist speech'.[143] Thus the applicants claimed that although Greece has anti-incitement legislation in place, Greek law is in practice interpreted in a way that deprives victims of incitement of the necessary protection against incitement.[144]

Strikingly, while the state party challenged the admissibility of parts of the complaint,[145] the sections of the complaint dealing with incitement were not procedurally rebutted. In fact, Greece provided ample comments on the merits of the part of the complaint that is premised on Article 20(2). The gist of Greece's defence in that respect was that the authors were exaggerating. The content of the letter would not be as hateful or inciting as the applicants presented it to be. According to Greece, '[t]he words "eviction" and "militant action" do not appear in the original letter ... the correct translation of the former would be "removal" and of the latter "dynamic mobilizations" which implies protests or demonstrations.'[146] Further, the Greek courts:

> did not consider that the letter "was not insulting" to the authors, but merely found that the legal condition, namely the offence of a "public, via

---

[140] *Maria Vassilari et al.* v. *Greece*, para. 2.3.
[141] *Maria Vassilari et al.* v. *Greece*, para. 2.4.
[142] *Maria Vassilari et al.* v. *Greece*, para. 2.6.
[143] *Maria Vassilari et al.* v. *Greece*, para. 3.1.
[144] *Maria Vassilari et al.* v. *Greece*, para. 3.1.
[145] I.e. the question of the alleged partiality of the judge. *Maria Vassilari et al.* v. *Greece*, para. 4.1.
[146] *Maria Vassilari et al.* v. *Greece*, para. 4.3.

the press, expression of offensive ideas against a group of people, by virtue
of their origin", is intentionally committed, was not met beyond reasonable
doubt. It so concluded, after hearing all witnesses and evaluating all of the
available evidence. While one may agree or disagree with the Court's evaluation of the evidence, there is no reason to regard its finding as arbitrary.[147]

Largely on account of the indistinctness of the facts, the Human Rights
Committee sided with Greece. The precise formulation used to establish
the inadmissibility of the incitement part of the complaint is very telling
indeed: 'Without determining whether article 20 may be invoked under the
Optional Protocol, the Committee considers that the authors have insufficiently substantiated the facts for the purposes of admissibility. Thus, this
part of the communication is inadmissible under article 2 of the Optional
Protocol.'[148]

The facts presented in this communication, however contested by
Greece, surely substantiated a prima facie case against this State party.
Clearly, the Committee's outspoken reluctance to settle the question of
'whether article 20 may be invoked under the Optional Protocol' in fact
clouded its admissibility judgment. The content of the letter and the vulnerable position of the verbally attacked minority seemed to at least warrant discussion of the merits – which is not the same, clearly, as saying that
a violation should have been determined by the Committee.[149] It is all the
more remarkable that the Committee dodged the Article 20(2) complaint
as Greece had not objected to the admissibility of this part of the communication. Dissenting member Amor elaborated on this point, contending
that '[t]he Committee's settled jurisprudence holds that, when the State
party raises no objection to admissibility, the Committee declares the
communication admissible unless the allegations are manifestly ground-
less or not serious or do not meet the other requirements set out in the
Protocol'.[150] He further pointed out that the Greek courts did rule on the
merits without raising questions of admissibility.[151]

Accordingly, both procedurally and substantively the communication
warranted a discussion on the merits of the complaint.[152] Furthermore,

---

[147] *Maria Vassilari et al.* v. *Greece*, para. 4.4.
[148] *Maria Vassilari et al.* v. *Greece*, para. 6.5 (emphasis added).
[149] A few individual members would have preferred to decide this case on the merits of
the Art. 20(2) complaint. See Individual opinion of Committee member Mr Abdelfattah
Amor (dissenting) and Individual opinion of Committee members Mr Ahmad Amin
Fathalla and Mr Bouzid Lazhari.
[150] Individual opinion of Amor, para. (2).
[151] Individual opinion of Amor, para. (3).
[152] See further section 7.3.4 of Chapter 7 and section 10.3 of Chapter 10.

the question of 'intent' appears to inform the entire domestic proceedings. The Greek courts indicated that it had not been proven – apparently they meant by the applicant – that the letter drafters and its signatories had intended discrimination or violence. Be that as it may, that was precisely the type of question that one would expect the Human Rights Committee to pronounce on in a decision on the merits.[153] In sum, the Committee more or less deliberately missed out on the opportunity to pronounce on the legal nature of Article 20(2) of the Covenant. In 2009 there was clearly no majority in the Committee willing to settle the question of victim status under the Covenant's incitement provision.

The nearly identical cases of *Fatima Andersen* v. *Denmark* and *A.W.P.* v. *Denmark* revolve around negative statements about Islam made by several members of the Danish Popular Party.[154] Some of the impugned statements were made in an article that discussed the fact that a candidate for Danish Parliament – Ms Fatima Andersen, main applicant in one of these two cases – had spoken in Parliament wearing a Muslim headscarf.[155] One politician remarked that 'just like the Nazis believed that everyone from another race should be eliminated it is the belief in Islam that everyone of another faith must be converted and if not eliminated'.[156] Another member of this far right party stated that 'Muslim societies are per definition losers. Muslims cannot think critically … and this produces losers.'[157] A third member argued in the same article that 'the idea that a fundamentalist with headscarf [sic] should become member [sic] of the Danish Parliament is sick. She (the candidate for Parliament) needs mental treatment.'[158]

The authors of the two communications filed criminal complaints, arguing, among other things, that the statements comparing Islam with Nazism were not only insulting to them as Muslims, but also created a hostile environment that might cause discrimination.[159] Both the Regional Prosecutor and, on appeal, the Public Prosecutor General dismissed the

---

[153] On the question of intent, see Chapter 9.
[154] Human Rights Committee, *A.W.P.* v. *Denmark*, Communication no. 1879/2009 (admissibility decision of 1 November 2013); and *Fatima Andersen* v. *Denmark*, Communication no. 1868/2009 (admissibility decision of 26 July 2010).
[155] *A.W.P.* v. *Denmark*, para. 2.1; and *Fatima Andersen* v. *Denmark*, para. 2.1. The article was published in *Jyllands-Posten*, the newspaper that first published the Danish Cartoons.
[156] *A.W.P.* v. *Denmark*, para. 2.1. Similar facts are described in *Fatima Andersen* v. *Denmark*, para. 2.1.
[157] *A.W.P.* v. *Denmark*, para. 2.1.
[158] *A.W.P.* v. *Denmark*, para. 2.1.
[159] *A.W.P.* v. *Denmark*, paras. 2.2–2.3; *Fatima Andersen* v. *Denmark*, para. 2.1.

complaints and decided not to prosecute, as the applicants had failed to show that they were an injured party in the meaning of Danish law on hate speech and discrimination.[160]

In their respective communications to the Human Rights Committee, the two complainants argued that Denmark had breached its positive obligation to take effective action against reported incidents of hate speech against Muslims in Denmark.[161] They submitted that this populist party was involved in a systematic hate speech campaign against Danish Muslims.[162] Both Mr A.W.P. and Ms Andersen expressly invoked, among other Articles, Article 20(2) ICCPR.[163] Mr A.W.P. formulated his complaint in the following terms: 'the comparison made in the incriminating statements between Islam and Nazism is just one example of the ongoing campaign by members of the DPP to stir up hatred against Danish Muslims. Some people who are influenced by such statements take action in the form of hate crimes against Muslims living in Denmark.'[164]

Realizing that there was no direct link between the activities complained of and direct harm done to the applicants, the authors of the Communications suggested that the Human Rights Committee should copy the flexible approach to standing that is practised by the Committee on the Elimination of Racial Discrimination in similar cases. As will be outlined in more detail in the next chapter, that monitoring body has held that simply belonging to the minority that is incited against can under certain circumstances be enough to satisfy the victim requirement.[165]

Denmark, to the contrary, argued that the impugned speech acts in no way incited to discrimination or violence so as to engage Article 20(2).[166] Further, Denmark reiterated that there was no evidence at all that the impugned statements negatively impacted either Mr A.W.P. or Ms Anderson in a way that would compel the state to interfere with these performances of free speech.[167] Accordingly, Denmark questioned their status as victims under Article 20(2).

---

[160] A.W.P. v. Denmark, para. 2.4; Fatima Andersen v. Denmark, para. 2.2. See Section 266 of the Criminal Code of Denmark 2009.
[161] A.W.P. v. Denmark, para. 3.1; Fatima Andersen v. Denmark, para. 3.1
[162] A.W.P. v. Denmark, para. 3.2; Fatima Andersen v. Denmark, para. 3.2.
[163] A.W.P. v. Denmark, paras. 1 and 3.1; Fatima Andersen v. Denmark, paras. 1 and 3.1.
[164] A.W.P. v. Denmark, para. 3.2. This complaint is followed by some data on hate crimes in Denmark. See also Fatima Andersen v. Denmark, para. 3.2.
[165] See, e.g., CERD, The Jewish Community of Oslo et al. v. Norway, Communication no. 30/2003 (15 August 2005). See section 6.4 of Chapter 6.
[166] A.W.P. v. Denmark, para. 4.5; and Fatima Andersen v. Denmark, para. 4.3.
[167] A.W.P. v. Denmark, para. 4.13; and Fatima Andersen v. Denmark, para. 4.9.

Unlike the Danish cartoons case,[168] in these two related communications concerning alleged incitement against Muslims in Denmark the applicants had exhausted domestic remedies. Nevertheless, the Human Rights Committee avoided a decision on the merits of the complaint. To that end, the Committee endorsed Denmark's arguments against granting victim status to the applicant. In the view of the Committee, 'the author has failed to establish that those specific statements had specific consequences for him or that the specific consequences of the statements were imminent and would personally affect him.'[169] In *A.W.P. v. Denmark* three individual Committee members were of the view that the 'lack of victim status due to the collective nature of the harm allegedly afflicted by the acts or omissions of the State party' was an incorrect ground for declaring this Communication inadmissible.[170]

It is quite apparent that the Human Rights Committee does for the time being not eagerly invite communications based on Article 20(2). This forms a sharp contrast to CERD's handling of cases brought by hate propaganda victims under Article 4 ICERD.[171] That said, the cases of *Fatima Andersen v. Denmark* and *A.W.P. v. Denmark* were quite weak – their facts point to insulting speech but not to incitement in the meaning of the Covenant.

5.4.4   The pending Wilders case

There is another incitement communication, currently still pending, that may shine a light on some of the unresolved questions about standing and victim status that flow from the above discussion. This communication, dealing with anti-Islam statements made by Dutch politician Geert Wilders, may be referred to as *M.R., A.B.S. and N.A. v. The Netherlands.*[172]

---

[168] See *Kasem Said Ahmad and Asmaa Abdol-Hamid* v. *Denmark* discussed above.

[169] *A.W.P.* v. *Denmark*, para. 6.4. A similar conclusion is reached with respect to Ms Anderson. *Fatima Andersen* v. *Denmark*, para. 6.4.

[170] Individual opinion by Committee members Mr Yuval Shany, Mr Fabian Omar Savlvioli and Mr Victor Manuel Rodríguez-Rescia (concurring), para. 3. (Member Savlvioli, who was also part of the Committee in the case of Andersen, did not append such an opinion in the latter's case.) They state that they would not have determined a violation of the Covenant, as the applicant in their eyes failed to substantiate his complaint in this particular case. Yet, considering previous case law, the granting of victim status as such would have been a significant development.

[171] See Chapter 6, particularly sections 6.2–6.4 thereof.

[172] *M.R., A.B.S. and N.A.* v. *The Netherlands*, CCPR Communication dated 15 November 2011 [pending]. This section's heading notwithstanding, this is not a case brought by, and in no means a case against, Geert Wilders. It is a case brought against the Netherlands by three individuals who claim to be victims of Wilder's alleged incitement.

Geert Wilders, leader of the rightist Party for Freedom (PVV), was, among other counts, tried in relation to (religious) group defamation and hate speech charges in Dutch criminal proceedings that lasted from 2009 to 2011. The following excerpts from interviews, a documentary (*Fitna*) and other public statements made by Wilders, are among the ones listed in the indictment:

- The demographic composition of the population is the biggest problem of the Netherlands. I am talking about what comes to the Netherlands and what reproduces here. If you look at the figures and the development therein Muslims will move from the big cities to the country. We must stop the tsunami of the Islamisation. This hits us in the heart, in our identity, in our culture. If we do not *defend ourselves* all other points from my programme will appear to be useless.
- Everybody adapts to our dominant culture. Who does not do so will no longer be here in twenty years' time. *They will be deported.*
- We have a gigantic problem with Muslims, in every respect it is going too far, and we present solutions that cannot even get a mouse to come out of its hole.
- In the Nederlands Dagblad of last Saturday Professor Ralphael Israeli is also quoted who predicts a 'Third Islamic Invasion of Europe' by means of 'penetration, propaganda, conversion and demographic changes'. In his eyes the Europeans are even committing 'demographic suicide' with the advancing Islam. The first Islamic invasion was stopped at Poitiers in the year 732 after the conquest of Spain, Portugal and the south of France and the second invasion attempt by the Ottoman Turks was stopped before the gates of Vienna where they were, fortunately, beaten in 1683. According to Prof. Israeli the third invasion attempt that is now going on in Europe has a much bigger chance of success. The man is absolutely right. The Muslim population doubles with every generation – 25 years – and the number of Islamics in each and every European country is taking disturbing forms.
- There is enough Islam in Europe and in the Netherlands. The PVV will *oppose* this third Islamic invasion attempt with man and might.
- *Close the borders, no more Islamics in the Netherlands, many Muslims deported from the Netherlands, denaturalisation of Islamic criminals.*
- This book incites to hatred and murder, and does therefore not fit in our legal system. If Muslims want to participate they must renounce the Quran. I understand this is much to ask, but we must stop making concessions.

- A moderate Islam does not exist. It does not exist because there is no distinction between Good Islam and Bad Islam. There is Islam and that is it. And Islam means the Quran and nothing but the Quran. And the Quran is the Mein Kampf of a religion that intends to eliminate others and that refers to those others – non-Muslims – as unfaithful dogs, inferior beings. Read the Quran, this Mein Kampf, again. In whatever version, you will see that all the evil that the sons of Allah commit to us and themselves originates from this book.
- The government wants you to respect the Islam, yet the Islam has no respect at all for you. The Islam wants to control, subdue and is out for the destruction of our Western civilisation. In 1945 Nazism was beaten in Europe. In 1989 communism was beaten in Europe. Now the Islamic ideology *must be beaten. Stop* the Islamisation. *Defend* our freedom [from *Fitna*].[173]

These statements resulted in a number of criminal complaints.[174] Geert Wilders was charged with five counts,[175] two of which are relevant for the present purposes. First, he was accused of inciting hatred against Muslims on grounds of their religion. Second, he was accused of inciting discrimination against Muslims on grounds of their religion.[176]

On 23 June 2011 Wilders was fully acquitted.[177] The Dutch Office of the Prosecution had in fact been prosecuting rather reluctantly. That is, the first prosecutor on the case had initially dismissed the criminal

---

[173] An English translation of the summons of the accused by Gatestone Institute, is available at www.gatestoneinstitute.org/951/summons-of-the-accused. The italics have been added to underscore the parts where Mr Wilders appears to appeal to certain actions, either to be instigated by himself or by the Dutch people in general or unidentified others.

[174] 'Hundreds', according to the authors of the Communication against the Netherlands. *M.R., A.B.S. and N.A. v. The Netherlands*, at 5.

[175] Not discussed here are the following charges: (religious) group defamation; inciting hatred against non-western immigrants and Moroccans because of their race; inciting discrimination against non-western immigrants and Moroccans because of their race. The group defamation charge draws on Art. 137c of the Criminal Code of the Netherlands 1881.

[176] These two charges draw on Art. 137d of the Criminal Code of the Netherlands 1881: '1. He who publicly, verbally or in writing or in an image, incites hatred against or discrimination of people or violent behaviour against the person or property of people because of their race, their religion or belief, their gender or hetero- or homosexual nature or their physical, mental, or intellectual disabilities, will be punished with a prison sentence of at the most one year or a fine of the third category. 2. If the offence is committed by a person who makes it his profession or habit, or by two or more people in association, a prison sentence of at the most two years or a fine of the fourth category will be imposed.'

[177] Amsterdam District Court, *Wilders*, Case no. 13-425046-09 (judgment of 23 June 2011).

complaints, concluding as early as 2008 that there was nothing in Wilders' statements or behaviour that might be deemed criminal under Dutch criminal law.[178] While deeming some of Wilders' statements 'insulting to Muslims', the prosecutor and the Amsterdam District Court agreed that the statements 'were done within the context of public debate'.[179]

In a unique twist, thus urged by a group of stakeholders under what in Dutch law is called the 'Article 12 SV-procedure',[180] the Amsterdam High Court overruled the Office of the Prosecution, forcing the latter's hand to start a case against Wilders after all.[181] Thus the High Court concluded that there were sufficient indications that Wilders may have breached Dutch criminal law on extreme speech, therefore deeming a prosecution viable.

This second time round the Office of the Prosecution again requested a full acquittal.[182] The prosecution came to this request, among other reasons, arguing that the fact that something is insulting does not make it criminal; also, all impugned statements targeted Islam or the Quran, not Muslims. The Amsterdam District Court subsequently did fully acquit Wilders, largely agreeing with the prosecutor, though it did not shy away from observing that the 'suspect balances on the border of what is accepted pursuant to criminal law'.[183]

A group of alleged victims brought a case against the Netherlands, requesting the Human Rights Committee to determine whether the Netherlands has breached Article 20(2) by, allegedly, not or not adequately implementing its own incitement legislation. Specifically, by not convicting Wilders, have the Netherlands failed to protect persons against incitement to discrimination, hostility and violence? To be precise, two Dutch lawyers of the international law-oriented Dutch firm Böhler Advocaten

---

[178] Dutch Office of the Prosecution, decision not to prosecute of 30 June 2008, presented to Arrondissementsparket Amsterdam (Amsterdam District Court).

[179] Dutch Office of the Prosecution, decision not to prosecute of 30 June 2008.

[180] A penal code procedure that enables victims and other stakeholders to appeal a prosecutorial dismissal of a case. Code of Criminal Procedure 1921 [Netherlands], Art. 12.

[181] Amsterdam High Court, decision of 21 January 2009.

[182] It did so on two occasions, on 15 October 2010, and – when the case was resumed with new judges after a successful substitution request – again on 25 May 2011.

[183] Amsterdam District Court, Case no. 13-425046-09 (judgment of 23 June 2011). This was observed with particular regard to his statement holding that 'a conflict is going on and we have to defend ourselves'. The court argued that such 'incitement to people to defend themselves has a subversive character, also by the vehement wording. The connection with the remainder of the interview does not take away the provocative character of these vehement words.'

brought the case against the Netherlands on behalf of three anonymous applicants, M.R., A.B.S. and N.A.[184] The applicants are Dutch citizens of Moroccan descent and all claim to have personally experienced the negative impact triggered by Wilders' statements, ranging from more general feelings of anxiety, to increasingly feeling threatened and marginalized, to very concrete incidents of hate crimes and discrimination.[185]

Unlike in *Kasem Said Ahmad and Asmaa Abdol-Hamid* v. *Denmark*, local remedies have been exhausted. And unlike the authors of the communications in *A.W.P.* v. *Denmark* and *Fatima Andersen* v. *Denmark*, the complainants seek to concretely substantiate their status as victims. That is, the impugned statements, it is argued by the applicants, have had a personal impact on their lives.

Besides other complaints, the applicants' principal claim is a breach of Article 20(2) ICCPR, taken in conjunction with the equality principle of Article 26 and minority rights as codified by Article 27.[186] The applicants are all too aware of the fact that they tread on uncharted territory. Already in one of the preliminary sections of the communications on the exhaustion of local remedies, the applicants start warming the Committee to the idea of invoking and applying Article 20(2). They submit that while Article 20 ICCPR is 'couched in terms of obligations of the state rather than in rights of individuals, this does not imply that these are matters to be left to the internal jurisdiction of state parties and as such immune from review under the individual communication procedure. If such were the case, the protection regime established by the Covenant would be weakened significantly.'[187] The applicants submit that '[a]s a consequence of the acquittal, the complainants are not only victims of the hate speech of Wilders but also victims of a violation of article 20 CCPR by the State of the Netherlands'.[188]

The applicants concede that incitement proceedings, when instigated, do not have to lead to a conviction. The Covenant does not provide a right to see another person prosecuted, let alone a right to see another person

---

[184] These are the same lawyers and law firm that assisted the victims in the domestic 'Article-12 SV procedure', leading to the prosecutor's decision not to prosecute being overruled by a court.

[185] *M.R., A.B.S. and N.A.* v. *The Netherlands* communication, at 3–4. See also the witness statement made by N.A. during the domestic proceedings (Annex 4).

[186] Other complaints are premised on Art. 2 and Art. 14 of the ICCPR.

[187] *M.R., A.B.S. and N.A.* v. *The Netherlands* communication, at 2. Note that this quote borrows a formula used by CERD in relation to Art. 4 of ICERD. See *The Jewish Community of Oslo et al.* v. *Norway*, Communication No. 30/2003 (15 August 2005), para. 10.6.

[188] *M.R., A.B.S. and N.A.* v. *The Netherlands* communication, at 2.

convicted.[189] Rather, they submit that the Dutch prosecutors and the judiciary made a number of errors in weighing the evidence in this case, hence suggesting that this particular acquittal was at odds with Article 20(2) ICCPR.[190] Thus the complaint does not claim that there is no legislation in the Netherlands corresponding to Article 20(2) ICCPR; nor that the existing provisions, notably Article 137d of the Dutch Criminal Code, would not fully accord with the said international standard. Rather the claim is that the prosecutorial and judicial authorities failed to properly assess the particulars of the case and failed to soundly apply incitement legislation.

In the light of what transpired in *Maria Vassilari et al. v. Greece*, it is uncertain whether the Committee will entertain the case. We know that some Committee members will be eager to do so, while others will not. Should the Committee declare the case admissible, the next question is how far the Committee's competence reaches. Generally speaking, the Committee has the following options when faced with an Article 20(2) complaint. It may generally assess the incitement legislation in question. Then it could find, for instance, that a State party's lack of legislation required by Article 20(2) amounts to a breach of the Covenant. Further, it could be that while the State party has relevant legislation in place, this legislation falls short of the requirements posed by Article 20(2). Alternatively, the Committee could find that the incitement legislation has no shortcomings when scrutinized in the light of the Covenant. Further, the Committee could hazard an opinion about a domestic incitement trial. The Committee may then, for instance find an arbitrary refusal to judicially enforce codified incitement laws to amount to a violation of the Covenant. Or, in the event that relevant incitement laws have been applied to the case, the Committee may find that particular judicial application to fall short of the requirements of Article 20(2) of the Covenant.

The authors of the 'Wilders' communication urge the Committee to make a pronouncement along the latter lines, to render the domestic incitement trial against Wilders as flawed. The authors admit that Article 137d of the Dutch Penal Code as such is fine and in compliance with Article 20(2).[191] They submit that '[t]he problem is not the law, but

---

189 See Human Rights Committee, *Leonardus Johannes Maria de Groot* v. *The Netherlands*, Communication no. 578/1994 (14 July 1995), para. 4.6; and *M.S.* v. *The Netherlands*, Communication no. 396/1990 (22 July 1992), para. 6.2.

190 *M.R., A.B.S. and N.A.* v. *The Netherlands* communication, at 9–13.

191 *M.R., A.B.S. and N.A.* v. *The Netherlands* communication, at 9, stating that this 'article [must] be seen as the implementation of both article 4 CERD and article 20 CCPR'. In

the way it was interpreted ... by the District Court so that the prohibition of hate speech was empty of any significance in this case'.[192] The authors of the communication also complain about the fact that the Office of the Prosecution repeatedly requested an acquittal, thus refraining from presenting evidence as to the adverse nature of Wilders' statements.[193] Accordingly, theirs is a combination of a complaint about the apparent reluctance on the part of the Dutch authorities to apply incitement legislation and a complaint about the alleged erroneous judicial interpretation of that same legislation.

One may wonder whether the Committee is competent to make such far-reaching assessments, essentially second-guessing a domestic trial. For the time being, we do not even have a jurisprudential precedent of the Committee reproaching a State party for not having incitement legislation corresponding with Article 20(2) in place. Hence, requesting an assessment of a domestic incitement trial is perhaps asking quite a lot from the Committee. The easy way out for the Committee would seem to be to insist on the fact that there is no right under the Covenant to have someone successfully prosecuted. The Dutch authorities did instigate criminal procedures against Wilders after all, the Committee might argue, and a prosecutorial or judicial dismissal of the criminal complaints is one possible outcome of a criminal procedure.[194]

That said, there certainly is precedent under international law of monitoring bodies reassessing domestic extreme speech cases in the light of international standards. The authors of the 'Wilders' communication rightly dwell on the fact that the Committee on the Elimination of Racial Discrimination does not only accept jurisdiction in similar cases, but actually goes as far as finding certain domestic hate propaganda cases

---

actual fact, a number of discrepancies between Art. 20(2) ICCPR and corresponding Dutch legal provisions can be discerned on close reading. For one thing, the Dutch legal threshold for 'hate speech' appears in fact to be lower than the threshold for 'incitement' under the ICCPR. We will return to questions of legal implementation of Art. 20(2) in Chapter 8.

[192] *M.R., A.B.S. and N.A. v. The Netherlands* communication, at 14.

[193] *M.R., A.B.S. and N.A. v. The Netherlands* communication, at 8–9.

[194] It may be noted that in its latest report on the Netherlands, the European Commission against Racism and Intolerance (ECRI) feels that Geert Wilders got off too lightly and that the domestic court's interpretation and application of national incitement standards may be at odds with international incitement standards and interpretations and applications thereof. ECRI, *Fourth Report on the Netherlands* (CRI(2013)39, adopted on 20 June 2013), para. 19. This report was not yet available when the applicants filed their communication with the Human Rights Committee.

to be in breach of ICERD for not combating extreme speech rigorously enough.[195]

Reflecting the trend described in this chapter, at times the applicants formulate their complaint expressly along the lines of the 'right to be protected from incitement to hatred, discrimination and violence in accordance with Article 20'.[196] Remarkably, the applicants make no mention of *Vassilari et al.* v. *Greece,* nor of the fact that a number of individual Committee Members had already declared themselves prepared to entertain this type of case.[197] The applicants do discuss relevant legal scholarship that accepts that Article 20 may be invoked by alleged victims, also accepting concomitant competence on the part of the Committee.[198]

5.5   Concluding remarks

The Committee's views on the question as to the exact legal status of Article 20(2) ICCPR read as an eclectic mix of arguments and confusing signals. The Committee has been torn between dodging the question and wishing to settle this score once and for all. Since this lack of legal clarity has been pointed out within legal doctrine,[199] and since the Committee has previously openly debated this issue,[200] the adoption of General Comment No. 34 was perhaps the ideal moment to settle the question of victim status under Article 20(2) and the related question of legal standing for alleged incitement victims. As the Committee then passed up on this opportunity, we can only refer to its other workings, most importantly its case law. Through the latter we can see a 'right to be protected against incitement' gradually being developed. However, for

---

[195] *M.R., A.B.S. and N.A.* v. *The Netherlands* communication, at 13–14. See CERD, *L.K.* v. *The Netherlands,* Communication No. 4/1991 (16 March 1993); and *Jewish Community of Oslo et al.* v. *Norway.* Both cases are discussed in Chapter 6.

[196] *M.R., A.B.S. and N.A.* v. *The Netherlands* communication, at 8 and 14.

[197] Moreover, the applicants erroneously claim twice that Art. 20 has never been invoked by alleged victims. *M.R., A.B.S. and N.A.* v. *The Netherlands* communication, at 13 and 20.

[198] Jakob T. Möller and Alfred M. de Zayas, *United Nations Human Rights Committee Case Law* (Kehl am Rhein: N. P. Engel Verlag, 2009), at 377, as cited by the authors of the communication, at 21.

[199] E.g. Möller and de Zayas, *UN Human Rights Committee Case Law,* at 377; Sarah Joseph, 'A Rights Analysis of the Covenant on Civil and Political Rights,' (1999) 5 *Journal of International Legal Studies* (1999) 57–94, at 73. Conversely, Nowak, *CCPR Commentary,* at 468, calling Art. 20 an 'alien element in the system of the Covenant' and implying that the provision exclusively entails state obligations, and not rights.

[200] *Maria Vassilari et al.* v. *Greece.*

the time being this 'right' does not quite serve as an autonomous 'invocable' right. Its main function lies in its capacity as limiting factor, that is as a 'right of others'. Perhaps the Committee will allow for an upgrade of this Article 20(2)-derived right in the 'Wilders' case. The Committee is rightly wary of opening up the floodgates to all types of undesirable hatred and insult litigation. CERD's treatment of Article 4 ICERD, however, shows that this need not necessarily be the case. On the interrelated question of victim status/rights status/legal standing, let us now compare the Human Rights Committee's treatment of Article 20(2) with other important players at the international level.

6

Comparative international perspectives: CERD and the European Court of Human Rights on the 'right to be free from incitement'

6.1 Introduction

The objective of this chapter is to contrast the Human Rights Committee's views on the legal nature of Article 20(2) ICCPR with the work in that area by the Committee on the Elimination of Racial Discrimination and the European Court of Human Rights. The question that concerns us specifically is whether those monitoring bodies have accepted a more full-fledged right to be protected against incitement or whether they are – even – more reserved in that respect. We will commence with CERD (sections 6.2–6.4) and subsequently discuss the European Court of Human Rights (sections 6.5–6.7).

6.2 A general introduction to Article 4 ICERD

Article 4 of the International Convention on the Elimination of All Forms of Racial Discrimination (ICERD) orders State parties to prohibit, among other things, incitement to racial discrimination and violence. The extensive prohibition reads in full:

> States Parties condemn all propaganda and all organizations which are based on ideas or theories of superiority of one race or group of persons of one colour or ethnic origin, or which attempt to justify or promote racial hatred and discrimination in any form, and undertake to adopt immediate and positive measures designed to eradicate all incitement to, or acts of, such discrimination and, to this end, with due regard to the principles embodied in the Universal Declaration of Human Rights and the rights expressly set forth in article 5 of this Convention, inter alia:
>
> (a) Shall declare an offence punishable by law all dissemination of ideas based on racial superiority or hatred, incitement to racial discrimination, as well as all acts of violence or incitement to such acts against any race or group of persons of another colour or ethnic

origin, and also the provision of any assistance to racist activities, including the financing thereof;

(b) Shall declare illegal and prohibit organizations, and also organized and all other propaganda activities, which promote and incite racial discrimination, and shall recognize participation in such organizations or activities as an offence punishable by law;

(c) Shall not permit public authorities or public institutions, national or local, to promote or incite racial discrimination.[1]

Article 4 of ICERD, like Article 20(2) ICCPR, is formulated in general terms of state obligations, not in terms of substantive rights. ICERD does not literally speak of a 'right to be free from racist incitement', but of a state duty to prohibit the latter. More clearly than Article 20(2) ICCPR, Article 4 ICERD leaves no doubts as to whether domestic legislative and other measures are optional or mandatory – the language of the latter article is very mandatory indeed. Also, the Committee on the Elimination of Racial Discrimination (CERD) reminds State parties of this fact in its General Recommendations, its case law[2] and in its concluding observations on State parties' periodic reports.[3]

---

[1] ICERD, Art. 4. Reservations or restrictive declarations in relation to Art. 4 have been adopted by: Antigua and Barbuda; Australia; Austria; Bahamas; Barbados; Belgium; Fiji; France; Grenada; Ireland; Italy; Japan; Malta; Monaco; Nepal; Papua New Guinea; Switzerland; Thailand; Tonga; United Kingdom; and United States of America. Some of these states reserve the right not to introduce new laws on this matter, while others have reserved the right not to consider all acts mentioned by Art. 4 as criminal offences.

[2] As discussed in detail below, see section 6.4 of this chapter.

[3] E.g. CERD, A/49/18 (1994) 37 para. 261 (Norway): 'It is reaffirmed that the provisions of article 4, paragraphs (a) and (b) are of a mandatory character ... These provisions have not been fully implemented in the State party; therefore, the State party should carry out each obligation under those mandatory provisions of the Convention.' Further, see A/57/18 (2002) 17, para. 51 (Belgium), emphasizing 'the mandatory nature of article 4 of the Convention'; and A/55/18 (2000) 60, para. 356 (UK), underscoring that 'all provisions of article 4 are of a mandatory character'. See also A/48/18 (1993) 95, para. 543 (Yugoslavia); A/49/18 (1994) 30, para. 202 (Sweden); A/49/18 (1994) 68, para. 474 (Sudan); A/51/18 (1996) 29, para. 175 (Finland); A/51/18 (1996) 41, para. 276 (Bolivia); A/52/18 (1997) 62, para. 476 (Poland); A/52/18 (1997) 69, para. 552 (Argentina); A/54/18 (1999) 14, para. 54 (Republic of Korea); A/54/18 (1999) 37, para. 374 (Chile); A/55/18 (2000) 29, para. 125 (Malta); A/56/18 (2001) 34, para. 168 (Japan); A/56/18 (2001) 50, para. 287 (Egypt); A/56/18 (2001) 58, para. 349 (Trinidad and Tobago); A/56/18 (2001) 64, para. 391 (USA); A/57/18 (2002) 30, para. 132 (Jamaica); A/57/18 (2002) 72, para. 444 (Senegal); A/57/18 (2002) 74, para. 461 (Yemen); A/58/18 (2003) 30, para. 117 (Ghana); A/58/18 (2003) 33, para. 140 (Morocco); A/58/18 (2003) 41, para. 210 (Saudi Arabia); A/58/18 (2003) 50, para. 274 (Uganda); A/58/18 (2003) 62, para. 362 (Cape Verde); A/58/18 (2003) 93, para. 556 (Malawi); A/59/18 (2004) 10, para. 30 (Bahamas); A/59/18 (2004) 21, para. 102 (Libya); A/60/18 (2005) 40, para. 197 (Luxembourg); A/60/18 (2005) 54, para. 292 (Nigeria).

Starting with the latter, the Committee has used the state reporting procedure time and again to closely monitor domestic legislative acts in the light of Article 4 ICERD. Thus the Committee does not shy away from pointing out to State parties if newly adopted laws or amendments are unfortunately still not fully in accordance with the requirements of Article 4 of ICERD.[4] If the domestic laws in place are found to be in accordance with the Convention, the Committee may still argue that State parties do not combat racist hate speech rigorously and proactively enough.[5] In that respect, the Committee has, for example, indicated that a State party's incitement laws have resulted in an alarmingly low number of convictions,[6] or that more active prosecution is

---

[4] E.g. CERD, A/50/18 (1995) 23, para. 71 (Cyprus): 'While welcoming the enactment of Law 11 of 1992, which created offences regarding acts amounting to racial discrimination, a question is raised about whether the wording of certain passages in section 2A meet completely the requirements of article 4(a) of the Convention.' Further, see A/54/18 (1999) 13, para. 33 (Austria): 'The fact that the condemnation of racist propaganda and incitement to racial hostility is qualified by a reference to public peace is of concern.' For another example, see A/54/18 (1999) 35, para. 350 (Iraq): '[Penal Code] provisions do not fully reflect the requirements of article 4 of the Convention'. See also A/55/18 (2000) 38, para. 197 (Zimbabwe); A/55/18 (2000) 17, para. 37 (Australia); A/56/18 (2001) 24, para. 92 (Georgia); A/56/18 (2001) 68, para. 415 (Vietnam); A/57/18 (2002) 50, para. 276 (Armenia); A/58/18 (2003) 47, para. 254 (Tunisia); A/58/18 (2003) 53, para. 311 (Albania); A/58/18 (2003) 58, paras. 336 and 338 (Bolivia); A/58/18 (2003) 65, paras. 381 and 382 (Czech Republic); A/58/18 (2003) 75, para. 446 (Latvia); A/58/18 (2003) 79, paras. 474 and 475 (Norway); A/58/18 (2003) 83, para. 494 (Republic of Korea); A/58/18 (2003) 88, para. 531 (UK); A/59/18 (2004) 41, paras. 214 and 220 (Sweden); A/59/18 (2004) 54, para. 286 (Kazakhstan); A/59/18 (2004) 61, paras. 339 and 340 (Mauritania); A/60/18 (2005) 40, para. 197 (Luxembourg); A/60/18 (2005) 46, para. 239 (Georgia).

[5] See also CERD's jurisprudence as discussed in section 6.4 below, from which it flows that State parties face a duty to investigate and prosecute relevant cases.

[6] E.g. CERD, A/51/18 (1996) 17, para. 63 (Denmark): 'It is noted with concern that only three convictions have been registered in the past six years against members of neo-Nazi groups, although instructions have been issued to prosecutors.' Further, see A/51/18 (1996) 22, para. 116 (Hungary): 'Grave concern is expressed at the persistence of expressions of racial hatred and acts of violence, particularly those by neo-Nazi skinheads and others, towards persons belonging to minorities, especially Gypsies, Jews and people of African or Asian origin ... In this regard, concern is expressed that the number of charges and convictions, including against neo-Nazi skinheads and others, is low relative to the number of abuses reported.' See also A/52/18 (1997) 39, para. 283 (Bulgaria); A/54/18 (1999) 39, para. 394 (Latvia).

required.[7] Conversely, the Committee is also known to emphatically praise State parties' active prosecution of relevant incidents.[8]

The fact that Article 4 is mandatory has also been firmly stated and confirmed throughout the Committee's General Recommendations. Even in the Committee's first Recommendation, sensing a degree of reluctance on the part of some State parties to implement this provision, CERD urged all State parties to supplement their legislation with provisions that conform to the requirements of Article 4 ICERD.[9] When a decade later the Committee still observed that some states took a half-hearted approach to implementing Article 4,[10] it responded in a bolder fashion. It requested from all states that had not yet done so to quote in their next periodic report the actual legal texts that purported to correspond with the requirements of Article 4 ICERD.[11] Going beyond the question of mere legal transposition of the norm into domestic law, the Committee, moreover, requested information concerning any decisions taken by the national tribunals and other state institutions reflecting the State party's actual enforcement policies with respect to Article 4.[12] Again a decade later, the Committee reiterated that Article 4 has always been deemed 'central to the struggle against racial discrimination', and in order to fulfil their obligations 'States parties have not only to enact

---

[7] CERD, A/59/18 (2004) 58, para. 316 (Madagascar): 'the perpetrators should be brought to justice in accordance with relevant domestic legislation, promulgated pursuant to article 4 of the Convention.' Further, see A/57/18 (2002) 69, para. 425 (New Zealand): 'The Committee takes note of the operation of Sections 131 and 134 of the Human Rights Act, according to which the institution of criminal proceedings against those accused of incitement to racial hatred is subject to the consent of the Attorney-General. Observing that the institution of such proceedings is rare, the State party is invited to consider ways and means of facilitating the institution of proceedings in this field.' See also A/58/18 (2003) 35, para. 159 (Poland); A/59/18 (2004) 14, para. 64 (Brazil); A/59/18 (2004) 29, para. 151 (Netherlands); A/60/18 (2005) 61, para. 317 (Turkmenistan).

[8] CERD, A/58/18 (2003) 19, para. 23 (Côte d'Ivoire): 'The Committee welcomes the State party's commitment to prosecute any media which incite hatred or racial discrimination.'

[9] CERD, *General Recommendation 1: States Parties' Obligations* (UN Doc. A/8718 at 37, Fifth session, 1972).

[10] It should be noted that Art. 4 ICERD is not self-executing. CERD, *General Recommendation 35: Combating Racist Hate Speech* (UN Doc. CERD/C/GC/35, 83rd session, 12–30 August 2013), para. 13.

[11] CERD, *General Recommendation 7: Measures to Eradicate Incitement to or Acts of Discrimination* (UN Doc. A/40/18 at 120, 32nd session, 1985), para. 2.

[12] CERD, *General Recommendation 7*, para. 3.

appropriate legislation but also to ensure that it is effectively enforced.'[13] The Committee reasoned that '[b]ecause threats and acts of racial violence easily lead to other such acts and generate an atmosphere of hostility, only immediate intervention can meet the obligations of effective response.'[14] In its 2013 General Recommendation, wholly dedicated to 'combating racist hate speech', the Committee once more underscored 'the mandatory nature of article 4'.[15] Appealing to State parties' sense of urgency in that regard, the Committee elaborated its position by positing that Article 4 of ICERD 'has an expressive function in underlining the international community's abhorrence of racist hate speech, understood as a form of other-directed speech which rejects the core human rights principles of human dignity and equality and seeks to degrade the standing of individuals and groups in the estimation of society.'[16]

Article 4 of ICERD is a comprehensive standard, ordering states to adopt measures, including criminal prohibitions,[17] in no less than seven areas: (1) dissemination of ideas based upon racial superiority or hatred; (2) incitement to racial hatred; (3) acts of violence against any race or group of persons of another colour or ethnic origin; (4) incitement to such acts; (5) the financing of racist activities; (6) racist organizations and other collective racist propaganda activities; (7) behaviour of public authorities or public institutions.

From the Committee's workings it transpires that any type of medium may fall under these prohibitions, ranging from radio,[18]

---

[13] CERD, *General Recommendation 15: Measures to Eradicate Incitement to or Acts of Discrimination* (UN Doc. A/48/18 at 114, Forty-second session, 1993), paras. 1–2. See also CERD, *General Recommendation 30: Discrimination against Non-citizens* (UN Doc. CERD/C/64/Misc.11/rev.3, 64th session, 2004), paras. 11–12.

[14] CERD, *General Recommendation 15*, para. 2.

[15] CERD, *General Recommendation 35*, para. 10.

[16] CERD, *General Recommendation 35*, para. 10.

[17] CERD, *General Recommendation 35*, para. 10, lists five offences that must be punished by law: '(a) All dissemination of ideas based on racial or ethnic superiority or hatred, by whatever means; (b) Incitement to hatred, contempt or discrimination against members of a group on grounds of their race, colour, descent, or national or ethnic origin; (c) Threats or incitement to violence against persons or groups on the grounds in (b) above; (d) Expression of insults, ridicule or slander of persons or groups or justification of hatred, contempt or discrimination on the grounds in (b) above, when it clearly amounts to incitement to hatred or discrimination; (e) Participation in organizations and activities which promote and incite racial discrimination.'

[18] E.g. CERD, A/55/18 (2000) 22, para. 64 (Denmark): 'In light of article 4 of the Convention, activities of organizations which promote racial hatred and discrimination are of concern, especially the influence of Radio Oasen. Radio Oasen is owned by a neo-Nazi association whose licence was renewed by the Ministry of Culture and which receives

television,[19] the Internet,[20] recorded music,[21] audio-visual media,[22] graphic media,[23] materials disseminated by the postal services,[24] school books[25] and printed or any other written publications.[26] In addition, the extreme speech prohibitions flowing from Article 4 ICERD in principle apply to every person, regardless of one's role in society. Accordingly, neither 'the press'/'national media'/'mass media' nor individual journalists are exempted.[27] Further, Article 4 must be enforced with respect to hateful politicians and political parties.[28] It may be reiterated that

---

financial support from the Government. It is recommended that the State party declare illegal and prohibit any organization which promotes and incites racial discrimination.' See also A/52/18 (1997) 59, para. 450 (Denmark); A/52/18 (1997) 77, para. 607 (Norway); A/57/18 (2002) 21, para. 70 (Costa Rica); A/57/18 (2002) 27, para. 116 (Denmark).

[19] E.g. CERD, A/53/18 (1998) 59, para. 318 (Croatia).

[20] E.g. CERD, A/59/18 (2004) 45, para. 245 (Argentina): 'The Committee is concerned about incidents of incitement to racial hatred and racist propaganda in the media, including on the Internet. The Committee recalls that article 4 of the Convention is applicable to the phenomenon of racism in the media, including on the Internet, and that the fundamental principle of respect for human dignity requires all States to combat dissemination of racial hatred and incitement to racial hatred. It recommends that the State party take appropriate measures to combat racist propaganda in the media.' See also A/57/18 (2002) 17, para. 44 (Belgium); A/58/18 (2003) 69, para. 407 (Finland); A/59/18 (2004) 14, para. 64 (Brazil); A/59/18 (2004) 29, para. 151 (Netherlands); A/59/18 (2004) 50, para. 264 (Belarus); A/60/18 (2005) 26, para. 98 (France); A/60/18 (2005) 40, para. 195 (Luxembourg).

[21] E.g. CERD, A/52/18 (1997) 65, para. 505 (Sweden): 'Concern is expressed at the ... increasing dissemination of recorded music, the lyrics of which promote hatred against ethnic minorities.' See also A/55/18 (2000) 57, para. 335 (Sweden), describing its concerns about 'white power music'.

[22] E.g. CERD, A/53/18 (1998) 59, para. 314 (Croatia).

[23] E.g. CERD, A/53/18 (1998) 59, paras. 318 and 325 (Croatia).

[24] E.g. CERD, A/57/18 (2002) 17, para. 43 (Belgium).

[25] E.g. CERD, A/59/18 (2004) 86, para. 452 (Saint Lucia): 'The Committee is concerned by reports of the alleged inclusion in certain school textbooks of racist passages concerning the Bethechilokono people. It urges the State party to delete all racist content from school textbooks, to take measures to punish those who make such references, to provide education that will eliminate racial prejudices and to promote understanding and tolerance among different racial and ethnic groups.'

[26] E.g. CERD, A/53/18 (1998) 59, para. 314 (Croatia); and A/52/18 (1997) 77, para. 607 (Norway). Interestingly, the Committee on the Rights of the Child has for their part added hateful 'video computer games' to this list. See CRC/C/146 (2005) 47, paras. 253 and 254 (Austria).

[27] E.g. CERD, A/48/18 (1993) 95, para. 543 (Yugoslavia); A/51/18 (1996) 17, para. 62 (Denmark); A/54/18 (1999) 30, para. 285 (Romania); A/57/18 (2002) 35, para. 177 (Lithuania); A/58/18 (2003) 35, para. 158 (Poland); A/58/18 (2003) 38, para. 193 (Russia); A/59/18 (2004) 10, para. 31 (Bahamas).

[28] E.g. CERD, A/59/18 (2004) 66, para. 366 (Portugal): 'the Committee is concerned about the activities of the National Renovation Party, which targets immigrants in its

Article 4, paragraph c expressly states that State parties must forbid public authorities or public institutions from promoting or inciting racial discrimination. Hateful speech by private persons not acting in any official capacity also comes within the ambit of this provision.[29]

Consequently, Article 4 ICERD in many respects goes significantly beyond Article 20(2) ICCPR. Qualifying extreme speech is not merely to be 'prohibited by law' (Article 20(2) ICCPR), but under the ICERD must be declared 'an offence punishable by law'. Hence, the ICERD leaves no doubt as to what type of law is required in this area – criminal law, with penal sanctions.[30] The Committee on the Elimination of Racial Discrimination has recently, however, toned down its position in this regard. In its General Recommendation on racist hate speech the Committee:

> recommends that the criminalization of forms of racist expression should be reserved for serious cases, to be proven beyond reasonable doubt, while less serious cases should be addressed by means other than criminal law, taking into account, inter alia, the nature and extent of the impact on targeted persons and groups. The application of criminal sanctions should be governed by principles of legality, proportionality and necessity.[31]

The fact remains that criminal laws against hate propaganda within the meaning of Article 4 ICERD must be in place in State parties. The above caveat made by the Committee is in regard to the application of those laws. This milder language concerning the enforcement of incitement laws resonates with the UN OHCHR-instigated Rabat Plan of Action.[32]

---

manifestos and campaigns'. See also A/48/18 (1993) 73, para. 416 (United Kingdom); A/51/18 (1996) 25, para. 150 (Russia); A/53/18 (1998) 33, para. 102 (Netherlands); A/53/18 (1998) 35, para. 121 (Czech Republic); A/57/18 (2002) 17, para. 51 (Belgium); A/57/18 (2002) 27, para. 115 (Denmark); A/57/18 (2002) 35, para. 177 (Lithuania).

[29] CERD, A/53/18 (1998) 33, para. 102 (Netherlands).

[30] See Stephanie Farrior, 'Molding the Matrix: The Historical and Theoretical Foundations of International Law Concerning Hate Speech' (1996) 14:1 *Berkeley Journal of International Law*, 1–98, at 51. See also CERD, A/58/18 (2003) 88, para. 524 (UK): 'The Committee commends the State party's efforts to address more stringently the issue of incitement to racial hatred, including … the increase in the maximum penalty for incitement to racial hatred from two to seven years' imprisonment under the Anti-Terrorism, Crime and Security Act 2001.'

[31] CERD, *General Recommendation 35*, para. 12.

[32] *Rabat Plan of Action on the Prohibition of Advocacy of National, Racial or Religious Hatred that Constitutes Incitement to Discrimination, Hostility or Violence* (Conclusions and recommendations emanating from the four regional expert workshops organized by OHCHR in 2011 and adopted by experts in Rabat, Morocco on 5 October 2012), at 7: 'Criminal sanctions related to unlawful forms of expression should be seen as last

CERD has also gone further than the Human Rights Committee by demanding that states redress breaches of Article 4 ICERD.[33] Accordingly, remedies must be made available to victims.[34] Further positive obligations that CERD has distilled from this standard include a duty to inform the public about the existence of extreme speech legislation.[35] The Committee has commended State parties for liaising with the media or with the postal authorities in order to prevent the distribution of hateful materials.[36]

Finally, while proposals by the drafters of Article 20(2) ICCPR to the effect that hateful organizations could also be prohibited were defeated,[37] Article 4 of the ICERD does force State parties to 'declare illegal and prohibit organizations, and also organized and all other propaganda activities, which promote and incite racial discrimination, and shall recognize participation in such organizations or activities as an offence punishable by law'.[38] With respect to hate-mongering organizations,[39] including political parties, the Committee has referred to 'financial sanctions',[40] but also to complete bans and dissolutions as appropriate sanctions.[41] CERD monitors this aspect of Article 4 closely.[42]

resort measures to be only applied in strictly justifiable situations. Civil sanctions and remedies should also be considered, including pecuniary and non-pecuniary damages, along with the right of correction and the right of reply. Administrative sanctions and remedies should also be considered, including those identified and put in force by various professional and regulatory bodies.'

[33] E.g. CERD, A/50/18 (1995) 53, para. 272 (Romania): 'Once such acts occur, it is not evident what remedies are available to victims and whether and how it is ensured that the guilty parties are prosecuted in an adequate and timely manner.'

[34] CERD, A/50/18 (1995) 48, para. 244 (Yugoslavia): 'It is further noted that the State party fails to take adequate action to either prosecute perpetrators of such acts or to attempt to redress injustices.'

[35] CERD, A/55/18 (2000) 43, para. 229 (Mauritius).

[36] A/57/18 (2002) 17, para. 43 (Belgium).

[37] E.g. A/AC.3/SR.291, para. 8 (Ukraine); E/SR.438, para. 59 (USSR); A/C.3/SR.569, para. 20 (Czechoslovakia).

[38] ICERD, Art. 4(b).

[39] For a more comprehensive analysis, see Chapter 12.

[40] E.g. A/57/18 (2002) 17, para. 42 (Belgium).

[41] A/58/18 (2003) 25, para. 91 (Fiji).

[42] E.g. CERD, A/48/18 (1993) 73, para. 416 (United Kingdom): 'By not prohibiting the British National Party and other groups and organizations of a racist nature, and by allowing them to pursue their activities, the State party is failing to implement article 4, which calls for a condemnation of all organizations attempting to justify or promote racial hatred and discrimination.' See also: A/48/18 (1993) 81, para. 449 (Germany); A/49/18 (1994) 30, para. 199 (Sweden); A/49/18 (1994) 68, para. 474 (Sudan); A/51/18 (1996) 25, para. 150 (Russia); A/51/18, (1996) 32, para. 209 (Spain); A/55/18 (2000) 41, para. 212 (Finland);

In the light of such seemingly rigorous supervision of Article 4 ICERD by the Committee on the Elimination of Racial Discrimination, one may start to wonder why a conceptualization of Article 20(2) ICCPR would at all be useful. In one important respect, though, Article 4 ICERD – including the workings of CERD – falls short of the potential protection offered by Article 20(2) ICCPR.

6.3   Article 4 ICERD and religious hatred constituting incitement

6.3.1   The place of religion in the ICERD

There is one area in which Article 4 ICERD is narrower than Article 20(2) ICCPR: the prohibited incitement grounds. Whereas Article 4 ICERD looks to racist propaganda and incitement against persons because of their race, colour or ethnic origin, Article 20(2) ICCPR looks to advocacy of national, racial and *religious* hatred. Thus the two articles' prohibited grounds partly overlap; yet the latter provision is in this respect wider for it also uniquely looks to religious hateful incitement.

The ICERD does mention 'religion' twice – once in the preamble,[43] and once so as to ensure that State parties undertake to prohibit and to eliminate racial discrimination in the enjoyment of, among other rights, the 'right to freedom of thought, conscience and religion'.[44] Crucially, however, this convention's key term – 'racial discrimination' – is defined as 'any distinction, exclusion, restriction or preference based on race, colour, descent, or national or ethnic origin which has the purpose or effect of nullifying or impairing the recognition, enjoyment or exercise, on an equal footing, of human rights and fundamental freedoms in the political, economic, social, cultural or any other field of public life'.[45]

This does not necessarily mean that ICERD cannot or does not play a role in promoting the rights of religious groups or individuals. However, as former CERD member Patrick Thornberry observes, the Committee always 'searches for an "ethnic" or other connection or element of

---

A/55/18 (2000) 50, para. 281 (Czech Republic); A/55/18 (2000) 67, para. 415 (Norway); A/57/18 (2002) 50, para. 276 (Armenia); A/57/18 (2002) 56, para. 335 (Canada); A/57/18 (2002) 63, para. 376 (Hungary).

[43] ICERD, preamble: 'one of the purposes of the United Nations which is to promote and encourage universal respect for and observance of human rights and fundamental freedoms for all, without distinction as to … religion'.

[44] ICERD, Art. 5(vii).   [45] ICERD, Art. 1(1).

intersectionality between racial and religious discrimination before it regards its mandate as engaged'.[46] The fact that the Committee on the Elimination of Racial Discrimination is nonetheless competent to deal with religion 'arises from the peculiarity that, although the Convention is structured to address racial discrimination, freedom of thought, conscience and religion figures ... among the protected rights in Article 5. Thus, the Convention requires conceptualization of racial discrimination in the enjoyment of religious freedom.'[47] Thornberry further shows that in its concluding observations on periodic reports submitted by State parties to the ICERD, the Committee has been quite outspoken on matters related to (protection of) religious groups, including extreme speech targeting religious minorities.[48]

Persons belonging to religious minorities have petitioned CERD, using the individual complaints procedure, to pronounce on their plight. Generally speaking, there are a number of reasons why they may pursue this legal avenue. First, discrimination is often of a 'multi-dimensional' nature. That is, distinctive treatment can occur, for example, on grounds of religion and ethnicity simultaneously. Second, an inciter might verbally base his or her hatred on one ground (e.g. religion, ethnicity) but really intend to target another. For instance, one might incite against 'Arabs' but in actual fact mean to spread hatred against 'Muslims', or vice versa. This type of often erroneous cross-identification may be on account of ignorance, but may also very well be a cunning way to circumvent the ramifications of domestic discrimination laws that prohibit incitement based on one ground but not on the other.[49] Third, as regards certain ethno-religious groups there may be an actual or at least perceived interface between race and religion.[50] Fourth, an argument of a procedural nature (thus referring back to our analysis in the previous chapter) is that the Human Rights Committee has thus far shown reluctance to

---

[46] Patrick Thornberry, 'Forms of Hate Speech and the Convention on the Elimination of all Forms of Racial Discrimination (ICERD)' (2010) 5 *Religion & Human Rights* 97–117, at 102.

[47] Thornberry, 'Forms of Hate Speech', at 102.

[48] E.g. A/58/18, para. 539 (United Kingdom); A/60/18, para. 142 (Ireland); A/60/18, para. 246 (Georgia); A/60/18, para. 295 (Nigeria); A/60/18, para. 323 (Turkmenistan); A/61/18, para. 418 (Ukraine). Thornberry, 'Forms of Hate Speech', at 102–3.

[49] Stephanie Berry, 'Bringing Muslim Minorities within the International Convention on the Elimination of All Forms of Racial Discrimination – Square Peg in a Round Hole?' (2011) 11:3 *Human Rights Law Review* 423–50, at 445–6.

[50] CERD, *P.S.N.* v. *Denmark*, Communication no. 36/2006 (admissibility decision of 8 August 2007), para. 6.3, referring to said 'interface'.

accept complaints under the heading of incitement. CERD has far more extensive experience in the area of extreme speech than does the Human Rights Committee. That is, CERD has conceptualized Article 4 of the ICERD much further than the Human Rights Committee has done in relation to Article 20(2) ICCPR.

That said, and contrary to the statements about the rights of religious minorities made during the state reporting procedure, the jurisprudence of the Committee on the Elimination of Racial Discrimination shows that it is hesitant to recognize 'religion' as part of its mandate – that is, hesitant to loosen the ICERD's required link to ethnicity.

6.3.2   Article 4 complaints concerning religious hatred

In *P.S.N. v. Denmark* a practising Muslim born in Pakistan but residing in Denmark complained about statements made by a Member of Parliament.[51] Specifically, the communication pertained to the reluctance on the part of the Danish authorities to prosecute Ms Louise Frevert, a member of the Danish People's Party, under Danish criminal law provisions on discriminatory and hate speech. The impugned statements were posted on a website, published in a book and made in a newspaper interview. The statements published on her website included the following: 'they think that we are the ones that should submit to Islam, and they are confirmed in this belief by their preachers and leaders ... [T]hey believe that they have a right to rape Danish girls and knock down Danish citizens.'[52] Another website message reads: 'We can spend billions of Kroner and hours in trying to integrate Muslims into the country, but the result will be what the doctor observes. The cancer spreads without hindrance while we are talking.'[53] The book in question accused Muslims of staging a secret holy war.[54] Furthermore, an excerpt of the impugned interview reads as follows: '(Reporter) In the chapter that you have now removed, you wrote that our laws forbid us to kill them. Is that what you would like the most? (Ms Frevert) No, but I am certainly allowed to write it. I am allowed to write exactly whatever suits me. If they rape and kill other people the way they do with suicide bombs, etc. – well, you aren't allowed to do so in our country, are you?'[55]

---

[51] *P.S.N. v. Denmark*, para. 2.1.   [52] *P.S.N. v. Denmark*, para. 2.1.
[53] *P.S.N. v. Denmark*, para. 2.2.   [54] *P.S.N. v. Denmark*, para. 2.3.
[55] *P.S.N. v. Denmark*, para. 2.4.

The Danish Documentary and Advisory Centre on Racial Discrimination filed on the petitioner's behalf criminal complaints, alleging violations of Danish criminal law. The complaints were dismissed by the police authorities as it was held that there was insufficient evidence in support of the view that unlawful acts had been committed.[56]

Before the Committee on the Elimination of Racial Discrimination the author of the communication complained that this omission to act amounted to a violation of Article 4 ICERD, among other provisions. Denmark challenged the admissibility of the case by pointing at the fact that the impugned speech acts concern 'persons of a particular religion and not persons of a particular "race, colour, descent, or national or ethnic origin" [i.e. see Article 1 ICERD]'.[57] The Committee agreed with Denmark. It held that:

> the impugned statements specifically refer to the Koran, to Islam and to Muslims in general, without any reference whatsoever to any race, colour, descent, or national or ethnic origin. While the elements of the case file do not allow the Committee to analyse and ascertain the intention of the impugned statements, it remains that no specific national or ethnic groups were directly targeted as such by these oral statements as reported and printed.[58]

The Committee substantiated this position by pointing out that Danish Muslims originate from many different countries, having diverse ethnic roots.[59] While acknowledging 'the importance of the interface between race and religion' and the problem of 'double discrimination', the Committee concluded that there could be no question of intersectionality in this case 'which exclusively relates to discrimination on religious grounds'.[60] As the ICERD's *travaux préparatoires* show that this convention was not meant to cover religion as a separate ground,[61] the Committee felt obliged to declare the complaint inadmissible.

This train of thought was confirmed in a similar case.[62] A.W.R.A.P., a Danish Muslim, had filed criminal complaints – again supported by the Danish Documentary and Advisory Centre on Racial Discrimination – about the way a member of the Danish People's Party had intervened in a debate on corporal punishment. This political party had previously been

---

[56] *P.S.N. v. Denmark*, paras. 2.5–2.10.
[57] *P.S.N. v. Denmark*, para. 4.1.   [58] *P.S.N. v. Denmark*, para. 6.2.
[59] *P.S.N. v. Denmark*, para. 6.2.   [60] *P.S.N. v. Denmark*, para. 6.3.
[61] *P.S.N. v. Denmark*, para. 6.3 (n. 10).
[62] CERD, *A.W.R.A.P. v. Denmark*, Communication no. 37/2006 (8 August 2007). Decided during the same CERD session as the previous case.

against abolishing corporal punishment, but now sided with the proponents of a ban. Søren Krarup explained his party's motives in the following terms:

> The problem is that the country unfortunately has been flooded with Muslim so-called culture, and according to Islam it is the right of the male to beat his children and wife yellow and blue. That form of violence which they are practising is of sadistic and brutal character. That is why we cannot reintroduce the act (on corporal punishment) and that is why it is important to make them sign it.[63]

A week later he added:

> What makes it so extremely difficult in relation to discussing the right to corporal punishment today is that we have been flooded by a culture to which violence – the holy right of the male to beat up his wife and children yellow and blue – is a natural thing. And that means that the Danish tradition for corporal punishment had become more or less compromised by a Muslim tradition which is much different.[64]

What followed next is largely a repetition of what occurred in *P.S.N. v. Denmark*. The Danish police and prosecution rejected the complaints of racial discrimination and incitement, causing Mr A.W.R.A.P. to seek satisfaction before CERD.[65] Denmark, however, argued that the subject matter fell outside the scope of the ICERD.[66] CERD agreed and declared the case inadmissible.[67]

Some older cases confirm that Article 4 complaints are not viable when applicants formulate their claim exclusively along the axis of religion.[68]

---

[63] *A.W.R.A.P.* v. *Denmark*, para. 2.3.

[64] *A.W.R.A.P.* v. *Denmark*, para. 2.4.

[65] *A.W.R.A.P.* v. *Denmark*, para. 2.7.

[66] *A.W.R.A.P.* v. *Denmark*, para. 4.1.

[67] *A.W.R.A.P.* v. *Denmark*, paras. 6.2–6.3.

[68] See, *mutatis mutandis*, *Kamal Quereshi* v. *Denmark*, Communication no. 27/2002 (19 August 2003), concerning hate speech against 'Mohammedans'. It should be noted that this case was in fact decided on the merits. The reason why the Committee could not find a violation of Art. 4 was because it could not be proven that a convicted inciter had provoked others to spread similar hateful messages (as was claimed by the applicant). See also the follow-up case of *Kamal Quereshi* v. *Denmark*, Communication No. 33/2003 (9 March 2005), finding no violation since the impugned speech acts verbally attacked 'foreigners', something that does not engage ICERD according to the Committee (para. 7.3). The impugned statements had in actual fact attacked both 'foreigners' as well as 'Mohammedans' (paras. 2.1–2.5, including the following excerpts: 'No to more Mohammedan rapes!'; 'Can the Mohammedans not show some respect for us Danish women'; 'Engage the military against the Mohammedan terror!'). The Committee chose to ignore the religious dimension to the case.

6.4   The right to be protected against racist hate propaganda

CERD's reluctance to grant standing to religious complainants notwithstanding, this Committee goes remarkably further than the Human Rights Committee in distilling individual protection from Article 4 of the ICERD. That is, on top of the state obligations that are clearly enshrined in this provision, this Committee also promotes protection against incitement to racial discrimination by employing this same article. In this section we explore exactly how far the Committee goes in that regard. Do alleged incitement victims have legal standing before this Committee?[69] If so, is this Committee prepared to pronounce an actual violation of Article 4 ICERD? And in the event that it does, what are the legal ramifications of such a breach of the ICERD's extreme speech provision?

6.4.1   Legal standing under Article 4 ICERD for racist hate speech victims

One of the legal questions in *Yilmaz-Dogan* v. *The Netherlands* was whether the ICERD requires a State party to actively prosecute all cases of alleged (incitement to) racial discrimination.[70] Such a duty is occasionally alluded to by the Committee in its concluding observations.[71] The backdrop of this case was that a Dutch employer had requested the termination of the contract of a Turkish national, the author of the communication to CERD. The termination request filed with a cantonal court included the following passage:

> When a Netherlands girl marries and has a baby, she stops working. Our foreign women workers, on the other hand, take the child to neighbours or family and at the slightest setback disappear on sick leave under the terms of the Sickness Act. They repeat that endlessly. Since we all must do our utmost to avoid going under, we cannot afford such goings-on.[72]

---

[69] I.e. other than those who formulate their claim exclusively on religious grounds. See section 6.3 above.

[70] CERD, *Yilmaz-Dogan* v. *The Netherlands*, Communication no. 1/1984 (10 August 1988).

[71] E.g. CERD, A/50/18 (1995) 36, para. 178 (Croatia): 'As a matter of urgency, the State party should comply with article 4 of the Convention and prohibit and *prosecute all incitement to ethnic hatred* in the media and elsewhere' (emphasis added). See also A/50/18 (1995) 48, para. 244 (Yugoslavia); and A/50/18 (1995) 53, para. 272 (Romania).

[72] *Yilmaz-Dogan* v. *The Netherlands*, para. 2.2.

Despite the bigoted language, the court agreed to the termination.

Mrs Yilmaz-Dogan's complaint pertains to both the court's endorsement of the termination request – amounting to an alleged endorsement of an act of racial discrimination and a breach of her equal right to work – as well as the fact that the Netherlands did not prosecute this employer, a duty that would flow from Article 4 ICERD.[73] In the latter respect, the applicant argued that it is not enough for a State party to have that provision transposed into domestic law – the Netherlands ought to have taken 'action to eliminate manifestations of racial discrimination', that is actively prosecute this type of racist message.[74]

The Netherlands challenged the admissibility of the Article 4-based complaint, arguing that the obligations arising from this article were met by incorporating extreme speech provisions into the Criminal Code. The responding state submitted, accordingly, that 'Article 4 cannot be read as obligating States parties to institute criminal proceedings under all circumstances with respect to actions which appear to be covered by the terms of the article'.[75]

CERD conceded that it cannot set aside or overrule the expediency principle (prosecutor's discretion to decide whether a case is worth prosecuting or not) as that doctrine is 'is governed by considerations of public policy' and since 'the Convention cannot be interpreted as challenging the raison d'être of that principle'.[76] Rather ambiguously it added that the principle should notwithstanding 'be applied in each case of alleged racial discrimination, in the light of the guarantees laid down in the Convention'.[77]

Accordingly, in this case the Committee did not find a violation of Article 4,[78] but for our present purposes what is more important is the fact that it actually investigated the complaint on the merits. From the very first case in which Article 4 was invoked by a petitioner, it transpires that the Committee on the Elimination of Racial Discrimination – unlike the Human Rights Committee – does not shy away from entertaining such cases. It is possible to conclude that Article 4 ICERD may provide standing to victims of hateful (racist) speech.

---

[73] *Yilmaz-Dogan* v. *The Netherlands*, para. 2.4, also listing additional claims.

[74] *Yilmaz-Dogan* v. *The Netherlands*, para. 2.4.

[75] *Yilmaz-Dogan* v. *The Netherlands*, para. 4.4.

[76] *Yilmaz-Dogan* v. *The Netherlands*, para. 9.4.

[77] *Yilmaz-Dogan* v. *The Netherlands*, para. 9.4.

[78] Note that a violation of her equal right to work was established and that the Netherlands did, consequently, breach the Convention (Art. 5).

6.4.2   The duty of effective investigation into
Article 4-related complaints

In another early Article 4 case brought against the Netherlands – *L.K. v. The Netherlands* – the Committee specified, if not revisited, its approach to the expediency principle.[79] Local xenophobia had given rise to this case. A Moroccan citizen residing in Utrecht went to visit a house for which a lease had been offered to him and his family.[80] Upon arrival he was met by local residents who had gathered outside the house, some of whom were shouting 'No more foreigners'. He was also threatened that should he take the lease, the house would be set on fire and his car would be damaged. Later that same day, twenty-eight of those residents signed a petition urging the Utrecht Housing Department to reallocate this man and his family. L.K. filed a complaint with the police claiming he had been the victim of racial discrimination in the meaning of the Dutch Criminal Code. This did not lead to a prosecution of the persons involved and various ensuing legal proceedings could not alter that.[81]

In his communication filed with CERD, L.K. complained that the Dutch prosecutorial and judicial authorities did not properly examine the relevant facts.[82] Further, the police were accused of not properly investigating the incidents described, while one of the prosecutors was blamed for being inactive.[83]

While the Netherlands invoked the expediency principle,[84] the Committee was not convinced this time that this principle excused the State party's passive attitude. Indeed, it held that the impugned speech acts 'constituted incitement to racial discrimination and to acts of violence against persons of another colour or ethnic origin' in the meaning of Article 4 of the ICERD.[85] Accordingly, Article 4 was engaged by the hateful incidents – the Committee essentially overruled the Dutch authorities' judgment on that point. And since the investigation by both the police and prosecutorial authorities into these incidents was 'incomplete', Article 4 was in fact breached.[86] Thus significantly

---

[79] CERD, *L.K. v. The Netherlands*, Communication no. 4/1991 (16 March 1993).
[80] *L.K. v. The Netherlands*, para. 2.1, describing these and following facts.
[81] *L.K. v. The Netherlands*, paras. 2.4–2.8.
[82] *L.K. v. The Netherlands*, para. 3.2.
[83] *L.K. v. The Netherlands*, para. 3.2.
[84] *L.K. v. The Netherlands*, paras. 4.5–4.6.
[85] *L.K. v. The Netherlands*, para. 6.3.
[86] *L.K. v. The Netherlands*, para. 6.3.

downplaying the status of the expediency principle, the Committee urged the Netherlands to review its prosecutorial policies. State parties to the ICERD are consequently under the obligation to 'investigate with due diligence and expedition' any incidents involving publicly made threats of racial violence.[87]

Accordingly, any time that domestic laws that are adopted to give effect to Article 4 ICERD are engaged, proper criminal investigations are called for. This line of reasoning was confirmed in *Mohammed Hassan Gelle* v. *Denmark*.[88] Mr Gelle, a Danish citizen of Somali origin, supported by the Danish Documentation and Advisory Centre on Racial Discrimination, filed a criminal complaint against Pia Kjærsgaard, leader of the Danish People's Party. This complaint pertained to a letter (a letter to the editor) the latter had published in a Danish newspaper. In the impugned letter, entitled 'A crime against humanity', this politician took a stance against consulting an Association of Danish Somalis on the issue of a bill on female genital mutilation. 'To me', she wrote, 'this corresponds to asking the association of paedophiles whether they have any objections to a prohibition against child sex or asking rapists whether they have any objections to an increase in the sentence for rape.'[89] According to Mr Gelle, this amounted to racist and discriminatory speech as prohibited by the Danish Criminal Code in an article giving effect to Article 4 ICERD.[90]

The Copenhagen police responded by letter that they had decided not to open an investigation since it was unlikely that a criminal offence had been committed.[91] The letter contained extensive reasoning in support of this decision, the most important argument being that Ms Kjærsgaard's criticism was aimed at the fact that the Minister wanted to consult Somalis on the matter at hand, not at Somalis per se. On appeal the Regional Public Prosecutor confirmed that the impugned statement was prima facie legal.[92]

---

[87] *L.K.* v. *The Netherlands*, para. 6.6. The same duty has been formulated in the Committee's concluding observations on state reports. E.g. CERD, A/52/18 (1997) 39, para. 283 (Bulgaria); A/53/18 (1998) 33, para. 102 (Netherlands); A/53/18 (1998) 59, paras. 314 (Croatia); A/56/18 (2001) 32, para. 153 (Iceland); A/57/18 (2002) 69, para. 425 (New Zealand).

[88] CERD, *Mohammed Hassan Gelle* v. *Denmark*, Communication No. 34/2004 (6 March 2006).

[89] *Gelle* v. *Denmark*, para. 2.1.

[90] Section 266(b) of the Danish Criminal Code 2009.

[91] *Gelle* v. *Denmark*, para. 2.3.   [92] *Gelle* v. *Denmark*, para. 2.4.

Before CERD, Mr Gelle alleged among other things a violation of Article 4 ICERD committed by Denmark for failing to carry out a proper investigation into the described incident.[93] CERD agreed with the petitioner. Contrary to the findings of the police and the prosecutorial authorities, the Committee found that 'Ms. Kjærsgaard's remarks can be understood to generalize negatively about an entire group of people based solely on their ethnic or national origin and without regard to their particular views, opinions or actions regarding the subject of female genital mutilation'.[94] Consequently, the ICERD – notably Article 4[95] – was engaged by the letter. In the light of that, only a complete and proper investigation of the incident would have sufficed.[96] The Committee concluded that among other provisions Article 4 ICERD was violated. Some four years later CERD pronounced an additional Article 4 violation over the same issue (in a radio interview a party member had endorsed the statements made by the leader of the Danish People's Party on Somalis).[97]

CERD has also developed this requirement of an effective investigation in cases wherein racist statements are not publicly disseminated but more privately expressed. The case of *Murat Er* v. *Denmark* revolved around employment discrimination.[98] Studying to become a carpenter at the Copenhagen Technical School, Murat Er would shortly be qualified to embark on a traineeship in a private company. On his teacher's list of companies offering these internships Mr Er had noticed the words 'not P' next to the name of one of the employers. Murat Er asked his teacher what this signified and the latter admitted that this literally meant 'no Pakis', while more generally boiling down to a request on the part of that particular employer not to receive trainees of non-Danish origin.[99] Er, who was of Turkish origin, filed complaints with the school inspector and the school board and later on, supported by the Danish Documentary and Advisory Centre on Racial Discrimination, also with the Complaints Committee on Ethnic Equal Treatment. While the latter Committee found a breach

---

[93] *Gelle* v. *Denmark*, para. 3.4.   [94] *Gelle* v. *Denmark*, para. 7.4.

[95] Earlier the Committee had already underscored that 'that it does not suffice, for purposes of article 4 of the Convention, merely to declare acts of racial discrimination punishable on paper. Rather, criminal laws and other legal provisions prohibiting racial discrimination must also be effectively implemented by the competent national tribunals and other State institutions.' *Gelle* v. *Denmark*, para. 7.3.

[96] *Gelle* v. *Denmark*, para. 7.4.

[97] CERD, *Saada Mohamad Adan* v. *Denmark*, Communication no. 43/2008 (13 August 2010).

[98] CERD, *Murat Er* v. *Denmark*, Communication no. 40/2007 (8 August 2007).

[99] *Murat Er* v. *Denmark*, para. 2.1.

of the Danish Equal Treatment Act,[100] this was later quashed in court proceedings wherein it was concluded that the applicant was in terms of his course load not yet eligible for the internship, that he hence could not be regarded as a victim, and further that it could not be proven whether the school had been willing to fulfil the discriminatory request made by the employer.[101] CERD, however, concluded that the mere fact that this practice existed at the school, apparently tolerated if not facilitated by one of the teachers, in itself amounted to racial discrimination of students other than ethnic Danes.[102] The fact that the applicant was not yet among the students who were at the material time eligible for the internships did not absolve Danish authorities from thoroughly investigating this incident.[103]

On the basis of this series of jurisprudence on investigative duties, one may then start wondering whether a full and proper investigation is always required, that is every time someone brings complaints of (incitement to) racial discrimination. In *Jama* v. *Denmark* CERD answered in the negative.[104] This case concerned yet further controversial statements made by Pia Merete Kjærsgaard, leader of the Danish People's Party.[105] She was assaulted in Copenhagen. Relating the particulars of the assault to the press, she referred to her attackers as suddenly having come out from their 'Somali clubs'.[106] Mr Jama, a Danish citizen of Somali origin himself, believed that no Somalis were involved in the incident. He believed that this was a false accusation by Kjærsgaard against the Somalis living in Denmark. Therefore, he filed a criminal complaint against her, alleging that she had committed an act of racist speech.[107] The police and subsequently different prosecutors dismissed the complaint, arguing that it was unlikely a crime had been committed. Before CERD the author of the communication claimed that the failure to start a proper investigation and to take other effective actions amounted to, among other provisions, a breach of Article 4.[108] Denmark denied that the statements made were of a racist nature. By claiming that her attackers had come out from 'Somali clubs' this politician had not verbally attacked 'persons of Somali

---

[100] *Murat Er* v. *Denmark*, para. 2.4.
[101] *Murat Er* v. *Denmark*, paras. 2.5–2.6.
[102] *Murat Er* v. *Denmark*, para. 7.3.
[103] *Murat Er* v. *Denmark*, para. 7.4.
[104] CERD, *Jama* v. *Denmark*, Communication no. 41/2008 (21 August 2009).
[105] See also *Gelle* v. *Denmark*.
[106] *Jama* v. *Denmark*, para. 2.1.
[107] *Jama* v. *Denmark*, para. 2.2.
[108] *Jama* v. *Denmark*, paras. 3.1–3.2.

origin.'[109] CERD, although finding the impugned speech act ambiguous, agreed with Denmark that Kjærsgaard's statement on its face did not engage Articles 2 and 4 of the ICERD.[110]

Accordingly, circumstances can be such that the police and prosecutorial authorities can legitimately decide that no full investigation is necessary. This is the case when relevant authorities could reasonably conclude,[111] without further investigation, that the speech act at hand did not come within the ambit of the ICERD.[112] However, whenever Article 4 ICERD is prima facie engaged, a complete investigation is required.[113]

6.4.3   Beyond 'effective investigation': a duty to convict hate speech offenders?

Accordingly, CERD grants standing to persons alleging non-compliance with the ICERD's anti-hate propaganda standards – the potential victims of hate speech. Further, decisions not to instigate proceedings against alleged hate speech offenders may under certain circumstances be construed as a breach of that same provision, that is when the investigation leading up to that police or prosecutorial decision did not meet the required standards – complete, proper, and expeditious.[114] But what if there were a full police investigation and an active prosecution, but a court decided the alleged hate speech offender must be acquitted? The

---

[109]   *Jama* v. *Denmark*, para. 4.8.   [110]   *Jama* v. *Denmark*, para. 7.4.

[111]   Note that in this respect, the Committee's decision in *Jama* v. *Denmark* is not fully convincing. The applicant had argued that the police's own records of the incident show that the attacker was a white male (para. 3.1), which, if true, makes Kjærsgaard's story a clear fabrication and reflects on her intentions. The fact remains that she did not, literally, accuse Somalis, but the apparent falsehoods arguably did provide a basis for further investigation into the nature of her statements.

[112]   See also CERD, *Zentralrat Deutscher Sinti und Roma et al.* v. *Germany*, Communication no. 38/2006 (22 February 2008), concerning complaints about hate speech against Sinti and Roma, allegedly disseminated by police officers by means of an article written for a specialized police journal, that were dismissed by the German authorities.

[113]   See also CERD, *TBB-Turkish Union in Berlin/Brandenburg* v. *Turkey*, Communication no. 48/2010 (26 February 2013), concerning alleged propaganda of racial superiority by a German former politician. CERD ruled that by not starting an investigation, Germany had breached Art. 4.

[114]   On the required expedient nature of criminal proceedings, see CERD, *Miroslav Lacko* v. *Slovak Republic*, Communication no. 11/1998 (21 October 1998). A restaurant manager – who, in his words, only served 'polite Roma' – was penalized only after three and a half years, due to the fact that regional prosecutorial authorities were reluctant to prosecute. These delays did not lead to a violation of ICERD.

question is whether CERD has the competence to second-guess the findings of domestic judges.

In *The Jewish Community of Oslo et al.* v. *Norway* this question was answered.[115] This case revolved around the acts of a group of neo-Nazis – the Norwegian 'Bootboys' – and especially the statements made by one of its leaders, Terje Sjolie. Thirty-eight members of the group, led by Sjolie, had held a march in the centre of Askim. At this event Sjolie addressed the Bootboys. Among other statements, he praised Rudolf Hess for attempting to free Europe from the Jews. Further, he accused immigrants of robbing, raping and killing Norwegians. He blamed Norwegian Jews for removing Norway's wealth and infecting Norwegians with their immoral thoughts. His speech concluded with the following fighting words: 'Our dear Führer Adolf Hitler and Rudolf Hess sat in prison for what they believed in, we shall not depart from their principles and heroic efforts, on the contrary we shall follow in their footsteps and fight for what we believe in, namely a Norway built on National Socialism.'[116]

Some witnesses to the scene filed complaints with the police. Sjolie was charged with extreme speech offences under the Norwegian Criminal Code.[117] In first instance he was acquitted by the City Court. Subsequently, he was convicted by the Court of Appeal. Yet in the final instance that conviction was overturned by the Norwegian Supreme Court, which definitively acquitted him. The latter court held 'the speech contained derogatory and offensive remarks, but ... no actual threats were made, nor any instructions to carry out any particular actions.'[118]

The authors of the communication to CERD were composed of a number of Jewish organizations, the Norwegian Anti-Racism Centre and a number of individuals, including Holocaust survivors. Among other claims, the petitioners alleged a violation of Article 4 ICERD. The Government of Norway challenged the admissibility of the communication because the applicants could not be regarded as victims.[119] CERD, however, agreed with the applicants' submission that the Norwegian Supreme Court's decision had exposed them 'to the effects of the dissemination of ideas of racial superiority and incitement to racial hatred,

---

[115] CERD, *The Jewish Community of Oslo et al.* v. *Norway*, Communication no. 30/2003 (15 August 2005).

[116] *Jewish Community of Oslo et al.* v. *Norway*, para. 2.1.

[117] Section 135a of the Criminal Code of Norway 1902.

[118] *Jewish Community of Oslo et al.* v. *Norway*, para. 2.7 (CERD's summary of the decision).

[119] *Jewish Community of Oslo et al.* v. *Norway*, paras. 4.1–4.5.

without being afforded adequate protection' and that the decision had 'contributed to an atmosphere in which acts of racism, including acts of violence, are more likely to occur'.[120]

On the merits Norway emphasized the 'due regard clause' embedded in Article 4 ICERD, that is the duties to prohibit certain types of extreme speech must be carried out with due regard of the right of freedom of expression.[121] The Norwegian Supreme Court, as was submitted by Norway, made a careful assessment of the rights and principles in question. The complainants argued that the precedent formed by the Supreme Court decision was already – at the time of the proceedings before CERD – casting a negative effect on Norwegian prosecutorial policies. Explicitly referencing the *Sjolie* case, the Oslo police had recently decided not to prosecute the leader of a neo-Nazi organization who among other things had stated that Jews were parasites, not human beings, and should be 'cleansed'.[122]

CERD disagreed with the Norwegian Supreme Court and with the Norwegian Government's subsequent defence of the former's reasoning. Making its own assessment of the impugned speech, the Committee concluded that it amounted to the dissemination of racial superiority and hatred. Moreover, the allusion of following in the 'footsteps' of Hitler amounted to 'incitement at least to racial discrimination, if not to violence'.[123] Accordingly, in the light of the particulars of the case, notably the extreme nature of the impugned speech act itself, the acquittal of Sjolie amounted to a violation of Article 4 ICERD.[124]

6.4.4   The freedom from racist incitement

Interestingly, in the case of *The Jewish Community of Oslo et al. v. Norway* CERD was outspoken on the question whether Article 4 ICERD contains 'rights' besides state obligations – more outspoken at any rate than in most of the other Article 4 cases. Paradoxically, the Human Rights Committee

---

[120] *Jewish Community of Oslo et al. v. Norway*, para. 7.3. Further, whereas the Optional Protocol to the ICCPR only permits communications from individuals, CERD may receive communications from individuals or groups of individuals (ICERD, Art. 14). Hence, CERD sees no problem in the fact that several organizations had joined the communication (para. 7.4).

[121] *Jewish Community of Oslo et al. v. Norway*, paras. 8.1–8.2.

[122] *Jewish Community of Oslo et al. v. Norway*, para. 9.4.

[123] *Jewish Community of Oslo et al. v. Norway*, para. 10.4.

[124] *Jewish Community of Oslo et al. v. Norway*, para. 10.5.

has gradually developed a right to be free from incitement while not accepting the legal standing ramifications that could come with such a right,[125] whereas CERD has accepted standing under Article 4 from the outset, but has been using 'rights' language rather sparsely in relation to Article 4. In *The Jewish Community of Oslo et al. v. Norway* CERD broke with that ambiguity and pronounced in no uncertain terms that Article 4 ICERD contains fundamental rights. Ironically, CERD's groundbreaking work in that regard was triggered by one of Norway's objections to the complaint brought by the applicant. Specifically, Norway had noted 'that the authors have not identified how the remarks of Mr Sjolie have had adverse effects on their enjoyment of any substantive rights protected by article 5 of the Convention'.[126] The Committee replied that this is not necessary, since its competence to consider communications:

> is not limited to complaints alleging a violation of one or more of the rights contained in article 5. Rather, article 14 states that the Committee may receive complaints relating to "any of the rights set forth in this Convention". The broad wording suggests that the relevant rights are to be found in more than just one provision of the Convention.[127]

The Committee moved on to elaborate on Article 4 specifically, noting that the fact that this provision 'is couched in terms of States parties' obligations, rather than inherent rights of individuals, does not imply that they are matters to be left to the internal jurisdiction of States parties, and as such immune from review under article 14. If such were the case, the protection regime established by the Convention would be weakened significantly.'[128] The Committee substantiated this position further by reference to Article 6 ICERD 'by which States parties pledge to assure to all individuals within their jurisdiction effective protection and a right of recourse against any acts of racial discrimination which violate their "human rights" under the Convention. In the Committee's opinion, this wording confirms that the Convention's 'rights' are not confined to article 5.'[129] All in all, the Committee was saying that Article 4 contains a right – the right to be protected against racist hate propaganda.[130]

---

[125] See Chapter 5.

[126] *Jewish Community of Oslo et al. v. Norway*, para. 8.7.

[127] *Jewish Community of Oslo et al. v. Norway*, para. 10.6.

[128] *Jewish Community of Oslo et al. v. Norway*, para. 10.6.

[129] *Jewish Community of Oslo et al. v. Norway*, para. 10.6.

[130] See, however, CERD's 2013 decision in *TBB-Turkish Union in Berlin/Brandenburg v. Turkey*, where it speaks (para. 12.7) largely in terms of state obligations (more specifically, 'State party's responsibility to protect the population against incitement to racial

6.5   The ECHR's lack of an incitement clause

The European Convention on Human Rights (ECHR), unlike the ICCPR and ICERD, and unlike other regional human rights instruments such as the American Convention on Human Rights,[131] lacks a provision specifically dealing with extreme speech. The ECHR provides for freedom of expression in Article 10. And 'since [this right] carries with it duties and responsibilities', freedom of expression may be subject to those restrictions that are prescribed by law and that are necessary 'in the interests of

---

hatred but also acts of racial discrimination by dissemination of ideas based upon racial superiority or hatred') rather than rights.

[131] See Art. 13 of the American Convention on Human Rights, OAS Treaty Series No. 36, 1144 UNTS 123, adopted 22 November 1969, entered into force 18 July 1978. Art. 13, para. (5) provides: 'Any propaganda for war and any advocacy of national, racial, or religious hatred that constitute incitements to lawless violence or to any other similar action against any person or group of persons on any grounds including those of race, color, religion, language, or national origin shall be considered as offenses punishable by law.' This sentence forms the final clause of the general freedom of expression Article (Art. 13) and thus does not form a separate provision as in the ICCPR. It is at the same time very clear that it draws heavily on Art. 20 of the ICCPR. In fact, it more or less merges the first and second paragraphs of Art. 20 ICCPR into one sentence. That said, the threshold of illegal incitement under the American Convention lies significantly higher: it forbids forms of hate propaganda that constitute 'incitements to *lawless violence or to any other similar action*' (emphasis added). It is clear that the drafters of the American Convention wanted to restrict the scope of the hate speech provision purely to instances where actual violence is incited (rather than more open-ended 'discrimination, hostility *or* violence'). For one case touching upon questions of Art. 13(5), see Inter-American Court of Human Rights, *Case of 'The Last Temptation of Christ' (Olmedo-Bustos et al.) v. Chile*, judgment of 5 February 2001. In this case the Inter-American Commission and subsequently the Court itself concluded that the film in question did not fall within the category of Art. 13(5) and that Chile had breached freedom of expression by censoring the film (see paras. 61 and 63–73 of the judgment). Whereas the American Convention contains an incitement provision and the European Convention does not, it is especially within the latter system that questions of extreme speech have repeatedly been put before the court (European Court of Human Rights). Accordingly, within the Inter-American system a judicial approach to hate speech questions is still to be developed. See, generally, Eduardo Bertoni and Julio Rivera Jr, 'The American Convention on Human Rights: Regulation of Hate Speech and Similar Expression', in Michael Herz and Peter Molnar (eds.), *The Content and Context of Hate Speech: Rethinking Regulation and Responses* (Cambridge University Press, 2012), 499–513. The African Charter on Human and Peoples' Rights, adopted 27 June 1981, OAU Doc. CAB/LEG/67/3 rev. 5, 21 ILM 58 (1982), entered into force 21 October 1986, does not contain an incitement provision. See also Henry Maina, *The Prohibition of Incitement to Hatred in Africa: Comparative Review and Proposal for a Threshold* (A study prepared for the regional expert meeting on Article 20, Organized by the Office of the High Commissioner for Human Rights, Nairobi, 6–7 April 2011), at 14. Hence, we will focus in this chapter chiefly on the European Convention system.

national security, territorial integrity or public safety, for the prevention of disorder or crime, for the protection of health or morals, for the protection of the reputation or the rights of others, for preventing the disclosure of information received in confidence, or for maintaining the authority and impartiality of the judiciary'.[132].

The European Convention does, however, formulate a general 'abuse of rights' clause in Article 17, stating that '[n]othing in this Convention may be interpreted as implying for any State, group or person any right to engage in any activity or perform any act aimed at the destruction of any of the rights and freedoms set forth herein or at their limitation to a greater extent than is provided for in the Convention'. This provision is clearly inspired by Article 30 of the Universal Declaration of Human Rights: the later adopted Article 5 ICCPR, discussed previously, contains a similar abuse of rights clause. Although the 'abuse of rights' doctrine holds significant relevance for freedom of expression, its ramifications are wider. For instance, the freedom of association may be affected by this clause too. In fact, the earliest instances in which State parties and the European Court of Human Rights successfully mobilized the clause concerned cases in which persons had sought to revitalize fascist or communist political parties.[133]

On the face of it, then, there is no *obligation* to introduce incitement laws for State parties to the ECHR.[134] This does not rule out, however, that incitement laws could be sanctioned by the European Court of Human Rights. Specifically, it does not rule out that this Court interprets the Convention as warranting incitement law restrictions inasmuch as those measures are necessary to promote one of the overriding goods recognized by the freedom of expression article itself, notably 'the protection of the reputation or the rights of others'.[135] We will see that the Court has construed the Convention so as to mean precisely that.[136]

However, before addressing the question of under which specific circumstances the European Court of Human Rights permits incitement restrictions (see Part IV of this book), let us first continue with the matter that preoccupied us in the previous pages. Although the ECHR lacks an

---

[132] Art. 10(2) of the [European] Convention for the Protection of Human Rights and Fundamental Freedoms, ETS No. 5 of 4 November 1950, entered into force 3 September 1953.

[133] E.g. European Commission of Human Rights, *Kummunistische Partei Deutschlands* v. *Germany*, Application No. 250/57, decision of 20 July 1957.

[134] Other Council of Europe instruments may and indeed do, as we will see, urge members to adopt hate speech laws, although the legal force of those instruments is significantly weaker than the Convention.

[135] ECHR, Art. 10(2).

[136] See section 9.6 of Chapter 9 and section 10.5 of Chapter 10.

express state duty to adopt anti-incitement legislation, can a *right* to be protected from incitement nonetheless be distilled from this Convention? And if so, do alleged incitement victims have standing before the European Court of Human Rights to complain about non-compliance with that right? Before we can answer this question, we must briefly reflect on this court's atypical extreme speech jurisprudence.

6.6   The European Court of Human Rights' atypical extreme speech jurisprudence

The said differences between the international and ECHR standards on incitement mean that the respective case law ensuing under those two regimes is fundamentally different. If a speech act engages Article 20(2) of the ICCPR, it is imperative that the Human Rights Committee takes stock of the State parties' duty to combat incitement when it rules on the permissibility of the restriction in question. In other words, if the impugned speech act amounted to incitement within the meaning of the Covenant, Article 20(2) ICCPR provides prima facie support to the legitimacy of the restriction imposed (the necessity of the restriction must still be assessed).[137] Consequently, for the Human Rights Committee, and also for CERD,[138] it is very pertinent indeed to make an assessment in relevant cases as to the precise nature of the impugned extreme speech act.

Conversely, the European Court of Human Rights has no extreme speech provision at its disposal. Among other things, this means that in extreme speech cases this Court is not likely to scrutinize in much detail the quality of the applied incitement law. That is, the Court will check whether the incitement restriction satisfied the regular tripartite test under Article 10 – whether the restriction was prescribed by law, whether it served a legitimate purpose (e.g. the reputation or the rights of others) and whether the restriction was necessary. But it will not assess whether the incitement restriction neatly mirrors the Convention for there is nothing to mirror it to. Accordingly, the Court has noted in relevant cases that:

> it is not for it to determine what evidence was required under [national] law to demonstrate the existence of the constituent elements of the offence of inciting to ... hatred. It is in the first place for the national authorities,

---

[137] That restriction must satisfy the regular limitation criteria posed by Art. 19(3) ICCPR. Human Rights Committee, *General Comment 34: Article 19: Freedoms of Opinion and Expression* (CCPR/C/GC/34, adopted at its 102nd session, Geneva, 11–29 July 2011), para. 48.

[138] The same applies, *mutatis mutandis*, for Art. 4 ICERD, containing mandatory restrictions on extreme speech.

notably the courts, to interpret and apply domestic law. The Court's task is merely to review under Article 10 the decisions they delivered pursuant to their power of appreciation.[139]

The Human Rights Committee and CERD would, on the contrary, be competent to make such quality assessments, and to check how the domestic incitement law is construed and how it functions in practice.

But there is more. The differences between the European Convention system and the international standards run deeper than that. Seeing as there is no equivalent to Article 20 ICCPR or Article 4 ICERD in the ECHR, that is no provision especially tailored to dealing with hateful incitement, there is nothing that prevents the European Court of Human Rights from claiming that certain types of extreme speech are simply not protected by the Convention at all under Article 17. Accordingly, the Court has developed two main approaches to extreme speech. One approach is to assess whether the restriction imposed on the impugned speech act satisfies the restrictions provided by the second paragraph of Article 10 of the ECHR. In the second approach the Court applies Article 17, the abuse of rights clause. If the speech act is of a nature as to negate the fundamental values of the Convention, the Court excludes the impugned speech act from the protection offered by the ECHR. One final difference between the Human Rights Committee and the European Court of Human Rights is that the latter monitoring body accepts low-threshold blasphemy or religious insult restrictions, whereas the former body has forbidden them.[140]

Let us now further chart these different approaches to dealing with extreme speech and ascertain how they differ from the workings of the Human Rights Committee.

---

[139] European Court of Human Rights, *Pavel Ivanov* v. *Russia*, Application no. 35222/04 (admissibility decision of 20 February 2007), section 'The Law', para. 1. See also e.g. *Lehideux and Isorni* v. *France*, Application no. 55/1997/839/1045 (23 September 1998), para. 50.

[140] Human Rights Committee, *General Comment 34*, para. 48 provides: 'Prohibitions of displays of lack of respect for a religion or other belief system, including blasphemy laws, are incompatible with the Covenant.' The Strasbourg Court has permitted such low-threshold religious insult provisions in many cases, including: European Commission of Human Rights, *X. Ltd. and Y.* v. *United Kingdom*, Application no. 8710/79 (7 May 1982); European Court of Human Rights, *Otto-Preminger-Institut* v. *Austria*, Application no. 13470/87 (20 September 1994); *Wingrove* v. *United Kingdom*, Application no. 17419/90 (25 November 1996); *Murphy* v. *Ireland*, Application no. 44179/98 (10 July 2003); *İ.A.* v. *Turkey*, Application no. 42571/98 (13 September 2005).

6.6.1   The guillotine approach

Let us start with the approach revolving around Article 17 of the ECHR. In this approach the abuse of rights doctrine has, as Cannie and Voorhoof put it, the effect of a guillotine.[141] Here the abuse clause prevents freedom of speech complaints brought by convicted hate speech offenders from being assessed on the merits by the European Court of Human Rights. The abuse clause, in other words, undermines the admissibility of such complaints.

Accordingly, the former European Commission of Human Rights declared white supremacists' complaints about free speech violations inadmissible in the early case of *Glimmerveen and Hagenbeek* v. *The Netherlands*.[142] Glimmerveen was the president of the Nederlandse Volks-Unie, a Dutch far-right political party. This party is premised on 'a world conception which grants each nation a proper state, as well as the belief that the general interest of a state is best served by an ethnical homogeneous population and not by racial mixing'.[143] Glimmerveen was convicted and sentenced to a two-week prison term for possessing, with a view to distributing, leaflets that announced that as soon as this political party seized power, it would start 'removing' foreigners from the Netherlands.[144] Subsequent court proceedings confirmed that this amounted to racist incitement as prohibited by the Dutch Criminal Code.

Before the European Commission of Human Rights, Glimmerveen argued that his freedom of expression had been violated by the Netherlands. A textual analysis of the leaflet led the Commission to conclude that Glimmerveen had incited to discrimination. According to the Commission, the possession and intended distribution of the leaflets constituted:

> an activity within the meaning of Article 17 of the Convention. The applicants are essentially seeking to use Article 10 to provide a basis under the Convention for a right to engage in these activities which are ... contrary to the text and spirit of the Convention and which right, if granted, would

---

[141] Hannes Cannie and Dirk Voorhoof, 'The Abuse Clause and Freedom of Expression in the European Human Rights Convention: An Added Value for Democracy and Human Rights Protection? (2011) 29:1 *Netherlands Quarterly of Human Rights* 54–83, at 58.

[142] European Commission of Human Rights, *Glimmerveen and Hagenbeek* v. *The Netherlands*, Application nos. 8348/78 and 8406/78 (admissibility decision of 11 October 1979).

[143] *Glimmerveen and Hagenbeek* v. *The Netherlands*, para. 2.

[144] *Glimmerveen and Hagenbeek* v. *The Netherlands*, para. 4.

contribute to the destruction of the rights and freedoms [of others]. Consequently, the Commission finds that the applicants cannot, by reason of the provisions of Article 17 of the Convention, rely on Article 10 of the Convention.[145]

As a result, the Commission declared the case inadmissible.

The Strasbourg Court has also been known to use the guillotine approach in cases revolving around Holocaust denial.[146] Following his convictions under the French Gayssot Act, Holocaust denier Roger Garaudy 'could not rely on the provisions of Article 10 of the Convention', according to the Strasbourg Court, since his publications – with such chapter titles as 'The Myth of the Holocaust' – 'had designs that fall into the category of aims prohibited by Article 17 of the Convention'.[147]

In *Pavel Ivanov* v. *Russia* the Court applied Article 17 to the complaint brought by an anti-Semitic owner and editor of a newspaper. The Court had 'no doubt as to the markedly anti-Semitic tenor of the applicant's views and it agrees with the assessment made by the domestic courts that he sought through his publications to incite hatred towards the Jewish people'.[148] Accordingly, the Strasbourg Court found that 'by reason of Article 17 of the Convention' the applicant could not 'benefit' from the right to freedom of expression.[149]

In *Norwood* v. *UK* Article 17 was again applied mercilessly. Norwood, a member of the far right British National Party, had displayed a poster in the window of his house with a photograph of the burning Twin Towers in New York and the words 'Islam out of Britain – Protect the British People'.[150] Further, the poster showed the Islamic symbols of the crescent and star placed in a prohibition sign. Having been convicted for an extreme speech offence under British law, his freedom of expression complaint was deemed inadmissible by the Strasbourg Court in the light of Article 17.

While the latter case shows that the Court has extended the guillotine approach outside the realm of anti-Semitism – it had been criticized

---

[145] *Glimmerveen and Hagenbeek* v. *The Netherlands*, para. 4.
[146] Below, in section 6.6.3, we will see that the Court occasionally takes a different approach to such cases. On Holocaust denial, see also Chapter 11.
[147] European Court of Human Rights, *Garaudy* v. *France*, Application no. 65831/01 (admissibility decision of 24 June 2003).
[148] European Court of Human Rights, *Pavel Ivanov* v. *Russia*, Application no. 35222/04 (admissibility decision of 20 February 2007).
[149] *Pavel Ivanov* v. *Russia*, 'The Law'.
[150] *Mark Anthony Norwood* v. *United Kingdom*, Application no. 23131/03 (admissibility decision of 16 November 2004).

over its one-sided application in earlier case law[151] – the Court has a lot to answer for when it comes to its unforgiving use of Article 17. In its Article 17 jurisprudence the European Court of Human Rights appears to be of the view that a speech act is either protected by the Convention or it is not. If a speech act is prima facie not protected by the Convention on account of Article 17, there is no need to address questions of the legitimacy and necessity for interference with free speech. This black-and-white view resembles the approach taken by the Human Rights Committee in its early case law. For instance, in *J.R.T. and the W.G. Party* v. *Canada* the Committee declared a case brought by a person convicted for spreading telephonic hate messages inadmissible.[152] The Committee reasoned that since the ICCPR obliged states to ban incitement, a claim brought by a convicted inciter does not merit assessment on the merits.[153] The Committee did, however, revisit that policy of automatically rendering cases brought by convicted inciters inadmissible.[154] Presently, the Committee holds that even those restrictions on speech that flow from Article 20(2) must satisfy the necessity test of Article 19(3) ICCPR.[155] This means that cases revolving around incitement law restrictions are always to be assessed on the merits.

The guillotine approach developed by the European Court of Human Rights, on the contrary, results in a situation wherein certain persons – persons with extreme views – cannot count on the protection the Convention guarantees to others. Their views are, when expressed, liable to be removed from the protection of Article 10 ECHR. This amounts to a type of 'content-discrimination' that specifically affects certain categories of persons: opinionated religious leaders, leaders of rightist political parties, deniers of historical atrocities. It is questionable whether such content-based criminal liability and sanctions are necessary or desirable.[156] The reasons that move the Court to apply Article 17 at the expense of a robust Article 10 assessment are quite obscure, leaving extreme speech cases quite unpredictable. In any event, freedom of speech complaints

---

[151] E.g. David Keane, 'Attacking Hate Speech under Article 17 of the European Convention on Human Rights' (2007) 25:4 *Netherlands Quarterly of Human Rights* 641–63.

[152] Human Rights Committee, *J.R.T. and the W.G. Party* v. *Canada*, Communication no. 104/1981 (6 April 1983).

[153] See also, *mutatis mutandis*, Human Rights Committee, *M.A.* v. *Italy*, Communication no. 117/1981 (21 September 1981).

[154] Human Rights Committee, *Robert Faurisson* v. *France*, Communication no. 550/1993 (19 July 1995).

[155] Human Rights Committee, *General Comment 34*, para. 48.

[156] On Holocaust denial, see Chapter 11.

ought not to be thrown out on the basis of such an opaque test – supposing an Article 17 application is indeed based on some sort of test.

For similar reasons, the guillotine approach has come under attack in the literature.[157] It is considered as unfathomable why the content of certain extreme speech should lead to certain speech acts being *ipso facto* removed from the protection of the Convention. There is no need to single out certain extremists in this way, since a substantive assessment of the free speech complaint could still lead to a conclusion that upholds the concrete restriction imposed by the State party. Only the latter approach can do justice both to robust freedom of expression and to the fact that this freedom 'carries with it duties and responsibilities' and may be subject to certain limitations.[158] Furthermore, since domestic courts take notice of the Strasbourg Court's Article 17 jurisprudence and may very well copy the guillotine approach,[159] there is a real risk that no judicial body, either at the national or at the international level, looks into the merits of free speech complaints brought by alleged extremists.

6.6.2   Indirect abuse of rights application

The Strasbourg Court's alternative for a clean-cut Article 17 application – inevitably leading to the inadmissibility of the individual complaint – is a judgment on the merits of the freedom of expression complaint brought. While a number of such substantive decisions are discernible in the Court's jurisprudence, it must be noted that there are misleading examples amongst those. This is the category of judgments wherein the supposedly substantive assessment of the merits of the Article 10 complaint is in actual fact significantly driven by Article 17.[160] Thus, whereas such decisions do not declare the case inadmissible from the outset, an Article 17-driven analysis of the claim is almost bound to lead to the complaint being declared manifestly ill-founded or otherwise unconvincing.

This indirect abuse of rights approach can be discerned in many Holocaust denial cases.[161] The case of *Udo Walendy* v. *Germany* serves

---

[157] Cannie and Voorhoof, 'The Abuse Clause'. The inconsistency of the European Court's approach was first pointed out by Keane, 'Attacking Hate Speech under Article 17'.

[158] ECHR, Art. 10(2).

[159] See e.g. the role of Art. 17 ECHR in the domestic proceedings that led up to *Garaudy* v. *France*, as described in the latter case in the section on the circumstances of the case.

[160] See Cannie and Voorhoof, 'The Abuse Clause', at 60, referring to this variant as the 'indirect application of Article 17'.

[161] Note that some of the early negationism cases were assessed in the light of Art. 10 and its regular restrictions, ignoring Art. 17 on abuse of rights. See e.g. European Commission

as a good illustration.[162] In ascertaining whether or not Germany was permitted under the Convention to start criminal proceedings, including a search and seizure order, against a Holocaust denier, the European Commission of Human Rights reasoned that because the negationist acts had engaged Article 17, the necessity of the interferences was a given.[163] In other words, the tripartite limitation test is seemingly followed and applied. Yet the necessity test is considered to be met merely by invoking Article 17. The effect is almost the same as declaring the case inadmissible on grounds of abuse of rights.[164] A similar indirect abuse of rights approach was taken in a number of other cases concerning negationism.[165]

6.6.3   Judgments on the merits of Article 10 complaints

The above criticism on the guillotine approach notwithstanding, be it in direct or indirect guise, the European Court of Human Rights does occasionally look into the merits of free speech complaints brought by convicted hate speech offenders.[166] Accordingly, in *Féret v. Belgium* the

---

of Human Rights, *T. v. Belgium*, Application no. 9777/82 (admissibility decision of 14 July 1983); and *X. v. Germany*, Application no. 9235/81 (admissibility decision of 16 July 1982).

[162] European Commission of Human Rights, *Udo Walendy* v. *Germany*, Application no. 21128/92 (11 January 1995).

[163] *Udo Walendy* v. *Germany*, 'The Law'.

[164] Cannie and Voorhoof, 'The Abuse Clause', at 58 and 67–8.

[165] E.g. European Commission of Human Rights, *D.I.* v. *Germany*, Application no. 26551/95 (admissibility decision of 26 June 1996); *F.P.* v. *Germany*, Application no. 19459 (admissibility decision of 29 March 1993); *Marais* v. *France*, Application no. 31159/96 (admissibility decision of 24 June 1996); *Friedrich Rebhandl* v. *Austria*, Application no. 24398/94 (admissibility decision of 16 January 1996); *Otto E.F.A. Remer* v. *Germany*, Application no. 25096/94 (admissibility decision of 6 September 1995); *Walter Ochensberger* v. *Austria*, Application no. 21318/93 (admissibility decision of 2 September 1994); *B.H., M.W., H.P. and G.K.* v. *Austria*, Application no. 12774/87 (admissibility decision of 12 October 1989). European Court of Human Rights, *Hans-Jürgen Witzsch* v. *Germany* [I], Application no. 41448/98 (admissibility decision of 20 April 1999); *Herwig Nachtmann* v. *Austria*, Application no. 36773/97 (admissibility decision of 9 September 1998). See also, *mutatis mutandis*, European Court of Human Rights, *Hans-Jürgen Witzsch* v. *Germany* [II], Application no. 7485/03 (admissibility decision of 13 December 2005); *Hans Jorg Schimanek* v. *Austria*, Application no. 32307/96 (admissibility decision of 1 February 2000); *Karl-August Hennicke* v. *Germany*, Application no. 34889/97 (admissibility decision of 21 May 1997); *Michael Kühnen* v. *Germany*, Application no. 12194/86 (admissibility decision of 12 May 1988).

[166] Details as to the precise reasoning adopted in those decisions that either uphold or reject extreme speech restrictions are discussed later. See section 9.6 of Chapter 9 and section 10.5 of Chapter 10.

Strasbourg Court applied Article 10(2) to the facts of the case. Belgian authorities had prosecuted and convicted Féret, a member of the Belgian House of Representatives, for his role in disseminating posters, leaflets and internet materials that verbally attacked immigrants and opposed the 'Islamization of Belgium'.[167] The Belgian Government expressly invoked Article 17 and, citing the *Glimmerveen* case, urged the European Court of Human Rights to declare the case inadmissible.[168] However, the Court, without explaining how this case differed from *Glimmerveen*, declared the complaint admissible and assessed the claim in the light of Article 10 and the limitations provided by the second paragraph of that provision.[169]

Similarly, Jean-Marie Le Pen, then president of the French National Front Party, was fined EUR 10,000 by a French court for 'incitement to discrimination, hatred and violence towards a group of people because of their origin or their membership or non-membership of a specific ethnic group, nation, race or religion' in 2005. This was a result of statements he made about Muslims in *Le Monde*. In *Le Pen* v. *France* the Strasbourg Court reflected exclusively on Article 10 and omitted assessments as to a possible 'abuse of rights' under Article 17.[170]

In *Seurot* v. *France*, concerning a schoolteacher who had used the school bulletin to agitate against immigration by North Africans, France invoked Article 17.[171] Yet the Strasbourg Court looked into the merits of the teacher's freedom of expression complaint,[172] as it did in the similar case of *Soulas and others* v. *France*.[173] The latter case revolved around a book in which the author argued against the immigration of Muslims into France. The French Government once again invoked Article 17, citing such cases as *Glimmerveen* and *Walendy*. Although the author was calling for no less than an 'ethnic civil war' against Muslims, the Strasbourg Court found that offending passages of the book were not of a nature so as to justify the application of Article 17 and moved on to address the complaint on its merits.[174]

---

[167] European Court of Human Rights, *Féret* v. *Belgium*, Application no. 15615/07 (16 July 2009).

[168] *Féret* v. *Belgium*, paras. 49–50.

[169] *Féret* v. *Belgium*, paras. 53 and 82.

[170] European Court of Human Rights, *Le Pen* v. *France*, Application no. 18788/09 (7 May 2010).

[171] European Court of Human Rights, *Jacques Seurot* v. *France*, Application No. 57383/00 (admissibility decision of 18 May 2004).

[172] Note that despite the Court's extensive considerations on the merits of the Art. 10 complaint, this is strictly speaking an admissibility decision.

[173] European Court of Human Rights, *Soulas and others* v. *France*, Application no. 15948/03 (10 July 2008).

[174] *Soulas and others* v. *France*, para. 48.

The alleged hate speech of Mr Gündüz, leader of the Islamic order of Aczmendi, was exclusively scrutinized by the Strasbourg Court in the light of Article 10 and the limitations formulated by the second paragraph of that provision.[175] The same goes for *Balsytė-Lideikienė* v. *Lithuania*, concerning the publication of a nationalistic calendar that Lithuanian authorities deemed hateful towards Poles, Russians and Jews.[176]

T. v. *Belgium* and *X* v. *Germany* are among the negationism cases in which the former European Commission of Human Rights does not engage, either directly or indirectly, with the abuse of rights doctrine contained in Article 17.[177] Further examples of cases in which the Strasbourg Court ventures into the merits of the Article 10 complaint brought by convicted extreme speech offenders include: *Giniewski* v. *France*, concerning a publication in which it was argued that the Catholic doctrine contained the seed for anti-Semitism and the horrors of Auschwitz;[178] *Nur Radyo Ve Televizyon Yayinciligi A.S.* v. *Turkey*, concerning a religious leader who had argued that a recent earthquake killing thousands had been a divine warning to non-believers;[179] *Güzel* v. *Turkey (No. 2)*, concerning alleged religious hate speech;[180] and *Yarar* v. *Turkey*, concerning speech against atheists.[181]

---

[175] European Court of Human Rights, *Gündüz* v. *Turkey*, Application no. 35071/97 (4 December 2003).

[176] European Court of Human Rights, *Balsytė-Lideikienė* v. *Lithuania*, Application no. 72596/01 (4 November 2008).

[177] European Commission of Human Rights, *T.* v. *Belgium*, Application no. 9777/82 (admissibility decision of 14 July 1983); *X.* v. *Germany*, Application no. 9235/81 (admissibility decision of 16 July 1982).

[178] European Court of Human Rights, *Giniewski* v. *France*, Application no. 64016/00 (31 January 2006).

[179] European Court of Human Rights, *Nur Radyo Ve Televizyon Yayinciligi A.S.* v. *Turkey*, Application no. 6587/03 (27 November 2007).

[180] European Court of Human Rights, *Güzel* v. *Turkey (No. 2)*, Application no. 65849/01 (27 July 2006). See further e.g. *Özgür Radyo-Ses Radyo Televizyon Yayın Yapım Ve Tanıtım A.Ş.* v. *Turkey (No. 2)*, Application no. 11369/03 (4 December 2007), concerning alleged incitement; *Lehideux and Isorni* v. *France*, Application no. 55/1997/839/1045 (Grand Chamber judgment of 23 September 1998), concerning alleged glorification of crimes against humanity; *Leroy* v. *France*, Application no. 36109/03 (2 October 2008), concerning alleged glorification of terrorism; *Asan* v. *Turkey*, Application no. 28582/02 (27 November 2007), concerning alleged extreme speech; *Willem* v. *France*, Application no. 10883/05 (16 July 2009), concerning alleged anti-Israeli incitement. See also, *mutatis mutandis*, *Jersild* v. *Denmark*, Application no. 15890/89 (Grand Chamber judgment of 23 September 1994).

[181] European Court of Human Rights, *Yarar* v. *Turkey*, Application no. 57258/00 (19 December 2006).

6.7   An emerging freedom from incitement?

The European Convention on Human Rights does not contain an incitement prohibition, let alone a *right* to be safeguarded against such speech. Furthermore, the above overview of approaches to extreme speech shows that almost all such cases have been brought to the Court by convicted extreme speech offenders. Thus politicians or other persons who have suffered the consequences of domestic extreme speech legislation have sought to invoke the European Convention on Human Rights to promote their freedom of expression. Whenever those claims are not dismissed by way of an Article 17 application, the Strasbourg Court is asked to assess the value of the free speech complaint in the light of colliding public interests, notably the 'reputation or rights of others'.[182] In that context, the Court has, unlike the Human Right Committee in similar cases,[183] not dwelt on the nature of those rights 'of others'. That is to say, the European Court of Human Rights has not generously distilled from the Convention a 'right to be protected from incitement'. In a recent case concerning neo-Nazi bullying of Roma and Jews the Court perhaps made a first step towards such a notion when it introduced a 'right to live without intimidation of the members of the target groups'.[184]

Since the ECHR does not contain an incitement provision, *victims* of extreme speech offences have not yet brought very many complaints to Strasbourg. And those who did thus far typically brought complaints that were straightforwardly and quite rightly dismissed by the European Court of Human Rights.[185] That said, the doctrine of 'positive obligations', applicable to many Convention rights, may change this. Specifically, the right to respect for one's private life could very well offer a point of departure for future successful claims against State parties.

The case of *Aksu* v. *Turkey* shows that alleged hate speech victims may very well attempt to persuade the Strasbourg Court to determine a

---

[182] ECHR, Art. 10(2).

[183] In *Robert Faurisson* v. *France* and *Malcolm Ross* v. *Canada*, Communication no. 736/1997 (18 October 2000), the Committee developed a right to be free from religious incitement.

[184] European Court of Human Rights, *Vona* v. *Hungary*, Application no. 35943/10 (9 July 2013), para. 66.

[185] E.g. European Commission of Human Rights, *Church of Scientology and 128 of its Members* v. *Sweden*, Application no. 8282/78 (admissibility decision of 14 July 1980), concerning an alleged act of 'agitation' against Scientology, which was rejected by the Commission. A complaint about the UK's unwillingness to prosecute Salman Rushdie over his *Satanic Verses* was rightly dismissed, too. See European Commission of Human Rights, *Abdal Choudhury* v. *United Kingdom*, Application no. 17439/90 (5 March 1991).

violation of Article 8 on private life.[186] Although in *Aksu* the European Court ultimately did not find a violation of this right, it did look into the complaint concerning a study about Roma and two dictionaries that contained passages negatively stereotyping Roma people.

Further on legal standing, the case of *Milanović* v. *Serbia* may provide further ammunition to extreme speech victims.[187] This case was brought by a member of Hare Krishna against Serbia. The applicant complained that the state authorities had not done enough to protect him from violent hate crimes. While no public incitement took place (making this case less relevant than *Aksu*), Mr Milanović received threatening telephone calls. A short time later he was repeatedly attacked in the street, beaten up and stabbed with knives. These threats and attacks were, according to the applicant, presumably carried out by members of far right organizations. Responding to the applicant's complaints about the inaction on the part of the police authorities after they had been informed of the threats against his person, the European Court pronounced violations of both Article 3 (degrading treatment) and Article 14 (equality). In relation to the former breach the Court argued that, in the light of the facts, the authorities could have anticipated these assaults yet did nothing to prevent them. In relation to the breach of the non-discrimination principle, the Court held that states should be extra vigilant when religious motives may have played a role in violent crimes, comparable to the treatment for racially motivated attacks.[188] The Court postulated that '[t]reating religiously motivated violence and brutality on an equal footing with cases that have no such overtones would be turning a blind eye to the specific nature of acts that are particularly destructive of fundamental rights'.[189] As the police authorities appeared more preoccupied with the applicant's

---

[186] *Aksu* v. *Turkey*, Application nos. 4149/04 and 41029/04 (Grand Chamber judgment of 15 March 2012). On the role of civil society organizations in exploring such novel Convention angles to cases of alleged incitement, see Dimitrina Petrova, 'Incitement to National, Racial or Religious Hatred: Role of Civil Society and National Human Rights Institutions' (expert paper presented at the UN OHCHR Expert workshop on the prohibition of incitement to national, racial or religious hatred, Vienna, 9–10 February 2011), paras. 19–22.

[187] *Milanović* v. *Serbia*, Application no. 44614/07 (14 December 2010). See also, *mutatis mutandis*, *Secic* v. *Croatia*, Application no. 40116/02 (31 May 2007), concerning hate crimes against Roma; and *Angelova and Iliev* v. *Bulgaria*, Application no. 55523/00 (26 July 2007), concerning hate crimes against Roma.

[188] *Milanović* v. *Serbia*, para. 96.

[189] *Milanović* v. *Serbia*, para. 97.

'strange appearance' than with finding the assailants, the Court found this additional violation of the Convention.[190]

Applicants have not yet successfully invoked Article 17.[191] Accordingly, the Strasbourg Court has not been in a position to elaborate on the question of whether a right to be free from incitement can perhaps be distilled from that provision. Although basing a complaint on Article 17 may not look very promising, it should be observed that there is a subtle difference between this provision and Article 5(1) of the ICCPR. Whereas the latter abuse of rights clause was inserted into Part II of that Covenant dealing with miscellaneous state obligations, the ECHR's abuse clause forms part of the section (Section I) listing substantive Convention rights.[192]

In sum, following *Aksu*, incitement victims' best strategy under the European Convention on Human Rights is to complain about interferences with the right to respect for their private life.

6.8   Concluding remarks

Contrary to the Human Rights Committee's practice under Article 20(2) ICCPR, hate speech victims have standing before CERD to complain about infringements of Article 4 ICERD. Each hateful incident that engages Article 4 must lead to a proper investigation. While an actual prosecution is not always required, CERD has drawn some limits to the expediency principle. Moreover, CERD does not shy away from overruling a national court's appreciation of complaints about racist incitement; the facts of a case can be such that CERD expects no less than a criminal conviction. Thus acquitting a racist incitement offender may amount to a breach of the Convention.

While it is therefore clear that at present CERD's protection of the right to be free from incitement is more robust than the protection offered by the Human Rights Committee, it must be observed that under the ICERD religious minorities more often than not come away empty-handed. If their complaints cannot be linked to racial discrimination, CERD is bound to declare their cases inadmissible. While CERD has paid lip-service to the

---

[190] *Milanović* v. *Serbia*, paras. 99–100.

[191] A complaint invoking Art. 17 against Denmark for tolerating the 'Danish cartoons' was rightly declared inadmissible. European Court of Human Rights, *Mohammed Ben El Mahi and others* v. *Denmark*, Application no. 5853/06 (admissibility decision of 11 December 2006).

[192] That said, Art. 35(3)(a) of the ECHR refers back to the abuse clause, making it quite clear that Art. 17's primary function is to serve as a bar to admissibility.

problem of 'double discrimination',[193] in practice it is often reluctant to accept the full ramifications of the phenomenon of intersectionality.[194] In a recent General Recommendation the Committee on the Elimination of Racial Discrimination announced that it will pay closer attention to intersectionality.[195] Further, in its recent Recommendation on racist hate speech the Committee underscored that:

> [i]n the light of the principle of intersectionality ... the Committee's attention has also been engaged by hate speech targeting persons belonging to certain ethnic groups who profess or practice a religion different from the majority, including expressions of Islamophobia, anti-Semitism and other similar manifestations of hatred against ethno-religious groups, as well as extreme manifestations of hatred such as incitement to genocide and to terrorism.[196]

The Ad Hoc Committee on the Elaboration of Complementary Standards, established by the Human Rights Council, considers the question about intersectionality so pertinent that it has requested CERD to draft a General Recommendation wholly dedicated to the issue.[197]

As long as CERD persists in its 'conservative' approach to cases that do not squarely fall into the category of racial discrimination,[198] Article 20(2)

---

[193] E.g. *P.S.N.* v. *Denmark*, para. 6.3.

[194] Berry, 'Bringing Muslim Minorities within ICERD'.

[195] CERD, *General Recommendation 32: The Meaning and Scope of Special Measures in the International Convention on the Elimination of All Forms Racial Discrimination* (CERD/C/GC/32, Seventy-fifth session, 3–28 August 2009), para. 7. On intersectionality in hate speech discourse, see Nazila Ghanea, 'Intersectionality and the Spectrum of Racist Hate Speech: Proposals to the UN Committee on the Elimination of Racial Discrimination' (2013) 32:4 *Human Rights Quarterly* 935–54; and Nazila Ghanea, 'The Concept of Racist Hate Speech and its Evolution Over Time' (paper presented at the United Nations Committee on the Elimination of Racial Discrimination, 81st session, 28 August 2012, Geneva), at 6–7. The United Nations Division for the Advancement of Women (DAW) provides the following definition: 'The idea of "intersectionality" seeks to capture both the structural and dynamic consequences of the interaction between two or more forms of discrimination or systems of subordination.' DAW, *Gender and Racial Discrimination: Report of the Expert Group Meeting* (2000). See also Kimberlé Crenshaw, 'Mapping the Margins: Intersectionality, Identity Politics, and Violence against Women of Color' (1991) 46:6 *Stanford Law Review* 1241–99.

[196] CERD, *General Recommendation 35*, para. 6.

[197] Human Rights Council, *Complementary International Standards, Compilation of Conclusions and Recommendations of the Study by the Five Experts on the Content and Scope of Substantive Gaps in the Existing International Instruments to Combat Racism Racial Discrimination, Xenophobia and Related Intolerance* (A/HRC/AC.1/1/CRP.4, 18 February 2008), para. 49.

[198] Berry, 'Bringing Muslim Minorities within ICERD', at 440.

ICCPR may well develop into the most important legal yardstick for the plight of victims of incitement to violence or discrimination. Yet for that to happen, the Human Rights Committee must copy CERD's approach to legal standing for victims of alleged incitement. In future cases we will see if the Human Rights Committee is prepared to go down that road.

The European Convention on Human Rights altogether lacks an incitement provision. In practice this means that it is hard to predict the European Court of Human Rights' case law on extreme speech. Occasionally, the Strasbourg Court employs Article 17 to throw out cases brought by convicted inciters. At other times, the Court considers those complaints on the merits. The abuse of rights approach must be criticized for needlessly stripping persons with extreme views of the Convention rights.

Since most of the extreme speech cases judged by the European Court of Human Rights have been brought by convicted inciters, this Court has no elaborate jurisprudential position on whether incitement victims have standing under the Convention to complain about non-protection by State parties. Following the *Aksu* case, incitement victims probably do best to complain about a breach of the right to respect for one's private life.

PART III

Legislative obligations: defining the scope of the offence of 'advocacy of religious hatred that constitutes incitement'

The *actus reus* of 'advocacy of religious hatred constituting incitement': threshold, definitions and concepts

7.1 Introduction

In the previous part two preliminary legal questions have been addressed. We have established that Article 20(2) of the ICCPR is mandatory: all State parties – save those that have entered reservations to this provision – are obliged to adopt laws prohibiting the advocacy of religious (and other) hatred that constitutes incitement to discrimination, hostility or violence. Second, although Article 20(2) ICCPR is clearly formulated as an obligation for State parties to adopt laws containing incitement prohibition, the Human Rights Committee in its jurisprudence has distilled a right to be free from/protected against incitement from this same article. Acknowledgement of that 'right' has, however, not yet moved the Committee to grant legal standing to alleged incitement victims. In this latter respect, the Human Rights Committee has shown itself to be more reserved than the Committee on the Elimination of Racial Discrimination.

It is now time to leave the rights discussion for the time being, and return to the mandatory 'prohibition' that is embodied by Article 20(2) ICCPR. Specifically, what acts set off the prohibition of incitement? In this chapter we seek to define the *actus reus* of the incitement offence that State parties to the ICCPR ought to enshrine in their domestic legislation.

State parties to the ICCPR have pledged to prohibit by law any 'advocacy' of 'national', 'racial' or 'religious' 'hatred' that constitutes 'incitement' to 'discrimination', 'hostility' or 'violence'.[1] In order to understand the *actus reus* of the incitement offence definitions of the constituent terms of Article 20(2) will be sought. In addition, once we have increased understanding of what these terms mean – and what they do not mean – it will be possible to create a checklist of criteria that must be met by domestic

---

[1] We have already seen that the words 'prohibit by law' point at a mandatory legislative assignment. See Chapter 4.

laws intended to implement this article. Comparative legal analysis will provide us with insights into good and bad legislative practice.

Thus this chapter focuses on the law of incitement. Formulating definitions and building a triangular model (see section 7.3 of this chapter) for the offence of incitement within the meaning of the ICCPR will serve to foster our subsequent discussion on how to *prove* incitement in a concrete case (see Part IV of this book). The key contention of this chapter is that State parties to the ICCPR are under no obligation to ban 'hate speech'. A textual analysis of Article 20(2) ICCPR supports the view that the threshold of the provision is very high indeed. This provision requires that legal prohibitions are in place to deal with *qualified* types of extreme speech; that is, only extreme speech that incites adverse responses – 'discrimination', 'hostility' or 'violence' – by others against a target group is to be banned.

7.2   Alternative definitions and concepts

Before specifically conceptualizing the key terms of Article 20's offence, let us chart some of the definitions previously offered by different stakeholders.

In its recent General Recommendation on racist hate speech CERD defines 'incitement' as follows: 'Incitement characteristically seeks to influence others to engage in certain forms of conduct, including the commission of crime, through advocacy or threats. Incitement may be express or implied, through actions such as displays of racist symbols or distribution of materials as well as words.'[2] It went on to observe that:

> [t]he notion of incitement as an inchoate crime does not require that the incitement has been acted upon, but in regulating the forms of incitement referred to in article 4, States parties should take into account, as important elements in the incitement offences … the *intention of the speaker*, and the *imminent risk or likelihood* that the conduct desired or intended by the speaker will result from the speech in question, considerations which also apply to the other offences listed in paragraph 13.[3]

The criteria of 'intent' and 'likelihood' will be discussed in a separate part of the book (Part IV). In relation to the form of speech that qualifies under Article 4 of the ICERD, the Committee basically keeps all options

---

[2] CERD, *General Recommendation 35: Combating Racist Hate Speech* (UN Doc. CERD/C/GC/35, 83rd session, 12–30 August 2013), para. 16.
[3] CERD, *General Recommendation 35*, para. 16 (emphasis added).

open, including speech directly attacking particular racial or ethnic groups as well as 'indirect language', speech by groups as well as individuals, whether disseminated orally or in print, and regardless of the medium used (e.g. electronic media, the Internet, social networking sites, non-verbal messages such as symbols and images).[4]

The UN Special Rapporteur on freedom of opinion and expression, the OSCE Representative on Freedom of the Media and the OAS Special Rapporteur on freedom of expression have elaborated on extreme speech in a joint statement.[5] By emphasizing what is *not* punishable speech under international law, these three independent experts say something about the legal threshold of incitement. They contend that 'no one should be penalized for statements which are true';[6] 'no one should be penalized for the dissemination of "hate speech" unless it has been shown that they did so with the intention of inciting discrimination, hostility or violence';[7] 'the right of journalists to decide how best to communicate information and ideas to the public should be respected, particularly when they are reporting on racism and intolerance';[8] 'no one should be subject to prior censorship';[9] 'any imposition of sanctions by courts should be in strict conformity with the principle of proportionality.'[10] Their second point affirms that while 'hate speech' per se is not prohibited by international law, extreme speech that amounts to incitement is.

The Council of Europe has at various times and by way of various bodies attempted to define not 'incitement' but 'hate speech'.[11] First of all, in some of its case law the European Court of Human Rights came close to defining this phenomenon. For instance, in the case of *Gündüz* v. *Turkey* the Strasbourg Court argued that 'all forms of expression which spread,

---

[4] CERD, *General Recommendation 35*, para. 7.

[5] *Joint Statement on Racism and the Media by the UN Special Rapporteur on Freedom of Opinion and Expression, the OSCE Representative on Freedom of the Media and the OAS Special Rapporteur on Freedom of Expression* (London, 27 February 2001).

[6] See section 3.2.2.3 of Chapter 3.

[7] On intent, see also Chapter 9.

[8] See also European Court of Human Rights, *Jersild* v. *Denmark*, Application no. 15890/89 (Grand Chamber judgment of 23 September 1994).

[9] See section 3.2.2.4 ('National legislative potential') of Chapter 3.

[10] On the proportionality of sanctions, see Chapter 13.

[11] For a more comprehensive analysis, see Tarlach McGonagle, 'A Survey and Critical Analysis of Council of Europe Strategies for Countering "Hate Speech"', in Michael Herz and Peter Molnar (eds.), *The Content and Context of Hate Speech: Rethinking Regulation and Responses* (Cambridge University Press, 2012), 456–98, also criticizing the uncertainty that arises from the myriad definitions used by different organs of this organization.

incite, promote or justify hatred based on intolerance (including religious intolerance)' may under circumstances be legitimately countered by State parties to the European Convention on Human Rights.[12]

Furthermore, according to a Recommendation adopted by the Council of Europe's Committee of Ministers, hate speech is to be understood 'as covering all forms of expression which spread, incite, promote or justify racial hatred, xenophobia, antisemitism or other forms of hatred based on intolerance, including: intolerance expressed by aggressive nationalism and ethnocentrism, discrimination and hostility against minorities, migrants and people of immigrant origin'.[13]

The Parliamentary Assembly of the Council of Europe followed suit and adopted a Recommendation in 2007 in which it sought to distinguish between blasphemy and other forms of insult on the one hand (to be decriminalized by member states) and 'hate speech' on the other (to be criminalized). Although it did not come up with a full-fledged definition, the Assembly did affirm that:

> hate speech against persons, whether on religious grounds or otherwise, should be penalised by law … For speech to qualify as hate speech in this sense, it is necessary that it be directed against a person or a specific group of persons. National law should penalise statements that call for a person or a group of persons to be subjected to hatred, discrimination or violence on grounds of their religion.[14]

Accordingly, the Assembly endeavoured to demarcate the difference between verbally attacking a religion and attacking religious believers.

---

[12] European Court of Human Rights, *Gündüz* v. *Turkey*, Application no. 35071/97 (4 December 2003), para. 40.

[13] Committee of Ministers, Recommendation No. R(97)20 on 'Hate Speech' (adopted on 30 October 1997). Other documents adopted by the Committee of Ministers emphasize specific contexts. See e.g. Recommendation No. R(97)21 on the Media and the Promotion of a Culture of Tolerance (adopted 30 October 1997); Declaration on Freedom of Political Debate in the Media (adopted on 12 February 2004); and the Declaration on Freedom of Communication on the Internet (adopted on 28 May 2003).

[14] Recommendation 1805 (2007) on 'Blasphemy, Religious Insults and Hate Speech against Persons on Grounds of Their Religion' (adopted on 29 June 2007), para. 12. See also its previously adopted Resolution 1510 (2006) on 'Freedom of Expression and Respect for Religious beliefs' (adopted on 28 June 2006), para. 12: 'The Assembly is of the opinion that freedom of expression as protected under Art. 10 of the European Convention on Human Rights should not be further restricted to meet increasing sensitivities of certain religious groups. At the same time, the Assembly emphasises that hate speech against any religious group is not compatible with the fundamental rights and freedoms guaranteed by the European Convention on Human Rights and the case law of the European Court of Human Rights.'

The European Commission against Racism and Intolerance (ECRI), a monitoring body of the Council of Europe, has advised on the *actus reus* of speech offences to be prohibited under (European) human rights standards: 'The law should penalise the following acts when committed intentionally: ... public incitement to violence, hatred or discrimination ... against a person or a grouping of persons on the grounds of their race, colour, language, religion, nationality, or national or ethnic origin.'[15] The criterion that incitement, for it to qualify, ought to be of a public nature resonates with Article 20(2) ICCPR's emphasis on 'advocacy' of hatred, which presupposes a degree of dissemination.[16]

A Venice Commission study of, among other things, incitement did not come up with a definition, but concluded that 'incitement to hatred, including religious hatred, should be the object of criminal sanctions'.[17]

In Europe, the European Union, too, has suggested definitions in this area.[18] The Council of the EU has urged all member states of the EU to ensure that criminal laws are in place to combat 'incitement to hatred'.[19] As per a Council Framework Decision, member states are to treat as punishable offences 'publicly inciting to violence or hatred directed against a group of persons or a member of such a group defined by reference to race, colour, religion, descent or national or ethnic origin' as well as the commission of that same act 'by public dissemination or distribution of tracts, pictures or other material'.[20] The preamble of the Framework Decision defines 'hatred', but does so in very abstract terms.[21]

---

[15] ECRI, *General Policy Recommendation No. 7 on National Legislation to Combat Racism and Racial Discrimination* (adopted on 13 December 2002), para. 18. On intent, see Chapter 9.

[16] Note that ECRI downplays this criterion subsequently in its *Explanatory Memorandum to ECRI General Policy Recommendation No. 7*, para. 38.

[17] Venice Commission, *Science and Technique of Democracy, No. 47: Blasphemy, Insult and Hatred – Finding Answers in a Democratic Society* (Strasbourg: Council of Europe Publishing, 2010), para. 89. This report was commissioned by the Parliamentary Assembly. See Resolution 1510 (2006), para. 18. The formal request was made by the Secretariat of the Parliamentary Assembly by way of a letter dated 11 October 2006.

[18] Freedom of expression is codified by the Charter of Fundamental Rights of the European Union (2000/C 364/01), Art. 11. The Charter does not contain specific rules on incitement.

[19] Council Framework Decision 2008/913/JHA of 28 November 2008 on 'Combating Certain Forms and Expressions of Racism and Xenophobia by Means of Criminal Law'.

[20] Council Framework Decision 2008/913/JHA, Article 1(a–d), in addition to other speech crimes.

[21] Council Framework Decision 2008/913/JHA, preamble points 8 and 9. For other instruments touching upon hate speech, see e.g. Directive 2010/13/EU of the European Parliament and of the Council of 10 March 2010 on the coordination of certain provisions

In 2009 the Fundamental Rights Agency (FRA) of the EU adopted the following definition of hate speech: 'Hate speech refers to public expressions which spread, incite, promote or justify hatred, discrimination or hostility towards minorities – for example statements by political or religious leaders appearing in the press or the Internet.'[22] In 2013 the Council of the EU adopted the *EU Guidelines on the Promotion and Protection of Freedom of Religion or Belief*,[23] which contain an extensive section on the intersection of freedom of expression and freedom of religion. Without providing a definition of incitement, the EU essentially adopts the terminology of Article 20(2) of the ICCPR.[24]

If anything, these widely differing definitions and concepts show the complexity of pinpointing the precise *actus reus* of punishable 'incitement'. Some of the definitions offered are quite narrow; others are frighteningly broad. Specifically, some of the above definitions fail to appreciate the difference between 'hate speech' and 'incitement' and are therefore of no use with respect to conceptualizing Article 20(2) of the ICCPR.

7.3   The triangle of incitement: reflections on the key terms of Article 20(2)

The Human Rights Committee has not offered a comprehensive definition of the *actus reus* of the incitement offence within the meaning of Article 20(2) of the ICCPR. On the basis of textual analysis, legal scholarship and the overall workings of this Committee, we can, however, piece together a model definition of 'advocacy of religious hatred that constitutes incitement'.

---

laid down by law, regulation or administrative action in member states concerning the provision of audiovisual media services (Audiovisual Media Services Directive).

[22] FRA, *Homophobia and Discrimination on Grounds of Sexual Orientation and Gender Identity in the EU Member States: Part II – The Social Situation* (2009), at 23, also quoting other definitions and emphasizing that there is no universal consensus as to an appropriate definition.

[23] *EU Guidelines on the Promotion and Protection of Freedom of Religion or Belief* (adopted by the Foreign Affairs Council meeting, Luxembourg, 24 June 2013). See particularly paras. 31–32.

[24] The EU Guidelines, possibly inadvertently, contain sentences that are hard to reconcile with Art. 20(2) ICCPR. For instance, the Guidelines posit that the EU may take certain actions '[w]hen critical comments are expressed about religions or beliefs and such expression *is perceived by adherents* as being so offensive that it may result in violence *towards or by* adherents' (para. 32, emphasis added). As we will see in this chapter, the way a speech act is perceived by the target group does not impact on the legality thereof. What matters is whether the speech act incites an audience.

7.3.1 'Advocacy'

From the *travaux préparatoires* it is not entirely clear why the term 'advocacy' was chosen and not 'propaganda', as is also used in the first paragraph of Article 20 on propaganda for war. Throughout the drafting debates delegates often used the term 'hate propaganda'. When the term 'advocacy' was introduced, some delegates maintained that 'advocacy' must be understood as 'systematic and persistent propaganda'.[25] Others submitted that advocacy means 'repeated and insistent expression'.[26] The latter would suggest that a one-off hateful statement could never qualify under Article 20(2). That is perhaps not correct. As we will see in the chapters to come, whether or not a form of 'advocacy' has the capacity to engage Article 20(2) also very much depends on the context – the latter can be such that a one-off statement is indeed not sufficient, while the context could also be such that it is. Since the question of 'incitement' significantly hinges on a contextual test,[27] it would be quite premature to rule out one-off instances of propagating hatred from the definition of 'advocacy'.

In its state reporting procedure the Human Rights Committee has not remarked on the exact terminology to be used in domestic incitement laws.[28] Since many State parties have opted for language different from 'advocacy' (e.g. 'dissemination' or 'propaganda'), one could infer that the Human Rights Committee is apparently not preoccupied with this matter. Alternatively, it may very well be that the Committee at this particular point in time is busy convincing State parties that national laws implementing prohibiting incitement are mandatory, leaving the technicalities for later. Indeed, the Committee's concluding observations on the question of compliance with Article 20(2) tend to be of a general nature, especially compared to detailed observations on domestic compliance made by CERD.[29]

---

[25] E/CN.4/SR.174, at 9 (Mr Malik, Lebanon).

[26] A/C.3/SR.1079, para. 2.

[27] See section 7.3.4 below and, more comprehensively, Chapter 10.

[28] The Committee has, however, repeatedly pointed out the more general point that a national law corresponding with Art. 20 ICCPR must be adopted, e.g. A/60/40 vol. I (2005) 74, para. 93(13) (Slovenia); A/50/40 vol. I (1995) 38, para. 181 (New Zealand); A/50/40 vol. I (1995) 57, para. 322 (Ukraine); A/59/40 vol. I (2003) 20, para. 64(20) (Russia).

[29] See section 6.2 of Chapter 6 on this Committee's observations made in the light of Art. 4 ICERD.

In its case law the Committee seems easily persuaded by responding states that the impugned speech act amounted to 'advocacy' in the
meaning of Article 20(2).[30] Accordingly, in *J.R.T. and the W.G. Party
v. Canada* the Committee accepted that the telephonically disseminated
anti-Semitic messages 'clearly' constituted advocacy.[31] In *Malcolm Ross
v. Canada* the author of the communication and the responding state in
fact firmly disagree as to whether the teacher's off-duty anti-Semitic pamphlets amounted to 'advocacy',[32] yet the Committee accepts that they did
without offering much in the way of argumentation.[33]

In its recent General Comment No. 34 on freedom of expression the
Committee was on the verge of providing a more robust definition of
'advocacy', but ultimately decided against including it. In an early draft
of the Comment 'advocacy' was defined as 'public forms of expression
that are intended to elicit action or response'.[34] This definition does not
cite Human Rights Committee case law,[35] or concluding observations or
travaux (while the General Comment does so throughout). Thus it can
be assumed that Professor O'Flaherty, the chief drafter of the Comment,
came up with this definition himself.[36]

The emphasis on *public* forms of expression makes sense. First, this
criterion taps into *travaux* discussion on this matter. Second, 'advocacy'
semantically clearly presupposes a degree of dissemination. This emphasis
presumably was not meant to imply that it is only public *authorities* that

---

[30] See Toby Mendel, *Study on International Standards Relating to Incitement to Genocide
or Racial Hatred for the UN Special Advisor on the Prevention of Genocide* (April 2006)
(hereafter *Study on Incitement*), 27.

[31] Human Rights Committee, *J.R.T. and the W.G. Party* v. *Canada*, Communication
no. 104/1981 (6 April 1983), para. 8(b).

[32] *Malcolm Ross* v. *Canada*, Communication no. 736/1997 (18 October 2000), paras. 6.2–6.3
(state) and para. 7.2 (applicant).

[33] *Malcolm Ross* v. *Canada*, para. 11.5.

[34] Draft General Comment No. 34: Article 19 (2nd revised draft, CCPR/C/GC/34/CRP.3,
28 June 2010), para. 53.

[35] As far as relevant case law is concerned, though, it can be observed that in all cases
in which Art. 20(2) played a role some form of *public* dissemination of hatred was
discernible, be it a publically available telephone service, pamphlets or newspaper
interviews.

[36] The Camden Principles' definition may have served as a source of inspiration. These principles provide that '[t]he term "advocacy" is to be understood as requiring an intention to
promote hatred publicly towards the target group'. ARTICLE 19, *Camden Principles on
Freedom of Expression and Equality* (2009), Art. 12(ii). The Camden Principles are a set
of benchmarks on freedom of expression drafted under the aegis of ARTICLE 19, having
consulted UN experts, civil society and academic experts.

can commit incitement (something that was occasionally suggested by drafters of the Covenant);[37] this criterion rather requires a minimal degree of public *dissemination* with respect to the speech or publication in question. While Article 20(2) was adopted against the backdrop of state-instigated hate propaganda by the Nazis, there was a majority among the drafters who felt that this clause ought to provide protection against incitement by private actors too.[38]

While private actors who commit public 'advocacy' (of hatred constituting incitement) come within the ambit of Article 20(2), the flip-side of the above definition is that purely private forms of hate speech do not. For example, a father who advocates hatred in front of his children would not engage Article 20(2). Or a letter or email to a friend in which one advocates hatred would also not set off the Covenant's incitement prohibition. Nowak goes even further and argues that State parties are not under an obligation to 'prohibit advocacy of hatred in private that instigates non-violent acts of racial or religious discrimination'.[39] This would, for instance, mean that hateful speeches made or inciteful music performed at a private gathering of neo-Nazis would not necessarily qualify as 'advocacy'.[40] The reverse would be the case only when that same gathering spread its messages to the outside world, for instance by means of a public march, internet postings and perhaps also by means of non-verbal messages such as cross burning. In that respect, 'advocacy' implies an effort of reaching out to a wider audience, possibly including the not-yet-like-minded, that is, persons whose minds can yet be poisoned by the hateful speech act in question. In further support of this reading, the widely endorsed *Camden Principles on Freedom of Expression and Equality* also define 'advocacy' as 'requiring an intention to promote hatred *publicly* towards the target group'.[41] The same goes for a definition formulated in a report of the UN Special Rapporteur on the promotion and protection of the right to freedom of opinion and

---

[37] Notably, the USA insisted on this. E/CN.4/SR.160, at 10.
[38] See e.g. E/CN.4/SR.160, at 13; E/CN.4/SR.160, at 12; E/CN.4/SR.163 at 11. See also Stephanie Farrior, 'Molding the Matrix: The Historical and Theoretical Foundations of International Law Concerning Hate Speech' (1996) 14:1 *Berkeley Journal of International Law* 1–98, at 23.
[39] Manfred Nowak, *U.N. Covenant on Civil and Political Rights: CCPR Commentary* (2nd rev. edn, Kehl: N. P. Engel., 2005), at 475.
[40] See, however, A/57/40 vol. I (2002) 57, para. 79(14), urging Sweden to take measures against 'white-power music'.
[41] *Camden Principles*, Art. 12(ii) (emphasis added).

expression, describing 'advocacy' as 'explicit, intentional, public and active support and promotion of hatred towards the target group'.[42]

The second part of O'Flaherty's (deleted) definition – 'are intended to elicit action or response' – further raises the threshold of the speech offence that State parties must prohibit as per the Covenant. While we return to the question of *mens rea* in a separate chapter,[43] what matters in terms of the *actus reus* of the offence is that 'advocacy' is more than merely spreading a message.[44] It is the act of spreading a message so as to evoke a certain outcome. Obviously, this point is more emphatically underscored by the provision's key term 'incitement'; therefore, we will return to this matter in due course.[45]

As for the form of the speech act, it would appear that any means of dissemination that makes the message public, thus reaching out to a wider audience, qualifies as 'advocacy'.[46] Accordingly, speech or written messages, use of the press, audio-visual media, books, and so on, in principle all qualify. This also means that different capacities can fulfil the role of the 'advocator', ranging from politicians, to religious leaders, to rally leaders or internet bloggers. That said, the precise medium used, its tone, the role of the advocator, as well as the general 'setting' – for example public debate, cinema film screening, rally, internet-based message exchanges – impact such factors as 'the extent of the speech act' and in turn 'the likelihood of harm' ensuing from it.[47] The line between the 'content' and 'context' of incitement, therefore, is oftentimes hard to draw (we will return to this matter in Chapter 10).

7.3.2 'Hatred'

The same early draft of General Comment No. 34 had attempted to define 'hatred'. This definition, which was ultimately also deleted, reads as

---

[42] UN Special Rapporteur on the Promotion and Protection of the Right to Freedom of Opinion and Expression, *Report of the Special Rapporteur to the General Assembly on Hate Speech and Incitement to Hatred* (A/67/357, 7 September 2012), para. 44(b).

[43] See Chapter 9.

[44] The Camden Principles further support this point ('an intention to promote hatred publicly towards the target group'). *Camden Principles*, Art. 12(ii).

[45] See section 7.3.4 below.

[46] *Rabat Plan of Action on the Prohibition of Advocacy of National, Racial or Religious Hatred that Constitutes Incitement to Discrimination, Hostility or Violence* (Conclusions and recommendations emanating from the four regional expert workshops organized by OHCHR in 2011 and adopted by experts in Rabat, Morocco on 5 October 2012), para. 22; ARTICLE 19, *Prohibiting Incitement to Discrimination, Hostility or Violence: Policy Brief* (2012) (hereafter *Incitement Policy Brief*), at 38.

[47] *Rabat Plan of Action*, para. 22; ARTICLE 19, *Incitement Policy Brief*, 34–40.

follows: 'By "hatred" is meant intense emotions of opprobrium, enmity and detestation towards a target individual or group.'[48] The UN Special Rapporteur on the promotion and protection of the right to freedom of opinion and expression uses a very similar formulation.[49] The said draft General Comment definition was clearly based on the Camden Principles.[50] In drafting this new General Comment, the Committee and Professor O'Flaherty in particular interacted with and consulted stakeholders to an unprecedented degree. Accordingly, the Committee invited written feedback on the different drafts of the General Comment and stakeholders, such as NGOs and academics, also had a chance to provide comments during conferences and meetings on the subject. One can see that free speech NGO ARTICLE 19 was particularly influential in this open consultation process.[51]

This definition sought to further emphasize the extreme nature of speech acts that engage Article 20(2) of the ICCPR. Only speech acts that convey intense emotions of 'opprobrium', 'enmity' and 'detestation' would come within the ambit of the Covenant's incitement clause. Perhaps the reason why it was deleted during a later reading by the Committee is that this definition would make it hard to combat extreme speech that is not explicitly accompanied by such 'emotions'. It is not unimaginable that a person would incite the most odious acts – including even crimes against humanity – ostensibly without conveying much emotion at all. Strictly, such 'emotionless' speech acts would not qualify under this definition of 'hatred'. Having said that, the definition certainly had some appeal to it,

---

[48] Draft General Comment No. 34: Article 19 (2nd revised draft), para. 53.

[49] UN Special Rapporteur on Freedom of Expression, *Report on Hate Speech and Incitement*, para. 44(a).

[50] See *Camden Principles*, Art. 12(i). These principles probably were on this point in turn influenced by a Canadian Supreme Court decision. In *R. v. Keegstra*, [1990] 3 S.C.R. 697, 13 December 1990, at 697 (Can.), para. 1, this Court held that the word 'hatred' under the Canadian criminal hate speech prohibition (s. 319(2) Criminal Code of Canada 1985) refers to 'only the most severe and deeply felt form of opprobrium'. This Court further speaks of 'extreme feelings of opprobrium and enmity against a racial or religious group' (*R. v. Keegstra*, section V). In this case the Canadian Supreme Court considered that this hate speech limitation is constitutional when proportionally applied.

[51] In addition to the Camden Principles, which were adopted under the aegis of ARTICLE 19, see also ARTICLE 19, *Towards an Interpretation of Article 20 of the ICCPR: Thresholds for the Prohibition of Incitement to Hatred* (A study prepared for the regional expert meeting on Article 20 organized by the Office of the High Commissioner for Human Rights, Vienna, 8–9 February 2010). The latter document was later further refined in ARTICLE 19, *Incitement Policy Brief*.

for it made it clear that weak, unqualified forms of 'hate speech' do not engage Article 20(2)'s prohibition.[52]

As already mentioned, the Camden Principles' definition of 'hatred' is similar. According to these principles, hatred 'refer[s] to intense and irrational emotions of opprobrium, enmity and detestation towards the target group'.[53] One subtle difference with the above definitions is that it is less evident that the said 'emotions' must, for the incitement clause to be engaged, actually be discernible in the speech act. Arguably, it would be sufficient that intense enmity (and so on) generally underlies or motivates the extreme speech act. That said, this definition also contains problematic terms, not least of which are 'irrational' and 'emotions'. However, by insisting on the intensity of the verbal attack that qualifies under Article 20(2), this definition also provides some insight into the provision's high threshold.

Again, the case law of the Human Rights Committee that touches upon Article 20(2) is not very instructive. The Committee tends to accept the responding State party's claim that impugned statements advocated 'hatred' in the meaning of Article 20(2) without much debate on this point.[54] While several members of the Committee would have preferred the contrary, in *Faurisson* v. *France* the Committee did not apply Article 20(2).[55] These individual opinions are most instructive on the question of 'hatred'. Elizabeth Evatt and David Kretzmer explain in their concurring opinion why Faurisson's statements can rightly be labelled advocacy of 'hatred' rather than merely insulting speech. They argue that not only did his negationist discourse in its own right amount to anti-Semitism, he further targeted Jews by blaming them for 'concocting' the Holocaust. He accused Jewish historians of pseudo-history or revisionism;

---

[52] An early version of the Comment made this more explicit. See Draft General Comment No. 34: Article 19 (2nd revised draft), para. 54. A slimmed down version of the Committee's concern about low-threshold 'hate speech laws' made it into the adopted General Comment: 'It is only with regard to the specific forms of expression indicated in article 20 that States parties are obliged to have legal prohibitions.' Human Rights Committee, *General Comment 34: Article 19: Freedoms of Opinion and Expression* (CCPR/C/GC/34, adopted at its 102nd session, Geneva, 11–29 July 2011), para. 52.

[53] *Camden Principles*, Art. 12(i). The same definition is used for 'hostility'. It is unclear why the Camden Principles lump together 'hatred' and 'hostility'. This does not flow logically from the system of Art. 20(2) ICCPR.

[54] E.g. *J.R.T. and the W.G. Party* v. *Canada*, para. 8(b); and *Malcolm Ross* v. *Canada*, para. 11.5.

[55] Human Rights Committee, *Robert Faurisson* v. *France*, Communication no. 550/1993 (19 July 1995).

the latter would have supported the 'dirty trick' committed by the victors of Nuremberg. Thus not only did Faurisson commit negationism, he further went on to accuse the very victims of National Socialism of committing historical revisionism. It was this vehemence that conveyed the type of enmity and detestation towards the target group – here Jewish persons – that qualifies as 'hatred' under Article 20(2).[56]

7.3.3 'Religious'

The ICCPR obliges State parties to prohibit advocacy of 'national', 'racial' or 'religious' hatred (to the extent such advocacy constitutes 'incitement', see sub-section 7.3.4). In this sub-section we focus on 'religious' hatred. The ICCPR is unique in covering this ground, while the other grounds are also covered by the ICERD.[57] A second objective of this sub-section is to discuss the question whether the prohibited grounds listed by the ICCPR are exhaustive.

As for 'religious' hatred, the first thing to observe is that it is compulsory for State parties to explicitly include this prohibited ground in their domestic incitement laws. Thus a national law implementing Article 20(2) must quite literally mention all three grounds.[58]

---

[56] Individual opinion (concurring) by Elizabeth Evatt and David Kretzmer, co-signed by Eckart Klein, para. 10.

[57] ICERD, Art. 1(1), defines racial discrimination as any 'distinction, exclusion, restriction or preference based on *race*, colour, descent, or *national* or *ethnic* origin which has the purpose or effect of nullifying or impairing the recognition, enjoyment or exercise, on an equal footing, of human rights and fundamental freedoms in the political, economic, social, cultural or any other field of public life' (emphasis added). See further Art. 4 of ICERD on hate propaganda, racial superiority and racist incitement, as discussed in Chapter 6 (particularly at sections 6.2–6.4 thereof). Nowak observes one possible difference between 'national' as used by ICERD and 'national' as used by ICCPR. Since ICCPR omits such caveats as the ones outlined by Art. 1, paragraphs 2 and 3 of ICERD, the former treaty covers hatred of aliens and foreigners and not only the state's own different (ethnic) nationals. Nowak, *CCPR Commentary*, at 475. Some of the drafters of the ICCPR, however, supported a restrictive interpretation of 'national'. The Brazilian delegate in the Third Committee, for instance, claimed that '[w]hile "national hatred" referred to hostility aimed against certain ethnic groups within a State, including minority groups, "racial or religious hatred" related to specific forms of hostility which might be independent of the national features of the peoples concerned'. A/C.3/SR.1082, para. 4.

[58] E.g. concerning laws in New Zealand the Committee held '[t]he Committee is concerned about the fact that, while the Human Rights Act contains a provision corresponding to article 20, paragraph 2, of the Covenant, this provision does not include a prohibition of advocacy of religious hatred'. A/50/40 vol. I (1995) 38, para. 181.

As for the meaning of 'religious', it stands to reason we turn to existing Covenant benchmarks on this notion. The concept of advocacy of 'religious' hatred is applicable to all religions and beliefs within the scope of Article 18 on freedom of religion.[59] That provision is very inclusive, for it 'protects theistic, non-theistic and atheistic beliefs, as well as the right not to profess any religion or belief'.[60] Moreover, the Human Rights Committee has held that '[t]he terms "belief" and "religion" are to be broadly construed. Article 18 is not limited in its application to traditional religions or to religions and beliefs with institutional characteristics or practices analogous to those of traditional religions.'[61] Accordingly, religion is broadly construed as covering metaphysical and non-metaphysical beliefs, old and new faiths, and in terms of membership numbers both large and small ones. This means that incitement against atheists is also covered by Article 20(2), as is incitement against new religious movements.

The combined phrase 'religious hatred' does raise one further semantic question, however – does 'religious hatred' merely mean all forms of *hatred targeting a religious group* (including non-theistic belief groups), or does it also include *religiously motivated hatred*? Hatred vis-à-vis a religious group is typically religiously motivated, while religiously motivated hatred is not necessarily aimed at a religious group.

From the historical background against which the incitement clause was adopted, it is evident that the first type of hatred is minimally covered. The incitement provision was intended as protection against express racial and religious intimidation and marginalization.

On the one hand, one might argue that the question of motivation is relevant, for if the latter is of a religious nature, the freedom of religious manifestation might be engaged. This is not to say that this freedom will trump other rights at stake, but it does generally speaking further complicate the assessment of incitement incidents. On the other hand, venturing into the question of whether the inciter's hatred was religiously motivated has a superfluous quality to it. For 'religious hatred' necessarily combines both intrinsic and extrinsic motivations. While one could in the abstract 'hate' (specific characteristics of) a religious group in and for itself, such hatred at the same time points at a minimum degree of

---

[59] See Nowak, CCPR Commentary, at 475.
[60] Human Rights Committee, *General Comment 22: Article 18* (Forty-eighth session, 1993), para. 2.
[61] Human Rights Committee, *General Comment 22*, para. 2.

intrinsic motivations of superiority. As this intrinsic motivation can be premised on any belief the inciter holds, including the absence of religious beliefs, it will become clear that religious hatred without a particular, personalized religious motive is bordering on the impossible.

Perhaps these considerations explain why the Human Rights Committee in its case law is not overly concerned with the question of how the convicted inciter's hatred was motivated. Accordingly, in its jurisprudence on anti-Semitism it is ultimately irrelevant whether anti-Semitic teachers or 'historians' expressed themselves in the way they did because they hate Jews in and for themselves or because they are Christian bigots who blame the Jews for crucifying Jesus. Put differently, the Committee does not seek to establish whether the inciter has religious motivations for his or her acts. The only thing that matters for the Committee in those cases is that Jews were in fact verbally attacked. For instance, in *Malcolm Ross* v. *Canada* the applicant and the responding state are engaged in a heated debate as to whether Ross' views can be deemed 'religious' or 'Christian'. Ross claims that his statements represent 'conflicts between Judaism and Christianity' and he made them in 'defence of the Christian religion'.[62] Canada responds that Ross had merely 'cloaked his views under the guise of the Christian faith'.[63] The Human Rights Committee concludes that Ross' statements were made against persons of Jewish faith and ancestry, but pretty much ignores whether Ross was religiously motivated when he made them.[64]

The question whether 'religious hatred' may mean more than hatred expressed against a religious target group is, however, not completely immaterial. As outlined just now, hatred against a religious target group is typically intrinsically religiously motivated. Still, if 'religiously motivated hatred' as such were also covered by Article 20(2), then the ramifications of the incitement clause may be much wider than the Committee's present case law suggests. Notably, religiously motivated hatred aimed at homosexuals or women could come within its ambit.

This matter touches upon the wider question of whether the prohibited grounds mentioned by Article 20(2) are exhaustive. Nowak argues that this is the case. Accordingly, incitement to violence against women would not fall under Article 20(2)'s prohibition.[65] Nowak does not comment on

---

[62] *Malcolm Ross* v. *Canada*, para. 2.1; see also paras. 4.2, 5.2, 5.4 and 7.3.
[63] *Malcolm Ross* v. *Canada*, para. 6.5; see also para. 6.4.
[64] *Malcolm Ross* v. *Canada*, para. 11.5.
[65] Nowak, *CCPR Commentary*, at 474–5.

the question of whether this would be any different if the incitement to violence were religiously motivated.

Of course, the prohibited incitement grounds – nationality, race and religion – were chosen against the backdrop of the Holocaust. Yet both from a historical as well as a contemporary perspective the drafters' choice can be accused of randomness. Homosexuals were also major victims of the Holocaust,[66] but this is entirely ignored in the drafting discussions concerning Article 20(2) ICCPR. And while there is no reason to presume that the words 'national, racial or religious' were not intended to be exhaustive, from a contemporary human rights perspective they appear overly limited. There are contemporary forms of incitement, for instance on grounds of hatred of certain sexual orientations, but think also of incitement of violence against women, that are just as objectionable as incitement based on the three grounds mentioned in the Covenant.

Thus the question is whether a dynamic treaty interpretation, taking account of contemporary challenges faced by the Covenant and the rights it contains, would warrant an inclusive reading of Article 20(2), including incitement on grounds of, for example, gender, sexual orientation and disability. Applying the 'living instrument doctrine' to the Covenant,[67] free speech NGO ARTICLE 19 has proposed such an upgrade.[68] Further, a number of State parties do expressly go beyond the three prohibited grounds, typically at a minimum adding the ground of sexual orientation.[69] Strikingly, the

[66] E.g. Richard Plant, *The Pink Triangle: The Nazi War Against Homosexuals* (New York: H. Holt, 1986).

[67] Notably, since such cases as *Toonen* v. *Australia*, Communication no. 488/1992 (31 March 1994) it is clear that sexual orientation discrimination engages the protection of the Covenant.

[68] ARTICLE 19, *Responding to Hate Speech against LGBTI People: Policy Brief* (2013). See also ARTICLE 19, *Incitement Policy Brief*, at 20–22.

[69] E.g. Section 283(1) of the Criminal Code of Austria 1974 (see also Anti-Discrimination Act 1977 [New South Wales]); Section 6 of the Anti-Discrimination Act of 25 February 2003, amending the Act of 15 February 1993 on the Establishment of a Centre for Equal Opportunities and Combating Racism [Belgium] (gender, sexual orientation, civil status, birth, wealth, age, religious or philosophical beliefs, current or future state of health, a disability or a physical characteristic); Art. 319 of the Criminal Code of Canada 1985 ('identifiable group' includes sexual orientation minorities); Anti-Discrimination Law 1482/2011 [Colombia]; Art. 266b of the Criminal Code of Denmark 2009 (race, colour, national or ethnic origin, religion, or sexual inclination; the latter ground was inserted as per Act No. 357 of 3 June 1987); Articles 225-1 and 225-2 of the Criminal Code of France 1992 (as amended through Law 2001/1066); Art. 233a of the General Criminal Code of Iceland 1940 (nationality, colour, race, religion or sexual inclination (the latter ground was inserter as per Act 135/1996)); Prohibition of Incitement to Hatred Act of 1989 [Ireland] (race, religion, nationality, or sexual orientation); Art. 170 of the Constitution

Human Rights Committee has not yet found fault, for instance in the context of its state reporting procedure, with these inclusive incitement laws.[70] While this as such does not mean that the Committee is inclined towards an inclusive interpretation of Article 20(2), this inaction on the part of the Committee can be taken to mean that those additional grounds are, if not obligatory under Article 20, at least permitted under Article 19(3). The latter view is, *mutatis mutandis*,[71] supported by the European Court of Human Rights, which held in *Vejdeland and others* v. *Sweden* that restrictions on homophobic incitement – here leaflets distributed in a school calling homosexuality a 'deviant sexual proclivity' – may under certain circumstances be legitimate.[72] The human rights NGO Interrights acted as third-party intervener in this case. In its *amicus curiae* brief, it held that '[s]exual orientation should be treated in the same way as categories such as race, ethnicity and religion which are commonly covered by hate-speech and hate-crime laws, because sexual orientation is a characteristic that is fundamental to a person's sense of self. It is, moreover, used as a marker of group identity.'[73] The Strasbourg Court implicitly endorsed this view.

The Human Rights Committee missed out on an excellent opportunity to settle this score when it adopted General Comment No. 34. It did

---

of Lithuania 1992 (sex, sexual, orientation, race, nationality, language, origin, social status, religion, conviction, or belief); Section 16 of the Freedom of Public Expression Act No. 1.299 of 15 July 2005 [Monaco] (origin, membership or non-membership of a particular ethnic group, nation, race or religion or actual or supposed sexual orientation); Art. 137d(1) of the Criminal Code of the Netherlands 1881 (race, religion or belief, gender or hetero- or homosexual nature or physical, mental, or intellectual disabilities); Art. 135a of the Criminal Code of Norway 1902 (skin colour or national or ethnic origin, religion or life stance, or homosexuality, lifestyle or orientation); Art. 19 of Law No. 48 of 16 January 2002 approving Government Ordinance No. 137/2000 Regarding the Prevention and Punishment of Every Form of Discrimination [Romania] (race, nationality, ethnic group, religion, social or non-favoured category or their beliefs, sex or sexual orientation); Art. 8(1) of the Mass Media Act of 26 May 2001 [Slovenia] (national, racial, religious, sexual); Articles 22 and 510 of the Criminal Code of Spain 1996 (ideology, religion or belief, race, national origin, gender, sexual orientation, illness or disability); Art. 216 of the New Criminal Code of Turkey 2004 (race, regional origin, religion, social class, sexual). For further examples, see ARTICLE 19, *Responding to Hate Speech against LGBTI People*, 31–44.

[70] Quite the contrary, the Committee welcomes legislative decisions to include sexual orientation among the prohibited grounds of discrimination (in the general context of criminal law). See ARTICLE 19, *Responding to Hate Speech against LGBTI People*, at 13, for examples of concluding observations in that regard.

[71] ECHR, Art. 10(2).

[72] European Court of Human Rights, *Vejdeland and others* v. *Sweden*, Application no. 1813/07 (9 February 2012).

[73] *Vejdeland and others* v. *Sweden*, para. 45.

not comment on the exhaustiveness of the prohibited grounds contained in Article 20(2). A future focus on intersectionality can partly remedy this historical oversight.[74] That is, if the Committee were to accept, as discussed above, that 'religious hatred' refers both to hatred aimed at a religious group as well as religiously motivated hatred, then hatred of the last type against, for instance, homosexuals or women may come within the ambit of the incitement clause. This will, however, be no remedy for incitement against sexual orientation minorities that is not religiously motivated, for instance, the incitement to violence against LGBTIs by neo-Nazis.

7.3.4 'Incitement'

Out of all the keywords of which Article 20(2) is composed, 'incitement' certainly is the most crucial, for it – rightly – raises the threshold of the extreme speech offence that State parties are expected to prohibit tremendously. Indeed, 'incitement' largely defines the Covenant's anti-extreme speech clause.[75]

The fact that this term was inserted into Article 20(2) ICCPR means that the latter is not concerned with 'hate speech'. Article 20(2) does not dictate national prohibitions of 'hate speech'. The term 'incitement' introduces a third required actor – the speech act's *audience*. 'Hate speech' can be defined, in the words of Susan Benesch,[76] as 'speech that attacks or disparages a group or a person, for characteristics purportedly typical of the group'.[77] Accordingly, 'hate speech' may have direct effects on the target group, possibly offending, outraging and hurting them. Incitement may have such direct effects on the target group too. But what distinguishes incitement, moreover, is that it is intended to mobilize other persons to

---

[74] On intersectionality, see Nazila Ghanea, 'The Concept of Racist Hate Speech and its Evolution Over Time' (paper presented at the United Nations Committee on the Elimination of Racial Discrimination, 81st session, 28 August 2012, Geneva); and Kimberlé Crenshaw, 'Mapping the Margins: Intersectionality, Identity Politics, and Violence against Women of Color' (1991) 46:6 *Stanford Law Review* 1241–99. For a discussion of intersectionality in the context of ICERD, see sections 6.3 and 6.8 of Chapter 6.

[75] See also UN Special Rapporteur on Freedom of Expression, *Report on Hate Speech and Incitement*, paras. 44–46.

[76] Formulating these benchmarks in her capacity as consultant to the UN Special Advisor on the Prevention of Genocide, Dr Francis Deng.

[77] Susan Benesch, 'Contribution to OHCHR Initiative on Incitement to National, Racial, or Religious Hatred' (expert paper presented at the UN OHCHR Expert workshop on the prohibition of incitement to national, racial or religious hatred, Vienna, 9–10 February 2011) (hereafter OHCHR Expert Paper), at 3.

harm the target group. Thus 'incitement' has as its focus a target group (e.g. a group characterized by religion or ethnicity), but its *real audience* consists of third persons whom the inciter hopes to arouse to respond to the message of hate to the extent that they would engage in hostile acts such as violence or discrimination vis-à-vis the target group.[78] 'Hate speech', as well as religious insult, defamation and all other types of gratuitously offensive speech – though potentially hurting the target group directly – do not have this indirect effect, or at least are typically unlikely to, and hence do not amount to 'incitement' within the meaning of Article 20(2) ICCPR.[79]

While there is accordingly most definitely no duty under this provision to ban this type of speech, it is possible to go further than that and claim that restrictions along the lines of such low-threshold 'hate speech' and 'religious insult' offences are also not legitimized by Article 19(3) of the ICCPR. The Human Rights Committee has offered support for that view in its recent General Comment on freedom of expression.[80]

Accordingly, the ICCPR does not prohibit extremist content per se; the Covenant's extreme speech prohibition is rather concerned with the potential consequences of hateful speech.[81] Indeed, only advocacy of religious (and other) hatred 'that constitutes incitement' is to be prohibited by State parties. Those words are premised, evidently, on the idea that there can be advocacy of religious hatred that constitutes incitement and advocacy of hatred that does not reach the level so as to potentially engage or mobilize others.[82]

Let us consider some further definitions and concepts that have been suggested with respect to 'incitement'. The second draft of General Comment No. 34 also hazarded a definition of this term (which again did not make the final draft). 'Incitement', this definition proposes, 'refers to the need for the advocacy to be likely to trigger imminent acts of discrimination, hostility or violence against a specific individual or group.'[83]

---

[78]   Benesch, 'OHCHR Expert Paper', at 4–5.
[79]   See Benesch, 'OHCHR Expert Paper', at 5.
[80]   Human Rights Committee, *General Comment 34*, para. 48: 'Prohibitions of displays of lack of respect for a religion or other belief system, including blasphemy laws, are incompatible with the Covenant.' 'Hate speech laws' will be further criticized in Chapter 8.
[81]   Benesch, 'OHCHR Expert Paper', at 4.
[82]   Also see UN Special Rapporteur on Freedom of Religion or Belief, *Tackling Manifestations of Collective Religious Hatred* (A/HRC/25/58, 26 December 2013), para. 56; and UN Special Rapporteur on Freedom of Expression, *Report on Hate Speech and Incitement*, para. 46.
[83]   Draft General Comment No. 34: Article 19 (2nd revised draft), para. 53.

This definition thus hinges on 'likelihood', which makes proof of incitement having taken place by definition a contextual matter. This is supported by the definition used by the UN Special Rapporteur on freedom of expression, positing that incitement 'refers to statements about national, racial or religious groups that create an imminent risk of discrimination, hostility or violence against persons belonging to those groups'.[84] Whether or not it was 'likely' that the speech act's audience would respond by way of hostile acts against the target group clearly cannot be distilled from the content of the speech act alone – it hinges on such questions as the size and composition of the audience, the position and status of the inciter, but also the position of the target group. This contextual conception resonates well with the Camden Principles. The latter propose that '[t]he term "incitement" refers to statements about national, racial or religious groups which create an imminent risk of discrimination, hostility or violence against persons belonging to those groups'.[85]

Hateful incitement in the meaning of Article 20(2) is by definition an inchoate offence.[86] What is prohibited is the act of inciting to discrimination, hostility or violence. For the offence to be committed, the latter hostile acts, perpetrated by third parties, do not actually need to occur. Accordingly, questions of causality do not necessarily play a role in incitement proceedings (one may of course conceptually distinguish between successful and unsuccessful incitement, and where the former has occurred, this may have ramifications for sanctions).[87] At the same time, the above definitions'

---

[84] UN Special Rapporteur on Freedom of Expression, *Report on Hate Speech and Incitement*, para. 44(c).

[85] *Camden Principles*, Art. 12(iii)

[86] See Toby Mendel, *Study on International Standards Relating to Incitement to Genocide or Racial Hatred for the UN Special Advisor on the Prevention of Genocide* (April 2006) (hereafter *Study on Incitement*), at 53. Note that other international incitement prohibitions, notably the ones contained in Art. 4 ICERD, could be of a different nature. Mendel (*Study on Incitement* at 28), distinguishes between three analytical species of incitement that could, in the abstract, be prohibited: (i) incitement to an illegal act that actually takes place; (ii) incitement to illegal acts that do not take place; and (iii) incitement to a certain state of mind. In relation to Art. 20(2) he concludes that for 'discrimination' and 'violence', category (ii) applies: the proscribed result does not need to occur for the sake of criminality. However, the Human Rights Committee occasionally seems to be using conception (iii) in relation to incitement to 'hostility'. Mendel criticizes this since this approach endangers free speech.

[87] In some jurisdictions the fact that incitement actually caused violence or discrimination is considered an aggravating factor, e.g. Art. 150 of the Criminal Code of the Federation of Bosnia and Herzegovina 1998 provides that 'if disorder, violence or other grave consequences for the living together of constitutional nations and others living in Bosnia and Herzegovina or the Federation resulted from' incitement, the inciter may be punished

insistence on the 'likelihood of (imminent) harm' makes sense. It would be rather contrary to the object and purpose of the Covenant, with its foundational focus on robust free speech, to stifle speech that cannot reasonably be expected to cause harm. Article 19(3)'s necessity principle, which integrally applies to Article 20(2), further supports that.[88]

Thus what is decisive is whether at the time of the incitement the risk of harmful acts, to be perpetrated by third parties against the speech act's target group, existed or not. Accordingly, in the *Malcolm Ross* case what mattered to the Human Rights Committee was not that this teacher's anti-Semitic publications denigrated the faith and beliefs of Jewish people, but the fact that he portrayed Jews as the 'enemy' of Canada and its predominantly Christian population and that he called upon 'true Christians' to join him in his fights against Jews.[89] Thus he reached out to others seeking to poison the mind of his audience, the recipients of his anti-Semitic pamphlet and writings. As his speech acts appear to remain short of calling for violence, they are probably best labelled as 'incitement to discrimination' (and/or hostility).[90]

In *Faurisson* v. *France* individual Committee members accepted that this Holocaust denier had committed 'incitement' in the meaning of Article 20(2) ICCPR,[91] something that was submitted by the responding state.[92] While the plenary Committee avoided any mention of Article 20(2) ICCPR, it did find that Faurisson's statements 'were of a nature as to raise or strengthen anti-semitic feelings', which could be construed as incitement to discrimination.[93] Furthermore, the Committee accepted France's argument that Holocaust denial fuels and serves 'as the principal vehicle

---

with eight (instead of maximally five) years' imprisonment. See also Art. 370 of the Criminal Code of Montenegro 2004, Art. 134 of the Criminal Code of Serbia and Art. 67 of the Criminal Code of Ukraine 2001.

[88] Human Rights Committee, *General Comment 34*, para. 50: 'a limitation that is justified on the basis of article 20 must also comply with article 19, paragraph 3.' First held in *Malcolm Ross* v. *Canada*, para. 10.6.

[89] *Malcolm Ross* v. *Canada*, para. 11.5.

[90] In this case there was some proof that his incitement was actually successful in causing incidents of discrimination against Jewish pupils, making substantiation of 'incitement' relatively straightforward (*Malcolm Ross* v. *Canada*, paras. 4.3 and 11.6). For the judicial art of weighing content and context factors so as to determine whether an advocator of hatred has committed incitement, see Chapter 10.

[91] Individual opinion by Elizabeth Evatt and David Kretzmer, co-signed by Eckart Klein, para. 4. See also the individual opinions by Cecilia Medina Quiroga (concurring), Rajsoomer Lallah (concurring) and Prafullachandra Bhagwati (concurring).

[92] *Robert Faurisson* v. *France*, paras. 7.5–7.7. Denied by Faurisson, para. 8.3.

[93] *Robert Faurisson* v. *France*, para. 9.6.

for anti-semitism'.[94] Thus it was accepted that such denial incites discrim-ination. A number of individual Committee members concurred with the plenary Committee's finding of no violation, yet they criticized the national law (Gayssot Act) that provided the basis for restrictions on extreme speech. The concerns expressed imply, *a contrario*, that national extreme speech lim-itations must link criminal liability directly to a speech act's risk of inciting discrimination, hostility or violence.[95] Consequently, these individual mem-bers were proponents of a 'likelihood'-oriented definition of incitement.

In *Maria Vassilari et al.* v. *Greece* the Committee – without much in the way of argumentation – rejected the claim that a letter to the editor con-taining anti-Roma sentiments amounted to 'incitement' in the meaning of the Covenant.[96] More accurately, according to the Committee the authors of that communication had, for the purposes of admissibility, 'insufficiently substantiated the facts' in relation to Article 20(2).[97] This conclusion is quite questionable in the lights of the facts. The letter, composed by the representa-tives of local associations, accused the Gypsies of a local Roma settlement of a number of crimes and called for their 'eviction', failing which these Roma people were to be threatened with 'militant action'.[98] Accordingly, this is a case of prima facie 'incitement' if ever there was one, certainly sufficient to engage Article 20(2) and discuss the case on the merits of the complaint.[99] The Committee was clearly hesitant to apply Article 20(2) and in fact bluntly stated that it refused to determine 'whether article 20 may be invoked under the Optional Protocol'.[100] This unwillingness to pronounce on the previ-ously discussed question of whether there exists an invocable 'right to be protected against incitement' seems to have clouded the Committee's judgment on admissibility. While the State party and the applicants disa-greed on the exact language used in the impugned letter, the latter seems to have been of a nature as to engage the Convention's incitement clause. Greece argued that the accurate translation of the crucial terms in the letter were not 'eviction' and 'militant action' but rather 'removal' and 'dynamic

---

[94] *Robert Faurisson* v. *France*, paras. 7.2–7.6 (France) and 9.7 (Committee).

[95] Individual opinion by Elizabeth Evatt and David Kretzmer, co-signed by Eckart Klein (concurring), para. 9. Similarly, Individual opinion by Rajsoomer Lallah (concurring), para. 6.

[96] *Maria Vassilari et al.* v. *Greece*, Communication no. 1570/2007 (19 March 2009).

[97] *Maria Vassilari et al.* v. *Greece*, para. 6.5.

[98] *Maria Vassilari et al.* v. *Greece*, para. 2.1.

[99] See also Individual opinion of Committee member Mr Abdelfattah Amor (dissent-ing). Two members associate themselves with Amor's views. See Individual opinion of Committee members Mr Ahmad Amin Fathalla and Mr Bouzid Lazhari.

[100] *Maria Vassilari et al.* v. *Greece*, para. 6.5.

mobilizations'.[101] A threat of 'dynamic mobilizations' against one's person or one's home or settlement does not sound too good, either, so even if true, the facts of the case provided more than enough material for the Committee to look at. Consequently, in *Maria Vassilari et al.* v. *Greece* the Committee missed out on an excellent opportunity to pronounce on the *actus reus* of 'incitement' within the meaning of the Covenant. In addition, the case provided an opportunity to elaborate on contextual questions such as the vulnerability of the target group.[102]

While 'incitement' is by definition relational – successful incitement involves a triangle of the inciter, the audience and acts committed by the latter against a target group – and hence hinges strongly on context, the content of the speech act per se remains tremendously important when it comes to assessing incidents of alleged incitement. The content of the speech provides us with the first prima facie answers as to whether the extreme level of incitement within the meaning of Article 20(2) is reached. As the Rabat Plan of Action formulates it, the:

> content of the speech constitutes one of the key *foci* of the court's deliberations and is a critical element of incitement. Content analysis may include the degree to which the speech was provocative and direct, as well as a focus on the form, style, nature of the arguments deployed in the speech at issue or in the balance struck between arguments deployed, etc.[103]

Thus, an assessment of the speech act's content may unveil a case of 'express incitement', that is extreme speech using 'fighting words', potentially going as far as directly calling for acts of violence or discrimination.[104] In addition, the assessment of the content may very well establish that a specific group, characterized by religion or other traits, was especially targeted.[105] Further, the speech act as such may reveal the use of dehumanizing or stereotyping language.[106] Accordingly, the intentions of the person carrying out the speech act may under circumstances be wholly or partly distilled from the content of the speech act.[107] Furthermore, the speech act's *tone* is strongly linked to its content. 'Tone' refers to the intensity of the statements made, and to underlying or motivating feelings of opprobrium, enmity and

---

[101] *Maria Vassilari et al.* v. *Greece*, para. 4.3.
[102] This argument is extended in section 10.3 of Chapter 10.
[103] *Rabat Plan of Action*, para. 22.
[104] ARTICLE 19, *Incitement Policy Brief*, at 34.
[105] ARTICLE 19, *Incitement Policy Brief*, at 34.
[106] ARTICLE 19, *Incitement Policy Brief*, at 34.
[107] Further on intent, see Chapter 9.

detestation on the part of the speaker.[108] While the question of the extent of the speech act (how far was it disseminated?) is a contextual question, the speech act's *form* is closely linked to its content. The form of the speech act – ranging from a rally speech, to artistic expression, to academic contributions, to religious preaching, and so on – could reveal something about the speaker's (lack of) intent to incite.[109]

7.3.5   Proscribed results: 'discrimination', 'hostility' or 'violence'

Article 20(2) ICCPR orders State parties to adopt incitement laws, not to ban hatred for the sake of banning hatred. That is, Article 20(2) wishes to outlaw advocacy of hatred if and only if such advocacy incites what Robert Post calls 'contingent harm' and 'measurable harm'.[110] The contingent harms listed by the ICCPR are narrower than the ones listed by the ICERD.[111] Yet the incitement offence of the ICCPR is in this respect broader than, for instance, the American Convention on Human Rights ('hatred that constitutes incitements to lawless violence').[112]

---

[108]   ARTICLE 19, *Incitement Policy Brief,* at 34, engaging with the 'how it was said' factor as follows: 'The degree to which the speech was provocative and direct – without including mitigating material and without drawing a clear distinction between the opinion expressed and the taking of action based on that opinion – should also be considered in this test. Courts should also examine whether the expression contained "something that is positively stimulatory of that reaction in others" and whether it was capable of stirring them towards the illegal action. The degree to which the speech was provocative and direct may also be relevant in this test. Courts should also examine whether "the speech contains phrases, words, or coded language that has taken on a special loaded meaning, in the understanding of the speaker and audience".'

[109]   For intent, see Chapter 9.

[110]   Robert Post, 'Hate Speech', in Ivan Hare and James Weinstein (eds.), *Extreme Speech and Democracy* (Oxford University Press, 2009), 123–38, at 127 and 133–5.

[111]   CERD, *General Recommendation 35,* para. 10, lists a number of offences that must be punished by law, including 'dissemination of ideas based on racial or ethnic superiority or hatred', 'incitement to hatred, contempt or discrimination against members of a group on grounds of their race, colour, descent, or national or ethnic origin', 'threats or incitement to violence against persons or groups', and 'expression of insults, ridicule or slander of persons or groups or justification of hatred, contempt or discrimination when it clearly amounts to incitement to hatred or discrimination'. See also Mendel, *Study on Incitement,* at 18–19.

[112]   Art. 13(5) of the American Convention on Human Rights. However, this provision goes on to refer to 'any other similar action against any person or group of persons', which leaves it more open-ended. The 'incitements to lawless violence' specification resonates well with the US Supreme Court's 'imminent lawless action' test adopted in *Brandenburg* v. *Ohio,* 395 U.S. 444 (1969). The latter was pronounced months before the adoption of the American Convention. See also Elizabeth Defeis, 'Freedom of Speech and International Norms: A Response to Hate Speech' (1992) 29 *Stanford Journal of International Law* 57–130, at 112.

In our discussion of the drafting history pertaining to Article 20(2) we have seen how some of the drafters wanted to narrow down the proscribed results – typically so as to exclusively include 'violence'[113] – while others sought to broaden them (e.g. so as to include 'racial exclusiveness').[114] Both those very broad as well as very narrow proposals were ultimately rejected in favour of the 'discrimination, hostility or violence' formula.

Thus the ICCPR's proscribed results are 'discrimination', 'hostility' or 'violence'. The Covenant is unclear as to whether the speech act must concretely incite to a specific proscribed result or if it is enough for the speech act to generally fall within the category of 'discrimination, hostility or violence'.[115]

The term 'discrimination' has direct counterparts in the Covenant. This proscribed result, therefore, presumably resonates with the equality and non-discrimination provisions of Articles 2 and 26 of the ICCPR and with the Committee's General Comment No. 18 on Non-Discrimination.[116] From those benchmarks we know that a distinction based on one of the 'suspect grounds' – such as race, colour, sex, language, religion, political or other opinion, national or social origin, property or birth – amounts to 'discrimination' unless the criteria for such differentiation are 'reasonable' and 'objective'.[117]

Mainstreaming several UN human rights treaties, ARTICLE 19 has come up with the most extensive definition of 'discrimination', formulating it (for the purposes of Article 20 ICCPR) as:

> any distinction, exclusion, restriction or preference based on race, gender, ethnicity, religion or belief, disability, age, sexual orientation, language political or other opinion, national or social origin, nationality, property, birth or other status, colour which has the purpose or effect of nullifying or impairing the recognition, enjoyment or exercise, on an equal footing, of human rights and fundamental freedoms in the political, economic, social, cultural or any other field of public life.[118]

---

[113] E.g. A/C.3/L.932.   [114] E.g. E/CN.4/SR.377.

[115] See Agnes Callamard, 'Combating Discrimination and Intolerance with a Free Speech Framework' (2010) 5 *Religion & Human Rights* 153–69, at 161; Sejar Parmar, 'How Human Rights Treaties Draw Borders between Freedom of Speech and Discrimination' (presentation at Media in the Media conference, London 28–29 March 2008).

[116] Human Rights Committee, *General Comment 18: Non-discrimination* (Thirty-seventh session, 1989).

[117] Human Rights Committee, *General Comment 18*, para. 13.

[118] ARTICLE 19, *Incitement Policy Brief*, at 19 (cf. ARTICLE 19, *Interpretation of Article 20 of the ICCPR*, at 7). See also UN Special Rapporteur on Freedom of Expression, *Report on Hate Speech and Incitement*, para. 45(d) for a similar definition.

In relation to 'religious discrimination' specifically, the 1981 UN Religious Tolerance Declaration contains concrete definitions.[119] According to this instrument, religious discrimination 'means any distinction, exclusion, restriction or preference based on religion or belief and having as its purpose or as its effect nullification or impairment of the recognition, enjoyment or exercise of human rights and fundamental freedoms on an equal basis'.[120]

'Hostility' and 'violence' do not have clear counterparts in the Covenant. The Human Rights Committee has not yet offered working definitions. The Camden Principles offer one and the same definition for 'hostility' and 'hatred'.[121] This defeats the purpose of the qualified nature of Article 20(2) ICCPR. 'Incitement to hostility', in that case, would be reached if the speech act's audience were merely to copy the inciter's 'hatred'. In other words, Article 20(2) would then ban the spreading of hatred per se and not be concerned with contingent harm being done to the target group. We must reject that reading for offering too low a threshold. The Covenant's incitement clause is not concerned with hatred per se, but with adverse actions flowing from hatred. It is not concerned with a state of mind, but with the tangible repercussions of the poisoned mind.

In 2012 ARTICLE 19 offered a revision of the Camden Principles on this point. In its Policy Brief on incitement it argued that 'hostility' can be defined as the 'manifestation of hatred'.[122] It also contended that hostility implies 'action'.[123] Since the difference between 'hostile action' and 'violence' appears to be but a matter of scale, this shift in terminology can be seen as an attempt to upgrade 'hostility' to 'violence'.

This upgrade makes sense. 'Hostility' is a problematic term. If (violent) actions are not read into this notion, the risk is that the Covenant's incitement clause will be abused to combat 'hate speech' or even 'hatred' or hateful states of mind per se;[124] in other words the term 'hostility' forms State parties' best excuse to prohibit 'hate speech' rather than qualified incitement. The UN Special Rapporteur on freedom of expression has,

---

[119]   Declaration on the Elimination of All Forms of Intolerance and of Discrimination Based on Religion or Belief, GA Resolution 36/55, adopted on 25 November 1981 (hereafter UN Religious Tolerance Declaration).

[120]   UN Religious Tolerance Declaration, Art. 2.

[121]   Camden Principles, Art. 12.1(i) ('intense and irrational emotions of opprobrium, enmity and detestation towards the target group').

[122]   ARTICLE 19, Incitement Policy Brief, at 19. Previously indicated in its Interpretation of Article 20 of the ICCPR.

[123]   ARTICLE 19, Incitement Policy Brief, at 19.

[124]   See Mendel, Study on Incitement, at 28.

however, confirmed that 'hostility' requires more than a state of mind. It requires a 'manifestation of hatred' in the form of actual harmful acts.[125]

Adapting a definition used by the World Health Organization, ARTICLE 19 defines 'violence' as 'as the intentional use of physical force or power against another person, or against a group or community that either results in or has a high likelihood of resulting in injury, death, psychological harm, maldevelopment, or deprivation'.[126]

The word 'or' in 'discrimination, hostility or violence' makes it quite clear that Article 20(2) is engaged when a speech act incites at a minimum to one of these adverse reactions. One draft of General Comment No. 34 spelled this out: 'It would be sufficient that the incitement relate to any of the three outcomes: discrimination, hostility or violence.'[127]

However, from the perspective of free speech it would have been quite preferable if the incitement clause had used 'and' instead of 'or'. As was observed above, 'hostility' specifically lacks specificity.[128] Proposals to use 'and' instead of 'or'[129] were, however, rejected – the cumulative effect thereof was apparently considered too high a threshold by some of the drafters and despite the scale differences, it was felt that 'incitement to hostility' and 'incitement to discrimination' deserved combating as much as 'incitement to violence' does.[130]

The latter notwithstanding, perhaps it would still have been better if the Covenant had included only 'violence' as the proscribed result. While both discrimination and violence are worth combating, the inherent imbalance between proscribed results remains problematic. Specifically, the respective *thresholds* – 'incitement to violence' versus 'incitement to hostility' and to 'discrimination' – quite simply cannot be compared. The seemingly lower thresholds required under 'incitement to discrimination' and 'incitement to hostility' largely remove the qualified nature of Article 20(2). For instance, as Nowak observes, is it even possible to advocate hatred without at least inciting to discrimination?[131]

---

[125] UN Special Rapporteur on Freedom of Expression, *Report on Hate Speech and Incitement*, para. 45(e).

[126] ARTICLE 19, *Incitement Policy Brief*, at 19 (cf. ARTICLE 19, *Interpretation of Article 20 of the ICCPR*, at 7). See also UN Special Rapporteur on Freedom of Expression, *Report on Hate Speech and Incitement*, para. 45(f).

[127] Draft General Comment No. 34, para. 53.

[128] See also Mendel, *Study on Incitement*, at 15.

[129] E/2447, at p. 9 (Chilean proposal).

[130] See section 3.2.2.4 of Chapter 3.

[131] Nowak, *CCPR Commentary*, at 475.

Thus, while it remains true that the Covenant does not ban advocacy of hatred but advocacy of hatred *that incites*, the latter qualification is at the same time undermined by the inserted low-threshold notions of 'hostility' and 'discrimination'. It is in that particular context that we must appreciate attempts to upgrade 'hostility' to the same level as 'violence'.[132] While potentially having the same effect, it would appear that this is a more viable exercise than upgrading Article 20's 'or' to 'and' – both a textual as well as a historical analysis clearly resists such a reading. In relation to 'incitement to discrimination' similar upgrades have been proposed. For instance, an additional test could be that 'incitement to discrimination' may only be penalized in cases where it is proven that lesser interfering measures would fail to secure the equality rights of the target group.[133] These kinds of additional tests would appear to touch upon the necessity of the interference and hence on the need to make an additional contextual assessment of the impugned speech act in addition to a content-based assessment.[134]

Other stakeholders have set the tone by simply ignoring in particular the proscribed outcome of 'hostility'.[135] The Human Rights Committee probably cannot circumvent the matter indefinitely. To ensure that the incitement clause's overly inclusive list of proscribed results is not abused by State parties, it would be best if the Committee seeks to ensure in all its anti-incitement workings a nexus with 'violence' as the principal proscribed result.

---

[132] As discussed above. See e.g. ARTICLE 19, *Incitement Policy Brief,* at 19.

[133] Nazila Ghanea, 'Expression and Hate Speech in the ICCPR: Compatible or Clashing' (2010) 5 *Religion & Human Rights* 171–90, at 175; and Robert Post, 'Religion and Freedom of Speech: Portraits of Muhammad' (2007) 14 *Constellations* 72–90, at 83, discussing European examples.

[134] We will return to this matter in Chapter 10.

[135] *Report of the Special Rapporteur on Freedom of Religion or Belief, Asma Jahangir, and the Special Rapporteur on Contemporary Forms of Racism, Racial Discrimination, Xenophobia and Related Intolerance, Doudou Diène, Further to Human Rights Council Decision 1/107 on Incitement to Racial and Religious Hatred and the Promotion of Tolerance* (UN Doc. A/HRC/2/3, 20 September 2006), para. 47: 'article 20 of the Covenant was drafted against the historical background of the horrors committed by the Nazi regime during the Second World War. The threshold of the acts that are referred to in article 20 is relatively high because they have to constitute advocacy of national, racial or religious hatred. Accordingly, the Special Rapporteur is of the opinion that expressions should only be prohibited under article 20 if they constitute incitement to *imminent acts of violence or discrimination* against a specific individual or group' (emphasis added).

7.4   Concluding remarks

The offence contained in Article 20(2) ICCPR goes beyond the relationship between an offender and an offended person or group. Article 20(2) is, crucially, premised on a triangular relationship between inciter, audience and target group. Thus Article 20(2) also goes beyond concerns about the direct harm extreme speech may cause to the target group – its prime concern lies in the harm a third party, the extreme speech's audience, may do to that group.

Accordingly, for Article 20(2) to be engaged we need the following. First, we need an inciter publicly addressing an audience. Second, content-wise the speech act must target a group on the basis of its religious (or racial or national) characteristics. Third, the speech act must constitute incitement, that is it must incite the audience to commit acts of (discrimination, hostility or) violence against the target group. For the speech act to amount to 'incitement' within the meaning of Article 20(2) a criterion of 'likelihood' must be satisfied. Accordingly, whether or not a speech act amounts to punishable incitement, and whether or not it can be said that it was necessary for the state to interfere with free speech using extreme speech restrictions, partly depends on *context*. We will return to this issue in Part IV of this book (see particularly Chapter 10).

8

National incitement law checklist

8.1 Introduction

Laws that do not strictly accord with Article 20(2) may lead to abuse. Such laws could stifle speech that ought to be protected, not combated, under international law. National incitement laws that do not neatly follow the gist of Article 20(2) ICCPR are likely to fall short, in and for themselves, of the Covenant's aims.[1] Having established the *actus reus* of the offence of 'advocacy of religious hatred that constitutes incitement to discrimination, hostility or violence', it follows that there are numerous ways in which State parties can miss the mark when it comes to adopting domestic legislation aimed at enshrining Article 20(2)'s offence in national law. Those inherent shortcomings are in addition to State practices of implementation that are at odds with international standards. Thus, while in the next part of this book we will delve into additional implementation, judicial and evidentiary issues surrounding the question of how to 'judge' incitement in concrete cases, here we concern ourselves for the time being purely with the 'law of incitement'.

8.2 Low-threshold speech offences

From the previous chapter it follows that Article 20(2) ICCPR is formulated in a rather qualified way: if corresponding national laws are not so formulated, such shortcomings are inevitable. The fact that the religious hateful incitement offence as embodied by international law deals with a

---

[1] See, however, Human Rights Committee, *Robert Faurisson* v. *France*, Communication no. 550/1993 (19 July 1995), finding no violation of freedom of speech despite having major reservations about France's Gayssot Act 1990. According to the Committee, judges may apparently be in a position to remedy inherent legal shortcomings of extreme speech laws. As we cannot safely assume that judges are always willing or able to mitigate the effects of bad laws, it remains valuable to make an inventory of legislative dos and don'ts.

triangular relationship implies that dissimilar 'extreme speech' offences are not to be combated under this heading.

8.2.1   No blasphemy, religious defamation or religious insult laws

One tremendously important ramification of the triangle of incitement is that blasphemy and many other forms of unqualified 'religious insult' offences do not come within the ambit of Article 20(2). Such speech acts may make the target group itself hostile towards the speaker, but that is not a scenario that the incitement clause looks to. This provision – and indeed international law generally – does not seek to protect religions or to accommodate religious sensitivities. The incitement clause is concerned with the question whether an audience is provoked to commit acts of discrimination, hostility or violence against a target group – incidents of blasphemy, defamation or religious insult fall way short of that threshold.

Proponents of blasphemy bans may argue that the fact that Article 20(2) ICCPR does not prescribe religious insult laws may mean that such restrictions could be justified under the regular exceptions to freedom of speech. However, since 2011 we can actually rule out that possibility. The Human Rights Committee has firmly postulated that the flip-side of the high-threshold offence flowing from Article 20(2) must be that low-threshold '[p]rohibitions of displays of lack of respect for a religion or other belief system, including blasphemy laws, are incompatible with the Covenant'.[2]

Unfortunately, such laws remain virtually universal practice in non-Western jurisdictions.[3] While some of those provisions are dead letters and occasionally even declared unconstitutional, some Western states also retain blasphemy as a criminal offence on their statutes.[4] Rather

---

[2] Human Rights Committee, *General Comment 34: Article 19: Freedoms of Opinion and Expression* (CCPR/C/GC/34, adopted 102nd Session, Geneva, 11–29 July 2011), para. 48.

[3] Paul Marshall and Nina Shea, *Silenced: How Apostasy & Blasphemy Codes are Choking Freedom Worldwide* (Oxford University Press, 2011).

[4] E.g. Section 115 of the Criminal Code of Austria 1974; Sections 138, 141 and 142 of the Criminal Code of Cyprus 1929; Section 140 of the Criminal Code of Denmark 2009 (Consolidated Act No. 1034 of 29 October 2009); Articles 198–199 of the Criminal Code of Greece 1950; Art. 36 of the Blasphemy Act 2009, Bill No. 43/2006, entry into force in July 2009 [Ireland]. Some states prohibit such offences as 'insulting religions' or 'insulting religious groups'. See e.g. Section 166 Criminal Code of Germany 1998; Art. 125 of the General Criminal Code of Iceland 1940; Section 173 of the Criminal Code of Israel 1996; Section 188 of the Criminal Code of Liechtenstein 1998; Art. 444 of the Criminal

unhelpfully, the European Court of Human Rights has sanctioned religious insult restrictions.[5] There are some indications that the Strasbourg Court is in the process of revisiting its problematic jurisprudence on blasphemy and 'gratuitously offensive' speech.[6] This judicial trend may guide European states to annul these free speech limitations.[7]

At the international level further momentum against blasphemy and religious defamation laws is mounting. Notably, the Rabat Plan of Action, which aims at conceptualizing Article 20(2) ICCPR, dismisses those laws as counter-productive and antithetical to international human rights.[8] The UN Special Rapporteur on freedom of religion and belief has made

Code of Luxembourg 2010 (inserted as per Act of 19 July 1997); Art. 238 of the Criminal Code of Monaco 1968 (several religious defamation offences are furthermore codified by the Freedom of Public Expression Act, No. 1.299 of 15 July 2005 [Monaco]); Art. 142 of the Criminal Code of Norway 1902; Art. 257 of the Criminal Code of Poland 1997; Arts. 251–252 of the Criminal Code of Portugal 2006 (Law No. 65/98 of 2 September 1998); Art. 260 of the Criminal Code of San Marino 1974; Art. 423 of the New Criminal Code of Slovakia 2005; Art. 525 of the Criminal Code of Spain 1996; Art. 261 of the Criminal Code of Switzerland 1937; and Arts. 125 and 216(3) of the New Criminal Code of Turkey 2004.

5 E.g. European Commission of Human Rights, *X. Ltd. and Y.* v. *United Kingdom*, Application no. 8710/79 (7 May 1982); European Court of Human Rights, *Otto-Preminger-Institut* v. *Austria*, Application no. 13470/87 (20 September 1994); *Wingrove* v. *United Kingdom*, Application no. 17419/90 (25 November 1996); *Murphy* v. *Ireland*, Application no. 44179/98 (10 July 2003); *İ.A.* v. *Turkey*, Application no. 42571/98 (13 September 2005). For a critical evaluation of these cases, see Jeroen Temperman, 'Blasphemy, Defamation of Religions and Human Rights Law' (2008) 26:4 *Netherlands Quarterly of Human Rights* 517–45. See also Ian Cram, 'The Danish Cartoons, Offensive Expression and Democratic Legitimacy', in Ivan Hare and James Weinstein (eds.), *Extreme Speech and Democracy* (Oxford University Press, 2009), 311–30.

6 E.g. European Court of Human Rights, *Klein* v. *Slovakia*, Application no. 72208/01 (31 October 2006); *Aydın Tatlav* v. *Turkey*, Application no. 50692/99 (2 May 2006); and *Nur Radyo Ve Televizyon Yayinciligi A.S.* v. *Turkey*, Application no. 6587/03 (27 November 2007). See also, *mutatis mutandis*, *Vereinigung Bildender Künstler* v. *Austria*, Application no. 68354/01 (25 January 2007).

7 Note that political bodies of the Council of Europe advise the abolition of blasphemy offences. See e.g. Parliamentary Assembly Resolution 1510 (2006) on 'Freedom of expression and respect for religious beliefs' (adopted during Assembly debate on 28 June 2006, 19th Sitting); and Parliamentary Assembly Recommendation 1805 (2007) on 'Blasphemy, religious insults and hate speech against persons on grounds of their religion' (adopted on 29 June 2007, 27th Sitting). A Venice Commission study, commissioned by the Parliamentary Assembly, further urges Council of Europe members to repeal blasphemy laws. See Venice Commission Study 406/2006 on 'Blasphemy, Religious Insults and Incitement to Religious Hatred' (adopted at the Commission's 70th Plenary Session, 16–17 March 2007), para. 89(c). This latter study is included in Venice Commission, *Science and Technique of Democracy, No. 47: Blasphemy, Insult and Hatred – Finding Answers in a Democratic Society* (Strasbourg: Council of Europe Publishing, 2010).

8 *Rabat Plan of Action on the Prohibition of Advocacy of National, Racial or Religious Hatred that Constitutes Incitement to Discrimination, Hostility or Violence* (Conclusions and

similar interventions.[9] At the regional level, too, benchmarking against blasphemy and religious defamation laws is ongoing. For instance, the recently adopted *EU Guidelines on the Promotion and Protection of Freedom of Religion or Belief* take a firm position against blasphemy laws.[10] The guidelines prescribe that the EU will 'at all appropriate occasions' advocate the position 'that laws that criminalize blasphemy restrict expression concerning religious or other beliefs; that they are often applied so as to persecute, mistreat, or intimidate persons belonging to religious or other minorities, and that they can have a serious inhibiting effect on freedom of expression and on freedom of religion or belief; and recommend the decriminalisation of such offences'.[11] This is an admirable cause, yet what is problematic in terms of public diplomacy is that a number of EU States themselves still have blasphemy restrictions in place.

8.2.2   No 'hate speech' or 'incitement to hatred' laws

Article 20(2) of the ICCPR is not concerned with the direct harm that may stem from 'hate speech'. The qualified nature of this provision – 'hatred that constitutes incitement' – ensures that the Covenant is focused on contingent harm emanating from extreme speech, that is harm done by an audience, having been stirred up by the inciter, to a target group that is characterized by its religion (or other traits). An early draft of General Comment No. 34 stated that there are 'many forms of "hate speech" that, although a matter of concern, do not meet the level of seriousness set out in article 20.'[12]

Accordingly, it is clear that Article 20(2) of the ICCPR does not impose 'hate speech laws'.[13] Again some may argue that this does not necessarily mean that the Covenant, especially Article 19(3), does not condone such

---

recommendations emanating from the four regional expert workshops organized by OHCHR in 2011 and adopted by experts in Rabat, Morocco on 5 October 2012), para. 17.

[9] *Report of the Special Rapporteur on Freedom of Religion or Belief, Asma Jahangir, and the Special Rapporteur on Contemporary Forms of Racism, Racial Discrimination, Xenophobia and Related Intolerance, Doudou Diène, Further to Human Rights Council Decision 1/107 on Incitement to Racial and Religious Hatred and the Promotion of Tolerance* (UN Doc. A/HRC/2/3, 20 September 2006), paras. 36–42.

[10] *EU Guidelines on the Promotion and Protection of Freedom of Religion or Belief* (adopted by the Foreign Affairs Council meeting, Luxembourg, 24 June 2013) (hereafter *EU Guidelines*).

[11] *EU Guidelines*, para. 32.

[12] Draft General Comment No. 34: Article 19 (2nd Revised Draft, CCPR/C/GC/34/CRP.3, 28 June 2010), para. 54.

[13] Note that even the otherwise carefully crafted Camden Principles make this error. See ARTICLE 19, *Camden Principles on Freedom of Expression and Equality* (2009), Principle 12, referring to 'incitement to hatred'.

restrictions, and that there would be a grey area of extreme speech not quite covered by the obligatory prohibitions flowing from Article 20(2) but nonetheless justifiable by reference to the regular grounds of restricting free speech. It is submitted that this reading is contrary to the object and purpose of the Covenant, notably its emphasis on robust free speech protection.[14] All hate speech may harm and hurt. All hate speech may incite further hatred. Yet there is a reason why the drafters of the Covenant went at great pains to come up with the qualified incitement formula: 'incitement' allows the judiciary to focus on contingent harm and hence on objective threats to the target group's rights. Early drafting proposals of Article 20(2) still spoke in terms of 'incitement to hatred'.[15] Yet offences of that type were rejected in favour of the qualified formula of 'advocacy of hatred that constitutes incitement' to concrete forms of contingent harm (namely discrimination, hostility or violence). 'Hate speech', 'incitement to hatred' and other extreme speech offences – not unlike 'blasphemy' and religious defamation offences in that respect – are overly preoccupied with the subjective (religious) feelings of the target group. Such offences lack legal specificity and cannot be enforced by state authorities without venturing into such doctrinal debates as to 'what constitutes a religious belief worth protection from offensive language' and 'what constitutes a punishable offence to that religion or its adherents'.

In support of the view that speech acts that do not reach the level of gravity of Article 20(2) cannot be legitimately restricted under Article 19 is the fact that the Human Rights Committee is busy erasing the said 'grey area'. Thus the Human Rights Committee has, as observed, taken an active stance against 'religious insult' restrictions,[16] but also for instance against 'memory laws', including laws that penalize the denial of the Holocaust.[17]

Unfortunately, numerous State parties to the ICCPR have adopted laws that do not neatly follow Article 20(2)'s structure. Rather than banning those forms of religious hate advocacy that constitute incitement

---

[14] See Toby Mendel, 'Does International Law Provide for Consistent Rules on Hate Speech?', in Michael Herz and Peter Molnar (eds.), *The Content and Context of Hate Speech: Rethinking Regulation and Responses* (Cambridge University Press, 2012), 417–29, at 420, arguing that the mandatory prohibitions under Art. 20(2) 'are extremely close to the permissions of 19(3), leaving little scope for restrictions on freedom of expression over and beyond the terms of Article 20(2)'. He bases this conclusion on the fact that the drafters of Art. 20(2) rejected both such overly broad proscribed results as 'racial inclusiveness' as well as an exclusive focus on incitement to 'violence'.

[15] See e.g. the 1953 proposal in E/CN.4/SR.379, at 13 ('incitement to hatred').

[16] HRC, *General Comment 34*, para. 48.

[17] HRC, *General Comment 34*, para. 49. On Holocaust denial, see further Chapter 11.

to contingent harms they have opted for banning 'incitement to hatred' per se.[18] Only in some cases has this shortcoming been repaired by the judiciary.[19]

[18] See e.g. Art. 265 of the Criminal Code of the Republic of Albania (Law No. 7895, 27 January 1995, consolidated version as of 1 December 2004); Art. 226(1) of the Criminal Code of Armenia (entry into force 1 August 2003); Art. 283 of the Criminal Code of Azerbaijan 2000 (see also Art. 1(2) of the Law on Freedom of Religious Faith 1992 [Azerbaijan] and Art. 10 of the Law on Means of Mass Media 1999 [Azerbaijan]); Art. 130 of the Criminal Code of Belarus (of 9 July 1999, amended 20 July 2007); Art. 20 of the Law of 30 July 1981 Criminalizing Certain Acts Inspired by Racism or Xenophobia (implementing ICERD) [Belgium]; Art. 281 quarter of the Criminal Code of Bolivia 1972; Art. 150 of the Criminal Code of the Federation of Bosnia and Herzegovina 1998 (also criticized by ECRI in its 2004 *Report on Bosnia and Herzegovina* (CRI(2005)2, paras. 10–12; see also Art. 390 Criminal Code of Republika Srpska 2003 and Art. 160 of the Criminal Code of Brcko District 2004 [Bosnia and Herzegovina]); Art. 164 of the Criminal Code of Bulgaria 1968 (amended in 2009); Art. 31 of Law No. 19.733 on Freedom of Opinion and Information and Journalism 2001 [Chile]; Art. 174(3) of the Criminal Code of Croatia 1997 (amended 1 October 2004) and Art. 39 of the Constitution of Croatia 1990 (amended 28 March 2001); Art. 356 of the New Criminal Code (40/2009) of the Czech Republic; Art. 12 of the Constitution of Estonia 2000 and Art. 151 of the Criminal Code of Estonia 2000; Art. R6257 of the Criminal Code of France 1992; Section 130 of the Criminal Code of Germany 1998; Art. 233a of the General Criminal Code of Iceland 1940; Section 2 of the Prohibition of Incitement to Hatred Act 1989 [Ireland]; Section 299 of the Criminal Code of Kyrgyzstan 1997; Sections 78 and 150 of the Criminal Code of Latvia 1998; Section 283 of the Criminal Code of Liechtenstein 1998; Art. 170 of the Criminal Code of Lithuania 2000; Art. 457-1 (and 454–455) of the Criminal Code of Luxembourg 2010 (inserted as per Act of 19 July 1997); Art. 82A.1 of the Criminal Code of Malta 1854 (amended 2014) (it should be noted that Malta made a reservation to Art. 20 ICCPR); Art. 9(xxvii) of the Federal law to Prevent and Eliminate Discrimination 2003 [Mexico]; Art. 346 of the Criminal Code of Moldova 2002 (see also Art. 4 of the Press Act 1994 [Moldova]); Section 16 of the Freedom of Public Expression Act, No. 1.299 of 15 July 2005 [Monaco]; Art. 43 of the Constitution of Montenegro 2007 and Art. 370 of the Criminal Code of Montenegro 2004; Art. 137d of the Criminal Code of the Netherlands 1881; Art. 135a of the Criminal Code of Norway 1902; Art. 256 of the Criminal Code of Poland 1997; Art. 30 of the Constitution of Romania 1991 and Art. 317 of the Criminal Code of Romania 2009; Art. 29 of the Constitution of the Russian Federation 1993 and Art. 282 of the Criminal Code of the Russian Federation 1996 (amended 2006); Art. 43 of the Constitution of Serbia 2006 and Art. 317 of the Criminal Code of Serbia 2005; Art. 424 of the New Criminal Code of Slovakia 2005; Art. 510 of the Criminal Code of Spain 1996; Chapter 16, Section 8 of the Criminal Code of Sweden 1962; Art. 261A of the Criminal Code of Switzerland 1937; Art. 3(iii) of the Sedition Act 1920 [Trinidad and Tobago]; Art. 161 of the Criminal Code of Ukraine 2001; and Art. 149 of the Criminal Code of Uruguay 1933. Note that occasionally 'incitement to hatred' is codified alongside incitement to one or more prescribed results as mentioned by the Covenant.

[19] For instance, in the case of Hungary (2012). Art. 332 of the Criminal Code of Hungary 2012 prohibits incitement to hatred against a religious group. The Hungarian judiciary has read into this prohibition a robust 'clear and present danger' test, turning the prohibition into a high-threshold incitement offence. See further section 10.6 of Chapter 10.

Accordingly, in those jurisdictions incidents of 'hate speech' clearly falling short of the ICCPR formula are liable to trigger domestic prosecutions and interfere with free speech. Far too many domestic extreme speech laws are not premised on measurable contingent harm, but on what Robert Post calls a 'bad tendency test'.[20] Whenever such 'hate speech' *tends* to have adverse results on the target group, it is considered justified to combat that speech. Incitement laws in the meaning of the Covenant, however, are premised on the need to establish a likelihood that harm will be done to the target group by the audience of the extreme speech.[21]

Good practice examples exist, but are quite rare. The incitement prohibition enshrined in the Constitution of South Africa speaks of 'incitement of imminent violence' and 'advocacy of hatred that is based on ... religion, and that constitutes incitement to cause harm'.[22] Although the 'harm' is not specified,[23] this qualified formulation is not far removed from Article 20(2) ICCPR. Italian criminal law speaks of 'incitement to commit acts of discrimination' and 'incitement to commit acts of violence', neatly following Article 20(2) ICCPR yet – perhaps sensibly[24] – avoiding incitement to 'hostility'.[25] In Brazil and Nicaragua the advocacy of hatred offence is inextricably linked with incitement to discrimination, thus expressly linking the advocacy of hatred offence to one of the proscribed results mentioned by Article 20 of the ICCPR.[26] In Peru, to give another example, incitement on religious grounds must, in order to be punishable, be made with a view towards nullifying the rights of others.[27] Since only incitement to violence or discrimination can arguably

---

[20] Robert Post, 'Hate Speech', in Hare and Weinstein (eds.), *Extreme Speech and Democracy*, 123–38, at 134.

[21] On how to evaluate and judge such 'likelihood', see Chapter 10.

[22] Art. 16, para. 2 of the Constitution of South Africa 1996, formulated as exceptions from freedom of expression. See also Law No. 4 of 2000 for the Promotion of Equality and Prevention of Unfair Discrimination [South Africa].

[23] I.e. as 'discrimination, hostility or violence' in the meaning of Art. 20(2) ICCPR.

[24] See the discussion on the vagueness of 'hostility' in section 7.3.5 of Chapter 7.

[25] Legislative Decree No. 122 of 26 April 1993, converted into Act No. 205 of 25 June 1993 on Urgent Measures in Respect of Racial, Ethnic and Religious Discrimination (amending Section 3 of Act No. 654 of October 1975) [Italy]. See ECRI, *Italy – General Overview: Legal Measures to Combat Racism and Intolerance in the Member States of the Council of Europe* (2004), at 12–13. Also see Venice Commission, *Science and Technique of Democracy, No. 47*, 21. The judiciary has interpreted this in such a way that these results do not actually have to materialize but need to have been likely at the material time.

[26] Art. 428 (read together with Art. 427) of the Criminal Code of Nicaragua 2007; Art. 20 of Law No. 7716, Act against Racism or 'Lei Caó' (of 5 January 1989) [Brazil].

[27] Art. 323 of the Criminal Code of Peru 1991.

reach that abject goal, the level of severity required under the Covenant is more or less secured. In Austria and Germany the incitement must be 'capable of endangering public order', while in Turkey the incitement must directly threaten public safety for it to be an offence.[28] Similarly, one extreme speech offence enshrined in the Canadian Criminal Code emphasizes that 'incitement to hatred' is a criminal offence 'where such incitement is likely to lead to a breach of the peace'.[29] This qualified type of incitement, however, does not apply to the 'wilful' promotion of hatred.[30]

It should be noted that these high-threshold offences are examples of 'good practice' in the light of the ICCPR specifically. Incorporating such stringent requirements into domestic extreme speech legislation may cause problems of compliance with the ICERD since the Committee on the Elimination of Racial Discrimination recommends the exact opposite of what is advocated and advised in the previous pages. That is, CERD increasingly finds fault with in-built 'likelihood of harm' requirements, arguing that the ICERD prohibits racist hate propaganda per se, regardless of the actual or potential damage done to public order or to the rights of the target group. Thus in the 2013 case of *TBB-Turkish Union in Berlin/ Brandenburg* v. *Turkey*, it rejected Germany's requirement that racist hate speech only become punishable if the impugned speech act is 'capable of disturbing public peace'.[31] Again, from the perspective of the ICCPR's necessity principle that requirement is ever so praiseworthy. In order to avoid fragmentation of international law, CERD may need to construe the 'due regard clause' in such a way that a similar necessity principle be mainstreamed with Article 4 ICERD.

[28] Section 283 of the Criminal Code of Austria 1974; Section 130 of the Criminal Code of Germany 1998; Art. 216 of the New Criminal Code of Turkey 2004. See also, *mutatis mutandis*, Art. 1(1) of Law 927/1979 (amended by Laws 1419/1984 and 2910/2001) on Punishing Acts or Activities Aimed at Racial Discrimination [Greece]; and Amending Laws 11/91, 6(III/95) and 28(III/99) implementing ICERD [Cyprus].

[29] Art. 319(1) of the Criminal Code of Canada 1985. See also Section 13 of the Human Rights Act 1985 [Canada], incorporating a likelihood criterion.

[30] Art. 319(2) of the Criminal Code of Canada 1985. The same partial recognition of a 'likelihood' factor, and thus of a qualified incitement prohibition, can be found in the incitement laws of Antigua and Barbados, Ireland, Malta, Santa Lucia and Singapore. See Section 2 of Prohibition of Incitement to Hatred Act (No. 19 of 1989) [Ireland]; Art. 82A.1 of the Criminal Code of Malta 1854 (amended 2014); Art. 359 of the Criminal Code of Santa Lucia 2003; Art. 298A of the Criminal Code of Singapore 1872; Art. 33 of the Public Order Act 1972 [Antigua and Barbados]. In all cases the likelihood factor functions as an alternative for proving intent rather than as a true requirement.

[31] CERD, *TBB-Turkish Union in Berlin/Brandenburg* v. *Turkey*, Communication no. 48/2010 (26 February 2013), para. 12.8 (a reference to Section 130 of the German Criminal Code).

8.3   Additional areas of concern

National lawmakers could potentially make a number of other choices
that are at odds with Article 20(2) of the ICCPR.

8.3.1   The public nature of incitement

From our analysis of the term 'advocacy' it follows that Article 20(2)
ICCPR is exclusively concerned with extreme speech that is publically
disseminated.[32] Extreme speech engages the Covenant only if the inciter
reaches out to others – an audience – with a view of mobilizing the latter
to commit hostile acts against a target group. The necessity principle further supports this view.

Nearly all national incitement laws require that the inciteful speech act
be made publicly. Where prohibitions use terms like 'advocacy', 'propaganda', 'dissemination' and so on, such is clearly presumed. Some laws
make it very clear that privately made hateful statements ought not to
be interfered with by the state. In Ireland and the UK, for example, the
fact that the speech act took place privately may serve as an express legal
defence against incitement charges.[33]

A few State parties to the ICCPR outlaw privately expressed forms
of incitement. For instance, Armenian criminal law considers publicly
expressed incitement an aggravating factor (providing for higher penalties),[34] implying that private incitement is also prohibited.[35]

---

[32] See section 7.3.1 of Chapter 7.

[33] Section 2 of the Prohibition of Incitement to Hatred Act 1989 [Ireland]: 'it shall be a
defence for the accused person … to prove that he was inside a private residence at the
relevant time and had no reason to believe that the words, behaviour or material concerned would be heard or seen by a person outside the residence.' Similarly, Section 29B,
para. 4 of the Racial and Religious Hatred Act 2006 [UK].

[34] Art. 226(2) of the Criminal Code of Armenia (entry into force 1 August 2003). The maximum prison sentence is thus lifted from three to six years.

[35] Further, French criminal law appears to ban private incitement too. See Art. R625-7 of
the Criminal Code of France 1992 ('La provocation non publique à la discrimination, à
la haine ou à la violence à l'égard d'une personne ou d'un groupe de personnes à raison
de leur … religion'). For the comprehensive body of law on extreme speech in France, see
Pascal Mbongo, 'Hate Speech, Extreme Speech, and Collective Defamation in French
Law', in Hare and Weinstein (eds.) *Extreme Speech and Democracy*, 221–26. The Venice
Commission further lists the following states as examples of jurisdictions where private
incitement may under circumstances be punishable: Albania, Estonia, Malta, Moldova,
Montenegro, Poland, Serbia, Slovenia and Ukraine. Venice Commission, *Science and
Technique of Democracy, No. 47*, para. 36.

8.3.2   Taking religion-based incitement seriously

Article 20(2) ICCPR specifies three grounds for prohibited incitement: 'national, racial or religious hatred'. The latter ground, hatred based on religion, is all the more precious since this one is omitted in other international extreme speech provisions, notably Article 4 ICERD. Therefore, the Human Rights Committee may, as it has done in the past (for example in relation to New Zealand)[36] reproach State parties for failing to include this ground in their domestic incitement legislation. A number of State parties, however, do omit 'religious hatred' from their incitement clauses. For example, Macedonia exclusively bans advocacy of racial hatred and spreading ideas of racial superiority.[37] By and large the same goes for Ecuador, Georgia, Guyana, Malta and Slovakia.[38]

Quite a different question is whether State parties are free to introduce incitement grounds that go *beyond* Article 20(2) of the ICCPR. There is no valid reason to hold that incitement stemming from hatred based on the trait of sexual orientation is less of a legal and societal problem than religious or racial incitement.[39] The same goes for incitement of violence against women. As Carolyn Evans argues:

[36] A/50/40 vol. I (1995) 38, para. 181 (New Zealand): 'The Committee is concerned about the fact that, while the Human Rights Act contains a provision corresponding to article 20, paragraph 2, of the Covenant, this provision does not include a prohibition of advocacy of religious hatred.' Accordingly, the Committee reproached New Zealand despite its reservation to Art. 20.

[37] Art. 417 of the Criminal Code of FYR Macedonia (23 July 1996). Art. 319 does mention religious hatred, but this provision does not serve as a proper incitement prohibition.

[38] See Art. 212A of the Criminal Code of Ecuador 1971 (a recently adopted amendment is to add religion as a prohibited ground shortly); Art. 142-1 of the Criminal Code of Georgia 1999 (this Article was inserted on 6 June 2003); Guyana's Racial Hostility Act 1964; Art. 424 of the New Criminal Code of Slovakia (L.300/2005); Art. 82A.1 of the Criminal Code of Malta 1854 (amended 2014) (it should be noted that Malta made a reservation to Art. 20 ICCPR). However, Art. 6 of the Press Act 1974 [Malta] does mention 'creed' as one of the prohibited hate speech grounds. See Malta Broadcasting Authority, Decision of 16 June 2004.

[39] See, however, Eric Heinze, 'Cumulative Jurisprudence and Human Rights: The Example of Sexual Minorities and Hate Speech', in Phil C. W. Chan (ed.), *Protection of Sexual Minorities since Stonewall: Progress and Stalemate in Developed and Developing Countries* (London/New York: Routledge, 2010), 62–78. It should be noted that Heinze is generally against incitement legislation, his argument against anti-gay hate speech being an extension of that position. Further, see Alon Harel, 'Hate speech and Comprehensive Forms of Life', in Herz and Molnar (eds.), *The Content and Context of Hate Speech*, 306–26, arguing that 'deeply rooted hate speech', including religiously motivated anti-gay speech, should be protected more stringently than hate speech that is not deeply rooted in a thick belief system. See also, *mutatis mutandis*, Ian Leigh, 'Hatred, Sexual Orientation,

> [d]omestic violence against women is at least as serious, costly, and wide-
> spread a social harm as violence based on religion or belief. There is no
> reason that similar measures to those that have been taken to protect
> racial and religious groups from hate that aims to stir violence against
> them should not equally be deployed against those who aim to stir hate or
> legitimize violence against women.[40]

Accordingly, while the language of Article 20(2) seems exhaustive in this
regard, the Human Rights Committee would do well to provide a more
inclusive interpretation of this provision's incitement grounds.[41]

8.3.3   Proscribed results

In section 8.2 of this chapter the phrase 'incitement to hatred' was criticized for not doing justice to qualified nature of the incitement offence in
the meaning of Article 20(2) ICCPR. The offence of 'hate speech' is not
focused enough on contingent harms. Other legislators, however, have
overstepped the mark by including contingent harms that appear at odds
with the ones mentioned by the Covenant ('discrimination', 'hostility' or
'violence').[42]

Thus such proscribed results as 'conflict' (Albania),[43] 'discord' (Belarus
and Bosnia and Herzegovina)[44] or 'degradation of national honour and
dignity' (Belarus)[45] must be dismissed for being susceptible to abuse.[46]

Free Speech and Religious Liberty' (2008) 10:3 *Ecclesiastical Law Journal* 337–44; and
Ian Leigh, 'Homophobic Speech, Equality Denial, and Religious Expression' in Hare and
Weinstein (eds.), *Extreme Speech and Democracy*, 375–99. Although accepting legislation penalizing the 'denial of sexual orientation equality', Leigh warns against overly
general legislation against expressing 'homophobia', for the latter could disproportionately affect religious expression.

[40] Carolyn Evans, 'Religious Speech that Undermines Gender Equality', in Hare and
Weinstein (eds.), *Extreme Speech and Democracy*, 357–74, at 371–2.

[41] See also ARTICLE 19, *Responding to Hate Speech against LGBTI People: Policy Brief* (2013);
and ARTICLE 19, *Prohibiting Incitement to Discrimination, Hostility or Violence: Policy
Brief* (2012), at 20–2. See the discussion at section 7.3.3 of Chapter 7.

[42] The former two results are problematic in their own right. See section 7.3.5 of Chapter 7.

[43] Art. 265 of the Criminal Code of the Republic of Albania (Law No. 7895, 27 January
1995, consolidated version as of 1 December 2004). This ground can also be translated as
'dispute'.

[44] Art. 130 of the Criminal Code of Belarus 1999 (amended 2007); and Art. 150 of the
Criminal Code of the Federation of Bosnia and Herzegovina 1998.

[45] Art. 130 of the Criminal Code of Belarus 1999 (amended 2007). 'Violence' is not listed as
a proscribed result but rather as an aggravating factor.

[46] See also, *mutatis mutandis*, Section 226b of the Criminal Code of Denmark 2009
('threatened, scorned, or degraded'); and Section 10 of the Criminal Code of Finland
1889 (amended 2012) ('threatened, defamed or insulted').

Furthermore, as the offence of incitement in the meaning of the Covenant is by definition an inchoate crime, national incitement laws may not require contingent harms to actually materialize. It should be likely at the material time that such harm ensues (proof of causality is therefore typically not required in incitement cases).[47] In some states the fact that the incitement has actually caused violence is considered an aggravating factor.[48] The ICCPR does not seem to resist such a practice.[49]

8.4   Concluding remarks

Deliberately or inadvertently, many domestic incitement laws do not follow Article 20(2) to the letter. The effect of this is that the *actus reus* of the domestic extreme speech offence may differ from the offence dictated by international law. Typically, this means that the domestic offence is wider, thus stifling free speech beyond what is required under international law. National lawmakers, hence, would do well to stick closely to the terminology used by the Covenant. Also, to ensure a nexus with Article 20(2) ICCPR, its high threshold and the free of expression safeguards provided by Article 19, the national law's *travaux* and possibly also the (preamble of the) implementation law adding the offence to the criminal code should reference the Covenant explicitly.

---

[47]   See Chapter 10 on 'likelihood'. Art. 151 of the Criminal Code of Estonia 2000 puts the bar quite high in this respect as it requires that the incitement 'results in danger to the life, health or property of a person'.

[48]   E.g. Art. 150(3) of the Criminal Code of the Federation of Bosnia and Herzegovina 1998; Art. 370 of the Criminal Code of Montenegro 2004; Art. 134 of the Criminal Code of Serbia 2005; Art. 161 of the Criminal Code of Ukraine 2001.

[49]   If anything, the fact that harm was directly caused by the inciteful speech act in question is bound to inform the necessity and proportionality of the sanction to be meted out in that particular case. On sanctions, see Chapter 13. In that chapter we will also discuss the question of whether State parties may designate different penalties for 'incitement to violence' as compared to 'incitement to discrimination'.

PART IV

Judging incitement

9

Intent

9.1 Introduction

So far we have established that the ICCPR's extreme speech clause is premised on a triangle of incitement. The *actus reus* of the incitement offence consists of elements that all point at a very high threshold. These objective elements of the crime require that a person publicly advocate hatred, thus reaching out to an audience, to such an extent that the speech amounts to proactively stirring that audience to commit hostile acts against a target group characterized by religion.

Article 20(2) of the ICCPR first and foremost requires that appropriate incitement laws are in place. National laws giving effect to the Covenant's incitement provision should do justice to its intrinsic high threshold. The necessity principle further requires that those laws are enforced at the expense of free speech only in cases where that is absolutely necessary. Thus in concrete incitement cases a case-by-case assessment is pivotal, so as to establish that the impugned speech act indeed reached the required gravity (see Chapter 10) and, as will be argued in this chapter, so as to ensure that the crime of incitement can be attributed to the alleged inciter.

In this chapter we will address the question of whether international incitement standards presuppose intent (or another degree of *mens rea*) on the part of the 'advocator'. The question of whether or not the incitement offence within the meaning of Article 20(2) ICCPR is premised on criminal intent is very pertinent for several reasons. First of all, it adds yet further meat to the definition of the crime that we were pursuing in Part III (see particularly Chapter 7). Second, any such requirement – be it full-fledged criminal intent or a weaker form of *mens rea* – is bound to impact the actual implementation practices, notably law enforcement and jurisprudence. Third, from the perspective of the accused it could also make all the difference whether proof of intent is required or whether, for instance, negligence or recklessness suffices – the latter case would clearly raise criminal liability tremendously. Finally, this discussion may also impact the legal position of the alleged incitement victim.

9.2   *Travaux préparatoires*

The Covenant's drafting history is far from clear on the point of intent. In fact, neither the text of Article 20(2) ICCPR nor the *travaux* make it clear whether this provision requires criminal incitement laws per se.[1] That particular question is now belied by the fact that the Human Rights Committee has pulled the prohibition into the spheres of criminal liability, notably in its concluding observations on state reports and in its jurisprudence.[2] Accordingly, at a minimum the clause requires criminal law responses to incitement – something that certainly does not rule out alternative, civil or administrative law responses and indeed non-legal responses as well.[3]

To return to the specific question of criminal intent, the scantiness of debates on this matter in the drafting history could point at oversight. Conversely, this omission could also be taken to mean that, to the extent that Article 20(2) does presuppose criminal laws, it was deemed self-evident that (proof of) criminal intent is required, since most jurisdictions require this for all or most criminal offences. Alternatively – and this is probably the best guess – this could imply that the drafters simply felt that this issue was something for the national legislative and judicial authorities to sort out in more detail in due course (an overview of comparative law is presented in section 9.7 of this chapter).

On the very few occasions that the question of *mens rea* was addressed, this did not lead to a definitive outcome or a majority position. In an early (1948) contribution New Zealand expressed its concern that 'the words "that constitutes an incitement to violence" do not imply any intent'.[4] In that way, it was argued, '[t]he dividing line between reasonable expressions of opinion on national, racial or religious matters, which should be

---

[1] Manfred Nowak, *U.N. Covenant on Civil and Political Rights: CCPR Commentary* (2nd rev. edn, Kehl: N. P. Engel, 2005), at 470.

[2] See section 4.5 of Chapter 4 and section 5.4 of Chapter 5.

[3] See *Rabat Plan of Action on the Prohibition of Advocacy of National, Racial or Religious Hatred that Constitutes Incitement to Discrimination, Hostility or Violence* (Conclusions and recommendations emanating from the four regional expert workshops organized by OHCHR in 2011 and adopted by experts in Rabat, Morocco on 5 October 2012), paras. 23–29. See further the sources and literature cited in the introduction (specifically at note 32).

[4] E/CN.4/82/Add.12, at 20.

permitted as part of the exercise of the right of freedom of expression, and statements which amount to advocacy of national, racial or religious hostility within the article proposed, will be difficult to draw.'[5] Accordingly, this was a strong argument in favour of an intent requirement, at the same time admitting that the incitement provision's formulation did not quite support such criterion.

In 1953 the Australian representative in the Commission on Human Rights raised similar concerns. In no uncertain terms he found it problematic that the draft incitement provision did not require criminal intent:

> In present-day circumstances a number of policies advocated in the Press, on the wireless and in public discussion, if taken at their face value, might be said to constitute incitement to some form of violence, and if States had rigidly to prohibit them, as they would under the [then debated draft] text, there would be danger of injustice. Jurisprudence always had to take intent into account. For instance, under the Australian Crimes Act the promotion of ill-will and hostility between different classes of Australian citizens constituted one form of sedition, but it was a legitimate defence for the accused person to prove good faith, and the charge of sedition was not sustainable unless the intention to foster ill-will and hostility could be proved. The [pending] proposal was therefore far too general in its terms and did not include those elements which were part of internationally recognized penal systems.[6]

While his argumentation draws on the particular experience of common law countries and the precise gist of his argument may not hold true for all penal law systems in the world, it is a point well made. A Brazilian delegate in the Third Committee went even further and argued that intention of the type required by this offence would 'easily' be established by 'any court'.[7]

While there are no records of representatives vehemently arguing *against* a proof of intent requirement, the rare examples of support at the same time seem to concede that whichever draft of the incitement provision was under consideration at the time was unclear on this point. All in all this leaves the *travaux* undecided on this matter.

9.3 Textual analysis, independent experts and scholarly teachings

On a textual level, some of the incitement provision's constituent terms may hint at a requirement of intent. Let us start with 'advocacy'. The

---

[5] E/CN.4/82/Add.12, at 21.   [6] E/CN.4/SR.379, at 4–5.
[7] A/C.3/SR.1079, para. 2.

ordinary meaning of 'advocacy' is necessarily premised on a minimal degree of intent.[8] One cannot unconsciously and unwillingly *advocate* something. While it is obviously possible to inadvertently cause offence, inadvertently *advocating hatred* seems impossible. Presumably, one could even inadvertently disseminate hateful messages, but then it would not amount to *advocacy* of hatred.[9]

Hatred and hate-inspired hostile actions such as violence or discrimination may result from a wider spectrum of actions than Article 20(2) strictly speaking looks to. Hatred can be accidentally or incidentally fostered.[10] Hatred can be the result of the controversial nature of the speech act's very subject matter, for instance scientific research output.[11] Hatred may be an unintended and even utterly surprising reaction to an act of communication even to the person responsible for the speech act. Thus hatred and hateful acts may emerge without anyone having expressly *advocated* hatred.

Hatred may very well be boosted by a speech act because of naivety, negligence or recklessness on the part of the speaker. Where the dissemination of hatred is somehow caused by the speaker's being ignorant, reckless or insensitive about his or her subject matter or audience, it is tempting to start applying more flexible concepts of criminal culpability. Of these negligent mind-sets 'recklessness' certainly seems the most culpable state of mind. And while under many domestic tort laws and also certain criminal laws this state of mind may lead to accountability and culpability, this low degree of *mens rea* may not suffice to prove the crime of incitement within the meaning of Article 20(2) ICCPR. For someone who makes a reckless statement does not *advocate* hatred, and does not quite engage in a deliberate act of promoting hatred against a certain group of people.[12] Many forms of provocative art or satire would be liable to suppression under a flexible requirement of 'recklessness' or 'insensitivity'. Yet, however shocking, insulting or disturbing, if any intention can at all be inferred from such expressions, it is typically a wish

[8] See ARTICLE 19, *Prohibiting Incitement to Discrimination, Hostility or Violence: Policy Brief* (2012) (hereafter *Incitement Policy Brief*), at 22: 'Although a requirement of intent is not explicitly stipulated in Article 20(2) ... ARTICLE 19 believes that the term "advocacy" necessarily implies intention.'

[9] Toby Mendel, *Study on International Standards Relating to Incitement to Genocide or Racial Hatred for the UN Special Advisor on the Prevention of Genocide* (April 2006) (hereafter *Study on Incitement*), at 47.

[10] Mendel, *Study on Incitement*, at 14.

[11] Mendel, *Study on Incitement*, at 14.

[12] See ARTICLE 19, *Incitement Policy Brief*, at 22.

to contribute to a certain debate. Under a robust criminal intent requirement such speech would be protected, which would appear to be most in line with the object and purpose of the Covenant, notably its strong focus on robust free speech protection.

Further, anything less than a criminal intent requirement could jeopardize genuine research and journalism, thus chilling free speech. Reports about extremism do, in the literal sense of the word, spread extremist views. Indeed, reports about hatred may fuel yet further hatred.[13] Yet obviously the law cannot blame all such woes on the messenger.[14] The law will have to face the fact that there may be high degrees of pre-existing intolerance on the part of some citizens. That is, more hate crimes occur than the sum of those that have been expressly advocated by hatemongering individuals. Worrying though that may be, it is not the law's function to blame all woes on extremists or to identify scapegoats. The law's task should be limited to allocating criminal culpability to those who actually 'advocate' hatred that amounts to incitement.

Accordingly, by way of the word 'advocacy' Article 20(2) seems to be premised on at least a minimal degree of intent, that is intent as far as the *dissemination of the hateful messages* goes. For an inciter to be convicted, it must be established that he or she was 'purposely striving to engage in advocacy of hatred'.[15] This also follows from a definition of 'advocacy' used by the UN Special Rapporteur on the promotion and protection of the right to freedom of opinion and expression.[16]

This begs the question if other elements of the incitement clause presuppose additional degrees of *mens rea*. In the light of the prohibited hatred grounds, it stands to reason that the 'advocator' must, moreover, purposefully target a particular group on the basis of its religion (or race or nationality).[17] Accordingly, a second type of *mens rea* must be proven

---

[13] Mendel, *Study on Incitement*, at 14.

[14] I.e. contrary to what Denmark did in the *Jersild* case. European Court of Human Rights, *Jersild* v. *Denmark*, Application no. 15890/89 (Grand Chamber Judgment of 23 September 1994), concerning Denmark's conviction of a reporter for 'aiding and abetting' the dissemination of hateful statements made by neo-Nazis during an interview with him.

[15] ARTICLE 19, *Incitement Policy Brief*, at 23 and 31, calling this degree of *mens rea* 'volition'.

[16] UN Special Rapporteur on the Promotion and Protection of the Right to Freedom of Opinion and Expression, *Report of the Special Rapporteur to the General Assembly on Hate Speech and Incitement to Hatred* (A/67/357, 7 September 2012), para. 44(b), defining 'advocacy' as 'explicit, *intentional*, public and active support and promotion of hatred towards the target group' (emphasis added).

[17] ARTICLE 19, *Incitement Policy Brief*, at 23 and 31, calling this degree of *mens rea* 'volition'.

and can be inferred from the inciter's seeking out a specific group characterized by such traits as religion or ethnicity.

Whether or not this double intent requirement could yet be further upgraded to no less than a triple intent criterion depends on the crucial question of whether the act of 'incitement' itself, too, is premised on criminal intent. The ordinary meaning of the words surrounding the term 'incitement' in Article 20(2) of the ICCPR certainly seem to resist that. The advocacy of religious hatred *that constitutes incitement* to the three proscribed results is to be prohibited. In the light of that particular formulation, both intended and unintended incitement seems to qualify (assuming that it is possible that one intentionally commits advocacy of hatred whilst not at the same time intending incitement to hostile acts). 'Unintended incitement', then, may be the result of ignorance, negligence, insensitivity or recklessness.

Again, weak types of *mens rea* such as 'negligence' and 'recklessness' are problematic from the perspective of freedom of speech. Such lenient requirements have a disproportionate chilling effect on free speech. Thus it is more than likely that the object and purpose of the ICCPR resist the interpretation that such flexible forms of *mens rea* are permitted. At the same time we cannot reasonably distil a full-fledged criminal intent requirement from the term 'incitement'. The dissemination of extreme speech 'that constitutes', that is that *amounts to*, 'incitement' does imply that certain lower degrees of *mens rea* may qualify. The present account proposes, therefore, to hold the middle ground. So as to ensure that we drop the bar not so low as to accept 'negligence' or 'recklessness', but at the same time remaining short of endorsing a requirement of specific intent to incite, a requirement of 'oblique intent' is proposed. Oblique intent means that the person at the material time knew and understood what would be the 'natural' consequences of or the consequences almost certainly following his or her acts.[18] A 'knowledge intent' requirement, which is one step further down the ladder of *mens rea*, has been proposed in the literature too.[19] According to this criterion, a person is criminally culpable of incitement if he or she had 'knowledge of the consequences of his/her action and [knew] that the consequences will occur *or might occur*

---

[18] See, generally, Glanville Williams, 'Oblique Intention' (1987) 46 *Cambridge Law Journal* 417–38.

[19] ARTICLE 19, *Incitement Policy Brief*, at 23 and 31. See also Mendel, *Study on Incitement*, at 45–49, arguing that proof of intent may be indirect, for instance based on the knowledge the inciter had at the material time.

in the ordinary course of events'.[20] The latter requirement will be easier to satisfy in incitement proceedings compared to oblique intent. As this requirement ensures that negligence or recklessness does not qualify, this criterion may also be compatible with the Covenant. However, barring full and specific criminal intent, 'oblique intent' provides the highest free speech guarantees.

In the context of incitement laws and their enforcement, staying clear of such flexible culpability factors as 'negligence' and 'recklessness' is important. It is precisely because not every 'hate speech' amounts to 'incitement' that state authorities must face the obligation to answer to a considerable extent the question *why* the advocator targeted a particular group. The seriousness of a criminal conviction for no less than stirring up a crowd to commit acts of discrimination, hostility or violence should be duly noted – it will not do to base such convictions on malleable notions of criminal negligence.

The Rabat Plan of Action also supports an intent requirement in relation to the incitement offence.[21] These benchmarks appear to require full-fledged criminal intent both in relation to the act of 'advocacy' *and* – thus quite in the face of the convoluted phrase 'hatred that constitutes incitement' – in relation to 'incitement'.

While some experts and stakeholders have proposed that proof of 'recklessness' may be sufficient in incitement proceedings,[22] arguments in favour of a more demanding intent requirement have been canvassed by a range of important players at the international level, outnumbering the former. In a joint statement the UN Special Rapporteur on freedom of opinion and expression, the OSCE Representative on Freedom of the Media, and the Special Rapporteur of the Organization of American

---

[20] ARTICLE 19, *Incitement Policy Brief,* at 23 and 31 (emphasis added). Note that at other times (at 22) ARTICLE 19 appears to argue in favour of a more full-fledged form of criminal intent: 'While many forms of speech might be offensive and shocking, the decisive factors should be that a speaker who incites others to discrimination, hostility or violence intends not only to share his/her opinions with others but also to compel others to commit certain actions based on those beliefs, opinions or positions.'

[21] *Rabat Plan of Action,* at 6, providing that 'Article 20 of the ICCPR requires intent. Negligence and recklessness are not sufficient for an article 20 situation which requires "advocacy" and "incitement" rather than mere distribution or circulation. In this regard, it requires the activation of a triangular relationship between the object and subject of the speech as well as the audience.'

[22] E.g. Venice Commission Study 406/2006 on 'Blasphemy, Religious Insults and Incitement to Religious Hatred' (adopted at the Commission's 70th Plenary Session, 16–17 March 2007), para. 89(a).

States on freedom of expression, postulated that 'no one should be penalized for the dissemination of "hate speech" unless it has been shown that they did so with the intention of inciting discrimination, hostility or violence'.[23] Furthermore, in a 2011 joint submission to one of the regional expert workshops that ultimately cumulated into the Rabat Plan by the UN Special Rapporteur on freedom of religion or belief, the UN Special Rapporteur on the promotion and protection of the right to freedom of opinion and expression and the UN Special Rapporteur on contemporary forms of racism, racial discrimination, xenophobia and related intolerance, it was similarly underscored that 'intent of inciting discrimination, hostility or violence must be present for hate speech to be penalized'.[24] Amnesty International, too, has argued strongly in favour of a robust requirement of intent.[25] While this NGO distils the requirement of intent chiefly from the term 'advocacy', it also speaks of 'a requirement of intent to bring about a prohibited result'.[26] Accordingly, Amnesty's intent requirement resonates well with the above proposed multiple intent requirement.

In sum, there is an emerging consensus that Article 20(2) requires strong degrees of *mens rea*, including at a minimum (1) the intent to advocate hatred, (2) the intent to target a specific group, and arguably also (3) an oblique intent or knowledge requirement in relation to the consequences of the incitement.

Turning from the principled question as to whether Article 20(2) ICCPR requires intent, let us proceed with the practical question of how such types of *mens rea* can be proven. Assuming that the intent to disseminate (a hateful message) is more readily proven, let us chiefly focus on the question of targeting and especially the question of incitement.

---

[23] *Joint Statement on Racism and the Media by the UN Special Rapporteur on Freedom of Opinion and Expression, the OSCE Representative on Freedom of the Media and the OAS Special Rapporteur on Freedom of Expression* (London, 27 February 2001).

[24] *Joint submission by Mr Heiner Bielefeldt, Special Rapporteur on freedom of religion or belief; Mr Frank La Rue, Special Rapporteur on the promotion and protection of the right to freedom of opinion and expression; and Mr Githu Muigai, Special Rapporteur on contemporary forms of racism, racial discrimination, xenophobia and related intolerance* (presented at the OHCHR expert workshops on the prohibition of incitement to national, racial or religious hatred, Vienna, 9–10 February 2011), at 11, quoting the outcomes of an earlier (2008) OHCHR workshop on the same issue.

[25] Amnesty International, *Written Contribution to the Thematic Discussion on Racist Hate Speech and Freedom of Opinion and Expression Organized by the United Nations Committee on Elimination of Racial Discrimination* (28 August 2012) (hereafter *Written Contribution on Racist Hate Speech*), at 4, also drawing on the ICCPR.

[26] Amnesty International, *Written Contribution on Racist Hate Speech*, at 2.

If the advocator does not confess his or her motivations, it will always be tremendously difficult to prove a speaker's (oblique) intent to incite acts of violence or discrimination against a target group.[27] ARTICLE 19 proposes three points of departure for making this assessment: (1) the language and content of the impugned speech; (2) the (underlying) objectives pursued by the speaker; and (3) the scale and repetition of the speech act.[28] Thus it is proposed that occasionally the content of the speech act itself reveals the speaker's motives. Otherwise, the speech act's underlying objectives may give insight into what moved the speaker. Any such unveiled implicit objectives – such as conveying news or research output, contributing to a public debate, or expressing oneself artistically or in a satirical or humorous way – could also serve to deny malicious intent on the part of the person responsible for the speech act. The notions of 'scale and repetition' aim to do justice to the *cumulative effect* of the multiple speeches. Thus the scale of the speech act may tell something about the ferociousness or tenacity of the speaker. While these qualities appear to be quite remote from the intentions of the speaker, in the context of spreading hatred the presence of a *systematic campaign* of verbally attacking a target group may be circumstantial evidence of someone's intention to incite.[29] It should be pointed out, though, that persons without any intention to incite discrimination or violence may be repetitive and ferocious in their communication too.

The work by Susan Benesch specifically elaborates on incitement to violence.[30] She composed the following test or checklist on how to determine a 'call to violence' – that is intentional incitement – from the speech act:

a. Was the speech understood by the audience as a call to violence? Inflammatory speech is often expressed in elliptical, indirect language, which can be variously interpreted. For this analysis, the only relevant meaning is the way in which the speech was understood by the audience most likely to react, at the time when it was made or disseminated.

---

[27] See ARTICLE 19, *Incitement Policy Brief*, at 32.

[28] ARTICLE 19, *Incitement Policy Brief*, 32–3.

[29] This is what the authors of the communication against the Netherlands argue in relation to statements made by Geert Wilders: while this politician's individual speech acts may appear to fall short of criminal intent to incite, the cumulative effect of his systematic campaign against 'Islamization' reaches that level. *M.R., A.B.S. and N.A.* v. *The Netherlands*, CCPR Communication dated 15 November 2011, at 10–11.

[30] Susan Benesch, 'Dangerous Speech: A Proposal to Prevent Group Violence' (World Policy Institute paper, 2012), at 4. See also Susan Benesch, 'Vile Crime or Inalienable Right: Defining Incitement to Genocide' (2008) 48:3 *Virginia Journal of International Law* 485–528.

b. Did the speech describe the victims-to-be as other than human, e.g. as vermin, pests, insects or animals? This is a rhetorical hallmark of incitement to genocide, and to violence, since it dehumanizes the victim or victims to be.

c. Did the speech assert that the audience faced serious danger from the victim group? Another hallmark of incitement, this technique is known as "accusation in a mirror". Just as self-defense is an ironclad defense to murder, collective self-defense gives a psychological justification for group violence, even if the claim of self-defense is spurious.

d. Did the speech contain phrases, words, or coded language that has taken on a special loaded meaning, in the understanding of the speaker and audience? Such coded language is typical of Dangerous Speech. It bonds the speaker and audience more tightly together.[31]

Thus, having acquired a sense of how independent experts and legal scholars propose to take intent into account in incitement proceedings, we will now turn to the Human Rights Committee to assess if and to what extent it treats the question of *mens rea* in its workings (section 9.4). By way of comparison we will subsequently look at CERD's practice in this area (section 9.5), as well as that of the European Court of Human Rights (section 9.6). Finally, this chapter will provide an overview of comparative state practice in the area in question (section 9.7).

9.4 The Human Rights Committee

At some point in its recent past the Committee was on the verge of expressly formulating a requirement of *mens rea* in relation to Article 20(2) of the ICCPR. Following the Camden Principles, the Committee inserted a requirement of intent into its definition of 'advocacy' in the early drafts of General Comment No. 34. Accordingly, this key term was temporarily defined as 'public forms of expression that are intended to elicit action or response'.[32] This definition of 'advocacy' more or less fuses the act of dissemination with the act of incitement and requires specific intent especially with respect to the latter act. The Camden Principles, more modestly, had required 'intention' with respect to the acts of publicly promoting

---

[31] Benesch, 'Dangerous Speech', at 4–5. Note that she also underscores the importance of such other factors as the person of the speaker, the audience, the socio-historical context and the mode of transmission. Such contextual factors will be extensively discussed in Chapter 10.

[32] Draft General Comment No. 34: Article 19 (2nd revised draft, CCPR/C/GC/34/CRP.3, 28 June 2010), para. 53. For further details, see section 7.3.1 of Chapter 7.

hatred and specifically targeting a certain group.[33] When taken in conjunction, these two definitions cover all three *mens rea* requirements as described in the previous section.[34]

At a later reading, however, the Committee deleted said definition and, in one fell swoop, the (explicit) *mens rea* requirement. The unofficial *travaux* do not shine a light on why this criterion was dropped, so we can only guess at the Committee's motives.[35] It could be that there was no consensus in the Committee on the point of a *mens rea*. It could be that Committee members differed on where *mens rea* should enter the equation, that is whether it should be posed in relation to 'advocacy', 'incitement', or both. Still further, it could be that members were amenable to a requirement of *mens rea* but that there was discord as to how specific or demanding such a requirement of intent should be. Finally, perhaps the majority of the members wished to leave such a complex issue to discretion of the State parties' legislators and judiciaries. What with the question of *mens rea* being so crucial, especially from the perspective of free speech promotion, the latter scenario would be quite ill advised and inexplicable.

In some cases the Committee altogether avoids the question of intent.[36] Take, for instance, the admissibility decision in *Vassilari* v. *Greece*. In the domestic proceedings leading up to this complaint being lodged with the Committee, the question of *mens rea* played an important role. In front of the Committee the Roma applicants and the responding state firmly differ on the relevant ramifications of Greek anti-racism law, notably

---

[33] ARTICLE 19, *Camden Principles on Freedom of Expression and Equality* (2009), Art. 12(ii): 'The term "advocacy" is to be understood as requiring an intention to promote hatred publicly towards the target group.'

[34] Note that a more modest type of 'oblique intent' was proposed in relation to the specific 'intent to incite'.

[35] The International Service for Human Rights (ISHR) and the Open Society Justice Initiative made a series of invaluable notes during the public sessions dedicated to the drafting of this General Comment. These records are available at www.ishr.ch/treaty-bodies/1128-human-rights-committee-adopts-general-comment-34-on-freedom-of-expression and www.freedominfo.org/2011/04/un-panel-revises-draft-comment-on-article-19/ and through the additional links posted there.

[36] See also the case of *Ernst Zündel* v. *Canada* [I], Communication no. 953/2000 (admissibility decision of 27 July 2003). While the applicant expressly denies he had any intention to incite hatred against Jewish people at his intended press conference (para. 6.5), neither Canada nor the Human Rights Committee deals with this argument, with Zündel's case ultimately being dismissed by the Committee on grounds of admissibility.

on the question of which racist (hate) crimes require proof of intent,[37] which party faces the burden of proof;[38] the precise degree of *mens rea* required,[39] and whether such proof was indeed available with respect to the anti-Roma newspaper publication in question.[40] This all confuses the Committee so much that it renders the communication inadmissible.[41] Yet, as dissenting member Amor argued:

> The [Greek] court hearing the case found no violation of that law, as 'doubts remained regarding the ... intention to offend the complainants by using expressions referred to in the indictment'. The authors took their case to the Committee, claiming to be the victims of a violation by the State party of article 20, paragraph 2 ... of the Covenant, because the court 'failed to appreciate the racist nature of the impugned letter and to effectively implement the [Greek anti-racism law] aimed at prohibiting dissemination of racist speech'. This allegedly 'discloses a violation of the State party's obligation to ensure prohibition of the advocacy of racial hatred that constitutes incitement to discrimination, hatred or violence'. Was it advocacy of racial hatred or just words? Was a racist offence committed or not? Was there the intention to offend, and who must prove this? These are questions that should be discussed, analysed and assessed on the merits.[42]

This case was a golden opportunity, if ever there was one, to settle the score on the question of *mens rea*.

In some of its decisions the Human Rights Committee has hinted at a requirement of *mens rea*, but it should be noted that it has done so only rather indirectly or implicitly. In addition, the Committee does not neatly specify to what particular act the intent requirement relates, thus leaving us in the dark as to whether single, double or triple intent as propagated above is what is required for an incitement conviction to meet the standards of Article 20(2) of the Covenant.

---

[37] *Maria Vassilari et al.* v. *Greece*, Communication no. 1570/2007 (19 March 2009), para. 4.4 versus para. 5.4.

[38] *Maria Vassilari et al.* v. *Greece*, para. 3.1.

[39] *Maria Vassilari et al.* v. *Greece*, para. 5.4 ('an incorrect notion of intent was applied by the court').

[40] *Maria Vassilari et al.* v. *Greece*, para. 2.6.

[41] *Maria Vassilari et al.* v. *Greece*, para. 7.2.

[42] Individual opinion of Committee member Mr Abdelfattah Amor (dissenting), para. 4 (the internal quotation marks reference the claims made by the authors of the communication). Two members associate themselves with Amor's views. See Individual opinion of Committee members Mr Ahmad Amin Fathalla and Mr Bouzid Lazhari.

For example, in *Faurisson* a robust requirement of criminal intent is not spelled out in detail in the decision.[43] Quite the contrary; the plenary views could be taken to mean that, if a criminal mind-set is at all required, forms of liability very low on the ladder of *mens rea* would suffice. Avoiding any assessment of the advocator's specific or even oblique intent leaves wide open the possibility of premising criminal liability on such flexible bases as recklessness or negligence. This indeed may have occurred in *Faurisson*. Specifically, the Committee concluded that France legitimately interfered with this Holocaust denier's speech since his negationist speech acts 'read in their full context, were of a nature as to raise or strengthen anti-semitic feelings'.[44] The Committee does not specify that this inciteful 'nature' of the speech acts was reached due to the intent of the speaker.

In addition, the Committee accepts the French argument that 'the denial of the existence of the Holocaust [serves] as the principal vehicle for anti-semitism'.[45] To the extent that everybody, including Faurisson, knows that to be the case, the Committee implicitly posits here that Faurisson had oblique intent to incite. Again, even if correct, this remains rather buried in the decision.

Individual members of the Committee are far more outspoken on the requirement of intent. From their vehement critique on the French Gayssot Act it transpires that members Evatt, Kretzmer and Klein advocate a more robust requirement of criminal intent.[46] Member Lallah also supports such a requirement,[47] as does Bhagwati.[48]

In *Malcolm Ross* v. *Canada* the applicant and the responding state in fact fiercely debate the question of *mens rea* through their respective submissions. That discussion is fuelled by the fact that Canadian criminal law requires proof of *mens rea* in cases of extreme speech. Notably, *mens rea* is an element of the offences of 'public incitement of hatred' and – as

---

[43] It may be reiterated that the Committee does not refer to Art. 20(2) in this case.

[44] Human Rights Committee, *Robert Faurisson* v. *France*, Communication no. 550/1993 (19 July 1995), para. 9.6.

[45] *Robert Faurisson* v. *France*, para. 9.7.

[46] Individual opinion by Elizabeth Evatt and David Kretzmer, co-signed by Eckart Klein (concurring), para. 9: this law does 'not link liability to the intent of the author' thus unnecessarily chilling free speech.

[47] Individual opinion by Rajsoomer Lallah, para. 6.

[48] Individual opinion by Prafullachandra Bhagwati (concurring), para. F, paraphrasing the plenary Committee's views on Faurisson's liability yet conspicuously inserting the word 'calculated' in relation to the latter's speech acts.

the crime suggests – 'wilful promotion of hatred'.[49] Not quite dealing with
a criminal incitement conviction, the *Ross* case more specifically concerned the question of whether it was right for the authorities to remove
this teacher from his position as a result of his off-duty anti-Semitic pam-
phleteering. Canada pointed out that in disciplining Ross, it had complied with a high burden of proof in relation to *mens rea*, borrowed from
criminal procedure. Specifically, the Human Rights Board of Inquiry that
monitored Ross' dismissal established an element of active and calculated – and thus 'wilful' – incitement.[50] Moreover, based upon a closer
assessment of Ross' writing techniques the Board of Inquiry ascertained
that the inciteful statements were his and that he fully understood their
meaning.[51] Thus it was held that Ross' 'primary purpose is clearly to attack
the truthfulness, integrity, dignity and motives of Jewish persons',[52] which
in the above outlined terminology can be construed as 'intent to advocate
hatred' and 'intent to target' a particular group characterized by religion
or ethnicity. In addition, the Supreme Court of Canada, in a final domestic instalment of this case, for its part placed special emphasis on the fact
that Ross had not merely spread hatred against Jews but had in fact called
upon 'true Christians' to 'hold those of the Jewish faith in contempt' and
to join him 'in the battle' against them.[53] These fighting words could be
construed as, if not specific, then oblique intent to incite to discrimination and/or hostility.

While Ross denied that he wilfully incited hostility or discrimination
against Jews,[54] the Human Rights Committee concurred with Canada.
Although it avoided any direct language on *mens rea* it paraphrased the
Canadian Supreme Court findings in particular. Accordingly, it adopted
the language that can be understood as accepting Ross' oblique intent to
incite discrimination against Jewish persons.[55]

---

[49] Sections 319(1) and 319(2) of the Criminal Code of Canada 1985. On extreme speech laws
in Canada, see Richard Moon, 'Hate Speech Regulations in Canada' (2009) 36 *Florida
State University Law Review* 79–97; and L. W. Summer, 'Incitement and the Regulation
of Hate Speech in Canada: A Philosophical Analysis', in Ivan Hare and James Weinstein
(eds.), *Extreme Speech and Democracy* (Oxford University Press, 2009), 204–20.

[50] Human Rights Committee, *Malcolm Ross* v. *Canada*, Communication no. 736/1997
(18 October 2000), para. 4.2.

[51] *Malcolm Ross* v. *Canada*, para. 4.2.

[52] *Malcolm Ross* v. *Canada*, para. 4.2.

[53] *Malcolm Ross* v. *Canada*, para. 6.2 (at para. 4.2 the Board of Inquiry makes a similar
point).

[54] *Malcolm Ross* v. *Canada*, para. 7.2.

[55] *Malcolm Ross* v. *Canada*, para. 11.5 ('the author's statements were discriminatory against
persons of the Jewish faith and ancestry and … denigrated the faith and beliefs of Jews

In sum, while circumventing direct pronouncements on a requirement of *mens rea*, the Committee has distilled notions of criminal liability from Article 20(2) of the ICCPR.

9.5   CERD and intent

By contrast, for a long time CERD's official position was that the extreme speech prohibitions contained in Article 4 ICERD should be enforced regardless of the precise intentions of the person responsible for the alleged racist hate speech. For instance, in a 1985 report on Article 4 the Committee bluntly and adamantly states that 'the mere act of dissemination is penalized, despite lack of intention to commit an offence and irrespective of the consequences of the dissemination, whether they be grave or insignificant'.[56] At that time, there were at least a couple of dozen State parties requiring intent under their criminal laws.[57] CERD based its argument against intent on the broad definition of discrimination contained in Article 1 of the ICERD. Mentioning the words 'purpose or effect', the Convention's discrimination definition covers both 'purposive or intentional discrimination and discrimination in effect'.[58] This inclusive definition, CERD has long believed, in turn frees the crime of propaganda of racial hatred in the meaning of Article 4 of ICERD from a requirement of *mens rea*. Indeed, the Committee has repeatedly reproached State parties for requiring criminal intent contrary to the – apparent – requirements of Article 4.[59]

CERD's early position on intent was not free from criticism. First of all, some State parties themselves have had a hard time accepting this.

and called upon true Christians to not merely question the validity of Jewish beliefs and teachings but to hold those of the Jewish faith and ancestry in contempt').

[56] *Positive Measures Designed to Eradicate all Incitement to, or Acts of, Racial Discrimination – Implementation of the International Convention on the Elimination of All Forms of Racial Discrimination, Article 4*, UN Doc. CERD/2 (1985) at 37, para. 221. There is also an earlier version of the report, prepared for the 1983 World Conference Against Racism (A/CONF.119/10). See also Stephanie Farrior, 'Molding the Matrix: The Historical and Theoretical Foundations of International Law Concerning Hate Speech' (1996) 14:1 *Berkeley Journal of International Law* 1–98, at 57.

[57] See section 9.7 of this chapter for the current state of play.

[58] CERD, *General Recommendation 32: The Meaning and Scope of Special Measures in the International Convention on the Elimination of All Forms of Racial Discrimination* (CERD/C/GC/32, Seventy-fifth session, 3–28 August 2009, para. 7.

[59] E.g. CERD, A/56/18 (2001) 34, para. 171 (Japan); A/54/18 (1999) 37, para. 374 (Chile); and A/61/18 (2006), para. 419 (Ukraine), first noticing this shortcoming as early as 1980 (see A/35/18, para. 426).

As mentioned, many State parties did and still do insist upon criminal intent, for that is the age-old legal and judicial practice within their jurisdiction, not only in respect of extreme speech offences but also possibly in relation to all criminal law offences.[60] In addition, other important stakeholders have agitated against the position on *mens rea* adopted by the Committee on the Elimination of Racial Discrimination. Notably, Amnesty International has called on the Committee to 'clarify that Article 4(a) requires an intention to disseminate ideas that advocate racial hatred before that dissemination is punishable by law', arguing that to do otherwise leads to inconsistencies amongst State parties, legal uncertainty and threats to free speech.[61] What seemed to have sparked major concern amongst key players at the international level was the fact that CERD was among the few monitoring bodies to actually welcome Denmark's conviction of a journalist who, by interviewing and broadcasting the interview of members of an openly racist Danish group, had committed the crime of 'aiding and abetting' the dissemination of hateful statements.[62] While it cannot be denied that by making this item for television the journalist in question had in the most literal sense of the word 'disseminated' extremist views, other monitoring bodies reproached Denmark, insisting that the objectives of the journalist ought to be taken into account, as in that way it can be guaranteed that only persons directly responsible for publicly uttering extremist views are punished.[63]

Moreover, individual CERD members have spoken out against the Committee's position on *mens rea*. Former member Patrick Thornberry has argued that CERD's indifference towards questions of *mens rea* 'approaches the domain of strict or absolute liability, and the total absence of culpability elements beyond the act of dissemination would do violence

---

[60] See also Farrior, 'Molding the Matrix', at 57. See section 9.7 of this chapter for more details.

[61] Amnesty International, *Written Contribution on Racist Hate Speech*, at 4.

[62] CERD, A/51/18 (1996) 17, para. 62 ('Noting the [chamber decision in the case of *Jersild v. Denmark*], it is affirmed that the "due regard" clause of article 4 of the Convention requires due balancing of the right to protection from racial discrimination against the right to freedom of expression'). Previously some Committee members had welcomed Denmark's conviction of Jersild as 'the clearest statement yet, in any country, that the right to protection against racial discrimination took precedence over the right to freedom of expression'. CERD, A/45/18 (1991), at 21 (para. 56; the same paragraph mentions that some members, however, disagreed with that view).

[63] See European Court of Human Rights, *Jersild v. Denmark*, Application no. 15890/89 (Grand Chamber judgment of 23 September 1994). This decision is discussed in more detail in section 9.6 of this chapter.

to basic principles of criminal liability in many if not most jurisdictions'.[64] Thornberry further posits that 'the element of striving to bring about a particular result is commonly built into the notion of incitement, whether or not the desired result is achieved'.[65] There is much to be said for Thornberry's views.[66] Obviously, a lax legal attitude towards *mens rea* fosters the successful prosecution of alleged inciters. Yet such could very well also foster abuse of extreme speech laws, thus stifling free speech and causing a chilling effect thereon.

Recently the Committee on the Elimination of Racial Discrimination has shown itself to be responsive to such critiques. In its 2013 General Recommendation on racial hate speech the Committee made a U-turn on the question of *mens rea* in relation to Article 4. In a paragraph specifically dedicated to the crime of 'incitement' the Committee postulates that State parties should recognize as 'important elements' of this offence 'the intention of the speaker and the imminent risk or likelihood that the conduct desired or intended by the speaker will result from the speech in question'.[67] From the references accompanying this change of heart it transpires that the Committee has been particularly influenced by the Rabat Plan of Action and the Human Rights Committee's interpretation of the necessity principle.[68] CERD also explicitly acknowledges the flip-side of posing an incitement requirement in relation to Article 4's speech offences; that is, from the apparent 'objectives of the speech' it may very well follow that the speaker should not be criminally liable under

---

[64] Patrick Thornberry, 'Forms of Hate Speech and the Convention on the Elimination of all Forms of Racial Discrimination (ICERD)' (2010) 5 *Religion & Human Rights*, 97–117, at 109.

[65] Thornberry, 'Forms of Hate Speech and ICERD', at 109.

[66] Note that rather than pleading for a full-fledged U-turn on the part of the Committee itself to the effect that the latter would impose a requirement of intent on all State parties, he argues in favour of granting State parties some discretion to retain their own rules of criminal procedure in this area. Thornberry, 'Forms of Hate Speech and ICERD', 109–10.

[67] CERD, *General Recommendation 35: Combating Racist Hate Speech* (UN Doc. CERD/C/GC/35, 83rd session, 12–30 August 2013), para. 16. Cross references used in that paragraph seem to indicate that this requirement applies to all extreme speech offences listed by Art. 4 ICERD and not only to racist incitement.

[68] See *Rabat Plan of Action*, para. 22. The Human Rights Committee has ruled that '[w]hen a State party invokes a legitimate ground for restriction of freedom of expression, it must demonstrate in specific and individualized fashion the precise nature of the threat, and the necessity and proportionality of the specific action taken, in particular by establishing a direct and immediate connection between the expression and the threat'. Human Rights Committee, *General Comment 34*, para. 35 (first held in *Hak–Chul Shin* v. *Republic of Korea*, Communication no. 926/2000, 16 March 2004, para. 7.3). CERD cites these sources in *General Recommendation 35*, para. 16 (at fn. 18).

incitement laws.[69] While CERD in this regard singles out 'speech protecting or defending the human rights of individuals and groups', it would appear that this point may be applicable to many different speech acts and speakers, for instance on account of their apparent journalistic, scientific or artistic motives.[70]

To sum up, while CERD originally positioned itself as a staunch opponent to a *mens rea* requirement in relation to the speech offences covered by Article 4 of the ICERD, recent practice indicates that it embraces the principle that a conviction for (racist) incitement requires proof of intent to incite.

9.6   The European Court of Human Rights and intent

From the outset it must be observed that for the Strasbourg Court the question of *mens rea* emerges in a somewhat different legal setting. As outlined in Chapter 6, the European Convention on Human Rights does not contain an anti-extreme speech provision that could serve as the equivalent of Article 20(2) ICCPR or Article 4 ICERD. Hence, State parties to the Convention are not *obliged* to combat extreme speech. Yet under the Convention they may be *permitted* to do so to the extent that such would be compatible with the limitations provided by the free speech article itself (Article 10 ECHR). More specifically, then, the question of *mens rea* may surface in the context of checking the necessity of a state's interference with a speech act.

From the European Court of Human Right's judgments in extreme speech cases it transpires that it indeed often raises the matter of intent (among other factors) so as to determine whether or not it was necessary in a democratic society for the state to penalize the impugned speech act. The best example of a case in which the apparent lack of criminal 'intent to incite' persuaded the Court to find in favour of the applicant is the previously mentioned case of *Jersild* v. *Denmark*.[71] The applicant had made a documentary about the Greenjackets, a group of openly racist youths based in Copenhagen. For that purpose, Jersild had conducted interviews with members of this group. Out of several hours of footage, the applicant used a couple of minutes in the final version of the documentary. The item was broadcast on Danish television as part of a programme consisting of

---

[69]   CERD, *General Recommendation 35*, para. 15 (final bullet), referencing the *Rabat Plan of Action*.

[70]   CERD, *General Recommendation 35*, para. 15 (final bullet).

[71]   European Court of Human Rights, *Jersild* v. *Denmark*, Application no. 15890/89 (Grand Chamber judgment of 23 September 1994).

various news items.[72] The brief introduction to the Greenjacket item stated that it was intended to investigate where racism in Denmark stems from, who 'the people who hate the minorities' are and what their mentality is like.[73] Subsequently, the item shows Jersild interviewing three members of the Greenjackets, who use abusive and racist language in relation to black persons and foreigners in general. At times they deny the humanity of their target groups ('A nigger is not a human being, it's an animal, that goes for all the other foreign workers as well, Turks, Yugoslavs and whatever they are called').[74] The Danish courts convicted Jersild for 'aiding and abetting' dissemination of the Greenjackets' racist views (he received a fine of 1,000 Danish kroner).[75]

Before the Strasbourg Court, the Danish Government argued that Jersild's item was of a sensational rather than newsworthy nature. In addition, Jersild knew full well that a spree of racist abuse would ensue from the way he had set up the interview with these hateful youths. Thus Jersild had abused a powerful medium such as television to all but facilitate a platform for racist propaganda.[76] Jersild denied all this and contended that he had sought to draw the public's attention to the societal problem that is racism. The context of the item made it sufficiently clear, he argued, that he had not aimed at disseminating racist views but to expose and even repudiate them.[77]

While the item could have underscored 'the immorality, dangers and unlawfulness of the promotion of racial hatred and of ideas of superiority of one race' much better,[78] the Strasbourg Court sided with Jersild. The Court distilled Jersild's intentions from the context in which the Greenjacket item was presented and from the item's ostensible 'purpose'. According to the Court he had, in his introduction to the item, sufficiently dissociated himself from the radicals' views.[79] It should be observed that no less than seven judges had doubts about the documentary maker's bona fide intentions, arguing that he should have included much more comprehensive disclaimers of personal disapproval.[80]

---

[72] *Jersild* v. *Denmark*, paras. 9–11.   [73] *Jersild* v. *Denmark*, para. 11.

[74] *Jersild* v. *Denmark*. para. 11. The comparison to animals is made a couple of times.

[75] *Jersild* v. *Denmark*, paras. 13–14.

[76] *Jersild* v. *Denmark*, para. 29.   [77] *Jersild* v. *Denmark*, para. 28.

[78] *Jersild* v. *Denmark*, para. 34.   [79] *Jersild* v. *Denmark*, para. 34.

[80] Joint dissenting opinion of Judges Ryssdal, Bernhardt, Spielmann and Loizou; and Joint dissenting opinion of Judges Gölcüklü, Russo and Valticos. As we have seen before, CERD also implicitly questioned this decision. See notably CERD, A/51/18 (1996) 17, para. 62 [Denmark], where the Committee on the Elimination of Racial Discrimination

In *Jersild* the controversy over questions of *mens rea* is fuelled by the peculiar way Danish anti-extreme speech law is phrased. At the basis of his domestic conviction lies the following offence:

> Any person who, publicly or with the intention of disseminating it to a wide circle of people, makes a statement, or other communication, threatening, insulting or degrading a group of persons on account of their race, colour, national or ethnic origin or belief shall be liable to a fine or to simple detention or to imprisonment for a term not exceeding two years.[81]

Setting aside the fact that the *actus reus* of this offence – insulting or degrading – is overly broad, the required *mens rea* pertains to the act of 'dissemination' per se. In the terminology developed above, this offence does not appear to be premised on multiple intent; notably a requirement of (oblique) intent in relation to the act of incitement – here 'threatening' – is omitted. Accordingly, all persons, including journalists or scientists, who publish or broadcast about extremism are criminally liable since they could be accused of 'disseminating' extremism in the literal sense of the word. Regardless of any misgivings one may have about the quality of the Greenjacket item, the domestic law and judicial proceedings that lay at the basis of the case of *Jersild* provide further arguments in firm support of a robust and multiple requirement of intent.

The *Jersild* judgment is in any event a strong indication that the European Court of Human Rights takes *mens rea* into account in the present context. This has been confirmed in subsequent decisions. Thus in *Lehideux and Isorni* v. *France* the Court distinguished the intention of the authors, who sought by way of a full-page advertisement in *Le Monde* to rehabilitate Marshal Pétain, from the intentions of those who more directly and unreservedly glorify the crimes of National Socialism and from those who deny the Holocaust and other Nazi crimes outright.[82] For a Holocaust denier such as Roger Garaudy, according to the European Court of Human Rights, 'the real purpose [is] to rehabilitate the National-Socialist regime'.[83] Lehideux (a minister in the Government of Pétain) and Isorni (the defence lawyer for Pétain at his

---

'notes' the European Court's judgment, yet reiterates that freedom of expression and protection against racial discrimination '[require] due balancing'.

[81] Art. 266(b) of the Danish Criminal Code (as it read at the material time). Aiding and abetting others to commit criminal offences is covered by Art. 23 of the Danish Criminal Code.

[82] European Court of Human Rights, *Lehideux and Isorni* v. *France*, Application no. 55/1997/839/1045 (Grand Chamber judgment of 23 September 1998).

[83] European Court of Human Rights, *Garaudy* v. *France*, Application no. 65831/01 (admissibility decision of 24 June 2003).

1945 trial in which he was sentenced to death), although their writings were effectively in support of Nazi collaborators, could not be accused of attempting to deny or revise Nazi atrocities. Calling Philippe Pétain's policies 'supremely skilful', Lehideux and Isorni were, in the words of the Strasbourg Court, 'rather supporting one of the conflicting theories in the debate about the role of the head of the Vichy government, the so-called "double game" theory'.[84] In an earlier decision on admissibility the former European Commission of Human Rights had already come to the conclusion that 'the advertisement which had given rise to the applicants' conviction did not contain any terms of racial hatred or other statements *calculated to destroy or restrict the rights and freedoms* guaranteed by the Convention'.[85] Thus the Commission had held, in so many words, that the advertisement lacked a clear aim of incitement. The Court endorsed that reading. While reproaching the authors of the advertisement for their polemical and clearly extremely one-sided depiction of Pétain,[86] ignoring all his objectionable conduct and the offences he had been accused of, the Court concluded that their advertisement amounted to protected speech under the Convention and that France had unjustifiably restricted their freedom. Like *Jersild*, it was a split decision with a number of judges being convinced that the speech act's clear distortions and omissions in relation to Pétain's regime were evidence of unsavoury aims – namely, Nazi apologetic – on the part of the applicants.[87] Thus, according to the latter judges, it was quite apparent that the impugned speech act did not amount to a genuine contribution of public or historical interest and should not have been treated like one.

Naturally, the Strasbourg Court's assessment of *mens rea* could also yield support for the domestic conviction of an inciter. Accordingly, in such cases as *Leroy* v. *France* and *Féret* v. *Belgium* the unveiled degrees of *mens rea* on the part of the applicant tipped the balance in favour of findings of no violation of free speech. The former case revolved around an act of apparent glorification of terrorist violence.[88] Leroy had published in a newspaper a cartoon depicting the burning Twin Towers in New York

---

[84] *Lehideux and Isorni* v. *France*, para. 47.

[85] European Commission of Human Rights, admissibility decision of 24 June 1996 (emphasis added).

[86] *Lehideux and Isorni* v. *France*, paras. 52–54, calling (at para. 54) the deliberate omission of criticism 'morally reprehensible'.

[87] Joint dissenting opinion of Judges Foighel, Loizou and John Freeland; and dissenting opinion of Judge Casadevall.

[88] European Court of Human Rights, *Leroy* v. *France*, Application no. 36109/03 (2 October 2008).

and adapting a well-known advertising slogan by adding the caption 'We
have all dreamt of it ... Hamas did it.'[89] In coming to their conclusion that
Leroy had thus committed the offence of condoning terrorism, French
judges had emphasized the combination of the drawing of the burning
towers, the word 'dream', which positively reflects on the event, and on
the use of the plural 'We', which appeared to justify recourse to terrorism
and even encourage it.[90] In front of the Strasbourg Court, the applicant
complained that this was too literal an assessment of his cartoon, lacking understanding of the trade of the cartoonist, which is to offer political, activist or satirical comments on the news. Specifically, he argued
that in creating this cartoon, he was not driven by terrorist motives, but
rather by anti-Americanism. His cartoon, as he had also pleaded before
the French courts, would have illustrated the decline of US imperial-
ism.[91] The European Court of Human Rights, however, could not see,
based on the cartoon, how the author could possibly have intended that
and agreed with France that the combination of images and text had a
condoning undertone.[92] The Court went on to admit that cartoons are
a form of artistic expression and social commentary that by definition
aims at exaggeration, the distortion of reality, satire and provocation; yet
this does not mean that it is impossible for a cartoon artist to overstep the
legal mark.[93] What appears to have tipped the balance, for the Court, was
the fact that publication of the cartoon occurred only days after the 9/11
attacks, while the whole world was trying to come to terms with it, and
that the newspaper was published in a particularly sensitive region where
it could easily stir up violence.[94] The Court seemed to imply that Leroy
was or should have been aware of both of these special circumstances.[95]
Thus, the Court implicitly bases Leroy's criminal culpability on a degree
of *mens rea* somewhere in between 'knowledge' and 'recklessness'.

Similarly, in *Féret v. Belgium* the European Court of Human Rights
concurred with the responding state on the question of criminal liability
of the inciter.[96] Chairman of a Belgian far right political party, Féret was
responsible for the creation and distribution of leaflets and posters agitat-
ing against immigrants and Muslims, as a result of which he was convicted

---

[89] *Leroy* v. *France*, para. 6.   [90] *Leroy* v. *France*, para. 42.

[91] *Leroy* v. *France*, paras. 10 and 42.

[92] *Leroy* v. *France*, para. 43.   [93] *Leroy* v. *France*, para. 44.

[94] Such context factors will be discussed in more detail in Chapter 10.

[95] *Leroy* v. *France*, para. 45.

[96] European Court of Human Rights, *Féret v. Belgium*, Application no. 15615/07
(16 July 2009).

of 'clear and deliberate incitation of discrimination, segregation or hatred, and even violence, for reasons of race, colour or national or ethnic origin'.[97] His parliamentary immunity being lifted, this resulted in a suspended prison sentence, a fine and being barred from public office for no less than ten years.[98] The European Court of Human Rights in yet another split decision – 4–3 in this case – permitted this conviction. The disagreement amongst judges was to a considerable extent concentrated on the requirement of *mens rea*. The majority decision stated that for a State party to legitimately combat extreme speech, it is not required that the hate speech in question includes an express aim of inciting to violence or to particular criminal acts.[99] Deliberately spreading hatred that amounts to 'incitement to discrimination' may be sufficient to incur criminal liability.[100] Subsequently, the Court determined that language employed by Féret had 'clearly incited discrimination'.[101] The dissenting judges argued that this remained very doubtful. According to them, Féret had certainly not incited to violence – in between the lines it was suggested that this should be the one and only *mens rea* requirement[102] – and the campaign posters and materials, though xenophobic and generally contrary to the 'spirit' of the Convention, could also not reasonably be construed as acts of deliberate incitement to racial or religious discrimination.[103]

A somewhat dissimilar series of case law that revolve around criminal convictions as a result of verbal, sometimes vehement attacks on religions and/or religious believers shed further light (*mutatis mutandis*) on the Court's dealing with *mens rea*. In some of those cases the Court found that the person in question should not have been penalized since the purpose of their speech act was to contribute to a genuine debate (e.g. *Giniewski* v. *France*, concerning a publication accusing the Catholic Church and Catholic doctrine of fostering anti-Semitism and the Holocaust; and *Klein* v. *Slovakia*, concerning a verbal attack on a church leader).[104] In other such cases the Court found fault with State parties' convictions of

---

[97] *Féret* v. *Belgium*, paras. 7–41.   [98] *Féret* v. *Belgium*, para. 34.

[99] *Féret* v. *Belgium*, para. 73 ('La Cour estime que l'incitation à la haine ne requiert pas nécessairement l'appel à tel ou tel acte de violence ou à un autre acte délictueux').

[100] *Féret* v. *Belgium*, para. 73.

[101] *Féret* v. *Belgium*, para. 78.

[102] Note that the dissent is written by Judge Sajó. In his country, Hungary, a high-threshold judicial doctrine of 'clear and present danger' is applicable to cases of extreme speech.

[103] Dissenting opinion of Judge Sajó, joined by Judges Zagrebelsky and Tsotsoria.

[104] European Court of Human Rights, *Giniewski* v. *France*, Application No. 64016/00, judgment of 31 January 2006; *Klein* v. *Slovakia*, Application no. 72208/01 (31 October 2006), particularly paras. 51–52. See, however, *Willem* v. *France*, Application no. 10883/05

speakers or authors, since it could not reasonably be claimed that the person in question, although using offensive language, had actually incited harm upon a target group (e.g. *Aydın Tatlav* v. *Turkey*, concerning an anti-religious publication; and *Gündüz* v. *Turkey*, concerning televized anti-secularist speech by a leader of the Islamic order of Aczmendi).[105] At the same time, the Court has occasionally permitted restrictions on speech acts that, although perhaps 'gratuitously offensive', by no means amounted to extreme speech and certainly not to 'incitement'.[106] Those decisions are very problematic. While the Convention lacks a legal yardstick of 'incitement', the Court would do well to revisit that jurisprudence by consistently assessing, in relevant cases, whether or not the impugned speech act truly put at jeopardy the 'rights of others', including their religious and equality rights, rather than assessing if and to what extent the speech act was intended to hurt the religious feelings of others and succeeded in doing so.[107]

In the context of its Article 17 jurisprudence *mens rea* plays a role too. There, proof of criminal intent serves as a mighty factor in determining an 'abuse of rights', causing certain free speech complaints to be inadmissible.[108] While the Court's heavy reliance on Article 17 in cases of extreme

---

(16 July 2009). In the latter case a mayor had called upon his municipality to boycott Israeli products. For this he was convicted of incitement to discrimination on national, racial and religious grounds. He argued that he had acted in this way so as to protest against anti-Palestinian policies carried out by the State of Israel. While this appears to be a contribution to a public debate, the Strasbourg Court sanctioned France's conviction, placing particular emphasis on his public role.

[105] European Court of Human Rights, *Aydın Tatlav* v. *Turkey*, Application no. 50692/99 (2 May 2006); *Gündüz* v. *Turkey*, Application no. 35071/97 (4 December 2003). See also, *mutatis mutandis*, European Court of Human Rights, *Nur Radyo Ve Televizyon Yayinciligi A.S.* v. *Turkey*, Application no. 6587/03 (27 November 2007), indirectly concerning statements made by a religious leader of the Mihr community who had suggested on the radio that a recent earthquake killing thousands amounted to an act of punishment of infidels by Allah. The broadcasting ban imposed on the radio station concerned was disproportionate according to the Court.

[106] E.g. European Commission of Human Rights, *X. Ltd. and Y.* v. *United Kingdom*, Application no. 8710/79 (7 May 1982); European Court of Human Rights, *Otto-Preminger-Institut* v. *Austria*, Application no. 13470/87 (20 September 1994); *Wingrove* v. *United Kingdom*, Application no. 17419/90 (25 November 1996); *Murphy* v. *Ireland*, Application no. 44179/98 (10 July 2003); *İ.A.* v. *Turkey*, Application no. 42571/98 (13 September 2005).

[107] For a more comprehensive account, see Jeroen Temperman, 'Blasphemy, Defamation of Religions and Human Rights Law' (2008) 26:4 *Netherlands Quarterly of Human Rights* 517–45.

[108] The 'guillotine' approach and more indirect uses of Art. 17 in the Court's extreme speech jurisprudence have been outlined in sections 6.6.1 and 6.6.2 of Chapter 6.

speech may be criticized,[109] this body of jurisprudence does show that *mens rea* is an important factor for the Strasbourg Court in its extreme speech jurisprudence. Notably, in the case of *Glimmerveen and Hagenbeek v. The Netherlands* the European Commission of Human Rights established an inciteful or at least plain racist intention on the part of the first applicant, the leader of a far right political party, who had been convicted for possession of flyers that criticized immigrants and non-whites. Specifically, the former Commission reasoned that 'the policy advocated by the applicants is inspired by the overall aim to remove all non-white people from the Netherlands' territory, in complete disregard of their nationality, time of residence, family ties, as well as social, economic, humanitarian or other considerations'.[110] Furthermore, the Commission agreed with the Dutch authorities that the xenophobic flyers in question would, when disseminated, 'certainly encourage' racial discrimination.[111] Accordingly, the apparent intent to incite on the part of the applicants was a crucial factor in deeming the complaint inadmissible.

Some cases show that the European Court of Human Rights occasionally directly (partly) distils *mens rea* from the submissions that applicants make before this Court. Thus, if in *W.P. and others v. Poland* the fiercely anti-Semitic intentions of the applicants were not already plainly evident from the national proceedings – concerning an association of 'victims of Zionism' that aimed at the abolition of 'the privileges of ethnic Jews' – the Strasbourg Court further noted 'the anti-Semitic tenor of some of their submissions made before the Court'.[112] Similarly, in *Hizb ut-Tahrir and others v. Germany*, a case concerning a fundamentalist group that seeks

---

[109] See Hannes Cannie and Dirk Voorhoof, 'The Abuse Clause and Freedom of Expression in the European Human Rights Convention: An Added Value for Democracy and Human Rights Protection? (2011) 29:1 *Netherlands Quarterly of Human Rights* 54–83.

[110] European Commission of Human Rights, *Glimmerveen and Hagenbeek v. The Netherlands*, Application nos. 8348/78 and 8406/78 (inadmissibility decision of 11 October 1979), at 'The law'. Also, their pamphlets 'would certainly encourage' acts of discrimination, and were thus thought to be inciteful.

[111] *Glimmerveen and Hagenbeek v. The Netherlands*, 'The law'.

[112] European Court of Human Rights, *W.P. and others v. Poland*, Application no. 42264/98 (admissibility decision of 2 September 2004), para. (iii) of 'The Law', deeming points 6 ('Taking action aimed at equality between ethnic Poles and citizens of Jewish origin by striving to abolish the privileges of ethnic Jews and by striving to end the persecution of ethnic Poles'), 12 ('Taking action aimed at improving the living conditions of Polish victims of Bolshevism/Bolsheviks and Zionism/Zionists') and 15 ('Claiming veteran benefits for Polish victims of Bolshevism/Bolsheviks and Zionism/Zionists') of the organization's statute as strikingly anti-Semitic and, in addition, holding that the applicants' 'racist attitudes' transpire from their submissions to the Strasbourg Court.

the worldwide overthrow of secular governments, the global introduction of Sharia law as well as the destruction of Israel, a finding of inadmissibility was significantly fuelled by the attitude of the applicants during the Strasbourg proceedings. Specifically, the Court observed that the impugned statements 'justified suicide attacks in which civilians were killed in Israel and that neither the first nor the second applicant distanced themselves from this stance during the proceedings before the Court'.[113]

The latter type of incitement is perhaps not typical. In cases of 'extreme speech' the speaker oftentimes avoids making explicit the precise – potentially inciteful – intentions he or she has. Considering the fact that Article 17 refers, in so many words, to the bad intentions on the part of the abuser ('any activity … *aimed at* the destruction of any of the rights and freedoms'), one would expect the Strasbourg Court to always monitor this factor closely whenever a responding state pleads that the complainant abused his or her rights. However, the Court has repeatedly taken this hurdle fairly uncritically, suggesting that it knows abuse when it sees it. Thus in *Pavel Ivanov* v. *Russia*, concerning a series of articles in which the Jews were accused of being the cause of all evil in Russia, the Court simply held that it had 'no doubt as to the markedly anti-Semitic tenor of the applicant's views', thus agreeing 'with the assessment made by the domestic courts that he sought through his publications to incite hatred towards the Jewish people'.[114] In *Norwood* v. *UK* the Court altogether omitted an assessment of the intentions of Mark Anthony Norwood, a member of the far right British National Party.[115] Norwood had displayed a poster in the window of his house with a photograph of the burning Twin Towers, together with the crescent and star symbol as part of a prohibited sign, and the words 'Islam out of Britain – Protect the British People'.[116] Thus Norwood's verbal attack on Islam is comparable to that of the earlier discussed Belgian right-wing politician, Féret. Yet while the latter's freedom

---

[113] European Court of Human Rights, *Hizb Ut-Tahrir and others* v. *Germany*, Application no. 31098/08 (admissibility decision of 12 June 2012), para. 73. The inciteful aims of the Hizb ut-Tahrir movement have been further dissected in the *Kasymakhunov and Saybatalov* case, where the Court in so many words said that State parties may ban this group and criminalize individual membership. See *Kasymakhunov and Saybatalov* v. *Russia*, Application nos. 26261/05 and 26377/06 (14 March 2013), in particular paras. 106–13.

[114] European Court of Human Rights, *Pavel Ivanov* v. *Russia*, Application no. 35222/04 (admissibility decision of 20 February 2007), para. 1 of 'The Law'.

[115] European Court of Human Rights, *Mark Anthony Norwood* v. *United Kingdom*, Application no. 23131/03 (admissibility decision of 16 November 2004).

[116] *Mark Anthony Norwood* v. *United Kingdom*, para. A of 'The facts'.

of expression complaint was discussed on the merits, Norwood's application was dismissed outright. While the Strasbourg Court observed that the poster 'amounted' to a public attack on the Muslims of Britain and, as such,[117] to an expression not protected by the Covenant, it did not dwell on the precise degree of *mens rea* on the part of Norwood. Perhaps his intentions were all too clear; yet further elaboration on Norwood's precise *aim* to destroy the rights of Muslims – to adopt the Article 17 formula – would have been in order.

9.7   State practice

The terms 'crimes' or 'offences' in most criminal law systems are systematically premised on a (strong) decree of culpability; accordingly, this does not always need to be spelled out separately for each criminal offence.[118] That said, incitement in the meaning of international law is a highly qualified offence. As outlined in this chapter, Article 20(2) is premised on various types of *mens rea* in relation to the specific elements of the incitement offence. In the light of that, it remains crucial for all State parties that in the process of adjudicating cases of alleged incitement, justice is given to Article 20(2)'s multiple *mens rea* requirement.

National incitement laws, purporting to generally implement Article 20(2) of the ICCPR, impact this aspect of the adjudication process. Those laws should either follow Article 20(2)'s terminology closely, or clearly reflect the fact that meeting a multiple *mens rea* criterion is required in order to convict incitement offenders. The Criminal Code of Moldova provides an example of a multiple *mens rea* requirement. It provides that '*[d]eliberate actions* or public statements spread by [a number of means] *with the aim* of fomenting national, racial or religious discord or hatred ... are to be punished'.[119] Accordingly, both the intent to publicly advocate and the intent to incite (here to 'foment') must be proven in order to reach a conviction. The incitement clause enshrined in the criminal law

---

[117] *Mark Anthony Norwood* v. *United Kingdom*, 'The Law', calling the poster a 'vehement attack against a religious group, linking the group as a whole with a grave act of terrorism'.

[118] See e.g. Art. 4(1) of the Criminal Code of Hungary 2012, providing that most 'criminal offences' listed in the Code must be committed 'intentionally' for them to be punishable.

[119] Art. 346 of the Criminal Code of Moldova 2002 (emphasis added). The word 'or' before 'public statements' implies that intent is a given when the impugned speech act is made in public. Since 'advocacy' in the meaning of Art. 20(2) ICCPR is chiefly characterized by an act of public dissemination, that formulation may be reconciled with the latter provision.

of Portugal also hints at a double intent requirement. In order to incur criminal liability, one must first have 'intended' to spread the statement publicly,[120] and second, one's intent must be expressly linked to one of the proscribed results listed by the ICCPR (namely 'discrimination').[121] The UK Racial and Religious Hatred Act is also premised on multiple requirements of intent. First, the person who uses 'threatening words' must have intended thereby to stir up religious (or racial) hatred.[122] Second, the speech act must have been disseminated deliberately to a wider public. A lack of the latter intention may be accepted as a defence to hate speech charges.[123]

Some national laws explicitly prescribe an intent requirement in relation to the element of 'advocacy', that is the act of disseminating the hateful message to a wider, non-private audience. The Danish hate speech provision, for instance, penalizes certain statements that threaten religious and other groups if they are made 'with the intention of wider dissemination'.[124] Latvian penal law also links a degree of *mens rea* ('knowingly') to the advocacy of hatred, not to the question of incitement.[125] While it is in line with Article 20(2) of the ICCPR to emphasize an intent requirement in relation to the act of 'advocacy', these formulations may be criticized inasmuch as they imply – *a contrario* – that no further *mens rea* is required for a criminal conviction.

While for reasons explained in this chapter it is best if national incitement laws and jurisprudence impose multiple *mens rea* requirements, if legislators decide on inserting a single reference to criminal intent, they are best to do so in relation to 'incitement', since the 'intent to advocate' and the 'intent to target' most likely inherently flow from the incitement offence anyway. That is, a degree of *mens rea* is in any event likely to follow from the requirement that the hateful message must, in order to qualify, be made publicly (something that is almost always required). Similarly, the

---

[120] Art. 240(2) of the Criminal Code of Portugal 2006 (Law No. 65/98 of 2 September 1998): 'Anyone who, in a public assembly, in a writing intended to be divulged or by means of mass communication…'.

[121] Art. 240(2)(b) of the Criminal Code of Portugal 2006: 'intending to incite to racial or religious discrimination or to encourage it'.

[122] Section 29B, para. 1 of the Racial and Religious Hatred Act 2006. It may be reiterated, however, that this is not a proscribed result in the meaning of Art. 20(2) ICCPR.

[123] Section 29B, para. 4 of the Racial and Religious Hatred Act 2006.

[124] Section 266b of the Criminal Code of Denmark (Consolidated Act No. 1034 of 29 October 2009).

[125] Section 78 of the Criminal Code of Latvia 1998: 'acts knowingly directed towards instigating hatred'.

'intent to target' a specific group tends to more or less automatically flow from most incitement provisions, since they typically (exhaustively) list the prohibited grounds – such as religion or ethnicity – for the incitement offence. The specific (oblique) 'intent to incite', however, is best indicated expressly, for otherwise it cannot at all be guaranteed that enforcement practices will do justice to this requirement. At present, however, only a small number of State parties have adopted incitement laws that explicitly require (direct or oblique) 'intent to incite'.[126] Some State parties have expressly settled for a lower degree of *mens rea*. For example, the Criminal Code of Norway provides that punishable incitement can be committed both 'wilfully' and 'through gross negligence'.[127]

An alternative for an express 'intent to incite' requirement is provided by the Irish Prohibition of Incitement to Hatred Act of 1989. Rather than inserting a degree of *mens rea* into the very definition of the incitement

---

[126] E.g. Art. 226, para. 1 of the Criminal Code of Armenia (entry into force 1 August 2003): 'actions aimed at incitement'; Art. 130 of the Criminal Code of Belarus (of 9 July 1999, amended through 20 July 2007): 'wilful actions aimed at incitement'; Art. 443 of the Criminal Code of Belgium 1867 (amended 2010): '*kwaadwillig*', i.e. malicious or malevolent (to be read in conjunction with Art. 444 of the same law and Art. 20 of the Law of 30 July 1981 Criminalizing Certain Acts Inspired by Racism or Xenophobia); Art. 174, para. 3 of the Criminal Code of Croatia 1997 (amended 1 October 2004): 'with the aim of inciting'; Art. 47(2) of the Criminal Code of Cyprus 1929: 'with the intention to promote feelings of ill-will and hostility' (note, however, that Amending Laws 11/92, 6(III)/95 and 28(III)/99) intend to loosen up the intent requirement; it may further be observed that the former proscribed result ('feelings of ill-will') cannot be squared with the Covenant; Art. 1, para. 1 of Law 927/1979 (amended by Laws 1419/1984 and 2910/2001) on Punishing Acts or Activities Aimed at Racial Discrimination [Greece]: 'wilfully ... incite to acts or activities which may result in discrimination, hostility or violence'; Section 299 of the Criminal Code of Kyrgyzstan 1997: 'actions aimed at incitement'; Section 131 of the Human Rights Act 1993 [New Zealand]: 'intent to excite hostility or ill-will' (note that the latter proscribed result cannot be squared with the Covenant; it should further be observed that this Act exclusively deals with inciting *racial* disharmony); Art. 323 of the Criminal Code of Peru 1991: 'with the object of destroying the rights of others'; Art. 161 of the Criminal Code of Ukraine 2001: 'wilful actions inciting ... religious enmity and hatred' (it should be observed that these proscribed results are not compatible with the ones mentioned in the Covenant); Art. 10, para. 1b of Law No. 4 of 2000 for the Promotion of Equality and Prevention of Unfair Discrimination [South Africa]: 'clear intention to be harmful or to incite harm' (alternative intent requirements, e.g. a 'clear intention to be hurtful', listed by the same provision, however, significantly lower the threshold); Art. 7 of the Equal Opportunities Act 2000 [Trinidad and Tobago]: 'intention of inciting'.

[127] Art. 135a of the Criminal Code of Norway 1902. See also Art. 298A of the Criminal Code of Singapore 1872, prescribing a 'knowledge intent' requirement ('any act which he knows is prejudicial to the maintenance of harmony between different religious or racial groups').

offence, it renders the lack of malicious intent a defence against incitement charges.[128] The incitement law of Liechtenstein also provides certain defences against charges of hate speech. If the impugned speech act 'serves the purpose of art or science, research or education, appropriate reporting on current events or history, or similar purposes', the relevant incitement clauses cease to apply.[129] In other words, a bona fide contribution on what will typically be a controversial subject related to, for instance, religion or ethnicity ought not to be combated.

Where the law is silent or ambiguous on *mens rea*,[130] prosecutorial and judicial authorities may read an intent requirement into an incitement prohibition. For example, in a case in Azerbaijan incitement charges were ultimately dropped against a person who had translated and inserted into his own publications – a paperback book and newspaper articles – parts of Hitler's *Mein Kampf*. While the experts consulted during the investigation phase had concluded that the extracts in and of themselves advocated hatred, the prosecutorial authorities concluded that the author of the impugned writings had bona fide objectives in pursuing these publications, namely to inform the public of the danger of racist ideologies.[131] The Canadian Supreme Court, to give a judicial example, rather

---

[128] Section 2 of the Prohibition of Incitement to Hatred Act 1989 [Ireland]: 'if the accused person is not shown to have intended to stir up hatred, it shall be a defence for him to prove that he was not aware of the content of the material or recording concerned and did not suspect, and had no reason to suspect, that the material or recording was threatening, abusive or insulting.' It should be noted, however, that under the Criminal Justice (Public Order) Act 1994 such intent does not need to be established. See David Cowhey, 'Racist Hate Speech Law in Ireland: The Need for Reform' (2006) 4 *Cork Online Law Review* 34–45.

[129] Section 283, para. III of the Criminal Code of Liechtenstein 1998. The same goes for Art. 256, para. 3 of the Criminal Code of Poland 1997.

[130] Examples of incitement laws that do not contain indications as to whether *mens rea* is required include the following: Art. 226 of the Criminal Code of Armenia (entry into force 1 August 2003); Art. 150 of the Criminal Code of Bosnia and Herzegovina 1998; Art. 31 of Law No. 19.733 on Freedom of Opinion and Information and Journalism 2001 [Chile]; Section 356 of the New Criminal Code of the Czech Republic (40/2009); Art. 151 Criminal Code of Estonia 2000; Section 10 of the Criminal Code of Finland 1889 (amended 2012); Art. R625-7 of the Criminal Code of France 1992; Art. 332 of the Criminal Code of Hungary 2012; Art. 233a of the General Criminal Code of Iceland 1940; Art. 170 of the Criminal Code of Lithuania 2000; Art. 457-1 of the Criminal Code of Luxembourg 2010 (inserted as per Act of 19 July 1997); Section 16 of the Freedom of Public Expression Act, No. 1.299 of 15 July 2005 [Monaco]; Art. 317 of the Criminal Code of Serbia 2005; Art. 300 of the Criminal Code of Slovenia 2008; Art. 149 of the Criminal Code of Uruguay 1933.

[131] ECRI, *Second Report on Azerbaijan* (CRI(2007)22, 15 December 2006), para. 14.

straightforwardly distilled a requirement of *mens rea* from Canadian criminal law on hate speech.[132]

Only a few State parties have explicitly ruled that the incitement offence does not necessarily require proof of intent. A number of criminal laws provide that criminal liability is incurred when incitement is either intended *or* 'likely' to follow from the speech act.[133] The either/or construction clearly points to the possibility of incitement convictions in the absence of proof of *mens rea*.

9.8   Concluding remarks

A consensus is gradually emerging – in the shape of relevant workings of the UN Human Rights Committee and the Rabat Plan of Action, as well as leading European Court of Human Rights cases such as *Jersild* – that criminal intent must be proven in order to convict a person of hateful incitement. Even CERD, which previously always agitated against intent requirements posed by the laws or jurisprudence of State parties to the ICERD, has recently joined this momentum in favour of a robust *mens rea* requirement in relation to incitement laws.

---

[132]   *R. v. Keegstra*, [1990] 3 S.C.R. 697, 13 December 1990, at 697 (Can.), para. 1: 'The word "wilfully" imports into the offence a stringent standard of *mens rea* which significantly restricts the reach of [the hate speech offence] by necessitating the proof of either an intent to promote hatred or knowledge of the substantial certainty of such a consequence.' Section 319(2) of the Criminal Code of Canada 1985 (R.S.C., 1985, c. C-46) provides: 'Everyone who, by communicating statements, other than in private conversation, wilfully promotes hatred against any identifiable group is guilty of: (a) an indictable offence and is liable to imprisonment for a term not exceeding two years; or (b) an offence punishable on summary conviction.'

[133]   E.g. Section 2 of the Prohibition of Incitement to Hatred Act of 1989, No. 19 of 1989 [Ireland]: 'intended or, having regard to all the circumstances ... likely to stir up hatred' (as was noted before, the apparent lack of intent may however be brought and accepted as a legal defence to incitement charges); Art. 82A.1 of the Criminal Code of Malta 1854 (amended 2014) ('with intent thereby to stir up racial hatred or whereby racial hatred is likely, having regard to all the circumstances, to be stirred up'); Art. 298A of the Criminal Code of Singapore 1872: whoever commits 'any act which he knows is prejudicial to the maintenance of harmony between different religious or racial groups and which disturbs or is likely to disturb the public tranquillity, shall be punished'; Art. 33 of the Public Order Act 1972 [Antigua and Barbados]; Art. 359 of the Criminal Code of Santa Lucia 2003. See also, *mutatis mutandis*, Section 282 of the Criminal Code of Austria 1974, banning certain hostile speech acts if they are carried out 'in a manner capable of endangering public order', thus prescribing a 'likelihood' criterion but seemingly omitting a specific requirement of *mens rea*.

In terms of Article 20(2) ICCPR specifically, this requirement means proof as to the act of *advocating* hatred, proof as to the *targeting* of a religious (or ethnic) group and, moreover, proof as to the (oblique) 'intent to incite' discrimination, hostility or violence. The consequence of not being able to prove any of that should mean prosecutorial dismissal or judicial acquittal.

State parties to the ICCPR would do well to reflect robust *mens rea* requirements in their incitement laws and enforcement practices.

While a *mens rea* requirement may not ensure that all potentially harmful speech is combated – certain forms of protected speech, as Post argues, may be far more damaging than 'the ranting of a street corner bigot'[134] – it does help to steer prosecutorial practices in meaningful directions. Proof of (multiple) *mens rea* is a significant hurdle for prosecutors to take. Consequently, prosecutorial practices in this area will revolve around the most flagrant and odious of hateful incitement cases. From the perspective of free speech protection, this is to be applauded.

---

[134]   Robert Post, 'Hate Speech', in Ivan Hare and James Weinstein (eds.), *Extreme Speech and Democracy* (Oxford University Press, 2009), 123–38, at 135.

The context of religious hatred

10.1 Introduction

In Chapter 7 we defined the *actus reus* of punishable incitement. It was argued that Article 20(2)'s offence is not a purely content-based ban.[1] It does not ban certain content per se. Extreme content may be punishable only if it 'constitutes' incitement to discrimination, hostility or violence. This leap from 'content' to 'action', that is from the content of the speech act to the likelihood of adverse responses of a third party, is relational and hence inherently context-dependent. One and the same speech or publication may in one situation constitute incitement while it does not in another. This depends on such contextual factors as: who is listening to the hateful speech act; what is the status of the advocator; what is the societal position of the speech act's target group, and so on.

As to the relative 'vulnerability' of the target group, it has been proposed in the literature that international law's incitement offence typically plays a unilateral role – that is, to protect members of oppressed or marginalized minorities.[2] From the perspective of 'likelihood' this certainly stands to reason. When societal circumstances are such that a certain group already faces threats, humiliation or even actual hate crimes, it is all the more likely that an act of hateful incitement hits the mark and successfully triggers further discrimination or violence. Thus the overall social, political and historical context is a paramount factor when it comes to making assessments of the necessity of extreme speech restrictions.

The 'likelihood of harm' criterion is tightly integrated with the Covenant's incitement provision. This also follows from the very system

---

[1] See Chapter 7, particularly section 7.3.4 on 'incitement'.
[2] Yared Legesse Mengistu, 'Shielding Marginalized Groups from Verbal Assaults Without Abusing Hate Speech Laws', in Michael Herz and Peter Molnar (eds.), *The Content and Context of Hate Speech: Rethinking Regulation and Responses* (Cambridge University Press, 2012), 352–77, excepting incitement to genocide from this criterion. See also Nazila Ghanea, 'Minorities and Hatred: Protections and Implications' (2010) 17 *International Journal on Minority and Group Rights* 423–36, at 425.

of the ICCPR. In its General Comment on freedom of expression the Committee underscores that the Covenant places the burden of proof, in relation to the likelihood of harm, on the state. In the words of the Committee, '[w]hen a State party invokes a legitimate ground for restriction of freedom of expression, it must demonstrate in specific and individualized fashion the precise nature of the threat, and the necessity and proportionality of the specific action taken, in particular by establishing a direct and immediate connection between the expression and the threat.'[3] As limitations on free speech based on Article 20(2) must satisfy the necessity test of Article 19(3),[4] it cannot be sufficient for a state to substantiate a casual link between the impugned speech act and harm done to the targeted group. It is not enough that the speech act under consideration would have what Robert Post calls a mere 'tendency' to cause harmful effects.[5] For the incitement prohibition to be enforced, it is necessary that the impugned speech act was at the material time *likely* to trigger *imminent* harm (see the Rabat Plan of Action).[6]

These paramount factors of likelihood and imminence presuppose a profound context-based assessment of extreme speech acts. As Peter Molnar observes:

> [w]hether danger caused by speech is imminent turns more on the context than the content of the speech … To determine whether speech causes imminent danger, thus justifying an exceptional prohibition of the respective communication, we have to take account of not only the immediately surrounding circumstances of the speech, but also its broader social environment, which obviously influences the immediate

---

[3] Human Rights Committee, *General Comment 34: Article 19: Freedoms of Opinion and Expression* (CCPR/C/GC/34, adopted at its 102nd session, Geneva, 11–29 July 2011), para. 35.

[4] HRC, *General Comment 34*, para. 50: 'a limitation that is justified on the basis of article 20 must also comply with article 19, paragraph 3.' First held in *Malcolm Ross v. Canada*, Communication no. 736/1997 (18 October 2000), para. 10.6.

[5] Robert Post, 'Hate Speech', in Ivan Hare and James Weinstein (eds.), *Extreme Speech and Democracy* (Oxford University Press, 2009), 123–38, at 133–4. Post criticizes hate speech laws as most such laws content themselves with this low threshold test.

[6] See *Rabat Plan of Action on the Prohibition of Advocacy of National, Racial or Religious Hatred that Constitutes Incitement to Discrimination, Hostility or Violence* (Conclusions and recommendations emanating from the four regional expert workshops organized by OHCHR in 2011 and adopted by experts in Rabat, Morocco on 5 October 2012), para. 22. See also CERD, *General Recommendation 35: Combating Racist Hate Speech* (UN Doc. CERD/C/GC/35, 83rd session, 12–30 August 2013), para. 16.

impact of speech that depending on its context can create a clear and present danger of violent action.[7]

Similarly, Kenan Malik contends that:

> [t]he meaning of "imminent danger" clearly depends upon circumstances. What constitutes imminent danger in, say, London or New York, where there exists a relatively stable, relatively liberal society, and a fairly robust framework of law and order, may be different from what constitutes imminent danger in Kigali or even in Moscow. And the meaning of imminent danger for a Jew in Berlin in 1936 was clearly different from that for a Jew – or a Muslim – in Berlin in 2011.[8]

'Imminence' is an important factor too (or perhaps rather a further qualification of 'likelihood'). If the possibility of harm being done to the extreme speech's target group is not imminent, there is less of a pressing need for the state to interfere now. More specifically, as long as harmful acts are not imminent, it is important to let counter-speech do its work.[9] As Barendt contends:

> [t]here is … a real public interest in hearing extreme views of this kind, not because we might consider them right, or might wish at some stage to act on them … but because it is vital to know that they are held and held sufficiently strongly that some people wish to communicate them to others … We can only respond intelligently to undesirable extremist attitudes, and remove or reduce the reasons why they are held, if we allow them, to some extent, to be disseminated.[10]

In sum, whether or not the advocacy of hatred 'is likely to trigger imminent acts' (see an early draft General Comment No. 34),[11] or whether an extreme statement 'creates an imminent risk' (see the Camden Principles),[12] or whether 'likelihood, including imminence' (see the Rabat Plan of Action) can be proven, strongly depends on the specific context in

---

[7] Peter Molnar, 'Responding to "Hate Speech" with Art, Education, and the Imminent Danger Test', in Herz and Molnar (eds.), *The Content and Context of Hate Speech*, 183–97, at 193.

[8] Peter Molnar and Kenan Malik, 'Interview with Kenan Malik', in Herz and Molnar (eds.),*The Content and Context of Hate Speech*, 81–91, at 87.

[9] See Eric Barendt, 'Incitement to, and Glorification of, Terrorism', in Hare and Weinstein (eds.), *Extreme Speech and Democracy*, 445–62, at 458, discussing imminence within the meaning of the *Brandenburg* test.

[10] Barendt, 'Incitement to, and Glorification of, Terrorism', at 453.

[11] Draft General Comment No. 34, Article 19, 2nd Revised Draft, CCPR/C/GC/34/CRP.3 (28 June 2010), para. 53.

[12] ARTICLE 19, *Camden Principles on Freedom of Expression and Equality* (2009), Art. 12 (iii).

which the speech was made as well as the wider socio-political context.[13] After a brief overview of context factors as proposed in recent benchmarks (section 10.2), we will scrutinize if and to what extent international monitoring bodies take context into account (sections 10.3–10.5). Towards the end of the chapter (section 10.6) examples of domestic jurisprudential reflections on the context of incitement are provided.

10.2   Context factors

Importantly influenced by the work of free speech NGO ARTICLE 19,[14] a number of international benchmarks in the area of extreme speech have recently touched upon the importance of taking into account context when it comes to judging cases of incitement. These include the Rabat Plan of Action and CERD's General Recommendation No. 35 on racist hate speech (which was adopted shortly after the Rabat Plan and expressly engages with it).[15]

These documents conceptualize the relevant contextual elements surrounding a speech act in the following ways. The Rabat Plan lists as the primary contextual element the overall socio-historical, economic and political context in which the speech act takes place, postulating that such:

> [c]ontext is of great importance when assessing whether particular statements are likely to incite to discrimination, hostility or violence against

---

[13] See also Mohamed Saeed M. Eltayeb, 'The Limitations on Critical Thinking on Religious Issues under Article 20 of ICCPR and its Relation to Freedom of Expression' (2010) 5 *Religion & Human Rights* 119–35, at 121 and 129, referring to such context factors as 'the local conditions, history, culture and political tensions'; Toby Mendel, 'Does International Law Provide for Consistent Rules on Hate Speech?', in Herz and Molnar (eds.), *The Content and Context of Hate Speech: Rethinking Regulation and Responses*, 417–29, at 423–4, arguing that context impacts the question whether extreme speech amounts to incitement and further concluding that a context-dependent test is consistent with universal human rights law.

[14] ARTICLE 19, *Prohibiting Incitement to Discrimination, Hostility or Violence: Policy Brief* (2012). The latter document draws on earlier documents such as ARTICLE 19, *Towards an Interpretation of Article 20 of the ICCPR: Thresholds for the Prohibition of Incitement to Hatred* (A study prepared for the regional expert meeting on Article 20 organized by the Office of the High Commissioner for Human Rights, Vienna, 8–9 February 2010). While the latter document proposed a seven-prong test (including content and intent), this has become a six-prong test in the former document. See also ARTICLE 19, *Responding to Hate Speech against LGBTI People: Policy Brief* (2013), further consolidating this test.

[15] Unlike the Human Rights Committee's General Comment No. 34 on freedom of expression, which predates the Rabat Plan.

the target group and it may have a bearing directly on both intent and/or causation. Analysis of the context should place the speech act within the social and political context prevalent at the time the speech was made and disseminated.[16]

CERD slightly adapts this factor so as to emphasize '[t]he economic, social and political climate prevalent at the time the speech was made and disseminated, including the existence of patterns of discrimination against ethnic and other groups, including indigenous peoples. Discourses which in one context are innocuous or neutral may take on a dangerous significance in another.'[17] This sharp focus on the speech act's overall societal context is to be applauded. As Molnar observes, to determine the question of imminent danger not only do the speech act's 'immediate surroundings' matter, but so also and in particular does the overall societal context.[18] To base a risk assessment only on the former, narrow context factors, would be tantamount to arguing that it does not matter if the target group's status in society is a strong or a precarious one. Obviously, that would not do.[19]

That is not to say that the speech act's immediate surrounding circumstances do not matter – they are very significant indeed. Both sets of benchmarks confirm this, first of all in relation to the *person* behind the impugned speech act.[20] The Rabat Plan provides that '[t]he position or status of the speaker in the society should be considered, specifically the individual's or organisation's standing in the context of the audience to whom the speech is directed'.[21] CERD adds to this by specifically emphasizing the responsibilities of 'politicians and other public opinion-formers', since they are in a strong position to create 'a negative climate towards groups'.[22]

---

[16] *Rabat Plan of Action*, para. 22, calling this factor simply 'context'.

[17] CERD, *General Recommendation 35*, para. 15, referencing its genocide indicators and its indicators of patterns of systematic and massive racial discrimination.

[18] Molnar, 'Responding to "Hate Speech"', at 193.

[19] Molnar, 'Responding to "Hate Speech"', at 193.

[20] Maitra argues that, for the hate speaker to exercise authority over their audience, it is not strictly necessary to act in an official capacity; moreover, authority does not derive only from one's social or hierarchical position. Ishani Maitra, 'Subordinating Speech', in Ishani Maitra and Mary Kate McGowan (eds.), *Speech & Harm: Controversies Over Free Speech* (Oxford University Press, 2012), 94–120.

[21] *Rabat Plan of Action*, para. 22.

[22] CERD, *General Recommendation 35*, para. 15, at the same time underscoring that these persons also have a right to freedom of expression.

While the precise form of the speech act could be considered to belong to its content, the *extent of the speech* is another important context factor. According to the Rabat Plan:

> this includes elements such as the reach of the speech, its public nature, magnitude and the size of its audience. Further elements are whether the speech is public, what the means of dissemination are, considering whether the speech was disseminated through one single leaflet or through broadcasting in the mainstream media or internet, what was the frequency, the amount and the extent of the communications, whether the audience had the means to act on the incitement, whether the statement (or work of art) was circulated in a restricted environment or widely accessible to the general public.[23]

CERD similarly emphasizes the fact that in the current time and age widely differing ways of communication are available with differing potential impacts.[24] More specifically, it postulates that the frequency and extent of the speech act may suggest 'the existence of a deliberate strategy to engender hostility towards ethnic and racial groups'.[25]

From the perspective of the 'necessity test', arguably the most important context factor is that of *likelihood, including imminence*.[26] The Rabat Plan posits that despite the fact that incitement is an inchoate crime, 'some degree of risk of resulting harm must be identified. ['Likelihood'] means the courts will have to determine that there was a reasonable probability that the speech would succeed in inciting actual action against the target group, recognising that such causation should be rather direct.'[27] CERD postulates that the offence of incitement means that someone 'seeks to influence others to engage in certain forms of conduct, including the commission of crime, through advocacy or threats'.[28] Such incitement 'may be express or implied', it may be committed 'through actions such as displays of racist symbols or distribution of materials as well as words',

---

[23] *Rabat Plan of Action*, at 22.

[24] CERD, *General Recommendation 35*, para. 15.

[25] CERD, *General Recommendation 35*, para. 15.

[26] *Rabat Plan of Action*, at 22. See also CERD, *General Recommendation 35*, para. 16, referring to the 'imminent risk or likelihood that the conduct desired or intended by the speaker will result from the speech in question'. It is not entirely clear why CERD reserved a separate paragraph for this factor, thus separating it from the other factors listed in paragraph 15 of the Recommendation (the cross references used in paragraph 16 imply that the factors of intent and likelihood/imminence apply to all speech offences listed in Art. 4 of ICERD).

[27] *Rabat Plan of Action*, para. 22.

[28] CERD, *General Recommendation 35*, para. 16

and while the incitement does not need to be acted upon for it to be punishable, in judging extreme speech cases State parties must take into account 'the imminent risk or likelihood that the conduct desired or intended by the speaker will result from the speech in question'.[29]

Notwithstanding what has been said about the importance of the other context factors, the factor of likelihood appears to be rather crucial from a human rights-based perspective. That is, this factor resonates clearly very well with the necessity test that is interwoven with the restrictions on freedom of expression under Article 19(3) of the ICCPR. Another way of looking at the different factors under consideration so far is that they all in one form or another influence the likelihood of harm coming the target group's way. That goes for the three contextual elements of the 'overall societal, economic, political and historical context', the 'person of the speaker', and the 'extent of the speech act', but also for the previously discussed factors of 'content' and 'intent'.

Finally, it should be observed that, in addition to such scholarly support as mentioned in the introduction of this chapter, a number of important stakeholders have either expressly endorsed the Rabat Plan including its emphasis on context factors (e.g. UN Special Rapporteur on freedom of religion or belief and UN Office on Genocide Prevention and the Responsibility to Protect),[30] or have otherwise endorsed context-based incitement tests (e.g. UN Special Rapporteur on the promotion and protection of the right to freedom of opinion and expression and the Venice Commission of the Council of Europe).[31]

---

[29] CERD, *General Recommendation 35*, para. 16, listing this factor in addition to the 'intention of the speaker'.

[30] UN Special Rapporteur on Freedom of Religion or Belief, *Tackling Manifestations of Collective Religious Hatred* (A/HRC/25/58, 26 December 2013), paras. 54–64, further endorsed in the report's executive summary by calling the Rabat Plan of Action a 'nuanced and practical framework for effective efforts in this area, which should be employed by all relevant stakeholders in a coordinated manner'. The importance of 'imminence' had already been accepted in an earlier report. See *Report of the Special Rapporteur on Freedom of Religion or Belief, Asma Jahangir, and the Special Rapporteur on Contemporary Forms of Racism, Racial Discrimination, Xenophobia and Related Intolerance, Doudou Diène, Further to Human Rights Council Decision 1/107 on Incitement to Racial and Religious Hatred and the Promotion of Tolerance* (UN Doc. A/HRC/2/3, 20 September 2006), para. 47. See also UN Office on Genocide Prevention and the Responsibility to Protect, *Preventing Incitement: Policy Options for Action* (2013), para. 21, embracing the Rabat Plan.

[31] UN Special Rapporteur on the Promotion and Protection of the Right to Freedom of Opinion and Expression, *Report of the Special Rapporteur to the General Assembly on Hate Speech and Incitement to Hatred* (A/67/357, 7 September 2012), endorsing, see paras. 45–46, ARTICLE 19's seven-prong incitement test that predates, and heavily influenced, the *Rabat*

Let us now scrutinize if and to what extent human rights monitoring bodies indeed consider those contextual elements surrounding the speech act in their jurisprudence on incitement.

10.3   Context considerations in Human Rights Committee jurisprudence

In some of the Human Rights Committee's jurisprudence we can discern a more or less balanced content–context assessment. For instance, in *Malcolm Ross* v. *Canada* the Committee concluded, on the basis of a content analysis of the impugned anti-Semitic pamphlets and other writings, that Ross had not merely sought to hurt the feelings of Jews directly but that he had explicitly called upon others to join him in his fight against Jews and to join him in holding Jews in contempt. Accordingly, the Committee distilled an aim of express incitement to discrimination on the part of Ross from the fighting words used in his writings.[32]

Yet in order to establish the criminal liability of Ross, the Committee went beyond this by engaging in a risk assessment of sorts. To a considerable extent the way had already been paved by the Canadian judicial authorities, which had, as emphasized by the Committee, established no less than a causal link between Ross' writings and a 'poisoned school environment experienced by Jewish children in the School district'.[33] The Committee concluded that '[i]n that context, the removal of the author from a teaching position can be considered a restriction necessary to protect the right and freedom of Jewish children to have a school system free from bias, prejudice and intolerance'.[34]

Thus the Committee's assessment was fostered by the fact that Ross' incitement had been going on for a while and had been quite successful in

---

Plan of Action. See also Venice Commission Study 406/2006 on 'Blasphemy, Religious Insults and Incitement to Religious Hatred' (adopted at the Commission's 70th Plenary Session, 16–17 March 2007), paras. 70–72, emphasizing in addition to 'content' the importance of such factors as 'context' per se, the 'public' (i.e. audience), the accessibility of the place where the speech act took place and the 'capacity' of the speaker.

[32] Human Rights Committee, *Malcolm Ross* v. *Canada*, Communication no. 736/1997 (18 October 2000), para. 11.5, essentially seconding the findings of the Canadian judicial authorities (see para. 4.2).

[33] *Malcolm Ross* v. *Canada*, para. 11.6, as established by the Canadian Supreme Court (paras. 4.6–4.7) and as previously established by the Board of inquiry (para. 4.3; see also the State party's submissions in paras. 6.4, 6.10, 6.12; rebutted by Ross in para. 7.1; sur-rebutted by Canada in para. 8.1).

[34] *Malcolm Ross* v. *Canada*, para. 11.6.

poisoning people's minds to the extent that they were persuaded to carry out hostile acts against the target group. The Canadian Board of Inquiry had, for example, established that Jewish pupils in the school district were increasingly harassed and intimidated and that swastikas were carved into the desks of Jewish children and on the blackboards. While Ross' off-duty anti-Semitic writings could not be blamed for all the intimidation, they were found to be 'a factor influencing some discriminatory conduct by the students'.[35] Such degrees of causality, clearly, are not always readily discernible – or made visible by the domestic authorities – for the Committee. While causality is not required by the inchoate crime of incitement, when present it obviously does help in assessing the gravity of the speech act (conversely, however, proof presented by the defendant that no actual adverse acts followed from his or her hateful speech does not necessarily release him or her from criminal culpability).[36]

Other context factors were briefly highlighted by the Committee in its views on the case of *Ross*. Specifically, the role and position of the inciter, a public school teacher, and the position and vulnerability of the target group, school children, were noted. To that effect the Committee emphasized that the right to freedom of expression comes with responsibilities and that '[t]hese special duties and responsibilities are of particular relevance within the school system, especially with regard to the teaching of young students'.[37] The judges in the domestic proceedings and the Canadian Government in its submissions to the Human Rights Committee emphasized time and again the important position of teachers as role models, implying that even their off-duty behaviour may influence pupils.[38] The Committee agreed, making the wider claim that 'the influence exerted by school teachers may justify restraints in order to ensure that legitimacy is not given by the school system to the expression of views which are discriminatory'.[39]

---

[35] *Malcolm Ross* v. *Canada*, para. 4.3.

[36] Ross questioned the causal link between his speech acts and the existence of a poisoned school environment (*Malcolm Ross* v. *Canada*, para. 7.1). Even if he were right, this does not imply that he did not commit incitement in the meaning of Art. 20(2) ICCPR. See also Human Rights Committee, *Robert Faurisson* v. *France*, Communication no. 550/1993 (19 July 1995), para. 8.3, where Faurisson attempts to dispel a causal link between his negationist remarks and acts of anti-Semitism perpetrated by others. Again, from the perspective of criminal culpability it strictly speaking does not matter if causality can be established or not.

[37] *Malcolm Ross* v. *Canada*, para. 11.6.

[38] *Malcolm Ross* v. *Canada*, paras. 4.1, 4.6–4.7, 6.6 and 6.12.

[39] *Malcolm Ross* v. *Canada*, para. 11.6.

In the Holocaust denial case of *Faurisson* v. *France* the Committee determined the likelihood of harm emanating from publicly made negationist remarks. Faurisson's statements made in interviews 'read in their full context, were of a nature as to raise or strengthen anti-semitic feelings'.[40] France had more unambiguously submitted to the Committee that Faurisson had incited to discrimination, hostility or violence against Jews.[41] While the plenary Committee approached the complaint from the perspective of Article 19, avoiding incitement terminology and mention of Article 20(2), individual Committee members accepted that Faurisson's negationist theses amounted to incitement. They suggest that besides the negationist content of the speech acts, the context in which they were made held particular significance.[42] Members Evatt, Kretzmer and Klein suggested that extreme speech statements, such as Holocaust denial, may form a 'pattern of incitement'.[43] That is, while the individual impugned statements, when assessed in isolation, may not reach the level of gravity of Article 20(2) each and every time, the cumulative effect of such statements may amount to punishable incitement.[44] They then proceeded to contend that Faurisson's negationist speech acts had particular significance in 'present-day France', thus alluding to the fact that contemporary anti-Semitism and ongoing anti-Semitic hate crimes were factors to be reckoned with.[45] Member Bhagwati spelled this out in more detail, arguing that 'in the context of the situation prevailing in Europe' the 'necessary consequence and fall-out' of publicly made negationist statements is the 'promotion and strengthening of anti-semitic feelings'.[46]

---

[40] *Robert Faurisson* v. *France*, para. 9.6.

[41] *Robert Faurisson* v. *France*, paras. 7.4–7.7. France further submits that the Gayssot Act 1990 was adopted with the aim of combating certain forms of incitement (paras. 2.8 and 4.1).

[42] As for the content of the impugned speech acts, Member Lallah comes to the conclusion, based on the reasoning provided by the French Courts, that Faurisson's statements amounted 'at the very least' to incitement to hostility and discrimination. Individual opinion by Rajsoomer Lallah (concurring), para. 9.

[43] Individual opinion by Elizabeth Evatt and David Kretzmer, co-signed by Eckart Klein (concurring), para. 4.

[44] Note that they argue this in the abstract and that these considerations are not applied to Faurisson specifically.

[45] Individual opinion by Elizabeth Evatt and David Kretzmer, co-signed by Eckart Klein (concurring), para. 6, while the speech act's content is analysed in detail in para. 10.

[46] Individual opinion by Prafullachandra Bhagwati (concurring).

The Committee's decisions in *A.W.P.* v. *Denmark* and *Fatima Andersen* v. *Denmark* shine some light on the requirement of 'imminence'.[47] As these are admissibility decisions, the questions of 'likelihood' and 'imminence' featured only indirectly, namely in relation to the victim requirement, and thus not in connection to the merits of the Article 20(2) complaints lodged with the Committee.[48] The authors of these communications had in fact presented context-based arguments, dwelling particularly on the risk of the hateful speeches made by Danish members of parliament about Islam. For instance, Mr A.W.P. argued before the Committee that '[s]ome people who are influenced by such statements take action in the form of hate crimes against Muslims living in Denmark. A study published by the Danish Board for Ethnic Equality in 1999 indicated that people from Turkey, Lebanon and Somalia (all of them mainly Muslims) living in Denmark suffer from racist attacks in the street.'[49] The complainant in *Fatima Andersen* v. *Denmark* similarly submitted that the societal context in Denmark at that time was such that people may actually be persuaded by the 'campaign' of anti-Islamic speech as carried out by politicians of the Danish far right.[50] Denmark rebutted that this risk was overly hypothetical and that evidence presented was too flimsy.[51] In addition, the authors of these communications had not presented proof substantiating that they themselves were attacked or any other evidence suggesting that they were at risk as a consequence of the alleged hateful speeches.[52] The

---

[47] Human Rights Committee, *A.W.P.* v. *Denmark*, Communication no. 1879/2009 (admissibility decision of 1 November 2013); and *Fatima Andersen* v. *Denmark*, Communication no. 1868/2009 (admissibility decision of 26 July 2010).

[48] See also, *mutatis mutandis*, Human Rights Committee, *Ernst Zündel* v. *Canada* [I], Communication no. 953/2000 (admissibility decision of 27 July 2003). This is another example – this time of a case brought not by an alleged incitement victim but by an alleged inciter – of an admissibility decision wherein 'likelihood' is only marginally discussed. Canada argues that denying Zündel the possibility to hold a press conference in the parliamentary precincts on the topic of his recent anti-Semitic hate speech conviction was necessary 'to protect the rights of the Jewish community, the dignity and integrity of Parliament, and the Canadian values of equality and cultural diversity. Compared to the potential harm of the author's planned press conference, the detrimental effects of hate propaganda on society at large, and the impression that such a press conference carried the official imprimatur of Parliament or the Government, the restriction on the author's freedom of expression was minimal and, therefore, proportionate' (para. 5.6). The Committee altogether omits a context-based risk assessment as it deems Zündel's complaint to fall outside the scope of protection offered by Art. 19 of the ICCPR.

[49] *A.W.P.* v. *Denmark*, para. 3.2.

[50] *Fatima Andersen* v. *Denmark*, paras. 3.1–3.2.

[51] *A.W.P.* v. *Denmark*, para. 4.13; *Fatima Andersen* v. *Denmark*, para. 4.9.

[52] *A.W.P.* v. *Denmark*, para. 4.13; *Fatima Andersen* v. *Denmark*, para. 4.9.

Committee concurred. Thus in *A.W.P.* v. *Denmark* it held that the applicant 'has failed to establish that those specific statements had specific consequences for him or that the specific consequences of the statements were imminent and would personally affect him', while concluding something similar with respect to the complaint filed by Fatima Andersen.[53]

On the face of the facts presented by the authors of the *Maria Vassilari* communication, their Article 20(2) complaint seems to satisfy both content and context criteria applicable to incitement.[54] That is, a content analysis of the impugned letter to the editor published in a newspaper suggests that the letter's authors and its signatories committed an act of express incitement. The latter accused nearby living Roma people of criminal behaviour and explicitly called for their 'eviction' (or for their 'removal' in the translation of the Greek Government) and threatened them with 'militant action' (or 'dynamic mobilizations' in the translation of the Greek Government). Accordingly, Roma persons were specifically targeted and hostile, potentially violent actions were explicitly incited against them. In terms of context, Roma people are a particularly vulnerable group in Greece (as they are throughout Europe). This point was presented in so many words by the authors of the complaint,[55] but in any event the Committee was familiar with this fact since it had observed that for itself and had reproached Greece over the precarious situation of Roma in this State party.[56] Accordingly, the Committee should not have declared this case inadmissible. An assessment of the merits, taking account of both content and context factors, may very well have led to a breach of Article 20(2) of the ICCPR.[57]

In sum, context factors such as the 'position or status of the speaker' and the 'extent' or 'reach of the speech' have occasionally been engaged

---

[53] *A.W.P.* v. *Denmark*, para. 6.5; *Fatima Andersen* v. *Denmark*, para. 6.4.

[54] *Maria Vassilari et al.* v. *Greece*, Communication no. 1570/2007 (19 March 2009), paras. 2.1–2.7.

[55] *Maria Vassilari et al.* v. *Greece*, paras. 2.1–2.7 and 5.3.

[56] Human Rights Committee, *Concluding Observations of the Human Rights Committee: Greece* (CCPR/CO/83/GRC, 25 April 2005), para. 9 ('Police violence against migrants and Roma appears to be recurrent'); para. 18(a) ('The Committee is concerned that the Roma people remain disadvantaged in many aspects of life covered by the Covenant ... The State party should intensify its efforts to improve the situation of the Roma people in a manner that is respectful of their cultural identity, in particular, through the adoption of positive measures regarding housing, employment, education and social services.'); para. 18(b) ('The State party should submit detailed information on the results achieved by public and private institutions responsible for the advancement and welfare of the Roma people').

[57] See also Individual Opinion of Committee member Mr Abdelfattah Amor (dissenting).

with by the Human Rights Committee. The vulnerable position of Jews has been addressed in anti-Semitic speech, specifically in the context of Holocaust denial.[58] While there was every reason to do so, it did not in a similar vein address the question of the vulnerability of Roma. It must furthermore be observed that the Committee could address the paramount context-dependent factor of 'likelihood' (including imminence) in much more detail in its incitement jurisprudence.[59]

10.4 Context considerations in CERD's Article 4 jurisprudence

We have seen that CERD endorses the Rabat Plan of Action, including its emphasis on the importance of taking into account contextual elements when judging cases of alleged incitement, in its recent General Recommendation on racist hate speech. Most of CERD's Article 4 ICERD case law predates that Recommendation. No context-based assessment terminology – the 'economic, social and political climate', the 'position or status of the speaker', the 'reach of the speech' and 'imminent risk or likelihood'[60] – can be discerned in the Committee's early jurisprudence.

For instance, in *The Jewish Community of Oslo et al.* v. *Norway* the Committee on the Elimination of Racial Discrimination makes an exclusive content-based assessment of the speech made by the leader of the Bootboys.[61] The authors of the communication repeatedly underscored the 'danger' and 'imminent risk' (of suffering racial discrimination or violence) Jews were exposed to as a result of the impugned speech, which was exacerbated, they claimed, by the Norwegian Supreme Court's acquittal of Sjolie, the leader of this neo-Nazi group.[62] The Committee carefully examined the text of the speech and came to the conclusion that it amounted to incitement to racial discrimination, perhaps even to

---

[58] On Holocaust denial, see further Chapter 11.

[59] In its general free speech jurisprudence the Committee occasionally applies a clear and present danger test of sorts. See e.g. Human Rights Committee, *Patrick Coleman* v. *Australia*, Communication No. 1157/2003 (17 July 2006), concerning an unlicensed public speech made at a mall. The Committee considered that the imposed fine was disproportionate since 'there was no suggestion that the author's address was either threatening, unduly disruptive or otherwise likely to jeopardise public order in the mall' (para. 7.3).

[60] CERD, *General Recommendation 34*, paras. 15–16.

[61] CERD, *The Jewish Community of Oslo et al.* v. *Norway*, Communication no. 30/2003 (15 August 2005).

[62] *Jewish Community of Oslo et al.* v. *Norway*, para. 3.9 ('danger') and paras. 3.2, 3.4, and 7.3 ('imminent risk').

violence.[63] The Committee, however, at no time considered the question if and to what extent it was likely that the racist speech's audience would commit acts of discrimination or violence against the speech's target group. In that respect, the Committee might have dwelt on the person of the inciter (Sjoile), the vulnerability of the target group (Jewish persons), the reach of the speech, and so on. In *L.K. v. The Netherlands*, too, the Committee omits any such context considerations from its analysis.[64] Here the fact that the State party had not sufficiently investigated an incident of racist intimidation amounted to a breach of Article 4.

Future Article 4 cases will show how the Committee incorporates the Rabat Plan-derived context tests into its extreme speech jurisprudence.

10.5   Context considerations in the European Court of Human Rights' extreme speech jurisprudence

In order to assess the legitimacy of state interferences with freedom of speech, the European Court of Human Rights typically analyses both 'the words used in the statement' (content) and the 'context in which they were made public' (context).[65] At the same time it must be observed that the body of jurisprudence of this Court is in this regard highly contradictory and incoherent.[66] Notably, while it applies extensive content and context tests to upper-level incitement cases, the Strasbourg Court has failed to do so in regard of low-threshold blasphemy and defamation restrictions. This has meant that it has sanctioned low-threshold restrictions in cases in which the likelihood of harm being done, by third parties, to the scorned or insulted target group was basically nil.[67] A robust context assessment would have pointed out that the restrictions in those

---

[63] *Jewish Community of Oslo et al.* v. *Norway*, para. 10.4.

[64] CERD, *L.K.* v. *The Netherlands*, Communication No. 4/1991 (16 March 1993).

[65] E.g. *Nilsen and Johnsen* v. *Norway*, Application no. 23118/93 (Grand Chamber judgment of 25 November 1999), concerning defamation proceedings.

[66] See also Louis-Léon Christians, *Study for the European Expert Workshop on the Prohibition of Incitement to National, Racial or Religious Hatred* (OHCHR expert seminar on Article 20(2) ICCPR, 9–10 February 2011, Vienna), at 5.

[67] See e.g. European Commission of Human Rights, *X. Ltd. and Y.* v. *United Kingdom*, Application no. 8710/79 (7 May 1982); European Court of Human Rights, *Otto-Preminger-Institut* v. *Austria*, Application no. 13470/87 (20 September 1994); *Wingrove* v. *United Kingdom*, Application no. 17419/90 (25 November 1996); *Murphy* v. *Ireland*, Application no. 44179/98 (10 July 2003); *İ.A.* v. *Turkey*, Application no. 42571/98 (13 September 2005).

cases were not necessary at all, but rather amounted to a blatant breach of freedom of expression.

Further, while context considerations increasingly matter for the Strasbourg Court in its extreme speech jurisprudence, in numerous cases the content of the impugned 'hate speech' remains decisive. First, the European Court deems certain topics per se to be unprotected speech (such as Holocaust denial).[68] Second, the Court occasionally pays lip-service to the importance of the 'context' of the speech, thus in reality not quite venturing too deeply into relevant contextual considerations.

Let us start off by looking into a number of cases in which 'content' seemed to be all-decisive. Subsequently, we will analyse in more detail some cases in which context factors appear to have tipped the balance.

10.5.1   Examples of content being all-decisive

It is particularly in those cases in which Article 17 is applied by the Court to altogether deny standing to the applicant – the alleged hate speaker – where the focus tends to be exclusively on the content of the impugned speech with little to no consideration of such context factors as the ones highlighted by the Rabat Plan of Action.[69] For instance, in *Glimmerveen* v. *Netherlands* the European Commission of Human Rights concluded, after a purely textual assessment, that the racist flyers in question 'would certainly encourage discrimination'.[70] However, no actual risk assessment as to whether the local residents in the city of Schiedam were likely to respond to this hateful propaganda was made – either by the Dutch authorities, or by the Commission. Hate crime monitors like the ones available today might still have been in their infancy, but the Netherlands could at least have been expected generally to substantiate the question of likelihood by elaborating on such context factors as the prevailing socio-historical, economic and political context in which the speech act occurred and the precarious position of the target group, in this case non-white Dutchmen of Turkish or Suriname origin and guest workers.

In *Karl-August Hennicke* v. *Germany* the former European Commission of Human Rights was called upon to determine whether the applicant's

---

[68] See Chapter 11.

[69] See also the Court's jurisprudence on Holocaust denial, as discussed in more detail in Chapter 11.

[70] European Commission of Human Rights, *Glimmerveen and Hagenbeek* v. *The Netherlands*, Application nos. 8348/78 and 8406/78 (admissibility decision of 11 October 1979), at 'The law'.

hate speech against Jews and his propaganda of racial superiority were protected by freedom of speech or excluded therefrom.[71] The applicant had distributed a brochure that he himself had edited, containing poems 'on his beliefs regarding the superiority of "higher races" and the inferiority of aliens, whom he compared to leeches, and that there could be no peace as long as Jews held power in this world'.[72] He was convicted for incitement to hatred by the German courts. The Commission concluded that the 'public interests in the prevention of crime and disorder in the German population due to incitement to hatred against foreigners and Jews, and the requirements of protecting their reputation and rights, outweigh, in a democratic society, the applicant's freedom to impart opinions such as those contained in the brochure at issue'.[73] Yet this sweeping balancing exercise tells us little on the question of whether it was likely that the recipients of these poems would harm Jews or foreigners.

In a case that borders on incitement to murder, it seems obvious that monitoring bodies would focus strongly on the content.[74] In *Michael Kühnen v. Germany* the applicant had not merely uttered anti-Semitic statements, but had also expressed his intention to reinstitute the NSDAP, while in an interview he had added that '[w]hoever serves this aim can act, whoever obstructs will be fought against and eventually eliminated'.[75] These statements, although clearly extreme, still beg the questions as to how close Kühnen was to achieving his aims, whether he had a considerable number of followers, whether they were likely to act upon his fighting words, and so on. Rather than elaborating on such contextual elements, the Commission simply endorsed the German courts' finding that the applicant's publications 'could revive antisemitic sentiments'.[76]

The 'vehement attack' by Norwood on British Muslims by means of displaying a poster stereotyping Muslims as terrorists and calling for their expulsion from the country certainly reeks of hateful speech.[77]

---

[71] European Commission of Human Rights, *Karl-August Hennicke v. Germany*, Application No. 34889/97 (admissibility decision of 21 May 1997).

[72] *Hennicke v. Germany*, 'The Facts'.

[73] *Hennicke v. Germany*, 'The Law'.

[74] European Commission of Human Rights *Michael Kühnen v. Germany*, Application no. 12194/86 (admissibility decision of 12 May 1988).

[75] *Kühnen v. Germany*, 'The Facts'.

[76] *Kühnen v. Germany*, 'The Law'.

[77] European Court of Human Rights, *Mark Anthony Norwood v. United Kingdom*, Application no. 23131/03 (admissibility decision of 16 November 2004). The guillotine approach used by the Court in effect endorsed the domestic judiciary conclusions reached in *Norwood v. DPP* [2003] EWHC 1564 (Admin), which judgment upheld Norwood's

Yet the responding state that fined this rightist politician could have been cross-examined much more on the question of likelihood of harm. Specifically, it may be questioned whether it was likely that the poster's audience would carry out hostile acts against Muslims in Britain. Striking in that respect is the fact that it concerned a single poster, which 'he displayed in the window of his first-floor flat'.[78] In terms of the 'extent' of the hate speech, this fact rather takes the edge off any likelihood argument the UK could have advanced.

In the case of *Aksu* v. *Turkey*, which was brought by an alleged hate speech victim, the Strasbourg Court missed an excellent opportunity to elaborate on relevant context factors.[79] The complaint concerned a book on Roma living in Turkey and dictionaries including entries concerning the word 'Gypsy'. While the applicant found fault with the book for linking Gypsies with criminal behaviour, the dictionaries were challenged by Mr Aksu as they rendered mostly negative, pejorative or prejudiced connotations to the word 'Gypsy'. With respect to the book the Strasbourg Court held that its author had made no unwarranted generalizations and that its publication accordingly did not breach the rights of Mr Aksu or other Roma.[80] As regards the dictionary entries, the Court held that 'it would have been preferable to label such expressions as "pejorative" or "insulting", rather than merely stating that they were metaphorical', yet despite this critique the Court ultimately also sanctioned the dictionaries.[81] With respect to the book, the Strasbourg Court ascertained that the author had not been driven by racist intentions and that he had carried out research.[82] A context assessment of sorts was carried out, too, but here for the Court 'context' largely referred to how the book was produced, not how it could be received within the prevailing socio-political climate and in the light of the vulnerable position of Roma people.[83]

---

conviction and imposed fines under the [UK] Public Order Act 1986. For a comprehensive critique of this national case law, see James Weinstein, 'Extreme Speech, Public Order, and Democracy: Lessons from The Masses,' in *Extreme Speech and Democracy*, 23–61, at 44–52. For a critique of the *Norwood* decision by the European Court of Human Rights, see Ivan Hare, 'Extreme Speech under International and Regional Human Rights Standards', in *Extreme Speech and Democracy*, 62–80, at 78–9.

[78] *Mark Anthony Norwood* v. *United Kingdom*, 'The circumstances of the case'.

[79] European Court of Human Rights, *Aksu* v. *Turkey*, Application nos. 4149/04 and 41029/04 (Grand Chamber judgment of 15 March 2012).

[80] *Aksu* v. *Turkey*, para. 70.   [81] *Aksu* v. *Turkey*, para. 85.

[82] *Aksu* v. *Turkey*, paras. 70–72.

[83] *Aksu* v. *Turkey*, para. 72 ('context of the book').

This critique must be more forcefully made with regard to the Court's assessment of the dictionaries. The publication of these dictionary entries containing pejorative stereotypes regarding Roma people was aggravated by a number of context factors. First and foremost, the dictionaries were partly financed by the Ministry of Culture. This gave an official stamp of approval to the publication and its contents, thus importantly adding weight to the context factor of what was earlier referred to as the *position or status of the speaker*. Secondly, one version of the dictionary was produced for school children (being entitled 'The Turkish Dictionary for Pupils').[84] Even though Turkey claimed that it did not formally recommend this publication as part of the curriculum,[85] the fact remains that it did finance it and essentially fostered its creation – a recommendation in its own right. In any event, the title of the book points to the fact that Turkish pupils formed the intended audience of the book. It has been internationally agreed by virtually all States that 'the education of the child shall be directed to ... [t]he preparation of the child for responsible life in a free society, in the spirit of understanding, peace, tolerance, equality of sexes, and friendship among all peoples, ethnic, national and religious groups and persons of indigenous origin'.[86] Within the Council of Europe, too, efforts are made to promote 'critical thinking among pupils and equipping them with the necessary skills to become aware of and react to stereotypes or intolerant elements contained in material they use', specifically also by 'removing from textbooks any racist material or material that encourages stereotypes, intolerance or prejudice against any minority group'.[87] It is therefore quite remarkable that the Strasbourg Court did not dwell more on the precarious position of the target group (Roma) in connection to Turkey's positive obligation to promote tolerance and fight negative stereotypes, especially among Turkish youths.

Obviously, 'content' may justly be all-decisive where a content-based assessment indicates that the impugned statement was nowhere near incitement. Thus in *Giniewski* v. *France* the European Court of Human Rights found Giniewski's writings on the role of Catholic doctrine in

---

[84] *Aksu* v. *Turkey*, para. 26.

[85] *Aksu* v. *Turkey*, para. 79.

[86] Art. 29(1)(d) of the Convention on the Rights of the Child, GA Res. 44/25, annex, 44 UN GAOR Supp. (No. 49) at 167, UN Doc. A/44/49 (1989), 20 November 1989, entered into force 2 September 1990.

[87] European Commission against Racism and Intolerance, *General Policy Recommendation No. 10 on Combating Racism and Racial Discrimination in and through School Education* (adopted on 15 December 2006). Referenced but thereafter ignored by the Court in *Aksu* (para. 85).

paving the way towards Europe's anti-Semitism, although doubtless offensive to many Catholics, to be a genuine contribution to an ongoing public debate and as such should have been protected by France.[88]

In a number of cases in which Turkey had convicted someone of 'incitement' or 'hate speech' the European Court of Human Rights has expressed its disagreement with this State party, essentially saying that based on the impugned text or speech, no necessity whatsoever to interfere with the speech act could be detected. Accordingly, in *Güzel* v. *Turkey (No. 2)* the Strasbourg Court second-guessed the hate speech conviction of a former minister and Member of Parliament (chairman of the Renaissance Party).[89] It was clear from the facts that Mr Güzel had done nothing more than take part, in his capacity as a politician, in a meeting about human rights organized by a municipality. Whilst discussing such issues as fundamental rights and social issues, he had criticized governmental policies. Convicting him of 'incitement to hatred and hostility', in sum, clearly amounted to an abuse by Turkey of its extreme speech laws with a view towards stifling political dissent. Similarly, in *Asan* v. *Turkey* the European Court of Human Rights disagreed fundamentally with the Turkish authorities as to how a book about Pontic culture could possibly be regarded as punishable speech.[90] In *Yarar* v. *Turkey*, too, the very content of the speech, made by the chairman of the Association of Independent Industrialists and Businessmen, against the 'atheistisation' of Turkey, could in no way have been regarded as extreme speech that is excluded from of protection.[91] Although the Court reiterated its often-used formula that it 'must look at the impugned interference in the light of the case as a whole, including the content of the speech and the context in which it was delivered',[92] in actual fact an exclusive content assessment led to the finding of a breach of freedom of expression. Whenever the Court did refer to 'context' in this case it meant the overall speech, not Rabat Plan-style context factors.[93]

---

[88] European Court of Human Rights, *Giniewski* v. *France*, Application no. 64016/00 (31 January 2006), paras. 45–50.

[89] European Court of Human Rights, *Güzel* v. *Turkey (No. 2)*, Application no. 65849/01 (27 July 2006).

[90] European Court of Human Rights, *Asan* v. *Turkey*, Application no. 28582/02 (27 November 2007).

[91] European Court of Human Rights, *Yarar* v. *Turkey*, Application no. 57258/00 (19 December 2006).

[92] *Yarar* v. *Turkey*, para. 41.

[93] E.g. *Yarar* v. *Turkey*, para. 43.

10.5.2   Examples of context tipping the balance

The above cases may be contrasted to the body of jurisprudence in which the Strasbourg Court in more detail assesses context factors. From its earliest jurisprudence, the European Court of Human Rights has been clear on the fact that speech acts that 'offend, shock or disturb the State or any sector of the population' are in principle covered by freedom of expression.[94] Accordingly, we should not think too lightly of 'potential harm to others' as a restriction ground. For such potential harm to legitimize interferences with free speech a robust risk analysis is in order. In what follows in this sub-section a breakdown of decisions is given that gives evidence of the Strasbourg Court's increasing consideration of context factors. While this is a trend that is to be applauded, we will see that, upon close scrutiny of these decisions, the Court's context-based assessment oftentimes remains half-hearted.

10.5.2.1   Socio-historical, economic and political context, including the position of the target group in society

The overall societal and political context in which a speech act is received may directly impact the question of likelihood of harm subsequently being done to the speech act's target group. The position of the target group, whether it is vulnerable or generally free from discrimination, is significant. Discrimination monitors and hate crime statistics can be indicators in relation to the target group's position in society. Occasionally, the European Court of Human Rights engages with these or related factors.

Thus in a case concerning a far right politician who scapegoated Muslims and other minorities, it mattered a great deal that this political intolerance correlated with increased societal intolerance.[95] Specifically, in the case of *Féret* v. *Belgium* the Strasbourg Court was concerned with growing racism and xenophobia in Belgian politics and society and to that effect it drew on existing reports and monitors (chiefly the workings of the European Commission against Racism and Intolerance).[96]

---

[94] European Court of Human Rights, *Handyside* v. *United Kingdom*, Application no. 5493/72 (7 December 1976), para. 49.

[95] European Court of Human Rights, *Féret* v. *Belgium*, Application no. 15615/07 (16 July 2009), paras. 44–47 and 76.

[96] *Féret* v. *Belgium*, paras. 45–47 and 72–74. See ECRI, *Second Report on Belgium* (21 March 2000); *Third Report on Belgium* (27 January 2004); and *Fourth Report on Belgium* (26 May 2009).

In *Leroy* v. *France* the volatile nature of the local political situation formed the fulcrum to the Court's reasoning.[97] Although much of the legal analysis was focused on the text of the impugned cartoon and its caption with which the 9/11 attacks were glorified, its possible meaning, and the underlying intentions of the artist, the Strasbourg Court especially emphasized that the speech act was made in the politically sensitive Basque region of France where such extreme statements may very well foster instability.[98] Arguably, the European Court of Human Rights could have cross-examined France more on how this risk was fostered by the impugned cartoon.

In *Balsytė-Lideikienė* v. *Lithuania*, concerning a nationalistic calendar that contained pejorative language vis-à-vis among others Jews and Poles, the European Court of Human Rights accepted the government's submission that in only recently independent Lithuania 'questions of territorial integrity and national minorities were sensitive'.[99] In the domestic proceedings leading up to this case, Lithuanian authorities had invited experts to report on the dangers emanating from this xenophobic calendar.[100] The latter had observed that the calendar 'could be characterised as promoting the radical ideology of nationalism, which rejected the idea of the integration of civil society, incited ethnocentrism, contained xenophobic and offensive statements, in particular with regard to the Jewish and Polish populations, and promoted territorial claims and national superiority vis-à-vis other ethnic groups'.[101] In finding that there was a pressing social need to interfere with the dissemination of this publication, the Strasbourg Court based itself on said expert findings, concluding that the experts had substantiated 'the gravity of the applicant's statements and the danger they posed to society'.[102] The Court, however, skipped the fact that those same experts had observed that 'the calendar did not directly incite violence against the Jewish population, nor did it advocate implementing discriminatory policy against this ethnic group.'[103]

In *Soulas and others* v. *France*, concerning a book against Muslim immigration, the Court dwelt extensively on the political context posed

---

[97] European Court of Human Rights, *Leroy* v. *France*, Application no. 36109/03 (2 October 2008).

[98] *Leroy* v. *France*, para. 45.

[99] European Court of Human Rights, *Balsytė-Lideikienė* v. *Lithuania*, Application no. 72596/01 (4 November 2008), para. 78.

[100] *Balsytė-Lideikienė* v. *Lithuania*, paras. 15–16.

[101] *Balsytė-Lideikienė* v. *Lithuania*, para. 16.

[102] *Balsytė-Lideikienė* v. *Lithuania*, para. 80.

[103] *Balsytė-Lideikienė* v. *Lithuania*, para. 16.

by France's immigration and integration challenges.[104] The author of the book went quite beyond portraying such immigration in 'catastrophic' terms by inciting to hostile, possibly violent acts – the author refers to a 'civil war' as a solution – against the target group.[105] But what mattered most was the 'special French context' of immigration and integration policies,[106] which could be harmed by inciteful, counterproductive extremist discourse like the one at hand.

The societal context can also be such that the likelihood of harm being done to the target group is, if not nil, extremely unlikely. Thus in *Aydın Tatlav* v. *Turkey*, the Strasbourg Court rightly underscored the fact the impugned book entitled *The Reality of Islam*, though potentially offensive to Muslims, was not likely to actually threaten the rights of the latter.[107] The fact that in predominantly Muslim Turkey the views of the author were clearly non-conformist made it, from the perspective of promoting free speech and diversity, all the more important to protect them.[108]

10.5.2.2   Role and position of the speaker

There are situations where the identity of the inciter implies an increased risk. In *Seurot* v. *France*, for instance, the Strasbourg Court underscored that the person who was penalized, a schoolteacher, held a position of authority vis-à-vis impressionable youths.[109] In the light of that it was all the more likely that his racist and hateful statements about North Africans, published in a bulletin meant for pupils and their parents, brought about harm. Having made this point *in abstracto*, the Court refrained from a more concrete risk assessment.

The possibility that politicians may foster hatred and incite discrimination or violence has led to a necessarily ambiguous attitude on the part of the Court. On the one hand, the Strasbourg Court's jurisprudence is clear on the fact that politicians should have a considerable licence to use strong

---

[104] European Court of Human Rights, *Soulas and others* v. *France*, Application no. 15948/03 (10 July 2008), paras. 37–39.

[105] *Soulas and others* v. *France*, paras. 41–43.

[106] *Soulas and others* v. *France*, para. 38 ('un context qui, en France, est particulier').

[107] European Court of Human Rights, *Aydın Tatlav* v. *Turkey*, Application no. 50692/99, (2 May 2006), para. 30.

[108] See also European Court of Human Rights, *Klein* v. *Slovakia*, Application No. 72208/01 (31 October 2006), paras. 51–52.

[109] *Jacques Seurot* v. *France*, Application no. 57383/00 (admissibility decision of 18 May 2004).

language.[110] Accordingly, the margin of appreciation granted to State parties to the Convention is narrow in the event of restrictions imposed on the freedom of expression of politicians.[111] On the other hand, the Court has stressed that 'the fight against all forms of intolerance is part of the protection of human rights' and that it is hence 'crucial that politicians in their public speeches avoid comments that might foster intolerance'.[112] Accordingly, politicians, too, could overstep the mark, as is evidenced by those cases such as *Le Pen v. France, Féret v. Belgium, Mark Anthony Norwood v. United Kingdom* and *Glimmerveen and Hagenbeek v. The Netherlands*, in which the European Court of Human Rights endorsed elected representatives' convictions resulting from anti-Muslim and/or anti-immigrant speech.[113]

The same difficult balance between the importance attached to their role in a democracy and the increased risk their influential messages may bring about can be found in the Court's case law on the mass media.[114] It is well-entrenched jurisprudence that the written press and other media have a vital role in any democratic society in their function as 'public watchdog'.[115] Accordingly, the Court will typically be extra vigilant when it comes to restrictions in this area, leaving a narrower margin of appreciation to State parties to the Convention. At the same time the Court

[110] *Castells* v. *Spain*, Application no. 11798/85 (23 April 1992), para. 42 (this case also confirmed that public figures and state organs may be expected to have a thicker skin when verbally attacked: para. 46). See also, *mutatis mutandis, Otegi Mondragon* v. *Spain*, Application no. 2034/07 (15 March 2011).

[111] E.g. European Court of Human Rights, *Incal* v. *Turkey*, Application no. 41/1997/825/1031 (Grand Chamber judgment of 9 June 1998), para. 46. See Anne Weber, *Manual on Hate Speech* (Strasbourg: Council of Europe Publishing, 2009), 37.

[112] European Court of Human Rights, *Erbakan* v. *Turkey*, Application no. 59405/00 (6 July 2006), para. 64 (unofficial translation from the French). See also Weber, *Manual on Hate Speech*, 37.

[113] *Le Pen* v. *France*, Application no. 18788/09 (admissibility decision of 7 May 2010); *Féret* v. *Belgium*; *Mark Anthony Norwood* v. *United Kingdom*; *Glimmerveen and Hagenbeek* v. *The Netherlands*.

[114] See Jacob Rowbottom, 'Extreme Speech and the Democratic Functions of the Mass Media', in Hare and Weinstein (eds.), *Extreme Speech and Democracy*, 608–30, particularly at 610–13.

[115] E.g. European Court of Human Rights, *The Sunday Times* v. *United Kingdom (No. 2)*, Application no. 13166/87 (plenary court judgment of 26 November 1991), para. 50; *Observer and Guardian* v. *United Kingdom*, Application no. 13585/88 (Grand Chamber Judgment of 26 November 1991), para. 59; *Pedersen and Baadsgaard* v. *Denmark*, Application no. 49017/99 (Grand Chamber judgment of 17 December 2004), para. 71; and more recently in e.g. *Von Hannover* v. *Germany (No. 2)*, Application nos. 40660/08 and 60641/08 (Grand Chamber judgment of 7 February 2012), para. 102.

has observed that the media, too, should avoid inciting violence or discrimination. Thus, while journalists have a licence to exaggerate or even provoke,[116] they should avoid becoming a 'vehicle for the dissemination of hate speech and the promotion of violence'.[117] Thus in *Sürek v. Turkey (no. 1)* the fact that the applicant in his capacity as owner of a weekly review could be said to be a member of the written press or the media did not exonerate him. To the contrary, 'as such [he] had the power to shape the editorial direction of the review', which made him partly responsible for the dissemination of the extreme views in question, which consisted of readers' letters published in the review.[118] Indeed, his negligence had provided an 'outlet for stirring up violence and hatred'.[119] The Court further contended that media professionals face greater responsibilities in 'situations of conflict and tension' (here Kurdish separatism).[120]

10.5.2.3   Extent/reach and 'setting' of the speech

The extent or reach of the speech may also impact the question of likelihood of harm. The European Court of Human Rights often treats the speech act's reach together with the question as to what medium was used and more generally what was the particular 'setting' or format chosen to disseminate the message in question.

While this journalist himself had not committed an act of punishable extreme speech according to the Court, in *Jersild v. Denmark* it did wish to emphasize that 'the audiovisual media have often a much more immediate and powerful effect than the print media'.[121] This means,

---

[116]   See Rowbottom, 'Extreme Speech and the Democratic Functions of the Mass Media', 611. See e.g. European Court of Human Rights, *Prager and Oberschlick v. Austria*, Application no. 15974/90 (26 April 1995), para. 38.

[117]   See Rowbottom, 'Extreme Speech and the Mass Media', 611. See e.g. European Court of Human Rights, *Erdoğdu and İnce v. Turkey*, Application nos. 25067/94 and 25068/94 (Grand Chamber judgment of 8 July 1999), para. 54; *Erdoğdu v. Turkey*, Application no. 25723/94 (15 June 2000), para. 62; *Sürek v. Turkey (No. 4)*, Application no. 24762/94 (Grand Chamber judgment of 8 July 1999), para. 60; *Sürek and Özdemir v. Turkey*, Application nos. 23927/94 and 24277/94 (Grand Chamber judgment of 8 July 1999), para. 63; *Şener v. Turkey*, Application no. 26680/95 (18 July 2000), para. 41. Note that in all these cases the Court ultimately held that journalistic freedoms were not abused, thus pronouncing freedom of expression violations.

[118]   European Court of Human Rights, *Sürek v. Turkey (No. 1)*, Application no. 26682/95 (Grand Chamber judgment of 8 July 1999), para. 63. Note that this was a split (11–6) decision. See also Weber, *Manual on Hate Speech*, 38.

[119]   *Sürek v. Turkey (No. 1)*, para. 63.   [120]   *Sürek v. Turkey (No. 1)*, para. 63.

[121]   European Court of Human Rights, *Jersild v. Denmark*, Application no. 15890/89 (Grand Chamber judgment of 23 September 1994), para. 31.

conversely, that there are many forms of dissemination of messages that do not typically bring about massive risks. Thus in *Klein* v. *Slovakia* the Strasbourg Court emphasized a point made by the applicant that the Slovakian Government ought not to exaggerate the potential impact of the impugned defamatory statements about a Catholic Church leader given the medium in which they were published, as well as given the readership concerned. Specifically, the European Court of Human Rights underscored the fact that Klein's article 'was published in a weekly journal aimed at intellectually-oriented readers', which was 'in line with the applicant's explanation that he had meant the article to be a literary joke' and that the relevant 'journal was then published with a circulation of approximately 8,000 copies'.[122] All in all, Klein's attack on the Catholic Church leadership could not be interpreted as a punishable attack on Catholic believers.[123]

In fact, in most cases revolving around blasphemy or 'gratuitously offensive' speech the applicants – sanctioned 'blasphemers' – rightly underscore the fact that the medium used, be it a short experimental video work, a satirical art-house film, a cartoon, paintings, and such like, was hardly going to be capable of undermining the rights of religious minorities.[124] While placing emphasis on the importance of the medium used and the reach of the speech in upper-tier extreme speech cases, the Strasbourg Court has time and again dismissed or ignored arguments made along these lines in cases concerning low-threshold blasphemy restrictions.[125]

---

[122] European Court of Human Rights, *Klein* v. *Slovakia*, Application no. 72208/01 (31 October 2006), para. 48 (underscoring the applicant's arguments made in para. 42).

[123] *Klein* v. *Slovakia*, para. 52. In other alleged defamation cases or cases of verbal attacks on church leaders and/or doctrines the Court additionally underscored that such critiques of religion contribute to public debate and that they are often largely premised on value statements (i.e. statements that, unlike statements of fact, cannot and do not need to be proven). See e.g. *Albert-Engelmann-Gesellschaft mbH* v. *Austria*, Application no. 46389/99 (19 January 2006), para. 31.

[124] E.g. European Court of Human Rights, *Wingrove* v. *United Kingdom*, Application no. 17419/90 (25 November 1996), para. 62, on the minor impact of an experimental video work.

[125] E.g. *Wingrove* v. *United Kingdom*, para. 63. See also *İ.A.* v. *Turkey*, Application no. 42571/98 (13 September 2005). The dissenting judges rightly argue that the medium used and the reach of the speech were such that the likelihood of harm was extremely low: 'The evidence before the Court does not indicate how many people actually read the novel but the number is probably small, as is suggested by the fact that the book was never reprinted. Moreover, the limited practical impact on society of the author's statements was not taken into account by the national authorities, which confined

While the reach of the speech obviously directly impacts the sheer size of the audience, the format or 'setting' of the speech act may tell something more about the intentions of the person or persons responsible for the disseminated messages and, in turn, about the level of gravity of the speech act as well as the risks emanating from it. The setting opted for may also reveal what audience was aimed at. Thus in *Gündüz* v. *Turkey* the Strasbourg Court found that a leader of a religious group should not have been convicted of hate speech charges as a result of statements he made on TV about secularism. Specifically, the Court emphasized that the applicant's views were embedded in a lively and 'pluralistic debate' on the topic.[126] Moreover, 'the applicant's extremist views were already known and had been discussed in the public arena and, in particular, were counterbalanced by the intervention of the other participants in the programme.'[127]

In *Jersild* v. *Denmark* it mattered a great deal that the journalist in question had not himself made racist remarks, although his programme on racist youths had formed a platform for their dissemination. While a number of dissenting judges doubted the good faith of the makers of a TV programme on racist youths, the majority felt that Jersild had sufficiently clearly introduced his TV item, announcing that a discussion about extremist persons and extremist views would ensue, which distanced the programme maker from the programme's content.[128] Moreover, the broadcast was part of 'a serious Danish news programme and was intended for a well-informed audience'.[129] In sum, the programme's setting took the edge off the risks emanating from it.

Similarly, in reaching the conclusion that the remarks made by a professor of theology about Scientology (referring to this Church as 'untruthful' and 'dangerous') that were reported in a Swedish newspaper article were not contrary to the Convention, the former European Commission of Human Rights emphasized the fact that the comments were made 'in the course of an academic lecture by a professor of theology and not in a context which could render the remarks inflammatory'.[130] Clearly, that

themselves to an abstract assessment of the statements (which were made, as has been noted, in a novelistic style).' Joint dissenting opinion of judges Costa, Cabral Barreto and Jungwiert, paras. 2–3.

[126] European Court of Human Rights, *Gündüz* v. *Turkey*, Application No. 35071/97 (4 December 2003), para. 51.

[127] *Gündüz* v. *Turkey*, para. 51.   [128] *Jersild* v. *Denmark*, para. 33.

[129] *Jersild* v. *Denmark*, para. 34.

[130] European Commission of Human Rights, *Church of Scientology and 128 of its Members* v. *Sweden*, Application no. 8282/78 (admissibility decision of 14 July 1980), para. 5. See also, *mutatis mutandis, ASBL Eglise de Scientology* v. *Belgium*, Application no. 43075/08

is not to say that a professor is incapable of inciting violence or discrimination. Yet the medium and setting opted for in combination with the intended audience made it rather unlikely that imminent acts of violence or discrimination would ensue.

10.5.2.4   Likelihood of harm

All previously discussed contextual elements impact the most crucial of all context factors – the likelihood of harm being done to the target group. Occasionally, the Strasbourg Court makes a more or less explicit risk assessment, sometimes also engaging with the question of the imminence of the harm that may come the target group's way. In Convention terms, the likelihood of harm being done to the target group obviously solidifies the existence of a 'pressing social need'.[131]

In *Féret v. Belgium* context factors steered the Court towards its finding that freedom of expression had not been breached.[132] The 'potential impact' of Féret's hateful flyers was deemed serious enough to sanction the hate speech penalties imposed on him by the Belgian authorities.[133] Unlike many similar judgments, the Strasbourg Court tried to specify the threat to the target group (immigrants) by linking the grounds for restriction – public order, rights of others – to existing data on rising intolerance vis-à-vis the target group. Specifically, the chamber refers to the then latest ECRI reports in which it was observed that racism in Belgium was fuelled by xenophobic politics, thus drawing on the precarious socio-political context in which the impugned statements were made.[134]

Nevertheless, for three of the seven chamber judges that was not quite enough. The overall socio-political context may have been alarming, but for the dissenting judges it was doubtful whether Féret's statements truly threatened the targeted group since it was not at all clear, according to them, whether he had incited to violence. This unveils a crucial difference in view among Strasbourg Court judges. While the majority of the

---

[admissibility decision of 19 September 2013], dismissing an application complaining that negative remarks made in the media would have prejudiced fundamental (fair trial) rights of this church.

[131] The European Court of Human Rights first defined the necessity test in terms of the existence of a pressing social need in such early cases as *Handyside v. United Kingdom* (para. 48, in relation to the restriction ground of 'the protection of morals') and *The Sunday Times v. United Kingdom*, Application No. 6538/74 (26 April 1979), para. 59 (in relation to the restriction grounds of 'maintaining the authority and impartiality of the judiciary' and 'the protection of the reputation or rights of others').

[132] *Féret v. Belgium*, para. 74–76.   [133] *Féret v. Belgium*, para. 76–78.

[134] *Féret v. Belgium*, para. 74 (these reports are extensively excerpted in paras. 45–47 of the judgment).

chamber believes that punishable extreme speech does not necessarily require a call to acts of violence,[135] these dissenters rather suggest that without such express incitement requirement we run the risk of banning 'crimes of opinion'. Thus express incitement must be part of the speech act for it to be punishable. And in order to substantiate the necessity of penalties imposed, states must go beyond speculative dangers by concretely showing that it was likely at the material time that the hate speech's audience would act upon the call for violence. In the dissenters' opinion this was far from proven by Belgium.[136]

In *Seurot* v. *France*, the Court briefly discussed the risk that emanated from a text, published by a teacher in the school's bulletin, that was hateful towards persons with Maghrebian origins.[137] Given the impressionable age group concerned – pupils – the likelihood of harm, and hence a pressing social need for the school authorities to interfere, was straightforwardly accepted by the Court.

In *Nur Radyo Ve Televizyon Yayinciligi A.S.* v. *Turkey* the Strasbourg Court concluded that deplorable though the impugned speech act may have been, it was 'unlikely' that it would have successfully incited religious discrimination or violence.[138] The case revolves indirectly around the remarks made by a leader of the Mihr religious community in Turkey, who had claimed that an earthquake killing thousands of persons in Izmit was 'a warning from Allah' against the 'enemies of Allah', by which he was referring to non-believers. As a result of these statements made on the radio, the broadcasting licence of the radio station was suspended. The Court went a long way to recognizing Turkey's concerns. It recognized the outrageous nature of the impugned statements, particularly in the light of the tragic context in which they were made.[139] It also noted that attributing religious significance to a natural disaster may inspire superstition and intolerance in some persons.[140] However, all in all the shocking and offensive statements were just that – shocking and offensive. The Court did not accept that they purported to incite violence or discrimination

---

[135] *Féret* v. *Belgium*, para. 73.

[136] Dissenting Opinion of Judge Sajó, joined by Judges Zagrebelsky and Tsotsoria.

[137] European Court of Human Rights, *Jacques Seurot* v. *France*, Application no. 57383/00 (admissibility decision of 18 May 2004), at 'The law' ('le risque avéré de diffusion du texte au sein de l'établissement scolaire').

[138] European Court of Human Rights, *Nur Radyo Ve Televizyon Yayinciligi A.S.* v. *Turkey*, Application no. 6587/03 (27 November 2007), para. 30.

[139] *Nur Radyo Ve Televizyon Yayinciligi A.S.* v. *Turkey*, para. 30 ('le contexte particulièrement tragique').

[140] *Nur Radyo Ve Televizyon Yayinciligi A.S.* v. *Turkey*, para. 30.

and still less that it was likely that hostile acts against non-believers would ensue following the radio programme.[141]

In *Klein* v. *Slovakia* the European Court of Human Rights accepted the argument by the applicant that it is very hard to see how unqualified defamatory statements about a church leader could threaten the religious freedoms of Catholics.[142] Klein had published a satirical article as a reaction to Archbishop Sokol's public criticism of and public request for a ban on Miloš Forman's film *The People vs. Larry Flynt*, including a request for a ban on the film poster with which it was advertised in the streets. Slovak courts convicted Klein of 'defamation of nation, race and belief'.[143] The courts found particular fault with the following excerpt from Klein's article: 'This principal representative of the first Christian church has not even as much honour as the leader of the last gypsy band in his bow! I do not understand at all why decent Catholics do not leave the organisation which is headed by such an ogre.'[144] Having assessed the risk stemming from these remarks, the Strasbourg Court rightly concluded that there was no indication whatsoever that the rights of religious believers were undermined by this type of criticism.[145]

In most cases in which the Court applies Article 17 a risk assessment is omitted. Thus it is largely the extreme content itself that leads to the

---

[141] *Nur Radyo Ve Televizyon Yayinciligi A.S.* v. *Turkey*, para. 30. See also, *mutatis mutandis*, *Özgür Radyo-Ses Radyo Televizyon Yayın Yapım Ve Tanıtım A.Ş.* v. *Turkey (No. 2)*, Application no. 11369/03 (4 December 2007), concerning the suspension of a radio station's broadcasting licence as a result of playing a protest song that mourned the deaths of members of the far-left People's Liberation Army of Turkey. While the Turkish authorities argued that the song incited violence, the Court emphasized that the likelihood of harm emanating from broadcasting this song was minimal, considering among other things that the song was widely known already and that the events narrated dated back thirty years.

[142] As also discussed above under the heading of extent of the speech.

[143] Art. 198(1) of the Criminal Code of Slovakia at the relevant time read: 'A person who publicly defames a) a nation, its language or a race or b) a group of inhabitants of the republic for their political belief, faith or because they have no religion, shall be punished by up to one year's imprisonment or by a pecuniary penalty.'

[144] *Klein* v. *Slovakia*, para. 14.

[145] *Klein* v. *Slovakia*, para. 51–54. See also European Commission of Human Rights, *Church of Scientology and 128 of its Members* v. *Sweden*, para. 5, holding that 'it has not been shown that either the Church of Scientology or its members have been prevented in any way as a consequence of these published remarks from "manifesting their beliefs" in the ways enumerated by this provision'. And see, *mutatis mutandis*, *Leela Förderkreis E.V. and Others* v. *Germany*, Application no. 58911/00 (6 November 2008) and *Jerusalem* v. *Austria*, Application no. 26958/95 (27 February 2001), in which the Court held that deeming certain religious groups to be 'sects' does not necessarily infringe upon the latter's rights.

conclusion that one is 'abusing' his or her right.[146] That said, occasionally the Strasbourg Court inserts a minimal risk assessment into its case law on abuse of rights. Accordingly, in *Le Pen* v. *France* the Court did elaborate a bit on the potential harm stemming from Le Pen's xenophobic statements.[147] In fact, on the face of it Jean-Marie Le Pen had merely given a warning to the French about future Muslim dominance. Among other things, he had claimed in an interview published in *Le Monde* that 'the day there are no longer 5 million but 25 million Muslims in France, they will be in charge.' This statement does not literally call for violence, hostility or discrimination. Also, Le Pen's exact intentions cannot be distilled from the content of this quote alone. The French courts had insisted that Le Pen's intentions went beyond the literal meaning of his chosen words. His comments would have suggested that France was endangered by an increasing Muslim presence, that France's security was on the line and that something needed to be done about that. Thus Le Pen's hidden agenda was to instil anxiety and fear in the French people about the Muslim presence. His message was also implicitly that the threats to France's security would decrease once the Muslim presence decreased.[148] The European Court of Human Rights agreed with this reading. It concurred with the French judges in holding that Le Pen's statements were likely to give rise to feelings of rejection and hostility among the French people. Accordingly, the apparent likelihood of harm here compensates the apparent lack of express incitement. While it is likely that both the French judges as well as the European Court of Human Rights took into account the general unsavoury nature of Le Pen's 'contributions' to public discourse, uncritically compensating for the missing elements of the offence of incitement may be quite ill advised from a free speech perspective.

Finally, in a number of free speech cases the European Court of Human Rights has adopted risk assessment tests influenced by judicial doctrines expounded by the US Supreme Court (which will be highlighted in the next section). For instance, in *Erbakan* v. *Turkey* we can discern formulas that are reminiscent of the 'clear and present danger' doctrine and the 'imminent lawless action' test.[149] The case revolved around a public speech given in Bingöl in south-east Turkey by Mr Erbakan, former

---

[146] See e.g. *Pavel Ivanov* v. *Russia*, Application no. 35222/04 (admissibility decision of 20 February 2007), altogether omitting a risk assessment.

[147] European Court of Human Rights, *Le Pen* v. *France*, Application no. 18788/09 (admissibility decision of 7 May 2010).

[148] *Le Pen* v. *France*, at section A.

[149] See next section for more details on these tests.

chairman of the dissolved Refah Partisi party,[150] in which he had allegedly – no recordings were made – made distinctions between 'believers'
and 'non-believers' and incited against the latter.[151] Turkey underscored
the volatile nature of the speech and generally emphasized the precarious situation in the region. However, the Strasbourg Court was not convinced by this. Specifically, it concluded that it had not been established
by Turkey that at the time of instigating the proceedings against Erbakan
the offending speech engendered a 'current risk' (*un risque actuel*) and
an 'imminent danger' (*un danger imminent*) to society.[152] Other case
law – not strictly dealing with religion-based incitement – confirms this
trend. In *Gül and Others* v. *Turkey* the Court held that Turkish courts
and authorities had not proven that the impugned slogans that were allegedly shouted by the applicants in favour of an illegal organization brought
about 'a clear and imminent danger'.[153] In yet another case against Turkey
the Turkish Government had not proven the 'clear and imminent danger' that would have emanated from pro-Öcalan slogans.[154] Individual
judges of the Strasbourg Court have expressed themselves in favour of
such stringent tests.[155]

---

[150] On the dissolution of this party, see European Court of Human Rights, *Refah Partisi (the Welfare Party) and Others* v. *Turkey*, Application nos. 41340/98, 41342/98, 41343/98 and 41344/98 (Grand Chamber judgment of 13 February 2003).

[151] European Court of Human Rights, *Erbakan* v. *Turkey*, Application No. 59405/00, judg-ment of 6 July 2006.

[152] *Erbakan* v. *Turkey*, para. 68.

[153] European Court of Human Rights, *Gül and Others* v. *Turkey*, Application no. 4870/02 (8 June 2010), para. 42. However, two dissenting judges, in the light of the terrorist con-text of the slogans, perceived a clear and imminent danger. See Dissenting Opinion of Judges A. Sajó and N. Tsotsoria.

[154] European Court of Human Rights, *Kılıç and Eren* v. *Turkey*, Application no. 43807/07 (29 November 2011), para. 29.

[155] E.g. Dissenting Opinion of Judge Pinto de Albuquerque in *Mouvement Raëlien Suisse* v. *Switzerland*, Application no. 16354/06 (13 July 2012), arguing that 'measures interfer-ing with freedom of expression which purport to safeguard public order, prevent crime and defend the rights of others require evidence of a clear and imminent danger'. See also Joint Dissenting Opinion of Judges Tulkens, Sajó, Lazarova Trajkovska, Bianku, Power-Forde, Vučinić and Yudkivska, arguing that the Swiss government had failed to show the existence of a clear and imminent danger in the same case. In *Sürek* v. *Turkey* (*No. 1*), Application no. 26682/95 (Grand Chamber judgment of 8 July 1999), Judge Bonello opined in his dissenting opinion that 'punishment by the national authorities of those encouraging violence would be justifiable in a democratic society only if the incitement were such as to create "a clear and present danger"' and that the 'guarantee of freedom of expression does not permit a state to forbid or proscribe advocacy of the use of force except when such advocacy is directed to inciting or producing imminent lawlessness and is likely to incite or produce such action', thus combining the *Schenck*

10.6   Context-dependent risk assessments in state practice

A number of states ensure that their extreme speech legislation does not degenerate into practices of 'content-discrimination', that is banning certain content per se. The opposite of content-discrimination is referred to as 'viewpoint neutrality', that is ensuring that speech is never banned on account of its – subjective – disagreeable content per se, but only on account of – objective – factors pointing at contingent harms.[156] This can, to a considerable extent, be ensured by the law itself. In addition, the judiciary may vouch for this by way of adopting judicial doctrines along the lines of 'likelihood' and 'imminence'. In this section a selection of legal and judicial examples is provided.

By way of notable legislative practices, particular attention may be focused on Austrian and German incitement law, which requires that the incitement must be 'capable of endangering public order'.[157] Similarly, Greek incitement law insists that only incitement 'to acts or activities which may result in discrimination, hatred or violence against individuals or groups' is to be prohibited.[158] In Cyprus incitement is punishable only if it is 'likely' to cause discrimination, hatred or violence.[159] One hate

---

and *Brandenburg* tests. See also his separate opinions in e.g. *Erdoğdu and İnce* v. *Turkey*, Application nos. 25067/94 and 25068/94 (Grand Chamber judgment of 8 July 1999); *Ceylan* v. *Turkey*, Application no. 23556/94 (Grand Chamber judgment of 8 July 1999); *Karataş* v. *Turkey*, Application no. 23168/94 (Grand Chamber judgment of 8 July 1999); *Başkaya and Okçuoğlu* v. *Turkey*, Application no. 23168/94 (Grand Chamber judgment of 8 July 1999).

[156] See, e.g., Corey Brettschneider, 'Value Democracy as the Basis for Viewpoint Neutrality: A Theory of Free Speech and Its Implications for the State Speech and Limited Public Forum Doctrines' (2013) 107:2 *Northwestern University Law Review* 603–46; and James Weinstein, 'Hate Speech, Viewpoint Neutrality, and the American Concept of Democracy', in Thomas R. Hensley (ed.), *The Boundaries of Freedom of Expression & Order in American Democracy* (Kent State University Press, 2001), 146–69.

[157] Section 283 of the Criminal Code of Austria 1974; and Section 130 of the Criminal Code of Germany 1998. In Turkey, the incitement must directly threaten public safety for it to be an offence. See Art. 216 of the New Criminal Code of Turkey 2004. From the above discussion we know, however, that Turkish Courts appear to take this hurdle rather uncritically.

[158] Art. 1(1) of Law 927/1979 (amended by Laws 1419/1984 and 2910/2001) on Punishing Acts or Activities Aimed at Racial Discrimination 1979 [Greece]. See e.g. Athens Court of Appeals, decision of 13 September 2007, concerning Konstantinos Plevris' anti-Semitic book entitled *Jews: The Whole Truth*. While Plevris was initially convicted of inciting hatred against Jewish persons, he was later acquitted (27 March 2009). See ECRI, *Fourth Report on Greece*, (CRI(2008)31, 2 April 2009), para. 16.

[159] Amending Laws 11/91, 6(III/95) and 28(III/99) [Cyprus] aimed at the implementation of ICERD.

speech offence enshrined in the Canadian Criminal Code emphasizes that incitement is a criminal offence 'where such incitement is likely to lead to a breach of the peace'.[160] A partial 'likelihood' requirement – it does not apply if it is clear that the incitement was carried out intentionally – can further be found in the incitement laws of Antigua and Barbados, Ireland, Malta, Santa Lucia and Singapore.[161]

Whether the law explicitly requires so or not, risk assessments can also be made on a case-by-case basis by the judiciary. Famously, the US Supreme Court has formulated relevant tests in its extreme speech jurisprudence. Initially, in a case taking place against the background of the First World War and revolving around incitement to insubordination and obstruction of the recruitment process of US armed forces, the Supreme Court developed a doctrine known as the 'clear and present danger' test.[162] The applicant (Schenck) had distributed leaflets to potentially drafted persons urging them to refuse to serve in the army, something that amounted to a crime according to the Espionage Act of 1917.[163] Writing for the Court, Justice Holmes emphasized the context of the speech act – the First World War – and considered that 'in many places and in ordinary times, the defendants, in saying all that was said in the circular, would have been within their constitutional rights. But the character of every act depends upon the circumstances in which it is done.'[164] In finding that Schenck's conviction was constitutional, Justice Holmes wrote the famous words:

> The most stringent protection of free speech would not protect a man in falsely shouting fire in a theatre and causing a panic … The question in every case is whether the words used are used in such circumstances and are of such a nature as to create a clear and present danger that they will bring about the substantive evils that Congress has a right to prevent. It is a question of proximity and degree.[165]

---

[160] Art. 319(1) of the Criminal Code of Canada 1985. This qualification does not, however, apply to the wilful promotion of hatred. See Art. 319(2) of the Criminal Code of Canada 1985. The latter provision was found to be constitutional by the Canadian Supreme Court in *R. v. Keegstra*, [1990] 3 S.C.R. 697, 13 December 1990, at 697 (Can.), defining it as a narrowly confined offence. Justices McLachlin, Sopinka and La Forest dissented.

[161] Art. 33 of the Public Order Act 1972 [Antigua and Barbados]; Section 2 of Prohibition of Incitement to Hatred Act of 1989, No. 19 [Ireland]; Art. 82A.1 of the Criminal Code of Malta 1854 (amended 2014); Art. 298A of the Criminal Code of Singapore 1872; Art. 359 of the Criminal Code of Santa Lucia 2003.

[162] *Schenck v. United States*, 249 U.S. 47 (1919).

[163] Espionage Act of 1917, 40 Stat. 217.   [164] *Schenck v. United States*, 249 U.S. 52.

[165] *Schenck v. United States*, 249 U.S. 52.

Accordingly, the Supreme Court held that the state cannot combat just any extreme speech, including inciteful speech. A context-based risk assessment is necessary to point out whether real harm is likely (a 'clear danger' that 'evil' will be brought about) and whether that harm is imminent ('present').

In a case concerning advocacy of hatred against Jews and 'Negroes' by a Ku Klux Klan member, the Supreme Court fine-tuned – if not partially overruled – the clear and present danger test set out in *Schenck* v. *United States* half a century earlier.[166] Thus in *Brandenburg* v. *Ohio* the Court reversed the conviction of said extremist since his hate speeches were not directed to inciting or producing imminent lawless action.[167] The judgment summarized recent jurisprudence on inflammatory speech as follows:

> constitutional guarantees of free speech and free press do not permit a State to forbid or proscribe advocacy of the use of force or of law violation *except where such advocacy is directed to inciting or producing imminent lawless action* and *is likely to incite or produce such action*. The mere abstract teaching … of the moral propriety or even moral necessity for a resort to force and violence, is not the same as preparing a group for violent action and steeling it to such action. A statute which fails to draw this distinction impermissibly intrudes upon the freedoms guaranteed by the First and Fourteenth Amendments. It sweeps within its condemnation speech which our Constitution has immunized from governmental control.[168]

This meant that the statute on which the conviction was based was overly intrusive and could no longer be sustained.[169] Accordingly, only the incitement of *imminent lawless action* that is, moreover, *likely* to incite or produce such action can be punished. This test is more stringent than the clear and present danger doctrine.[170] Subsequent jurisprudence shows

---

[166] *Brandenburg* v. *Ohio*, 395 U.S. 444 (1969).

[167] *Brandenburg* v. *Ohio*, 395 U.S. 444, 449.

[168] *Brandenburg* v. *Ohio*, 395 U.S. 444, 447 (internal quotation marks removed; emphasis added).

[169] *Brandenburg* v. *Ohio*, 395 U.S. 444, 448: 'The Act punishes persons who "advocate or teach the duty, necessity, or propriety" of violence "as a means of accomplishing industrial or political reform"; or who publish or circulate or display any book or paper containing such advocacy; or who "justify" the commission of violent acts "with intent to exemplify, spread or advocate the propriety of the doctrines of criminal syndicalism"; or who "voluntarily assemble" with a group formed "to teach or advocate the doctrines of criminal syndicalism." Neither the indictment nor the trial judge's instructions to the jury in any way refined the statute's bald definition of the crime in terms of mere advocacy not distinguished from incitement to imminent lawless action.'

[170] The judgment, which was delivered *per curiam* in the final version, omits altogether the clear and present danger test. According to Justices Black and Douglas, the latter test has

that this test is not easily satisfied and hate speech restrictions tend to get struck down by the Supreme Court as well as lower courts.[171]

Nearly a century after *Schenck* and nearly half a century after *Brandenburg*, these likelihood and imminence doctrines are still not only hugely influential within the USA but also, increasingly, outside. We have seen before that at the international level the European Court of Human Rights, and to a lesser extent the Human Rights Committee, adopt similar language.[172] National judges, too, have been influenced by the tests laid down in *Schenck* and/or *Brandenburg*. Notably, Hungarian case law reflects somewhat of a mixture of a clear and present danger doctrine and the imminent lawless action doctrine.[173] In the first instance the Municipal Court of Budapest found Lóránt Hedegûs Jr, author of an anti-Semitic journal article, as well as the publisher of the journal, guilty of the crime of incitement against the Jewish community.[174] This decision

not been adjusted but rather altogether overruled by the imminent lawless action test. See Concurring opinion of Justice Black and Concurring opinion of Justice Douglas. The judgment expressly overrules *Whitney* v. *California*, 274 U.S. 357 (1927), which still drew on the clear and present danger test in confirming a conviction (in fact going beyond that test by introducing a 'bad tendency' test); but it implicitly also casts doubt if not de facto overrules such cases as *Abrams* v. *United States*, 250 U.S. 616 (1919) (in which Justice Holmes fine-tuned his clear and present danger test through his dissenting opinion by, among other things, placing a stronger emphasis on the imminence of harmful and unlawful acts), *Beauharnais* v. *Illinois*, 343 U.S. 250 (1952) (in which a group defamation offence was upheld), and *Dennis* v. *United States*, 341 U.S. 494 (1951) (the latter is referenced in *Brandenburg*).

[171] E.g., *R.A.V.* v. *City of St. Paul*, 505 U.S. 377 (1992), unanimously striking down a Minnesota crime ordinance that had led to the conviction of the applicant who had burned a cross on the lawn of a black person. See also, *mutatis mutandis*, *Snyder* v. *Phelps*, 562 U.S. ___ (2011); and *National Socialist Party of America* v. *Village of Skokie*, 432 U.S. 43 (1977). See, however, *Virginia* v. *Black*, 538 U.S. 343 (2003), fine-tuning *R.A.V.* v. *City of St Paul*. At a lower level, see the infamous case of a group of Nazis who wished to hold a march in Skokie, Illinois, where many Jews live. US Court of Appeals for the Seventh District, *Collin* v. *Smith*, 578 F.2d 1197 (1978), concluding that the intended march amounted to protected speech under the First Amendment of the US Constitution. See also James Weinstein, 'An Overview of American Free Speech Doctrine and its Application to Extreme Speech', in Hare and Weinstein (eds.), *Extreme Speech and Democracy*, 81–91, at 83; and, generally, Samuel Walker, *Hate Speech: The History of an American Controversy* (Lincoln, NE: University of Nebraska Press, 1994).

[172] E.g. Human Rights Committee, *Patrick Coleman* v. *Australia*; European Court of Human Rights, *Gül and Others* v. *Turkey* and *Kılıç and Eren* v. *Turkey*.

[173] For a more comprehensive account, see Peter Molnar, 'Toward Improved Law and Policy on "Hate Speech" – The "Clear and Present Danger" Test in Hungary', in Hare and Weinstein (eds.), *Extreme Speech and Democracy*, 237–64.

[174] Municipal Court of Budapest, *Lóránt Hedegûs Jr.*, Case no. 13.B.423/2002/7 (6 November 2002).

was based on a nearly exclusive content-based assessment of the impugned speech act. Expressly referencing Article 20(2) of the ICCPR,[175] the court of first instance came up with the following definitions of 'hatred' and 'incitement': 'In colloquial usage, the word "hatred" means a vehement, hostile emotion. Incitement is a statement or series of statements which are aimed at inducing a malicious and hostile behaviour which is not based primarily on reasoned, rational and consciously considered views, but on rage and base instincts.'[176] In the light of these definitions, this court found particular fault with this excerpt: 'Exclude them! For if you do not exclude them, they will exclude you!'[177] In that respect, the municipal court held that '[t]he call to the exclusion of a certain part of the society and their stigmatization thereby, in other words, the arousing of hatred in itself may be suitable to disturb the social order, peace and public tranquillity'.[178] Obviously, these observations fell short of ascertaining the precise degree of risk flowing from the publication. In that regard the Court solely mentioned the fact that the act was committed 'in great publicity', noting the circulation of 12,000 copies of the journal in question.[179] While this tells us something about the extent or reach of the speech, this fact alone does not substantiate the likelihood of harm.

Based on these and other concerns, in second instance the Municipal High Court of Appeal of Budapest reversed the first decision, thus acquitting the accused.[180] Specifically, the High Court found fault with the first court's lack of attention to contextual elements that reflect on the actual risk emanating from the hateful article. The High Court found that it is crucial in such cases of extreme speech to establish whether the hateful statements amount to 'incitement' and to ascertain precisely how 'dangerous' the impugned speech act was.[181] The High Court firmly distinguished between insulting and inciting speech and concluded that only the latter should be penalized.[182] The High Court generally described

---

[175] Translation of this case included in: Tibor Szeszlér (ed.), *Anti-Semitic Discourse in Hungary in 2002–2003: Report and Documentation* (Budapest: B'nai B'rith Elso Budapesti Kozosseg, 2004), 321–33, ICCPR reference at 327–8.

[176] *Lóránt Hedegûs Jr.* (first instance) in Szeszlér, *Anti-Semitic Discourse in Hungary*, at 329.

[177] *Lóránt Hedegûs Jr.* (first instance) in Szeszlér, *Anti-Semitic Discourse in Hungary*, at 330.

[178] *Lóránt Hedegûs Jr.* (first instance) in Szeszlér, *Anti-Semitic Discourse in Hungary*, at 331.

[179] *Lóránt Hedegûs Jr.* (first instance) in Szeszlér, *Anti-Semitic Discourse in Hungary*, at 332.

[180] Municipal High Court of Appeal of Budapest, *Lóránt Hedegûs Jr.*, Case no. 3. Bf.111/2003/10 (6 November 2003).

[181] *Lóránt Hedegûs Jr.* (second instance) in Szeszlér, *Anti-Semitic Discourse in Hungary*, at 339.

[182] According to this reading, anti-Semitic speech that falls short of incitement should not be penalized. Note that ECRI has criticized this interpretation. See ECRI, *Report on*

incitement as 'an emotional preparation to violence'.[183] More precisely, 'incitement' is committed by a person who 'calls to violent acts' or 'calls to the performance of such an action or conduct' where 'the danger is not only assumed but there are actual rights endangered and there is a direct threat of a violent act'.[184] When applied to the case at hand, these principles meant that however 'offensive, astonishing and also alarming' the article was, and while Lóránt Hedegûs Jr could clearly be accused of being an anti-Semite, he could not be convicted for 'incitement' in the meaning of Hungarian criminal law.[185] First of all, it was questionable whether he had expressly incited.[186] And moreover it was questionable whether the impugned speech act was dangerous enough for the state to step in with penalties of law. The last consideration is accompanied by a fairly extensive risk assessment:

> It follows from the (immaterial) endangering nature of the criminal act that the assumed existence of the danger (abstract endangerment) is not sufficient for its performance. Danger means the realistic possibility of the occurrence of the injury, that is, the prevalence of a situation where the possibility of the development of the process in the direction of the occurrence of the injury has to be reckoned with. The conclusion of the Municipal Court of Budapest that it is sufficient that the offender has the foresight that the aroused hatred might as well emerge from the enclosed

Hungary (2008); and ECRI, *Conclusions on the Implementation of the Recommendation in Respect of Hungary* (CRI(2012)8 adopted on 8 December 2011).

[183] *Lóránt Hedegûs Jr.* (second instance) in Szeszlér, *Anti-Semitic Discourse in Hungary*, at 340.

[184] *Lóránt Hedegûs Jr.* (second instance) in Szeszlér, *Anti-Semitic Discourse in Hungary*, at 340–1. The High Court goes on to explain the meaning of incitement as follows (at 341): 'The content of incitement to hatred – as a concept used in criminal law – has been formulated by the practice of judicature. The person who in large public [*sic*] incites to hatred against particular groups of people, shares not only his antipathy, unfavourable or offending views and ideas arousing concern with other people, by setting the mood of the public, but also he displays a rebellious conduct generating tension, which is suitable to arouse the rage of the people and to violate the social order and peace. The heated hatred may turn into extreme activity, ultimately into the eruption of violent acts. The incitement against the community is basically not a political but a legal crime, and as such, has been listed among the crimes against public tranquillity. The person who provokes active, efficient hatred in others, performs incitement to hatred.'

[185] *Lóránt Hedegûs Jr.* (second instance) in Szeszlér, *Anti-Semitic Discourse in Hungary*, at 341.

[186] *Lóránt Hedegûs Jr.* (second instance) in Szeszlér, *Anti-Semitic Discourse in Hungary*, at 341. Specifically, the impugned speech act did 'not call upon the performance of any activity or conduct or some violent act. It is not even suitable to stimulate the active effective hatred in the reader or in the listener which is required for the facts as described in the statutory provision.'

world of emotions and manifest itself in a manner perceivable also for outsiders is not substantiated; it must satisfy also the triple requirements detailed above [a call; action; danger]. Nor was the reasoning shared by us in respect of the statement that the invitation for exclusion by itself constitutes a criminal act, as no such provision is contained in the Criminal Code currently in force, or was contained in the Criminal Code in force at the time of the performance of the act. On the other hand, in its judgement the Municipal Court of Budapest failed to address the extent of the danger, the tangibility thereof, as well as the degree of violence. From the call 'Exclude them! For if you do not exclude them, they will exclude you' it does not follow and cannot be assumed that it was the intention of the accused to encourage its readers/listeners to conduct violent acts.[187]

Consequently, the Hungarian judiciary has adopted a remarkably stringent clear and imminent danger test. According to European Commission against Racism and Intolerance, Hungary has in fact overstepped the mark in this respect and would currently fail to protect incitement victims sufficiently.[188] In fairness to that view it should be observed that while in the second instance the Hungarian High Court in *Lóránt Hedegûs Jr.* had much more of an eye for contextual elements surrounding Hedegûs' anti-Semitic remarks, at the same time it failed to appreciate other context factors, notably the fact that Jewish people are a relatively vulnerable target group considering the fact that anti-Semitism and anti-Semitic hate crimes are on the rise in Hungary.[189]

In a case of negationism spread through the Internet, the German Federal Court of Justice overruled previous jurisprudence on public incitement to hatred.[190] The extermination of Jews during the Holocaust was referred to by an Australian of German origin as '*Auschwitzlüge*', the Auschwitz lie. While the Federal Court admitted that all the elements of the *actus reus* of the offence of incitement may have been present, it was

---

[187] *Lóránt Hedegûs Jr.* (second instance) in Szeszlér, *Anti-Semitic Discourse in Hungary*, at 341–2.

[188] ECRI, *Conclusions on the Implementation of the Recommendation in Respect of Hungary* (CRI(2012)8, adopted on 8 December 2011).

[189] See e.g. Human Rights Committee, *Concluding Observations Concerning Hungary* (CCPR/C/HUN/CO/5, 16 November 2010), para. 18; ECRI, *Report on Hungary* (2008), para. IV; CERD, A/51/18, para. 116.

[190] Federal Court of Justice of Germany, '*Auschwitzlüge*' *im Internet*, BGH 1 StR 184/00 (12 December 2000). Public incitement is prohibited pursuant to Section 130 of the German Criminal Code 1998. For a general overview of hate speech legislation in Germany, see Winfried Brugger, 'The Treatment of Hate Speech in German Constitutional Law' (2003) 4:1 *German Law Journal* 1–44.

still necessary to separately ascertain concretely if and to what extent the impugned speech act was capable of disturbing public order.[191]

The incitement clause in Estonian criminal law presently requires that the incitement 'results in danger to the life, health or property of a person' for it to be punishable.[192] This requirement was spelled out as a result of lower court case law in which low thresholds were formulated in relation to the crime of incitement. The National Court of Estonia overruled one such case – revolving around hatred against Jews and Christians disseminated through the Internet – emphasizing that the office of the prosecution and lower court judges had failed to sufficiently appreciate context factors that impact the risk of incitement.[193] The response of the Estonian legislator appears quite drastic, considering that the present standard is in fact far more stringent than Article 20(2) of the ICCPR.

In a 2007 Holocaust denial case the Spanish Constitutional Court declared the denial of genocide offence enshrined in the Spanish Criminal Code unconstitutional.[194] Among other things it argued that the crime, as formulated,[195] was at odds with freedom of expression since it cannot be automatically implied that such speech incites ethnic or religious discrimination or violence. In other words, a content-based ban, with no consideration for the actual risks at stake, is contrary to constitutionally protected free speech in the eyes of the Spanish Constitutional Court.[196]

In sum, a number of states have incorporated into their extreme speech offences and jurisprudence more or less stringent requirements along the lines of 'likelihood' and 'imminence'.

10.7   Concluding remarks

Upon close scrutiny Article 20(2) of the ICCPR appears to be carefully formulated so as not to amount to a content-based ban. Advocacy of hatred

---

[191] For more details on this case, see ECRI, *National Legal Measures to Combat Racism and Intolerance in the Member States of the Council of Europe: Germany (General Overview)* (2002).

[192] Art. 151 Criminal Code of Estonia 2000. If the incitement actually 'causes the death of a person or results in damage to health or other serious consequences', the penalty may be increased (to three years' imprisonment).

[193] National Court of Estonia, Case no. 3-1-1-117-05 (10 April 2006).

[194] Constitutional Court of Spain, Sentence no. 235/2007 (7 November 2007).

[195] Art. 607(2) of the Criminal Code of Spain 1996.

[196] Trying to 'justify' genocide, however, enshrined in the same Criminal Code provision, remains punishable, since incitement is considered to be inextricably linked with that offence.

is to be prohibited by law only if it constitutes incitement. The necessity test, moreover, requires that inciteful speech only be punished if the extreme speech was likely to produce imminent acts of discrimination or violence against the speech's target group. Thus, in order to determine if extreme speech constitutes incitement, and especially in order to determine the concrete and imminent risks that may ensue from the speech act, we need to know what the circumstances directly surrounding the impugned speech act were, in addition to requiring deeper knowledge of the wider socio-political and historical context in which the speech act took place. The Rabat Plan of Action has made a tremendous contribution to the development of a full-fledged context-oriented risk assessment. The content of a speech and the speaker's intent may be very telling, but it is especially by means of additionally assessing the overall societal context of the speech act, the role and status of the speaker, the position of the target group, in addition to other factors that impact the likelihood and imminence of harm coming the target group's way, that we can appreciate an extreme speech act's risks. Therefore it is positive that such important stakeholders as CERD, the UN Special Rapporteur on freedom of religion or belief, as well as the UN Special Rapporteur on freedom of expression embrace and further conceptualize those context factors in their monitoring work. In case law predating the Rabat Plan, notably in *Ross* v. *Canada*, the question of concrete and imminent harm plays an important role in the Human Rights Committee's views. In some decisions the Committee may have elaborated more comprehensively on contextual elements of the case. Future case law will show how devoted this Committee is to a Rabat Plan-style risk assessment. The extreme speech case law of the European Court of Human Rights is incoherent. In most cases lip-service is paid to the importance of context factors, yet the Court all too easily and uncritically accepts that offensive or shocking speech acts will lead to harm being done to the target group.

Holocaust denial and glorification of religious violence

11.1 Introduction

In the previous chapters we have come across numerous examples of incitement and other verbal attacks on religious groups.[1] In this chapter we will look more closely at two special types of extreme speech. The reason for singling out Holocaust denial and the act of glorifying religious violence or terrorism is that these offences are oftentimes perceived as justified content-based restrictions par excellence – the substance of such speech is so abhorrent that it should be punishable in and for itself. If context enters the equation at all, it is typically to generally underscore the state's special history that in and of itself would make denial laws necessary.[2] Thus historical awareness functions as a perpetual state of heightened alert, supporting the view that negationism is always dangerous. Others have pointed at inherent problems of denial laws. Fraser, for example, posits that:

> [t]here is no real, practical doubt, in the world of Holocaust denial as a political and ideological position and strategy, that Jews are the target. But the idea that such statements as 'There is no Hitler order' or 'No one was gassed at Auschwitz' fit into established criminal law categories such as assault or that they create the likelihood of a specific harm to foreseeable

---

[1] This chapter draws on Jeroen Temperman, 'Laws against the Denial of Historical Atrocities: A Human Rights Analysis' (2014) 9 *Religion & Human Rights* 151–80.

[2] E.g. Klaus Guenther, 'The Denial of the Holocaust: Employing Criminal Law to Combat Anti-Semitism in Germany' (2000) 15 *Tel Aviv University Studies in Law* (2000) 51–66, arguing that Germany has a special licence to combat Holocaust denial. He posits that since 'one cannot deal with the problem of antisemitism in Germany without regard to the horrific legacy of Nazi atrocities, restrictions on freedom of expression in this context are essentially not comparable to similar restrictions on other countries'. See also Julie C. Suk, 'Holocaust Denial and the Free-Speech Theory of the State', in Michael Herz and Peter Molnar (eds.), *The Content and Context of Hate Speech: Rethinking Regulation and Responses* (Cambridge University Press, 2012), 144–63, arguing, in the light of among other things the defeat of the Vichy regime, that Holocaust denial laws are significant to France's very legitimacy as a state.

victims such as Holocaust survivors, or that they are likely to incite others to acts of antisemitic violence, is each extremely problematic, without even entering into issues of free speech or good faith.[3]

In this chapter we will address the question of whether such restrictions – 'memory laws' on the one hand, and anti-glorification limitations on the other – are compatible with international law. Again, our main legal yardstick will be Article 20(2) of the ICCPR, but we will also compare and contrast the workings of the Human Rights Committee in this regard with those of CERD and the European Court of Human Rights.

11.2   Examples of memory laws

Holocaust denial can be defined as:

> an attempt to negate the established facts of the Nazi genocide of European Jews, Roma, gays and lesbians as well as political opponents. Key denial assertions include that the murder of approximately six million Jews during the Second World War never occurred, that the Nazis had no official policy or intention to exterminate the Jews, and that the extermination camps such as Auschwitz-Birkenau never existed.[4]

Typically, Jews themselves are implicated by such denial, allegedly having concocted the Holocaust so as to further Zionist causes.[5] After the Second World War the Allied Powers imposed – interestingly, some of these powers today vehemently argue against such content-based bans – as per the 1947 Paris Peace Treaties on Austria, Bulgaria, Hungary, Finland and Italy the duty to outlaw fascist propaganda, including negationist speech.[6] By way of illustration of memory laws in this section we will highlight a few

---

[3] David Fraser, 'On the Internet, Nobody Knows You're a Nazi: Some Comparative Legal Aspects of Holocaust Denial', in Ivan Hare and James Weinstein (eds.), *Extreme Speech and Democracy* (Oxford University Press, 2009), 511–37, at 519.

[4] Special Rapporteur on contemporary forms of racism, racial discrimination, xenophobia and related intolerance, *Report of the Special Rapporteur on the Implementation of General Assembly Resolution 68/150* (A/HRC/26/50, 10 April 2014), para. 35.

[5] See also Andrew Altmen, 'Freedom of Expression and Human Rights Law: The Case of Holocaust Denial', in Ishani Maitra and Mary Kate McGowan (eds.), *Speech & Harm: Controversies Over Free Speech* (Oxford University Press, 2012), 24–49, at 26–8, outlining twelve of the most common characteristics of Holocaust denial.

[6] Egon Schwelb, 'The International Convention on the Elimination of All Forms of Racial Discrimination' (1966) 15 *International and Comparative Law Quarterly* 996–1068, at 1022; and Stephanie Farrior, 'Molding the Matrix: The Historical and Theoretical Foundations of International Law Concerning Hate Speech' (1996) 14:1 *Berkeley Journal of International Law* 1–98, at 27.

pieces of contemporary legislation prohibiting Holocaust denial specifically or, more generally, the denial or trivialization of historical atrocities.[7]

In the preceding chapters we have repeatedly come across France's Gayssot Act,[8] which made it a criminal offence to contest the existence of crimes against humanity as defined in the London Charter of 8 August 1945,[9] on the basis of which Nazi leaders were tried and convicted by the International Military Tribunal at Nuremberg in 1945–1946.[10] On the basis of this Act such infamous Holocaust deniers as Robert Faurisson and Roger Garaudy have been prosecuted and convicted. The French Constitutional Council struck down a law against the denial of the Armenian genocide in 2012, leaving intact the denial offences enshrined in the Gayssot Act.[11]

In some states the act of denying Nazi crimes in general is considered a criminal offence. This tends to include the denial of the Holocaust. Accordingly, in Austria the judiciary have for a long time held that the National Socialism Prohibition Act 1947 (amended 1992), which prohibits any attempt at revitalizing Nazism and threatens Nazi activity with prison sentences of up to twenty years, was also applicable to the act of negationism. However, so as to put an end to any remaining legal uncertainty, the offence of publicly 'denying, grossly playing down, approving or trying to excuse' the Holocaust or other Nazi crimes was inserted into the Act.[12] In Israel, too, the denial of Nazi crimes in general and Holocaust denial specifically are both banned.[13]

---

[7] See also Art. 6 of Emergency Ordinance No. 31 of 13 March 2002 [Romania], which prohibits the public denial of the Holocaust; and Art. 300 of the Criminal Code of Slovenia 2008, which prohibits denying, advocating, approving or diminishing the significance of genocide.

[8] For an interesting historical take on this law, see Patrick Weil, 'The Politics of Memory: Bans and Commemorations', in Hare and Weinstein (eds.), *Extreme Speech and Democracy*, 562–79 (siding with the critics of the law at 574–5).

[9] Charter of the International Military Tribunal – Annex to the Agreement for the Prosecution and Punishment of the Major War Criminals of the European Axis (Nuremberg Charter or London Charter) of 8 August 1945.

[10] Law No. 90–615 of 13 July 1990 on the Punishment of Racist, Xenophobic or Anti-Semitic Acts, commonly referred to as the 'Gayssot Act'. This Act inserted Art. 24Bis into the Freedom of the Press Act of 29 July 1881. For a comprehensive historical analysis of French Holocaust denial and wider anti-racism legislation, see Suk, 'Holocaust Denial and the Free-Speech Theory of the State', 144–63.

[11] Constitutional Council of France decision of 28 February 2012.

[12] See Jacqueline Lechtholz-Zey, 'The Laws Banning Holocaust Denial' (revised version) (2012) 9 *Genocide Prevention Now* (online).

[13] See also Articles 2 and 3 of the Denial of Holocaust (Prohibition) Law 1986 [Israel], No. 5746-1986.

Holocaust denial also appears to be covered by the general denial of Nazi crimes offence recently codified by the Lithuanian legislator.[14] Interestingly, Lithuania has introduced this crime in direct response to an EU call to that effect. In 2008 the Council of the EU adopted a Framework Decision urging EU member states to take measures necessary to ensure, among other things,[15] that 'publicly condoning, denying or grossly trivialising crimes of genocide, crimes against humanity and war crimes' be punishable.[16] In Lithuania the new offence has led to a number of prosecutions.[17]

It should be observed that said EU contribution to the legal discourse on denial of historical atrocities perfectly reflects the current schism in Europe on this issue. That is, there are those countries that prioritize free speech and reject the idea that Holocaust denial should be punishable. Then there are the states discussed here that prohibit Holocaust denial. Still further, there are those countries, like Germany and Portugal, where the denial of crimes against humanity is punishable only if it amounts to incitement to discrimination or violence or if it is likely that such denial disturbs the public peace.[18] This means that denial *simpliciter* does not necessarily constitute a punishable offence.[19] The EU Framework Decision accepts this. In a formulation that clearly reeks of compromise

---

[14] Art. 170(2) of the Criminal Code of Lithuania 2000, criminalizing 'public endorsement of international crimes, public endorsement of crimes committed by USSR or Nazi Germany against the Lithuanian Republic or its residents, denying or grossly diminishing such crimes'. See Justinas Žilinskas, 'Introduction of "Crime of Denial" in the Lithuanian Criminal Law and First Instances of its Application' (2012) 19:1 *Jurisprudence* 315–29.

[15] It should be noted that the Framework Decision calls on the EU member states to criminalize overly broad 'incitement to hatred' offences. Those recommended offences go significantly beyond what is required by Art. 20(2) of the ICCPR and other relevant international law.

[16] Art. 1(1)(c) of the Council Framework Decision on Combating Certain Forms and Expressions of Racism and Xenophobia by Means of Criminal Law (2008/913/JHA of 28 November 2008).

[17] Žilinskas, 'Introduction of "Crime of Denial"', at 322–6.

[18] Section 130(3) of the Criminal Code of Germany (1998), requiring that the denial (or approval or belittlement of acts committed during the rule of National Socialism) be made 'in a manner capable of disturbing the public peace'. Art. 240(2) of the Criminal Code of Portugal 2006 requires that the denial is made 'with intent to incite to racial, religious or sexual discrimination or to encourage it'.

[19] Compare such cases as Oberlandesgericht Celle, decision of 17 February 1982 (NJW 1982, 1545); Bundesgerichtshof, decision of 26 January 1983 (BGHSt 31, 231); Bundesgerichtshof, decision of 15 March 1994 (NJW 1994, 1421); Bundesgerichtshof, decision of 6 April 2000 (NJW 2000, 2217); Bundesgerichtshof, decision of 10 April 2002 (5 Str 485/01); Bundesgerichtshof, decision of 18 September 1979 (BGHZ 75, 160); and Bayerisches Oberstes Landesgericht, decision of 17 December 1996 (NStZ 1997, 283).

it is stipulated that 'Member States may choose to punish only conduct which is ... carried out in a manner likely to disturb public order'.[20]

The Czech denial law is interesting in that it prohibits the denial (or approval or justification) of both Nazi and 'Communist genocide'.[21] While denial crimes were declared unconstitutional in Hungary,[22] a newly adopted offence similarly equates crimes perpetrated by National Socialism to those committed during the Communist regime.[23] This law has already resulted in convictions.[24] The 'national remembrance offences' prohibited by Poland also cover the denial both of the Holocaust and of 'communist crimes'.[25]

Most inclusive are those laws that ban the denial of all historical crimes against humanity. Liechtenstein and Luxembourg, for example, do not single out the Holocaust but ban the denial of any genocide.[26] A politician in Switzerland was convicted for denying the Armenian Genocide under a similar denial offence.[27] In Portugal, denying historical war crimes is banned in addition to denying crimes against humanity, while Slovakia prohibits the denial of committed crimes against humanity within the meaning of the Rome Statute.[28]

---

[20] Art. 1(2) of the Council Framework Decision on Combating Racism and Xenophobia. Further caveats are made in the third and fourth paragraphs of the same article. These caveats were added to appease states – notably, the UK, Ireland, Scandinavian states and Italy – that had objected, on grounds of freedom of expression, against a blanket ban on Holocaust denial. See Michael Whine, 'Expanding Holocaust Denial and Legislation Against It', in Hare and Weinstein (eds.), *Extreme Speech and Democracy*, 538–56, at 548.

[21] Section 261a of the Law against Support and Dissemination of Movements Oppressing Human Rights and Freedoms (2001) [Czech Republic].

[22] Constitutional Court of Hungary, Decision no. 30/1992 (26 May 1992). On this judgment, see András Sajó, 'Militant Democracy and Transition Towards Democracy,' in András Sajó (ed.), *Militant Democracy* (Utrecht: Eleven International Publishing, 2004), 209–30, at 220 and 228.

[23] Subsection (2) of Section 2 of Act XLVIII of 2013, amending the Criminal Code of Hungary, which seeks to punish 'those, who deny the genocides committed by national socialist or communist systems, or deny other facts of deeds against humanity' (a previous draft had mentioned the word Holocaust, but this was dropped).

[24] Budapest Court, *Case of Gyorgy Nagy* (judgment of 31 January 2013), resulting in a suspended eighteen-month prison sentence and other sanctions.

[25] Act of 18 December 1998 on the Institute of National Remembrance [Poland].

[26] Section 283, para. I(5) of the Criminal Code of Liechtenstein 1998; Art. 457-3 of the Criminal Code of Luxembourg 2010 (inserted as per Act of 19 July 1997). The first paragraph refers to the crimes against humanity committed during the Second World War while the second paragraph penalizes the denial or minimization of any genocide.

[27] Art. 261A of the Criminal Code of Switzerland 1937. See Lausanne District Court, judgment of 9 March 2007.

[28] Art. 240(2) of the Criminal Code of Portugal 2006; Art. 424a of the New Criminal Code of Slovakia 2005.

The Belgian Holocaust denial law reserves a special role for the Belgian Centre for Equal Opportunities and Opposition to Racism by authorizing it to instigate proceedings.[29] The maximum prison sentence for the offence of grossly minimizing, attempting to justify or approving the genocide committed by the German National Socialist Regime is one year. Belgian jurisprudence shows that in addition to prison sentences and fines, stripping a negationist of their political rights is considered an appropriate penalty too.[30]

In the absence of explicit memory laws, the denial of historical atrocities can nevertheless come within the ambit of criminal law through jurisprudence. For example, Dutch courts have held that Holocaust denial may constitute 'group defamation' vis-à-vis Jews within the meaning of the Criminal Code of the Netherlands.[31] In Australia, vilification offences enshrined in anti-racism legislation have been successfully mobilized against negationists.[32] Prior to the 1994 amendment to the Criminal Code of Germany, which introduced the denial offence,[33] the Federal Court of Justice of Germany (Bundesgerichtshof) had already accepted that Holocaust denial could be punished through the enforcement of such dissimilar crimes as defamation of the dead or generic libel or slander offences.[34]

In other countries regulations against Holocaust denial have been declared unconstitutional infringements upon the right to freedom of expression. For example, while Spain formally bans Holocaust denial (and denial of other genocides) as per Article 607 of its Criminal Code, in 2007

---

[29] Art. 4 of Act of 23 March 1995 on Punishing the Denial, Minimisation Justification or Approval of the Genocide Perpetrated by the German National Socialist Regime during the Second World War. Certain other associations are entitled to fulfil this role too.

[30] Antwerp Court of Appeal, *Centre for Equal Opportunities and Opposition to Racism and the Auschwitzfoundation* v. *Siegrid Verbeke* (14 April 2005). Verbeke was fined, imprisoned and stripped (for a period of ten years) of his political rights.

[31] Articles 137c and 137e of the Criminal Code of the Netherlands 1881. E.g. Netherlands Supreme Court, *Auswitchcartoon*, Case no. 10/03978 (27 March 2012); and *Openbaar Ministerie* v. *Krick*, Case no. 01362/02 U (5 November 2002). See also Court of Den Bosch, decision of 21 December 2004.

[32] Notably, in Federal Court of Australia, *Toben* v. *Jones* (2003) 129 FCR 515. See Racial Discrimination Act 1975 [Australia].

[33] Section 130(3) of the Criminal Code of Germany 1998.

[34] See, e.g., Bundesgerichtshof, BGHZ 75, 160, 162–3 [1980] (judgment of 18 September 1979). See also German Constitutional Court, 'Auschwitzlüge', BVerfGE 90, 241 [1994] (judgment of 13 April 1994). On these cases and other relevant German jurisprudence, see Dieter Grimm, 'The Holocaust Denial Decision of the Federal Constitutional Court of Germany', in Hare and Weinstein (eds.), *Extreme Speech and Democracy*, 557–61.

the Spanish Constitutional Court declared this provision unconstitutional.[35] The Canadian Supreme Court has declared the criminal offence of
spreading false information or news – which had formed the basis for proceedings against Holocaust denier Ernst Zündel – to be at odds with freedom of expression within the meaning of the Canadian Charter of Rights
and Freedoms.[36] In the USA it is commonly held that a statute prohibiting
the denial of the Holocaust would be liable to be struck down as contrary to
the First Amendment.[37]

11.3   The Human Rights Committee and Holocaust denial

The Human Rights Committee has recently revised its position on Holocaust
denial. Initially, it sided with certain State parties, deeming such denial *ipso
facto* unprotected speech (see section 11.3.1). The Committee took the opportunity to revisit that jurisprudence in the course of drafting a new General
Comment on freedom of speech (see section 11.3.2).

11.3.1   Early case law

In *Faurisson* the Committee implicitly accepted the position that all
Holocaust deniers, to some extent, aim to promote anti-Semitism and
that therefore such speech is categorically excluded from protection.[38]
Negationism, it was contended, in today's world serves as the 'principal
vehicle' for anti-Semitism.[39] Thus where the Holocaust is concerned, there

[35] Constitutional Court of Spain, Sentence no. 235/2007 (7 November 2007). Attempting to
'justify' genocide remains punishable.

[36] *R. v. Zundel* [1992] 2 S.C.R. 731. Note that later on proceedings were lodged against
Zündel on a dissimilar legal basis. See, e.g., Canadian Human Rights Tribunal, *Citron
v. Zündel*, TD 1/02 (18 January 2002).

[37] E.g. Frederick Schauer, 'Freedom of Expression Adjudication in Europe and the
United States', in George Nolte (ed.), *European and US Constitutionalism* (Cambridge
University Press, 2005), 49–69, at 61; Frederick Schauer, 'Social Epistemology, Holocaust
Denial, and the Post-Millian Calculus', in Herz and Molnar (eds.), *The Content and
Context of Hate Speech*, 129–43, at 130; Jonathan D. Varat, 'Deception and the First
Amendment: A Central, Complex, and Somewhat Curious Relationship' (2005–2006)
53 *UCLA Law Review* 1107–41, at 1116–19; James Weinstein, 'An Overview of American
Free Speech Doctrine and its Application to Extreme Speech', in Hare and Weinstein
(eds.), *Extreme Speech and Democracy*, 81–91, at 89.

[38] Human Rights Committee, *Robert Faurisson v. France*, Communication no. 550/1993
(19 July 1995). On Holocaust denial, see also, *mutatis mutandis, Ernst Zündel v. Canada*
[I], Communication no. 953/2000 (admissibility decision of 27 July 2003).

[39] *Faurisson v. France*, para. 9.7, thus accepting the argument made by the French Minister
of Justice.

can be no such thing as 'simple denial'; denial of this type in the view of the Committee is premised on intent to incite and therefore is *ipso facto* 'qualified denial'.[40] In principle this is an ever so laudable position, especially when considering that the contemporary human rights movement stems from the Holocaust – a denial thereof amounts to a denial of the human rights discourse. The UN Special Rapporteur on contemporary forms of racism has recently stated in this regard:

> Holocaust denial and distortion are generally motivated by strong anti-Semitism, and build on the claim that the Holocaust was invented or exaggerated as part of a plot to advance Jewish interests. That view perpetuates long-standing anti-Semitic prejudices and stereotypes, accusing Jews of conspiracy and world domination and of hateful charges that were instrumental in laying the groundwork for the Holocaust.[41]

Equating Holocaust denial with incitement to discrimination is one thing, yet in *Faurisson* the Committee further accepted, as a matter of course, the necessity of the interference with freedom of expression.[42] Again, while the first leap in the argument – denial equals incitement – is understandable,[43] this second leap must be criticized. It amounts to unduly reversing the burden of proof. The Committee literally expected Faurisson to falsify France's submission that his negationist acts had fostered anti-Semitism in France, failing which he would lose the case.[44] Thus, given the nature of the impugned speech act, express incitement is considered a given and on top of that, the necessity to punish such speech is deemed self-evident too. All in all, such reasoning leans heavily toward a content-based ban, that is a proscription of certain speech regardless of concrete risks. Member Lallah admitted as much when he, in his concurring opinion, engaged

---

[40] Christian Tomuschat, 'Prosecuting Denials of Past Alleged Genocides', in Paola Gaeta (ed.), *The UN Genocide Convention: A Commentary* (Oxford University Press, 2009), 513–30, at 519–20, using this terminology in relation to historical genocides in general.

[41] Special Rapporteur on contemporary forms of racism, racial discrimination, xenophobia and related intolerance, *Report on Implementation of GA Resolution 68/150*, para. 36. See also UN General Assembly, Resolution 61/255 on Holocaust denial (UN Doc. A/RES/61/255, 26 January 2007).

[42] *Faurisson* v. *France*, para. 9.7.

[43] See also Natan Lerner, 'Freedom of Expression and Advocacy of Group Hatred: Incitement to Hate Crimes and Religious Hatred' (2010) 5 *Religion & Human Rights* 137–45, at 144–5, arguing that banning anti-Semitic incitement forms the philosophy of denial laws.

[44] *Faurisson* v. *France*, para. 9.7: '*In the absence in the material before it of any argument undermining the validity* of the State party's position as to the necessity of the restriction, the Committee is satisfied that the restriction of Mr Faurisson's freedom of expression was necessary within the meaning of article 19, paragraph 3, of the Covenant' (emphasis added).

with Article 20(2) ICCPR. He argued that '[i]n so far as restrictions or prohibitions in pursuance of article 20, paragraph 2, are concerned, *the element of necessity is merged with the very nature of the expression* which may legitimately be prohibited by law'.[45] Thus, his argument goes, speech that engages Article 20(2) may always be restricted by the state.

The above views completely disregard contextual elements. In theory, the context surrounding an act of negationism could be such that it is in fact rather unlikely that the target group will face harm. For example, the target group could be a well-respected rather than a vulnerable one; or the denial could be expressed by a person who does not have the reputation or influence required for successful incitement; and so on. The denial of historical atrocities may very well be punishable in a concrete case on account of factors substantiating the likelihood of adverse acts being committed against the target group. Yet the entire rationale of the necessity test is that the state faces the burden to prove the existence or applicability of those special factors.

The previous considerations precisely pinpoint the inherent problem of most domestic memory laws – with the exception of those few laws that insist on proof of harm,[46] they ban content per se or in any event leave too little room for a context-based risk assessment. At the time of *Faurisson* the Committee had not yet come to the insight that Article 20(2)-derived restrictions must satisfy the necessity test and other requirements imposed by Article 19(3).[47] The Committee did criticize the Gayssot Act for being overly broad and vague.[48] While one would assume that this indicates that less intrusive measures were available, the Committee went on to accept the necessity of the interference.[49]

11.3.2   Faurisson *overruled*

The case of *Malcolm Ross* v. *Canada* contains elements of Holocaust denial, yet the content of Ross' negationist pamphlets alone did not justify Canada's restrictions of his speech.[50] What tipped the balance, according to the Human Rights Committee, was that the impugned statements

---

[45] Individual Opinion by Rajsoomer Lallah (concurring), para. 4 (emphasis added).
[46] See the German and Portuguese examples in the previous section.
[47] Note that the plenary Committee avoids any direct mention of Art. 20(2), unlike the individual members in their separate opinions.
[48] *Faurisson* v. *France*, para. 9.3. For extensive criticism see also the separate opinions.
[49] *Faurisson* v. *France*, para. 9.7.
[50] Human Rights Committee, *Malcolm Ross* v. *Canada*, Communication no. 736/1997 (18 October 2000).

amounted to express incitement – he had called upon 'true Christians' to join him in his fight against Jews – and that his anti-Semitic writings had created a poisoned atmosphere at local schools in which Jewish children faced a real risk of being bullied or marginalized. Thus *Ross* can be seen as the first step away from content-based bans towards a more holistic context-based risk assessment. Crucially, the Committee revisited old case law by postulating that 'restrictions on expression which may fall within the scope of article 20 must also be permissible under article 19, paragraph 3, which lays down requirements for determining whether restrictions on expression are permissible'.[51] This implies that Article 20-derived bans and measures must satisfy the principle of necessity.

In its 2010 concluding observations regarding compliance with the Covenant by Hungary, the Human Rights Committee expressed its concern that the 'evolution of the so-called "memory laws" in the State party risks criminalizing a wide range of views on the understanding of the post-World War II history of the State party ... The State party should review its "memory laws" so as to ensure their compatibility with articles 19 and 20 of the Covenant.'[52] This call on Hungary to 'review' this law may seem to suggest that it could be fixed, and that its full annulment was not necessary. Such a reading would prove to be premature.

A full, unambiguous revision of *Faurisson* was carried out by the Committee in 2011. General Comment No. 34 on freedom of expression provides that:

> [l]aws that penalize the expression of opinions about historical facts are incompatible with the obligations that the Covenant imposes on States parties in relation to the respect for freedom of opinion and expression. The Covenant does not permit general prohibition of expressions of an erroneous opinion or an incorrect interpretation of past events. Restrictions on the right of freedom of opinion should never be imposed and, with regard to freedom of expression, they should not go beyond what is permitted in paragraph 3 or required under article 20.'[53]

---

[51] *Ross* v. *Canada*, para. 10.6, thus overruling *J.R.T. and the W.G. Party* v. *Canada*, Communication no. 104/1981 (6 April 1983). This requirement was subsequently firmly enshrined in Human Rights Committee, *General Comment 34: Article 19: Freedoms of Opinion and Expression* (CCPR/C/GC/34, adopted at its 102nd Session, Geneva, 11–29 July 2011), para. 51.

[52] CCPR/C/HUN/CO/5 (2010), para. 19.

[53] HRC, *General Comment 34*, para. 49. Confusingly, the Comment refers in a footnote to *Faurisson*. In fact, it says 'see *Faurisson*', suggesting that these remarks are compatible with previous jurisprudence. In actual fact, this excerpt must be considered as a radical departure from *Faurisson*.

The final sentence of this excerpt does not offer an escape. Although a concrete extreme speech conviction as a result of Holocaust denial may be sanctioned under Article 20(2) – that is, if the regular requirements of incitement are met, including content, intent and context criteria and especially the 'likelihood of harm' factor – generic memory laws as such cannot be brought in line with Articles 19 and 20 ICCPR. The reference to Article 20 is clearly not intended as a clawback,[54] but rather so as to indicate the difference to speech that may be punishable under the Covenant, namely incitement to discrimination, hostility or violence.[55] According to the chief drafter of the Comment, Michael O'Flaherty, as per the Comment the Committee's stance on memory laws has been adjusted 'to the effect that they are never compatible with the ICCPR (thus overruling *Faurisson*)'.[56]

In sum, whereas under *Faurisson* memory laws were permissible and ensuing restrictions would almost automatically be deemed 'necessary' based on the egregious content of the speech act, under General Comment No. 34 generic content-based bans are incompatible with the Covenant. In its thematic report on incitement, the UN Special Rapporteur on freedom of expression has endorsed this position.[57]

---

[54] It can be questioned, however, if it was wise to include this final sentence, as apologists of denial laws are bound to seize upon it in defence. See, e.g., German Institute for Human Rights, *Written Contribution to the Thematic Discussion of the Committee on the Elimination of Racial Discrimination on Racist Hate Speech* (2012), at 7, stating that memory laws 'are compatible with human rights if they are justified under Article 19(3) or Article 20 ICCPR. This is why the Committee, in its General Comment No. 34 cited above, continues by stating that "[r]estrictions on the right of freedom of opinion should … not go beyond what is permitted in paragraph 3 or required under article 20".'

[55] In this respect, the composition of this paragraph is very similar to that of paragraph 48 of the General Comment, dealing with blasphemy: it starts out with robust language against blasphemy laws and ends with a general caveat that states 'except in the specific circumstances envisaged in article 20, paragraph 2, of the Covenant' (*General Comment No. 34*, para. 48). This final part does not mean that blasphemy laws can be made compatible with the Covenant. Rather, this final observation is meant to indicate that extreme speech that may be punishable under the Covenant is of an entirely different nature – viz., incitement in the meaning of Art. 20.

[56] Michael O'Flaherty, 'Freedom of Expression: Article 19 of the International Covenant on Civil and Political Rights and the Human Rights Committee's General Comment No 34' (2012) 12 *Human Rights Law Review* 627–54, at 653.

[57] Special Rapporteur on the Promotion and Protection of the Right to Freedom of Opinion and Expression, *Report of the Special Rapporteur to the General Assembly on Hate Speech and Incitement to Hatred* (A/67/357, 7 September 2012), para. 55: 'With regard to discussion of history, the Special Rapporteur is of the view that historical events should be open to discussion and, as stated by the Human Rights Committee, laws that penalize the expression of opinions about historical facts are incompatible with the obligations

11.4   CERD and memory laws

CERD has not dealt with the issue of Holocaust denial in its decisions on individual communications. It has occasionally touched upon the issue in the process of scrutinizing state reports. For example, it noted that Belgian denial law was 'too restricted' by exclusively prohibiting 'the denial, minimization, justification or approval of the genocide committed by the German national socialist regime during the Second World War'.[58] The Belgian denial law, CERD recommended, 'should be broadened to cover the different types of genocide'.[59] Clearly, CERD does not criticize Belgium's wish to prohibit denying historical atrocities per se; CERD rather finds fault with the one-sided focus of the Belgian denial offence. This implies that if Belgium were to make adjustments, this memory law could be made permissible under the ICERD. Indeed, the Committee appears to welcome such a law.[60]

In its recent General Recommendation on racist hate speech the Committee leaves no doubt about this issue. It explicitly 'recommends that public denials or attempts to justify crimes of genocide and crimes against humanity, as defined by international law, should be declared as offences punishable by law, provided that they clearly constitute incitement to racial violence or hatred'.[61] The Committee was strongly lobbied by states with denial laws in place to pronounce itself more favourably on the subject

that the International Covenant on Civil and Political Rights imposes on States parties in relation to the respect for freedom of opinion and expression ... By demanding that writers, journalists and citizens give only a version of events that is approved by the Government, States are enabled to subjugate freedom of expression to official versions of events.'

58   CERD, A/52/18 (1997) 31, para. 217.
59   A/52/18 (1997) 31, para. 226.
60   At the February 2014 CERD session Belgium's Holocaust denial law was questioned. One expert asked, 'Given that it was prohibited to deny the Holocaust, was it prohibited to deny genocides, such as the one in Srebrenica?' Belgium responded that for the time being 'legislation referred only to the denial of the Holocaust and crimes of the Nazi Party', but that a draft law was under review that would cover any genocide. See OHCHR, *Committee on the Elimination of Racial Discrimination Considers Report of Belgium* (press release, 7 February 2014).
61   CERD, *General Recommendation 35: Combating Racist Hate Speech* (UN Doc. CERD/C/GC/35, 83rd session, 12–30 August 2013), para. 14. Citing the Human Rights Committee as an authority, CERD adds that 'the expression of opinions about historical facts should not be prohibited or punished.' The latter comment clearly fails to distract from the fact that CERD has embarked on a fundamentally different path than the Human Rights Committee.

of memory laws than its colleague, the Human Rights Committee, had recently done (i.e. as per the latter's General Comment No. 34).[62]

The UN Special Rapporteur on contemporary forms of racism has also recently argued that Holocaust denial comes within the ambit of Article 4 ICERD and hence must be punished by State parties.[63]

11.5   The Council of Europe and memory laws

The European Court of Human Rights has long and extensive experience with memory laws and cases of Holocaust denial. Before turning to the Court (see section 11.5.2), let us observe that the Council of Europe has adopted a wider toolbox of instruments aimed at combating Holocaust denial.

11.5.1   Instruments against Holocaust denial

While the European Convention on Human Rights is silent on the issue of denial of historical atrocities – as it is on speech offences in general – other treaties adopted by the Council of Europe do contain relevant standards. The most important treaty in that regard is the 2003 Additional Protocol to the Convention on Cybercrime, Concerning the Criminalisation of Acts of a Racist and Xenophobic Nature Committed through Computer Systems.[64] More than twenty Council of Europe members have ratified it, while two non-members, Canada and South Africa, have signed it. Interestingly, this Protocol caters to all possible positions regarding memory laws. Article 6 of this convention calls on State parties to adopt laws prohibiting the denial, gross minimization, approval or justification of genocide or crimes against humanity. According to the explanatory report this is necessary since:

---

[62] E.g. German Institute for Human Rights, *Written Contribution to the Thematic Discussion of the Committee on the Elimination of Racial Discrimination on Racist Hate Speech* (2012), at 7, stating that the Human Rights Committee's 'General Comment No. 34 can be misunderstood or misconstrued as expressing an absolute bar to laws penalizing the denial of the Shoah. In fact, persons denying the Shoah have started in Germany to make this argument. For this reason, it would be advisable for CERD to clarify the issue in a General Recommendation on racist hate speech.'

[63] Special Rapporteur on contemporary forms of racism, racial discrimination, xenophobia and related intolerance, *Report on Implementation of GA Resolution 68/150*, para. 39.

[64] Additional Protocol to the Convention on Cybercrime, Concerning the Criminalisation of Acts of a Racist and Xenophobic Nature Committed through Computer Systems, ETS No. 189, adopted on 28 January 2003, entered into force 1 March 2006.

[i]n recent years, various cases have been dealt with by national courts where persons (in public, in the media, etc.) have expressed ideas or theories which aim at denying, grossly minimising, approving or justifying the serious crimes which occurred in particular during the second World War (in particular the Holocaust). The motivation for such behaviours is often presented with the pretext of scientific research, while they really aim at supporting and promoting the political motivation which gave rise to the Holocaust. Moreover, these behaviours have also inspired or, even, stimulated and encouraged, racist and xenophobic groups in their action, including through computer systems. The expression of such ideas insults (the memory of) those persons who have been victims of such evil, as well as their relatives. Finally, it threatens the dignity of the human community.[65]

The drafters deliberately went beyond Holocaust denial per se. The genocide offence in the meaning of this Protocol covers all historical genocides that have occurred since the Second World War, and also allows State parties to criminalize the denial of future genocides recognized by international courts.[66]

Quite unusual for international human rights law,[67] the protocol explicitly indicates that states may reserve this provision in whole or in part.[68] Moreover, the Protocol spells out yet a third alternative, further suggesting that the issue of denial offences is far from crystallized in Europe. This third, intermediate position aims at accommodating those states that, though willing to ban the denial of genocide and crimes against humanity, wish to raise the offence's threshold of criminal liability somewhat.[69] Specifically, the clause at hand provides that a State party 'may ... require that the denial or the gross minimisation referred to in paragraph 1 of

---

[65] *Explanatory Report Pertaining to the Additional Protocol to the Convention on Cybercrime*, para. 39. The report further embeds (at para. 41) this provision in the case law of the European Court of Human Rights, particularly the case of *Lehideux and Isorni v. France*, Application no. 55/1997/839/1045 (Grand Chamber judgment of 23 September 1998).

[66] *Explanatory Report Pertaining to the Additional Protocol to the Convention on Cybercrime*, para. 40.

[67] If nothing had been indicated on this matter, a reservation would nevertheless have been possible inasmuch as such can be deemed compatible with the object and purpose of the Protocol. Explicit agreements on reservations would typically be included in the miscellaneous section of the treaty. It is striking that the substantive provision itself provides the opt-out.

[68] Art. 6, para. 2(b) of the Additional Protocol to the Convention on Cybercrime. Denmark and Finland have made a reservation to Art. 6.

[69] Accordingly, the compromise reached in this Protocol is reminiscent of the compromise reached by the EU on related matters. See the discussion on the Council Framework Decision on Combating Racism and Xenophobia at section 11.2 above.

this article is committed with the intent to incite hatred, discrimination or violence against any individual or group of individuals, based on race, colour, descent or national or ethnic origin, as well as religion if used as a pretext for any of these factors'.[70] Accordingly, those states that do not want to criminalize 'simple denial' but only 'qualified denial' – namely inciteful denial – can do so. A number of State parties have availed themselves of this possibility.[71]

At the political level, the Parliamentary Assembly of the Council of Europe in 2007 called upon the governments of the member states to 'actively and vigorously condemn all states sponsoring anti-Semitism, Holocaust denial and incitement to genocide'.[72] Clearly, this recommendation relates to foreign policy and does not amount to a call to adopt memory laws.

Conversely, the Council of Europe's monitoring body on racism, the European Commission against Racism and Intolerance (ECRI), has expressly called on all member states to penalize 'the public denial, trivialisation, justification or condoning, with a racist aim, of crimes of genocide, crimes against humanity or war crimes'.[73]

11.5.2   The European Court of Human Rights and Holocaust denial

We have already seen that the Strasbourg Court has developed a rather fragmented approach to the issue of standing in its extreme speech case law.[74] Occasionally convicted inciters are denied standing altogether by

---

[70] Art. 6, para. 2(a) of the Additional Protocol to the Convention on Cybercrime.

[71] Lithuania has declared that 'criminal liability for denial or gross minimisation arises if it has been committed "with the intent to incite hatred, discrimination or violence against any individual or group of individuals, based on race, colour, descent or national or ethnic origin, as well as religion if used as a pretext for any of these factors"', thus literally quoting the interpretative option provided by the Protocol itself. Montenegro and Ukraine have done the same. The Netherlands declared, to more or less the same effect, that it 'will comply with the obligation to criminalise the denial, gross minimisation, approval or justification of genocide or crimes against humanity laid down in Article 6, paragraph 1, of the Protocol where such conduct incites hatred, discrimination or violence on the grounds of race or religion'. Norway has reserved the right not to apply this Article 'except for hatred offences'.

[72] Parliamentary Assembly, Resolution 1563 (2007) Combating anti-Semitism in Europe (adopted at its 24th Sitting on 27 June 2007).

[73] ECRI, General Policy Recommendation No. 7 on National Legislation to Combat Racism and Racial Discrimination (adopted on 13 December 2002), para. 18(e). According to the chapeau of the provision, this offence is to be made punishable when committed intentionally.

[74] See section 6.6 of Chapter 6.

the Court. In those cases the European Court of Human Rights mobilizes the abuse of rights clause of Article 17 of the European Convention on Human Rights (the guillotine approach, i.e. direct application of Article 17). In other cases the Strasbourg Court does look into the merits of the free speech complaint, yet lets such seemingly substantive assessment be strongly informed by the gist of Article 17 (indirect abuse of rights approach). In still other cases, the Court ignores Article 17 and assesses whether the restrictions imposed on the person responsible for the extreme speech were justifiable under Article 10(2). We can see each of these alternatives in the Court's jurisprudence on Holocaust denial.

11.5.2.1   Holocaust denial as an abuse of rights

Commonly regarded as one of the landmark cases – because it is most extensively reasoned – is that of *Garaudy v. France*.[75] Despite its relative length, this decision falls squarely within the first category – the guillotine approach. Garaudy had published a book entitled *The Founding Myths of Israeli Politics*. This book includes a chapter with the title 'The Myth of the Holocaust', in which he among many other things claims that no gas chambers existed in the Nazi extermination camps and that if many Jews had died, this was due to the deportations – which he did not deny – and on account of malnourishment and epidemics.[76] He also denied that the Nazis had an official policy of extermination of the Jews and disputed that Hitler's 'final solution' necessarily meant the killing of Jews – the so-called missing Hitler order. In different sets of proceedings he was charged and convicted for 'aiding and abetting the denial of crimes against humanity', 'denial of crimes against humanity' (under the Gayssot Act)[77] and 'publishing racially defamatory statements'.[78] As a result of this he received a number of fines and a suspended prison sentence.

In a famous formulation, the Strasbourg Court sided with France and declared Garaudy's freedom of expression complaints inadmissible:

> There can be no doubt that denying the reality of clearly established historical facts, such as the Holocaust, as the applicant does in his book, does not constitute historical research akin to a quest for the truth. The aim and the result of that approach are completely different, the real purpose

---

[75] *Garaudy* v. *France*, Application no. 65831/01 (admissibility decision of 24 June 2003).
[76] *Garaudy* v. *France*, 'Circumstances of the case'.
[77] I.e. the same law that is at the heart of the Human Rights Committee's decision in *Faurisson* v. *France*.
[78] See Sections 23, 24, 29 and 32 of the Freedom of the Press Act of 29 July 1881 [France].

being to rehabilitate the National-Socialist regime and, as a consequence, accuse the victims themselves of falsifying history.[79]

Accordingly, the Court equates Holocaust denial with express and intentional incitement to discrimination. Moreover, the necessity of France's interference is a given according to the Court. On this point it postulates:

> [d]enying crimes against humanity is ... one of the most serious forms of racial defamation of Jews and of incitement to hatred of them. The denial or rewriting of this type of historical fact undermines the values on which the fight against racism and anti-Semitism are based and constitutes a serious threat to public order. Such acts are incompatible with democracy and human rights because they infringe the rights of others. Their proponents indisputably have designs that fall into the category of aims prohibited by Article 17 of the Convention.[80]

In sum, Holocaust denial constitutes *ipso facto* incitement and an abuse of rights in the meaning of Article 17, while combating such denial by the state is self-evidently deemed necessary for the protection of public order and the rights of Jews. Together these premises imply that State parties to the European Convention on Human Rights are entitled to adopt content-based speech bans in this area. That is, the Court's decision in Garaudy does not urge making a context-based assessment of the actual risks emanating from a concrete act of denial.[81]

It is striking, however, that the French courts had convicted Garaudy of everything he was charged with – denial of crimes against humanity, publishing racist statements, and so on – except incitement. The French judiciary had in fact acquitted Garaudy of the charge of 'incitement to racial discrimination, hatred or violence'. Specifically, the Paris Tribunal had reasoned that '[although] the author singled out ... the Jewish community on account of its allegedly excessive influence on the media and its power to "manipulate" public opinion ... for the offence of incitement ... it [was] necessary for the impugned text, both in terms of its significance and its impact, to incite the public to discrimination, hatred and violence'.[82] Applied to the case of Garaudy, it was found that there was nothing in the impugned publication that 'incite[d] or even

---

[79] *Garaudy* v. *France*, 'The law'.   [80] *Garaudy* v. *France*, 'The law'.

[81] Note that Garaudy had in fact questioned the necessity of France's memory law inasmuch as it 'did not amount to a "necessary" measure and did not satisfy a "pressing social need" under the Convention'. *Garaudy* v. *France*, 'The law'.

[82] Tribunal de Grande Instance de Paris, judgment of 27 February 1998.

encourage[d] readers to adopt the behaviour or sentiments punishable under [French law]'.[83]

In the light of the absence of express incitement, one would expect the European Court of Human Right to be all the more vigilant with respect to the necessity principle. Yet, as mentioned, since the Court determined that Garaudy's speech was of a nature to engage Article 17, no concrete risk assessment followed.

In those cases in which the Court applies Article 17 more indirectly, there is a bit more scope for consideration of the necessity of the interference – but not much. Accordingly, in *Udo Walendy* v. *Germany*, concerning an editorial in which this infamous German Holocaust denier had claimed that no gas-asphyxiation techniques had been used at the concentration camps of Auschwitz, Birkenau and Majdanek, the Court's assessment of the necessity of Germany's interferences with his freedom of speech largely boils down to invoking and explaining the relevance of Article 17.[84] At no point does the decision address the question of how the act of denial made it likely that the target group, Jewish persons, would face imminent harm.

The case of *Hans Jorg Schimanek* v. *Austria* offered an excellent opportunity for the Strasbourg Court to elaborate on the risk emanating from negationism and other neo-Nazi activities.[85] Indeed, it transpires from the facts that there may have been a strong sense of urgency motivating Austria's interferences with this extremist's freedoms. Not only had

---

[83] Tribunal de Grande Instance de Paris, judgment of 27 February 1998.

[84] European Commission of Human Rights, *Udo Walendy* v. *Germany*, Application no. 21128/92 (decision of 11 January 1995), holding as follows: 'It remains to be ascertained whether the measure in question was necessary in a democratic society and proportionate to the aims pursued ... In this respect the Commission refers to Article 17 of the Convention ... Article 17 covers essentially those rights which will facilitate the attempt to derive therefrom a right to engage personally in activities aimed at the destruction of any of the rights and freedoms set forth in the Convention. In particular the Commission has repeatedly found that the freedom of expression as expressed in Article 10 of the Convention may not be invoked in a sense contrary to Article 17 ... As regards the circumstances of the present case the Commission notes that the publication in question did according to the German appellate court deny historical facts about the mass murder committed by the totalitarian Nazi régime and therefore constituted an insult to the Jewish people and at the same time a continuation of the former discrimination against the Jewish people. These findings which were confirmed by the Federal Constitutional Court do not disclose any arbitrariness. The Commission therefore concludes that the interference at issue can be considered as "necessary in a democratic society" within the meaning of Article 10 para. 2 of the Convention.'

[85] European Court of Human Rights, *Hans Jorg Schimanek* v. *Austria*, Application No. 32307/96 (admissibility decision of 1 February 2000).

Schimanek denied the Holocaust, he was in fact convicted for leading an association that sought to revitalize the National Socialist regime contrary to the Austrian National Socialism Prohibition Act.[86] A jury had found that he had 'recruited new members, organised special events where the members of the association were familiarised with a historical view glorifying the dictators of the Third Reich, its army, the SA and the SS'.[87] Moreover, this jury had found that Schimanek had started organizing paramilitary training camps where the members could sport their uniforms and tactically prepare for the violent conflict ahead. Schimanek, like Hitler, aimed at the incorporation of Austria into an 'Enlarged Germany'.[88] These facts seem to lend themselves particularly well to a context-based risk assessment. The Strasbourg Court, however, largely fell back on the indirect Article 17 approach, thus in no way whatsoever distinguishing this case from other cases concerning negationism.

In numerous other decisions the former Commission and the Court, following a similar stratagem by leaning heavily on Article 17, content themselves that the necessity of the interferences with free speech were self-evident.[89]

11.5.2.2   Moderate risk assessment

In those (older) negationism cases in which the former European Commission of Human Rights omitted Article 17 from its analysis, the assessment is slightly more rigorous. Thus in *T. v. Belgium* it accepts that

---

[86] Section 3a(2) of the National Socialist Prohibition Act 1947 (amended in 1992).

[87] *Hans Jorg Schimanek* v. *Austria*, 'The facts'.

[88] *Hans Jorg Schimanek* v. *Austria*, 'The facts'.

[89] E.g. European Commission of Human Rights, *D.I.* v. *Germany*, Application no. 26551/95 (admissibility decision of 26 June 1996); *F.P.* v. *Germany*, Application no. 19459 (admissibility decision of 29 March 1993; *Marais* v. *France*, Application no. 31159/96 (admissibility decision of 24 June 1996); *Friedrich Rebhandl* v. *Austria*, Application no. 24398/94 (admissibility decision of 16 January 1996); *Otto E.F.A. Remer* v. *Germany*, Application no. 25096/94 (admissibility decision of 6 September 1995); *Walter Ochensberger* v. *Austria*, Application no. 21318/93 (admissibility decision of 2 September 1994); *B.H., M.W., H.P. and G.K.* v. *Austria*, Application no. 12774/87 (admissibility decision of 12 October 1989). European Court of Human Rights, *Hans-Jürgen Witzsch* v. *Germany* [I], Application no. 41448/98 (admissibility decision of 20 April 1999); *Herwig Nachtmann* v. *Austria*, Application no. 36773/97 (admissibility decision of 9 September 1998). See also, *mutatis mutandis*, European Court of Human Rights, *Hans-Jürgen Witzsch* v. *Germany* [II], Application no. 7485/03 (admissibility decision of 13 December 2005); European Commission of Human Rights, *Karl-August Hennicke* v. *Germany*, Application no. 34889/97 (admissibility decision of 21 May 1997); and *Michael Kühnen* v. *Germany*, Application no. 12194/86 (admissibility decision of 12 May 1988).

interferences were 'necessary for the prevention of disorder', but does not provide much in the way of argumentation.[90] The Commission's observation that 'present events demonstrate that anti-democratic ideologies, resembling those that inspired such atrocities, have not disappeared from Europe', strikes as overly abstract to justify a limitation on free speech.[91] More to the point is the Commission's argument that while there are fewer and fewer Holocaust survivors, 'the family of those survivors continue to be entitled to the protection of their relatives' memory'.[92] However, one may question whether this point truly substantiates the necessity of the encroachment of memory laws on free speech. Obviously, Holocaust survivors (and their relatives) may be tremendously hurt by someone denying their horrific experience. Understandable though the urge to legally ban such grotesque speech may seem, mental distress – while a profound *malum in se* – does not provide a solid basis for the codification and justification of speech offences.[93]

In *X. v. Germany*, concerning someone who was forbidden by the authorities to display pamphlets alleging that the assassination of millions of Jews during the period of the Third Reich was a Zionistic swindle, the Commission accepted that this interference was necessary to protect the reputation of others (namely Jewish persons).[94] Strikingly, the Commission speaks of the 'tendency' of the pamphlets to not only provide a distorted picture of history but also to attack the reputation of Jews. Indicating a 'tendency' falls short of substantiating that harm may imminently befall the target group. The Committee did, however, rightly dwell on the vulnerable nature of the target group.[95]

11.5.2.3   No legal defence of 'truth'

In a fair number of German, Austrian and French Holocaust denial cases the former European Commission of Human Rights accepted in so many words that national judicial authorities do not need to grant the defendant's request to raise a legal defence of 'truth', for example to

---

[90] European Commission of Human Rights, *T. v. Belgium*, Application no. 9777/82 (admissibility decision of 14 July 1983), at 'The law'.

[91] *T. v. Belgium*, 'The law'.   [92] *T. v. Belgium*, 'The law'.

[93] See Fraser, 'On the Internet, Nobody Knows You're a Nazi', at 519.

[94] European Commission of Human Rights, *X. v. Germany*, Application no. 9235/81 (admissibility decision of 16 July 1982), at 'The law'.

[95] *X. v. Germany*, 'The law', postulating that '[t]he protection of these principles [of tolerance and broadmindedness] may be especially indicated vis-à-vis groups which have historically suffered from discrimination.'

present 'proof' that no gas chambers existed in Auschwitz.[96] Of course, normally evidence of truth may have the potential of dismantling allegations of malicious defamation. In the area of defamation it is well-established Strasbourg jurisprudence that statements or allegations of fact are susceptible of proof, whereas value statements are not;[97] that is, a value judgment cannot be proven and proof of accuracy may accordingly not be required by courts. However, a minimal factual basis may be required to support certain (defamatory) value statements.[98] Statements of fact, on the contrary, may be proven to be right or wrong. Accordingly, an allegation of fact regarding something or someone that proves to be wrong may cause an instance of defamation, whereas a restriction placed on a certain accusatory speech act that proves to be correct may cause an instance of a breach of freedom of expression. The onus is, naturally, on the person responsible for the speech act to substantiate the statement.

Accordingly, not granting the defendant the possibility to dispel allegations of defamation made against them would under any other circumstances appear to be unfair. In the particular context of Holocaust denial the European Court of Human rights has reasoned

---

[96] See, e.g., European Commission of Human Rights, *X. v. Germany*, Application No. 9235/81 (admissibility decision of 16 July 1982); *Otto E.F.A. Remer v. Germany*, Application no. 25096/94 (admissibility decision of 6 September 1995); *D.I. v. Germany*, Application no. 26551/95 (26 June 1996); *Friedrich Rebhandl v. Austria*, Application no. 24398/94 (admissibility decision of 16 January 1996); *Marais v. France*, Application no. 31159/96 (admissibility decision of 24 June 1996).

[97] The landmark case is European Court of Human Rights, *Lingens v. Austria*, Application no. 9815/82 (8 July 1986), paras. 46–47. See also, e.g., *Nilsen and Johnsen v. Norway*, Application no. 23118/93 (Grand Chamber judgment of 25 November 1999), paras. 48–50; *Pedersen and Baadsgaard v. Denmark*, Application no. 49017/99 (Grand Chamber judgment of 17 December 2004), para. 76; *Oberschlick v. Austria*, Application no. 11662/85 (23 May 1991), para. 63.

[98] European Court of Human Rights, *Jerusalem v. Austria*, Application no. 26958/95 (27 February 2001), paras. 43–46, concerning a case in which an organization was accused of being a 'sect' – here the value judgment was not considered excessive. See also, e.g., *De Haes and Gijsels v. Belgium*, Application no. 19983/92 (24 February 1997), para. 47, concerning criticism of judges, which was not deemed to be excessive; *Prager and Oberschlick v. Austria*, Application no. 15974/90 (26 April 1995), paras. 36–38, in which criticism of judges was considered to be 'unnecessarily prejudicial'; *Lindon, Otchakovsky-Laurens and July v. France*, Application nos. 21279/02 and 36448/02 (Grand Chamber judgment of 22 October 2007), in which the Court upheld the need to support value judgments by showing a sufficient factual basis even if those value judgments are made in a novel (if those novelistic works include real-life characters, here Jean-Marie Le Pen). Four judges dissented. See Joint Partly Dissenting Opinion of Judges Rozakis, Bratza, Tulkens and Šikuta.

that granting evidentiary requests would only provide deniers with a further platform on which to spread their hateful messages, while 'the gassing of Jews in Auschwitz [is] a historically proven fact and therefore common knowledge'.[99] This certainly stands to reason – there is no need to put the spotlights on Holocaust deniers when this can be avoided. Considering that those evidentiary attempts are bound to be futile, these rejections are not likely to impede a fair trial. The defendant must, however, remain in a position to raise a meaningful defence. Obviously, requests to bring evidence that the impugned speech act did not incite must be granted. The same goes for evidence as to the intentions of the speaker and the likelihood of harm as perceived by the speaker. These concerns once again point at the fact that narrowly tailored incitement laws are to be preferred over memory laws, since laws of the former type steer the parties to an incitement case to meaningful legal battles.

Interestingly, there is one case wherein the Austrian judicial authorities did go to remarkably great pains, not so much to allow the defendant to present proof that he was right, but to obtain expert information demonstrating that the Holocaust denier under consideration, Gerd Honsik, was – obviously – utterly wrong and hence had committed 'National Socialist activities' within the meaning of the Austrian National Socialist Prohibition Act,[100] so much so that Honsik's complaint to the European Commission of Human Rights chiefly raised fair trail issues, notably concerning the question of 'reasonable time'. Honsik was the writer and editor of various periodicals in which he had cast doubt as to the existence of gas chambers in concentration camps. An investigating judge of the Vienna Regional Court, who had instituted criminal investigations against Honsik, in January 1987 appointed an expert on contemporary history to prepare a report on the existence of gas chambers and their role in the mass extermination of Jews. It was only in 1992 that Honsik, on the basis of the long overdue expert report, could be sentenced to serve a prison sentence. For the Commission this was sufficient reason to declare the case admissible on the point of reasonable time.[101]

---

[99] *D.I.* v. *Germany*, 'The law' (approvingly paraphrasing the words of a German regional court).

[100] European Commission of Human Rights, *Gerd Honsik* v. *Austria*, Application no. 25062/94 (admissibility decision of 27 February 1997).

[101] Yet it never came to a judgment on the merits as Honsik did not follow up from here. See Committee of Ministers Resolution DH (98) 93, Application No. 25062/94.

11.5.2.4 Non-public denial as punishable speech

International incitement prohibitions, specifically Article 20(2) of the ICCPR, aim at banning *public* incitement to discrimination, hostility or violence.[102] 'Advocacy' of hatred suggests that the person responsible for the hateful speech must be deliberately reaching out to others for the speech act to become punishable. The European Court of Human Rights has adopted a different approach in this regard.

For example, at the heart of the case of *F.P. v. Germany* were statements that the applicant, a member of the German army, had made on the occasion of a private party. In the presence of German and American soldiers he had said, among other things, 'that the Holocaust was a lie of Zionists while in reality Jews had never been persecuted and killed'. He further claimed to have evidence 'showing that allegations about persecutions of Jews in Germany were a part of a strategy of Zionism and Communism in order to discredit Germany', that 'some Concentration Camps had been constructed only after the war for the purposes of anti-German propaganda' and that 'the educational system was used to give pupils a wrong picture of German history'.[103] As a result, German military courts and on appeal, administrative courts, established a series of disciplinary offences – breaches of 'political loyalty', 'supporting ideals that endanger the free democratic order' – and imposed disciplinary sanctions (demotion). The European Commission of Human Rights applied its combined Article 17/Article 10 approach and concluded that as F.P. had abused his rights, the interferences with his freedom of speech were deemed to be necessary in a democratic society.[104]

In the (two) cases of *Witzsch v. Germany* the Strasbourg Court again accepted that negationist speech uttered in private may amount to punishable speech under the Convention. But whereas in *F.P. v. Germany* the reputation of the army was at stake, in *Witzsch* the acts of denial merely implicated the applicant. In addition, whereas in *F.P. v. Germany* there was an audience, albeit a private gathering, *Witzsch I* revolved around an unspecified number of 'written letters to Bavarian politicians' and *Witzsch II*

---

[102] See section 7.3.1 of Chapter 7 and section 8.3.1 of Chapter 8.
[103] European Commission of Human Rights, *F.P. v. Germany*, Application no. 19459 (admissibility decision by of 29 March 1993), at 'The facts'.
[104] *F.P. v. Germany*, 'The Law'.

concerned a single letter sent to a history professor.[105] Moreover, whereas in
F.P. v. *Germany* the negationism statements resulted in administrative penalties, Witzsch incurred criminal sanctions.

More specifically, the first *Witzsch* case concerned letters the applicant
had sent to politicians complaining about the intended amendment of the
Penal Code that would make the approval, trivialization or denial of the
atrocities perpetrated by the National Socialists a crime. In those same letters Witzsch had managed to do precisely that – he denied the existence of
the gas chambers, the mass killing by the Nazis, and so on. As a result of that
he was sentenced to four months' imprisonment for 'disparaging the dignity of the deceased'.[106] His Article 10 complaint failed in Strasbourg as the
European Court of Human Rights applied Article 17.[107]

While in *Wizsch I* the impugned letters, although sent to public figures,
presumably formed a private correspondence, this was undoubtedly the
case in *Witzsch II*. This time he transmitted his unremitting negationist sentiments – on this occasion he challenged the idea that Hitler had author-
ized the extermination of Jews (the 'Hitler order') – by means of a personal
reply to a history professor who had published an article about the murder
of the Jews by Hitler and the Nazis in a German review. The history professor concerned, Professor W., submitted Witzsch's letter to the police.
Professor W. himself left it at that and refused to press charges. The police, in
turn, informed one Mr or Mrs H. – 'whose grandparents', as the facts indicated, 'had died in a concentration camp' – about the letter, who on the same
day lodged a criminal complaint.[108] Subsequently, Witzsch was again convicted of the crime of disparaging the dignity of the deceased and this time
he was sentenced to three months' imprisonment.[109]

Before the Strasbourg Court Witzsch emphasized that the impugned
statements were made in a private correspondence.[110] Yet the Court held
that '[t]he fact that they were made in a private letter and not before a
larger audience is irrelevant'.[111] While acknowledging that the German
police had been instrumental in giving wider attention to his views, the

---

[105] European Court of Human Rights, *Hans-Jürgen Witzsch* v. *Germany* [I], Application
no. 41448/98 (admissibility decision of 20 April 1999); and European Court of Human
Rights, *Hans-Jürgen Witzsch* v. *Germany* [II], Application no. 7485/03 (admissibility
decision of 13 December 2005).

[106] Pursuant an older crime contained in Art. 189 of the Criminal Code of Germany 1998.

[107] *Witzsch* v. *Germany* [I], 'The law'.

[108] *Witzsch* v. *Germany* [II], 'The facts'.

[109] *Witzsch* v. *Germany* [II], 'The facts'. This was upheld in the several appeals that followed.

[110] *Witzsch* v. *Germany* [II], 'The law', para. 1.

[111] *Witzsch* v. *Germany* [II], 'The law', para. 3.

Court agreed with Germany that the offence of disparaging the dignity of the dead had in any event already been committed simply by virtue of composing and sending the impugned letter, thus accepting the scope of the German criminal offence in issue.[112]

This broad offence of disparaging the deceased certainly covers the present scenario, but the question is if an international monitoring body should permit the width of such a crime. Initially, when Witzsch sent his letter to Professor W., other than the latter there was no audience taking notice of Witzsch's hateful views. Thus the likelihood that the rights of the target group, here Jewish people, were going to be undermined was nil. Only later on, when Witzsch's letter was forwarded to H. by the police, was (one member of) the target group itself confronted with Witzsch's hatred. Disturbing as that may have been for H., no triangle of incitement – consisting of an inciter, a target group and an audience capable of acting upon a call to violence or discrimination – was set in motion by Witzsch's hateful speech act.

Even aside from comparisons with plausible reasonings under Article 20(2) of the ICCPR, the Strasbourg Court has a lot to answer for. In dismissing this complaint, once again the Court strongly depended on Article 17. Yet the Court fails to explain how the rights of others could be 'destroyed' if no one else sees the impugned letter.

11.6   Glorification of religious violence or terrorism

There is a subtle difference between the denial or trivialization of historical atrocities and the glorification of past or ongoing violence. Although both forms of extreme speech are bound to hurt the feelings of the target group immensely, by 'glorifying' historical crimes against humanity someone more or less expressly incites to similar crimes being perpetrated in the near future against the same group. Even short of a direct call for action, the person who glorifies atrocities obviously makes it explicit that he or she did not quite mind that they occurred in the past and thus implies that he or she would not mind if they were to occur again. Accordingly, the glorifier's malicious intent may be relatively transparent. Also, a person glorifying historical violence ostensibly abuses his or her rights.

For these and related reasons, some states have enshrined 'glorification' offences in their criminal law. For example, Germany prohibits 'glorifying,

---

[112] *Witzsch* v. *Germany* [II], 'The law', para. 1.

or justifying National Socialist rule of arbitrary force'.[113] This is only a punishable offence if the public speech act 'disturbs the public peace'.[114] The UK prohibits the encouragement of terrorism.[115] One indirect way of committing this crime is by making a statement that 'glorifies the commission or preparation (whether in the past, in the future or generally) of [terrorist acts]'.[116] This constitutes a punishable offence if the speech act 'is a statement from which those members of the public could reasonably be expected to infer that what is being glorified is being glorified as conduct that should be emulated by them in existing circumstances'.[117] Russia has banned, as part of a wider law that aims at 'combating extremist activity', the act of offering justifications for terrorism.[118]

The question remains whether international law permits bans on glorifying content per se, or whether with respect to such instances a case-by-case assessment of the actual risk emanating from such speech is in order. If the latter holds true, then the application of narrowly tailored incitement law again is preferable over combating 'glorification' offences.[119]

While political UN bodies have expressed some support for this type of legal measure,[120] the expert bodies have expressed concern. Notably, the Human Rights Committee, having reviewed UK's terrorism legislation,

---

[113] Art. 130(4) of the Criminal Code of Germany 1998.

[114] Art. 130(4) of the Criminal Code of Germany 1998.

[115] Section 1 of the Terrorism Act 2006 [UK] c. 11.

[116] Section 1(3)(a) of the Terrorism Act 2006 [UK].

[117] Section 1(3)(b) of the Terrorism Act 2006 [UK].

[118] Section 1 of Federal Law No. 114-FZ of 25 July 2002 on Combating Extremist Activity (as amended on 27 July 2006, 10 May and 24 July 2007, and 29 April 2008) [Russia].

[119] See S. Chehani Ekaratne, 'Redundant Restriction: The U.K.'s Offense of Glorifying Terrorism' (2010) 23 *Harvard Human Rights Journal* 205–21, rejecting the broadness and vagueness of the British glorification offence. See also Eric Barendt, 'Incitement to, and Glorification of, Terrorism', in Hare and Weinstein (eds.), *Extreme Speech and Democracy*, 445–62; and Tufyal Choudhury, 'The Terrorism Act 2006: Discouraging Terrorism', in Hare and Weinstein (eds.), *Extreme Speech and Democracy*, 463–87.

[120] The General Assembly of the United Nations has called upon member states to take measures, including legal prohibitions, to combat the 'glorification of Nazism'. See General Assembly, Resolution 67/154 'Glorification of Nazism: Inadmissibility of Certain Practices that Contribute to Fuelling Contemporary Forms of Racism, Racial Discrimination, Xenophobia and Related Intolerance' (UN Doc. A/RES/67/154, 20 December 2012); see also Resolution 68/150 (UN Doc. A/RES/68/150, 18 December 2013). These Resolutions claim that such acts of glorification come within the ambit of both Art. 4 of ICERD as well as Art. 20(2) of the ICCPR (Resolution 67/154, paras. 7 and 20; Resolution 68/150, paras. 8 and 23). The Resolutions were tabled by Russia. The USA and Canada, alarmed by the freedom of expression and freedom of assembly ramifications, voted against them, while, among other states, all members of the European Union abstained from voting on them.

criticized the encouragement/glorification of terrorism offence for being 'broad and vague'.[121] The Committee particularly found fault with the fact that 'a person can commit the offence even when he or she did not intend members of the public to be directly or indirectly encouraged by his or her statement to commit acts of terrorism, but where his or her statement was understood by some members of the public as encouragement to commit such acts'.[122] Accordingly, the Committee suspects this offence to disproportionately affect freedom of expression. Similarly, the Committee dismissed Russian anti-extremism legislation for being vague and overly intrusive.[123] In its 2011 General Comment on freedom of expression the Committee summed up its concerns by postulating that 'States parties should ensure that counter-terrorism measures are compatible with paragraph 3 [of Article 19 ICCPR]. Such offences as "encouragement of terrorism" and "extremist activity" as well as offences of "praising", "glorifying", or "justifying" terrorism, should be clearly defined to ensure that they do not lead to unnecessary or disproportionate interference with freedom of expression.'[124]

Indeed, enforcement of such broad speech offences is bound to be in contravention of the Johannesburg Principles on National Security, Freedom of Expression and Access to Information, a set of benchmarks adopted by international law experts and endorsed by the UN Special Rapporteur on freedom of expression.[125] According to these Principles, 'expression may be punished as a threat to national security only if a government can demonstrate that: (a) the expression is intended to incite imminent violence; (b) it is likely to incite such violence; and (c) there is a

---

[121] CCPR/C/GBR/CO/6 (2008), para. 26.
[122] CCPR/C/GBR/CO/6 (2008), para. 26.
[123] A/59/40 vol. I (2003) 20, para. 64(20), as reiterated in 2009: CCPR/C/RUS/CO/6, para. 24.
[124] HRC, *General Comment 34*, para. 46.
[125] *The Johannesburg Principles on National Security, Freedom of Expression and Access to Information, Freedom of Expression and Access to Information* (1996). See Report of the Special Rapporteur on the promotion and protection of the right to freedom of opinion and expression (E/CN.4/1996/39, 22 March 1996), endorsing them in para. 4 and appending them (see Annex). See also ARTICLE 19, *Camden Principles on Freedom of Expression and Equality* (2009). These principles somewhat cryptically indicate that states 'should prohibit the *condoning* or denying of crimes of genocide, crimes against humanity and war crimes', yet 'only where such statements constitute hate speech' (principle 12.2, emphasis added). Since hate speech is defined by reference to Art. 20(2) ICCPR (see footnote pertaining to principle 12), essentially what the Principles say is do not prohibit negationism, unless the speech act amounts to punishable speech in the meaning of the ICCPR.

direct and immediate connection between the expression and the likelihood or occurrence of such violence.'[126]

At the regional level of the Council of Europe, attention must again first be drawn to the work of ECRI. We have seen before that this anti-racism watchdog recommends legislation criminalizing denial offences. In addition, ECRI urges members of the Council of Europe to penalize the act of 'justification' or 'condoning' crimes of genocide, crimes against humanity or war crimes.[127]

The Council of Europe Convention on the Prevention of Terrorism requires each State party to declare as a punishable crime the act of 'public provocation to commit a terrorist offence'.[128] This offence is committed through 'the distribution, or otherwise making available, of a message to the public, with the intent to incite the commission of a terrorist offence, where such conduct, whether or not directly advocating terrorist offences, causes a danger that one or more such offences may be committed'.[129] As the explanatory report outlines, the words 'whether or not directly advocating terrorist offences' were included to ensure that such indirect provocation as for instance through 'the dissemination of messages praising the perpetrator of an attack' was also covered.[130]

The European Court of Human Rights has repeatedly dealt with the question of whether State parties to the European Convention on Human Rights were justified in interfering with alleged instances of glorification of terrorism and past or ongoing religious or ethnic violence. Increasingly, the Court moves away from accepting content-based bans of glorification and tends to apply a context-based risk assessment, more or less concisely charting the potential harm that emanated from the impugned extreme speech act.

Thus in *Leroy* v. *France*, concerning a cartoon published in a newspaper with which the applicant allegedly had condoned and glorified the 9/11 attacks, the Court's analysis goes beyond the content of the cartoon and the intentions of the cartoon artist. The Court places much emphasis on the politically sensitive (Basque) region, suggesting that France

---

[126] *Johannesburg Principles*, Principle 6.

[127] ECRI, *General Policy Recommendation No. 7*, para. 18(e).

[128] Art. 5 of the Council of Europe Convention on the Prevention of Terrorism, ETS no. 196, adopted on 16 May 2005, entry into force 1 June 2007.

[129] Art. 5 of the Convention on the Prevention of Terrorism.

[130] *Explanatory Report Pertaining to the Additional Protocol to the Convention on Cybercrime*, para. 95 (quoting suggestions made to that effect by the Parliamentary Assembly and the Commissioner for Human Rights of the Council of Europe).

could reasonably have anticipated that violent acts would be stirred up.[131] Admittedly, that conclusion would have benefited from a more comprehensive argumentation.

The landmark decision in the area of glorification of Nazism is the case of *Lehideux and Isorni* v. *France*.[132] This is in fact a rather ambiguous case of glorification of historical atrocities. Rather than directly glorifying acts perpetrated by the Nazis, these two – respectively a former minister in Pétain's Vichy Government and Pétain's defence lawyer during his post-war trial – sought to rehabilitate Pétain. In so doing they had publicly glorified the collaboration with the Nazis, and through still further implication the atrocities perpetrated by the Nazis. In condemning the two of the crime of condoning Nazi collaboration, the French judiciary had concentrated on the one-sided nature of their writing (an advertisement in *Le Monde*).[133] In front of the Strasbourg Court, France defended its prohibition of this speech offence and the enforcement thereof in the present case. The French Government conceded that these two men had not committed Holocaust denial, yet 'in order to glorify Philippe Pétain's record during the Second World War they had been impelled to deny, by deliberately omitting to mention it, the existence of his policy of collaboration with the Third Reich'.[134] The European Court of Human Rights was unable to agree with France. First of all, no malicious intent was established.[135] Second, contextual elements persuaded the Court to find in favour of a freedom of speech violation. In relation to likelihood specifically, the Court found that 'ten or twenty years previously' the statements made would have made a more severe impact.[136] This lapse of time argument, which has featured in the Court's freedom of expression jurisprudence on other occasions too,[137] is interesting since in relation to clear-cut

---

[131] European Court of Human Rights, *Leroy* v. *France*, Application no. 36109/03 (October 2008), para. 45.

[132] European Court of Human Rights, *Lehideux and Isorni* v. *France*, Application no. 55/1997/839/1045 (Grand Chamber judgment of 23 September 1998).

[133] *Lehideux and Isorni* v. *France*, para. 21.

[134] *Lehideux and Isorni* v. *France*, para. 42.

[135] *Lehideux and Isorni* v. *France*, para. 37 (views of the Commission), paras. 47 and 53 (Court). Some judges dissented, arguing it was clear that the two were trying to recruit adherents to their objectionable cause. See Joint dissenting opinion of Judges Foighel, Loizou and John Freeland; and dissenting opinion of Judge Casadevall.

[136] *Lehideux and Isorni* v. *France*, para. 55.

[137] E.g. European Court of Human Rights, *Monnat* v. *Switzerland*, Application no. 73604/01 (21 September 2006), para. 64, concerning a journalist who had argued that Switzerland's role in the Second World War was not as rosy as is often portrayed.

forms of negationism the Court is not willing to consider a similar argument for the time being.

The fact that the Court is gradually coming to terms with contextual elements in cases of alleged glorification or condoning of violence is particularly visible in the numerous Turkish cases of alleged propaganda of separatism and nationalist violence.[138] In *Sürek v. Turkey (No. 1)* the Grand Chamber was requested to consider whether the publication by a weekly review of two inflammatory letters justified interference with freedom of expression.[139] The letters had been written by readers of the review and vehemently condemned acts by the Turkish authorities against the Turkish Kurds, accusing the former of perpetrating massacres and other brutalities.[140] In assessing whether the penalties imposed (fines) on the applicant, who acted as the major shareholder of said review, were legitimate, the Grand Chamber contended that:

> there is a clear intention to stigmatise the other side to the conflict by the use of labels such as 'the fascist Turkish army', 'the TC murder gang' and 'the hired killers of imperialism' alongside references to 'massacres', 'brutalities' and 'slaughter'. In the view of the Court the impugned letters amount to an appeal to bloody revenge by stirring up base emotions and hardening already embedded prejudices which have manifested themselves in deadly violence.[141]

The Court found that the review for which Sürek was responsible functioned as an outlet to stir up violence and accordingly no violation of free speech could be established.[142] Judge Palm argued that the majority's emphasis on the content of the letters was rather beside the point. Specifically, she wrote that:

> the majority has attached too much weight to the admittedly harsh and vitriolic language used in the impugned letters and insufficient attention to the general context in which the words were used and their likely impact. Undoubtedly the words in question shock and disturb the reader with their general accusatory tone and their underlying violence. But in a

---

[138] For a case predating the ones discussed here, see European Court of Human Rights, *Incal v. Turkey*, Application no. 41/1997/825/1031 (Grand Chamber Judgment of 9 June 1998), finding that the penalties imposed on the author of a pro-Kurdish leaflet amounted to a violation of Art. 10.

[139] European Court of Human Rights, *Sürek v. Turkey (No. 1)*, Application no. 26682/95 (Grand Chamber Judgment of 8 July 1999).

[140] *Sürek v. Turkey (No. 1)*, para. 11.   [141] *Sürek v. Turkey (No. 1)*, para. 62.

[142] *Sürek v. Turkey (No. 1)*, para. 63.

democracy, as our Court has emphasised, even such 'fighting' words may be protected by Article 10.[143]

She went on to contend that:

> [t]he question in the present case concerns the approach employed by the Court to decide the point at which such 'violent' and offensive speech ceases to be protected by the Convention. My answer to this question is to focus less on the vehemence and outrageous tone of the words employed and more on the different elements of the contextual setting in which the speech was uttered. Was the language intended to inflame or incite to violence? Was there a real and genuine risk that it might actually do so? The answer to these questions in turn requires a measured assessment of the many different layers that compose the general context in the circumstances of each case.[144]

Applying these context factors, Judge Palm establishes a violation of Article 10, concluding that there was no real likelihood that the published letters would stir up violence. Her comparison of *Sürek* to the older case of *Zana* v. *Turkey* is most illuminating and proves a powerful explanation of the necessity for a context-based risk assessment in this type of cases.[145] Zana, a former mayor, had remarked in an interview with journalists that he supported the PKK national liberation movement. Whilst he was 'not in favour of massacres', he added rather ambiguously that 'Anyone can make mistakes, and the PKK kill women and children by mistake.'[146] He was sentenced to twelve months' imprisonment for condoning violent acts. The Strasbourg Court emphasized that 'the interview coincided with murderous attacks carried out by the PKK on civilians in south-east Turkey, where there was extreme tension at the material time', which meant that an interview 'by the former mayor of Diyarbakır, the most important city in south-east Turkey' that was 'published in a major national daily newspaper' could reasonably have been regarded by Turkey 'as likely to exacerbate an already explosive situation in that region'.[147]

Thus, in *Zana* Turkey, and subsequently the European Court of Human Rights in its own assessment, could determine a host of contextual elements that pointed to an increased degree of likelihood of harm (here

---

[143] Partly dissenting opinion of Judge Palm.
[144] Partly dissenting opinion of Judge Palm.
[145] European Court of Human Rights, *Zana* v. *Turkey*, Application no. 69/1996/6888/880 (Grand Chamber Judgment of 25 November 1997). See Partly dissenting opinion of Judge Palm.
[146] *Zana* v. *Turkey*, para. 12.   [147] *Zana* v. *Turkey*, paras. 59–60.

potential violence). Notably, there was the special status of the speaker. Zana, as a former mayor and public figure, could be said to exercise a degree of influence on public opinion. This constitutes an important difference with Sürek, who merely acted as the major shareholder of the impugned review. Further, there is the factor of the medium used and the particular setting in which the speech acts are made public. Zana ventilated his views in a national newspaper. The impugned letters by readers published in Sürek's review arguably were less likely to have an adverse impact, not only on account of the review's more moderate circulation, but also as Judge Palm argues since 'letter-writing by readers does not occupy a central or headline position in a review and is by its very nature of limited influence. Moreover some allowance must be made for the fact that members of the public expressing their views in letters for publication are likely to use a more direct and vehement style than professional journalists.'[148] Last but not least, Zana's (ambiguous) condoning of murder occurred during a peak of regional violence.[149]

Palm's dissent struck a chord with some of the other judges. In a series of judgments delivered by the Court that same day on cases brought against Turkey, this contextual approach is expressly shared by a number of other judges, but also generally impacted the approach taken by the plenary Court in some cases. For instance, in *Arslan* v. *Turkey*, concerning a book that according to the Turkish authorities 'glorified the acts of insurgents in south-east Turkey',[150] the Grand Chamber unanimously held that freedom of expression was in fact breached. While the Court came to this conclusion having argued that the book did not contain express incitement and on account of the book having only limited potential of achieving the harm that Turkey had attributed to it,[151] Judge Palm and four other judges – this time in the form of a concurring opinion – urged their colleagues to assess contextual elements even more rigorously. 'It is

---

[148] Partly dissenting opinion of Judge Palm.

[149] Note that these observations do not mean that to say the Court got it completely right in *Zana*, but merely to show how context factors help to distinguish meaningfully between cases in which 'fighting words' are used. In *Zana*, no less than seven judges dissented with the finding of no violation of Art. 10 on account of the interference (prison sentence) being disproportionate. See Partly Dissenting Opinion of Judge Van Dijk, joined by Judges Palm, Loizou, Mifsud Bonnici, Jambrek, Kūris and Levits. Judge Thór Vilhjálmsson, moreover, could not detect express incitement to violence in the dubious words used by Zana. See Dissenting Opinion of Judge Thór Vilhjálmsson.

[150] European Court of Human Rights, *Arslan* v. *Turkey*, Application no. 23462/94 (Grand Chamber Judgment of 8 July 1999), para. 10.

[151] *Arslan* v. *Turkey*, para. 48.

only by a careful examination of the context in which the offending words appear', they emphasized, 'that one can draw a meaningful distinction between language which is shocking and offensive – which is protected by Article 10 – and that which forfeits its right to tolerance in a democratic society.'[152] This opinion is also appended to most of the dozen additional freedom of expression decisions concerning Turkey – mostly revolving around alleged instances of glorification of separatist violence – that were handed down that same day.[153] In that body of case law, the Court among other things held that insurgent poetry, even when 'very aggressive in tone' and calling 'for the use of violence', inherently has limited potential to cause harm given its small audience.[154] Turkey's anti-extremism policies had furthermore overstepped the mark by undermining academic freedom (scholarship in relation to the Kurdish plight),[155] uninhibited news reporting (in relation to the Kurdish plight)[156] and journalism in general.[157]

The contextual approach then set in motion is reiterated and further conceptualized in subsequent decisions against Turkey involving

---

[152] Joint Concurring Opinion of Judges Palm, Tulkens, Fischbach, Casadevall and Greve, final paragraph. Judge Bonello for his part also emphasized the need to make a concrete risk assessment. See Concurring Opinion of Judge Bonello, engaging with the 'clear and present danger' doctrine and the 'imminent lawless action' doctrine as formulated in US Supreme Court jurisprudence.

[153] See European Court of Human Rights, *Sürek and Özdemir v. Turkey*, Application nos. 23927/94 and 24277/94 (Grand Chamber Judgment of 8 July 1999); *Sürek v. Turkey (No. 2)*, Application no. 24122/94 (Grand Chamber Judgment of 8 July 1999); *Sürek v. Turkey (No. 3)*, Application no. 24735/94 (Grand Chamber Judgment of 8 July 1999); *Sürek v. Turkey (No. 4)*, Application no. 24762/94 (Grand Chamber Judgment of 8 July 1999); *Ceylan v. Turkey*, Application no. 23556/94 (Grand Chamber Judgment of 8 July 1999); *Gerger v. Turkey*, Application no. 24919/94 (Grand Chamber Judgment of 8 July 1999); *Polat v. Turkey*, Application no. 23500/94 (Grand Chamber Judgment of 8 July 1999); *Karataş v. Turkey*, Application no. 23168/94 (Grand Chamber Judgment of 8 July 1999); *Erdoğdu and İnce v. Turkey*, Application nos. 25067/94 and 25068/94 (Grand Chamber Judgment of 8 July 1999); *Başkaya and Okçuoğlu v. Turkey*, Application nos. 23536/94 and 24408/94 (Grand Chamber Judgment of 8 July 1999); *Okçuoğlu v. Turkey*, Application no. 24246/94 (Grand Chamber Judgment of 8 July 1999).

[154] *Karataş v. Turkey*, para. 52.

[155] *Başkaya and Okçuoğlu v. Turkey*, para. 65. See also, *mutatis mutandis*, *Polat v. Turkey* and the previously discussed *Arslan v. Turkey*, which both revolved around books that, although not of an academic nature, contained historical passages.

[156] See specifically *Sürek v. Turkey (No. 2)*; *Sürek v. Turkey (No. 4)*; *Ceylan v. Turkey*; and *Gerger v. Turkey*.

[157] *Erdoğdu and İnce v. Turkey*, concerning sentences imposed on the editor of a monthly review and an interviewee.

instances of alleged glorification,[158] also impacting later cases of alleged *religion*-oriented instances of incitement.[159]

In sum, unlike its case law on denial of historical atrocities, the Strasbourg Court's jurisprudence on glorification/justification/condoning past or ongoing violence appears to be moving towards a more context-dependent approach.

11.7   Concluding remarks

The argument that most if not all Holocaust denial is a form of express or covert – often hidden under the cloak of pseudoscience – incitement to anti-Semitic discrimination stands to reason. Yet the position that negationism is always and everywhere, purely on account of its excruciating content, likely to trigger hostile acts against its target group is not tenable. Despicable though negationism is, law-makers and judges ought not to let emotions cloud sound judgment. Content-based bans may very well overestimate the impact of negationist speech acts, while underestimating the capacity of a liberal democracy to dismantle grotesque statements through counter-speech. Glorification of religious violence or terrorism *in abstracto* raises tremendous public order issues. Yet in that area of extreme speech too the necessity principle ought to be taken seriously, meaning that judges must closely scrutinize whether the alleged glorification at the material time posed a real risk that violent or other harmful acts would ensue.

---

[158] See also, e.g., European Court of Human Rights, *Erdoğdu* v. *Turkey*, Application no. 25723/94 (15 June 2000); *Kizilyaprak* v. *Turkey*, Application no. 27528/95 (2 October 2003); *Alinak* v. *Turkey*, Application no. 40287/98 (29 March 2005); *Ergin* v. *Turkey (No. 1)*, Application no. 48944/99 (16 June 2005); *Ergin* v. *Turkey (No. 2)*, Application no. 49566/99 (16 June 2005); *Ergin* v. *Turkey (No. 3)*, Application no. 50691/99 (16 June 2005); *Ergin* v. *Turkey (No. 4)*, Application no. 63733/00 (16 June 2005); *Ergin* v. *Turkey (No. 5)*, Application no. 63925/00 (16 June 2005); *Ergin* v. *Turkey (No. 6)*, Application no. 47533/99 (4 May 2006); *Ergin and Keskin* v. *Turkey (No. 1)*, Application no. 50273/99 (16 June 2005); *Ergin and Keskin* v. *Turkey (No. 2)*, Application no. 63926/00 (16 June 2005); *Başkaya* v. *Turkey*, Application no. 68234/01 (3 October 2006); *Halis Dogan and Others* v. *Turkey*, Application no. 50693/99 (10 January 2006); *Halis Dogan* v. *Turkey (No. 2)*, Application no. 71984/01 (25 July 2006); *Refik Karakoç* v. *Turkey*, Application no. 53919/00 (10 January 2006); *Bingöl* v. *Turkey*, Application no. 36141/04 (22 June 2010); *Şener* v. *Turkey*, Application no. 26680/95 (18 July 2000); *Erdal Tas* v. *Turkey*, Application no. 77650/01 (19 December 2006); *Faruk Temel* v. *Turkey*, Application no. 16853/05 (1 February 2011).

[159] E.g. European Court of Human Rights, *Erbakan* v. *Turkey*, Application no. 59405/00 (6 July 2006).

There is a strong counter-argument against the critique of denial laws presented in this chapter: Surely states cannot be expected to passively wait until the accumulative effect of negationist acts effectively shapes a poisoned atmosphere, that is an atmosphere in which the previously benign incitements gradually become successful incitements to discrimination? The alternative for content-based bans is narrowly tailored incitement laws. A concrete instance of extreme speech could at one moment in time not be justifiably punishable by the state, while the exact same words used could at another moment, or within another setting, be punishable – that is precisely what the paramount context factor is all about. Thus under narrow incitement laws with high legal thresholds for criminal liability, the prosecutorial authorities will indeed need to be on top of their game, which means closely monitoring the situation and timing their intervention well. The right to freedom of speech warrants such close, careful and diligent scrutiny.

This position is not given in by a notion that such denial does not hurt – it is importantly driven by public diplomacy. Holocaust denial laws raise the question of double standards. Non-Western states may very well wish to know why Western taboos are more pertinent than theirs. Rather than compare pains, we must identify objective indicators that help to dissect inflammatory speech acts with a view to ascertaining whether it is truly necessary for the state to step in. Thus those indicators will help shape our judgment as to which speech acts do amount to punishable hateful incitement versus those speech acts, however outrageous, that we will have to stomach.

PART V

Aggravating factors and sanctions

12

Organized hatred

12.1 Introduction

In his thematic report entitled *Tackling Manifestations of Collective Religious Hatred* the UN Special Rapporteur on freedom of religion or belief warned against group hatred. He argued that collective hatred is never a natural or spontaneous phenomenon, but very much man-made, through deliberate actions and omissions of hate-mongers. He postulates:

> Manifestations of collective hatred, including religious hatred can set in motion a seemingly unstoppable negative dynamic. However, manifestations of hatred do not 'erupt' like a volcano. Rather, they are caused by human beings ... For instance, populist politicians attract followers by offering simplistic explanations for complex societal problems; advocates of hatred poison intergroup relations by stirring up resentment for short-sighted political or economic gains; lack of trust in public institutions may exacerbate an existing atmosphere of suspicion in society; and parts of the population may be all too willing to replace political common sense with the snappy slogans of hatred.[1]

The Special Rapporteur has defined collective hatred as 'any joint manifestations of intense and irrational emotions of opprobrium, enmity and animosity towards a specific target group or individual that are proclaimed in the name of a particular religion or belief'.[2] Anti-religious sentiments could also be channelled through group hatred, since not only religious but also all belief-related (including secular) truth claims could be marshalled against real or imagined threats emanating from the religious views of others.[3]

---

[1] Special Rapporteur on Freedom of Religion or Belief, *Tackling Manifestations of Collective Religious Hatred* (A/HRC/25/58, 26 December 2013), para. 19.

[2] Special Rapporteur on Freedom of Religion or Belief, *Collective Religious Hatred*, para. 16.

[3] See Special Rapporteur on Freedom of Religion or Belief, *Collective Religious Hatred*, para. 16. See also Special Rapporteur on Freedom of Religion or Belief, *Early Warning Signs of Discrimination and Violence on the Grounds or in the Name of Religion or Belief* (A/HRC/13/40, 21 December 2009).

Policies of hatred can be appealing because 'in the eyes of their follow-ers ... they provide scapegoats on whom to project multiple fears'.[4] These hate policies combine fear with contempt, which in turn may translate into a 'toxic mix' of aggression vis-à-vis the powerful-yet-contemptible other and propaganda as to one's own collective superiority.[5]

The objective of this chapter is to investigate if and to what extent group hatred is treated as an area of particular concern under international standards on extreme speech. Specifically, we will address the question of whether international law contains standards on the basis of which 'organized hatred', that is, more or less formally institutionalized hatred, can or must be combated by states.

12.2   Organized hatred under the ICCPR

On its face, Article 20(2) of the ICCPR significantly differs from Article 4 of the ICERD in one – or rather, yet another – respect. While both provi-sions order State parties to ban certain types of hate propaganda, only the latter provision expressly requires states to also prohibit organizations that disseminate hateful messages.[6] From the drafting debates we can dis-til that this was not oversight on the part of the drafters. Earlier proposals to equip the freedom of association clause of the Universal Declaration on Human Rights with an express limit on 'fascist or anti-democratic organizations' had stranded.[7] Likewise, the wish on the part of some of the Covenant drafting partners to extend the hateful incitement prohib-ition to hate-mongering organizations was defeated in the voting.[8]

---

[4] Special Rapporteur on Freedom of Religion or Belief, *Collective Religious Hatred*, para. 20.
[5] Special Rapporteur on Freedom of Religion or Belief, *Collective Religious Hatred*, paras. 22–24. On the policy of fear, see Martha C. Nussbaum, *The New Religious Intolerance: Overcoming the Politics of Fear in an Anxious Age* (Cambridge, MA, Harvard University Press, 2012).
[6] On ICERD, see further section 12.3 below.
[7] E/800. This USSR draft entailed the twofold proposal insisting that the freedom of expres-sion clause explicate that this right 'should not be used for purposes of propagating fascism, aggression and for provoking hatred as between nations' whilst 'fascist or anti-democratic' organizations were to be excluded from the protection of the freedom of association. See Johannes Morsink, *The Universal Declaration of Human Rights: Origins, Drafting & Intent* (Philadelphia:University of Pennsylvania Press, 1999), 68. Panama at one point also intro-duced a proposal for a limitation on the right to freedom of assembly, affecting 'organiza-tion of parties seeking to establish a dictatorship' (E/HR/3, at 16). See Stephanie Farrior, 'Molding the Matrix: The Historical and Theoretical Foundations of International Law Concerning Hate Speech' (1996) 14:1 *Berkeley Journal of International Law* 1–98, at 13.
[8] E.g. A/AC.3/SR.291, para. 8 [Ukraine]; E/SR.438, para. 59 [USSR]; A/C.3/SR.569, para. 20 [Czechoslovakia].

Accordingly, an express ban on fascist-like or other extremist organizations did not make its way into the Covenant. The question remains, however, if the Covenant nevertheless sanctions such bans. One abstract argument in favour of that view is premised on the fact that the Covenant's incitement clause is contained in a separate article. That is, while the incitement provision was inserted immediately after the freedom of expression clause – thus suggesting a close nexus – it is significant that it was not actually merged with that provision. Accordingly, its autonomous existence may imply that its ramifications not only impact the right to freedom of expression but also freedoms contained in other provisions, notably the rights to freedom of association and freedom of assembly contained in Articles 21 and 22 of the Covenant.[9]

If the latter holds true, the Covenant would not merely permit restrictions in the area of association, it would actually require it,[10] just as the incitement clause forces State parties to adopt extreme speech legislation. While the Committee expresses its concerns about hateful organizations, it does not tend to explicitly call for their dissolution. For instance, reviewing Swedish compliance with the Covenant, the Committee urged this State party to 'take steps to review its policy towards the establishment and operation of racist, xenophobic and, especially, neo-Nazi organizations'.[11] What 'taking steps' precisely entails is left open, but it is clear that the Committee is concerned that Sweden is too lenient vis-à-vis racist and Neo-Nazi organizations.[12] In its Concluding Observations regarding the Belgian state report, it elaborated on possible steps by suggesting that the public funding to in this case hatred-propagating political parties be ceased.[13] The Committee,

---

[9] See Manfred Nowak, *U.N. Covenant on Civil and Political Rights: CCPR Commentary* (2nd rev. edn, Kehl: N. P. Engel, 2005), 468.

[10] See Nowak, *CCPR Commentary*, 505 and 507–8. See, however, Dominic McGoldrick, *The Human Rights Committee: Its Role in the Development of the International Covenant on Civil and Political Rights* (Oxford: Clarendon Press, 1991), 483, arguing that Art. 20 'proscribes certain propaganda rather than the organizations engaging in such propaganda'.

[11] A/57/40 vol. I (2002) 57, para. 79(14).

[12] A/57/40 vol. I (2002) 57, para. 79(14) [Sweden].

[13] A/59/40 vol. I (2004) 56, para. 72(27) [Belgium]: 'It is concerned that political parties urging racial hatred can still benefit from the public financing system, and observes that a bill designed to put an end to that situation is still being considered by the Senate (art. 20). The State party should take all necessary steps to protect communities resident in Belgium against racist, xenophobic, anti-Semitic and anti-Muslim acts. It should have the above-mentioned bill passed as soon as possible, and consider sterner measures to prevent individuals and groups from seeking to arouse racial hatred and xenophobia, in pursuance of article 20, paragraph 2, of the Covenant.'

furthermore, praised Russia's efforts in banning and prosecuting racist groups.[14]

Accordingly, under its state reporting procedure the Committee has on occasion called for or endorsed measures against hateful groups, but its findings fall short of an outright call for their dissolution. While it cannot be denied upfront that bans could in certain circumstances be permissible under the Covenant, it appears that prohibitions specifically targeting hateful organizations are not deemed mandatory by the Committee. By contrast, it has emphatically and consistently deemed incitement law applicable to hateful individuals to be mandatory.[15]

The Committee's views on individual communications do not provide definitive answers as to whether and under which circumstances bans on extremist organizations are permitted under the Covenant. In 1984 the Human Rights Committee was presented with the opportunity to pronounce on the question as to whether State parties may, under the Covenant, prohibit fascist organizations. In *M.A. v. Italy* the Human Rights Committee applied Article 5(1) on abuse of rights for the first and only time, which is hardly indicative of a crystallized judicial doctrine.[16] M.A., 'a 27-year-old Italian citizen and right-wing political militant and publicist',[17] was convicted and served a prison sentence for committing the crime of 'reorganizing the dissolved fascist party', something prohibited in Italy as per penal legislation dating back from 1952. M.A. complained that he had accordingly been deprived of his right to express his political beliefs. The Italian Government did not invoke Article 5(1) or Article 20(2). It rather suggested that the regular restrictions on freedom of expression (Article 19, paragraph 3) and freedom of association (Article 22, paragraph 2) applied, pleading that any interference was necessary to protect public order.[18] A ban on reorganizing the fascist party ensured that movements that had as their object 'the elimination of

---

[14] A/59/40 vol. I (2003) 20, para. 64(20), while also vehemently criticizing other aspects of Russia's law against 'extremist activity'.

[15] E.g. Human Rights Committee, *General Comment 11: Article 20* (Nineteenth session, 1983); and Human Rights Committee, *General Comment 34: Article 19: Freedoms of Opinion and Expression* (CCPR/C/GC/34, adopted at its 102nd Session, Geneva, 11–29 July 2011), para. 51. See also the following concluding observations on state reports A/60/40 vol. I (2005) 74, para. 93(13) [Slovenia]; and A/50/40 vol. I (1995) 38, para. 181 [New Zealand]. See Chapter 4 for more details, particularly at section 4.5.

[16] Human Rights Committee, *M.A. v. Italy*, Communication no. 117/1981 (21 September 1981).

[17] *M.A. v. Italy*, para. 1.1.

[18] *M.A. v. Italy*, para. 7.2. In addition to several dissimilar objections to admissibility.

the democratic freedoms and the establishment of a totalitarian regime' could not grasp power. M.A. found this law to be discriminatory, since 'not all allegedly "anti-democratic" movements (anarchistic, Leninist, etc.)' were subject to it but exclusively 'movements with fascist leanings'.[19] Therefore, according to M.A., the ban could be said to 'persecute' or discriminate 'on the basis of ideology'.[20]

The Committee concluded that 'the acts of which M.A. was convicted (reorganizing the dissolved fascist party) were of a kind which are removed from the protection of the Covenant by article 5 thereof', thus rendering the complaint inadmissible.[21] While this application of the abuse of rights clause stood in the way of a more robust assessment on the merits of the complaint, the Committee did say by way of *obiter dictum* that the restrictions imposed 'were in any event justifiably prohibited by Italian law having regard to the limitations and restrictions applicable to the rights in question under the provisions of articles 18 (3), 19 (3), 22 (2) and 25 of the Covenant'.[22] Thus *M.A. v. Italy* indicates that the limitation clauses under, among others, freedom of expression and freedom of association – interestingly the Committee makes no mention of Article 20(2) in this regard – have the capacity of justifying bans on extremist organizations.

Again, it cannot be said with any degree of certainty that the Committee would rule similarly if presented with a similar complaint. On the one hand, it cannot be denied that the application of Article 5(1) as in *M.A. v. Italy* is how the drafters envisaged it. The *travaux* state that this provision is 'aimed at checking the growth of nascent nazi, fascist or other totalitarian ideologies; groups with such tendencies [may] not invoke the covenants to justify their activities'.[23] The drafting discussions on the proper position of Article 5(1) within the Covenant are significant, too. Proposals to incorporate the abuse of rights clause with Article 19 on freedom of expression were rejected 'because it was felt that paragraph 1 [of Article 5] also affected other articles of the covenants such as the articles relating to assembly and association'.[24] Article 5(1) is, unlike Article 20(2), not part of the Covenant's section on substantive rights.[25] Thus the provision has a purely 'accessory character',[26] meaning that unlike under

---

[19] *M.A. v. Italy*, para. 9(b).   [20] *M.A. v. Italy*, para. 9(b).
[21] *M.A. v. Italy*, para. 13.3.   [22] *M.A. v. Italy*, para. 13.3.
[23] A/2929, para. 55.   [24] A/2929, para. 56.
[25] Nowak, *CCPR Commentary*, at 111. According to Nowak, the abuse clause should have been included in Part V of the Covenant, which contains other such general caveats.
[26] See Nowak, *CCPR Commentary*, 115.

Article 20(2) no legislation is required under Article 5. Accordingly, its main relevance lies in the area of (blocking) international legal standing.[27]

On the other hand, the criticism as formulated earlier with respect to the Committee's decision in *J.R.T. and the W.G. Party* v. *Canada*,[28] and with respect to the European Court of Human Rights' dependence on Article 17 of the European Convention on Human Rights,[29] should be reiterated. This type of hyper-marginal review deprives certain persons – extremists – from the protection other persons do receive. The required standard of proof for purposes of deciding the admissibility of cases brought by persons potentially having 'abused' their rights is utterly unclear, while the consequences for the applicant are severe, considering that their cases will not be assessed on the merits. In addition, the application of the abuse of rights doctrine makes the law on which the restrictions in question are based more or less immune from human rights scrutiny. Although M.A.'s objections to the 'discriminatory' nature of anti-fascist laws were obviously rather unseemly, the risk that anti-extremist laws are abused is very real.[30] Consequently, substantive assessment of those laws, whenever enforced, is vital.[31]

12.3   Organized hatred under the ICERD

Unlike the ICCPR, the ICERD looks expressly to the scenario of collective hate propaganda campaigns. Flowing neatly from the general standard that in addition to discrimination by individuals, discrimination by organizations must also be tackled by State parties,[32] under this Convention incitement to racial discrimination is to be combated whether perpetrated by individuals or by organizations. Article 4 of the ICERD generally provides that State parties 'condemn' all organizations

---

[27] The Optional Protocol to the ICCPR on individual communications supports that view. Art. 3 of this Protocol provides that the Committee shall consider inadmissible any communication 'which it considers to be an abuse of the right of submission of such communications or to be incompatible with the provisions of the Covenant'.

[28] See section 5.4.3 of Chapter 5.

[29] The same criticism applies to cases thrown out by the European Court of Human Rights on the basis of Art. 17 of the European Convention on Human Rights. See Chapter 6.

[30] As observed by the Committee itself, for instance in relation to Russia. See A/59/40 vol. I (2003) 20, para. 64(20).

[31] See also Nowak, *CCPR Commentary*, at 455; McGoldrick, *The Human Rights Committee*, 167; and Sarah Joseph, Jenny Schultz and Melissa Castan, *The International Covenant on Civil and Political Rights* (Oxford University Press, 2000), 400.

[32] ICERD, Art. 2(b) and (d).

that are based on ideas of racial superiority or that promote racial hatred and discrimination.[33] More specifically it is stipulated that State parties 'declare illegal and prohibit organizations, and also organized and all other propaganda activities, which promote and incite racial discrimination, and shall recognize participation in such organizations or activities as an offence punishable by law'.[34]

Notwithstanding the fact that this provision is clearly significantly more robust than the ICCPR on the point of combating organized hatred, Article 4 ICERD is also the result of a compromise between states that wanted a categorical ban on hate-mongering collective entities and those that wanted to hold on to strong freedom of expression and association clauses.[35] The drafting debates reveal similar concerns and political divisions to the ones encountered in ICCPR *travaux*.[36] It was a Nigerian proposal that resolved the impasse. The proposed formula has come to be known as the 'due regard clause'. State parties were to condemn all racist propaganda and adopt measures designed to eradicate racist propaganda 'with due regard to the principles embodied in the Universal Declaration of Human Rights and the rights expressly set forth in article 5 of this Convention'.[37] The French would have preferred a due regard clause exclusively mentioning Articles 19 and 20 of the ICCPR.[38] Yet there the problem would have been that parties to the ICERD have not necessarily all ratified the ICCPR. The Americans proposed an alternative due regard clause generally referring to the freedoms of expression and association.[39] Ultimately, the Nigerian proposal referencing the entire UDHR – including freedom of expression and all other Declaration freedoms – was adopted. Significantly, Article 4 ICERD was adopted much more universally than Article 20(2) ICCPR. Many Western states – including the USA – voted in favour.[40] That said, Article 4 ICERD has triggered many

---

[33] ICERD, Art. 4 (chapeau).
[34] ICERD, Art. 4(b).   [35] See Farrior, 'Molding the Matrix', 48–50.
[36] The United Kingdom, for instance, manifested itself as one of the more staunch defenders of free speech during these debates. Farrior, 'Molding the Matrix', 49.
[37] ICERD, Art. 4 (chapeau).
[38] See Farrior, 'Molding the Matrix', 49.
[39] See Farrior, 'Molding the Matrix', 49.
[40] Explaining his vote, the US representative insisted on making an interpretative declaration, stating that the due regard clause is taken to mean 'not imposing on a State party the obligation to take any action impairing the right to freedom of speech and freedom of association' (A/C.3/SR.1318). The final vote on this Article was: 76 to 1, with 14 abstentions (A/6181). See Farrior, 'Molding the Matrix', at 50.

reservations, more than Article 20(2) ICCPR, also by States that supported the draft article.[41]

In 1993 CERD underscored the importance of combating organized hatred through a General Recommendation. Explaining the original rationale of the ICERD in this regard, the Committee wrote:

> When the International Convention on the Elimination of All Forms of Racial Discrimination was being adopted, article 4 was regarded as central to the struggle against racial discrimination. At that time, there was a widespread fear of the revival of authoritarian ideologies. The proscription of the dissemination of ideas of racial superiority, and of organized activity likely to incite persons to racial violence, was properly regarded as crucial. Since that time, the Committee has received evidence of organized violence based on ethnic origin and the political exploitation of ethnic difference. As a result, implementation of article 4 is now of increased importance.[42]

More specifically, the Committee faulted those State parties that, in the opinion of the Committee, waited too long before declaring hate-mongering organizations illegal. As the Committee pointed out:

> Some States have maintained that in their legal order it is inappropriate to declare illegal an organization before its members have promoted or incited racial discrimination. The Committee is of the opinion that article 4(b) places a greater burden upon such States to be vigilant in proceeding against such organizations at the earliest moment. These

---

[41] Reservations or restrictive declarations in relation to Art. 4 have been made by: Antigua and Barbuda; Australia; Austria; Bahamas; Barbados; Belgium; Fiji; France; Grenada; Ireland; Italy; Japan; Malta; Monaco; Nepal; Papua New Guinea; Switzerland; Thailand; Tonga; United Kingdom; and the United States of America. Most reservations aim at underscoring that the state in question reserves the right not to introduce additional laws in this area or the right not to consider all acts mentioned by Art. 4 as criminal offences. A number of states underscore that the due regard clause shall more particularly be taken to mean that the standards contained in Art. 4 may not impede freedom of expression or association rights under national or international law.

[42] Committee on the Elimination of Racial Discrimination, *General Recommendation 15: Measures to Eradicate Incitement to or Acts of Discrimination* (UN Doc. A/48/18 at 114, Forty-second session, 1993), para. 1. See also *General Recommendation 31: Prevention of Racial Discrimination in the Administration and Functioning of the Criminal Justice System* (Sixty-fifth session, 2005), para. 4(a). On organized forms of discrimination in general, see *General Recommendation 27: Discrimination against Roma* (Fifty-seventh session, 2000), para. 2; *General Recommendation 32: The Meaning and Scope of Special Measures in the International Convention on the Elimination of All Forms Racial Discrimination* (CERD/C/GC/32, Seventy-fifth session, 3–28 August 2009), para. 9; *General Recommendation 34: Racial Discrimination against People of African Descent* (Seventy-ninth session, 2011), para. 11.

organizations, as well as organized and other propaganda activities, have to be declared illegal and prohibited. Participation in these organizations is, of itself, to be punished.[43]

In its recently adopted General Recommendation on racist hate speech the Committee reiterates the ICERD's role in combating organized hatred. Not only is participation in organizations and activities that promote and incite racial discrimination to be declared a criminal offence,[44] the Committee underscored that that Article 4(b) actually 'requires that racist organizations which promote and incite racial discrimination be declared illegal and prohibited'.[45] Moreover, it is the Committee's understanding, according to the General Recommendation, 'that the reference to "organized ... propaganda activities" [in Article 4b] implicates improvised forms of organization or networks'.[46]

In its Concluding Observations, the Committee has indeed repeatedly pointed out that State parties are violating the terms of the treaty by not prohibiting certain racist organizations, including racist political parties. The Committee reproached the UK for breaching Article 4 by 'not prohibiting the British National Party and other groups and organizations of a racist nature'.[47] Similarly, while welcoming Belgium's imposition of 'financial sanctions' on anti-democratic, racist or xenophobic political parties,[48] the Committee insists that the State party enacts legislation that 'declares illegal and prohibits any organization which promotes or incites to racism and racial discrimination'.[49] The Committee, deeming Article 4(b) a non-negotiable matter of legal principle, does not accept as an excuse that banning organizations would be counter-productive or otherwise

---

[43] *General Recommendation 15*, para. 6.
[44] *General Recommendation 35: Combating Racist Hate Speech* (UN Doc. CERD/C/GC/35, 83rd session, 12–30 August 2013), para. 13(e).
[45] *General Recommendation 35*, para. 21.
[46] *General Recommendation 35*, para. 21, further defining that 'all other propaganda activities' as used in Art. 4(b), 'may be taken to refer to unorganized or spontaneous promotion and incitement of racial discrimination'. Further mention of the 'the organizational context for the production of speech' is made in para. 10 of the Recommendation.
[47] A/48/18 (1993) 73, para. 416 (and 421). The gist of this statement was reiterated in later concluding observations: A/55/18 (2000) 60, para. 356.
[48] A/57/18 (2002) 17, para. 42. Note that other UN treaty-monitoring bodies have expressed similar concerns with respect to this state. Committee on Economic, Social and Cultural Rights, E/2001/22 (2000) 77, para. 482: 'The State party should adopt measures to ensure that xenophobia, racism and activities of racist organizations, groups or political parties are outlawed, with a view to complying with the principle of non-discrimination, set forth in article 2.2 of the Covenant.'
[49] A/57/18 (2002) 17, para. 51.

ineffective.[50] With respect to certain states the Committee has emphasized that it is not enough to enshrine prohibitions and bans in criminal law – those laws must also be rigorously enforced.[51] The Committee has also complained that some State parties are overly preoccupied with combating specific criminal activities employed by hateful organizations, while what they could and under the Covenant should do, in its view, is ban the organizations concerned altogether.[52] The same goes for individual participation within xenophobic and hate-mongering organizations. Under Article 4(b), State parties are not to merely combat active participation but also make sure to penalize any such involvement.[53]

Many other State parties have, in a similar vein, been urged to tighten up their fight against xenophobic organizations and parties as well as membership thereof.[54] Conversely, the Committee does not shy away from

[50] See A/58/18 (2003) 79, para. 475: 'The Committee takes note of [Norway's] observation that a formal ban on organizations might not be very effective in combating racism, owing to the fact that the groups involved in most of the racist activities are loose networks and not formal organizations. In this respect, the Committee draws that State party's attention to its general recommendation XV according to which all provisions of article 4 of the Convention are of a mandatory character, including declaring illegal and prohibiting all organizations promoting and inciting racial discrimination.'

[51] E.g. with respect to Latvia it 'noted with concern that, although the State party has adopted new legislation with respect to article 4 of the Convention … no organization involved in such activities [e.g. advocacy of violence] has been prohibited, even though the existence of such cases has been widely reported' A/54/18 (1999) 39, para. 394. The gist of this statement was reiterated in later concluding observations: A/58/18 (2003) 75, para. 446.

[52] A/57/18 (2002) 56, para. 335 [Canada].

[53] A/58/18 (2003) 65, para. 382 [Czech Republic]. Similar observations were made with respect to Sweden: A/59/18 (2004) 41, para. 220; and Luxembourg: A/60/18 (2005) 40, para. 197.

[54] E.g. A/48/18 (1993) 81, para. 449 (Germany); A/48/18 (1993) 90, para. 505 (Croatia); A/53/18 (1998) 59, para. 320 (Croatia); A/49/18 (1994) 30, para. 199 (Sweden) as reiterated in A/52/18 (1997) 65, para. 505 and A/55/18 (2000) 57, para. 340; A/49/18 (1994) 68, para. 474 (Sudan); A/51/18 (1996) 25, para. 150 (Russia); A/51/18, (1996) 32, para. 209 (Spain); A/51/18, (1996) 32, para. 209 (Spain); A/51/18 (1996) 29, para. 175 (Finland) as reiterated in A/55/18 (2000) 41, para. 212 (see also the Committee against Torture: A/55/44 (2000) 12, para. 55); A/52/18 (1997) 59, para. 450 (Denmark), as reiterated in: A/55/18 (2000) 22, para. 64 and A/57/18 (2002) 27, para. 116; A/52/18 (1997) 69, para. 552 (Argentina); A/54/18 (1999) 14, para. 54 (Republic of Korea); A/54/18 (1999) 35, para. 350 (Iraq); A/54/18 (1999) 37, para. 374 (Chile); A/55/18 (2000) 50, para. 281 (Czech Republic); A/52/18 (1997) 77, para. 607 (Norway), as reiterated in: A/55/18 (2000) 67, para. 415; A/53/18 (1998) 33, para. 102 (Netherlands); A/56/18 (2001) 58, para. 349 (Trinidad and Tobago); A/57/18 (2002) 50, para. 276 (Armenia); A/57/18 (2002) 63, para. 376 (Hungary); A/57/18 (2002) 30, para. 132 (Jamaica); A/58/18 (2003) 25, para. 91 (Fiji); A/58/18 (2003) 35, para. 158 (Poland); A/58/18 (2003) 50, para. 274 (Uganda); A/58/18 (2003) 53, para. 311 (Albania); A/58/18 (2003) 58, para. 338 (Bolivia); A/59/18

congratulating State parties that adopt tougher laws or measures in this area.[55]

12.4 Organized hatred under the European Convention on Human Rights

It may be reiterated that the European Convention on Human Rights, unlike several UN human rights treaties, does not impose a duty to prohibit extreme speech. This holds true whether such speech is disseminated by an individual or by an organization. That said, the European Court of Human Rights has employed its two familiar approaches in this area – occasionally it relies on Article 17 on abuse of rights,[56] while in other cases concerning states' banning of hateful organizations it engages in more comprehensive analysis of the merits of the Article 11 (freedom of association) complaint.

Accordingly, in the eyes of the European Court of Human Rights Poland did not need to tolerate the National and Patriotic Association of Polish Victims of Bolshevism and Zionism.[57] This organization had listed in its statute, among other aims, such objectives as 'striving to abolish the privileges of ethnic Jews' and 'taking action aimed at improving the living conditions of Polish victims of Zionism/Zionists'.[58] The Court concluded that the association's memorandum of association contained ideas that 'can be seen as reviving anti-Semitism'.[59] That aim constituted an abuse of rights within the meaning of Article 17, making the complaint against its prohibition by Poland inadmissible.

Similarly, the European Court of Human Rights sanctioned Germany's prohibition order regarding the Hizb Ut-Tahrir association.[60] This group, whose name literally means Liberation Party, considers itself a global

---

(2004) 14, para. 64 (Brazil); A/60/18 (2005) 46, para. 239 (Georgia); A/60/18 (2005) 54, para. 292 (Nigeria); and A/60/18 (2005) 75, para. 404 (Zambia).

[55] E.g. A/59/18 (2004) 66, para. 364 (Portugal): 'The Committee … notes with satisfaction the prohibition, as a result of the fourth revision of the Constitution, of racist organizations (organizations adopting a fascist ideology having already been banned).'

[56] The first time the European Commission of Human Rights applied Art. 17 was in a case brought by a dissolved (political) association. See *Kummunistische Partei Deutschlands* v. *Germany*, Application no. 250/57 (admissibility decision of 20 July 1957).

[57] European Court of Human Rights, *W.P. and others* v. *Poland*, Application no. 42264/98 (admissibility decision of 2 September 2004).

[58] *W.P. and others* v. *Poland*, 'The Facts' (para. 3).

[59] *W.P. and others* v. *Poland*, 'The Law' (para. 2).

[60] European Court of Human Rights, *Hizb Ut-Tahrir and others* v. *Germany*, Application no. 31098/08 (admissibility decision of 12 June 2012).

Islamic political party and was established in 1953. It advocates the 'overthrow of governments throughout the Muslim world and their replacement by an Islamic State in the form of a recreated Caliphate'.[61] For that purpose members had made statements – through a magazine closely connected to the group, through statements in the media and in the form of pamphlets – inciting violence, more particularly calling for the destruction of the State of Israel and to kill Jewish people.[62] The Strasbourg Court agreed with Germany that in the light of Article 17 this group 'may not benefit from the protection afforded by Article 11 of the Convention'.[63]

In another case the European Court of Human Rights in fact went as far as permitting the criminalization of individual membership of the same international pan-Islamic organization – Hizb Ut-Tahrir – again importantly basing its reasoning on the abuse of rights doctrine.[64] Having consulted ample expert opinions on the Hizb ut-Tahrir group as well as literature produced by the group itself, the Court arrived at the conclusion that this group's aims were contrary to the Convention.[65] From both the expert reports as well as the Court's own assessment of Hizb ut-Tahrir's literature, it transpired that this organization engaged in comprehensive campaigns of incitement to religious violence, incitement to discrimination (especially through the promotion of gender inequality), glorification of warfare in the form of jihad, incitement to violently overthrow governments, while occasionally it incited to murder (of citizens of enemy states, such as Israel, the USA, and the UK).[66]

In other cases the Court assesses such prohibition or dissolution cases through the lens of Article 11 and its regular grounds for restriction.[67]

---

[61] *Hizb Ut-Tahrir and others* v. *Germany*, para. 2.

[62] *Hizb Ut-Tahrir and others* v. *Germany*, paras. 15–22

[63] *Hizb Ut-Tahrir and others* v. *Germany*, para. 74. Germany had invoked Art. 17 (para. 63).

[64] European Court of Human Rights, *Kasymakhunov and Saybatalov* v. *Russia*, Application Nos. 26261/05 and 26377/06 (14 March 2013).

[65] *Kasymakhunov and Saybatalov* v. *Russia*, paras. 44–53 outlining expert reports on Hizb ut-Tahrir and Hizb ut-Tahrir's literature.

[66] *Kasymakhunov and Saybatalov* v. *Russia*, paras. 107–113.

[67] See also, *mutatis mutandis*, the famous case of European Court of Human Rights, *Refah Partisi (the Welfare Party) and Others* v. *Turkey*, Application nos. 41340/98, 41342/98, 41343/98 and 41344/98 (Grand Chamber judgment of 13 February 2003). This Turkish Islamic political party (literally, the 'Welfare Party') was dissolved at the very height of its success: it had just become the largest party in the country. The Principal State Counsel at the Court of Cassation had applied to the Turkish Constitutional Court to have Refah dissolved chiefly on account of the fact that leaders of this party had called for the abolition of secularism and the introduction of Sharia law, the establishment of a theocratic system based on the supremacy of the Koran through a holy war, if necessary by force (*Refah Partisi*, para. 12). While referencing Art. 17 once (para. 96), the European Court

The case of *Vona v. Hungary* is interesting since the Court engaged in a fairly extensive context-based risk assessment.[68] That is, while in *W.P. and others v. Poland* and *Hizb Ut-Tahrir and others v. Germany* the flagrant anti-Semitic and the express inciteful aims of the associations' mission statements were apparently decisive, in the case of *Vona* the Court went out of its way to establish the existence of a poisoned atmosphere in which anti-Roma and anti-Jewish violence was likely. The applicant in this case was a member of Magyar Gárda, the Hungarian Guard Association. This organization was dissolved by the Hungarian judiciary on account of hateful speech acts against Roma and Jews made by its members and due to its unacceptable nature (a paramilitary force).[69] Finding no violation of Article 11, the European Court of Human Rights observed that there were a number of factors that made the situation particularly acute from the perspective of the Hungarian authorities. Notably, Magyar Gárda members had targeted the populations of villages in ways – marching with as many as 200 members in a town with a population of 1,800 – that had turned the latter into a 'captive audience'.[70] Thus their paramilitary intimidation in the style of the Arrow Cross Party – the party that had facilitated the Nazi mass murder of Hungarian Roma and Jews – brought about a 'true threat'.[71] The Strasbourg Court would have done well to

of Human Rights considered the merits of the complaints. The Court agreed with the assessment made by the Turkish Constitutional Court that the Party posed a real risk to democracy and fundamental rights, specifically underscoring the potential introduction of a plurality of legal systems, the introduction of Sharia and the possibility of recourse to force as advocated by high-profile Refah members. This judgment has been strongly criticized in the literature. See, e.g., Kevin Boyle, 'Human Rights, Religion and Democracy: The Refah Party Case' (2004) 1 *Essex Human Rights Review* 1–16. Turkish dissolutions of political parties have led to a number of Art. 11 violations, e.g. *United Communist Party of Turkey and others v. Turkey*, Application no. 133/1996/752/951 (Grand Chamber judgment of 30 January 1998); *Socialist Party and Others v. Turkey*, Application no. 20/1997/804/1007 (Grand Chamber judgment of 25 May 1998); *Freedom and Democracy Party (ÖZDEP) v. Turkey*, Application no. 23885/94 (Grand Chamber judgment of 8 December 1999).

[68] European Court of Human Rights, *Vona v. Hungary*, Application no. 35943/10 (9 July 2013).

[69] *Vona v. Hungary*, paras. 15–16.   [70] *Vona v. Hungary*, para. 61.

[71] *Vona v. Hungary*, paras. 65–66, quoting from US Supreme Court jurisprudence. See *Virginia v. Black*, 538 U.S. 343 (2003). Note that in certain other cases concerning the dissolution of associations on account of alleged incitement, the Court has conceptualized context by means of a 'present and imminent threat' test. See *Association of Citizens Radko and Paunkovski v. the former Yugoslav Republic of Macedonia*, Application no. 74651/01 (15 January 2009), para. 75. Often no such threat can be discerned by the Court. See also, e.g., *Stankov and the United Macedonian Organisation Ilinden v. Bulgaria*, Application nos. 29225/95 and 29221/95 (2 October 2001).

dwell on other contextual elements. This section of the judgment would have lent itself particularly well to elaboration on the position of the target group – here the position of Roma and Jews in Hungary, two groups that are particularly liable to suffer hate crimes.[72] Judge Pinto de Albuquerque remedied this striking omission by raising this point as an 'issue of crucial importance' in his concurring opinion. He extensively documented anti-Semitic and anti-Roma sentiments in Hungarian public life and public expression, as well as societal discrimination.[73]

12.5   State practice

In this section we will discuss some of the contemporary domestic laws aimed at banning hateful organizations. Again it may be observed that the victors of the Second World War had a hand in some early forms of state bans on extremist groups. The Paris Peace Treaties imposed on a number of states – among others, Italy and Hungary[74] – the obligation to outlaw fascist organizations and counter through various legal means the potential revival of Nazism.[75] Post-war denazification, as formalized by the Potsdam Agreement,[76] implied similar obligations for Germany and Austria with respect to the Nazi party and movement.[77] The German Constitution has upheld the denazification measures up until the current time.[78] It also allows for the banning of both political parties as well as general associations if their aims are contrary to constitutional or democratic order.[79] While the former possibility has only rarely occurred since

[72] See e.g. Human Rights Committee, *Concluding Observations Concerning Hungary* (CCPR/C/HUN/CO/5, 16 November 2010), para. 18; ECRI, *Report on Hungary* (2008), para. IV; CERD, A/51/18, para. 116.
[73] Concurring Opinion of Judge Pinto de Albuquerque.
[74] In Italy a law is still in place prohibiting the revitalization of the fascist party. Law No. 645/1952, as applied in e.g. Constitutional Court of Italy, Sentence No. 74/1958. See also the background to the Human Rights Committee's case of *M.A.* v. *Italy*.
[75] Egon Schwelb, 'The International Convention on the Elimination of All Forms of Racial Discrimination' (1966) 15 *International and Comparative Law Quarterly* 996–1068, at 1022; and Farrior, 'Molding the Matrix', at 27.
[76] A result of the Potsdam Conference (17 July–2 August 1945).
[77] The Allied Control Council abolished the Nazi party as per Allied Control Council Laws Nos. 2 and 16. See Andreas Stegbauer, 'The Ban of Right-Wing Extremist Symbols According to Section 86a of the German Criminal Code' (2007) 8:2 *German Law Journal* 173–84, at 177.
[78] Art. 139 of the Basic Law of the Federal Republic of Germany 1949. See, generally, G. Lübbe-Wolff, 'Zur Bedeutung des Art. 139 GG für die Auseinandersetzung mit Neonazistischen Gruppen' (1988) *Neue Juristische Wochenschrift* 1289–94.
[79] Articles 21(2) and 9(2) of the Basic Law of the Federal Republic of Germany 1949 respectively.

the denazification process (the Sozialistische Reichspartei was banned by the Federal Constitutional Court in 1952),[80] non-public far right organizations have frequently been banned.[81] The Criminal Code of Germany, more specifically, proscribes the use of Nazi symbols and the use or dissemination of Nazi propaganda (e.g. historical Nazi writings). The former offence targets Nazi flags, swastikas, insignia, uniforms, slogans and forms of greeting (Nazi salute), while the latter crime bans the use of propaganda intended to further the aims of organizations that have been banned, including the National Socialist organization.[82] In Austria the Nazi party was banned pursuant to Verbotsgesetz 1947. It is still in force, having since been updated and employed to suppress any revival of (organized) National Socialism.[83]

The following are among the states that have laws in place generally proscribing organized hatred. The Constitution of Albania prohibits political parties and other organizations 'which incite and support racial, religious, regional or ethnic hatred'.[84] Italian incitement law similarly prohibits organizations whose aims consist of inciting discrimination or violence.[85] In 2003 Moldova adopted a law that serves to outlaw 'extremist organizations', including those that incite religious hatred.[86] The Constitution of Poland bans Nazi or fascist groups, but also, more generally, those organizations whose programme or activities consist of inciting hatred.[87] In Romania, organizations can be banned under an Emergency Ordinance, when necessary 'for the prevention and control of incitement to national, racial or religious hatred'.[88] Russia bans groups that incite religious or other hatred through a myriad of overlapping and complementary laws, including relevant provisions of its constitution, its criminal code, as well as through its Public Associations Law and the Law

---

[80] Federal Constitutional Court, *Sozialistische Reichspartei*, BVerfGE 2, 1 (judgment of 23 October 1952).

[81] For further details, see Stegbauer, 'The Ban of Right-Wing Extremist Symbols', at 178–84.

[82] Articles 86a and 86 of the Criminal Code of Germany 1998 respectively.

[83] National Socialism Prohibition Act 1947 [Austria], as amended in 1992.

[84] Art. 9(2) of the Constitution of Albania 1998.

[85] Legislative Decree No. 122 of 26 April 1993, converted into Act No. 205 of 25 June 1993 on Urgent Measures in Respect of Racial, Ethnic and Religious Discrimination (amending Section 3 of Act No. 654 of October 1975) [Italy].

[86] Art. 6 of the Extremist Activity Law, No. 54-XV of 21 February 2003 [Moldova]. See also Art. 4 of the Law on Public Associations 1996 [Moldova]. See ECRI, *Third Report on Moldova* (CRI(2008)23), 14 December 2007, for a brief assessment of the former law.

[87] Art. 13 of the Constitution of Poland 1997.

[88] Emergency Ordinance No. 31 of 13 March 2002 Regarding the Ban of Organisations and Symbols with a Fascist, Racist or Xenophobic Character [Romania].

on Political Parties.[89] Armenia has laws in place to dissolve both political parties as well as NGOs that engage in acts of incitement.[90]

The width of some of these laws clearly gives cause for concern. Human rights monitoring bodies have observed that some of these anti-extremism policies may well overstep the mark, thus abusing rather than protecting civil and political rights.[91] Hence, if State parties to the Covenant insist that collective forms of hatred be penalized, it would appear to be preferable that they deem this organizational element an aggravating factor. That is, short of outlawing allegedly extremist groups, the organizational context can enter the equation by allowing this factor to impact the appropriate sanction to be meted out in concrete instances of incitement. For instance, in the Netherlands the maximum penalty for incitement is lifted from one to two years when the offence is perpetrated in an organized fashion.[92] Thus, based also on other particulars of the case, judges may – though are not forced to – consider if it is proportionate to allow for a higher penalty. A number of other states similarly deem organized forms of incitement to be an aggravating factor.[93]

12.6   Concluding remarks

The International Convention on the Elimination of All Forms of Racial Discrimination contains the most outspoken condemnations

---

[89]   Art. 13 of the Constitution of the Russian federation (12 December 1993); Art. 239 of the Criminal Code of the Russian Federation 1996 (amended 2006); Art. 23 of the Public Associations Law 1995; and Art. 9 of the Law on Political Parties 2001. See also Federal Law No. 114-FZ of 25 July 2002 on Combating Extremist Activity (as amended on 27 July 2006, 10 May and 24 July 2007, and 29 April 2008).

[90]   Art. 3 of the Law of the Republic of Armenia on Non-Governmental Organizations (4 December 2001); and Art. 3 of the Law of the Republic of Armenia on Political Parties 1992 (amended 2003).

[91]   See, e.g., Human Rights Committee, CCPR/C/RUS/CO/6 (2009), para. 24; and A/59/40 vol. I (2003) 20, para. 64(20), concerning Russia's anti-extremism laws.

[92]   Art. 137D(2) of the Criminal Code of the Netherlands 1881.

[93]   E.g. Art. 213ter of the Criminal Code of Argentina 1984 and Art. 3 of Law No. 23.592 (1988) adopting measures against those who arbitrarily impede the full exercise of fundamental rights and guarantees recognized in the National Constitution [Argentina]; Art. 283 of the Criminal Code of Azerbaijan 2000, lifting the maximum prison sentence from three to five years; Section 356(3)(b) of the New Criminal Code of the Czech Republic (40/2009), lifting the maximum prison sentence from two to three years (establishing a hatred-inciting movement is punishable separately with five years' imprisonment under Section 403); Art. 151(3) Criminal Code of Estonia 2000; and Section 299 of the Criminal Code of Kyrgyzstan 1997, lifting the maximum prison sentence from three to five years. Some states have codified organized incitement as a separate offence, typically with

of organized dissemination of hatred. Article 20(2)'s role in combating hate-mongering organizations remains ambiguous. While a textual interpretation may point at an actual obligation to ban such groups, the Human Rights Committee's concluding observations on state compliance sensibly draw the contours of a fight against extremism that is not based on outright prohibitions and bans of collective forms of hatred. That said, in their case law both the Human Rights Committee and the European Court of Human Rights depend strongly on the abuse of rights doctrine, thus granting near-infinite discretion to states. While this is a tempting stratagem, monitoring bodies would do well to decide cases brought by alleged extremists on the merits of the freedom of association and/or freedom of speech complaint. Laws adopted under the cloak of the fight against extremism are liable to abuse and should hence not be shielded from close scrutiny. Like all other incitement cases, a context-based focus on the question of likelihood of harm is vital.

higher penalties than for plain incitement, thus amounting to roughly the same as an aggravating factor. See, e.g. Art. 162(3) of the Criminal Code of Bulgaria 1968 (amended 2011) (this provision was amended in 2009 and penalizes the founder and/or leader of groups or organizations that propagate hatred, while the next paragraph penalizes members of such groups: maximum penalties for these two offences are six and three years respectively); Art. 214(13) of the Law of the Republic of Lithuania of 18 November 1997 on Supplementing the Code of Administrative Violations; Art.457-1(3) of the Criminal Code of Luxembourg 2010 (inserted as per Act of 19 July 1997); Art. 515 of the Criminal Code of Spain 1996; and Art. 161 of the Criminal Code of Ukraine 2001 (see also Art. 37 of the Constitution of Ukraine 1996). See also the following examples: Art. 130(3) of the Criminal Code of Belarus (of 9 July 1999, amended through 20 July 2007), lifting the maximum prison sentence from five to twelve years; Sections 78 and 150 of the Criminal Code of Latvia 1998, lifting the maximum prison sentence from three to ten years. These latter penalties, however, appear disproportionate (see further Chapter 13).

13

Sanctions

13.1 Introduction

Article 20(2) ICCPR begs one more question – that of penalties. Remarkably, the question of what the international law-sanctioned 'prohibition' of incitement really means in terms of sanctions has largely been absent from most of the free speech debate. It is, however, by no means a straightforward matter. The fact that the Human Rights Committee has declared Article 20(2) fully compatible with Article 19 on freedom of expression is, though convenient, of course not free from complications.[1] The general rules on restrictions pertaining to Article 19, including the necessity principle, force assessment of the precise nature of the free speech restriction. More particularly, this article demands to know whether less interfering means were imaginable to safeguard whichever public good was at stake at the time of the interference – be it public order or the rights of others. At the same time, Article 20(2) requires State parties to take far-reaching measures in the event of incitement – namely its 'prohibition by law'. The necessity principle is integrally applicable to Article 20(2)-based prohibitions.[2] This begs the question as to how State parties can live up to the necessity principle if their hands are, in this respect, forced – it is, after all, mandatory to ban incitement within the meaning of the Covenant.

The answer to this conundrum could possibly only lie in disentangling the legislative and enforcement duties that emanate respectively from the ICCPR. That is, while all State parties that have made no reservation to

[1] Human Rights Committee, *General Comment 34: Article 19: Freedoms of Opinion and Expression* (CCPR/C/GC/34, adopted at its 102nd session, Geneva, 11–29 July 2011), para. 51. This was first held in *General Comment 11: Article 20* (Nineteenth session, 1983), para. 2; and later confirmed in *Malcolm Ross* v. *Canada*, Communication no. 736/1997 (18 October 2000), para. 10.6.

[2] See HRC, *General Comment 34*, para. 50: 'a limitation that is justified on the basis of article 20 must also comply with article 19, paragraph 3.' This was first held in *Malcolm Ross* v. *Canada*, para. 10.6.

Article 20(2) must have laws in place prohibiting any advocacy of religious hatred that constitutes incitement to discrimination or violence, the actual enforcement of such incitement laws must, in each and every concrete case, still meet the necessity principle. An important aspect of such law enforcement is meting out proportionate penalties.

The question of appropriate sanctions is twofold. First, there is the general question as to what types of sanction are generally envisaged by the ICCPR. That is, what categories of penalties are generally allowed, or indeed ordered, by the Covenant? This question relates to the potential range of sanctions – civil, criminal or administrative – that may be incorporated into domestic incitement laws. Part of this investigation into the general appropriateness of different sorts of penalties is the sub-question of whether or not international law envisages maximum (prison) sentences for the crime of incitement. In that regard we will also compare and contrast state practice in this field.

Second, what penalties should judges mete out in concrete extreme speech cases? What factors (should) impact the concrete penalty imposed on the inciter? When is a penalty imposed on the inciter necessary and proportionate? This is where the interplay of Articles 19 and 20 comes to life to the full extent.

13.2   Types of penalties permitted

The text of Article 20 ICCPR does not envisage required or permitted penalties for the crime of incitement. As has already been indicated,[3] the ICERD is far more specific as to the question of which types of penalty are envisaged – criminal ones. Farrior has noted that the ICERD's 'phrase "offense punishable by law" has been interpreted by the Committee to mean a criminal offense, in part because the long delays that might accompany a civil suit would not provide the punitive effect necessary to protect the community effectively from racial discrimination'.[4] The Committee on the Elimination of Racial Discrimination once expressly held that 'the imposition of civil liability falls short of the requirement of article 4 to declare certain acts or activities "as an offence punishable by law".'[5] Indeed, CERD has in fact distilled from Article 4 ICERD a duty

---

[3] See Chapter 6, particularly sections 6.2–6.4 thereof.

[4] Stephanie Farrior, 'Molding the Matrix: The Historical and Theoretical Foundations of International Law Concerning Hate Speech' (1996) 14:1 *Berkeley Journal of International Law* 1–98, at 51.

[5] CERD, *Positive Measures Designed to Eradicate all Incitement to, or Acts of, Racial Discrimination – Implementation of the International Convention on the Elimination of*

to enact a full criminal investigation into allegations of hate propaganda that prima facie engage Article 4 ICERD.[6] Moreover, and quite in the face of the expediency principle, under certain circumstances this Committee expects no less than criminal punishment of inciters.[7] This approach is further solidified through its reflections on state reports in which the Committee expressed its concern that State parties' hate speech laws result in an alarmingly low number of convictions, insisting on more active prosecutions in this area.[8] In other concluding observations CERD has demanded harsher penalties.[9] Further, in the specific context of organized hatred (including incitement by political parties) the Committee has made concrete recommendations such as 'financial sanctions'[10] and has on numerous occasions called for express bans and dissolutions of racist or otherwise hateful organizations.[11]

Recently, CERD seems to have alleviated its insistence on rigorous prosecution of hate speech offenders. In its General Recommendation on racist hate speech it postulated that:

All Forms of Racial Discrimination, Article 4 (UN Doc. CERD/2 (1985) at 37), at 39. See Farrior, 'Molding the Matrix', 57.

[6] E.g. CERD, *L.K.* v. *The Netherlands*, Communication No. 4/1991 (16 March 1993) and *Mohammed Hassan Gelle* v. *Denmark*, Communication No. 34/2004 (6 March 2006). However, if Art. 4 is not prima facie engaged, no such investigations may be required. See, e.g., *Jama* v. *Denmark*, Communication no. 41/2008 (21 August 2009) and *Zentralrat Deutscher Sinti und Roma et al.* v. *Germany*, Communication no. 38/2006 (22 February 2008). See Chapter 6 for more details.

[7] See CERD, *The Jewish Community of Oslo et al.* v. *Norway*, Communication no. 30/2003 (15 August 2005). See section 6.4.3 of Chapter 6 for more details.

[8] See e.g. CERD, A/51/18 (1996) 17, para. 63 (Denmark): 'It is noted with concern that only three convictions have been registered in the past six years against members of neo-Nazi groups, although instructions have been issued to prosecutors.' See also A/51/18 (1996) 22, para. 116 (Hungary); A/52/18 (1997) 39, para. 283 (Bulgaria); A/54/18 (1999) 39, para. 394 (Latvia); A/59/18 (2004) 58, para. 316 (Madagascar); A/57/18 (2002) 69, para. 425 (New Zealand); A/58/18 (2003) 35, para. 159 (Poland); A/59/18 (2004) 14, para. 64 (Brazil); A/59/18 (2004) 29, para. 151 (Netherlands); and A/60/18 (2005) 61, para. 317 (Turkmenistan). Conversely, the Committee praised those states that stepped up their game in this area. See, e.g., A/58/18 (2003) 19, para. 23 (Côte d'Ivoire); and A/52/18 (1997) 25, para. 157 (Germany).

[9] See, e.g., CERD, A/52/18 (1997) 22, para. 140 (Luxembourg); A/52/18 (1997) 59, para. 450 (Denmark). Conversely, the Committee expressed its encouragement to those states that increased their penalties in this area. See, e.g., A/58/18 (2003) 88, para. 524 (UK): 'The Committee commends the State party's efforts to address more stringently the issue of incitement to racial hatred, including ... the increase in the maximum penalty for incitement to racial hatred from two to seven years' imprisonment under the Anti-Terrorism, Crime and Security Act 2001.'

[10] E.g. CERD, A/57/18 (2002) 17, para. 42 (Belgium).

[11] See section 12.3 of Chapter 12.

the criminalization of forms of racist expression should be reserved for serious cases, to be proven beyond reasonable doubt, while less serious cases should be addressed by means other than criminal law, taking into account, inter alia, the nature and extent of the impact on targeted persons and groups. The application of criminal sanctions should be governed by principles of legality, proportionality and necessity.[12]

Be that as it may, Article 20(2) does, when it comes to sanctions, appear to allow for more discretion to be granted to State parties than the ICERD does.[13] While Article 4 of the latter treaty demands that State parties 'declare' as an 'offence punishable by law' the several racist speech offences listed, Article 20(2) of the ICCPR requires that incitement be 'prohibited by law'. The former formulation leaves little doubt – CERD's recently adopted less stringent tone in this regard notwithstanding – as to criminal law-based prosecution and sanctioning being the preferred *modus operandi*. Article 20(2) of the ICCPR can, on its face, be met through laws of a different nature, including administrative and civil law-based measures. Moreover, it is commonly accepted that Article 20(2)'s toolkit consists of a host of non-legal measures, including policies and other positive measures promoting tolerance through education, sensitization and awareness-raising,[14] with criminal sanctions merely being the *ultimum remedium*.[15]

---

[12] CERD, *General Recommendation 35: Combating Racist Hate Speech* (UN Doc. CERD/C/GC/35, 83rd session, 12–30 August 2013), para. 12.

[13] See Nazila Ghanea, 'Nature and Means of Effective Remedies' (expert paper presented at the UN OHCHR Expert workshop on the prohibition of incitement to national, racial or religious hatred, Vienna, 9–10 February 2011), at 3. See also Manfred Nowak, *U.N. Covenant on Civil and Political Rights: CCPR Commentary* (2nd rev. edn, Kehl: N. P. Engel, 2005), 470, arguing that an older draft of the incitement clause did not require criminal laws and that later drafts have left the matter open to controversy.

[14] See, e.g., *Rabat Plan of Action on the Prohibition of Advocacy of National, Racial or Religious Hatred that Constitutes Incitement to Discrimination, Hostility or Violence* (Conclusions and recommendations emanating from the four regional expert workshops organized by OHCHR in 2011 and adopted by experts in Rabat, Morocco on 5 October 2012), paras. 23–29; CERD, *General Recommendation 35*, paras. 30–44 listing a comprehensive set of positive measures; Special Rapporteur on Freedom of Religion or Belief, *Tackling Manifestations of Collective Religious Hatred* (A/HRC/25/58, 26 December 2013), particularly paras. 31–53; Special Rapporteur on the Promotion and Protection of the Right to Freedom of Opinion and Expression, *Report of the Special Rapporteur to the General Assembly on Hate Speech and Incitement to Hatred* (A/67/357, 7 September 2012), particularly paras. 56–74; ARTICLE 19, *Prohibiting Incitement to Discrimination, Hostility or Violence: Policy Brief* (2012) (hereafter *Incitement Policy Brief*), at 41–45 ('Sanctions and other measures').

[15] See, e.g., *Rabat Plan of Action*, at 7 (see recommendations following para. 22). See further section 13.4 of this chapter. Note that the Rabat Plan does not, however, rule out criminal

In most of its workings, the Human Rights Committee has not challenged or overruled the expediency principle to the same degree as CERD has done in some of its decisions and observations. In that respect, it is also telling that the phrase used in an old draft of General Comment No. 34, in which it was insisted that '[a]ll allegations of violations of the law should be vigorously investigated and the perpetrators prosecuted',[16] was ultimately dropped by the Committee.

Particularly in its views on individual communications, the Human Rights Committee has shown itself not to be as prepared as CERD to go down the road of recommending rigorous prosecutions and compulsory criminal penalties. Notably, while the latter Committee on occasion accepted that a State party had breached the ICERD by not prosecuting and punishing ostensible hate-mongers,[17] the Human Rights Committee has been reluctant to do the same.[18]

That is not to say, however, that criminal sanctions are not permitted by the Human Rights Committee in the area of extreme speech – they are. For instance, following private criminal actions brought against him by associations of resistance fighters and survivors of concentration camps, Robert Faurisson was convicted of the crime of 'contesting proven crimes against humanity'.[19] As a consequence, a criminal sanction – more specifically a fine – was imposed on him pursuant to the Gayssot Act.[20] By finding no violation of Faurisson's freedom of expression, the Committee sanctioned the imposed fine.

The case of *Ross* v. *Canada* shows that the Committee does accept penalties of a non-criminal nature, too. In fact, while the Committee accepts that the imposed restrictions on Ross' free speech 'derive support from the principles reflected in article 20(2) of the Covenant',[21] the fact that

penalties. See the recommendations following para. 19 ('expression that constitutes a criminal offence') and para. 22 ('criminally prohibited').

[16] Human Rights Committee, *Draft General Comment No. 34* (UN Doc. CCPR/C/GC/34/ CRP.2, dated 29 January 2010), para. 51.

[17] Again, see particularly *The Jewish Community of Oslo et al.* v. *Norway*.

[18] Notably, see Human Rights Committee, *Maria Vassilari et al.* v. *Greece*, Communication no. 1570/2007 (19 March 2009). See, generally, Chapter 5 on the position of alleged incitement victims under the ICCPR.

[19] Human Rights Committee, *Robert Faurisson* v. *France*, Communication no. 550/1993 (19 July 1995), para. 2.5.

[20] *Faurisson* v. *France*, para. 2.5 (this fine was increased upon appeal: para. 2.7). Note that he was furthermore 'removed from his chair' held at Sorbonne University (para. 2.1). However, this appears to have been an internal university matter and does not feature as part of Faurisson's complaints (paras. 3.1–3.4).

[21] Human Rights Committee, *Malcolm Ross* v. *Canada*, Communication no. 736/1997 (18 October 2000), para. 11.5.

the sanctions in question are not of a criminal law nature is at no point mentioned by any party to the case, let alone extensively discussed by the Committee. The penalties imposed do not stem from Canadian criminal law, but rather from Canadian human rights law, more specifically from the New Brunswick Human Rights Code in conjunction with Canadian constitutional law.[22] To be specific, as a result of this schoolteacher's anti-Semitic statements, a human rights board of inquiry had ordered that the local school board:

(a)   immediately place Malcolm Ross on a leave of absence without pay for a period of eighteen months;
(b)   appoint Malcolm Ross a non-teaching position, if a non-teaching position becomes available in School District 15 for which Malcolm Ross is qualified.
(c)   terminate his employment at the end of the eighteen months leave of absence without pay if, in the interim, he has not been offered and accepted a non-teaching position.[23]

Not finding a breach of Ross' free speech, the Committee allowed these repercussions. Moreover, unlike in *Faurisson*, the Committee expressly referenced Article 20(2) in coming to its conclusions.[24]

In *J.R.T. and the W.G. Party* v. *Canada* the imposed penalties on the person responsible for telephonically disseminated anti-Semitic messages were also – initially – not of a criminal nature.[25] The curtailment of the applicant's telephone 'service' and interferences with his correspondence stemmed again from Canadian human rights law, more specifically the Canadian Human Rights Act 1985 in conjunction with the Canadian Post Office Act 1867. The latter law forbids the transmission of 'scurrilous material' and, according to the Canadian Government, therefore, 'gives effect to article 20 of the Covenant'.[26] The former law, the Canadian Human Rights Act, led

---

[22] *Ross* v. *Canada*, paras. 3.1–3.6, 4.1–4.8 and 6.4.
[23] *Ross* v. *Canada*, para. 4.3. An additional order was quashed by the Canadian Supreme Court (para. 4.8).
[24] *Ross* v. *Canada*, para. 11.5. Note that member Hipólito Solari Yrigoyen would have preferred to move Art. 20(2) even more to the centre of the Committee's reasoning. See Individual Opinion of Hipólito Solari Yrigoyen.
[25] Human Rights Committee, *J.R.T. and the W.G. Party* v. *Canada*, Communication no. 104/1981 (6 April 1983). That is, up until the moment that contempt of court proceedings were instigated against the applicant (see paras. 2.8–2.9). The latter, separate, proceedings resulted in fines and a prison sentence imposed on the Western Guard Party and John Ross Taylor respectively.
[26] *J.R.T. and the W.G. Party* v. *Canada*, para. 6.3, Section 7 of the Post Office Act 1867 [Canada]. Restrictions flowing from this law are not assessed by the Committee as the applicant did not exhaust remedies in that regard. In an *obiter dictum* – see para. 8(c) – the

to the curtailment of the applicant's telephone usage. With respect to those interferences specifically, the Committee concluded that Canada had in fact 'an obligation under article 20(2) of the Covenant' to act in the way that it did, thus sanctioning the repercussions of the extreme speech in question.[27]

In its concluding observations on periodic state reports the Committee uses more aggressive language, suggesting that criminal laws, criminal investigations and criminal penalties are envisaged by Article 20(2).[28] Thus it has, for example, urged State parties to 'take the necessary action to investigate, prosecute and punish [acts of hateful incitement] in order to ensure respect for article 20, paragraph 2, of the Covenant'.[29] Prosecution clearly implies criminal liability. On occasion, the Committee has – like CERD – called for 'sterner measures' to be imposed on convicted inciters.[30]

Thus far we have established that the ICCPR, in the view of the Committee, permits both criminal and non-criminal sanctions. The Committee's case law suggests that in the criminal law sphere fines are permitted (*Faurisson*), while in the non-criminal law sphere job dismissals (*Ross*) and restrictions of one's use of communication technology (*J.R.T. and the W.G. Party v. Canada*) have been sanctioned. The biggest issue here is clearly whether or not prison sentences are permitted. In the literature it has been suggested that prison sentences 'for hate speech may well violate the principle of proportionality'.[31] The question still remains whether prison sentences are categorically excluded or whether that type of penalty tends to be disproportionate in concrete incitement cases (which forms a separate discussion, see section 13.4).

The Rabat Plan of Action omits altogether any mention of prison sentences, suggesting that, if not ruled out, such penalties for speech offences are highly controversial at best. The Human Rights Committee did not use the opportunity presented by drafting General Comment No. 34 on freedom of expression to pronounce specifically on permitted penalties under Article 20(2). It did, however, take a position as to the permissibility

---

Committee indicates, however, that the restrictions imposed pursuant this law are rather broad in scope and raise questions of compatibility with freedom of expression.

[27] *J.R.T. and the W.G. Party v. Canada*, para. 8(b).

[28] For more details, see section 5.4.2 of chapter 5.

[29] A/58/40 vol. I (2003) 64, para. 85(20) (Israel). For similar observations, see, e.g., A/59/40 vol. I (2004) 68, para. 75(25) (Serbia and Montenegro); CCPR/CO/78/SVK (2003), para. 17 (Slovakia); A/57/40 vol. I (2002) 44, para. 76(8) (Switzerland); and A/58/40 vol. I (2002) 31, para. 77(18) (Egypt).

[30] A/59/40 vol. I (2004) 56, para. 72(27) (Belgium).

[31] Farrior, 'Molding the Matrix', at 11.

of sanctions in relation to dissimilar speech offences. Notably, while generally recommending the decriminalization of 'defamation' offences, the Committee added that in that area 'the application of the criminal law should only be countenanced in the most serious of cases and imprisonment is never an appropriate penalty.'[32] The Committee did not expressly extend the ramifications of that comment to the offence of incitement.

UN Special Rapporteurs on freedom of expression have been somewhat more outspoken on this point than the Human Rights Committee.[33] In one report it was held that in the area of restrictions on free speech the actual 'deprivation of liberty is clearly a disproportionate sanction'.[34] However, the one caveat that is made is in relation to 'wholly exceptional cases in which there is a clear and present danger of violence'.[35] Obviously, this phrase has a bearing on the permissibility of sanctions under Article 20(2) of the ICCPR, suggesting the ambiguous conclusion that prison sentences are typically yet not necessarily barred in the area in question.

The UN Human Rights Committee's own position remains equally ambiguous. While on occasion it has called for 'sterner measures',[36] the Committee has neither through its concluding observations nor by way of its views in individual communications expressly called for prison sentences. It has on occasion more or less indirectly sanctioned them, but one may very well wonder how representative that body of case law is. Notably, in *M.A. v. Italy* the Committee indirectly endorsed a four-year prison sentence imposed on the applicant who had endeavoured to reorganize the dissolved Italian fascist party.[37] Several caveats are in order, though. First and foremost, this was not a decision on the merits of a freedom of expression/association complaint, but an admissibility decision in which the Committee heavily leaned on the abuse of rights doctrine enshrined in Article 5 of the Covenant. Second, the Committee makes no mention of Article 20(2) in its reasoning; thus in any event it cannot be said that the imposed penalties were justified by virtue of that provision. Third, M.A. was sentenced

---

[32] HRC, *General Comment 34*, para. 47.

[33] See Farrior, 'Molding the Matrix', 92–3.

[34] *Final Report by Mr Danilo Türk and Mr Louis Joinet, Special Rapporteurs, on the Right to Freedom of Opinion and Expression* (UN Doc. E/CN.4/Sub.2/1992/9, 14 July 1992), para. 83: further postulation that 'deprivation of liberty carries the inherent risk of leading to numerous violations of human rights'.

[35] *Report of Special Rapporteurs on the Right to Freedom of Opinion and Expression*, para. 83.

[36] A/59/40 vol. I (2004) 56, para. 72(27) (Belgium).

[37] Human Rights Committee, *M.A. v. Italy*, Communication No. 117/1981 (21 September 1981), para. 2.3.

prior to the entry into force of the Covenant in Italy. This implies that the Human Rights Committee was never competent to declare a violation in this regard even if it were so inclined.[38] For reasons already indicated,[39] the case of *J.R.T. and the W.G. Party* v. *Canada*, while indirectly sanctioning a prison sentence, cannot be said to form a precedent either.

Turning to regional human rights organizations, a document adopted within the Council of Europe postulates that 'prison sentences for hate speech should remain the exception', thus reluctantly accepting the possibility of this penalty in extreme cases.[40] Again, as there is no incitement provision or other extreme speech offence to be found in the European Convention on Human Rights, there can be no question of mandatory penalties, only of generally permitted ones under the limitation clause pertaining to the right to freedom of expression. Thus from the case law of the European Court of Human Rights it transpires that many categories of sanctions are generally permitted in the area of extreme speech, ranging from civil remedies (including civil damages awards),[41] seizures, confiscations and forfeitures of publications,[42] fines,[43] to actual prison

---

[38] *M.A.* v. *Italy*, para. 13.3.

[39] J.R.T.'s prison sentence was, strictly speaking, the result of contempt of court. For more details, see n. 25.

[40] Committee of Ministers, Recommendation No. R(97)20 on 'Hate Speech' (adopted on 30 October 1997), para. 37 of the Appendix.

[41] Suggested by the Court, notwithstanding its finding of a violation of Art. 10 of the Convention, in *Lehideux and Isorni* v. *France*, Application no. 55/1997/839/1045 (Grand Chamber judgment of 23 September 1998), para. 57 (symbolic civil damages were awarded by the French judiciary, see para. 21). See Anne Weber, *Manual on Hate Speech* (Strasbourg: Council of Europe Publishing, 2009), at 45.

[42] See, e.g., European Commission of Human Rights, *Udo Walendy* v. *Germany*, Application no. 21128/92 (admissibility decision of 11 January 1995), at 'The Facts'; *Glimmerveen and Hagenbeek* v. *The Netherlands*, Application nos. 8348/78 and 8406/78 (admissibility decision of 11 October 1979), at 'The Facts' (Part A, para. 3); European Court of Human Rights, *Otto-Preminger-Institut* v. *Austria*, Application no. 13470/87 (20 September 1994), paras. 12–16; and *Balsytė-Lideikienė* v. *Lithuania*, Application no. 72596/01 (4 November 2008), paras. 17 and 20.

[43] See, e.g., European Commission of Human Rights, *Karl-August Hennicke* v. *Germany*, Application no. 34889/97 (admissibility decision of 21 May 1997), at 'The Facts'; European Court of Human Rights, *İ.A.* v. *Turkey*, Application no. 42571/98 (13 September 2005), para. 13 (the initial prison sentence was commuted to a fine); *Garaudy* v. *France*, Application no. 65831/01 (admissibility decision of 24 June 2003), at 'The Facts' (Garaudy received, in addition to a suspended prison sentence, a number of fines); *Sürek* v. *Turkey* (*No. 1*), Application no. 26682/95 (Grand Chamber judgment of 8 July 1999), para. 14; *Le Pen* v. *France*, Application No. 18788/09, decision of 7 May 2010, at 'The Facts'; *Soulas*

sentences. As early as 1979, in one of the first hate speech cases filed with the Strasbourg Court by a convicted inciter, the former European Commission of Human Rights indirectly sanctioned a prison sentence – albeit a short one (two weeks) – by declaring Glimmerveen's complaint against the Netherlands inadmissible.[44] Prison sentences have since been endorsed by the Strasbourg Court in a number of cases.[45]

13.3   Comparative state practice

The lack of univocal guidance from international monitoring bodies explains the widely diverse state practice in the area of sanctions for incitement offences. Some states enforce prison sentences; some do not. Some states have stipulated aggravating factors; others have not, while still others have commenced imposing 'educational' sentences on intolerant persons. In this section we will discuss the main trends.

13.3.1   Prison sentences

Most states with incitement laws in place allow for prison penalties. States differ widely on the question as to what the maximum prison sentence for this offence ought to be. The spectrum ranges from a maximum three months' sentence (New Zealand) to fifteen years' imprisonment (Santa Lucia). A maximum penalty of two or three years' imprisonment appears to be most common. The following table gives a concise overview of state practice in this area:

and others v. *France*, Application no. 15948/03 (10 July 2008), at 'The Facts'; and *Leroy* v. *France*, Application no. 36109/03 (2 October 2008), para. 11.

[44] European Commission of Human Rights, *Glimmerveen and Hagenbeek* v. *The Netherlands*, Application nos. 8348/78 and 8406/78 (admissibility decision of 11 October 1979), at 'The Facts' (Part A, para. 3).

[45] E.g. European Commission of Human Rights, *Hans Jorg Schimanek* v. *Austria*, Application no. 32307/96 (admissibility decision of 1 February 2000), at 'The Facts'; *Garaudy* v. *France*, Application no. 65831/01 (admissibility decision of 24 June 2003), at 'The Facts' (Garaudy received, in addition to a number of fines, a suspended prison sentence); European Court of Human Rights, *Hans-Jürgen Witzsch* v. *Germany* [I], Application no. 41448/98 (admissibility decision of 20 April 1999), at 'The Facts' (para. A); *Hans-Jürgen Witzsch* v. *Germany* [II], Application no. 7485/03 (admissibility decision of 13 December 2005), at 'The Facts' (para. A); and *Zana* v. *Turkey*, Application no. 69/1996/6888/880 (Grand Chamber judgment of 25 November 1997), para. 26.

Maximum prison sentence	Countries
15 years	Santa Lucia[46]
10 years	Albania[47]
7 years	United Kingdom[48]
5 years	Belarus, Bolivia, Bosnia and Herzegovina, Cyprus, Germany, Monaco, Portugal, Serbia and Ukraine[49]
4 years	Armenia and Bulgaria[50]

[46] Art. 359 of the Criminal Code of Santa Lucia 2003.
[47] Criminal Code of the Republic of Albania (Law No. 7895, 27 January 1995, consolidated version as of 1 December 2004), Art. 265.
[48] Section 29L of the Racial and Religious Hatred Act 2006 [UK].
[49] Art. 130 of the Criminal Code of Belarus 1999 (amended 2007) (containing a number of aggravating factors); Art. 281quarter of the Criminal Code of Bolivia 1972; Art. 150 of the Criminal Code of Bosnia and Herzegovina 1998 (containing a number of aggravating factors; note, moreover, that according to ECRI, Bosnia and Herzegovina's incitement laws are not enforced sufficiently – see ECRI, *Report on Bosnia and Herzegovina* (CRI(2005)2, 25 June 2004), para. 12); Section 47 of the Criminal Code of Cyprus 1929; Section 130 of the Criminal Code of Germany 1998; Section 16 of the Freedom of Public Expression Act, No. 1.299 of 15 July 2005 [Monaco]; Art. 240(2) of the Criminal Code of Portugal 2006 (Law No. 65/98 of 2 September 1998); Art. 317 of the Criminal Code of Serbia 2005; Art. 161 of the Criminal Code of Ukraine 2001.
[50] Art. 226 of the Criminal Code of Armenia (entry into force 1 August 2003). The case law suggests that such sentences are indeed occasionally handed down. ECRI reports a couple of incitement cases, including one in which a three-year suspended prison sentence for an anti-Semitic statement was imposed on the head of an ultranationalist organization. ECRI, *Second Report on Armenia* (CRI(2007)1, 30 June 2006), para. 24. Art. 164 of the Criminal Code of Bulgaria 1968 (amended 2011) (thus increased by amendment in 2009). The Bulgarian Law against Discrimination gives alleged discrimination (including harassment or incitement) victims the possibility to file complaints with either the Commission for Protection against Discrimination (CPD), or to submit a complaint before the courts. There are recent examples of both. See, e.g., CPD Decision of 20 June 2008 (fining a mayor for anti-Roma speech on the radio); CPD Decision of 25 July 2008 (concerning anti-Roma speech on TV, and imposing self-regulation mechanisms within Bulgarian broadcasting); CPD Decision of 23 December 2008 (also finding incitement to discrimination and imposing media self-regulation); and, as an example of the second type, Sofia City Court, *Yuliana Metodieva* v. *Volen Siderov*, Case no. 847/2007, judgment of 26 May 2008 (sentencing for the first time an MP over anti-Semitic and anti-Roma speech).

(continued)

Maximum prison sentence	Countries
3 years	Armenia, Brazil, Croatia, Estonia, Hungary, Italy, Kyrgyzstan, Latvia, Moldova, Norway, Peru, Singapore, Slovakia, Spain and Turkey[51]
2 years	Austria, Canada, Czech Republic, Denmark, Finland, Greece, Iceland, Ireland, Liechtenstein, Lithuania, Luxembourg, Poland, Russia, Slovenia and Sweden[52]

---

[51] Art. 20 of Law No. 7,716, Act against Racism or '*Lei Caó*' of 5 January 1989 [Brazil]; Art. 174, para. 3 of the Criminal Code of Croatia 1997 (amended 1 October 2004) (containing a number of aggravating factors); Art. 151 of the Criminal Code of Estonia 2000 (containing certain aggravating circumstances); Art. 332 of the Criminal Code of Hungary 2012; Legislative Decree No. 122 of 26 April 1993, converted into Act No. 205 of 25 June 1993 on Urgent Measures in Respect of Racial, Ethnic and Religious Discrimination (amending Section 3 of Act No. 654 of October 1975) [Italy], as enforced in, e.g., Court of Justice of Verona, Sentence No. 2203/04 (judgment of 2 December 2004, imposing a six-month prison sentence, among other penalties, on six Lega Nord members for incitement to discrimination); Section 78 of the Criminal Code of Latvia 1998; Art. 346 of the Criminal Code of Moldova 2002; Art. 135a of the Criminal Code of Norway 1902 (as enforced in, e.g., Supreme Court judgment of 21 December 2007, concerning anti-Semitic statements made by the spokesman of a right-wing group; reported by ECRI, *Fourth Report on Norway* (CRI(2009)4, 20 June 2008), paras. 11–12); Art. 323 of the Criminal Code of Peru 1991; Art. 424 of the New Criminal Code of Slovakia (L.300/2005); Art. 510 of the Criminal Code of Spain 1996; Art. 216 of the New Criminal Code of Turkey 2004; Section 299 of the Criminal Code of Kyrgyzstan 1997; and Art. 298A of the Criminal Code of Singapore 1872.

[52] Section 283 Criminal Code of Austria 1974; Art. 319 of the Criminal Code of Canada 1985; Section 356 of the New Criminal Code of the Czech Republic (40/2009); Section 226b of the Criminal Code of Denmark (Consolidated Act No. 1034 of 29 October 2009); Section 10 of the Criminal Code of Finland 1889 (amended 2012); Art. 1(1) of Law 927/1979 (amended by Laws 1419/1984 and 2910/2001) on Punishing Acts or Activities Aimed at Racial Discrimination [Greece] (enforced in, e.g., Athens Court of Appeals, Judgment of 19 September 2008, concerning an anti-Semitic newspaper column, resulting in a five-months' suspended sentence; and Athens Court of Appeals, Judgment of 13 September 2007, concerning an anti-Semitic book, resulting in a fourteen-months' suspended sentence, which was later lifted; see ECRI, *Fourth Report on Greece*, (CRI(2008)31, 2 April 2009), para. 16); Art. 233a of the General Criminal Code of Iceland 1940; Section 2 of the Prohibition of Incitement to Hatred Act 1989 [Ireland]; Section 282 of the Criminal Code of Liechtenstein 1998 (as enforced in, e.g., Supreme Court of Liechtenstein, Decision 1 JG 2005.32 (Judgment of 2 August 2006)); Art. 170 of the Criminal Code of Lithuania 2000 (containing aggravating factors; ECRI has lamented the fact that Lithuanian incitement law is not sufficiently enforced: ECRI, *Third Report on Lithuania* (CRI(2006)2, 24 June 2004), para. 55); Art. 457-1, to be read

(continued)

Maximum prison sentence	Countries
1.5 years	Malta and Uruguay[54]
1 year	Antigua and Barbados, Belgium and the Netherlands[53]
3 months	New Zealand[55]

It is of course possible to prohibit incitement while not making perpetrators liable to serve time in prison. For instance, certain incitement offences in Chile and France subject offenders to fines only.[56]

13.3.2   Other penalties

Virtually all incitement laws allow for the imposition of a fine instead of or in addition to a prison sentence. Some laws expressly allow for additional measures such as the confiscation of the publications in question.[57]

in conjunction with Articles 454 and 455 of the Criminal Code of Luxembourg 2010 (inserted as per Act of 19 July 1997; enforced in, e.g., Court of Appeal (5th chamber), Case No. 263/05 V (judgment of 7 June 2005, imposing a six-month prison sentence on an eighteen-year-old person for, among other things, incitement to hatred and violence); Art. 256 of the Criminal Code of Poland 1997; Art. 239 of the Criminal Code of the Russian Federation 1996 (amended 2006); Art. 300 of the Criminal Code of Slovenia 2008; and Chapter 16, Section 8 of the Criminal Code of Sweden 1962.

[53] Art. 33 of the Public Order Act 1972 [Antigua and Barbados]; Art. 20 of the Law of 30 July 1981 Criminalizing Certain Acts Inspired by Racism or Xenophobia 1981 [Belgium] (see, e.g., Appeal Court of Antwerp, *F.A., K.U., M.K., M.B., B.U. & Centre for Equal Opportunities and Opposition to Racism v. B.D.*, judgment of 31 January 2008; and Belgian Court of Cassation, *B.D. v. F.A., K.U., M.K., M.B., B.U. & Centre for Equal Opportunities and Opposition to Racism*, judgment of 27 May 2008); and Art. 137d(2) of the Criminal Code of the Netherlands 1881.

[54] Art. 82A.1 of the Criminal Code of Malta 1854 (amended 2014); and Art. 149 of the Criminal Code of Uruguay 1933.

[55] Section 131 of the Human Rights Act 1993 [New Zealand] (exclusively dealing with incitement to racial disharmony).

[56] Art. R625-7 of the Criminal Code of France 1992, categorizing incitement as a fifth class (i.e. minor) offence that may lead to the imposition of a EUR 1,500 fine; and Art. 31 of Law No. 19.733 on Freedom of Opinion and Information and Journalism 2001 [Chile]. Note that in France prison sentences may be imposed under dissimilar incitement offences, namely, the denial crimes prohibited by the Gayssot Act 1990. (Suspended) prison sentences have been enforced under that law.

[57] E.g. Art. 214(12) of the Law of the Republic of Lithuania of 18 November 1997 Supplementing the Code of Administrative Violations; Art. 457-1(3) of the Criminal

Monaco's incitement clause is quite unique in allowing for an additional 'shame and blame' strategy: judges may rule that at the offender's expense the sentence be publicized and disseminated in the form of a press release.[58] In that event, the hate speech victim's identity is only to be included if the latter so wishes.

Recently, Hungarian judges have shown themselves to be creative in their sentencing practice. In the case of *Gyorgy Nagy*, this Holocaust denier was ordered – in addition to receiving a suspended prison sentence – to visit either Auschwitz in Poland, Yad Vashem in Jerusalem or the Budapest Holocaust memorial museum.[59] A minimum of three visits was required. Nagy, moreover, was requested to write a report describing his experiences.

13.3.3 Aggravating factors

As was noted in the previous chapter, some states accept an organizational or systematic element as an aggravating factor in their extreme speech offences.[60] That is, higher sentences may be imposed on those hate-mongers who perpetrate this crime in an organized capacity. Article 20(2) of the ICCPR does not resist that, and in any event that approach is to be preferred over altogether proscribing 'extremist organizations'.

Other aggravating factors are discernible in state practice. For instance, some states allow higher penalties in cases where the incitement offence is committed by someone in an official capacity.[61] Again, Article 20(2) of the ICCPR does not seem to resist this. We have seen before that someone's official capacity also impacts the question of likelihood of harm, since a public figure may exercise a considerable degree of influence. Accordingly, such public positions may come with increased responsibilities, which implies that increased sanctions in this area are not contrary to the gist of the Covenant's incitement clause.

Occasionally certain factors are legally declared an 'aggravating factor' while they should be deemed a standard requirement of the incitement

Code of Luxembourg 2010; and Art. 300(3) of the New Criminal Code of Slovenia 2008. In other countries, this prerogative may of course also flow from the criminal law system itself without being spelled out in the incitement provision.

[58] Section 16, para. 3 of the Freedom of Public Expression Act No. 1.299 of 15 July 2005 [Monaco].

[59] Budapest Court, *Case of Gyorgy Nagy* (judgment of 31 January 2013).

[60] See section 12.5 of Chapter 12.

[61] E.g. Art. 161(4) of the Criminal Code of Montenegro 2004; Art. 424(3) of the New Criminal Code of Slovakia 2005; Art. 134, final sentence of the Criminal Code of Serbia 2005; Art. 67 and Art. 161(2) of the Criminal Code of Ukraine 2001.

offence within the meaning of Article 20(2) ICCPR. For example, a few jurisdictions consider it an aggravating factor that the incitement is made 'publicly'.[62] This is at odds with Article 20(2) of the Covenant since this is actually a condition for the speech act to amount to punishable incitement.

Finally, Article 20(2) ICCPR does not seem to resist attaching a heavier penalty to 'incitement to violence' as opposed to, for instance, 'incitement to discrimination', as long as both proscribed results mentioned by Article 20(2) are covered. It stands to reason that states deem certain outcomes graver than others; hence maximum sentences may be tailored to that effect. Lithuania is a good example here, since it raises the maximum penalty from two years – that is, in case of incitement to discrimination – to three years in case of incitement to violence.[63] Again, 'incitement' as such may never be deemed an aggravating factor, as that would imply that extreme speech that falls short of incitement is also punishable – when it is not.[64]

13.4   Proportionality in incitement case law

In section 13.2 we established that monitoring bodies have accepted different categories of penalties, ranging from criminal sanctions – including prison sentences, according to the case law of the European Court of Human Rights – to job dismissals, to seizure and forfeiture orders. We now consider the more specific question of when a penalty in a concrete incitement case can be considered necessary and proportionate.

The Human Rights Committee has declared that the measures taken pursuant Article 20(2) of the ICCPR must nevertheless satisfy Article 19's rules on 'regular' restrictions. This, then, must apply to the sanctions emanating from Article 20(2), too. The Rabat Plan of Action supports this reading.[65] Given the intrusive nature of criminal sanctions, and

---

[62] E.g. Art. 226 of the Criminal Code of Armenia 2003.

[63] Art. 170 of the Criminal Code of Lithuania 2000.

[64] On unqualified 'hate speech laws' and their incompatibility with international law, see section 8.2.2 of Chapter 8.

[65] *Rabat Plan of Action*, para. 18, postulating that 'the three part test for restrictions (legality, proportionality and necessity) also applies to incitement cases, i.e. such restrictions must be provided by law, be narrowly defined to serve a legitimate interest, and be necessary in a democratic society to protect that interest. This implies, among other things, that restrictions: are clearly and narrowly defined and respond to a pressing social need; are the least intrusive measures available; are not overly broad, in that they do not restrict speech in a wide or untargeted way; and are proportionate in the sense that the benefit to the protected interest outweighs the harm to freedom of expression, including in respect to the sanctions they authorise.'

their inherent 'chilling effect' on free speech, it follows that criminal penalties in many extreme speech cases run the risk of being disproportionate. Hence, criminal sanctions are increasingly considered to be a last resort, that is, in the words of the Rabat Plan, only to be applied 'in strictly justifiable situations'.[66] The Rabat Plan adds that '[c]ivil sanctions and remedies should also be considered, including pecuniary and non-pecuniary damages, along with the right of correction and the right of reply. Administrative sanctions and remedies should also be considered, including those identified and put in force by various professional and regulatory bodies'.[67] In other words, states should not assume that criminal penalties must be imposed on each and every perpetrator of national incitement laws – the necessity principle would still force states to look out for possible, less interfering alternatives.

13.4.1   The Human Rights Committee on proportionate sanctions

The Human Rights Committee has stipulated in a General Comment that '[w]hen a State party invokes a legitimate ground for restriction of freedom of expression, it must demonstrate in specific and individualized fashion the precise nature of the threat, and the necessity and proportionality of the specific action taken, in particular by establishing a direct and immediate connection between the expression and the threat'.[68] This

---

[66] *Rabat Plan of Action*, at 7 (see recommendations following para. 22). ARTICLE 19, similarly, argues on the basis of the necessity test that '[r]ecourse to criminal law should ... not be the default response to instances of incitement if less severe sanctions would achieve the same effect. Moreover, the experience of many jurisdictions shows that civil and administrative law sanctions are better suited as responses to the harm caused by "hate speech".' ARTICLE 19, *Incitement Policy Brief*, at 41 (with a reference to Brazilian state practice). See also, Venice Commission, *Science and Technique of Democracy, No. 47: Blasphemy, Insult and Hatred – Finding Answers in a Democratic Society* (Strasbourg: Council of Europe Publishing, 2010), para. 55 (speaking of a 'last resort'); Committee of Ministers, Recommendation No. R(97)20 on 'Hate Speech' (adopted on 30 October 1997), at Principle 5, holding that 'the imposition of criminal sanctions generally constitutes a serious interference with that freedom. The competent courts should, when imposing criminal sanctions on persons convicted of hate speech offences, ensure strict respect for the principle of proportionality', while Principle 2 refers to alternatives for penal sanctions; the appendix to the recommendation, moreover, repeatedly refers to 'disciplinary sanctions' and 'other sanctions' as alternatives for criminal law sanctions (e.g. in paras. 26 and 28, while paras. 29, 33, 37 and 48 contain further notes of caution as to criminal sanctions).

[67] *Rabat Plan of Action*, at 7 (see recommendations following para. 22).

[68] HRC, *General Comment No. 34*, para. 35 (first held in *Hak–Chul Shin* v. *Republic of Korea*, Communication no. 926/2000, 16 March 2004, para. 7.3).

clearly extends to the nature of the penalty imposed. For the time being we cannot, however, perceive much of a consistent approach on insisting that criminal penalties are the *ultimum remedium* in the case law of the Human Rights Committee, as the Committee's extreme speech jurisprudence predates these recent benchmarks (i.e. General Comment No. 34 and the Rabat Plan of Action). The Committee's existing jurisprudence, though generally overly brief on the important question of the proportionality of the imposed sanction,[69] tells us the following.

In *Ross v. Canada*, revolving around administrative (disciplinary) sanctions imposed on an anti-Semitic public school teacher, the Committee praised Canada's guarded approach. It emphasized 'that the author was appointed to a non-teaching position after only a minimal period on leave without pay and that the restriction thus did not go any further than that which was necessary to achieve its protective functions'.[70] Previously, the Canadian Supreme Court had quashed part of the order imposed by a Board of Inquiry on the local School Board (urging the latter to take a range of measures against Ross). This concerned clause (d) of the order, which urged the school board to:

> [t]erminate Malcolm Ross' employment with the School Board immediately if, at any time during the eighteen month leave of absence or of at any time during his employment in a non-teaching position, he: (i) publishes or writes for the purpose of publication, anything that mentions a Jewish or Zionist conspiracy, or attacks followers of the Jewish religion, or (ii) publishes, sells or distributes any of the following publications, directly or indirectly: Web of Deceit, The Real Holocaust (The attack on unborn children and life itself), Spectre of Power, Christianity vs Judeo-Christianity (The battle for truth).[71]

The Supreme Court found that that part of the order was not justified 'since it did not minimally impair the author's constitutional freedoms, but imposed a permanent ban on his expressions'.[72] The parts of the order that placed Ross on a temporary leave of absence without pay and reappointed him to a non-teaching position – or fire him should such a position not become available – were upheld by the Supreme Court. While not explicitly considering the question of whether even lighter penalties

---

[69] Still less may we distil from such early cases as *J.R.T. and the W.G. Party v. Canada* and *M.A. v. Italy* since they were handed down as admissibility cases, not judgments on the merits of a freedom of expression complaint. The question of proportionality of penalties is altogether ignored in those cases.

[70] *Malcolm Ross v. Canada*, para. 11.6.

[71] *Malcolm Ross v. Canada*, para. 4.3.   [72] *Malcolm Ross v. Canada*, para. 4.8.

had been available, the Human Rights Committee found this sanction package to be proportionate.[73]

The Committee's decision in *Faurisson* sanctioned a heavy fine.[74] Faurisson and the editor of the magazine in which the former's negationist remarks were published were fined 326,832 French Francs, which was upheld and slightly raised to FRF 374,045.50 upon appeal (i.e. some EUR 57,000).[75] The fine was not punitive per se, but also included compensation for the associations of Holocaust survivors and resistance fighters that had filed the private criminal actions that had triggered the whole process.[76] In finding no violation of Faurisson's free speech, the Committee did not elaborate on the proportionality of the fine.[77] The absence of a robust assessment in that area is remarkable since the Committee had great reservations about the Gayssot Act.[78] It decided to set those concerns aside, arguing that the Committee 'is not called upon to criticize in the abstract laws enacted by States parties', but rather 'to ascertain whether the conditions of the restrictions imposed on the right to freedom of expression are met in the communications which are brought before it'.[79] Obviously, the latter task must include a robust assessment of the proportionality of penalties imposed for speech offences.

13.4.2   CERD on proportionate sanctions

Given the nature, goals and objectives of ICERD, Article 4 cases typically do not revolve around complaints brought by convicted hate speakers, but around complaints brought by alleged victims of racist hate speech. Thus this body of case law only provides a very indirect picture as to appropriate penalties.[80] In fact, in those cases in which the Committee on the Elimination of Racial Discrimination finds a violation of the ICERD

---

[73] It should be noted that the ultimate dismissal from his job was not reflected upon by the Committee as that part of Ross' complaint was deemed inadmissible for failure to exhaust domestic remedies. *Malcolm Ross* v. *Canada*, para. 10.3.

[74] It may be reiterated that this is not, strictly, an Art. 20(2) case since the Committee engages exclusively with Art. 19 and its limitations. Individual members do elaborate on Art. 20(2) in their separate opinions.

[75] *Faurisson* v. *France*, paras. 2.5 and 2.7.   [76] *Faurisson* v. *France*, para. 2.7.

[77] *Faurisson* v. *France*, paras. 9.6–9.7.   [78] *Faurisson* v. *France*, para. 9.3.

[79] *Faurisson* v. *France*, para. 9.3.

[80] In *Miroslav Lacko* v. *Slovak Republic*, CERD indirectly accepted a fine of SKK 5,000 (some EUR 165) for discriminating speech and acts against Roma people (the alternative for paying the fine was a prison term of three months). See *Miroslav Lacko* v. *Slovak Republic*, Communication no. 11/1998 (21 October 1998), para. 7.10.

attributable to the fact that the State party in question did not sufficiently investigate and combat alleged instances of incitement, the Committee typically does not indicate what could or should have been the penalty for the person responsible for the racist speech. Accordingly, in such cases as *L.K.* v. *Netherlands* (xenophobic speech against a Moroccan man),[81] *Gelle* v. *Denmark* (hateful remarks vis-à-vis Somalis),[82] *Adan* v. *Denmark* (facts similar to *Gelle*)[83] and *Er* v. *Denmark* (discrimination of Pakistanis),[84] the Committee found that the responding state failed to carry out its duties to instigate a full, diligent and prompt investigation into the extreme speech in question, yet it stopped short of indicating what type of penalties would have been appropriate. That is of course logical – finding that a full investigation was in order is not quite the same as finding that the person responsible for the impugned speech acts was guilty of racist hate speech or incitement in the meaning of Article 4 ICERD. Yet, also in the exceptional case law in which the Committee fully overrules the findings of the State party by holding that an acquitted hate speaker ought to have been convicted, it refrains from dictating what penalty would have been appropriate. Thus in *The Jewish Community of Oslo et al.* v. *Norway* it concludes that the leader of a neo-Nazi group should have been convicted over a speech in which he glorified Hitler, yet it stops short of indicating how this person should have been punished.[85] In this case Norway did indicate what penalties would have been available,[86] yet the Committee decided not to comment on this.[87]

The case of *Zentralrat Deutscher Sinti und Roma et al.* v. *Germany* – yet another case not brought by a convicted hate speaker but by alleged victims of racist speech – contains a remarkable *obiter dictum* on sanctions.[88] The case revolves around a letter, written by a high-ranking police

---

[81] CERD, *L.K.* v. *The Netherlands*, Communication No. 4/1991 (16 March 1993).

[82] CERD, *Mohammed Hassan Gelle* v. *Denmark*, Communication No. 34/2004 (6 March 2006).

[83] CERD, *Saada Mohamad Adan* v. *Denmark*, Communication no. 43/2008 (13 August 2010).

[84] CERD, *Murat Er* v. *Denmark*, Communication no. 40/2007 (8 August 2007).

[85] CERD, *The Jewish Community of Oslo et al.* v. *Norway*, Communication no. 30/2003 (15 August 2005).

[86] *Jewish Community of Oslo et al.* v. *Norway*, para. 2.5, indicating that the Norwegian Criminal Code stipulates fines or a prison sentence of up to two years for the offence of hate speech.

[87] CERD simply urges Norway to 'take measures to ensure that statements such as those made by Mr. Sjolie in the course of his speech are not protected by the right to freedom of speech under Norwegian law'. *Jewish Community of Oslo et al.* v. *Norway*, para. 12.

[88] CERD, *Zentralrat Deutscher Sinti und Roma et al.* v. *Germany*, Communication No. 38/2006 (22 February 2008).

detective, concerning the Sinti and Roma minorities in Germany, that was published in a police journal. The authors of the communication allege that the letter was an expression of racism on account of it attributing criminal behaviour to Sinti and Roma people. German authorities did not prosecute the author of the letter since its contents did not reach the high threshold for criminality under German incitement offences.[89] CERD accepted that position.[90] In finding no violation of Article 4 ICERD, the Committee added that 'the article in "The Criminalist" has carried consequences for its author, as disciplinary measures were taken against him'.[91] Indeed, the facts of the case show that the police officer had been suspended.[92] Now there are two ways to interpret this remark. First, this was a mere afterthought. The facts of the case did not engage Article 4, hence the decision not to instigate criminal proceedings against the author of the letter were immaterial. Then the fact that the author was nonetheless reprimanded was appreciated by the Committee as a sign of good faith on the part of Germany, showing that it takes the fight against racism within the police force seriously. An alternative reading is as follows: the letter did engage Article 4 and Germany showed that it took appropriate actions. While not instigating criminal proceedings, it applied sanctions, namely in the form of a suspension. Thus Article 4 was not breached precisely because of the fact that the German authorities discharged the punitive obligations flowing from this provision. If the latter reading holds true, then, in retrospect, *Zentralrat Deutscher Sinti und Roma et al. v. Germany* can be seen as paving the way towards the Committee's later announcement that criminal penalties should be reserved for the most serious of extreme speech cases.[93]

13.4.3 The European Court of Human Rights on proportionate sanctions

Generally speaking, the Strasbourg Court tends to more closely scrutinize the nature and gravity of the imposed penalty than do its international counterparts.[94] While the European Convention on Human Rights does not decree extreme speech restrictions, the latter may be compatible with

---

[89] *Zentralrat Deutscher Sinti und Roma et al. v. Germany*, para. 4.5.
[90] *Zentralrat Deutscher Sinti und Roma et al. v. Germany*, para. 7.7.
[91] *Zentralrat Deutscher Sinti und Roma et al. v. Germany*, para. 7.7.
[92] *Zentralrat Deutscher Sinti und Roma et al. v. Germany*, para. 2.3 (as dwelt upon by Germany at para. 4.5).
[93] CERD, *General Recommendation 35*, para. 12.
[94] See also Weber, *Manual on Hate Speech*, 43–6.

the Convention if deemed necessary to protect the rights of others. As part of the latter test, the European Court of Human Rights often – yet not always nor, as we will see below, always sufficiently – inquires into the proportionality of the penalty imposed on the hate speaker.

13.4.3.1   Prison terms

It has already been indicated that for the European Court of Human Rights, generally speaking, prison sentences could be acceptable penalties in cases of extreme speech.[95] Let us now address the question as to how the Court assesses the proportionality of that type of severe sanction in specific cases.

In Article 17-driven admissibility decisions the Strasbourg Court hardly ever pays sufficient attention to the severity of the penalty. Thus in the early racist speech case of *Glimmerveen* v. *the Netherlands*, the former European Commission of Human Rights endorsed a relatively short prison term of two weeks, but at no point considered the fact that a prison sentence is a heavy penalty for a 'speech offence'.[96] Since Glimmerveen – by virtue of Article 17 – could not rely on his freedom of expression in the first place, a proportionality test was apparently held to be superfluous.

The decision in *Hans Jorg Schimanek* v. *Austria* is another case in point.[97] The European Court of Human Rights sanctioned a prison sentence of no less than eight years. In fact, a lower court had initially sentenced him to fifteen years' imprisonment for carrying out activities contrary to the National Socialism Prohibition Act, but the Austrian Supreme Court found mitigating circumstances such as the fact that he had confessed and had renounced the incriminated activities.[98] Thus, whilst a fifteen-year prison term 'appeared disproportionate' according to the Supreme Court, eight years' imprisonment was deemed 'commensurate to the applicant's guilt'.[99] Clearly the Austrian Government should have been probed more on the proportionality of this long prison

---

[95] See section 13.2 of this chapter. In fact, even in plain blasphemy cases (suspended) prison sentences have been accepted. See, e.g. European Commission of Human Rights, *X. Ltd. and Y.* v. *United Kingdom*, Application no. 8710/79 (7 May 1982), sanctioning a fine of GBP 1,000 imposed on the publisher of *Gay News* and a fine of GBP 500 and a suspended prison sentence of nine months imposed on the editor responsible for publishing the blasphemous poem. Blasphemy bans are objectionable in general; sanctioning these penalties was frankly absurd.

[96] *Glimmerveen and Hagenbeek* v. *The Netherlands*.

[97] *Hans Jorg Schimanek* v. *Austria*.

[98] *Hans Jorg Schimanek* v. *Austria*, 'The Facts'.

[99] *Hans Jorg Schimanek* v. *Austria*, 'The Facts'.

sentence, yet the Article 17-based marginal assessment by the Strasbourg Court prevented that from happening.

Holocaust denier Roger Garaudy received five suspended prison sentences, ranging from three months to three years.[100] As the Paris Court of Appeal ordered the suspended sentences to run concurrently,[101] they boil down to a three years' suspended prison term. The Government of France submitted that the imposed sentences were fully proportionate.[102] The Strasbourg Court omitted – once more significantly fuelled by Article 17 – checking the proportionality of the penalties imposed.[103] This body of case law illustrates perfectly the shortcoming of the Article 17 ('guillotine') approach – basic safeguards, notably necessity and proportionality, flowing from the second paragraph of Article 10 on possible restrictions of freedom of expression, are undermined.[104]

In extreme speech cases wherein Article 10 complaints are wholly discussed on the merits, the Strasbourg Court's assessment of the imposed sentence's proportionality tends to be somewhat more meticulous. Accordingly, in *Zana v. Turkey* the Court addressed at length why Turkey's interference with this mayor's pro-PKK speech was answering to a pressing social need.[105] This included an assessment of whether the

---

[100] *Garaudy* v. *France*. These sentences were on top of heavy fines and damages payable to civil parties.

[101] The yet to be discussed fines, however, were ordered to be cumulative, thus amounting to some EUR 25,000.

[102] *Garaudy* v. *France*, 'The Law'.

[103] It should be noted that the Court does say something about the imposed penalties under the heading of the fair trial complaint (Garaudy had questioned the fact that he had received five separate sentences rather than one flowing from a joint case). This section of the judgment reads: 'Lastly, regarding the penalties, the Court notes that the Court of Appeal decided of its own motion to order the prison sentences to run concurrently and that the total length did not exceed the statutory maximum custodial sentence imposable for the most serious offence had the five cases been joined. As regards the fines, although they were not subsumed within the largest individual amount, it should be pointed out that the aggregate amount of the fines imposed in the five cases was FRF 170,000, which was far less than the statutory maximum fine imposable for the most serious offence (FRF 300,000).' Obviously, the fact that the imposed sentence under national law could have been even higher tells us little about the proportionality of the sentence from the perspective of freedom of expression.

[104] See also *Hans-Jürgen Witzsch* v. *Germany* [I] and *Hans-Jürgen Witzsch* v. *Germany* [II]. In these cases the Court sanctioned prison sentences of four months and three months respectively. In deciding on these sentences, on both occasions the German judiciary took into account the fact that Witzsch had been convicted previously for similar negationist offences. In both decisions by the European Court of Human Rights, Art. 17 stands in the way of a thorough assessment of the proportionality of these sentences.

[105] *Zana* v. *Turkey*, paras. 52–61.

sentence imposed, a prison term of one year, was proportionate to the aims pursued – maintaining national security and public safety. Here the Court seemed to imply that the same reasons that substantiated a pressing social need can reasonably be regarded as proof of proportionality.[106] While there is something to be said for this, it amounts to a fairly abstract proportionality test. Notably, such a test does not scrutinize whether less interfering measures were imaginable at the material time. Furthermore, the Strasbourg Court placed great emphasis on the fact that the applicant ultimately served only one-fifth of his sentence.[107] This seems quite beside the point – if suspended prison sentences and fines can have a chilling effect, then, surely, partly served prison sentences do too.

In some cases the imposed prison sentence is the turning point towards finding a breach of the Convention. For instance, in *Arslan v. Turkey* the Strasbourg Court went out of its way to note that the socio-political context in which the Kurdish separatist speech act occurred made for a precarious situation from the perspective of the Turkish Government.[108] While the Court expressed its doubts as to whether the impugned speech act amounted to incitement,[109] the final blow to the responding state's pleadings came in the form of considerations as to the proportionality of the penalty imposed on Arslan. The Strasbourg Court concluded that it:

> is struck by the severity of the penalty imposed on the applicant – particularly the fact that he was sentenced to one year and eight months' imprisonment – and the persistence of the prosecution's efforts to secure his conviction ... The Court notes in that connection that the nature and severity of the penalties imposed are also factors to be taken into account when assessing whether the interference was proportionate ... In conclusion, Mr Arslan's conviction was disproportionate to the aims pursued and accordingly not 'necessary in a democratic society'. There has therefore been a violation of Article 10 of the Convention.[110]

---

[106] *Zana* v. *Turkey*, paras. 61–62.   [107] *Zana* v. *Turkey*, para. 61.

[108] European Court of Human Rights, *Arslan* v. *Turkey*, Application no. 23462/94 (Grand Chamber Judgment of 8 July 1999), para. 47, noting 'the background to the cases submitted to it, particularly problems linked to the prevention of terrorism ... On that point, it takes note of the Turkish authorities' concern about the dissemination of views which they consider might exacerbate the serious disturbances that have been going on in Turkey for some fifteen years ... In that connection, it should be noted that the second edition of the book was published shortly after the Gulf War, at a time when, fleeing repression in Iraq, a large number of people of Kurdish origin were thronging at the Turkish border.'

[109] *Arslan* v. *Turkey*, para. 48.   [110] *Arslan* v. *Turkey*, paras. 49–50.

Similarly, in *Incal* v. *Turkey*, *Karataş* v. *Turkey* and *Erbakan* v. *Turkey* the imposed prison sentences importantly tip the balance in favour of finding a violation of freedom of expression. In *Incal* v. *Turkey* the Court found fault with a sentence of six months and twenty days' imprisonment, imposed on top of the censorship and seizure of the pro-Kurdish leaflets (called a 'radical' interference by the Court),[111] a heavy fine and a host of other penalties.[112] In *Karataş* v. *Turkey* the Court was 'struck by the severity of the penalty imposed on the applicant – particularly the fact that he was sentenced to more than thirteen months' imprisonment – and the persistence of the prosecution's efforts to secure his conviction'.[113] In *Erbakan* v. *Turkey* the Court reasoned that a prison sentence imposed on a politician, here the chairman of Refah Partisi, in itself has a strong chilling effect (*un effet dissuasif*).[114]

Furthermore, there are cases wherein the Court briefly criticizes the severity of the penalty applied by way of *obiter dictum*. In such cases the Court does not enter into much detail on the question of penalties since it has already found a violation, for example stemming from the lack of a legitimate aim or for failing to pass the necessity test per se. Accordingly, in *Gündüz* v. *Turkey*,[115] revolving around criticism expressed on the subject of secularism and Kemalism by a leader of an Islamic group, the two-year prison sentence imposed on the applicant following a conviction for religious hate speech was deemed 'an extremely harsh penalty'.[116] Interestingly, the harshness of the penalty resurfaces once more in this judgment, namely when it comes to establishing what just satisfaction must be afforded by Turkey to Gündüz. In the light of the hardship endured, the latter was awarded a sum of EUR 5,000.[117] Similarly, in

---

[111] European Court of Human Rights, *Incal* v. *Turkey*, Application no. 41/1997/825/1031 (Grand Chamber judgment of 9 June 1998), para. 56, further noting that '[i]ts preventive aspect by itself raises problems under Article 10'.

[112] *Incal* v. *Turkey*, para. 57. The fine amounted to 55,555 Turkish liras (some EUR 25,000). Moreover, he was barred from driving for fifteen days (see para. 16) as well as 'debarred from the civil service and forbidden to take part in a number of activities within political organisations, associations or trade unions' (paras. 56 and 22).

[113] European Court of Human Rights, *Karataş* v. *Turkey*, Application no. 23168/94 (Grand Chamber judgment of 8 July 1999), para. 51. See also Weber, *Manual on Hate Speech*, at 44.

[114] European Court of Human Rights, *Erbakan* v. *Turkey*, Application no. 59405/00 (6 July 2006), para. 69. See also Weber, *Manual on Hate Speech*, at 44.

[115] European Court of Human Rights, *Gündüz* v. *Turkey*, Application no. 35071/97 (4 December 2003).

[116] *Gündüz* v. *Turkey*, para. 52.

[117] *Gündüz* v. *Turkey*, para. 57. The latter is criticized by dissenting Judge Türmen. While he makes clear why in his view the impugned speech acts were more hateful than his

Güzel v. *Turkey (No. 2)*, revolving around a speech on political, social and human rights issues in Turkey given by the chairman of the Renaissance Party, the Strasbourg Court fundamentally disagreed with Turkey as how to appreciate the facts – according to the Court no extreme speech whatsoever could be discerned.[118] Moreover, the sentence of one year's imprisonment was deemed too severe.[119] The fact that that sentence was ultimately suspended by Turkish authorities had, in the view of the Court, the undesirable effect of de facto censoring Güzel's activities for the period of the suspension.[120]

13.4.3.2   Fines

The European Court of Human Rights has on numerous occasions accepted fines as proportionate penalties for speech offences.[121] For instance, moderate to heavy fines have been accepted in Holocaust denial cases, for example in *Marais* v. *France* (FRF 10,000, some EUR 1,500),[122] *Hennicke* v. *Germany* (DEM 6,000, some EUR 3,000)[123] and *Garaudy* v. *France* (the aggregate fine amounted to FRF 170,000, some EUR 25,000).[124] Again, since these are largely Article 17-type admissibility cases the proportionality of the fine is never properly assessed.

---

colleagues were prepared to accept, at no point in his opinion does he take stock of the extremely severe penalty imposed by Turkey. See Dissenting Opinion of Judge Türmen.

[118] European Court of Human Rights, *Güzel* v. *Turkey (No. 2)*, Application no. 65849/01 (27 July 2006), para. 26.

[119] *Güzel* v. *Turkey (No. 2)*, para. 28.   [120] *Güzel* v. *Turkey (No. 2)*, para. 28.

[121] Again, even in cases concerning plain blasphemy criminal penalties, including prison sentences, but also fines have been endorsed by the Strasbourg Court. Thus in *İ.A.* v. *Turkey* the Court accepted a fine of Turkish lira 3,291,000, calling this penalty 'insignificant' (para. 32), thereby completely ignoring the chilling effect such blasphemy laws may have on protected speech. This is a 'symbolic' fine only in the sense that it shows that the blasphemy law concerned is very much alive. Similarly, in *X. Ltd. and Y.* v. *United Kingdom* a GBP 1,000 fine imposed on the *Gay News* magazine and a GBP 500 fine on the responsible editor who published a blasphemous poem were permitted by the European Commission of Human Rights (on top of the previously mentioned suspended prison sentence imposed on the editor). For an extensive assessment by the Court on the appropriate height of libel or defamation awards, see the case of *Tolstoy Miloslavsky* v. *United Kingdom*, Application no. 18139/91 (13 July 1995).

[122] European Commission of Human Rights, *Marais* v. *France*, Application no. 31159/96 (admissibility decision of 24 June 1996).

[123] *Karl-August Hennicke* v. *Germany*.

[124] *Garaudy* v. *France*. This fine is imposed on top of the previously discussed three years' suspended prison sentence and damages (FFR 220,021, some EUR 33,000) payable to civil parties.

In incitement cases, too, the Strasbourg Court has sanctioned fines. Le Pen was ordered to pay a EUR 10,000 fine as a result of his anti-Semitic slurring.[125] The Court's marginal assessment of the proportionality thereof is not convincing. It said – in so many words – that considering the fact that under France law he was liable to imprisonment, he should count himself lucky that he received merely a fine.[126] Similarly, in *Soulas and others* v. *France* the Court deemed the EUR 7,500 fine, in combination with symbolic damages to be paid to civil parties (two French anti-racism organizations), on the heavy side; however, since the applicants might have been imprisoned over their anti-immigration publication, the Court reasoned, the fine must be considered proportionate.[127]

At other times the Court has expressly deemed certain fines to be 'modest' and therefore proportionate. Thus in *Leroy* v. *France* a EUR 1,500 fine imposed on the person responsible for a cartoon glorifying the 9/11 attacks was considered to be modest.[128] Similarly, in *Sürek* v. *Turkey (No. 1)* the Court accepted a fine of TRL 83,333,333 (some EUR 30).[129] Calling the latter 'a relatively modest fine' is in fact in shrill contrast to Turkish law, which labelled this a 'heavy fine' at the material time.[130]

A more principled approach on the part of the Court can be found in the case of *Giniewski* v. *France*. Giniewski had been convicted of the offence of 'publicly defaming a group of persons on the ground of membership of a religion', in this case Christians, the result of an article he had written alleging a causal link between Catholic doctrine, European anti-Semitism and the Holocaust. While his criminal conviction was later quashed, a civil damages claim – brought by an association named the General Alliance against Racism and for Respect for the French and Christian Identity – was granted (1 French Franc) and enforced. Giniewski furthermore was ordered to publicize this verdict at his own expense in a national newspaper. This time the Court held that these

---

[125] *Le Pen* v. *France*, 'The Facts'.

[126] *Le Pen* v. *France*, 'The Law' ('En outre, et même en tenant compte de l'importance du montant de l'amende mise à la charge du requérant, étant précisé toutefois qu'il encourait en principe une peine d'emprisonnement, cette condamnation ne saurait être regardée comme disproportionnée dans les circonstances de l'espèce').

[127] *Soulas and others* v. *France*, para. 46.

[128] *Leroy* v. *France*, para. 47 ('une amende modérée').

[129] *Sürek* v. *Turkey (No. 1)*, para. 64.

[130] Art. 19 of the Criminal Code of Turkey 2004 reads as follows: 'The term "heavy fine" shall mean payment to the Treasury of from twenty thousand to one hundred million Turkish liras.' Note that the Turkish lira is now obsolete.

penalties were disproportionate, precisely because of the chilling effect they may have.[131]

Similarly in *Aydın Tatlav v. Turkey*, concerning the conviction of an author of a book heavily criticizing the role and function of religion in society (namely as a false 'legitimizer' of social injustice), the Strasbourg Court held that even though the Turkish judiciary had reduced the initially imposed prison sentence to merely a minor fine, the extreme speech conviction nevertheless breached Article 10.[132] Tatlav was fined TRL 2,640,000, which amounted to about EUR 10 at that time.[133] In this case the Strasbourg Court said what it should have said in the host of other 'religious insult' cases,[134] namely that such convictions, fines and other interferences show that blasphemy laws apparently are very much alive, something that may of course very well deter opinionated authors and publishers to publish opinions that are not conforming to the dominant religious mores.[135] The Court furthermore pointed out that the Turkish religious insult laws hinder pluralism.[136]

In sum, the Court quite selectively emphasizes or, conversely, minimizes the deterrent impact of fines. Whenever the Court is inclined to accept the overall necessity of the interference, it tends to sign off on the fine imposed too. Whenever, conversely, the Court already has major reservations about an interference with free speech, the severity of the fine tends to be mobilized as yet another pertinent reason to find in favour of a violation. While dutifully reiterating in most cases that the nature and severity of the penalties imposed are factors to be taken into account, the upshot of this is that in only a few cases the severity of the penalty is truly decisive.

13.4.3.3   Seizures and confiscations, including prior restraint

The European Court of Human Rights has sanctioned, in addition to prison terms and fines, a range of other restrictions of freedom of

---

[131] European Court of Human Rights, *Giniewski v. France*, Application no. 64016/00 (31 January 2006), para. 55.

[132] European Court of Human Rights, *Aydın Tatlav v. Turkey*, Application no. 50692/99 (2 May 2006).

[133] *Aydın Tatlav v. Turkey*, para. 14.

[134] This would have been in order in such cases as *X. Ltd. and Y. v. United Kingdom*; *Otto-Preminger-Institut v. Austria*; *Wingrove v. United Kingdom*, Application no. 17419/90 (25 November 1996); *Murphy v. Ireland*, Application no. 44179/98 (10 July 2003); and *İ.A. v. Turkey*.

[135] *Aydın Tatlav v. Turkey*, para. 30.   [136] *Aydın Tatlav v. Turkey*, para. 30.

expression, including seizures, confiscations and forfeitures. Occasionally, such seizure or forfeiture orders amounted to actual prior restraint. Far-reaching – if not draconian – though such *ex ante* bans are, they have been permitted by the Court.[137]

---

[137] These far-reaching measures have been sanctioned by the Strasbourg Court in its questionable jurisprudence on blasphemy bans. In *I.A.* v. *Turkey* the Strasbourg Court emphasized, in the context of a discussion of the proportionality of a fine imposed on the author of an allegedly blasphemous book, that it was 'mindful of the fact that the domestic courts did not decide to seize the book', thus finding the interference (a fine imposed on the author) proportionate (para. 32). It would hence be tempting to reason *a contrario* that seizures of blasphemous publications are a bridge too far. However, the Court has time and again sanctioned seizures and forfeitures of such materials. Notably, the film *Das Liebeskonzil* was both seized and forfeited by Austrian authorities in the case of *Otto-Preminger-Institut* v. *Austria*. This happened at the request of a diocese of the Roman Catholic Church (para. 11). Since accordingly none of the six planned screenings could take place, the measures imposed amounted to a total ban on the film. Such acts of prior restraint – that is preventing a speech act from being expressed or disseminated altogether – are clearly among the most severe free speech restrictions imaginable. Nevertheless, in *Otto-Preminger* the European Court of Human Rights in a split six-to-three decision held that neither the seizure nor the forfeiture was disproportionate and hence no violation of Art. 10 was established. It is, however, blatantly clear that the measures imposed were anything but proportionate. What is more, the cinema concerned had proposed, and in fact implemented, a range of less interfering measures to accommodate concerns over the film's content (para. 10). These measures included warnings about the film's potential to offend religious sensitivities and special regulations to ensure that young persons (those under 17) were barred from the screenings. As the dissenting judges (see Joint Dissenting Opinion of Judges Palm, Pekkanen and Makarczyk, para. 9) rightly observe, this made the screening of *Das Liebeskonzil* different from the sexually explicit art exhibition in *Müller and others* v. *Switzerland*, Application no. 10737/84 (24 May 1988). (That being said, the confiscation of the paintings in the latter case – for nearly eight years – should be severely criticized for being disproportionate too.) The refusal to issue a licence for the video work entitled *Visions of Ecstasy* (blending religious and erotic motifs), at the heart of *Wingrove* v. *United Kingdom*, also effectively amounted to prior censorship. Again the applicant had in fact proposed ways to prevent the video from being watched by persons beyond the desired audience. For instance, in accordance with the Video Recordings Act 1984 its distribution could have been limited to licensed sex shops only (para. 23). The Strasbourg Court did not accept this (para. 63). Yet the UK certainly should have been probed on the question as to why it decided not to grant such a limited licence but instead went as far as to ban the film, in the words of dissenting Judge De Meyer, 'absolutely ab initio' (Dissenting Opinion of Judge De Meyer, para. 3). Dissenting Judge Lohmus, moreover, stated that prior restraint measures are 'based on the opinion of the authorities that they understand correctly the feelings they claim to protect. The actual opinion of believers remains unknown. I think that this is why we cannot conclude that the interference corresponded to a "pressing social need"' (Dissenting Opinion of Judge Lohmus, para. 3). Yet another example of prior restraint sanctioned by the Strasbourg Court is the case of *Murphy* v. *Ireland*, concerning religious advertising.

At other times, the fact that the impugned publication was seized or confiscated tipped the balance in favour of finding that the interference with free speech was disproportionate. Thus, in finding that the measures imposed on the applicants in the case of *Sürek and Özdemir v. Turkey* were disproportionate, the Strasbourg Court stressed, among other things, that 'the copies of the reviews in which the impugned publications appeared were seized by the authorities'.[138]

Ex post seizure and confiscation orders have furthermore been permitted in cases of Holocaust denial. In *Udo Walendy v. Germany* the seizure of a periodical with the title *Historische Taisachen* (Historical Facts) was ordered by a court.[139] The applicant, editor of the periodical, had written an editorial on the testimony he had given at the trial of fellow Holocaust denier Ernst Zündel,[140] the protagonist in many international and domestic Holocaust denial cases.[141] By narrating his oversees adventures Walendy effortlessly committed the same crime Zündel was accused of – negationism. While at the time of the seizure of the periodical the outcome of his criminal trial was in fact still pending, the necessity of the former measure was accepted by the European Commission of Human Rights (the German authorities had reasoned that it was very likely that Walendy would be convicted).[142]

13.4.3.4   Dismissals and alternative penalties

In *Seurot v. France* the contract of the schoolteacher who had, (ab)using the school bulletin, spread hatred against North Africans was terminated.[143] This was sanctioned as being proportionate by the Strasbourg Court, putting emphasis on the influential position of the hate speaker.[144] This is very much in the style of *Malcolm Ross v. Canada*, in which case

---

[138] European Court of Human Rights, *Sürek and Özdemir v. Turkey*, Application nos. 23927/94 and 24277/94 (Grand Chamber judgment of 8 July 1999), para. 62.

[139] *Walendy v. Germany*, 'The Facts'.

[140] *Walendy v. Germany*, 'The Facts', referring to the latter as 'E.Z.'

[141] E.g. Human Rights Committee, *Ernst Zündel v. Canada* [I], Communication no. 953/2000 (admissibility decision of 27 July 2003); *Ernst Zündel v. Canada* [II], Communication no. 1341/2005 (admissibility decision of 20 March 2007); and Regional Court of Mannheim, *Zündel* judgment (14 February 2007).

[142] *Walendy v. Germany*, 'The Facts' and 'The Law'.

[143] European Court of Human Rights, *Jacques Seurot v. France*, Application no. 57383/00 (admissibility decision of 18 May 2004). Note that Seurot was also criminally prosecuted.

[144] *Jacques Seurot v. France*, section 'The Law' ('Concernant plus spécialement les enseignants, ceux-ci étant symbole d'autorité pour ses élèves dans le domaine de l'éducation, les devoirs et responsabilités particuliers qui leur incombent valent aussi dans une certaine mesure pour leurs activités en dehors de l'école'). See also, *mutatis mutandis*, *Vogt v. Germany*, Application no. 17851/91 (Grand Chamber judgment of 26 September

the UN Human Rights Committee permitted the firing of a schoolteacher for similar reasons.[145]

The Strasbourg Court has furthermore sanctioned an extreme speech verdict sentencing a xenophobic Belgian politician to 250 hours of community work – aptly in the area of integration of foreign nationals – and to a symbolic fine. Moreover, he was stripped of his right to stand for election for a period of no less than ten years.[146] While the Court uncritically glances over the question of proportionality,[147] the dissenting judges in this case of *Féret* v. *Belgium* found the latter political excommunication rather too harsh.[148]

Finally, in the case of *Lehideux and Isorni* v. *France*, concerning convictions for 'publicly defending the crime of collaboration', the Strasbourg Court contemplated in a general fashion the merits of 'civil remedies' as opposed to criminal sanctions.[149] The Court found a criminal conviction unwarranted since Lehideux and Isorni had not explicitly denied Nazi crimes, nor had they expressly incited violence or discrimination. The Court seemed to suggest that if only civil damages had been awarded – the two applicants, in addition to their criminal conviction were ordered to pay 1 French Franc to French organizations of members of the resistance[150] – the applicants' penalty would have been proportionate. That approach raises questions, though. It would rather seem that if no speech offence – that is, one that is sanctioned by international law – can be proven, then no sanctions whatsoever should be imposed, be it criminal or civil ones. After all, civil damage awards may also have a chilling effect on free speech, as the Court itself has indicated.[151]

1995), para. 60, on the special duties and obligations of teachers who may not indoctrinate their pupils (the Court, however, found that Vogt's dismissal amounted to a violation since it was not sufficiently proven by Germany that her membership of the Communist Party adversely impacted her teaching tasks).

[145] *Malcolm Ross* v. *Canada*. The Human Rights Committee dwelt more extensively on the proportionality of this restriction (paras. 11.5–11.6) than does the Strasbourg Court.

[146] European Court of Human Rights, *Féret* v. *Belgium*, Application no. 15615/07 (16 July 2009), para. 34.

[147] *Féret* v. *Belgium*, para. 80.

[148] Dissenting Opinion of Judge Sajó, joined by Judges Zagrebelsky and Tsotsoria.

[149] *Lehideux and Isorni* v. *France*, paras. 51 ('the State could have used means other than a criminal penalty') and 57 ('the Court notes the seriousness of a criminal conviction for publicly defending the crimes of collaboration, having regard to the existence of other means of intervention and rebuttal, particularly through civil remedies').

[150] *Lehideux and Isorni* v. *France*, para. 21.

[151] *Giniewski* v. *France*, in which case the applicant was also ordered to pay FRF 1 to civil parties, something that was not accepted by the Court (para. 55).

13.4.3.5   Remedies for wrongful hate speech convictions

The flip-side of the present debate is expressed in the question as to how a person wrongfully convicted of extreme speech must be remedied. However, no coherent patterns can be distilled from the Court's case law.

For example, in their respective cases Jersild, Castells and Giniewski did not receive non-pecuniary damages awards,[152] while Arslan, Incal and Zana received modest awards. More specifically, in *Arslan* v. *Turkey*, ordering FRF 30,000 (some EUR 4,500) to be paid by Turkey towards non-pecuniary damages, the Court reasoned that 'the applicant must have suffered distress on account of the facts of the case'.[153] Incal received the same in the light of 'a certain amount of distress' he must have suffered due to the facts of the case,[154] while Zana received slightly more – FRF 40,000 (some EUR 6,000).[155] In the latter case the Court stated that the mere finding of a violation could not in itself compensate him, but did not dwell more on the question why this was a just award.

Typically, if applicants do receive awards at all, they get a mere fraction of what they themselves had suggested. Thus, Gündüz received 1 per cent of his EUR 500,000 claim. The Strasbourg Court, although emphasizing that the imposed penalty – a two-year prison sentence – 'was extremely harsh',[156] made its own assessment 'on an equitable basis' (amounting to EUR 5,000).[157] Similarly, Klein – wrongfully convicted for defaming an archbishop – claimed non-pecuniary damages to the tune of EUR 90,000,

---

[152] European Court of Human Rights, *Jersild* v. *Denmark*, Application no. 15890/89 (Grand Chamber judgment of 23 September 1994). He had requested 20,000 kroner in compensation, yet the Court held that the finding of a violation in itself amounted to sufficient just satisfaction (paras. 42–43). *Castells* v. *Spain*, Application no. 11798/85 (23 April 1992), para. 56. In *Giniewski* v. *France* the applicant had in fact not submitted any claim for just satisfaction. See also, *mutatis mutandis*, *Vereinigung Bildender Künstler* v. *Austria*, Application no. 68354/01 (25 January 2007), paras. 42 and 44; and *Albert-Engelmann-Gesellschaft mbH* v. *Austria*, Application no. 46389/99 (19 January 2006), para. 38. The latter two cases concern wrongful free speech interferences, though not strictly extreme speech convictions. The bottom line in any event was that awards were requested by the applicants but not granted by the Court.

[153] European Court of Human Rights, *Arslan* v. *Turkey*, Application no. 23462/94 (Grand Chamber Judgment of 8 July 1999), paras. 59–61. Arslan had requested FRF 100,000.

[154] European Court of Human Rights, *Incal* v. *Turkey*, Application no. 41/1997/825/1031 (Grand Chamber judgment of 9 June 1998), para. 82.

[155] European Court of Human Rights, *Zana* v. *Turkey*, Application no. 69/1996/6888/880 (Grand Chamber judgment of 25 November 1997), para. 40.

[156] European Court of Human Rights, *Gündüz* v. *Turkey*, Application no. 35071/97 (4 December 2003), para. 57.

[157] *Gündüz* v. *Turkey*, para. 57.

contending 'he had suffered stress as a result of his prosecution, that he had experienced difficulties in finding suitable employment following his conviction and that his social status had been harmed. As a result, he suffered from bouts of depression, insomnia, hypoactivity and anxiety and he had to consult a professional psychiatrist.'[158] The Court awarded him EUR 6,000 in respect of non-pecuniary damage to be paid by Slovakia.[159]

13.5 Concluding remarks

International monitoring bodies' reflection on appropriate sanctions for extreme speech offences in general and on the proportionality of sanctions meted out in domestic cases is for the time being somewhat of a mishmash. Most urgently, firm pronouncements on whether incitement offences could ever justify prison sentences and prior restraint are in order. It would rather appear that in relation to speech offences those are excessive measures in and for themselves. The workings of the Human Rights Committee do not justify these measures, although this body could take a more outspoken stance against harsh penalties in general,[160] while in its case law on domestic extreme speech convictions it could more meticulously check the proportionality of the sanctions imposed.

Specifically on prior censorship, the impossibility thereof under Article 20 has repeatedly been suggested in the literature.[161] Furthermore, three Special Rapporteurs and independent experts have endorsed incitement laws as long as 'no one [shall] be subject to prior censorship'.[162] Conversely, the Strasbourg Court – although paying lip-service to the dangers of *ex ante* banning of

---

[158] European Court of Human Rights, *Klein* v. *Slovakia*, Application no. 72208/01 (31 October 2006), para. 57 (pecuniary damage was claimed in addition).

[159] *Klein* v. *Slovakia*, para. 59.

[160] The Committee (*General Comment 34*, paras. 13 and 20) has more generally confirmed that Art. 19 precludes censorship in relation to press and media freedom.

[161] E.g. Agnes Callamard, 'Conference Paper #2' (paper presented at the Expert seminar on 'Freedom of expression and advocacy of religious hatred that constitutes incitement to discrimination, hostility or violence – the links between Articles 19 and 20 of the International Covenant on Civil and Political Rights', organized by the Office of United Nations High Commissioner for Human Rights, 2–3 October 2008, Geneva, Switzerland), at 24, arguing that 'prior censorship should not be used as a tool against hate speech'. See also Nowak, *CCPR Commentary*, at 474 and 457–8.

[162] *Joint Statement on Racism and the Media by the UN Special Rapporteur on Freedom of Opinion and Expression, the OSCE Representative on Freedom of the Media and the OAS Special Rapporteur on Freedom of Expression* (London, 27 February 2001), at 'Civil, Criminal and Administrative Law Measures'.

the expression of certain ideas[163] – interprets the European Convention on Human Rights as not categorically excluding prior restraints.[164] Other regional human rights conventions, notably the American Convention on Human Rights, are far more outspoken against the possibility of censorship. The freedom of expression article therein is expressly declared not to be 'subject to prior censorship' but only to 'subsequent imposition of liability'.[165] The Strasbourg Court would be well advised to interpret the European Convention on Human Rights in that same spirit.

---

[163] E.g. European Court of Human Rights, *Observer and Guardian* v. *United Kingdom*, Application no. 13585/88 (Grand Chamber judgment of 26 November 1991), para. 60: 'the dangers inherent in prior restraints are such that they call for the most careful scrutiny on the part of the Court. This is especially so as far as the press is concerned, for news is a perishable commodity and to delay its publication, even for a short period, may well deprive it of all its value and interest.' For the dissenting judges these dangers inherent in prior restraint mean that prior restraint ought to be rejected altogether. See Partly Dissenting Opinion Concerning Prior Restraint of Judge De Meyer, joined by Judges Pettiti, Russo, Foighel and Bigi.

[164] In addition to the cases discussed in this chapter so far, see also, e.g., *Observer and Guardian* v. *The United Kingdom*, para. 60; and, *mutatis mutandis*, *The Sunday Times* v. *United Kingdom*, Application no. 6538/74 (Plenary Court judgment of 26 April 1979); and *Markt Intern Verlag GmbH and Klaus Beermann* v. *Federal Republic of Germany*, Application no. 10572/83 (20 November 1989).

[165] American Convention on Human Rights 1969, Art. 13(2). See, however, Art. 13(4). For a discussion of whether this Convention's incitement clause – Art. 13(5) – permits prior censorship, see Michael Kearney, *The Prohibition of Propaganda for War in International Law* (Oxford University Press, 2007), at 175–83.

PART VI

Conclusion

14

Conclusion

By adopting Article 20(2) of the ICCPR the drafters of this Covenant did something unique. They adjudicated an abstract clash of fundamental rights and settled on an a priori balance. Accordingly, protection against violence and discrimination triumphed over absolute free speech. The *travaux préparatoires* pertaining to this article are a narrative of fear. A number of states dreaded future hate propaganda, condemning such abuse of free speech at the expense of vulnerable minorities. Other states were wary rather about the potential for abuse of anti-incitement legislation in the hands of illiberal or ill-disposed states. States were not completely unselfish in their interventions. Cold War dialectics were not eschewed in the drafting chambers.

That said, those historical discussions on the incitement provision do unveil a meaningful human rights debate – a controversy as pertinent now as it was sixty years ago. Should the state be able to take measures against a speech act that is purported to incite violence or discrimination against people on account of the latter's religion or other traits? In addition, for all the polemics around the drafting tables and the clear voting pattern – 'the West' largely rejecting the incitement clause, 'the rest' endorsing it – subsequent state practice tells a different story. First of all, only a handful of Western states took their reluctance or outright criticism so far as to enter an express reservation to Article 20(2) of the ICCPR. Second, numerous states, including Western ones, have incitement laws in place more or less corresponding to the Covenant's ground rules on incitement.

The fact that a separate article was reserved for a ban on incitement is legally relevant in many ways. For starters, the text of Article 20(2) ICCPR itself – in addition to the drafters' views, subsequent state practice and the opinion of the UN Human Rights Committee – suggests that the Covenant's incitement provision is mandatory. This means that State parties, unless they have made a reservation to the opposite effect, are required to enact legislation prohibiting any advocacy of hatred that constitutes incitement to discrimination, hostility or violence. Thus Article

20(2) is not yet another limitation ground – it imposes an autonomous and additional state duty upon parties to the Covenant.

Article 20(2) stands out inasmuch as this standard prescribes a prohibition instead of a fundamental right. Be that as it may, the Human Rights Committee has gradually derived from that standard a right to be free from or protected against incitement. For the time being that 'right' does not live the life of autonomous right that can be invoked by applicants against their state. It is mostly construed as a 'right of others', thus as a limiting factor with respect to the freedom of expression. Future case law may upgrade this right to a full-fledged legal entitlement, providing legal standing in cases in which State parties to the Covenant are alleged to have failed to uphold the protection offered by this standard.

If so, that would bring the Human Rights Committee in line with the judicial practice of the Committee on the Elimination of Racial Discrimination. The latter Committee offers more robust protection to the right to be free from racist incitement, protection inherent to Article 4 ICERD. From the outset CERD granted legal standing to persons who claim to be a victim of racist hate speech and who have not been protected by State parties. This Committee has derived far-reaching state obligations in this regard. States are to instigate a complete and proper criminal investigation into each incident that engages Article 4 ICERD. The Committee has gone so far as suggesting that states ought to have prosecuted certain cases and occasionally even that a State party ought to have convicted a racist hate speech offender. While these state obligations, combined with legal standing for incitement victims, are clear indications that CERD considers Article 4 to be at the heart of its mandate, protection for religious groups or individuals under that same article has proven to be burdensome. The Committee will only accept such cases where ethnicity and religion are clearly intersected. This apparent gap shows that Article 20(2) of the ICCPR is all the more important to the plight of victims of religion-based incitement to discrimination or violence.

The European Convention on Human Rights, by contrast, does not contain a provision expressly dealing with extreme speech. This has led to a somewhat unpredictable body of jurisprudence, wherein occasionally Article 17 on abuse of rights is mobilized to throw out complaints made by convicted hate speakers, while at other times those complaints are assessed on the merits, using the limitation methodology enshrined in Article 10(2) of the ECHR. As most of those extreme speech cases have been brought by convicted inciters and other extreme speech offenders,

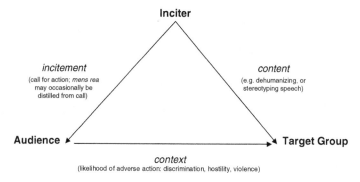

Figure 1   Triangle of incitement

the European Court of Human Rights has not elaborated extensively on the question of whether the Convention also provides standing to alleged incitement victims. Following the *Aksu* case, incitement victims may in the future successfully employ Article 8 on respect to private life as a legal weapon against hateful incitement.

In terms of the *actus reus* of the incitement offence within the meaning of Article 20(2) of the ICCPR, this offence distinguishes itself from other 'speech offences' by insisting on a triangular relationship; that is, incitement requires an inciter, an audience and a target group. Thus incitement is not first and foremost concerned with direct harm done by extremists to target groups. Incitement is much more preoccupied with contingent harm, that is the possibility of harm vis-à-vis the target group stemming from a third party – the extreme speech act's audience. Accordingly, while Article 20(2)'s constituent term 'hatred' relates to the nature and degree of enmity propagated by the inciter (e.g. the question to what extent he or she dehumanizes or stereotypes the target group), the key term 'incitement' really points to the question as to whether other persons are mobilized to commit acts of discrimination or violence against the target group.

The *actus reus* of the speech offence contained in Article 20(2) ICCPR is schematically summarized in Figure 1.

A large number of national incitement laws do not neatly transpose Article 20(2) of the ICCPR. The most worrying shortcoming can be perceived in those laws that ban 'hate speech' or 'incitement to hatred'. The ICCPR prohibits a highly qualified offence of advocacy of hatred that constitutes incitement to concrete contingent harms, notably 'incitement to violence' and 'incitement to discrimination'. Those 'hate speech' offences fall short of that, thus critically broadening the *actus reus* of the speech offence. The effect is that citizens are liable to be prosecuted for speech that should not be combated under international standards.

State parties to the ICCPR would do well to ensure that incitement laws and/or jurisprudence contain a strong focus on criminal intent. From Article 20(2) ICCPR a triple intent requirement can be distilled. First, this provision requires that the intent to 'advocate', that is to publicly disseminate hatred, be proven. Second, intent to target a group based on religion (or other traits such as ethnicity) must be proven. Third, in order to be convicted of incitement, a specific or oblique 'intent to incite' must be proven. At the moment, State practices vary widely on this issue. Free speech is unduly threatened by incitement laws that do not require criminal intent or those that require weak forms of *mens rea* such as 'negligence' or 'recklessness'.

While the content of a speech act and its author's intentions may go a long way in establishing that someone committed an extreme speech offence, the offence of incitement within the meaning of Article 20(2) of the ICCPR always requires an additional context-dependent risk assessment. The Covenant bans advocacy of religious hatred when and only when it constitutes incitement. The necessity test, which is integrally applicable to Article 20(2), moreover requires that incitement only result in criminal punishment if it was likely that harm would shortly – imminently – befall the speech act's target group. In order to make that determination we need, first of all, knowledge of the speech act's overall societal context. In particular, we need to establish the position of the target group in terms of its vulnerability, as evidenced by, for instance, recorded hate crimes and discrimination monitors. Further, we need to establish the speech act's directly surrounding circumstances, such as the position, role and status of the speaker, the extent or reach of the speech, the composition of his or her audience, and suchlike. This information, together with the speech act's content (possibly containing e.g. fighting words, or acts of stereotyping or dehumanization) and its tone (possibly being inflammable) as well as the speaker's intent, will provide a fuller picture of the risk emanating from the hateful speech. The Human Rights Committee has engaged with contextual elements in some of its jurisprudence. Future case law will show if it intends to meticulously implement and further conceptualize the Rabat Plan of Action's useful focus on context. The European Court of Human Rights is on paper committed to a context-based risk assessment, yet all too often it uncritically accepts that harm may flow from defamatory or shocking speech acts.

Whereas the European Court of Human Rights expressly accepts (and CERD does so by implication) restrictions on negationism, the UN Human Rights Committee no longer permits such forms of content-discrimination. The latter approach is to be preferred. Narrowly tailored incitement legislation does more justice to contextual elements surrounding extreme speech acts. It is only on that basis that a proper risk assessment of extreme speech can be made, mapping the harm that is likely to flow from such speech. Many generic memory laws are not responsive to such contextual considerations, thus threatening speech that ought to be protected under international free speech standards. The offence of glorification of past or ongoing acts of terrorism or religious, national or ethnic violence, as codified by some countries, is also oftentimes overly preoccupied with the egregious content of such speech. While the public order issues emanating from such extreme speech may seem evident in the abstract, judges must nevertheless closely scrutinize the necessity of interferences with alleged instances of glorification. Ultimately, it is again only by assessing contextual elements surrounding the speech act that the actual risk of such speech can be ascertained.

A number of states have outlawed extremist organizations, including those accused of inciting religious discrimination or violence in an organized fashion. International monitoring bodies have granted State parties to human rights conventions significant discretion to do so. However, it is vital that complaints about interferences with the freedoms of association and expression are analysed on their merits. Anti-extremism laws may in practice very well overstep the mark and lead to abuses of civil and political rights, rather than protect such freedoms. Those states that insist that collective forms of incitement ought to be penalized more severely would do well to treat the organizational element as an aggravating factor when meting out sentences rather than imposing blanket bans on extremist groups.

International monitoring bodies are far from unanimous on which penalties are generally permitted for speech offences. Specifically, it is urgent that they take a coherent stance against prior restraints and draconian prison sentences. The lack of uniform guidance may well explain the extremely diverse state practice in this area. As for sanctions meted out in concrete incitement cases, monitoring bodies have adopted approaches of checking the proportionality thereof, but those checks tends to be rather minimalistic. A more coherent and principled approach is in order, one that does justice to the proportionality principle.

BIBLIOGRAPHY

Altmen, A., 'Freedom of Expression and Human Rights Law: The Case of Holocaust Denial', in Ishani Maitra and Mary Kate McGowan (eds.), *Speech & Harm: Controversies Over Free Speech* (Oxford University Press, 2012), 24–49.

Amor, A., 'Considérations sur le Paragraphe 3 de l'Article 19 du Pacte International Relative aux Droits Civils et Politique' (paper presented at the Expert seminar on 'Freedom of expression and advocacy of religious hatred that constitutes incitement to discrimination, hostility or violence – the links between Articles 19 and 20 of the International Covenant on Civil and Political Rights', organized by the Office of the United Nations High Commissioner for Human Rights, 2–3 October 2008, Geneva, Switzerland).

Baker, C. E., 'Autonomy and Hate Speech', in Ivan Hare and James Weinstein (eds.), *Extreme Speech and Democracy* (Oxford University Press, 2009), 139–57.

Barendt, E., *Freedom of Speech* (2nd rev. edn, Oxford University Press, 2007).

'Incitement to, and Glorification of, Terrorism', in Ivan Hare and James Weinstein (eds.), *Extreme Speech and Democracy* (Oxford University Press, 2009), 445–62.

'Religious Hatred Laws: Protecting Groups or Belief?' (2011) 17 *Res Publica* 41–54.

Belnap, A. G., 'Defamation of Religions: A Vague and Overbroad Theory that Threatens Basic Human Rights' (2010) *Brigham Young University Law Review* 635–85.

Benesch, S., 'Contribution to OHCHR Initiative on Incitement to National, Racial, or Religious Hatred' (expert paper presented at the UN OHCHR Expert workshop on the prohibition of incitement to national, racial or religious hatred, Vienna, 9–10 February 2011).

Benesch, S. 'Dangerous Speech: A Proposal to Prevent Group Violence' (World Policy Institute paper, 2012).

'Vile Crime or Inalienable Right: Defining Incitement to Genocide' (2008) 48:3 *Virginia Journal of International Law* 485–528.

Berry, S., 'Bringing Muslim Minorities within the International Convention on the Elimination of All Forms of Racial Discrimination – Square Peg in a Round Hole?' (2011) 11:3 *Human Rights Law Review* 423–50.

Bertoni, E., and Rivera, J., 'The American Convention on Human Rights: Regulation of Hate Speech and Similar Expression', in Michael Herz and Peter Molnar (eds.), *The Content and Context of Hate Speech: Rethinking Regulation and Responses* (Cambridge University Press, 2012), 499–513.

Blitt, R. C., 'Defamation of Religion: Rumors of Its Death are Greatly Exaggerated' (2011) 62 *Case Western Reserve Law Review* 347–97.

Bossuyt, M. J., *Guide to the 'Travaux Préparatoires' of the International Covenant on Civil and Political Rights* (Dordrecht/Boston/Lancaster: Martinus Nijhoff Publishers, 1987).

Boyle, K., 'Human Rights, Religion and Democracy: The Refah Party Case' (2004) 1 *Essex Human Rights Review* 1–16.

Brettschneider, C., 'Value Democracy as the Basis for Viewpoint Neutrality: A Theory of Free Speech and Its Implications for the State Speech and Limited Public Forum Doctrines' (2013) 107:2 *Northwestern University Law Review* 603–46.

Brugger, W., 'The Treatment of Hate Speech in German Constitutional Law' (2003) 4:1 *German Law Journal* 1–44.

Callamard, A., 'Combating Discrimination and Intolerance with a Free Speech Framework' (2010) 5 *Religion & Human Rights* 153–69.

'Conference Paper #2' (paper presented at the Expert seminar on 'Freedom of expression and advocacy of religious hatred that constitutes incitement to discrimination, hostility or violence – the links between Articles 19 and 20 of the International Covenant on Civil and Political Rights', organized by the Office of United Nations High Commissioner for Human Rights, 2–3 October 2008, Geneva, Switzerland).

Cannie, H., and Voorhoof, D., 'The Abuse Clause and Freedom of Expression in the European Human Rights Convention: An Added Value for Democracy and Human Rights Protection? (2011) 29:1 *Netherlands Quarterly of Human Rights* 54–83.

Choudhury, T., 'The Terrorism Act 2006: Discouraging Terrorism', in Ivan Hare and James Weinstein (eds.), *Extreme Speech and Democracy* (Oxford University Press, 2009), 463–87.

Christians, L. L., *Study for the European Expert Workshop on the Prohibition of Incitement to National, Racial or Religious Hatred* (OHCHR expert seminar on Article 20(2) ICCPR, 9–10 February 2011, Vienna).

Cotler, I., 'State-Sanctioned Incitement to Genocide: The Responsibility to Prevent', in Michael Herz and Peter Molnar (eds.), *The Content and Context of Hate Speech: Rethinking Regulation and Responses* (Cambridge University Press, 2012), 430–55.

Cowhey, D., 'Racist Hate Speech Law in Ireland: The Need for Reform' (2006) 4 *Cork Online Law Review* 34–45.

Cram, I., 'The Danish Cartoons, Offensive Expression and Democratic Legitimacy', in Ivan Hare and James Weinstein (eds.), *Extreme Speech and Democracy* (Oxford University Press, 2009), 311–30.

Crenshaw, K., 'Mapping the Margins: Intersectionality, Identity Politics, and Violence against Women of Color' (1991) 46:6 *Stanford Law Review* 1241–99.

Defeis, E., 'Freedom of Speech and International Norms: A Response to Hate Speech' (1992) 29 *Stanford Journal of International Law* 57–130.

Dobras, R. J., 'Is the United Nations Endorsing Human Rights Violations?: An Analysis of the United Nations' Combating Defamation of Religious Resolutions and Pakistan's Blasphemy Laws' *Georgia Journal of International & Comparative Law* 37 (2009) 339–80.

Dworkin, R. 'A New Map of Censorship' (2006) 1 *Index on Censorship* 130–3.

'Foreword', in Ivan Hare and James Weinstein (eds.), *Extreme Speech and Democracy* (Oxford University Press, 2009), v–ix.

Edger, R., 'Are Hate Speech Provisions Anti-Democratic? An International Perspective' (2010) 26:1 *American University International Law Review* 119–55.

Ekaratne, S. C., 'Redundant Restriction: The U.K.'s Offense of Glorifying Terrorism' (2010) 23 *Harvard Human Rights Journal* 205–21.

Eltayeb, M. S. M., 'The Limitations on Critical Thinking on Religious Issues under Article 20 of ICCPR and its Relation to Freedom of Expression' (2010) 5 *Religion & Human Rights* 119–35.

Evans, C., 'Religious Speech that Undermines Gender Equality', in Ivan Hare and James Weinstein (eds.), *Extreme Speech and Democracy* (Oxford University Press, 2009), 357–74.

Farrior, S., 'Molding the Matrix: The Historical and Theoretical Foundations of International Law Concerning Hate Speech' (1996) 14:1 *Berkeley Journal of International Law* 1–98.

Fraser, D., 'On the Internet, Nobody Knows You're a Nazi: Some Comparative Legal Aspects of Holocaust Denial', in Ivan Hare and James Weinstein (eds.), *Extreme Speech and Democracy* (Oxford University Press, 2009), 511–37.

Gelber, K., 'Reconceptualizing Counterspeech in Hate Speech Policy', in Michael Herz and Peter Molnar (eds.), *The Content and Context of Hate Speech: Rethinking Regulation and Responses* (Cambridge University Press, 2012), 198–216.

'"Speaking Back": The Likely Faith of Hate Speech Policy in the United States and Australia', in Ishani Maitra and Mary Kate McGowan (eds.), *Speech & Harm: Controversies Over Free Speech* (Oxford University Press, 2012), 50–71.

Ghanea, N., 'The Concept of Racist Hate Speech and its Evolution Over Time' (paper presented at the United Nations Committee on the Elimination of Racial Discrimination, 81st session, 28 August 2012, Geneva).

'Expression and Hate Speech in the ICCPR: Compatible or Clashing' (2010) 5 *Religion & Human Rights* 171–90.

'Intersectionality and the Spectrum of Racist Hate Speech: Proposals to the UN Committee on the Elimination of Racial Discrimination' (2013) 32:4 *Human Rights Quarterly* 935–54.

'Minorities and Hatred: Protections and Implications' (2010) 17 *International Journal on Minority and Group Rights* 423–36.

'Nature and Means of Effective Remedies' (expert paper presented at the UN OHCHR Expert workshop on the prohibition of incitement to national, racial or religious hatred, Vienna, 9–10 February 2011).

Graham, L. B., 'Defamation of Religions: The End of Pluralism?' (2009) 23 *Emory International Law Review* 69–84.

Greenawalt, K., *Fighting Words* (Princeton University Press, 1996).

Speech, Crime, and the Uses of Language (Oxford University Press, 1989).

Greene, J., 'Hate Speech and the Demos', in Michael Herz and Peter Molnar (eds.), *The Content and Context of Hate Speech: Rethinking Regulation and Responses* (Cambridge University Press, 2012), 92–115.

Grimm, D., 'The Holocaust Denial Decision of the Federal Constitutional Court of Germany', in Ivan Hare and James Weinstein (eds.), *Extreme Speech and Democracy* (Oxford University Press, 2009), 557–61.

Guenther, K., 'The Denial of the Holocaust: Employing Criminal Law to Combat Anti-Semitism in Germany' (2000) 15 *Tel Aviv University Studies in Law* (2000) 51–66.

Haraszti, M., 'Hate Speech and the Coming Death of the International Standard Before It Was Born (Complaints of a Watchdog)', foreword in Michael Herz and Peter Molnar (eds.), *The Content and Context of Hate Speech: Rethinking Regulation and Responses* (Cambridge University Press, 2012), xiii–xviii.

Hare, I., 'Extreme Speech under International and Regional Human Rights Standards', in Ivan Hare and James Weinstein (eds.), *Extreme Speech and Democracy* (Oxford University Press, 2009), 62–80.

Hare, I. and Weinstein, J., 'Free Speech, Democracy, and the Suppression of Extreme Speech Past and Present', in Ivan Hare and James Weinstein (eds.), *Extreme Speech and Democracy* (Oxford University Press, 2009), 1–7.

Harel, A., 'Hate speech and Comprehensive Forms of Life', in Michael Herz and Peter Molnar (eds.), *The Content and Context of Hate Speech: Rethinking Regulation and Responses* (Cambridge University Press, 2012), 306–26

Heinze, E., 'Cumulative Jurisprudence and Human Rights: The Example of Sexual Minorities and Hate Speech', in Phil C. W. Chan (ed.), *Protection of Sexual Minorities since Stonewall: Progress and Stalemate in Developed and Developing Countries* (London/New York: Routledge, 2010), 62–78.

'Viewpoint Absolutism and Hate Speech' (2006) 69:4 *Modern Law Review* 543–82.

Heyman, S. J., 'Hate Speech, Public Discourse, and the First Amendment', in Ivan Hare and James Weinstein (eds.), *Extreme Speech and Democracy* (Oxford University Press, 2009), 158–82.

Jacobson, A. and Schlink, B., 'Hate Speech and Self-Restraint', in Michael Herz and Peter Molnar (eds.), *The Content and Context of Hate Speech: Rethinking Regulation and Responses* (Cambridge University Press, 2012), 217–41.

Joseph, S., 'A Rights Analysis of the Covenant on Civil and Political Rights', (1999) 5 *Journal of International Legal Studies* (1999) 57–94.

Joseph, S., Schultz, J. and Castan, M., *The International Covenant on Civil and Political Rights* (Oxford University Press, 2000).

Keane, D., 'Attacking Hate Speech under Article 17 of the European Convention on Human Rights' (2007) 25:4 *Netherlands Quarterly of Human Rights* 641–63.

Kearney, M. G., *The Prohibition of Propaganda for War in International Law* (Oxford University Press, 2007).

Kretzmer, D., 'Freedom of Speech and Racism' (1986–1987) 8 *Cardozo Law Review* 445–513.

Langer, L., *Religious Offence and Human Rights* (Cambridge University Press, 2014).

Lechtholz-Zey, J., 'The Laws Banning Holocaust Denial' (revised version) (2012) 9 *Genocide Prevention Now* (online).

Leigh, I., 'Hatred, Sexual Orientation, Free Speech and Religious Liberty' (2008) 10:3 *Ecclesiastical Law Journal* 337–44.

'Homophobic Speech, Equality Denial, and Religious Expression' in Ivan Hare and James Weinstein (eds.), *Extreme Speech and Democracy* (Oxford University Press, 2009), 375–99.

Lerner, N., 'Freedom of Expression and Advocacy of Group Hatred: Incitement to Hate Crimes and Religious Hatred' (2010) 5 *Religion & Human Rights* 137–45.

Lübbe-Wolff, G., 'Zur Bedeutung des Art. 139 GG für die Auseinandersetzung mit Neonazistischen Gruppen' (1988) *Neue Juristische Wochenschrift* 1289–94.

McGoldrick, D., *The Human Rights Committee: Its Role in the Development of the International Covenant on Civil and Political Rights* (Oxford: Clarendon Press, 1991).

McGonagle, T., 'A Survey and Critical Analysis of Council of Europe Strategies for Countering "Hate Speech"', in Michael Herz and Peter Molnar (eds.), *The Content and Context of Hate Speech: Rethinking Regulation and Responses* (Cambridge University Press, 2012), 456–98.

Maina, H., *The Prohibition of Incitement to Hatred in Africa: Comparative Review and Proposal for a Threshold* (A study prepared for the regional expert meeting on Article 20, Organized by the Office of the High Commissioner for Human Rights, Nairobi, 6–7 April 2011).

Maitra, I., 'Subordinating Speech', in Ishani Maitra and Mary Kate McGowan (eds.), *Speech & Harm: Controversies Over Free Speech* (Oxford University Press, 2012), 94–120.

Maitra, I. and McGowan, M. K., 'Introduction and Overview', in Ishani Maitra and Mary Kate McGowan (eds.), *Speech & Harm: Controversies Over Free Speech* (Oxford University Press, 2012), 1–23.

Malik, M., 'Extreme Speech and Liberalism', in Ivan Hare and James Weinstein (eds.), *Extreme Speech and Democracy* (Oxford University Press, 2009), 96–120.

Marshall, P. and Shea, N., *Silenced: How Apostasy & Blasphemy Codes are Choking Freedom Worldwide* (Oxford University Press, 2011).

Mbongo, P., 'Hate Speech, Extreme Speech, and Collective Defamation in French Law', in Ivan Hare and James Weinstein (eds.), *Extreme Speech and Democracy* (Oxford University Press, 2009), 221–36.

Mendel, T., 'Does International Law Provide for Consistent Rules on Hate Speech?', in Michael Herz and Peter Molnar (eds.), *The Content and Context of Hate Speech: Rethinking Regulation and Responses* (Cambridge University Press, 2012), 417–29.

Study on International Standards Relating to Incitement to Genocide or Racial Hatred for the UN Special Advisor on the Prevention of Genocide (April 2006).

Mengistu, Y. L., 'Shielding Marginalized Groups from Verbal Assaults Without Abusing Hate Speech Laws', in Michael Herz and Peter Molnar (eds.), *The Content and Context of Hate Speech: Rethinking Regulation and Responses* (Cambridge University Press, 2012), 352–77.

Mill, J. S., *On Liberty* (London: John W. Parker & Sons, 1859).

Möller, J. T., and de Zayas, A., *United Nations Human Rights Committee Case Law* (Kehl am Rhein: N. P. Engel Verlag, 2009).

Molnar, P., 'Responding to "Hate Speech" with Art, Education, and the Imminent Danger Test', in Michael Herz and Peter Molnar (eds.), *The Content and Context of Hate Speech: Rethinking Regulation and Responses* (Cambridge University Press, 2012), 183–97.

'Toward Improved Law and Policy on "Hate Speech" – The "Clear and Present Danger" Test in Hungary', in Ivan Hare and James Weinstein (eds.), *Extreme Speech and Democracy* (Oxford University Press, 2009), 237–64.

Molnar, P. and Malik, K., 'Interview with Kenan Malik', in Michael Herz and Peter Molnar (eds.), *The Content and Context of Hate Speech: Rethinking Regulation and Responses* (Cambridge University Press, 2012), 81–91.

Moon, R., 'Hate Speech Regulations in Canada' (2009) 36 *Florida State University Law Review* 79–97.

Report to the Canadian Human Rights Commission Concerning Section 13 of the Canadian Human Rights Act and the Regulation of Hate Speech on the Internet (October 2008).

Morsink, J., *The Universal Declaration of Human Rights: Origins, Drafting & Intent* (Philadelphia: University of Pennsylvania Press, 1999).

Nielsen, L. B., 'Power in Public: Reactions, Responses, and Resistance to Offensive Public Speech', in Ishani Maitra and Mary Kate McGowan (eds.), *Speech & Harm: Controversies Over Free Speech* (Oxford University Press, 2012), 148–73.

Nowak, M., *U.N. Covenant on Civil and Political Rights: CCPR Commentary* (2nd rev. edn, Kehl: N. P. Engel, 2005).

Nussbaum, M. C., *The New Religious Intolerance: Overcoming the Politics of Fear in an Anxious Age* (Cambridge, MA, Harvard University Press, 2012).

O'Flaherty, M., 'Freedom of Expression: Article 19 of the International Covenant on Civil and Political Rights and the Human Rights Committee's General Comment No 34' (2012) 12 *Human Rights Law Review* 627–54.

Parekh, B., 'Is there a Case for Banning Hate Speech', in Michael Herz and Peter Molnar (eds.), *The Content and Context of Hate Speech: Rethinking Regulation and Responses* (Cambridge University Press, 2012), 37–56.

Parmar, S., 'The Challenge of "Defamation of Religions" to Freedom of Expression and the International Human Rights System' (2009) 3 *European Human Rights Law Review* 353–75.

'How Human Rights Treaties Draw Borders between Freedom of Speech and Discrimination' (paper presented at Media in the Media conference, London 28–29 March 2008).

Petrova, D., 'Incitement to National, Racial or Religious Hatred: Role of Civil Society and National Human Rights Institutions' (expert paper presented at the UN OHCHR Expert workshop on the prohibition of incitement to national, racial or religious hatred, Vienna, 9–10 February 2011).

Plant, R., *The Pink Triangle: The Nazi War Against Homosexuals* (New York: H. Holt, 1986).

Post, R., 'Hate Speech', in Ivan Hare and James Weinstein (eds.), *Extreme Speech and Democracy* (Oxford University Press, 2009), 123–38.

'Religion and Freedom of Speech: Portraits of Muhammad' (2007) 14 *Constellations* 72–90.

Richards, D., *Free Speech and the Politics of Identity* (Oxford University Press, 1999).

Rosenfeld, M., 'Hate Speech in Constitutional Jurisprudence: A Comparative Analysis' (2003) 24 *Cardozo Law Review* 1523–67.

Rowbottom, J., 'Extreme Speech and the Democratic Functions of the Mass Media', in Ivan Hare and James Weinstein (eds.), *Extreme Speech and Democracy* (Oxford University Press, 2009), 608–30.

Sajó, A., 'Militant Democracy and Transition Towards Democracy,' in András Sajó (ed.), *Militant Democracy* (Utrecht: Eleven International Publishing, 2004), 209–30.

Schabas, W. A., 'Hate Speech in Rwanda: the Road to Genocide' (2000) 46 *McGill Law Journal* 141–71.

Schauer, F., 'Freedom of Expression Adjudication in Europe and the United States', in George Nolte (ed.), *European and US Constitutionalism* (Cambridge University Press, 2005), 49–69.

'Social Epistemology, Holocaust Denial, and the Post-Millian Calculus', in Michael Herz and Peter Molnar (eds.), *The Content and Context of Hate Speech: Rethinking Regulation and Responses* (Cambridge University Press, 2012), 129–43.

Schwelb, E., 'The International Convention on the Elimination of All Forms of Racial Discrimination' (1966) 15 *International and Comparative Law Quarterly* 996–1068.

Stegbauer, A., 'The Ban of Right-Wing Extremist Symbols According to Section 86a of the German Criminal Code' (2007) 8:2 *German Law Journal* 173–84.

Suk, J. C., 'Holocaust Denial and the Free-Speech Theory of the State', in Michael Herz and Peter Molnar (eds.), *The Content and Context of Hate Speech: Rethinking Regulation and Responses* (Cambridge University Press, 2012), 144–63.

Summer, L. W., 'Incitement and the Regulation of Hate Speech in Canada: A Philosophical Analysis', in Ivan Hare and James Weinstein (eds.), *Extreme Speech and Democracy* (Oxford University Press, 2009), 204–20.

Szeszlér, T. (ed.), *Anti-Semitic Discourse in Hungary in 2002–2003: Report and Documentation* (Budapest: B'nai B'rith Elso Budapesti Kozosseg, 2004).

Taylor, P. M., *Freedom of Religion: UN and European Human Rights Law and Practice* (Cambridge University Press, 2005).

Temperman, J., 'Blasphemy, Defamation of Religions and Human Rights Law' (2008) 26:4 *Netherlands Quarterly of Human Rights* 517–45.

'Blasphemy Versus Incitement', in Christopher Beneke *et al.* (eds.), *Profane: Sacrilegious Expression in a Multicultural Age* (University of California Press, 2014), 401–25.

'The Emerging Counter-Defamation of Religion Discourse: A Critical Analysis' (2010) 4 *Annuaire Droit et Religion* 553–9.

'Freedom of Expression and Religious Sensitivities in Pluralist Societies: Facing the Challenge of Extreme Speech', (2011) 3 *Brigham Young University Law Review* 729–57.

'Laws against the Denial of Historical Atrocities: A Human Rights Analysis' (2014) 9 *Religion & Human Rights* 151–80.

'A Right to be Free from Religious Hatred? The Wilders Case in the Netherlands and Beyond', in Peter Molnar (ed.), *Free Speech and Censorship Around the Globe* (New York/Budapest: Central European University Press, 2014), 509–30.

Thornberry, P., 'Forms of Hate Speech and the Convention on the Elimination of all Forms of Racial Discrimination (ICERD)' (2010) 5 *Religion & Human Rights*, 97–117.

Timmermann, W., 'Incitement in International Criminal Law' (2006) 864 *International Review of the Red Cross* 823–52.

Tomuschat, C., 'Prosecuting Denials of Past Alleged Genocides', in Paola Gaeta (ed.), *The UN Genocide Convention: A Commentary* (Oxford University Press, 2009), 513–30.

Tirrell, L. 'Genocidal Language Games', in Ishani Maitra and Mary Kate McGowan (eds.), *Speech & Harm: Controversies Over Free Speech* (Oxford University Press, 2012), 174–221.

Varat, J. D., 'Deception and the First Amendment: A Central, Complex, and Somewhat Curious Relationship' (2005–2006) 53 *UCLA Law Review* 1107–41.

Verkhovsky, A., *Data-Collection and Fact-Finding* (OHCHR expert seminar on Article 20(2) ICCPR, 9–10 February 2011, Vienna).

Waldron, J., 'Dignity and Defamation: The Visibility of Hate' (2010) 123 *Harvard Law Review* 1596–657.

The Harm in Hate Speech (Cambridge, MA: Harvard University Press, 2012).

Walker, S., *Hate Speech: The History of an American Controversy* (Lincoln, NE: University of Nebraska Press, 1994).

Weber, A., *Manual on Hate Speech* (Strasbourg: Council of Europe Publishing, 2009).

Weil, P., 'The Politics of Memory: Bans and Commemorations', in Ivan Hare and James Weinstein (eds.), *Extreme Speech and Democracy* (Oxford University Press, 2009), 562–79.

Weinstein, J., 'Extreme Speech, Public Order, and Democracy: Lessons from The Masses,' in Ivan Hare and James Weinstein (eds.), *Extreme Speech and Democracy* (Oxford University Press, 2009), 23–61.

'Hate Speech, Viewpoint Neutrality, and the American Concept of Democracy', in Thomas R. Hensley (ed.), *The Boundaries of Freedom of Expression & Order in American Democracy* (Kent State University Press, 2001), 146–69.

Hate Speech, Pornography, and the Radical Attack on Free Speech Doctrine (Boulder: Westview Press, 1999).

'An Overview of American Free Speech Doctrine and its Application to Extreme Speech', in Ivan Hare and James Weinstein (eds.), *Extreme Speech and Democracy* (Oxford University Press, 2009), 81–91.

West, C., 'Words that Silence? Freedom of Expression and Racist Hate Speech', in Ishani Maitra and Mary Kate McGowan (eds.), *Speech & Harm: Controversies Over Free Speech* (Oxford University Press, 2012), 222–48.

Whine, M., 'Expanding Holocaust Denial and Legislation Against It', in Ivan Hare and James Weinstein (eds.), *Extreme Speech and Democracy* (Oxford University Press, 2009), 538–56.

Williams, G., 'Oblique Intention' (1987) 46 *Cambridge Law Journal* 417–38.

Žilinskas, J., 'Introduction of "Crime of Denial" in the Lithuanian Criminal Law and First Instances of its Application' (2012) 19:1 *Jurisprudence* 315–29.

INDEX

CAMBRIDGE STUDIES IN INTERNATIONAL AND
COMPARATIVE LAW

BOOKS IN THE SERIES

CPSIA information can be obtained
at www.ICGtesting.com
Printed in the USA
LVOW04*1111130816
500250LV00008B/51/P